Third Edition

PRODUCTION AND OPERATIONS MANAGEMENT

Third Edition

PRODUCTION AND OPERATIONS MANAGEMENT

Manufacturing and Nonmanufacturing

James B. Dilworth
University of Alabama in Birmingham

Random House
Business Division
New York

Dedicated with love
to Ginger, Jimmy, Caroline,
Jessica Leigh, and Michael,
and to the memory of my father,
my mother, and Andrew

Third Edition
987654321
Copyright © 1979, 1983, 1986 by Random House, Inc.

Library of Congress Cataloging-in-Publication Data

Dilworth, James B., 1939-
    Production and operations management.

    Bibliography: p.
    Includes index.
    1. Production management.   I. Title.
TS155.D545   1986   658.5   85-28148
ISBN 0-394-35111-8

Cover, Part and Chapter Opening photos by Paul Silverman

Text design: Suzanne Bennett

Cover design: Lorraine Hohman

Manufactured in the United States of America

PREFACE
TO THE THIRD EDITION

The third edition of *Production and Operations Management: Manufacturing and Nonmanufacturing,* and the ancillaries that are available to use with it, should provide valuable tools for teaching operations management to students today. The text has been revised to reflect recent developments in a field which is changing rapidly and becoming more widely recognized for its strategic importance. Although there are many smaller changes throughout the text, some of the more important changes are mentioned below.

First of all, plant tours have been added to provide some introduction to what happens in manufacturing operations, since most students have been in banks, restaurants, hospitals or other nonmanufacturing operations, but many have never been in a factory. The text also incorporates many new current topics, including just-in-time manufacturing, the growing use of computers and automation, the use of group technology or cellular manufacturing, and the idea of flexible manufacturing systems, that incorporate all of these factors. A new chapter on scheduling service operations has been provided, and all of the chapters have been updated and improved. The material within the quality assurance and aggregate planning chapters has been resequenced to improve the presentation. The supplements have been retained, but the material on investments and the time value of money has been deleted because our user survey indicated that this material was not used, since it was covered in finance and accounting courses.

Ancillary Materials   For the convenience of teachers and students, a number of ancillary materials are available to supplement this book:

A *Study Guide with Problems and Cases* by Larry Ettkin and myself can be purchased by students as an addition to the text. In addition to standard self study features such as learning objectives, detailed chapter summaries and true–false and multiple-choice questions, the guide provides further examples of solved problems (reinforcing this approach in the text), unsolved problems for working, and additional readings and cases on current and important issues in operations management.

The *Solutions Manual,* which is available to professors, provides detailed solutions to all end-of-chapter questions and problems. It also contains solutions to unsolved problems and suggested responses to discussion questions in the study guide.

The *Instructor's Resource Manual* helps the instructor use the text effectively. It provides Learning Objectives, Lecture Outlines and Notes, and Transparencies, along with an Instructor's Test File of problems and solutions to test students' knowledge.

Software that can be used with this text is also available from Random House. A set of Lotus templates is available with extensive macro programs to perform operations management calculations. Also, an operations management "tool kit," which is software for solving operations management problems of many different types, such as those the practitioner might face, can be purchased through Random House.

Structure of the Text   The book is designed to describe different types of operations and then discuss early in the book the importance of operations in a company's pursuit of its strategic goals and objectives. In developing its strategy a company defines what business it is in—that is, what goods or services it offers in what territories and by what methods they are to be provided. After doing so, a company is better able to forecast the demand for these products and, hence, to estimate the level of operations the company should be prepared to provide. Part I of the book is designed to present these concepts.

A demand forecast, or projection of future demand, is the basis for two major categories of decisions about operations: (a) designing the operations system and (b) planning and controlling the efforts of that system. Part II of the book discusses management issues related to planning and controlling operations efforts. Part III discusses design-related issues and contains a concluding chapter.

Although the material in this course can be covered in various sequences, I chose to provide more material related to running an operations system and to present it before design-related material because of several considerations.

- This sequence fits the life cycle of the *student* who is preparing for the world of work. Most students will be employed initially in a position that relates to an ongoing system and may later be involved in designing one. Few will have an initial assignment to design some type of production and operations system.

- The greatest percentage of students who take the introductory production and operations management course will interface with an ongoing production system. For those who go into marketing or finance and those whose only interaction with a production system is as consumers, it will be most important to understand how the production system works. The smaller percentage of students who will become involved in designing production and operations systems will receive training beyond the course for which this text is used.

- In terms of design logic, one must first understand the functions of a system in order to develop the most appropriate design for that system.

One would not design an automobile or airplane without first developing an understanding of how the machine operates.

The material within each chapter is structured to provide flexibility. Generally, the first part of each chapter introduces a topic, discusses why it is important, and relates it to the field of operations management. The application of tools, methods, and techniques generally is discussed in the latter part of a chapter or in a chapter supplement. This structure enables a professor to teach a descriptive course by omitting, or not emphasizing, the latter parts of the chapters and the quantitative supplements and using mostly discussion questions and cases, instead of problems. For a more quantitative course, one can devote more class time to the tools and problems and let the students read the chapters' introductory discussion material outside of class.

Acknowledgments This book has drawn on the talents, advice, and encouragement of more people than I can possibly acknowledge. I would, however, like to recognize the contributions of many who have helped. First, I want to thank my family, who have persevered with me even though we grew a little weary before this project was completed. I want to thank Gene Newport, Robert Ford, and my other colleagues at UAB for their encouragement and interest. The assistance of David Dannenbring of Columbia University, who carefully checked all the quantitative material in the text, *Solutions Manual,* and test file, was an invaluable help in ensuring the accuracy of this text. I am very grateful to June Smith, Susan Badger, Niels Aaboe, Anne Mahoney, Andrew Roney, and the other staff members at Random House who have worked so hard to make this project a success.

I greatly appreciate the comments and splendid advice of the academics who reviewed this edition: Frank C. Barnes, University of North Carolina at Charlotte; Thomas E. Callarman, Arizona State University; C. W. Dane, Oregon State University; Gene K. Groff, Georgia State University; Peter Haug, University of Washington; Yunus Kathawala, Eastern Illinois University; John F. Kottas, College of William and Mary; Bruce J. McLaren, Indiana State University; J. Roberta Minifie, Texas Tech University; C. Carl Pegels, State University of New York—Buffalo; and R. Daniel Reid, Bowling Green State University. I am grateful as well to those individuals, too numerous to mention by name, who responded to a survey which formed the basis for the revision of the text.

I also want to express my gratitude to Betty Smith, who typed the material for the ancillaries and who assists our department in so many kind ways.

Finally, I want to thank you, THE READER, for taking time to read this far. I hope that you will read the book and use it to benefit many. As with the first and second editions, I welcome your comments about how this book can be improved.

JAMES B. DILWORTH
Birmingham, Alabama
October, 1985

CONTENTS IN BRIEF

CONTENTS
IN DETAIL

PART I
FOUNDATION MATERIAL

Part I of this book contains three chapters and four in-
formational supplements. Together they provide a
foundation for the further study of production and operations management. Chapter 1 introduces the operations
function in manufacturing and nonmanufacturing settings
and briefly reviews some of the activities of operations managers. Two types of manufacturing operations introduced in
the first chapter are continuous- and intermittent-production
plants. Supplement A, the first supplement to follow Chapter
1, provides a verbal tour of a plant engaged in continuous production, and Supplement B, the next one, provides a tour of a
plant engaged in intermittent production—providing further insight into these two types of operations. Supplement C briefly
reviews the history of, and current developments in, production
and operations management in the United States.

The operations function is a vital component of a business, making
major contributions to achievement of the company's strategic plans.
Chapter 2 discusses how operations relate to the long-range, strategic
decisions that managers make to guide a company. Supplement D,
which follows Chapter 2, provides an overview of the decision-making
process and the use of models in decision making.

Managers must make decisions based on inferences about the future. They
must attempt to answer such difficult questions as What future developments do we need to be planning for and reaching decisions about? What
will be the outcome of each possible course of action we might take? Forecasting, the basis for much of management's planning and control activities,
is the subject of Chapter 3.

Forecasts may reveal a need for decisions in either of the two major categories
that constitute Parts II and III of the book. Forecasts help managers make decisions relating to the short- to intermediate-term *operation* of the production
system—issues that are discussed in Part II. Forecasts also are the basis for
decisions pertaining to longer-term changes in the *design* of the production
system—issues that are discussed in Part III.

Chapter Outline
ZEROING IN ON OPERATIONS

THE OPERATIONS FUNCTION

Operations Management In Action   SCHOOLS AGAIN OFFER COURSES ON PRODUCTION

OTHER FUNCTIONS

Marketing / Finance / Supporting Functions / Interdependence of Functions

TODAY'S BROADER VIEW OF THE OPERATIONS FUNCTION

Operations: Providing a Product or Service / Operations Are of Many Types / Manufacturing Operations / Nonmanufacturing Operations / The Challenges of Service Operations

MANAGERS' ROLES IN OPERATIONS

Skills Needed by Operations Managers / Activities of Operations Managers to Support Company Success

OVERVIEW OF THE BOOK AND ISSUES DISCUSSED

Summary / Discussion Questions / Bibliography

KEY TERMS

Operations function
Production function
Marketing function
Finance function
Manufacturing operations
Nonmanufacturing operations

Make-to-stock producer
Make-to-order producer
Assemble-to-order producer
Continuous production
Repetitive manufacturing

Process industries
Intermittent production
Job shop
Project
Service operations
Standard services

Custom services
Technical competence
Behavioral competence
Quality
Productivity

Chapter I

ZEROING IN ON OPERATIONS

THE OPERATIONS FUNCTION

The *operations function* is performed by that group of persons in a business who are responsible for producing the goods or providing the services that the business offers to the public. The operations function, also called the *production function,* is one of three primary functions within a business, the other two being finance and marketing. But in a typical business, it is the operations function that employs the greatest number of people and is responsible for the greatest portion of the firm's controllable assets. You can quickly see, then, that operations is a very important function and certainly worthy of study. Our purpose in this text is to study the various activities that take place in the operations function, the factors that influence the operations function, and the actions that are required to manage this function well.

For a few moments imagine what life would be like if there were no organized groups other than the family unit to provide goods or services. Each family would have to build its own home. Most family members would have to work to raise food with whatever crude implements they could fashion for themselves. Transportation would be limited: people would have to travel by horseback or in horse-drawn carts, on rafts or simple boats, or on their own two feet. Communication would be limited to word of mouth or letters carried by someone who happened to be going to the desired destination. Heating the

3

home and cooking would require many hours of cutting wood. The activities required to obtain the necessities of life would consume so much time that great composers, artists, surgeons, and inventors would have little opportunity to develop. None of the advances in medicine, communications, law, and transportation that we have today would exist. There would be no cities, and rural life would be very different from what we know today.

Fortunately, the world today is quite unlike the one described above. Many organizations produce goods and provide services for us to use. The increased skills, efficiency, and productivity that are achieved within these organizations are much greater than individuals could achieve by working alone. Even though we sometimes think the things they produce are not as well made as we would like them to be, we must admit that they are better than we could make for ourselves in the amount of time required to earn what we pay for them. We not only have more and better goods and services than we could produce ourselves, we have more leisure time to enjoy books, television programs, concerts, travel, ball games, and so on. We profit from exposure to broader expanses of the world, have better health care, and enjoy more material wealth because there are businesses that provide us with goods and services.

Both manufacturing and nonmanufacturing operations make important contributions to increasing our standard of living. We live in what is said to be an information age. Yet information is just another resource, enabling us to live better and manage better; people cannot eat, ride in, wear, or hit a tennis ball with information. And the same is true of the many new and growing types of services. People are rediscovering the vital importance of factories and the valuable jobs and goods they provide.

The past few decades have shown the vital power and importance of operations to businesses and to entire national economies. Developed and developing nations can add to their wealth and standard of living by supplying goods to the world marketplace—as has been demonstrated by Japan in recent years. One major reason the Japanese economy has flourished is that many Japanese businesses are very good at the production function. You probably have seen numerous articles and television programs that compare production in Japan with production in the United States. Many other countries have entered this race for a share of the world market, and the collective power of the production function within those nations will be an important key in determining how much of a share each wins.

Work in operations will become even more exciting and challenging in the years ahead: careers and fortunes will be made or lost; economies of entire nations will improve or decline. Much of the outcome will depend on how well operations are managed.

To meet these challenges, companies are adopting new methods and applying new technology. For example, during a visit to an electronics plant in Japan, the author noticed an interesting and somewhat amusing sight. A robot with a bank card was inserting the card into the proper slot and typing various messages on the keyboard of a recently produced automatic teller machine

(ATM). No, the ATM was not dispensing money to the robot. Signals from the circuits in the ATM were being sent to a computer, where they were being analyzed to determine if all of the circuits in the ATM were working properly. But Japan is not the only country using robots. At a General Motors assembly plant a robot guides a laser measurement device into door and window openings of cars as they come down the line. From this device, data are relayed to a computer that analyzes them to determine if the openings are the proper size and if the processing equipment is working properly.

In addition to adopting new technology, companies in the United States, Japan, and other countries are trying to gain or retain market share by offering customers better value. To this end, they are working to improve product quality and to raise productivity—objectives that must be met primarily by the operations function. In this book we will be examining in detail some of the things that are being done to make operations better able to meet these challenges.

OPERATIONS MANAGEMENT IN ACTION

Schools Again Offer Courses On Production

Manufacturing, a subject that long ago fell from favor among graduate students and professors at many business schools, is making a comeback.

Academicians are recruiting teachers and creating courses to treat manufacturing-related topics. MBA candidates who a year ago wouldn't have thought of getting their hands dirty on a factory floor are vying for top grades and recommendations that will land them jobs as plant managers. Manufacturing companies are showing up on Ivy League campuses to recruit not just marketing and finance executives, but also the best and brightest students majoring in what college course catalogs now call "production and operations management."

Making Things Better

It's all the result of the embarrassment and trouble U.S. manufacturers are suffering at the hands of foreign competitors. For 20 years, the highest salaries and the fastest promotions have gone to marketing and finance students. Now, says Robert Mayer, vice president for operations-management services at the consulting firm of Booz, Allen & Hamilton, "we're beginning to realize that we can finance anything and sell anything, but we can't make it very well. We've got to get back to making things better."

Manufacturing began to lose its position in business schools in the early 1960s. The main reason was the view that there wasn't much more to be learned about manufacturing. At the time, the nation had the world's most modern, well-equipped industrial base, and the computer was still in its infancy.

Students, too, shunned manufacturing then. "That was the time when you were supposed to be helping society by doing 'countercultural' things," recalls Harvard Business School Prof. Robert Hayes. "One of the least countercultural things you could do was go into a dirty factory and make people work harder."

Second-Class Status

High salaries, rapid promotions and prestige went to the students of finance and marketing who then joined consulting firms, investment bankers or consumer-products companies. At many prestigious business schools, manufacturing students were relegated to second-class status. Some schools dropped all but an introductory course on manufacturing. Companies tended to ignore the manufacturing end of their businesses, hiring engineers to run their factories.

The result, says Columbia University professor Martin Starr, is that the nation's industrial base "is going from hell-in-a-handbasket to worse, and the economists don't have the slightest idea what to do about it."

What the country needs, says Prof. Starr, is a trained cadre of managers who can go into factories, analyze what's wrong, and then take steps to correct it. Engineers can't do that because they don't have the management and finance background, and finance specialists can't do it because they lack the technical knowledge. Only by producing managers who can apply a broad knowledge of business and technical processes to manufacturing problems will U.S. industry regain its competitive edge, he says.

Developing a Curriculum

Getting there won't be easy. The first step is for business schools to re-establish manufacturing as a central part of their curricula, and that will take time. At Stanford University, a six-member faculty committee is spending a year studying how to develop a manufacturing curriculum and the research base to support it. Once that's established, the next obstacle will be recruiting qualified faculty members, of which there already is a shortage.

"There probably are open positions in operations management at just about every major business school," says Charles Holloway, dean of academic affairs at Stanford's Graduate School of Business. "It's a seller's market."

Most schools are looking for teachers who have both academic and industrial credentials. "You just don't teach a course in operations management without having had some successful exposure to the real world," says Prof. Starr. When such talent is found, it's expensive. "The compression of salaries is causing

a lot of trouble all over the country," he adds. "You have junior faculty whose salaries are beginning to knock at the bottom range of the salaries for full professors."

Once a program is started, a school must attract enough students to keep it going. That's done mostly by getting companies interested in hiring the graduates. At Harvard, where manufacturing never was abandoned, the business school publishes annually a book of resumes of 150 to 200 students who are interested in manufacturing-management jobs. The book is sent to companies that have expressed interest in hiring such students. In the last six years or so, the mailing list has grown to 300 or more, and, it includes such concerns as General Motors Corp., General Electric Co. and Bendix Corp.

A Job-Market Edge

In addition, more companies are helping to create manufacturing courses and to convince students that manufacturing is a good career choice. General Motors, for instance, sends some of its top executives to the best business schools to talk about opportunities in manufacturing. At Columbia, an advisory committee of 24 corporations is starting a program in which each will sponsor a student's MBA studies in manufacturing.

Columbia's Prof. Starr says students are beginning to understand that "you have an edge in the job market if you understand productivity and how to improve it." He admits that one of the most difficult obstacles will be long-standing attitudes about manufacturing.

"But most of our students still want to go into the glass towers on Wall Street or Madison Avenue. They're afraid that if they study manufacturing they'll be sent to places like Erie, Pa."

OTHER FUNCTIONS

The operations function is only one part of a larger system—the entire organization. As such, it is interrelated with other functions within the organization. Plans and actions of all components of the business must be kept in concert if the total organization is to achieve its full potential. Before we discuss the operations function in greater detail, let us briefly review the other primary functions of a business—marketing and finance—as well as some secondary or supporting functions.

Marketing

The *marketing function* consists of the group of people who are responsible for discovering or developing a need or demand for the company's goods and services. They also seek to maintain a responsive working relationship with consumers or potential consumers. Profit-seeking companies cannot long survive without a market for their goods or services. Nonprofit organizations, such as governmental agencies, may survive without a genuine need or demand for their services, but such situations represent a misapplication of economic resources. Nonbusiness enterprises are performing a marketing activity when they determine the extent and location of the need for their services and when they make the availability of their services known to the public.

Finance

The *finance function* primarily concerns those activities aimed at obtaining funds for an organization and guiding the wise use of those funds. The finance function exists in nonbusiness enterprises and may include lobbying for support or seeking public contributions through the efforts of volunteers. Included in the finance function are budgeting and allocation of funds to the various subdivisions of the firm and review of their expenditures.

Supporting Functions

Naturally functions other than operations, marketing, and finance exist within organizations, and they receive varying emphasis, depending on the organization's purposes, its external environment, and the persons within the organization who shape its responses to the environment. If a company produces a tangible product, some product development, design, and engineering functions must be performed. Similar functions must be performed in nonmanufacturing companies, but in these organizations such functions consist of deciding on the services to offer and the manner in which they will be provided. A restaurant, for example, must decide whether to provide food for patrons through service at tables or at self-service cafeteria counters.

Since organizations require human effort, they must recruit personnel, train them, and distribute benefits to them so that they may share in the profits from the organization's work. Some authors treat the personnel function as a fourth major function; others contend that employee relations are an inherent part of all the other functions of an organization. Our objective is not to debate such issues but to recognize that operations depend on people, whether or not we call personnel considerations a separate function. We shall discuss some human relations and behavioral concepts when they are appropriate to our discussions of operations.

Interdependence of Functions

Public relations are important to all the primary and secondary functions. Public attitude affects the success of attempts to sell stock or to borrow money. The public's attitude also affects the company's ability to sell its product and to obtain competent employees to produce the goods and services that the company exists to provide.

Public relations activities illustrate some of the interrelationships among functions within businesses. We may divide a company into smaller units so that each unit is within the human capacity to understand and to supervise, but the parts still are only *parts*. They must work together if the total organization is to function properly.

The three major functions within a business are interdependent. Having the financial resources and the ability to produce a product are of little value if there is no market for the product. Having the finances and a market for a product are of little value if one cannot provide the product. The ability to produce a product and a market for the product are not sufficient if one does not have the necessary capital to employ personnel, buy raw material, and put the other capabilities into action. All of the functions within an organization both contribute to the whole and depend on the remainder of the organization. We consider each function separately so that we may study a manageable unit, but it is important to keep in mind that the other functions are at the same time necessary to and dependent on the function being studied. Figure 1.1 illustrates the interrelatedness of some functions within businesses.

Coordinating the endeavors of the various functional subdivisions of the enterprise is the job of general managers at the top management level. Much of the coordination of the functions is accomplished by establishing consistent objectives and a strategy for achieving these objectives. Corporate policy[1] is established to guide and coordinate the entire organization. In the next chapter we shall discuss some considerations of the operations function in the establishment of corporate strategy and see how the operations function relates to corporate strategy.

It is clear that businesses have more functions than the three primary ones. No attempt will be made here to discuss all functions in detail because our primary interest is in only one of them—operations. The discussion of other functions serves to show how the operations function interacts with other activities within the organization.

TODAY'S BROADER VIEW OF THE OPERATIONS FUNCTION

The operations function is sometimes called the production function, or the

---

[1]The term *corporate* is used as meaning "of or pertaining to the whole," without regard to whether the entity is organized legally as a corporation or a partnership or is individually owned.

FIGURE 1.1

Functions within Organizations

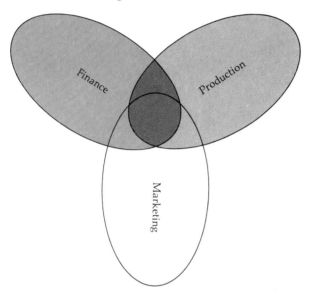

production and operations function. In the past, the term *production* was considered by some persons to connote only the manufacture of tangible items; later the term *operations* was added or substituted to include references to nonmanufacturing operations. Today the term *production* is often used with a broader meaning to refer to the production of goods or the production of services. We have stated earlier that the operations function is responsible for producing goods or providing services. In this book the terms *production, operations,* or *production and operations* are used to refer to the function in either manufacturing or nonmanufacturing settings. Where a distinction or a more restricted focus is intended, we will add an adjective, referring to *manufacturing operations* or *nonmanufacturing operations.*

Manufacturing operations perform some physical or chemical processes such as sawing, sewing, machining, welding, grinding, blending, or refining to convert some tangible raw materials into tangible products. We will classify all other operations that do not actually make goods as *nonmanufacturing* or *service operations.* Customers deal with some of these nonmanufacturing companies to obtain purely intangible services such as advice or instruction; customers may seek help in completing tax forms, for example. Customers deal with other nonmanufacturing companies, such as wholesalers or retailers, to obtain goods—but these companies do not make the goods. These companies primarily serve their customers by transporting, packaging, storing, etc. rather than by performing manufacturing processes. Thus, our major criterion for classifying operations lies in whether these operations manufacture goods or provide some type of service operation, even though they may provide tangible goods or some less tangible service to customers.

Operations: Providing a Product or Service

When viewed at a general or conceptual level, all types of production operations have some common characteristics. The most obvious common ground is the system's purpose or function; that is, the production system is responsible for providing the goods or services offered by the organization. The production system must transform some set of inputs into a set of outputs. This is the element that all production systems have in common; it is illustrated schematically in Figure 1.2. The types of inputs, transformations, and outputs will vary between operations.

Manufacturing operations transform or convert such inputs as raw materials, labor skills, management skills, capital, and sales revenue into some product, which is then sold. Other outputs are wages that flow into the economy, environmental effects, social influences, and other, even less obvious factors. The production system is a part of the larger system—the company. The company is a part of a larger system—the community. As the system boundaries expand, it becomes more difficult to determine all of the inputs, outputs, and transformations.

Service operations also transform a set of inputs into a set of outputs. A restaurant uses such inputs as meat, potatoes, lettuce, the chef's skills, servers' skills, and many others. Some of the transformation processes involve storing supplies, blending ingredients into desirable combinations, and altering the form of the inputs by cooking, freezing, heating, and transporting them to the proper tables at the proper time. Less tangible operations involve the provision of a pleasant atmosphere, perhaps even by offering entertainment. The outputs include, one hopes, a satisfied patron. Other outputs include wages and purchase payments sent into the economy and refuse sent into the refuse collection system (which is yet another service system).

Educational institutions use such inputs as books, students, and instructional skills to produce knowledgeable and skilled individuals as their output. Hospitals use scientific equipment, professional skills, and tender loving care to transform sick people into well ones. Repair shops use repair parts, equipment, and worker skills to transform malfunctioning inputs into properly functioning outputs. All types of operations, then, transform inputs into outputs.

When the output is a tangible product, the transformations performed by the operations function are intended to increase the utility of the inputs by changing either the physical form of the inputs or the time or place at which

FIGURE 1.2

Conceptual Diagram of a Production System

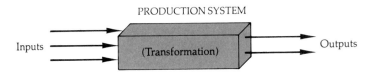

the outputs are available. Operations that change the physical form of the inputs include factories, landscapers, restaurants, upholstery shops, ice cream shops, and laundries. Some operations provide special skills or convenience by providing services for customers. Operations such as wholesalers, retailers, transporters, and the postal system provide materials-handling operations to change the place at which the output is made available. Banks, public warehouses, and cold storage plants for food or fur storage perform an inventory function to make the output available at a different time. Even though the inputs, transformations, and outputs may vary, the general characteristic of transformation of inputs into more usable outputs holds true for all operations.

Operations Are of Many Types

Operations can be classified according to several schemes, such as whether they are part of for-profit or not-for-profit businesses. Operations are sometimes classified according to the particular industry in which their product falls—such as the steel industry, the chemical industry, or the health-care industry. Our studies will not go into the detailed management problems that are peculiar to one particular industry or type of product. We will focus on more general operations management issues that exist in various types of companies. Operations will be subdivided into several categories to show the breadth of types of operations and because some of the issues and methods of dealing with these issues are more consistent within the subdivisions.

A distinction has already been made between manufacturing and non-manufacturing operations. Let us first discuss some of the differences within the category of manufacturing operations.

Manufacturing Operations

The type of production facility and production methods that a manufacturing company uses are sometimes referred to as its production system. The production system that a company finds most appropriate is frequently related to the way in which the company conducts its business. More specifically, it is related to the stage at which the company plans to hold inventory so it can serve its customers more quickly than the full lead time required to purchase all of the materials and convert them into the final product. At the time a customer's order is received, the items used to fill that order might intentionally be (1) held as finished goods, (2) held as standard modules waiting to be assembled, or (3) held or ordered as basic inputs without any processing performed on them. The terms presented in the following paragraph are used to characterize the degree of processing that is done after the customer's order is received.

Some companies are *make-to-stock producers,* that is, they make items that are completed and placed in stock prior to receipt of the customer's order. The end item is shipped "off the shelf" from finished-goods inventory after receipt of a customer order. In contrast, some companies make to order. In the case of a *make-to-order producer* the end item is completed after receipt of the customer's order for the item. If the item is fully a unique, custom-designed item, the customer will probably have to wait for many of the materials to be purchased and for the production work to be performed, because the producer cannot anticipate what each customer might want and have the necessary raw materials and components on hand to shorten the production lead time. If some components or materials are frequently used by the business, however, the producer might keep some of them in stock—particularly if the lead time to purchase or produce these items is long. When the company produces standard-design, optional modules ahead of time and assembles a particular combination of these modules after the customer orders it, the business is said to be an *assemble-to-order producer*.[2] An example of an assemble-to-order producer is an automobile factory that, in response to a dealer's order, provides an automatic or manual transmission, air conditioner, sound system, interior options, and specific engine options as well as the specified body style and color. Many of the components would already have been ordered or started into production when the dealer placed the order. Otherwise the lead time to deliver the automobile would be much longer. With these terms in mind, we will now discuss the two major categories of production facilities and methods.

Continuous Production   A *continuous production* system is one in which the equipment and work stations are arranged in a sequence according to the steps used to convert the input raw materials into the desired component or assembly. The routings of jobs are fixed, and the setup of the equipment is seldom changed from one product to another. The flow of materials is relatively continuous during the production process. This type of production is sometimes called *repetitive manufacturing*—which is high-volume production of discrete units, usually with a fixed sequence of material flow. Since the material flow path and processing steps are fixed, this type of production is frequently used with standard products that are make-to-stock items. Examples are production lines or assembly lines for the production of radios, televisions, refrigerators, or other products that may be produced and stocked in perhaps a few standard models. The customer selects the particular standard model he or she wants. Continuous production might be used for items that are made to order or assembled to order if the volume is sufficient to justify having a fixed, special-purpose production system for the items. Supplement A, at the end of this chapter, provides an overview of the operations that occur in one continuous production factory.

Some continuous production operations produce a product that blends together in bulk rather than being in discrete units. Some products of this type of operation include petroleum products, flour, cement, and liquid chemicals. The industries that produce these types of products are sometimes called *process industries*, particularly if some physical or chemical reaction is used. (Chemical processing can also occur with batches of material, and this is sometimes called batch-process production.)

[2]Terms from *APICS Dictionary*, 5th ed. Thomas F. Wallace (Falls Church, Va.: American Production and Inventory Control Society, 1984).

Intermittent Production or Job Shop   An *intermittent production* system or *job shop* differs greatly from the continuous system, in that it is designed to provide much more flexibility. This type of production system is one in which the production equipment or work stations are grouped and organized according to the function or process they perform. Different types of products flow in batches corresponding to individual orders. Each batch or lot might have a different routing through the functional work centers, depending on the requirements of the type of product being made. Products could be made for stock or to order, but generally this type of production is associated with make-to-order businesses.

Continuous and intermittent production systems are points near opposite ends of a continuum representing the degree of specificity of the production system (see Figure 1.3). At one end of the continuum are production facilities designed specifically to produce one particular standard item and optimized for the materials movement and production steps required to make that item. Near the other end of the continuum are job shops; they are not ideal for any single product but are capable of producing a wide variety of items. Many production facilities embody features of both of these production approaches. That is, they lie somewhere on the continuum between a job shop and continuous production. We will discuss some hybrid production facilities in Chapter 13, where we discuss facility arrangement in greater detail.

Lying at the flexibility end of the continuum is the low-volume type of operation often referred to as a *project*. Usually, projects are of relatively long duration, and the same personnel often are assigned to a project for a significant part of this time. In the manufacturing category, projects include such items as ships, bridges, buildings, and large, special machines.

Nonmanufacturing Operations

Nonmanufacturing operations—also known as *service operations*—are operations that do not produce tangible outputs. Like manufacturing operations, nonmanufacturing operations can be subdivided according to the degree of standardization of their outputs—that is, whether they are *standard services* or *custom services*—and/or the processes they perform. Some nonmanufacturing activities might be thought of as projects because they involve the activities of a team of people over a period of time. In the nonmanufacturing category, a project might be a software package or a training program. Table 1.1 displays a classification

FIGURE 1.3

Degree of Specificity of Production Systems

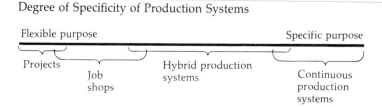

Table 1.1
CLASSIFICATION OF TYPES OF OPERATIONS

Types of Operations	Manufacturing, or Goods-Producing, Operations	Nonmanufacturing, or Non-Goods-Producing, Operations
Project: activities of long duration and low volume	Building a bridge, dam, house, preparing for a banquet	Research projects, development of software
Unit or batch: activities of short duration and low volume, producing custom goods or services	Job shop: making industrial hardware; printing personalized stationery; making drapes	Custom service: offering charter air or bus service; cleaning carpets; repairing autos; providing health care or counseling services; providing hair care; translating a foreign-language book for a publisher; designing costumes for a theatrical production; public warehousing; providing special delivery mail service
Mass production: activities of short duration and high volume, producing standard goods or services	Continuous operation: making light bulbs, refrigerators, television sets, automobiles	Standard service: providing fast food, standard insurance policies, scheduled air or bus service, dry cleaning, personal checking accounts, regular mail service, distribution and wholesaling of standardized products, processing photographic film
Process industries: continuous processing of a homogeneous material	Continuous operation: processing chemicals, refining oil, milling flour, manufacturing paper	

system for manufacturing and nonmanufacturing operations based on the degree of standardization of their output.

Nonmanufacturing operations can be divided into catetories according to another classification scheme that provides useful insights into the management issues they face. Some nonmanufacturing operations deal primarily with tangible outputs, even though these operations do not manufacture the items. These types of operations include wholesale distributors and transportation companies, and they can utilize many of the materials management principles and techniques that a manufacturing operation might use. The ideas of materials handling are also important in some operations that deal with tangible items.

Other nonmanufacturing operations deal in intangible products, or services, as their primary outputs. We will call these *service operations,* but one should recognize that an operation does not necessarily provide *only* services or *only* goods. Facilitating goods may be provided with services and facilitating services may be provided with goods. For example, we can obtain the same goods (although in a different form) from a grocery store or from a restaurant. We think of a grocery store as primarily providing goods. We trade with a restaurant primarily for the services it provides in selecting, preparing, and serving food, which is actually a tangible good. When we have a car "serviced," the process may include the installation of some parts. The service is provided by someone who knows which parts to replace and how to replace them and who spends the time to perform this service.

Operations that deal primarily in services can be further divided according to the degree to which the customer is a participant in the process. Many services are custom services, so the customer often has some contact with the service provider. The customer, however, does not have to be present during the process for some types of service, such as having clothes laundered or a watch repaired. Professor Richard Chase states that systems with a greater percentage of customer contact are more difficult to rationalize and control.[3] Table 1.2 displays a

[3]Richard B. Chase, "Where Does the Customer Fit in a Service Operation?" *Harvard Business Review,* November–December, 1978, p. 138.

Table 1.2
A CLASSIFICATION OF NONMANUFACTURING OPERATIONS

NONMANUFACTURING (NON-GOODS-PRODUCING) OPERATIONS

Providers of Tangible Products	Providers of Services	
Mail service	Services in which the customer is not a participant.	Services in which the customer is a participant.
Library service	Examples:	Examples:
Wholesale and retail distributors	Preparing tax forms	Health care
Examples:	Architectural design	Hair care
Television sets	Landscaping	Travel
Radios	Cleaning clothes	Legal advice
Watches	Repairing watches, automobiles, appliances, etc.	Financial advice
Refrigerators	Rating and issuing insurance	Marriage counseling
Air conditioners		

classification of nonmanufacturing operations, with some examples of each type of operation.

Dan Thomas provides a useful breakdown of service operations according to whether they are equipment- or people-based. His spectrum of service businesses is shown in Figure 1.4.[4]

The Challenges of Service Operations

Each type of operation has its unique characteristics. When they are viewed in sufficient detail, the problems of any operations system are found to be unique and dynamic, that is, changing through time. Detailed operations of any type are so perplexing that several books could be and possibly have been written about them.

Even at a general level, however, four differences between manufacturing and service operations can be recognized:

1. Productivity generally is more easily measured in manufacturing operations than in service operations because the former provides tangible products, whereas the products of service operations are generally intangible. A factory that produces automobile tires can readily count the number of tires that were produced in a day. Repair service operations may repair or replace portions of a tangible product, but their major service is the application of knowledge and skilled labor. Advisory services may provide only spoken words, an entirely intangible product and very difficult to measure.

2. Quality standards are more difficult to establish and product quality is more difficult to evaluate in service operations. This difference is directly related to the previous one. Intangible products are more difficult to evaluate because they cannot be held, weighed, or measured. We can evaluate a repair to a tangible product by comparing the product's performance after the repair with its performance before the repair. It is more difficult to know the worth of such a service as legal defense. No one knows for certain how the judge would have ruled had the attorney performed in some different manner.

3. Persons who provide services generally have contact with customers, whereas persons who perform manufacturing operations seldom see the consumer of the product. The marketing and customer relations aspects of a service often overlap the operations function. The doctor–patient relationship, for example, is often considered to be a very important component of the physician's services. In the service of hair care, the hairdresser–patron contact is necessary. The impact of discourteous salespersons or restaurant employees is of great concern in many establishments.

4. Manufacturing operations can accumulate or decrease inventory of finished products, particularly in standard product, continuous production operations. A barber, in contrast, cannot store up haircuts during slack times so that he or she can provide service at an extremely high rate during peak demand time. Providers of services often try to overcome this limi-

[4]Dan R. E. Thomas, "Strategy Is Different in Service Businesses," *Harvard Business Review*, July–August 1978, p. 161.

FIGURE 1.4

A Spectrum of Types of Service Businesses

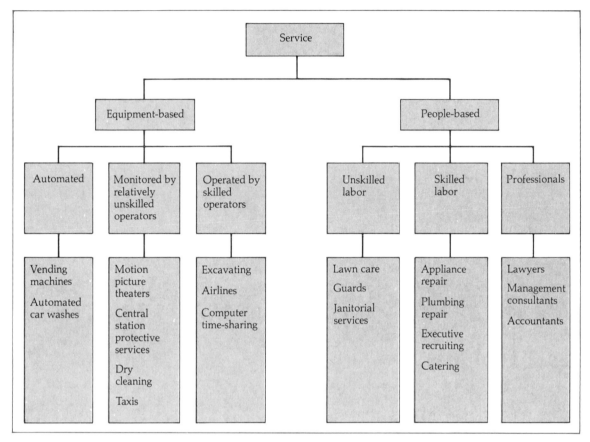

tation by leveling out the demand process. Telephone systems, for example, offer discount rates during certain hours to encourage a shift in the timing of calls that can be delayed.

There are several other general differences between manufacturing and nonmanufacturing operations. Generally, the proportion of expenses required for materials handling is smaller for nonmanufacturing than for manufacturing operations. Exceptions are such organizations as wholesale distributors and mail delivery services, which are primarily materials-handling operations. The transformation they perform is one of place rather than of physical form, so handling represents their major cost. Usually a manufacturing operation has a greater percentage of its assets invested in facilities, equipment, and inventory than a service organization. Since they have more equipment, manufacturing operations generally depend more heavily on maintenance and repair work. Health care institutions are probably an exception to this generality because of the importance that their equipment perform satisfactorily.

MANAGERS' ROLES IN OPERATIONS

Some companies have an executive with a title such as operations manager, production manager, vice-president of operations, or director of operations. In a sizable company, many persons serve in managerial roles within the operations function, even though they may not have one of these titles. Many managers, from the top executive to the foremen or supervisors of direct workers, play vital roles in planning the right things for operations to do and in seeing that these things are done well. These people include line managers and others in such activities as planning, quality control, scheduling, and maintenance. We will discuss some of the decisions and activities of these persons in a later section; but first we should mention some important skills that these persons should have.

Skills Needed by Operations Managers

In trying to work through others to accomplish the objectives of operations, managers must possess and employ a variety of skills. Two major categories of management skills are discussed below.

Technical Competence.   Since managers make decisions about the tasks that other people are to perform, they must understand two major aspects of an organization: They need a basic understanding of the technology with which the production system works, and they need adequate knowledge of the work they are to manage. *Technical competence* can be obtained through training and experience or through the use of staff specialists and consultants. Today's highly technical processes and the trend toward conglomerates have brought with them an increase in the use of staff organizations specializing in various aspects of operations.

Behavioral Competence.   Many group activities exist because people find that they can achieve more, both in work accomplished and in rewards achieved, by working as a group rather than by working alone. Humans generally are gregarious animals and fulfill some of their needs in social interaction. Management must therefore consider the social as well as the physical aspects of work and workers. Since managers work through others, their work necessarily involves a great deal of interpersonal contact. A good manager should have *behavioral competence*—the ability to work with other people.

Activities of Operations Managers to Support Company Success

Managers are responsible for seeing that their companies are successful. There are at least three basic requirements for a successful company:

1. It must provide a product (goods or services) that is suited to the company's capabilities and for which there is a sufficient market.
2. It must provide the product with consistent quality at a level that appeals to intended customers and serves their needs.
3. It must provide the product at a cost that allows an adequate profit and a reasonable sales price.

The operations function plays a major role in accomplishing all three of the requirements listed above. Higher-level operations managers must ensure that company objectives are consistent with operations capabilities and that the appropriate strengths are developed within operations to be consistent with broad, companywide strategy. Since the operations function produces the goods or services, it is largely responsible for the level of quality. The operations function also has a great effect on costs, since in many companies it uses the greatest portion of the company's resources.

Quality and *productivity* are two factors that are frequently featured in newspaper articles on the challenges facing American companies in today's international market. Peter Drucker has stated that "making resources productive is the specific task of management."[5] This idea of productivity is broader than just achieving the highest output per worker hour. It means balancing all factors of production so that the greatest output is achieved for a given total input of all resources. Achievement of high quality relates very closely to productivity. Making defective items that have to be remade definitely is not a productive use of resources. Making inferior products that no one will buy is also a waste of resources. In fact it can waste the entire company. The central theme throughout this book is how to make resources productive—that is, how to plan and control the use of resources to achieve their wisest use in accomplishing company objectives.

A survey of operations managers in manufacturing and nonmanufacturing operations in Canada and the United States supports the importance of quality and the productive use of resources. These managers were asked to rank 25 activities in terms of the amount of their time required by the activities and how important the activities were to their company's success. The three activities that most consistently appeared at the top were personnel relations, quality control, and cost control. These findings might be summarized by saying that it is important to keep qualified and motivated employees working to provide quality goods or services at a cost that will be competitive and provide a reasonable profit. Many decisions and actions must be performed by managers to achieve these objectives.

Often the decisions and activities of managers are grouped into major categories referred to as the functions of managers. Some of the functions of managers, which are often presented in introductory management courses, are listed in Table 1.3. Presented below each major function or category are several of the decisions or activities that managers in operations might perform in dis-

---

[5]Peter F. Drucker, *Managing in Turbulent Times* (New York: Harper & Row, 1980), p. 14.

Table 1.3
**DECISIONS AND ACTIVITIES OF MANAGERS
IN OPERATIONS (GROUPED ACCORDING
TO FAMILIAR MANAGEMENT FUNCTIONS)**

Planning

Establish the mix of products or services
Set the master schedule of what products to make when
Plan the capacities of plants and work centers
Plan the locations of facilities
Arrange facilities and equipment
Decide how many shifts and work hours
Establish improvement projects or other projects
Decide what production methods to use for each item
Organize changes to new processes or procedures
Plan acquisitions of equipment

Organizing

Centralize or decentralize operations
Organize by functions, products, or hybrid
Establish work center assignments
Assign responsibility for every activity
Arrange supplier and subcontractor networks
Establish maintenance policies

Controlling

Encourage pride in performing as expected
Compare costs to budgets
Compare actual labor hours to standards
Inspect quality levels
Compare work progress to schedule
Compare inventory level to targets

Directing

Establish provisions of union contracts
Establish personnel policies
Establish employment contracts
Issue job assignments and instructions
Issue routings and move tickets
Issue dispatch lists

Motivating

Challenge through leadership examples, specific objectives and expectations
Encourage through praise, recognition, and other intangibles
Motivate through tangible reward system
Motivate through enriched jobs and challenging assignments

Coordinating

Coordinate through use of common forecasts and master schedules
Coordinate through common, standardized data bases
Observe actual performance and recommend needed performance
Report, inform, communicate
Coordinate purchases, deliveries, design changes, maintenance activities, tooling
Respond to customer inquiries about status of orders

Training and Developing Personnel

Show a better way
Encourage employees to seek a better way
Give more advanced job assignments
Support employees in training programs

charging the specific management function. The table provides some information about the types of decisions and activities that are discussed in this book. Table 1.3 also relates the activities that we will be discussing to the functions of management with which you may already be familiar.

OVERVIEW OF THE BOOK AND ISSUES DISCUSSED

Figure 1.5 provides an overview of the structure of this book and of the types of issues we will be discussing. This information, intended as an alternative to

FIGURE 1.5

Types of Issues Discussed in the Book

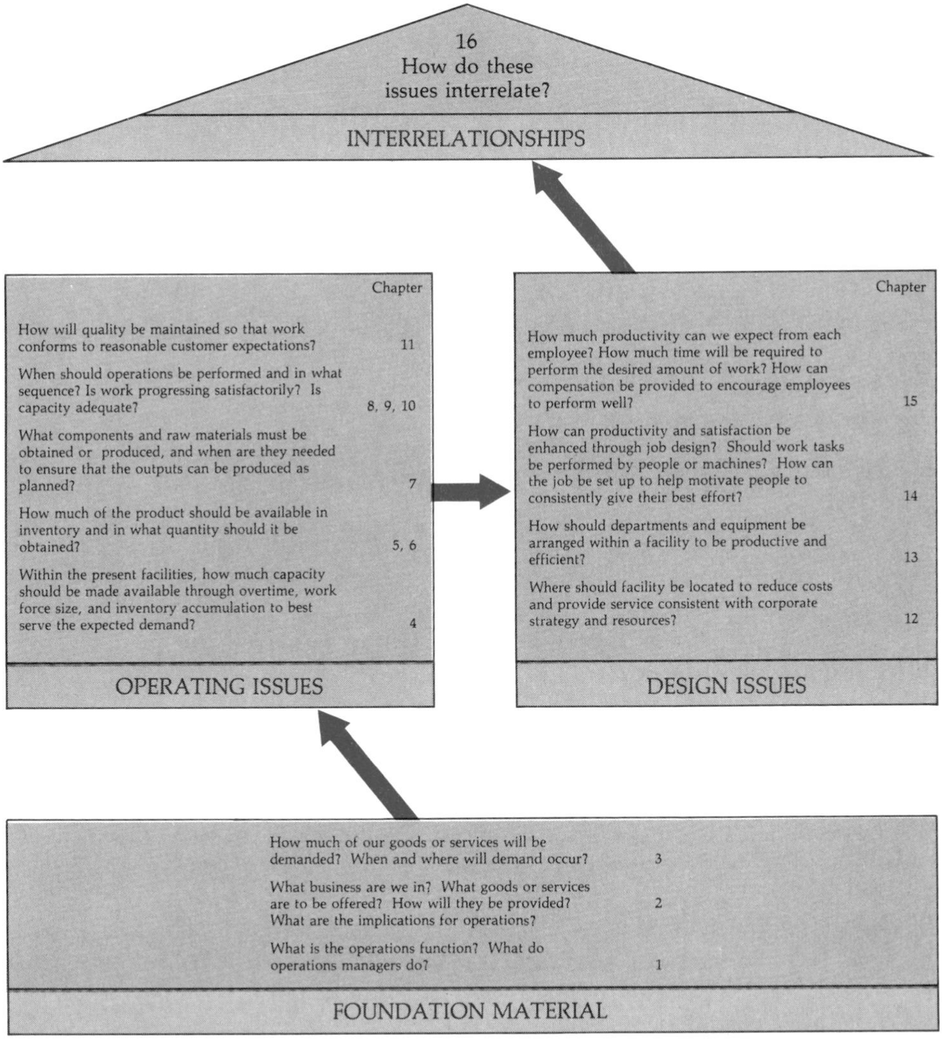

16
How do these
issues interrelate?

INTERRELATIONSHIPS

	Chapter
How will quality be maintained so that work conforms to reasonable customer expectations?	11
When should operations be performed and in what sequence? Is work progressing satisfactorily? Is capacity adequate?	8, 9, 10
What components and raw materials must be obtained or produced, and when are they needed to ensure that the outputs can be produced as planned?	7
How much of the product should be available in inventory and in what quantity should it be obtained?	5, 6
Within the present facilities, how much capacity should be made available through overtime, work force size, and inventory accumulation to best serve the expected demand?	4

OPERATING ISSUES

	Chapter
How much productivity can we expect from each employee? How much time will be required to perform the desired amount of work? How can compensation be provided to encourage employees to perform well?	15
How can productivity and satisfaction be enhanced through job design? Should work tasks be performed by people or machines? How can the job be set up to help motivate people to consistently give their best effort?	14
How should departments and equipment be arranged within a facility to be productive and efficient?	13
Where should facility be located to reduce costs and provide service consistent with corporate strategy and resources?	12

DESIGN ISSUES

How much of our goods or services will be demanded? When and where will demand occur?	3
What business are we in? What goods or services are to be offered? How will they be provided? What are the implications for operations?	2
What is the operations function? What do operations managers do?	1

FOUNDATION MATERIAL

the table of contents, provides the reader with a schematic representation of the book.

The book is divided into three major sections, each of which is represented by a rectangular block in the figure. One or more questions relating to the types of issues addressed in each chapter are presented to show the type of issues discussed in the chapter.

The lower block, titled "Foundation Material," refers to the material in Part I (the first three chapters), which deals with general background material. Forecasting the demand, the subject of Chapter 3, is the basis for the two major categories of decisions that constitute the other two parts of the book.

The first major category—operating issues—comprises issues that relate to the short or intermediate lead time decisions in a currently existing operations system. Operating issues are discussed in Part II. We discuss operating issues ahead of design issues because that is consistent with the career pattern of the majority of persons who study an introductory operations text. That is, most readers already work for or will go to work for ongoing businesses and will deal with operating issues first and most often.

Part III of the book discusses issues that primarily relate to the design of an operations system. These types of issues usually involve longer lead time decisions and are made less often. They are nevertheless important decisions for operations, and several chapters are devoted to this material. Some people prefer to approach these two categories of issues in a sequence consistent with the life of a production facility, that is, they prefer to discuss design-related issues before operating issues. The material in Part III can be read before the material in Part II without any loss of understanding.

The final chapter, Chapter 16, is a brief discussion of some interrelationships between the various subjects that have been presented in the book.

SUMMARY

This chapter has introduced a variety of topics. The initial discussion pointed out the primary functions and some secondary functions that take place within organizations. All of these functions depend on one another for effective performance of the organization's activities.

The operations function was discussed in detail to indicate the similarities of operations in manufacturing and nonmanufacturing organizations. Four general differences between manufacturing and service operations were mentioned: Manufacturing operations can better measure productivity, can better measure quality, have less contact with the consumer, and can use finished goods inventory to smooth their work loads.

Operations managers, like other managers, work through others to establish and achieve the objectives of their organizational units. Important activities of managers include planning, organizing, directing, motivating, coordinating, and controlling activities plus training and developing subordinates. To be successful in these activities a manager should possess both technical and behavioral skills. Operations managers must apply these skills to achieve productivity and quality while providing goods or services on time.

DISCUSSION QUESTIONS

1. What are the three primary functions that must be performed in all organizations? Define each one and explain how they are interrelated.
2. Define *continuous production* and *job shop*. How are the two terms related?
3. Define *standardized* and *custom service* as they relate to service operations. In what ways are these two types of service operations similar to continuous production and job shop manufacturing operations?
4. List and briefly describe the four major differences between manufacturing operations and service operations.
5. Find a recent magazine or newspaper article that discusses one or more of the problems currently facing manufacturing operations today. What is being done about the problem? Be prepared to discuss the problem(s) and attempted solution(s) in class.
6. Briefly describe some of the ways you have observed in which nonmanufacturing operations are trying to improve productivity.
7. Why are quality and productivity generally more difficult to measure in service operations as compared to manufacturing?
8. What are two major goals operations managers must achieve in the operations function in order to keep their companies competitive?
9. What is the central theme of the book?

BIBLIOGRAPHY

Buffa, Elwood A. *Meeting the Competitive Challenge.* Homewood, Ill.: Irwin, 1984.

Drucker, Peter F. *Managing in Turbulent Times.* New York: Harper & Row, 1980.

Fitzsimmons, James A., and Robert S. Sullivan. *Service Operations Management.* New York: McGraw-Hill, 1982.

Levitt, Theodore. "Production Line Approach to Service." *Harvard Business Review,* September–October 1972, pp. 41–52.

Sasser, W. Earl, R. Paul Olsen, and D. Daryl Wyckoff, *Management of Service Operations: Text, Cases and Readings.* Boston: Allyn and Bacon, 1978.

Supplement A Outline
TOUR OF A CONTINUOUS PRODUCTION PLANT: NISSAN MOTOR MANUFACTURING CORP., U.S.A.

SCHEDULING

SUPPLIERS AND MATERIAL MANAGEMENT

STAGES OF FABRICATION

Frame Production / Sheet Metal Stamping / Cab and Bed Buildup / Painting / Assembly / Testing

QUALITY

TOUR OF A CONTINUOUS PRODUCTION PLANT: NISSAN MOTOR MANUFACTURING CORP., U.S.A.

Nissan Motor Manufacturing Corporation U.S.A. stands on some 782 acres near Smyrna, Tennessee, that as late as February of 1981 were used as grazing land for cattle. By June of 1983, 78 of those acres were covered by one of the most modern automotive factories in the world—combining the management approaches and production technology of both Japan and the United States. The total investment for this facility stands at about $660 million. Originally, the plant's sole product was seven models of light trucks, and in October 1984, the company celebrated production of its 100,000th truck. In early 1985, with an employment level of about 2,000 persons, the plant began production of Sentra model automobiles in addition to light trucks. Employment is expected to increase to 3,000 as Sentra automobile production is scaled up and a second shift is added during 1985.

The plant is shaped like a giant E, with the long edge of the E being about three-quarters of a mile long and each of the three extensions from it being about one-quarter of a mile long. Approximately seventeen miles of conveyors move parts through the plant, some at

FIGURE A.1

General Layout—Nissan

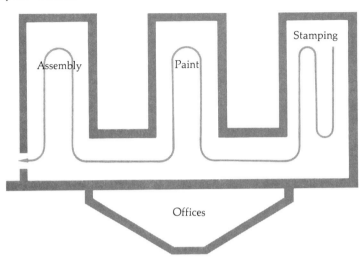

floor level, some overhead, and a small amount below the floor. The overall factory is divided into three major plants: the body, frame, and stamping plant; the paint plant; and the trim and chassis plant. We will discuss the work in these plants in the order they were mentioned, along with other information related to the overall operation of the plant.

SCHEDULING

Output of the plant is purchased by Nissan Motor Corporation U.S.A., headquartered in California, which is responsible for distributing the product and supplying dealers. The sales organization forecasts demand and provides the plant with information about its requirements for a planning horizon of three months into the future. The plant uses this information as a basis for planning procurement and for scheduling production.

A great deal of information processing is required to coordinate operations in such a vast facility. The plant makes extensive use of au-

tomation and robots, many of which have small computers or microprocessors to control their movements. Other computers are located in various zones of the factory to communicate with the process controllers and to coordinate conveyor speeds and processing equipment in various portions of the plant. A central control computer schedules and coordinates operation of the three major sections of the plant by communicating with the computers in various parts of the factory. In addition, coordination with the plant's suppliers is given high importance.

SUPPLIERS AND MATERIAL MANAGEMENT

The plant site is serviced by both rail and truck transportation. The plant is supplied with major components—such as major frame parts, engines, and transmissions—from factories in Japan. But many components are supplied from domestic manufacturers, some of which are located within a thirty-minute drive of the plant. The plant receives frequent shipments from some of its suppliers, as often as every two hours in some cases. Nissan strives to keep a close working relationship with such suppliers and makes its production schedule available to them so the supplier can develop accurate plans and can better coordinate their plans with Nissan's requirements. For example, about every two hours, seats are delivered to the plant from a nearby vendor. The seats are received in carts that can be towed to the work station where seats are installed. The vendor has the seats stacked in the carts so they can be removed in the order called for in the assembly schedule for that portion of the day.

STAGES OF FABRICATION

Frame Production

Let us trace the build-up of a light truck as it proceeds through the facility. Basic fabrication begins with production of a vehicle's frame in the body, frame, and stamping plant. Here, there are two conveyor lines, one to produce frames for four-wheel-drive trucks and one to produce frames for two-wheel-drive trucks. Each frame line can produce options, such as long- or short-wheelbase frames. The right and left frame sides are automatically loaded onto the conveyor in response to a command from the frame-line coordinating computer, which calls for production of the type of frame that has just been withdrawn from the stock of frames in the overhead at the end of the frame line. The side rails are fed to a work station, where workers place and tack weld the frame cross members between the side rails. The frame is then conveyed to the next station on the frame production line, where a fixture holds it in the correct shape while a battery of robots weld the seams more solidly to form a rigid frame. At a final stage, workers inspect the robots' work and weld on a few brackets that would have been in the robots' way if the brackets had been attached earlier. The frames are then shipped to the paint plant.

Sheet Metal Stamping

Large coils of sheet steel, weighing up to 20 tons, arrive at the plant by rail and by truck. A coil of the appropriate thickness and width is fed through a set of rollers to level it as it is uncoiled and fed into a blanking press that cuts the metal into the proper size sheets for each part that is to be made. These sheets are then fed into a large press that holds the metal around the outside edges between a protruding die half and a cavity die half, each shaped like the part to be made. The upper die half, or punch, comes down with great pressure. The drawing action caused by this die pressure makes the sheet of metal take on the desired shape, which is built into the die—such as the shape of a hood, door, fender, roof, half of the bed, etc. Sometimes the metal sheet is fed through a series of a half-dozen or so presses to form the final shape and to trim off the metal around the edges. The resulting parts are inspected and conveyed to a hold area, where they are held until they are used in assembly.

Cab and Bed Buildup

Several major subassemblies are made from stamped parts before they are all assembled into a truck. Numerous large stamped parts and even more small parts and brackets are spot welded together to form these subassemblies and to unite the subassemblies into a truck cab and bed. Spot welding involves clamping two overlapping sheets of metal between two protruding electrodes, about a quarter inch in diameter, and running a heavy electrical current between the electrodes. The sheets of metal are quickly heated to a red glow, mashed together, and released. This process welds the two pieces of metal together at the spot where the electrodes pinched; but the electrodes are cooled so they do not get hot enough to stick to the metal. Most of the parts handling is automated, and almost all of the spot welding is performed by robots.

Many of the subassemblies are made at work stations beside the production line on which the cab is built. One station makes right doors by assembling an inner panel, outer panel, and window frame. Another station makes left doors, and another makes hood subassemblies. A major body subassembly that is not normally observable is the engine compartment, composed of two inner fenders on the sides, the radiator support on the front, and the dash panel (the sloping part of the floorboard where one's feet are placed) at the back. At the first station on the cab production line, the engine compartment is welded to a long or short cab floor—depending on whether it will form a standard-size or a "king cab." The cab floor is then transferred to the next station on the production line, where the cab back is welded to the floor. At the next station, the left and right cab halves, each of which has been assembled from several parts at a subassembly area, are added. Then a top is added—standard or sunroof—at the next work station. Hundreds of finishing spot-welds are added to strengthen the cab, then it is moved to the metal area. In the metal area, the doors, front fenders, and hood are added; then the seams are filled and the welds are ground smooth to prepare the completed cab for painting.

Truck beds are produced in short, long, and deluxe models. The bed is formed from a floor, a front, an inner and outer side panel on each side, and numerous small braces and brackets. The tailgate is added as the bed moves through the metal area. The bed and cab are not connected but will each be mounted on a frame in the assembly operation at the chassis line. The completed cabs and beds go into an overhead hold area to await painting.

Painting

The central control computer calls a matching combination of cab and bed out of the overhead to move through the paint plant so they can be assembled into a finished product. The paint plant is a long, winding series of conveyors, with numerous spray booths and dip tanks along the way. The frame moves along one line where it is dipped in a series of tanks to degrease, phosphate etch, and coat it with electro-deposited paint. The cab and bed move along another line and receive the same three initial treatments. The body and cab then receive chip-resistant primer paint along the front and sides, where pebbles or other objects might strike the paint. Any runs or specks are sanded smooth, then the cab and bed are primer painted all over. Vehicles are "blocked"--that is, grouped in several holding lines depending on the color they are to receive—so that three or more can be painted without changing the color of paint in the spray guns. The primer is sanded smooth, and the final color is applied. Metallic colors receive an additional clear coat over the color coat. Two-tone vehicles make a second pass through the paint booth for the second color. Most of the painting is performed by robots and rotary spray atomizers, which results in a more uniform coat of paint and more efficient paint application. More paint is deposited on the vehicles and less paint is lost into the air through these processes.

Assembly

After being painted, the frame, cab, and bed are transported by separate overhead conveyors to different zones in the trim and chassis plant, where they will eventually be reunited for final assembly. Vehicles are scheduled onto the assembly line in such a way that the sequence provides a relatively consistent level of work. For example, a unit with high work content—such as a four-wheel-drive truck with air conditioning—would be followed by a unit that requires much less work—such as a two-wheel-drive truck without air conditioning. A broadcast, or list of operations to be performed on each truck, is printed by the computer at nu-

Spot welding robots on the Cab Main Respot Line.

Painting robots.

Trim Line 2 in the Trim and Chassis Plant.

Electrostatic rotary spray atomizers painting truck.

Trucks coming off the Final Line.

Photos courtesy of Nissan Manufacturing Corp., U.S.A.

merous zones in the assembly area. This paper is taped to the vehicle part and moves with it down the assembly line to instruct technicians regarding what parts are to be installed on the vehicle or subassembly as it passes through the zone.

The frame starts down the assembly line where previously assembled front and rear axles are installed on the frame. Shock absorbers, brake lines, and (if required) a four-wheel-drive transfer case and front differential are installed. A spare tire is bolted on below where the truck bed will be. At the time that the spare tire is mounted, four other matching tire-and-wheel sets are mounted and balanced by a highly automated process and are sent into the assembly area on overhead conveyors. (Thus the spare is delivered here, but the other tires are delivered at a later station, where they will be installed on the truck.) The driveshaft, gas tank, engine, and transmission are attached to the frame. The bed, which has had the tail lights and wiring installed on it at an earlier station, is transported through the overhead, lowered onto the frame, and secured in place.

While work is progressing on the frame and bed, the cab is also receiving further assembly operations on another assembly line. First the wiring is installed; then the headliner, sunroof (if called for), sunvisors, and rear window; then the instrument panel (which has been assembled in a subassembly area); then the radiator and headlight units; then the windshield, door hardware, and steering column are installed. The electrical system is connected to a power source and tested. The cab is then transported by a "drop-lift" into the overhead and to the station where it is lowered onto the chassis. Four wheels and tires that match the spare are received from an overhead conveyor and are installed on the truck at the next station. The seats are installed, and then fluid reservoirs—such as the radiator and brake system—are filled and tested. The front wheels

are aligned, and the completed truck is then started and driven to a test area.

Testing

At the test area, the trucks are run with the wheels on rollers as the trucks are test "driven." The trucks are run in all gears to check the engine and transmission and handling. The front end alignment, steering wheel alignment, brake performance, emission certification, and turn angle are checked. The foot pedals, cigarette lighter, radio, gauges, and speedometer are also tested. The headlights are aligned, and the truck is driven to a water spray booth where it is tested for leaks. The final operation is to spray the bottom of the truck and the engine compartment with a sealant. Trucks that do not pass all tests are taken to an area where any problems are corrected. When trucks have passed all tests, they are checked and accepted by representatives of the sales company, then driven to a loading area to be transported to dealer locations throughout the country.

QUALITY

Quality is encouraged at all stages of the operation. Only a small percentage of employees hold jobs as inspectors. All employees are extensively trained in their jobs and are told that they are responsible for the quality of their work. Workers who spot a problem can stop the operation, and people then immediately begin trying to solve the problem. Employees and their supervisors meet each morning to discuss the day's work, any problems they had the day before, and how they are going to accomplish the day's assignment. Some groups also have longer meetings once a week, as involvement circles, to identify problems and work together to solve them. Four completed vehicles are randomly selected each day, thoroughly inspected and parked in a display area that many employees pass. Employees can see the vehicles and their quality scorecards, to note any problems that were detected. All employees seem to have an interest in the VES, vehicle evaluation score, and work to keep a good score. This rapid feedback keeps all parts of the team informed about how well they are performing.

Supplement B Outline
TOUR OF AN INTERMITTENT PRODUCTION PLANT: TELEDYNE BROWN ENGINEERING FABRICATION AND ASSEMBLY PLANT I

COMPANY PRODUCTS

INDIVIDUALIZED JOB PLANNING

MATERIALS HANDLING

GENERAL PURPOSE EQUIPMENT

TOUR OF AN INTERMITTENT PRODUCTION PLANT: TELEDYNE BROWN ENGINEERING FABRICATION AND ASSEMBLY PLANT I

Most people are familiar with standardized manufactured items that are made in high volume—examples are televisions, refrigerators, and bicycles, in addition to automobiles. When we are in the market for a particular item of this type, we decide whether we want to buy the item and often we are able to select a particular set of standard-design options that we want with the product. The Nissan plant is an excellent example of a facility producing this type of product. However, needs exist also for manufactured goods that are not standard items and that are needed in only small volume. Facilities that are used to make these types of

products require versatile equipment and plant arrangements, and they need people who can perform a variety of tasks in the course of a week's work. Teledyne Brown Engineering provides an outstanding example of such an operation.

Teledyne Brown Engineering (TBE) has a job shop manufacturing operation that produces small-volume, unique items for aerospace companies and government agencies, primarily in support of the U.S. space program. TBE's predecessor was moved to Huntsville, Alabama, in the early 1950s to provide manufacturing support for the fledgling rocket and space program, which was being developed around a group of German space scientists and engineers that the U.S. government had located there. The company grew as the National Aeronautics and Space Administration (NASA) developed programs at the nearby Marshall Space Flight Center and as other space efforts advanced, with TBE performing such work as research and engineering support in addition to manufacturing. During the 1960s, TBE employed several hundred persons in manufacturing, many of whom worked in support of the manned lunar landing. A number of subsidiaries or separate companies have been spawned from this manufacturing operation. The original manufacturing operation, now called Fabrication and Assembly Plant 1, has about 60 employees involved in mechanical manufacturing. Another part of the company also produces custom electronic components and systems that may be used separately or may sometimes be incorporated into systems produced in mechanical manufacturing.

COMPANY PRODUCTS

The company bids on "design-and-build" work and prototype production from other designs; therefore the volume is low. Many of the products are flight hardware, launch support equipment, and handling equipment for space items. NASA and the U.S. Air Force are two major customers. Work comes to the manufacturing operation as a set of blueprints and specifications prepared by TBE's engineers or those from other companies. For some jobs, the company submits a fixed-price bid for the work. Design-and-build work may be done on a cost-plus-fixed-fee basis, because it is difficult to estimate the cost to produce something that has not yet been fully designed. The hourly rate is bid, and the hours may be audited to see that they were actually spent on the authorized project. Some products may be unusual shapes that are complex to produce, particularly for flight items. To lighten these items, any unnecessary material is removed from the

FIGURE B.1

General Layout—TBE

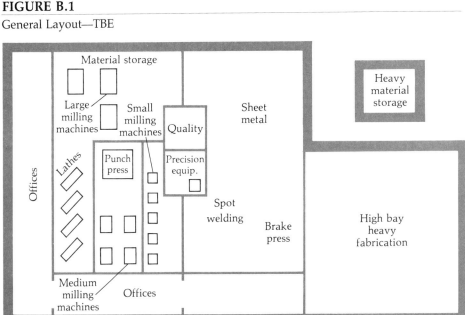

places where stress is low. Some parts, such as a telescope mount, are very delicate and require close-tolerance work, i.e., the size must be within a few thousandths of an inch, or less, of the desired dimensions. Other parts may be large structural members that are machined from a block of aluminum originally weighing almost a ton; the material is machined away until only the final item, weighing about 120 pounds, is left. A few representative products are shown in Figure B.2.

INDIVIDUALIZED JOB PLANNING

The set of blueprints for a job is studied by a planner, who determines the sequence of operations required to convert a standard available mill shape, a special ingot, or a special casting into the desired final product. These operations are specified on a route sheet to tell the shop what work to do. The route sheet, blueprint, and any special instructions accompany the material through the shop to instruct workers about what work is to be done at each location and where the part should next be moved. Work that is performed in support of design often has several engineering change orders (ECOs) during fabrication. That is, the design is changed before the part is completed. This condition makes it difficult to plan the amount of work to be done in a particular week or to schedule a definite completion date for some jobs.

Although the space industry is relatively young, changing technology has had an effect on TBE's manufacturing operations and on other parts of the business as well. For instance, ten or more years ago, a large portion of the mechanical manufacturing work was in fabricating sheet metal into chassis, control panels, and cabinets to hold electronic devices. But microminiaturization has advanced to the point where a function previously performed by equipment housed in three large cabinets can now be performed by a few chips con-

tained in a device that can be held in one's hand. Today, a small portion of TBE's business involves electronic cabinets or other sheet metal work. In an enterprise such as this, it is important that the company have versatile equipment and personnel so that most of the required operations can be performed and so that the company can adapt to the requirements of its market.

MATERIALS HANDLING

There is no need for automatic material movement between operations because the produc-

Photos courtesy of Teledyne Brown Engineering

FIGURE B.2

TBE Products

tion volume is so low that little movement is required and because there is no set path through which items move. Small parts can be carried by hand, and some larger parts can be rolled manually on wheeled carts. Occasionally a crane or forklift may be required to move large parts in the machine shop. Heavy fabrication and structural steel weldments often must be moved with a forklift and an overhead crane, which are available in the heavy fabrication area.

GENERAL PURPOSE EQUIPMENT

A wide variety of operations can be performed at various locations in the plant. The equipment must be of adequate size and must work to sufficiently close tolerances to perform to various levels of required accuracy. Operations might consist of drilling, tapping (cutting threads in a hole into which a bolt can then be screwed), milling a flat surface, turning a cylindrical shape, shearing or bending flat sheets of metal, bending material to various angles, welding machined or formed parts into more complex shapes, and assembling parts or subassemblies into custom items or major subassemblies. Each section of the plant is equipped and staffed to perform a particular type of

FIGURE B.4

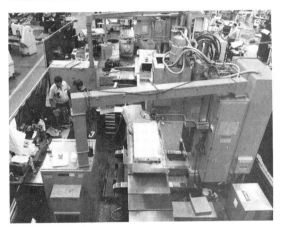

FIGURE B.5

FIGURE B.3

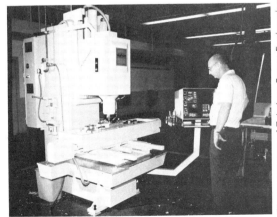

FIGURE B.6

operation. Figure B.3 shows small milling machines equipped with optical measuring devices to locate the workpiece accurately. Figure B.4 shows a group of lathes for turning cylinders so that the outer surface can be cut away to produce an object that has a round cross section. Figure B.5 shows larger milling machines with computer controls to locate the workpiece. With this type of machine, a parts programmer studies the blueprint and programs a few key coordinates and instructions concerning the size of the block of metal from which the part is to be made, the depth of each cut that is to be made in the metal, and the size cutter to be used. A computer develops the detailed instructions, which are then transferred to the machine. The machine's small computer then controls every movement of the machine. Some machines of this type have automatic tool changers, but they are primarily useful in higher-volume operations in which one operator tends multiple machines that are making identical parts. Figure B.6 shows a machine with a feature that is highly desirable in design-and-build and prototype work in which design changes are common. The machine has its own cathode ray tube (CRT), which shows the design it plans to build. The operator can rotate, enlarge, or modify the part's design at the machine. The production equipment then follows the design that has been established. This figure illustrates in one device a unique integration of computer-aided design (CAD) and computer-aided manufacturing (CAM).

You can see that the type of manufacturing business pursued by TBE requires a versatile plant arrangement and types of equipment that can accurately perform a variety of operations. Also important are skilled workers who can operate sophisticated equipment. All critical operations are carefully inspected to ensure that quality is controlled to meet the necessary standards.

KEY TERMS

Industrial Revolution
Division of labor or
    specialization

Mechanization
Interchangeable parts
Scientific management

Human relations era
Management science
Just-in-time production

Stockless production
Zero inventory

HISTORICAL BACKGROUND AND CURRENT PERSPECTIVES

Cooperative endeavors for production have probably existed as long as human beings, and operations management has existed equally long. Surprisingly, little or no theory of management was recorded until the eighteenth century. Before that time, productive activities were not complicated and involved relatively small groups, with a few notable exceptions. Ancient ruins provide evidence that the early Egyptians and Sumerians systematically organized and directed the efforts of many people in the production of goods. In Europe, the church, the military, and governments were the major administrative organizations before industrialization. These organizations used some of the concepts recognized today as management principles. For example, early military leaders coordinated large groups of people through a chain of command extending from the supreme commander to the front line leader.[1]

During the Middle Ages (fifth through fourteenth centuries) and the Renaissance (fourteenth through sixteenth centuries) the methods of production differed enormously from those of today. Workshops were small, as was the typical work force, which may have consisted of a craftsman and an apprentice or two. The craftsman was the equivalent of today's manager and could observe the entire work force during most of its activities. The tasks carried out by the employees involved relatively low levels of technology and hence were not complicated to direct. Verbal instruc-

[1]Theo Haimann and William G. Scott, *Management in the Modern Organization* (Boston: Houghton Mifflin, 1974), p. 19.

39

tions could be provided through direct face-to-face communication but probably were not often necessary. The apprentice could learn by observing the master craftsman.

The evolution of production from the small workshops of that era to the vast factories of today is often referred to as the *Industrial Revolution*. It is this movement that brought about the need for more formal and sophisticated methods of management. During the Renaissance such men as Galileo, Kepler, and Newton had helped to further the understanding of the principles of science and mechanics. The printing press had been developed and put to use so that the dissemination of knowledge was much broader than at any previous time. Master mechanics and skilled craftsmen working in small shops learned of useful new methods and materials. Many small inventions and improvements to existing inventions were made possible, and in turn gave birth to the machine age and the Industrial Revolution.

THE INDUSTRIAL REVOLUTION

The Industrial Revolution began in England in the late eighteenth century and spread to other parts of Europe and to the United States. In 1776, Adam Smith's *The Wealth of Nations* praised the advantages of *division of labor* or *specialization* (1) because the reduced scope of one person's operations allowed the worker to develop dexterity quickly, (2) because it saved time otherwise required to shift from one operation to another, and (3) because specialists were more likely to find or develop specialized mechanical devices to assist their operations. Smith early recognized the increased productivity offered by *mechanization,* or the use of machines.

It is significant that the development of the United States as a nation coincided with the development of the factory system of production. Smith's ideas on industry and division of labor were of interest to early American political leaders. Alexander Hamilton stressed the importance of establishing manufacturing in the newly founded nation.

THE FIRST U.S. FACTORY

During the years before the American Revolution, England had prohibited the export of such items as textile manufacturing machinery or plans from which such machines could be made. However, Samuel Slater, who served an apprenticeship in an English textile mill, came to the United States with the necessary plans for a mill stored in his phenomenal memory. In December 1790, near Providence, Rhode Island, Slater produced the first cotton yarn made automatically in America. The superiority of the process he introduced was recognized and was applied so rapidly that by the end of the War of 1812 there were 165 mills in Massachusetts, Connecticut, and Rhode Island alone.[2] The factory system flourished in New England and the American textile industry was well under way.

SPECIALIZED LABOR AND STANDARDIZED PARTS

In 1790 Eli Whitney made a phenomenal proposal: Within two years he would supply the army with 10,000 muskets at $13.40 each. He proposed to accomplish this feat by the use of specialized labor producing *interchangeable parts.* In order to fulfill the contract given him by the Congress, Whitney established a factory near New Haven, Connecticut. He had to improve the existing metalworking machines and develop new ones to achieve the required dimensional accuracy. Through these efforts,

[2]Edward C. Bursk, Donald T. Clark, and Ralph W. Hidy, *The World of Business* (New York: Simon & Schuster, 1962), vol. 2, p. 1085.

Whitney did much to establish America's metalworking industry.[3] Ironically, Whitney had earlier developed the cotton gin, the device that helped tie the South's economy to cotton and agriculture. His New Haven factory, by stimulating the industrial growth of the North, widened the gap between the interests of the North and the South and contributed to the industrial strength that enabled the North to win the resulting war.

THE FACTORY SYSTEM IN AMERICA

Conditions in America were well suited to the development and spread of the factory system. Capital was available to provide the investments necessary to form large production companies, and those who controlled the capital—wealthy merchants, bankers, and landowners—were willing to invest in business. The lack of tariff barriers between the new states and the development of canals and turnpikes facilitated mass marketing of mass-produced goods. Raw materials for the developing manufacturing system were abundant. The development of the steel plow and the reaper opened the Great Plains to agricultural production, and the factories that produced these and other machines provided jobs that enabled large numbers of people to live in industrial cities rather than being tied to the land for survival.

The early settlers of America were not, generally speaking, people who owned a great deal or had businesses in the old country. Most of them were relatively unskilled and were better suited to factory work than to craftwork. Since older economies, with an abundance of skilled craftsmen, had a lesser need for standardized, factory-made products and replacement parts, the growth of the factory system was less spectacular in Europe. The United States, however, had little in the way of an established production system to be supplanted by new methods, so the factory system became a basic part of the country almost from its beginning.

The spread of industry led to mass employment, which provided incomes that made mass consumption possible. Mass consumption provided the demand that enabled mass production to prosper. The improvement of agricultural techniques, which freed a large part of the work force from food production, was necessary for industrial growth. With abundant fertile land and industrial raw materials, the United States developed a balance of agriculture and industry.

THE NEED FOR NEW MANAGEMENT SKILLS

The Industrial Revolution was characterized by a shift of the production process to large factories, which was a significant departure from the small shops of earlier periods. Larger groups of people were employed, each working on only a small portion of the total product and having little contact with those who were making other parts of the same product. Specialization of labor brought about new requirements for management, since coordination was crucial and much more difficult to achieve. In view of this increased need for management skills, it is surprising that few management studies were produced.

The first hundred years of the Industrial Revolution were almost devoid of recorded management developments. It is likely that managers discussed common problems among themselves and improved their skills, but there were no management societies or journals to facilitate the exchange of ideas. In England in 1832, Charles Babbage wrote about some of his ideas on management, but he is more noted for developing a "difference engine" that was

[3]Mitchell Wilson, *American Science and Invention* (New York: Simon & Schuster, 1954), pp. 82–83.

a forerunner of today's computer.[4] It is significant that Babbage is associated with a mechanical device. During the first century of the Industrial Revolution much of the emphasis was on mechanization and the development of new tools and devices. Engineers played a prominent role in the industrial progress during that era, and the American Society of Mechanical Engineers became a forum for the exchange of ideas on both mechanical and management matters.

THE MANAGEMENT MOVEMENT

The second hundred years of the Industrial Revolution might be called the century of the management movement. In 1886, Henry R. Towne presented a classic paper, "The Engineer as an Economist," before the American Society of Mechanical Engineers (ASME). "The matter of shop management," he said, "is of equal importance with that of engineering." Towne stimulated interest in management and began the management movement, which can be divided into three major eras.

The Scientific Management Era

Frederick W. Taylor, a young member of the ASME, was stimulated by Towne's statement to become involved in changing the concepts and practices of management. In his work at the Midvale Steel Company in Philadelphia, Taylor had observed that workers were left relatively free to carry out their job assignments at their own pace by their own methods. He used the scientific method of logical inquiry and idea testing to experiment with work methods in search of the best way to perform a job. In 1906 he presented a paper, "On the Art of Cutting Metals," in which he stated that management had four major duties:

1. To develop a science of management for each element of a job to replace the old rule-of-thumb methods.
2. To select the best worker for each job and to provide workers with training in order to develop their skills.
3. To develop a hearty cooperation between management and the people who carried out the work.
4. To divide work between managers and workers in almost equal shares, each doing what he was best suited to do, instead of placing most of the responsibility on the worker, as was customary.[5]

Although not all of the ideas that came to be known collectively as *scientific management* originated with Taylor, he synthesized them, made them operational, verified that they worked, and publicized them in a book called *The Principles of Scientific Management* and in other works. He remained active in the movement until his death in 1915. Taylor stressed that his concepts were not merely a set of tools but a philosophy of the sharing of responsibility and cooperation between labor and management. Despite these efforts, scientific management was widely misunderstood and some "efficiency experts" exploited and increased this misunderstanding.

Taylor is called the father of scientific management, but he was not alone in his pioneering efforts. Among others, Frank and Lillian Gilbreth shared in the search for the "one best way" to perform a job and developed the principles of motion study, through which jobs were broken into component movements and studied so that wasted motions and fatigue could be reduced. Henry L. Gantt worked with Taylor and invented the "Gantt chart" for the scheduling of work and the checking of actual progress against plans. Harrington Emerson,

---

[4]Carl Heyel, ed., *The Encyclopedia of Management* (New York: Reinhold, 1963), p. 47.

[5]Frederick W. Taylor, *The Principles of Scientific Management* (Norwood, Mass.: Plimpton Press, 1911; reprinted New York: Norton, 1967); also reprinted in *Scientific Management* (New York: Harper, 1947), p. 36.

a demon for railroad efficiency, did much to advance scientific management when he testified before the Interstate Commerce Commission in 1910 that the railroads could save $1 million a day through the use of scientific management. His statement resulted in newspaper headlines that helped popularize the scientific management movement.

Not all of the management pioneers were in the United States. Similar activities were taking place in Poland, Russia, France, and England. Henri Fayol was chief executive of a large French mining and metallurgical combine from 1888 to 1918. Unlike Taylor, who had studied management from the bottom up, with emphasis on shop management, Fayol studied it from the top down, with emphasis on overall administration. In 1916 he published a book on general and industrial administration, and other works followed. He retired in 1918, at the age of seventy-seven, and spent his remaining seven years spreading his theory and pointing out governmental and other nonbusiness applications.[6]

The Human Relations Era

The pioneers of scientific management recognized the human element in management and addressed its psychological aspects in some of their writings.[7] Most of their emphasis, however, was on efficiency. The most noted recognition of workers' social needs occurred with the investigations at the Hawthorne plant of the Western Electric Company (1927–1932), under the direction of Elton Mayo of Harvard. The experiments emphasized the need to take workers' attitudes and sentiments into account and to give workers a sense of being contributing members of the company.[8] Since the

Hawthorne studies, management theorists have done much to incorporate the findings of psychologists and anthropologists in management studies.

This new emphasis did not exclude the previous interest in efficiency; it simply added a new consideration to the field of management. Management should be interested in getting the work done, but it should also be interested in the people who do the work. Later writings have delineated a technical system for performing work and a social system of interactions among the persons involved. The term *sociotechnical systems* has been coined to describe this merger.

The Management Science Era

Management science had its beginnings during World War II under the labels *operational research* and *operations research*. Today the terms are used interchangeably. During World War II mathematical analysis of military data led to new decisions that improved the effectiveness of the military effort. Soon after the war these analytical methods were applied to problems of government and industry, with promising results. *Management science* is concerned with the application of mathematical and statistical theory to business situations. It involves the use of models (often equations or formulas) to describe and provide an understanding of a problem and its alternative solutions. The objective is to achieve the best, or optimum, solution.

Management science is not a redirection in management but a change in the approach to management problems. Computers and mathematical tools available today are capable of dealing with large problems so that many related aspects of a problem can be considered at the same time. In this computer age it is not surprising that managers have come to recognize that quantitative skills can assist them as they perform their jobs.

[6]Heyel, ed., *Encyclopedia of Management*, p. 218.
[7]See, for example, Taylor, *Principles of Scientific Management*, pp. 49–51.
[8]F. V. Roethlisberger and W. J. Dickson, *Management and the Worker* (Cambridge: Harvard University Press, 1939).

Considerable progress has been made in the development of management concepts and practices. International organizations have been formed to study and exchange ideas on management. Each year new types of business are developed and new goods and services are offered by existing businesses. Technology becomes increasingly challenging and sophisticated. Multinational companies have added the complications of foreign cultures, languages, and currencies to the obvious logistic problems of dealing with broad geographical areas. The field of management will continue to change as the world in which it functions continues to change.

THE GROWTH OF TECHNOLOGY

As managers' knowledge of the behavioral aspects of management was being further developed, so were many facets of technology. Some of these changes have affected the ways in which the work that managers supervise is performed. More recently, technology has had a greater impact on the way that managers themselves work. Early production tasks were performed with humans providing both the energy to perform the work and the control of the process. At the next stage, people had to control the operation of machines directly but the energy was provided by another source—such as an animal, water wheel, or steam engine. The following stage provided automation or automatic control, in which the machine could sense its output, compare it to some preset level, and adjust itself to the desired level. Today, automation is capable of varying the instructions to machines, and the machines will adjust the values they are trying to achieve as well as comparing feedback to see if the target is being met.

Probably no one development has changed all of management and operations as greatly as the development of the electronic computer. Computer applications have diversified and spread broadly since the early business applications of the 1950s. Many of these early applications were to mechanize routine clerical operations such as payroll and accounting. Computers also made it possible for management scientists to analyze and solve large-scale problems, and software for these applications became more common. Computer applications were extended to support operations, but these systems required operations personnel to interact with the system—for example, an automatic airline ticket reservations system. Now, automatic tellers can provide service by interacting directly with the customer. In manufacturing, computers perform numerous functions—such as processing inventory records, scheduling, keeping up with the status of jobs, and keeping maintenance records.

Programmable logic also has greatly affected the way that manufacturing processes per se are performed. Modern equipment, with stored logic that enables it to make decisions depending on certain signals or conditions, has led to a reversal of the trend that began with the Industrial Revolution. Until the 1970s the trend of automation was generally tied to more standardization of design and specialization of equipment. Automatic material handling equipment generally traveled in a single, fixed path. Today, material handling systems can move objects to various locations depending on the computer signals they receive. Computer-controlled robots can execute various manipulations of work objects or tools. Production machines are equipped with racks of tools and automatic tool changers so that they can execute various commands without human assistance and can operate as unmanned machining centers. Combinations of automatic material handling systems and automatic machines, coordinated under the control of a computer, are being operated as unstaffed factories during part of the day. With computer-aided design, designers can use computer graphics and powerful simulation programs to develop and test designs. These designs can then be translated into instructions to operate automatic equipment in the type of factory just described. Much remains to be done to make this type of processing broadly available, but the technology is at hand.

JAPANESE INFLUENCE ON OPERATIONS MANAGEMENT

While technology can be used to some extent to improve efficiency and productivity, much can be gained from new management practices and operating methods. The concepts of *just-in-time (JIT)* production, which originally were practiced in Japan, are continuing to be employed more broadly in other parts of the world. These concepts, also called *stockless production* or *zero inventory programs,* rely on employing only a minimum of inventories or other resources to make products. Companies operating under this philosophy coordinate their operations so that one work center produces only what is required by subsequent work centers, and this production occurs just when the necessary components are needed. The method characteristically produces items in small lots, which means setup costs must be low and workers must have multiple skills so they can shift back and forth between various items. Successful implementation of JIT also requires that companies develop reliable supplier networks, sound preventive maintenance programs, and excellent quality control programs to avoid defective components.

THE RISE OF THE SERVICE SECTOR

As changes have taken place in the field of management, the types of operations being managed have changed as well:

1. Operations have become dispersed over wider geographical areas.
2. Operations have come to use more and increasingly varied technology.
3. Operations have become increasingly diversified.
4. The aggregate mix of operations has changed, with service operations assuming increasing importance.

During this century, management, labor, and science have brought about great increases in productivity per worker-hour in industry and other sectors of the economy. The number of persons needed to produce food, for example, has decreased dramatically. In 1900, approximately 10.5 million people were employed in agriculture, forestry, and fishing; in 1981, the number was about 4.5 million. Even though the United States now has many more mouths to feed than it had at the turn of the century, approximately 6 million fewer people are now employed in this sector of the economy.

Where have all the former agricultural workers gone? How do they earn a living? The number of city dwellers has greatly increased as literally millions of people have left the farms. While the work force has grown spectacularly, from approximately 29 million to approximately 105 million, the decline in the percentage of people employed in extractive enterprises has been even more stunning, as can be seen in Figure C.1. There also has been significant growth in the percentage of workers employed in communications, utilities, transportation, and trade between 1900 and 1930, and there has been another significant increase in the past 15 years.

In contrast to the change that occurred in extractive industries, the percentage of workers employed in the production of tangible items has changed little during this century. In 1900, approximately 25 percent of the workers were employed in manufacturing and construction, not a great deal less than the approximately 26 percent who were so employed in 1984. The

FIGURE C.1

Percentage of the Work Force in Four Sectors of U.S. Economy, 1900–1984

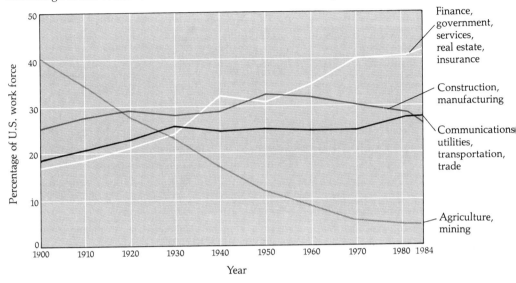

Source: "Employment and Earnings," U.S. Department of Labor Bureau of Labor Statistics, January 1982, p. 167; and January 1985, p. 183, "Long-Term Economic Growth, 1860–1970," U.S. Department of Commerce, Bureau of Economic Analysis, June 1973, p. 76; and "People and Jobs," U.S. Department of Labor, Bureau of Labor Statistics, April 1975, pp. 12–13.

number of persons employed in the production of tangible items, however, grew from 7 million to more than 27 million during this period. Coupled with a fivefold increase in productivity, this employment increase indicates that Americans have increased their consumption of tangible goods enormously.

The most dramatic increase in the composition of the work force has been in the service sector. The proportion of the work force involved in finance, government, services, real estate, and insurance has more than doubled, from approximately 17.2 percent in 1900 to about 41.7 percent in 1984. When percentages are translated into numbers, we find that approximately 5 million people were engaged in these fields in 1900 and over 43 million in 1984. The increase in service jobs was almost three times as great as the decline in extractive industries—enough to absorb displaced farm workers and provide many of the additional jobs required by a growing work force.

This change in employment structure has been accompanied by changes in operations management. The early studies of management in this country dealt with shop management—how to cut metal, how to lay bricks, and so on. In Frederick Taylor's time, many people were employed in manufacturing, and much of it was labor-intensive. As automation and mechanization have multiplied the effectiveness of human efforts, interests within management have broadened. People are interested in finance and marketing management as well as in operations, which have become largely nonmanufacturing endeavors.

DISCUSSION QUESTIONS

1. Why did the factory system experience such a dramatic growth in the United States as compared with the older economies of Europe?
2. Who was called the father of scientific management? Was he really alone in his pioneering efforts? If not, who also contributed? Briefly describe scientific management.
3. What is management science? When did it develop and why?
4. How have computers been employed in manufacturing operations and in what two major types of applications?
5. What influence have Japanese production management practices had on manufacturing operations in the United States and in other countries?
6. How did the work force composition change between 1900 and 1984? Which areas of the work force experienced the largest growth? Which areas experienced the greatest loss? Which, if any, remained relatively stable?

Chapter Outline
OPERATIONS STRATEGY

STRATEGY PROVIDES FOCUS

STRATEGY FORMULATION
External Conditions / Internal Conditions

Operations Management In Action   OPERATIONS IMPACT OF NISSAN'S STRATEGY

DIFFERENT OPERATIONS, DIFFERENT STRATEGIES

OPERATIONS: A VITAL ELEMENT IN STRATEGY

Operations Management In Action   HOW GM TAKES PLANNING INTO THE TRENCHES

STRATEGY DECISIONS FOR OPERATIONS
Positioning Decisions / Other Decisions /

Application: Retaining a Consistent Position / Other Strategy Factors in Services

PRODUCT DESIGN: AN IMPORTANT STRATEGY FACTOR
Product Design in Nonmanufacturing Operations / Product Design in Manufacturing Operations / Computer-Aided Design and Computer-Aided Manufacturing / Simplification and Standardization

Summary / Discussion Questions / Bibliography

KEY TERMS

Strategic decisions	External conditions	Quality	Computer-aided
Mission	Internal strengths	Dependability	manufacturing
Strategic business units	Internal weaknesses	Flexibility	(CAM)
Strategy	Competitive strategy	Computer-aided design	Simplification
Objectives	Positioning	(CAD)	Standardization
Policies	Cost efficiency		

Chapter 2

OPERATIONS STRATEGY

Companies spend a great percentage of their income and employee hours carrying out activities that stem from decisions in various parts of the company. As these activities continue, they help to shape the destiny of the entire company. The accomplishments of a company can be astounding if all its parts work together toward the same carefully established, appropriate goals. But if different parts work toward different goals or if the entire company cooperates toward inappropriate goals, efforts are wasted. The results may even spell disaster for the company.

Top managers are responsible for making the vital decisions that set the company's overall goals and keep all parts of the company pulling together toward these goals. Decisions that have a long-range impact on the general direction and basic character of a company are called *strategic decisions.* Through strategic planning, managers evaluate the company's relationship to its external environment and establish the basic directions for the company.

The broadest expression of the direction in which a company will apply its efforts is a statement of its *mission,* which explains the fundamental purpose of the enterprise. The company's mission statement describes in general terms what key decision makers want the company to accomplish and what kind of company they want it to become. A company's mission is its very long-range purpose and, consequently, is changed infrequently. Developing a statement of mission helps to identify the company's *strategic business units* (SBUs), parts of the business that focus on distinct markets. A specific mission focuses the scope of the company's search for opportunities in the marketplace, further defines the types of organizations with which it must compete, and helps the company identify threats it must guard against. That is, the company's intended mission will identify the parts of the total environment that are most relevant to the company's decisions.

STRATEGY PROVIDES FOCUS

Top managers formulate strategy to provide more definitive direction and guidance to the organization. *Strategy* is a long-term master plan of how the company will pursue its mission; it establishes the general direction in which the company will move. In formulating strategy, top managers establish corporate objectives and make broad-reaching decisions on such matters as the breadth of the product line the company will choose to offer, the geographical scope it will try to serve, the types of competitive actions it will employ and to what extent it will use them, the types of social involvement in which the company will engage, the amount of resources that will be committed to various company endeavors, and performance *objectives* for such matters as the company's market share, growth, and profitability.

General policies and subunit objectives guide and coordinate decisions at the lower levels of an organization. *Policies* are official statements, expressed or implied, that guide decisions and actions of company members in a consistent general direction. Sometimes a company's overall strategy is explicitly defined and circulated to lower-level managers to provide unified direction for decisions on short-term matters or on problems of more limited scope. Subunits of the company, such as operations, develop strategies to accomplish the objectives assigned to their particular unit. It is logical that decisions and actions within a company will be better coordinated internally and will be more consistently directed toward the company's strategic goals if the company's strategy is explicitly recognized, if objectives and policies consistent with the overall strategy are formulated, and if these objectives are communicated and recognized throughout the organization.

Strategy formulation within an organization must be considered from two directions. The capabilities and limitations of each subunit down though the organization must be evaluated by top-level managers before a realistic strategy can be formulated. Also, the lower-level managers must take top-level corporate strategy into account as they make decisions for the various subunits within the organization. Operations managers and managers in all other parts of the organization must formulate plans and make decisions within the context of the corporate strategy and policies to achieve a unified effort toward corporate objectives. Strategies for the functional areas must be formulated to be consistent with corporate objectives and strategy. This forms a hierarchy of lower-level objectives aligned to carry out corporate strategy. This chapter provides an overview of some key elements in strategy formulation and the interrelationship between corporate strategy and the operations functions. Supplement D, at the end of this chapter, reviews some details of the decision-making process.

STRATEGY FORMULATION

Because strategy deals with broad issues and long-range plans, strategy formulation is a multifaceted activity. Managers must evaluate information about many diverse elements of the company's environment to determine what overall course a company should pursue. In the process of formulating strategy, managers must evaluate information about conditions in the company's external and internal environments.

External Conditions

The following are some of the major *external conditions* that might influence a company's strategy:

1. *Economic conditions.* Levels of consumer and capital spending; GNP; number of households, and growth patterns, in the target markets; current stage of the business cycle; interest rates; and employment levels.
2. *Political conditions.* War or peace; tariffs; foreign trade restrictions; monetary exchange rates; political stability in nations of interest and in neighboring countries; national, state, and local government spending in various budget categories; labor policies; environmental policies; and fiscal and monetary actions.
3. *Social conditions.* Trends toward more leisure time and casual life styles; trends away from conspicuous consumption to more efficient living; greater awareness of physical fitness; increase in number of single parents; changes in status of women and minorities; appearance of more breadwinners per family; trends toward more dining out.
4. *Technological conditions.* New products to offer or compete against, such as word processors and storage through shared logic, digital watches and clocks, calculators, home computers, office computers, electronic controls for automobile engines; new formulations of plastics, metals, fabrics, and chemicals; new processes to use or to compete against, such as automated process control, robots, continuous casting of basic metals, long-wall mining equipment, computerized medical diagnostic equipment, satellite transmission of information, laser printing, synfuels, nuclear power, solar energy, and electron beam welding.
5. *Market conditions.* Functions of a potential product, needs and desires of customers, primary concentrations of present and potential customers, possible distribution methods; potential competitors, their location, their strategies, their vulnerable points; barriers to entering the market, either for the company or its competitors; cost structure of product (high fixed cost or variable cost), availability and cost of necessary materials and equipment; price structure of product, sensitivity of market to price, potential volume of sales and profitability over the product's life cycle.

Internal Conditions

While the company is evaluating the environment to determine market opportunities or threats, it must also evaluate its *internal strengths and weaknesses* to determine what opportunities best suit its unique capabilities. There must be an adequate fit between the key requirements of the market and the competence of the enterprise. The enterprise must at least be able to assemble the resources and develop the skills necessary to successfully implement a strategy. Mergers and acquisitions are sometimes used as a way to obtain internal capabilities to implement growth strategies and to reduce competition. The internal conditions that should be evaluated could include:

Market understanding and appropriate marketing capabilities

Existing products (goods and/or services)

Existing customers and relationships

Existing distribution or delivery systems

Existing supplier networks and relationships

Human resources:
  Management capabilities
  Current worker skills and motivation
  Access to necessary worker skills

Ownership of or access to natural resources

Current facilities, equipment, processes, and locations

Mastery of special technology

Patent protection for products or processes

Available capital and financial strength

In evaluating the match between its capabilities and the demands imposed by potential opportunities or threats, a company will consider such questions as: What advantages do we have in serving present and future customer needs? What are our weaknesses? How can we strengthen these weaknesses? Can we attract and train sufficient workers and develop managers fast enough to grow at the desired rate? Can our available capital be better invested in different programs or projects? What are the internal limitations for improving any of these weaknesses or capitalizing on any of these strengths?

The basic objective of evaluating internal conditions is to determine where the opportunities or threats are, then to determine how the company's resources can best be used to capitalize on the opportunities or counteract the threats. Because conditions change and competitive actions and reactions occur, strategy development is a continuing activity. A company's managers must constantly study information about the factors outlined in the previous discussion, re-evaluating and perhaps reformulating the company's strategy from time to time. Strategic changes must be communicated throughout the appropriate parts of the organization if they are to be effective.

After clearly defining its strategy, a company is better able to establish policies and objectives that will guide all subunits of the organization. The efforts of each part of the company operating under the guidance of these policies and objectives can be more effectively and efficiently channeled toward the common strategy. Figure 2.1 outlines the relationships between the elements and activities involved in formulating and implementing corporate strategy. It shows that various external and internal conditions influence the selection of the company's mission. A company's mission would seldom be changed; but it it were, it would then become another factor to be considered in formulation of the company's strategy. Since activities in any part of the company can change internal conditions over time, and since external conditions can and do change,

FIGURE 2.1

The Desired Relationship between Strategy Formulation and Company Activities

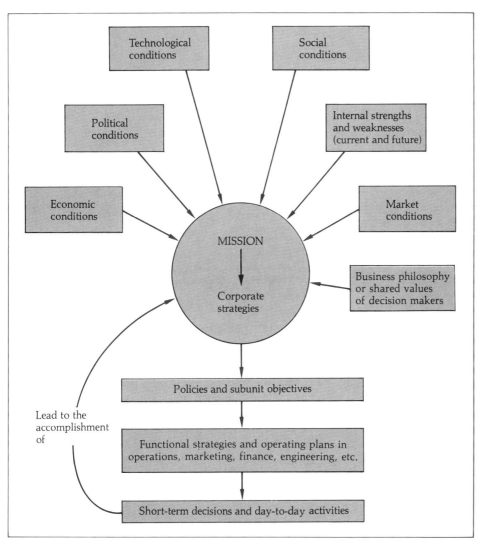

OPERATIONS MANAGEMENT IN ACTION

Operations Impact of Nissan's Strategy

Japan's automobile producers are now competing in what has become an enlarged and more competitive world car market. Nissan, maker of Datsun cars and trucks, appears to have effected a change of strategy in response to certain changes in the external environment, as outlined below:*

1. Social Conditions: High unemployment among United States automobile workers.
2. Political Conditions: U.S. Congress under pressure to erect trade barriers such as import quotas and higher tariffs.
3. Technological Conditions: Aluminum used in lightweight, high-mileage automobiles, requires large amounts of energy to produce.

4. Economic Conditions: Japan's trade balance endangered because it imports 88 percent of its energy, and energy costs have multiplied in recent years; high costs of shipping coal, oil, and other resources to Japan, and engines back to the United States.
5. Strategic Decision: Produce engines in Mexico and assemble pickup trucks in the United States.
6. Operations Implications: Engine production workers with lifetime employment must be retrained and assigned to other jobs. Production control becomes more difficult to coordinate when operations are scattered over several countries. Lead times to get engines for units assembled in Japan are longer. Higher inventories must be maintained to ensure that operations will not be interrupted.

*Louis Kraar, "Japan's Automakers Shift Strategies," Fortune, August 11, 1980, pp. 106–111. A description of Nissan's U.S. plant is provided in Supplement A at the end of Chapter 1.

the company's strategy must be reevaluated regularly. Strategic changes can also change the objectives and activities of various components of the organization and affect development of strategies within functions such as operations.

As an example of how a broad array of external conditions can influence overall strategy, consider the following brief application. Notice that the operations function had an important part to play in implementing this strategy adjustment.

DIFFERENT OPERATIONS, DIFFERENT STRATEGIES

The preceding application clearly shows how a change in the company's strategy affects the operations function. We will discuss some of the relationships between a company's strategy and the operations function in more depth in this and the next section of the chapter. A company's overall strategy addresses many broad issues and can even include plans for social involvement, stockholder relations, and employee relations. One important aspect of the overall direction of a firm is its *competitive strategy* for marketing. At a very general level, one can identify some characteristics of marketing strategies often associated with the types of operations functions introduced in the previous chapter. Pri-

Table 2.1
MARKETING STRATEGIES ASSOCIATED WITH VARIOUS TYPES OF OPERATIONS

Type of Operation	Type of Product	Typical Process Characteristics	Typical Characteristics of Market Strategy
Service Project Job shop	Make to order as customer specifies	Use of broadly skilled workers and general purpose equipment; emphasis on good initial planning of work, quality, flexiblity	Selling diversity of capabilities and ability to provide features customers desire, ability to perform a quality job, ability to achieve reasonable delivery times
Continuous Process	Make for inventory product designed to have features desired by many potential customers	Use of workers with narrower skills, specialized equipment, perhaps automation; emphasis on efficiency and cost control; good distribution system to make items readily available	Selling the desirability of features that are already designed into the product plus the desirability of the price, availability, service. Market research is important to ensure that product features are appropriate for the market

marily, strategies of companies with a custom product will tend to differ from those of companies with a more standardized product. Table 2.1 shows some general features of marketing strategy for various types of operations.

Generally, companies can compete on three primary features of their goods or services:

1. Quality. Do all of the characteristics of a product make it suitable and reliable for the customer's intended use?
2. Price. Is the cost to the customer over the life of the product affordable and considered reasonable when compared to the quality of the product and other quality-to-price ratios available in the marketplace?
3. Availability. Can the product be obtained within a reasonable and competitive time?

To succeed in the marketplace, the product must be judged as at least adequate by all three measures.

OPERATIONS: A VITAL ELEMENT IN STRATEGY

The operations function has great value as a competitive weapon in a company's strategy. Because it is the part of the firm that must produce the goods or provide the services that the consumer buys, the operations function plays an important role in implementing strategy. The operations function establishes the level of quality as a product is manufactured or as a service is provided. The operations function often is responsible for the largest part of a company's human and capital assets. Thus much of a product's cost is incurred within operations, and this cost affects the price that must be charged and the profit margin that can be achieved. Finally, the ability of the operations function to perform determines to a great extent the ability of the company to have sufficient products available to meet delivery commitments.

It is clear then that the operations function has an important influence on cost, quality, and availability of the company's goods or services. Operations' strengths and weaknesses can have a great impact upon the success of the company's overall strategy. Therefore, the capabilities of operations must be carefully considered when corporate strategy is formulated, and operations decisions must be consistent with corporate strategy so that the full potential of operations' resources can be harnessed in pursuit of the company's goals. In fact, the capabilities of operations can be aimed and developed so that this

OPERATIONS MANAGEMENT IN ACTION

How GM Takes Planning into the Trenches

Only eight years ago, General Motors Corp. had no strategic planners in its divisions, let alone in a lowly car plant. But as Raymond K. Fears, the strategic planner for GM's Buick City complex in Flint, Mich., amply demonstrates, times have changed. Fears, who turns 30 in mid-September, moved from GM's corporate strategic-planning group in 1983 to Buick City—the trio of 60-year-old plants that GM aspires to turn into the world's most efficient auto factory. His assignment: "To get [operating managers], who are used to thinking in terms of nuts and bolts, to think in strategic terms." That, he concedes, "is a major educational job."

Fears's transfer is part of GM Chairman Roger B. Smith's master plan to integrate strategic planning "into our daily lives." In Smith's book, that means "true integration with the operating organization."

Marching in Step.

Fears served as a product planner for three years in GM's Chevrolet Motor Div. before moving in 1982 to corporate, where he worked as a business-plan consultant to nine GM divisions. At Buick City, which will begin cranking out full-size 1986 cars a year from now, Fears's job is to aid in devising and implementing its piece of Buick Motor Div.'s strategy.

Chairman Smith insists that "the guy in charge of strategic planning is the general manager." Indeed, Fears's job will probably be phased out next year when the plant manager assumes all strategic-planning duties. One of Fears's tasks is to coordinate the strategic committee charged with insuring that all corporate groups involved in pilot production are marching in step. He also has helped to scout the competition to make sure Buick City will not be made obsolete—even by newer GM plants that adopt the facility's manufacturing practices.

Does he have regrets about moving from headquarters to the down-in-the-trenches atmosphere of a car plant? Absolutely none, says Fears, who aspires to an operating job. "I see the move as getting closer to the action."

Reprinted from the September 17, 1984 issue of Business Week *by special permission, © 1984 by McGraw-Hill, Inc.*

function contributes to the competitive strength of the company. This concept will be discussed further in the next section.

An approach to strategic planning that many companies are using is to have line managers in various units involved in strategic planning (see box).

STRATEGY DECISIONS FOR OPERATIONS

Positioning Decisions

Strategy decisions at the top management level and within the operations function affect how well the operations function will contribute to the competitive effectiveness of a company. One broad strategy decision that is important in guiding and coordinating the actions of operations relates to positioning. *Positioning* establishes the extent to which the production system will emphasize certain characteristics in order to achieve the greatest competitive advantage. Regardless of how desirable it may sound, a company cannot simultaneously have a product that is lowest in cost, highest in quality, and instantly available in abundance at numerous convenient locations. Professor Steven Wheelwright recommends that a manufacturing company explicitly establish the relative priorities it will give to the four performance characteristics: cost efficiency, quality, dependability, and flexibility.[1] These performance characteristics can be briefly described as follows:

> *Cost efficiency.* A company that emphasizes cost efficiency will see that its capital, labor, and other operating costs are kept low relative to other similar companies.
>
> *Quality.* A company that emphasizes quality will consistently strive to provide a level of quality that is significantly superior to that of its competitors, even if it has to pay extra to do so.
>
> *Dependability.* A company that stresses dependability can be relied upon to have its goods available for customers or to deliver its goods or services on schedule, if it is at all possible.
>
> *Flexibility.* A company that develops flexibility can quickly respond to changes in product design, product mix, or production volume.

Positioning might be visualized as selecting a particular volume within a pyramid, such as the one shown in Figure 2.2, that the company consistently operates within. The pyramid defines the relative priorities that can be assigned to each of the four performance characteristics. However, the portion of the pyramid that a company will try to occupy is a strategic decision that must rest with the top management. If each part of a company tries to move in any direction in which that part of the company believes a competitor is outperforming it, then overall the company's money, talents, and efforts will not be effectively expended. By trying to move in several directions simultaneously,

---

[1]Steven C. Wheelwright, "Reflecting Corporate Strategy in Manufacturing Decisions," *Business Horizons*, February 1978, pp. 57–66.

FIGURE 2.2

Possible Positions of an Operations Function

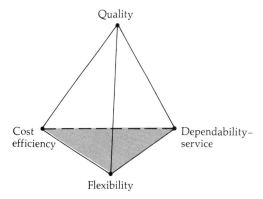

such a company would not be recognized as having a distinctive competence that would attract and retain customers, and customers could not rely upon it for consistent treatment.

Although a company cannot be simultaneously at all corners of the pyramid shown in Figure 2.2, a company can expand the range of the pyramid that it covers. This is quite different from the company or parts of the company bouncing inconsistently from one location to another within the pyramid. Expanding the range within the pyramid that a company consistently covers can be thought of as shortening one or more legs of the pyramid or making the pyramid smaller (i.e., shrinking their pyramid). The effect is that a company can then cover a larger relative percentage of its pyramid than its competitors and leave less space for a competitor to develop a distinctive competence.

An example of shrinking the pyramid can be found in the operation of numerous Japanese companies. Through very careful and diligent efforts, these companies have controlled processes to prevent defects and have achieved greatly improved quality. These actions have reduced the cost of screening and repairing defective work in the factory and the cost of warranty work in the field. In effect, the companies simultaneously improve quality and cost, so that they cover a larger relative portion of the cost-quality leg of their pyramid. We can think of this as reducing the length of the cost-quality leg of the pyramid, as shown in Figure 2.3a. Many Japanese manufacturers have provided extensive training and cross training of their workers so that they will have multiskilled workers. This versatile work force, coupled with plant arrangements and equipment that can easily be changed over from one product to another, provide greater flexibility without a significant increase in cost. The flexibility-cost leg of the pyramid is thereby shortened, as shown in Figure 2.3b. Companies can employ these or other means to shrink various legs of their pyramids. Companies that are resourceful and succeed in shrinking their pyramids can serve their markets well. And their competitors will have difficulty finding a spot in which to try to establish their own distinctive competence.

FIGURE 2.3

Shrinking the Pyramid

(a)

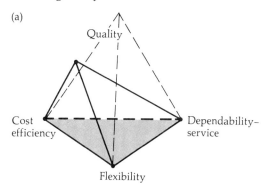

(b)

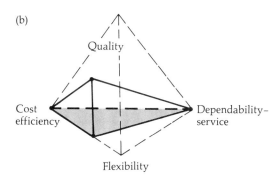

Other Decisions

Once a company has selected its intended position and internally communicated this intention, all parts of the company can be more consistent in their decisions. That is, the decisions of any given part of the company will be more consistent with its own decisions over time and more consistent with the decisions made in other parts of the company. The company will be more likely to achieve its strategic objectives when all parts of the company are making concerted efforts to support these objectives in all of their decisions and activities.

Numerous decisions within the operations function are related to the positioning decision as well as to each other. Hayes and Wheelwright present eight major categories of strategy decisions for a manufacturing company, as shown in Table 2.2.[2] The first four categories are normally recognized as long-term decisions that are difficult to reverse and therefore more likely to be considered strategic. The last four categories appear to deal with "tactical" matters, that is, with decisions that are more concerned with day-to-day operating mat-

[2]Robert H. Hayes and Steven C. Wheelwright, *Restoring Our Competitive Edge* (New York: Wiley, 1984), p. 31.

Table 2.2
CATEGORIES OF STRATEGY DECISIONS
IN MANUFACTURING OPERATIONS

1. **Capacity**—amount, timing, type
2. **Facilities**—size, location, specialization
3. **Technology**—equipment, automation, linkages
4. **Vertical Integration**—direction, extent, balance
5. **Work force**—skill level, wage policies, employment security
6. **Quality**—defect prevention, monitoring, intervention
7. **Production planning/materials control**—sourcing policies, centralization, decision rules
8. **Organization**—structure, control/reward systems, role of staff groups

ters. It is important to recognize, however, that even these matters have long-run strategic impact.

John Puttick, a British management consultant, noted in regard to Japanese companies: "The idea of manufacturing strategy is at heart a simple one—setting up process, organization, and information systems so a company can respond in the most appropriate way to the market."[3] Recent international competition has shown that quality control methods show up in competitive advantage and that efficient scheduling and control of work affect the cost competitiveness and delivery dependability of manufacturing companies. Many of the topics in Table 2.2 will be discussed in greater detail later in the text.

Strategy considerations in nonmanufacturing companies are in some ways similar to those in manufacturing companies. The concept of trading off priorities to select the appropriate position is valuable to almost any company. Consider the following application, for example.

APPLICATION

Retaining a Consistent Position

A local chain of fast food restaurants wants to extend its performance in the flexibility characteristic and is considering broadening its menu to offer chicken, fish, or veal platters in addition to its normal, limited-menu sandwich items. The new platters will not be ordered in large volume as are its standard items, and the company is therefore evaluating alternative decisions regarding whether or not the platters will be prepared ahead of time. If the company chooses not to prepare platters ahead of demand, it will move away from the dependability-service characteristic for these items. If these items are prepared ahead and held, the platters might not appear so fresh and be so tasty. This option would cause the company to move away from a high-quality emphasis. If the items are prepared at some rate of reasonable expected demand and thrown away if not demanded, the company's cost performance will suffer. The company elected to employ technology—rapid microwave cooking—so as to remain consistent with its position.

[3]Stephen P. Fitzpatrick and John Puttick, "Manufacturing Strategies—Lessons from Japan," *Production Engineering*, October 1983, p. 36.

Table 2.3
OPERATIONS FEATURES THAT SUPPORT PARTICULAR
PERFORMANCE CHARACTERISTICS

Performance Characteristic to Be Emphasized	Features that Manufacturing Operations Might Provide	Applicability to Service Operations
Cost efficiency	Low overhead	Yes
	Special purpose equipment and facilities	Yes
	High utilization of capacity	Yes
	Close control of materials	Maybe
	High productivity	Yes
	Low wage rates	Yes
Quality	Skilled workers	Yes
	Adequate precision of equipment	Maybe
	Motivation for pride of workmanship	Yes
	Effective communication of standards or job requirements	Yes
Dependability	Effective scheduling system	Yes
	Low equipment failure	Yes
	Low absenteeism, turnover; no strikes	Yes
	High inventory investment	Maybe
	Commitment of personnel to perform as required	Yes
Flexibility	Dependable, rapid suppliers	Yes
	Reserve capacity	Yes
	Multiskilled workers who can be shifted	Yes
	Effective control of work flow	Yes
	Versatile processing equipment	Yes
	Low setup time and cost	Maybe
	Integration of design and production	Maybe

The ability of operations to achieve various performance characteristics and the cost associated with doing so must apply to both manufacturing and non-manufacturing operations. Table 2.3 shows the four performance characteristics mentioned earlier and some of the supporting features that are desirable in the operations function of a manufacturing company to help achieve a particular performance characteristic. Comments in the third column of the table indicate the degree to which this feature might also be appropriate to support the performance characteristic in a nonmanufacturing company.

Other Strategy Factors in Services

Professor Dan Thomas of the Harvard Business School has pointed out certain differences between strategy formulation in companies whose primary products are tangible objects and in companies whose primary products are services. He says that several general differences should be considered in the development of a competitive strategy for a service company. Fewer barriers prevent competitors from entering the service-oriented market, since a service product is often not patentable and the capital investment is usually lower than for a manufacturing company. Proprietary technology is more difficult to achieve, particularly in the types of services classified as people-based in the scheme presented in Figure 1.4. Costs of specific elements of services are difficult to measure, so a rational basis for pricing and price competition in services is less clear. Acquisitions carry more risk as a growth strategy for people-based services, because key personnel can leave whereas in a manufacturing company equipment and patents would remain.

Location is generally more important in services than in manufacturing, so acquisition of good locations can be a key strategic move for service business. Some services, particularly people-based services, can be varied at the request of the consumer, so flexibility can be a key element in competitive strategy. It is sometimes possible to "value engineer" service products and offer a no-frills version of the primary service, such as a moderate-priced motel with basic furnishings and no swimming pool.[4]

PRODUCT DESIGN: AN IMPORTANT STRATEGY FACTOR

One of the basic decisions a company must face is what goods or services it will offer in the marketplace. Identification of the general type of product helps narrow the search for a niche in the market where the company might stimulate sufficient demand to achieve success. Beyond the broad question of what business it will be in, the company must address many details regarding what specific product or service it will offer and how. Decisions about the product's design specifications affect the selection of process technology (one of the decision categories in Table 2.2), which in turn affect the company's expenditures for equipment and facilities. Product design also affects the ease with which the product can be fabricated and assembled, so that it has an effect on operating costs. Design also affects the ease with which a product can be produced with few defects, so that it has an effect on market acceptance and the customer's perception of the company. Product design, then, has serious implications for the company's long-range success and therefore is of strategic importance. Let us now consider the relationship between design and operating decisions in manufacturing and nonmanufacturing operations.

Product Design in Nonmanufacturing Operations

The product, or output, desired from the operations system of a nonmanufacturing firm will certainly affect the type of inputs needed and the capabilities that must be available to transform the inputs into the desired goods or services. The processing technology and kinds of skills that must be available in the operations function may be significantly affected even by what appear to be small differences in the characteristics of the product or of the way it is delivered. The decision of a food establishment to provide buffet meals rather than

[4]Dan R. E. Thomas, "Strategy Is Different in Service Businesses," *Harvard Business Review,* July–August 1980, pp. 158–165.

cafeteria-style service, for example, will mean that fewer people will be needed behind the counter to serve patrons. It will, however, require the establishment to have extra food available, or to be able to prepare additional food quickly, because management will no longer be able to control the size of each portion.

Levitz Furniture Corporation operated for years with cavernous 170,000-square-foot buildings that were combination warehouse-showrooms located near rail sidings in large cities. Customers could select furniture and haul it home. More recently, the company has added a chain of satellite stores that serve only as showrooms; the warehouses are located about twenty-five miles away. As a result of this change in merchandising strategy, the company must keep better inventory records so the people at the showrooms know what is available at various locations, and the company must have a more extensive fleet of vehicles and personnel to move the product between locations and make deliveries to the customers.

To take another example of the operating implications that result from a product characteristic, consider a decision by Wendy's Old-Fashioned Hamburgers chain. Wendy's had the choice of serving fresh or frozen french-fried potatoes. Serving fresh potatoes would have required each location to select, purchase, store, peel, store again, then cook and serve the potatoes. The use of preprocessed and frozen potatoes would have required each location only to store, then cook and serve the potatoes. Preprocessed potatoes also provide a more uniform product. Therefore, preprocessed frozen french fries were selected, reducing the number of employees and the amount of space required at each location and reducing quality control and waste-disposal problems at each location.

Product Design in Manufacturing Operations

A manufacturing firm must balance the need to make its product marketable with the need to produce it economically. Product design can affect appearance, so the designer must work for an appealing look. Because some aspects of the product design may necessitate particular processes and equipment in production, the best time to begin a cost-reduction program is while the product is on the drawing board. As the product is designed, a cost-benefit evaluation should be performed, taking into account the kind and amount of materials, labor, and processing equipment that each alternative design will require. The company must also recognize that the potential consumer will also perform some sort of cost-benefit evaluation before deciding whether to purchase the product. Some processes and materials are more expensive and should be used only if the functions of the product make them necessary or the aesthetic appeal of the results justifies the expense.

Myriad alternative designs for a product are usually possible, and alternative production methods may be possible even after the product is designed. Production engineers often serve as advisers to designers, helping them develop product designs that are reasonably economical to produce. A brief discussion of product design ideas will provide some appreciation of the complex nature of this topic. In selecting the raw material for a product, the designer must consider such properties as hardness, wear resistance, fatigue strength, tensile strength, weight, transparency, and ductility. Although a designer might consider the use of an inexpensive raw material, a more expensive material such as a free-machining alloy might result in a net saving when the processing costs are considered. After the material is selected, other design parameters must be evaluated. Economy can result from such ideas as:

Using a different process to achieve basic shape, e.g., casting instead of machining

Requiring machined surfaces only where necessary

Requiring close tolerances only where necessary

Ensuring that surfaces are easily accessible to the types of processes to be used

Considering less costly ways of joining materials, such as spot welding rather than riveting

Requiring thinner materials or less severe bends so that light-capacity machines can be used for forming operations

As indicated earlier, the most effective time to consider a product's manufacturability is while the product is being designed. Close coordination between the design and manufacturing departments is desirable if a company wants to develop economical and effective designs. One characteristic that was found to be in common during a comparison of some of America's best-managed factories was a close linkage between design and manufacturing departments so that easily producable designs could be rapidly developed. (Other similarities noted were that the companies excelled in the ability to "build in quality, [to] make wise choices about automation, [to] get close to the customer and [to] handle their work forces.")[5]

Computer-Aided Design and Computer-Aided Manufacturing

Effective organization and information systems make it easier for a company to respond rapidly and appropriately to the market. One very effective tool to help achieve the close integration of design and manufacturing, and of other activities as well, is computer-aided design (CAD) and manufacturing (CAM). When CAD and CAM (both discussed below) are linked together they can electronically exchange data from common data bases to provide rapid and accurate information on the current design of each part. This technology (called CAD/CAM) helps to achieve a close linkage between design and manufacturing.[6]

Computer analysis can be used to evaluate the consequences of a series of design alternatives by performing engineering calculations and graphical manipulations. Today's technology has made it possible for a designer working with a light pen to sketch ideas on a cathode ray tube and receive a response from the computer after the design has been evaluated. Computers can calculate the stress

[5]Gene Bylinsky, "America's Best-Managed Factories," *Fortune,* May 28, 1984, pp. 16–24.
[6]"CAD/CAM—The Factory Integrator," *Production Engineering,* April 1983, p. 65.

imposed on various sections of the product and assist in determining the necessary material strengths and thicknesses to meet the specified load requirements. The computer can then draw the object from different angles for further evaluation by the designer. This process of interaction between a designer and a computer is called *computer-aided design* (CAD) and will probably find new applications as the technology and user acceptance grows (see Figure 2.4).

Computers also are being used to develop the electronic signals that control production processing equipment. Once a component has been designed, some types of computers can analyze the necessary steps that a machine must make to produce the part. The computer can then encode into a punched paper or magnetic tape the instructions that will control certain types of processing equipment so that they perform the appropriate production steps to produce the part. This is called *computer-aided manufacturing* (CAM), and it too will probably find new applications as the technology progresses and user acceptance grows.

Simplification and Standardization   The total costs to a company over the life cycle of one of its products can often be reduced through simplification and standardization. In *simplification* a product is designed to have as few parts and components as are necessary to perform its intended function. Because there are fewer parts to fail, one indirect benefit of simplification may be to increase the product's reliability. In *standardization* less variety is used in the configuration of a product or a common component is used in more than one type of product (e.g., using the same type of electrical cord on an entire line of small electric appliances). The use of common components will increase the volume of each component used and can result in economies of scale in purchasing or producing the component. Fewer new components must be designed, produced, distributed, and stored. Through simplification and standardization, fewer blueprints and specifications will be needed, and preparing and updating parts catalogs and price lists will be simplified. Simplification and standardization are desirable goals if they do not reduce a product's sales appeal.

We have seen that numerous decisions about issues ranging from very broad, general strategy to specific aspects of product design can have long-range effects on the operations function. Conversely, many decisions that must be made within the operations function can affect the company's long-range

FIGURE 2.4

Computer-Aided Design (CAD)

Photo courtesy of Computervision, Corp.

capabilities and success. It is important that operations capabilities and the requirements imposed on the operations function be carefully considered when strategy is formulated. Supplement D, which follows this chapter, is devoted to a discussion of the decision-making process.

SUMMARY

In this chapter we have discussed several aspects of a company's strategy. Strategy is the pattern of decisions that determines a company's basic direction and character. We began with an overview of the types of broad external factors that top managers must monitor and evaluate so that they are apprised of the opportunities and threats that their company faces over the course of time. Companies must also evaluate their internal strengths and weaknesses relative to their competitors so they can develop strategies that exploit their competitive advantages.

As a company formulates strategy, capabilities of the operations function must be evaluated and taken into consideration. The operations function has to produce the goods or provide the services that the customer will either elect to purchase or ignore. The operations function often controls a large portion of the physical and human resources within a company. It is important that these resources be coordinated and directed toward company strategic objectives.

Multidivisioned companies or companies with diverse product lines may compete in several distinct markets, each of which is called a strategic business unit, SBU. The strategy a company selects for each particular SBU determines the degree of emphasis to be placed on each of four performance criteria: cost efficiency, dependability, flexibility and quality. Several of the capabilities that the operations function must possess in order to achieve each of these criteria were mentioned, and the implications of several types of strategy decisions for the operations function were also reviewed. Even the details of product design can have an impact on the operations function, and some factors that should be considered in product design were presented.

A broad array of decisions must be made by managers throughout a company. Supplement D discusses decision making and the use of models as an approach to the decision-making process.

DISCUSSION QUESTIONS

1. What does the term *corporate strategy* refer to?
2. What level of management is responsible for development of a company's overall strategy?
3. List five external conditions that might exert an important influence on the process of shaping the strategic plans of a company.
4. How does the operations function play a significant role in ensuring the success of a company's strategy?
5. List four major performance characteristics that a company can elect to emphasize to give it a distinctive strategy.
6. Explain and discuss the concept of *positioning*. Why would a company not want to keep changing so its competition would always be confused?
7. In addition to the positioning decision, what are six categories of strategy decisions for a manufacturing company?
8. What are some of the capabilities that it is

desirable for the operations function to have in a manufacturing company that elects to emphasize cost efficiency?

9. What are some of the capabilities that it is desirable for the operations function to have in a nonmanufacturing company that elects to emphasize quality?

10. What are some of the capabilities that it is desirable for the operations function to have in a manufacturing company that elects to emphasize dependability of delivery?

11. What are some of the capabilities that it is desirable for the operations function to have in a nonmanufacturing company that elects to have flexibility in its volume of work?

12. What are some of the possible advantages of standardization of at least some of the components in a company's product line?

13. How can a company gain some of the advantages of standardization without having to accept an undesirable degree of lack of variety in the products it offers to potential customers?

14. What are some of the ways in which the availability of computer-aided design (CAD) and computer-aided manufacturing (CAM) will have a great impact on manufacturing companies?

15. (a) In your opinion, where are most hospitals positioned within the pyramid discussed in the chapter and presented in Figure 2.2? What is the reason for your answer? (b) If you know of any hospitals that are positioned differently, discuss these differences.

16. Compare an automobile shop near your school or the repair shop you use to the service department of a local Mercedes dealer, in terms of where they are positioned within the pyramid shown in Figure 2.2.

17. Visit a fast food establishment. Do any items on the menu appear to be inconsistent with the degree of quality, flexibility, and service that you typically would expect to be offered? If so, and if the staff are not busy, ask how they prepare this item quickly with high quality and low cost.

BIBLIOGRAPHY

Buffa, Elwood S. *Meeting the Competitive Challenge*. Homewood, Ill.: Dow Jones-Irwin, 1984.

Hayes, Robert H., and Steven C. Wheelwright. *Restoring Our Competitive Edge*. New York: Wiley, 1984, chap. 2.

Hobbs, John M., and Donald F. Heany. "Coupling Strategy to Operating Plans." *Harvard Business Review*, May–June 1977, pp. 119–126.

Lubar, Robert. "Rediscovering the Factory." *Fortune*, July 13, 1981, pp. 52–64.

Skinner, Wickham. "Manufacturing: the Missing Link in Corporate Strategy." *Harvard Business Review*, May–June 1969, pp. 136–145.

———. "The Focused Factory." *Harvard Business Review*, May–June 1974, pp. 113–121.

———. "Reinventing the Factory: A Manufacturing Strategy Response to Industrial Malaise." Chap. 24 in *Competitive Strategies Management*. Englewood Cliffs, N.J.: Prentice-Hall, 1984.

Thomas, Dan R. E. "Strategy Is Different in Service Businesses." *Harvard Business Review*, July–August 1979, pp. 158–165.

Thompson, Arthur A., Jr., and A. J. Strickland III. *Strategy and Policy: Concepts and Cases*. 3rd ed. Plano, Tex.: Business Publications, 1984.

Wheelwright, Steven C. "Reflecting Corporate Strategy in Manufacturing Decisions," *Business Horizons*, February 1979, pp. 57–66.

———. "Japan—Where Operations Really Are Strategic." *Harvard Business Review*, July-August 1981, pp. 67–74.

Supplement D Outline
DECISION MAKING

PHASES OF DECISION MAKING
Recognition of the Need for a Decision / Identification of Objectives / Search for
Reasonable Alternatives / Evaluation of Alternatives / Selection of the Best
Alternative / Implementation

MODELING
Types of Models / The Modeling Process / The Value of Models

MODELS OF DECISION MAKING
Statistical Decision Theory / Application: Example of a Decision Matrix / Decision
Trees / Application: Example of a Decision Tree

Summary / Discussion Questions / Problems / Bibliography

KEY TERMS

Decision making
Models
Modeling
Validation of a model

Statistical decision
  theory
Alternative acts
States of nature
Decision matrix
Payoff matrix

Certainty
Risk
Uncertainty
Maximax
Expected monetary
  value (EMV)

Maximin
Decision trees

Supplement D

DECISION MAKING

Decision making is the act of selecting a preferred course of action among alternatives. The act of decision making enters into almost all of a manager's activities. Managers must reach decisions about objectives and plans for their organizational units. They must decide how to direct, how to organize, how to control. They must not only make many decisions but also guide subordinates in reaching decisions of their own. Much of a manager's time is spent in gathering and evaluating information so that he or she will know if a decision is needed and so that the necessary background information will be available if it is.

Since decisions are so frequently made in all areas of life, one may wonder why so much has been written about decision making in management. The answer is very simple, though it may appear harsh: Businesses and other organizations survive by making and implementing enough of the right decisions; they fail either because they make the right decisions but are unsuccessful in implementing them or because they make the wrong deci-

sions and succeed in implementing them. The success of business and nonprofit organizations hinges on their ability to make good decisions and to implement their decisions well.

Implementation may involve the manager's competence in working with others. Depending on the particular decision, implementation may range from very simple to impossible. It may merely require communicating the decision to one individual who recognizes its wisdom (that is, finds it consistent with his or her view of the world) and performs the required acts. Or it may require long-term programs that will revise the organization's complete method of operation. New people, equipment, responsibilities, organization components, and/or communications patterns may be necessary.

Making and implementing decisions are crucial parts of management. The making of decisions is the major focus of the mathematical and statistical tools of the management sciences. Implementation involves influence, leadership, gaining acceptance of ideas, and other important capabilities dealt with in the behavioral school of management thought. Management sciences attempt to improve the decision-making process. One should understand that management does not consist of mathematical models; the models are tools to aid management in reaching decisions. The management science school and the behavioral school are two sides of the same coin; both help to improve management's chances of success. Much of the material written on operations management deals with methods of making good decisions in planning and controlling the use of resources.

PHASES OF DECISION MAKING

Decisions are made by many methods. No doubt some successful decisions have been made by illogical processes, and some poor decisions have been made by very sophisticated logic. Psychological, emotional, and nonrational factors influence the process. The predominant factor in many decisions is probably experience: "We've done it this way in the past and it worked, so we'll go on doing it this way." Some decisions are based on a follow-the-leader approach: "If they can do it, so can we." Ego may be involved in a decision: "I'll never buy from him again." If a manager walks into a workplace and has a feeling of being crowded or almost trips over a large object protruding from a small space, he may immediately decide that he needs to enlarge or rearrange the workplace.

A detailed study of decisions based on some of the preceding factors would be interesting and perhaps amusing, but it would teach us little about improving the process of reaching decisions. Study of an approach that can be identified, learned, and improved is a much better investment of time for a potential manager. Such an approach requires a structured,

organized, and logical view of decision making. The processes of discovery, analysis, and exploration involved in decision making have been divided into a series of phases to provide this desired expository structure. The actual mental processes and behavior are quite complex. Decision making is a series of interrelated, often overlapping phases, each representing a different point of emphasis rather than a distinctly separate step. The major phases of decision making are discussed in the following sections.

Recognition of the Need for a Decision

Recognizing the need for a decision is not so simple as it may seem. The need arises when actions do not meet objectives and/or objectives need to be reestablished.[1] Frequently either of these situations is termed a problem. The objective of the first phase of decision making can be interpreted as recognizing that there is a problem and defining it. *Problem* in this context can mean an opportunity to change or improve as well as a failure to achieve some intended objective.

Good managers should always be searching for problems and potential problems. Their technical and behavioral competence will provide valuable insights into the operations under their supervision. By understanding the situation, managers are better able to spot potential problems before they develop into more serious problems requiring more difficult decisions. One purpose of the reporting and control systems in a company is to make managers aware of problems that need management attention.

It is imperative that the problem be properly defined once its symptoms have been recognized. Obviously, solving the wrong prob-

[1]Max D. Richards and Paul S. Greenlaw, *Management: Decisions and Behavior*, rev. ed. (Homewood, Ill.: Irwin, 1972), p. 37.

lem is unlikely to give the desired result. The problem-definition phase requires a look behind the scenes. In order to solve a problem, one needs to look beyond the symptoms to discover the causes.

Identification of Objectives

Obviously one cannot make the right decision unless one knows what "right" is. Some criterion or criteria for judging alternatives should be developed in the decision-making process. Sometimes two people facing the same situation reach totally different decisions. It would appear that they have different value systems; that is, they wish to accomplish different objectives. Organizations are more likely to be successful—at least, they will require less coordination effort—if the members agree on what they are seeking to accomplish. Managers can reduce wasted time and uncertainty for their subordinates by keeping them informed about objectives.

An understanding of objectives is desirable in searching for and identifying solutions to a problem. This understanding is by no means essential, however; some managers (and other persons as well) do not want to be very explicit in setting objectives. They may not be able to describe what they are looking for, but if they look at enough alternatives they can tell you which they like best. They identify the desirable features in alternatives as they study the alternatives.

Subordinates are often frustrated when expected to aid in decision making or to seek alternatives under these conditions. It is desirable to have at least general guidelines or objectives to assist associates. Obviously, the final choice must be based on some criteria, explicit or implicit. Subordinates often learn their boss's desires by inferring them from past decisions. Small, informal organizations typically operate in this manner.

Search for Reasonable Alternatives

It is seldom possible to identify and explore all possible alternatives due to limitations of time and money. Talent may also be limited. Certainly creative thinking is a valuable asset in the search for alternatives. Marginal analysis also offers some guidance. The search should proceed only if the incremental gain from an additional alternative is expected to be greater than the incremental cost of further search. One should bear in mind that in conservative organizations, exotic or extreme alternatives are unlikely to be accepted, and such alternatives can therefore be expected to offer little gain.

Use of highly skilled or expert people in the decision-making process can reduce the search activities. Such people have presearched many of the alternatives and have some of the more promising ones in their memory. However, they would seldom have all of the possible alternatives already in mind. Furthermore, no one is likely to discover and identify all of the possible alternatives within a reasonable amount of time. The search process is usually exceedingly complex and is probably a heuristic process. Examination of alternatives may lead to a change in the direction of search for other alternatives. As one identifies alternatives with desirable characteristics, the search is directed toward finding other alternatives with these types of characteristics. If weak points are found in some alternatives, then the search will seek alternatives that lack these shortcomings.

Evaluation of Alternatives

The objective of the fourth phase, evaluation of alternatives, is to compare the consequences one can expect as a result of selecting particular alternatives. A formal, explicit computation of the expected consequences considers both the possible outcomes and the likelihood that they will occur. Such an approach is taken in decision theory, to be discussed later in the supplement. Some preliminary evaluation should have occurred in the preceding phase of decision making as unreasonable alternatives were discarded. Those alternatives that were retained should now be subjected to further scrutiny.

Because each alternative may have several possible outcomes to be evaluated, determining the outcomes and estimating the likelihood of their occurrence can be a time-consuming process. Considerable data collection may be a necessary part of the process. Dealing with a large number of alternatives, each with several possible outcomes, and large amounts of data on each possible outcome is a challenging task. For this reason formal, well-organized approaches to evaluation are of great assistance. Some people find models and quantitative techniques the most valuable tools to use in approaching this task.

Evaluation of alternatives should include the consideration of factors other than the possible outcomes. Often there are differences in the methods and costs necessary to undertake alternatives. Therefore, consideration must also be given to the cost of implementation, the amount of time required to put each alternative into effect, and the likelihood that one can obtain the necessary resources to attempt a particular alternative.

The objective is to select the "best alternative," that is, the one whose expected consequences are most consistent with the objective. If at any stage of evaluation we find that an alternative could not be the best, that alternative requires no further evaluation. For example, one alternative may cause us to lose $200,000, although this outcome is very unlikely. If one of our criteria is that we are willing to risk losing no more than $100,000, this alternative is rejected without further examination. It is apparent that decision making does not consist of distinctly separable steps but is really a process, during which emphasis is placed on various parts of the whole. The phase of evaluating alternatives overlaps selection (which is discussed next) because in some instances alternatives are "selected out" (eliminated from further consideration) before the final decision is reached.

Selection of the Best Alternative

This phase of the decision process is sometimes confused with decision making per se. Granted, one can make a decision by randomly selecting any possible alternative, but only by chance would such a procedure achieve the best alternative. One may not always achieve the best decision even after expending all available effort on the preceding phases, but the greater the effort in the previous phases, the more satisfactory the decision is likely to be.

Selection may be based on the degree to which an alternative appears to achieve the objectives. Sometimes, however, the objective may be simply to surpass some minimum threshold—that is, to find a satisficing solution—and several alternatives may meet this criterion. In such cases one may establish further criteria to select the acceptable alternative with the minimum cost or the minimum time to accomplish or some other objective. Perhaps no alternative meets the criterion. The selection may then be based on how near the alternative comes to achieving the objective sought. A potential scheme may be completely abandoned because no alternative is found to achieve the objective. The decision in this case is to select the alternative not to act. This, of course, is often a feasible alternative.

Implementation

Decision making often is considered primarily a mental process. But if we include all the phases preceding resolution or selection, the process may also involve much physical action in data collection and analysis. The point was made earlier that merely making a decision seldom accomplishes the intended goal. A decision usually must be implemented before it becomes effective—unless the objective of the decision is to determine one's attitude toward a particular subject. When such a decision is made, uncertainty is removed and the objective is accomplished. Management decisions, however, usually involve actions to be taken or discontinued.

Part of the evaluation phase involves preliminary consideration of procedures necessary to implement possible decisions. The implementation phase involves the many subdecisions required to plan and carry out the selected alternative. Who must do what, at what time, in what manner, at what place? Decisions and plans must be made and communicated to everyone who must contribute to the implementation. Further, anyone who, through being uninformed, could interfere with the implementation should be informed of the plans.

Planning the implementation of a selected alternative should also be included in the development of control procedures. A broad outlook might include in this phase developing control procedures for the decision being implemented. Managers frequently plan to have periodic reporting and performance reviews. Determining the types and amount of data to be reported is another subdecision to be made about the selected alternative. Control procedures help to keep the alternative performing properly until its preplanned discontinuance or until a decision is made to change it.

MODELING

Decision making involves extensive mental processing. The analysis and comparison of alternatives involves suppositions. Only very rarely will all possible alternatives actually be tried. More often the alternatives will be considered abstractly, in thought or imagination. The decision maker may visualize them in operation and visualize the possible outcomes. Sometimes these concepts can be expressed in words so that they can be communicated to others. Often other forms of expression, called *models*, are useful in depicting alternatives and in analyzing their performance.

A model is an abstract representation of some real-world process, system, or subsystem. Models are used in all aspects of life. We think and speak with models rather than with actual tangible objects. Accountants do not collect actual dollars in different containers to keep track of various accounts. Instead they write numbers in various locations to represent amounts in the accounts. Words and numbers are symbols that stand for something else; that is, they are abstractions of reality, or models. We carry in our memories a vast array of useful models. When we construct a paragraph to describe something, we are producing a model of the aspects or features that we feel are pertinent and wish to convey. We are accustomed to dealing in abstractions, so the *modeling* process is certainly not a new, incomprehensible mystery.

Types of Models

Beyond our basic representations of reality such as words, numbers, and symbols, there are three general categories of complex models that are useful in analyzing and understanding real-world situations.

Schematic Models A schematic model is a representation in the form of lines and colors, usually on some flat surface, that provides an image of a real-world situation. Graphs, maps, and charts are schematic models.

Physical Models Physical models are usually three-dimensional representations of other objects. They are tangible objects made to look and perform like some aspects of the system being modeled. A globe is a simple physical model of the planet earth. Small model airplanes are tested in wind tunnels to determine the expected aerodynamic characteristics of larger aircraft.

Mathematical Models Mathematical models use arrangements of symbols to depict the process or system being modeled. These symbols are arranged to form equations or mathematical expressions in the same way that the more familiar word symbols are arranged to form sentences to express concepts. This kind of model is the least familiar to most people, but it can provide a high degree of abstraction and it serves as a powerful analytic tool. The equation $A = B + C$ is a mathematical model stating that the object we symbolize by A is the simple sum of the thing we are calling B and the thing we are calling C.

The Modeling Process

Models are developed when the need for a decision is recognized and when one seeks to understand how the real world works. When real-world situations are exceedingly complex, models are necessarily incomplete. Time limitations, expense, and complexity usually preclude the development of a model of every aspect of the real world. Consequently, a model is usually a simplification of the real-world situation; otherwise, it would be just as easy to work with the real world as to work with the model.

Several procedures may be used in simplifying a real-world situation and developing a model. Often the model developer attempts to include in the model only those aspects of the real world that are relevant to the decision at hand. Other simplifying measures may also be taken to reduce the complex real-world situation to a manageable form. Higher-degree mathematical relationships may be simplified to linear (straight-line) relationships. Some components of a complex system may be grouped into larger subsystems to reduce the number of items that must be manipulated. Conditions of certainty may be assumed even though the actual conditions may be probabilistic.

When a simple model has been developed, it is then tested to see if it is adequate for the intended use. If it is not, it may be improved by the abstraction of additional features of the real world until the model is considered valid. *Validation of a model* means gaining confidence that the information it provides about the real world is accurate for its intended purposes. The iterative nature of modeling is indicated by the loop in the left-hand portion of Figure D.1. The model can be put to use once it appears to be a reliable representation of the real world. Application of the model is shown in the right-hand section of the figure.

The Value of Models

The results of the modeling process can sometimes be very useful to decision makers. As an analogy, consider the testing of a small model airplane in a wind tunnel. Such a test provides information with much less expenditure of time and money than a test of a full-scale plane would require. Further, the test can be made with much less risk. Very little property damage or human injury would result from a failure of the test model. Similarly, management can use models to reduce the time, cost, and risk involved in decision making. Any attempt to operate a real business by every reasonable alternative in an attempt to find the best method would be extremely risky, expensive, and time-consuming. Such erratic changes in procedure would frustrate employees and reduce their confidence in management. After one alternative had been tried, it would be difficult or impossible to restore the identical conditions so that the second alternative could be tried.

FIGURE D.1

The Modeling Process and Use of Modeling in Decision Making

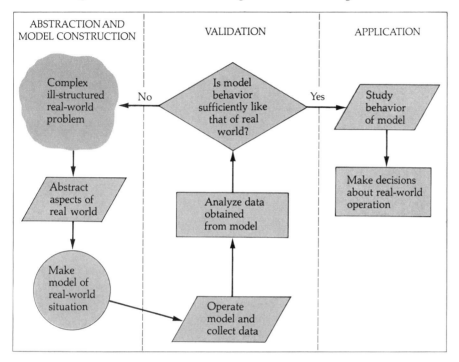

Once an alternative leading to failure had been attempted, further experimentation would be impossible. Models provide managers with some understanding of a system so that they may manage it with reasonable expectation of success.

MODELS OF DECISION MAKING

Models of real-world systems assist decision makers by identifying some of the feasible alternatives and displaying their estimated consequences. Having obtained information, the decision maker still must select the preferred alternative. The final selection is a perplexing challenge and often is the most crucial phase of decision making. Models of the decision process are of great assistance in displaying known data. Two of the models used by managers are decision matrices and decision trees.[2]

Statistical Decision Theory

Statistical decision theory has become recognized as a model of rational selection from alternative courses of action. This model is intended to represent a process of decision making that will lead to the best selection in accordance with an established criterion. Like any other model or process, it does not guarantee the wisdom of the criterion; it merely leads to the alternative that meets the criterion.

[2]Rex V. Brown, ''Do Managers Find Decision Theory Useful?'' *Harvard Business Review*, May–June 1970, p. 79.

General Features Certain basic elements are common to decision making in all situations:

1. Alternative courses of action, sometimes called alternative *acts* or alternative *strategies*. As mentioned previously, the objective is to select the best of these alternatives from among the total set.
2. Conditions outside the control of the decision maker that will determine the consequences of a particular act. These conditions, sometimes termed *events* or *states of nature*, must be mutually exclusive and all possible conditions must be listed (i.e., they must be collectively exhaustive).
3. Payoff or loss, as a measure of the benefit to the decision maker of a particular state of nature resulting from a particular course of action.
4. Some criterion or measure of what constitutes the objective being sought by the decision maker.
5. An environment representing the extent of knowledge about the state of nature that will occur.

The Decision Matrix The first three elements listed above are often displayed in a *decision matrix* to organize some of the features of a situation into an orderly format. The alternatives, A_i, are listed as row headings, the events E_j, are listed as column headings, or vice versa. The consequences, C_{ij}, (payoffs or losses), are then displayed within the body of the matrix at the intersection of the appropriate alternative and the appropriate event. Table D.1 illustrates a decision matrix (sometimes called a *payoff matrix*, payoff table, or loss table).

Decision Environments The environment within which a decision is to be made arises from the degree of certainty about the state of nature that may occur. The environments can be:

1. *Certainty:* The decision maker knows which state of nature will occur.

Table D.1
ILLUSTRATIVE DECISION MATRIX

Alternative Acts or Strategies	STATES OF NATURE (EVENTS)			
	E_1	E_2	$\cdots$	E_N
A_1	C_{11}	C_{12}	$\cdots$	C_{1N}
A_2	C_{21}	C_{22}	$\cdots$	C_{2N}
A_3	C_{31}	C_{32}	$\cdots$	.
.	.	.	$\cdots$	.
.	.	.	$\cdots$	.
.	.	.	$\cdots$	.
A_M	C_{M1}	C_{M2}	$\cdots$	C_{MN}

2. *Risk:* The decision maker does not know which state of nature will occur but can estimate the probability that any one state will occur.
3. *Uncertainty:* The decision maker lacks sufficient information even to estimate the probabilities of the possible states of nature.

Under conditions of certainty, the decision maker needs only one column of the matrix—the one corresponding to the state of nature that will occur. The highest payoff or the smallest loss in this column leads to the best decision—if the best alternative is in the set being examined and if the forecast of consequences is correct. The most common environment for decision making is that of risk. The decision maker may have past data from similar circumstances or subjective estimates of the probabilities.

Decisions Under Uncertainty When the decision maker has no estimates of the probability of events or does not wish to use expected monetary value as a decision criterion, some other selection guide must be used. The *maximax* criterion selects the alternative with the maximum possible return. Under such a criterion the decision maker would examine the payoff matrix, find the largest payoff, and se-

APPLICATION

Example of a Decision Matrix

Larry Locke has been in business, in a city which shall remain nameless, for the past two years. He and his partner, Kirk Key (the mayor's son-in-law), have a sideline business selling used road machinery and paving equipment, which they buy at very good prices from a city agency. The mayor has received some uncomplimentary publicity and his chances of being reelected are rather slim.

Larry and Kirk are considering an opportunity to sell all or part of their business. The potential buyer has made three offers: to pay $60,000 for the entire business, to pay Larry $30,000 for his half of the business, or to pay Larry and Kirk $10,000 each so that each of them would own one third of the company. A matter of risk pertains to the chances that the mayor will be reelected. Larry estimates that the odds are two to one that the mayor will be defeated in the upcoming mayoral race (i.e., the probability is two thirds that he will lose). Larry constructed the payoff table shown in Table D.2. The numbers in the table represent the present worth of the money he will receive if a particular event-act combination occurs.*

Table D.2
POSSIBLE PAYOFFS FOR LARRY LOCKE

Alternative Acts	STATES OF NATURE (EVENTS)		Expected Monetary Value (EMV)
	S_1, Mayor Reelected $P(S_1) = 1/3$	S_2, Mayor Defeated $P(S_2) = 2/3$	
A_1, keep a 1/2 interest	$50,000	$12,000	$24,667
A_2, keep a 1/3 interest	40,000	10,000	20,000
A_3, sell all of his interest	30,000	30,000	30,000

The *expected monetary value (EMV)* was calculated for each alternative. The EMV gives weight to each payoff for an alternative in proportion to the likelihood that the payoff will occur. Larry calculated the EMV for an alternative by multiplying the payoff in the second column by the probability of the first event ($1/3$) and adding to it the payoff in the third column for that alternative times its probability ($2/3$). If there had been more than two possible events, this summation would have been continued until all events had been included. The expression for the expected monetary value, EMV, is

$$EMV_i = \sum_{i=1}^{n} C_{ij} \cdot P(S_j) \tag{D.1}$$

Where EMV_i = the expected monetary value of the ith alternative act
C_{ij} = the payoff or loss for the ith alternative and jth event or state of nature
$P(S_j)$ = the probability that the jth event or state of nature will occur.

Larry used equation D.1 to calculate the expected monetary values for each alternative, as shown in Table D.2. He showed the result to his partner, Kirk Key. They agreed that the expected monetary value was the criterion they should use as a basis for the decision. After considerable discussion, they decided to sell the Locke and Key Machinery Company, lock, stock, and barrel.

*Income that will be received in the future has been discounted to its present value. That is, it has been converted to an equivalent amount of money at the present time so we can compare amounts at the same point in time. This conversion allows for the fact that if we have money, it can earn interest for the use of it.

lect the alternative associated with it. This is a criterion of extreme optimism. The *maximin* is a more pessimistic criterion, under which the decision maker examines only the worst possible outcome of each act and selects the act that will give the largest payoff if the worst circumstances occur.

There are other possible reasons for choosing an alternative. For further discussion of this subject the reader should consult a text on decision theory or statistics.

Decision Trees

A decision matrix might be considered a mathematical model of the decision situation. It seems appropriate to consider it in this way when the calculations of *EMV* are used to represent a measure of an alternative's desirability.

Decision trees also use calculations of *EMV* to measure the attractiveness of alternatives. Decision trees, however, use graphical models as well to display several relevant aspects of a decision situation. These graphical models consist of treelike structures (hence the name) with branches to represent the possible action-event combinations. The conditional payoffs are written at the end of each branch. A tree gives much the same information as a matrix, but in addition it can be used to depict multiple-stage decisions, that is, a series of decisions over time.

The conventions used to represent a situation by a decision tree are shown in Figure D.2. Decision points usually are represented by square blocks with branches representing all alternative decisions emanating from the square. When a decision has been made not to follow one of the branches, that branch can be "sawed off" the tree by two short lines marked across it. Actions not under the control of the decision maker are represented by circular event nodes. Branches from the circles represent the possible states of nature or events that may occur. The probability of each event branch—represented by $P(E_i)$—is shown on each branch. The sum of the probabilities on all branches emanating from an event node must be 1.

It is useful to visualize that the decision maker is going to progress in time from left to right and will end up at one end of one branch of the tree. At some points (squares) he can select the branch he will take. At other junctions, chance will determine the direction in which he must go.

One solves the problem represented by a decision tree by working from right to left. Each outcome at the end of an event branch is multiplied by the probability that it will occur, and these products are summed to obtain the *EMV* at the event node. This *EMV* represents the expected gain (or loss) if the sequence of decisions and events results in the decision maker's reaching this point in the tree.

FIGURE D.2

Symbolic Example of a Decision Tree

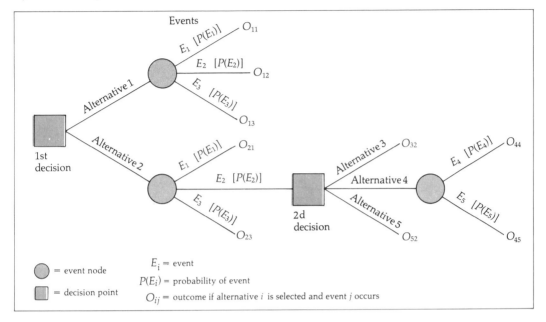

APPLICATION

Example of a Decision Tree

Carl Bright has operated Bright Cleaners ("Service with a Bright Smile") for ten years. He purchased a small cleaning plant when he was discharged from the army and has subsequently added a second location. The business has grown until both plants are being used to their full capacity and there is no room for enlargement. Bright does not want to relocate either business because he feels a major reason for his success is the convenient locations he has acquired.

Bright recognizes that his cleaning operations are very crowded and he would like to improve the way items are moved between the various stages of processing (sorting, cleaning, pressing, and so on). He is considering having an overhead conveyor system installed that will free some floor space currently occupied by dollies used to roll the material between processes. An out-of-town company has proposed to come in and install the conveyor, but Bright is undecided about the work he wants done. The company will equip either location and replace the dollies at the other location for $25,000. If it equips both locations while its work crew and equipment are in town, the cost will be only $45,000. If a conveyor is not installed, Bright must spend $1,000 to replace the dollies that are now used to move material.

Bright feels that the conveyor will save time for his employees, resulting in a present worth (PW) of savings that he estimates at $16,000 per plant. The real potential economic gain resulting from the conveyor is the possibility of increased business resulting from faster service and increased usable work space. There is no absolute guarantee, however, that any new business will materialize. If the conveyor is slower than Bright has estimated or if it breaks down often Bright Cleaners may lose its reputation for service. Bright has estimated the present worths (*PW*s) of increased profits at each location and the probabilities that they will be achieved, shown in Table D.3.

Table D.3
PRESENT WORTHS AND PROBABILITIES
OF INCREASED PROFITS FOR BRIGHT CLEANERS

Increase in Business (Percent)	Present Worth of All Future Profits per Location	Probability of Occurrence
0	$16,000	0.30
3	30,000	0.50
6	50,000	0.20

FIGURE D.3

Decision Tree for Bright Cleaners

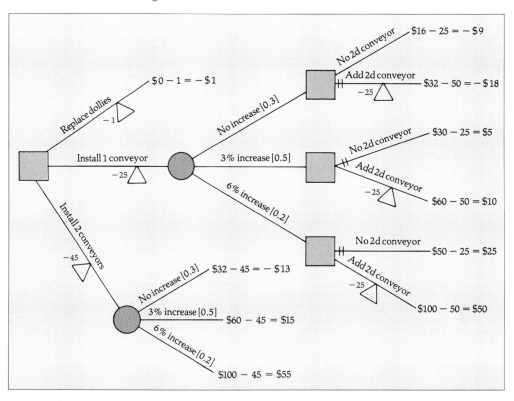

The town is small enough that advertising and a reputation for prompt service are assumed to affect the success of both locations in the same way. So, for simplicity, the same probabilities are used for single or joint results at the two locations. Actually, he could consider the probabilities of a large increase in business at one location and no increase, a moderate increase, or a large increase in business at the other. The decision tree could also be used to consider revising the probability estimates for the level of business at the second location after Bright sees how things turn out at the first installation. (These features are not considered because our objective is to illustrate the features of a decision tree without adding complications that may obscure the basic method.)

Bright constructed the decision tree shown in Figure D.3. His analysis showed the expected values of the three alternative decisions that could be made, shown in Table D.4.

Bright considered the expected values and decided he is definitely interested in the conveyors, but he is still not sure that he wants to risk an extra $20,000 on the initial installation when the increase in expected value for initially installing two conveyors instead of one is only $2,300. Carl Bright is not from Missouri, but his favorite uncle lived there for six years. Carl has decided he will spend $50 or $60 on long-distance calls to talk with other people who have installed conveyors. He wants to recalculate the expected values after he gets more information on the

Table D.4
EVALUATION OF ALTERNATIVE DECISIONS FOR BRIGHT CLEANERS

Alternative Strategies or Acts		STATE OF NATURE			Expected Monetary Value of Each Strategy (Σ Payoff × Probability of Payoff)
		No Increase in Business	3 Percent Increase in Business	6 Percent Increase in Business	
Replaces dollies	Probability of State of Nature	0.3	0.5	0.2	
	Payoff ($)	− 1,000	− 1,000	− 1,000	
	Payoff times Probability of Payoff ($)	− 300	− 500	− 200	− 1,000
Install one conveyor initially; evaluate and install second conveyor if indicated	Payoff ($)	− 9,000	10,000	50,000	
	Payoff times Probability of Payoff ($)	− 2,700	5,000	10,000	12,300
Install two conveyors initially	Payoff ($)	− 13,000	15,000	55,000	
	Payoff times Probability of Payoff ($)	− 3,900	7,500	11,000	14,600

reliability of conveyors, the probability of increases in business, and so on. If Carl buys new dollies, he will have a $1,000 out-of-pocket expense. He may also have an opportunity cost between 0 and $55,000, depending on the amount of future business he would forgo. The uncertainty of the future prevents his being sure that there is any opportunity loss.

If Bright buys one conveyor, he may have a net out-of-pocket cost of $9,000 or a gain of $10,000 or $50,000 if his estimates of cost and volume are correct. His estimates are based on 0, 3 percent, and 6 percent increases in business. Actually the percentage increase in business is a continuous variable. The discrete case is a simplification of the actual situation.

At any decision point immediately prior to an event node, it is assumed that the decision maker will proceed along the branch with the highest *EMV*, so the other branches to the right of the decision point can be sawed off. The *EMV* of the remaining branch from the decision point is transferred to the decision point. This process is continued until the amounts at the right-hand ends of all event branches have been multiplied by their probabilities and summed to the event nodes, and all of the event nodes have been either sawed off or transferred to the left. Eventually the leftmost decision block is reached, and the decision is considered to be the one indicated by the branch with the highest *EMV*.

SUMMARY

Operations managers are required to make decisions as they plan, organize, direct, and control operations activities. Many techniques discussed in this supplement can be used in the course of decision making, even though the decision maker may not consciously develop each step of the process in some formal procedure. Certainly, not all operations management problems can be reduced to models, but many models have been developed and applied in operations management. Two general types of models, the decision matrix and the decision tree, were presented in this section. They were selected for presentation because they depict the decision process itself. They show that one must identify alternatives, forecast the outcome for each alternative, and determine which alternatives seem most appropriate for the objectives. When conditions are not certain, probability can be used to guide the decision maker, who must identify his or her objective or criterion. The decision maker who does not identify an objective is unlikely to find the best way to accomplish it. Even though a decision tree or decision matrix may not be used, decision makers try to estimate the results of various alternatives and make some adjustments according to the likelihood that those results will occur.

Models other than decision trees or decision matrices are presented in future chapters. Some of these models also evaluate alternatives and include probabilities that various outcomes or states of nature will occur. Forecasts frequently are the means by which managers become aware that decisions about the future should be made. Forecasts also help in determining the conditions under which alternative solutions to problems will be implemented and the outcomes expected. The following chapter discusses forecasting and some tools for forecasting.

DISCUSSION QUESTIONS

1. Why is delaying a decision a form of making a decision? Can managers today avoid the decision-making process?
2. Is making the right decision enough to ensure success for a manager? Why, or why not?
3. Why is it popular today to allow subordinates to participate in the decision-making process?
4. The idea of optimization implies that we can identify all possible alternatives and evaluate them from the viewpoint of the total system. *Suboptimization* refers to the fact that we can optimize only a subset of a total system. Discuss some reasons that suboptimization is a fact of life.
5. Name the six phases of the decision process.
6. Explain the role of models in the decision process. Name and describe the three types of model used.
7. On what strength would the accuracy of statistical decision theory rely?
8. What is the most common environment for decision making?

PROBLEMS

1. A young company has been successful in its first two years of operation and is planning to open a second location. Its management is trying to decide whether to build a small, medium, or large facility. The level of demand at the new facility can be described as poor, moderate, or good, with the probability for poor 0.20, for moderate 0.55, and for good 0.25.

   If a large facility is built and business is good, the net present worth (*PW*) of the after-tax earnings is estimated to be $175,000. If business is moderate for the large facility, the *PW* will be $100,000, and if business is poor the facility will lose a *PW* of $50,000.

   A medium-sized facility will lose a *PW* of $20,000 if business is poor and will make a *PW* of $110,000 if business is moderate. If business is good, the medium-sized facility is expected to earn a *PW* of $120,000, or it can be enlarged at a cost of $50,000 to earn

   a *PW* of $165,000 before the cost of the expansion is deducted.

   A small facility is estimated to earn a *PW* of $15,000 if business is poor. If business is moderate, the small facility is expected to earn a net *PW* of $60,000, or it can be enlarged moderately at a cost of $40,000 to earn a *PW* of $90,000 before the cost of the enlargement is deducted. If business is good, the small facility will earn a *PW* of $60,000, or it can be enlarged moderately at a cost of $40,000 to earn $90,000 (as above) or greatly at a cost of $60,000 to earn a *PW* of $160,000 before the cost of the expansion is deducted.

   (a) Draw the decision tree for this decision.
   (b) Decide what the company should do to achieve the highest *EMV*.

2. Demand for electric power in a region appears to be growing at a rate of 6 percent

per year and a new generating plant is being designed to serve this demand. The company feels that there is 0.70 probability that the demand will continue to grow at this rate and a probability of 0.30 that the demand growth may slow to about 5 percent. A smaller plant costing $290 million and a larger plant costing $340 million are being considered. If the smaller plant is built and demand remains high, the generating capacity can be expanded.

The net present worth of all future annual operating revenues minus disbursements other than those for recovery of the plant investment is $485 million if the larger plant is built and demand is high. If demand is low, the company will have used valuable capital in excess capacity and will have to follow uneconomical alternatives in other operating decisions within the company so that the PW will be only $375 million.

Should the company elect to build a smaller plant and the demand be low, the PW will be $410 million. If the demand is high under this condition, the company has the option of purchasing power so that the PW will be $370 million, or it can expand the plant generating capacity for $90 million. With expansion programs there will be some inefficiencies and lost revenues so that the PW will be $480 million.

(a) Draw a decision tree for this analysis.
(b) Which decision should the company make to maximize the expected present worth after the cost of the plant is deducted?

3. The Flying Turkey Airline runs a gambling junket flight from a midwestern city to Las Vegas. Passengers are charged $100 in advance. This amount is refunded if the passenger does not show for the flight. The airline thus loses $100 in revenue for each empty seat. If the flight is overbooked, however, the airline has to pay $160 (the cost of a ticket on a commercial flight) to each passenger it cannot accommodate. The probabilities of no-shows are shown in the decision matrix below. How many passengers should the airline overbook for each flight?

Alternative Strategies	STATES OF NATURE (NUMBER OF NO-SHOWS)			
	0	1	2	3
Probability	0.5	0.25	0.15	0.10
Overbook 0				
Overbook 1				
Overbook 2				
Overbook 3				

4. A company is considering modifying its method of production. Their options include introducing two relatively new methods (Method A or Method B) or continuing their present method. Demand for their finished product is described as low, medium, and high. If demand is low, Method A would result in net present worth (PW) of $0 for the after-tax earnings; Method B would result in a PW of $4,000; the present method would earn a PW of $3,500. If demand is medium, the PW of the after-tax earnings for Methods A and B would be $5,000 and for the present method $4,000. If demand is high, Method A would earn a PW of $10,000, Method B and the present method would each earn a PW of $6,000. The company has decided to use the EMV as the sole criterion for their decision. The estimated probability of low demand is 0.2; medium demand, 0.7; and high demand, 0.1. Construct the decision matrix that describes the events and alternatives and decide which investment the company should choose.

,

BIBLIOGRAPHY

Bierman, Harold, Charles P. Bonini, and Warran H. Hausman. *Quantitative Analysis for Business Decisions.* 6th ed. Homewood, Ill.: Irwin, 1981, Chaps. 1–6.

Brown, Rex V. "Do Managers Find Decision Theory Useful?" *Harvard Business Review,* May–June 1970.

Lee, Sang M., and Laurence J. Moore. *Introduction to Decision Science.* New York: Petrocelli/Charter Publishers, 1975. Chaps. 1 and 3.

Simon, Herbert A. *The New Science of Executive Decision Making.* New York: Harper & Row, 1960.

Smith, David Eugene. *Quantitative Business Analysis.* New York: Wiley, 1977. Chaps. 3 and 4.

Chapter Outline
FORECASTING DEMAND

ASPECTS OF FORECASTING

What Is Forecasting? / Types of Forecasts / Factors that Influence Demand / Dilemmas of Forecasting / Forecast Time Spans and Update Frequencies / Two General Approaches: Buildup versus Breakdown

QUALITATIVE VERSUS QUANTITATIVE METHODS

Qualitative or Subjective Forecasting / Quantitative or Statistical Forecasting Methods

TIME SERIES SMOOTHING

Simple Moving Average / Weighted Moving Average / Exponential Smoothing

MEASURES OF FORECAST ERROR

The Mean Absolute Deviation (MAD) / Mean Square Error (MSE) / Mean Forecast Error (MFE) / The Mean Absolute Percentage Error (MAPE) / *Application: Example of Exponential Smoothing*

TIME SERIES DECOMPOSITION

Multiplicative and Additive Models / *Application: Example of Time Series Decomposition*

CAUSAL MODELS

Regression Methods / *Application: An Example of Simple Linear Regression*

USING COMPUTERS TO FORECAST

Operations Management in Action   HOW PERSONAL COMPUTERS ARE CHANGING THE FORECASTER'S JOB

MONITORING AND CONTROLLING FORECASTS

Summary / Solved Problems / Discussion Questions / Problems / Bibliography

KEY TERMS

Forecasting	Irregular component	Mean forecast error (MFE)	Regression methods
Forecast	Simple moving average		Leading indicator
Prediction	Stability	Mean square error (MSE)	Dependent variable
Technological forecast	Responsiveness		Independent variable
Economic forecast	Weighted moving average	Time series decomposition	Coefficient of linear correlation
Demand forecast	Exponential smoothing	Turning point	Tracking signal
Business cycle	Mean absolute deviation (MAD)	Multiplicative model	Running sum of forecast errors (RSFE)
Product life cycle		Additive model	
Time series	Mean absolute percentage error (MAPE)	Causal models	Adaptive smoothing
Trend component			
Seasonal component			
Cyclical component			

Chapter 3

FORECASTING DEMAND

Many of the decisions managers make require forecasts or estimates about the future. A company must have some estimate of demand in the near and inter-mediate-term future if wise decisions are to be made about how to use its current resources in operating the production system. (Operating the production system is discussed in Part II of this book.) And a company must have some estimate of the demand that will exist over the long term in various territories as a basis for long-range decisions about the location and design of its operations facilities, as well as for other long-range decisions. (Design of the production system is discussed in Part III of this book.) In this final chapter of Part I, we consider forecasting because it is the foundation for many of the decisions to be discussed later.

Various aspects of forecasting are presented in the chapter. The primary focus is on demand forecasts, because demand directly affects the plans and decisions of the operations function. Several forecasting methods and models, ranging from subjective opinions to mathematical computations, are examined.

ASPECTS OF FORECASTING

What Is Forecasting?

Forecasting, in simple terms, is attempting to state beforehand what will happen in the future. In this book, a forecast is considered to be a prediction or estimate of future conditions. Authors sometimes make a distinction between a forecast and a prediction. They sometimes use *forecast* to mean calculations from or extrapolation of a previous pattern by mathematical means, and they use *prediction* to mean conjecture or the use of subjective knowledge or experience to arrive at an estimate of the future. Some dictionaries offer definitions that suggest reverse meanings. No distinctions between forecasts and predictions will be made in this book. Purely subjective forecasts are considered to be possible. And a scientifically calculated forecast can be adjusted to incorporate subjective estimates without losing its right to be called a forecast.

Types of Forecasts

Businesses and other organizations may use several types of forecasts, depending on the objective and the situation for which a forecast is to be used. Three types are discussed below, with primary consideration given to demand forecasts.

Technological Forecasts   A *technological forecast* is an estimate of rates of technological progress. Certainly electric utilities are interested in the rates of technological advancement in solar and nuclear power. Chemical and petroleum companies want to know about the development of processes to make usable fuel from oil shale. Technological changes will provide many companies with new products and materials to offer for sale, while other businesses will be faced with competition from those companies. Even if the product remains unchanged, a new process for producing it can be developed, thus rendering large capital investments obsolete. Technological forecasting is probably best performed by specialists in the particular technology. Although technological developments affect operations management, the forecasting of these developments is not within the focus of managing operations and will not be considered specifically.

Economic Forecasts   Governmental agencies and other organizations publish *economic forecasts*, or statements of expected future business conditions. Expectations of the general business climate are of interest to governmental agencies in anticipating tax revenues, levels of employment, the needs of the economy for money, and other matters. Business can obtain ideas about long-range and intermediate-range business growth from this type of forecast. The details of general business or economic forecasting, however, are outside the scope of our study.

Demand Forecasts   The *demand forecast* gives the expected level of demand for the company's goods or services throughout some future period and is usually an instrument in the company's planning and control decisions. Since the operations function is responsible for providing the company's goods and services, operations decisions are greatly influenced by demand forecasts. We will assume in this chapter that the company intends to make and is successful in making the level of sales equal to the demand. Thus the demand forecast and the sales forecast are assumed to be the same.

Factors that Influence Demand

The portion of total demand that actually flows to a particular company is a result of many factors. Basically, it depends on the size of the total market for the particular good or service and the share of the market that the company is successful in capturing. A number of forces that are beyond the company's control, as well as some that the company can at least influence, act to determine the level of demand that the company receives. Some of these factors are discussed below.

The Business Cycle   Sales are influenced by demand and demand is influenced by a large number of factors. One factor that influences demand is the status of the economy as the *business cycle* goes through the phases of recovery, inflation, recession, and depression. Government actions and reactions are intended to mitigate the severity of this variation, but it is still a fact of life in much of the business world.

Product Life Cycle   A product, whether goods or services, is not sold to the same percentage of the population or target market every day of its existence. Normally, each successful product may be considered to pass through five stages in its *product life cycle,* as shown in Figure 3.1.

If a product has market appeal and enters the rapid-growth stage, competitors will usually introduce similar products in an attempt to capture part of the market. The result is changing competitive pressures, which may slow the growth rate. A product that has a long life eventually reaches a point when almost everyone who desires to own it and can purchase it has already done so. At such a point demand diminishes. Consumable items (toothpaste, clothes) and some services (haircuts, car washes) do not reach such a point in the life cycle, as they are "consumed" and repurchased. Market research and product improvement efforts are undertaken to modify nonconsumable products so that

FIGURE 3.1

Stages of Product Life Cycle

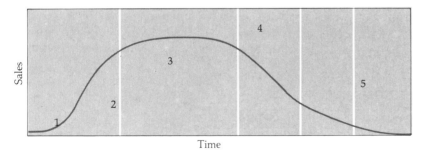

1. product development   2. testing and introduction   3. rapid growth of demand
4. steady-state demand   5. phase out

FIGURE 3.2

Some Factors That Affect Demand for a Company's Product or Service

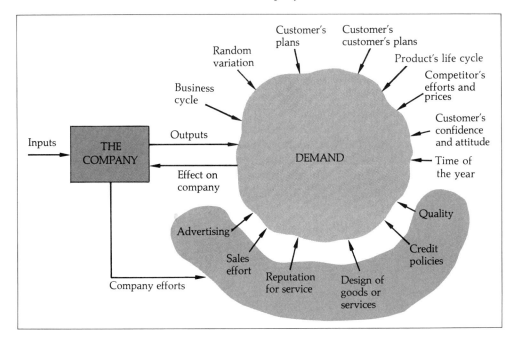

their appeal in the marketplace lasts longer than it otherwise would. In the meantime research and product development activities should be under way so that new goods or services can be introduced to maintain the company's existence when other offerings are phased out.

It is probably a rare occurrence for a product to experience several years of steady-state (or unchanging) conditions that affect demand for it. One can readily see that there is a danger in extrapolating trends very far.

Other Factors   A large number of other factors influence demand (see Figure 3.2), particularly when one considers secondary influences, that is, factors that affect the customer's demand for goods and services, which in turn affects demand for the company's product or service. Figure 3.2 shows schematically some of the factors that affect demand.

Dilemmas of Forecasting

After reviewing some of the forces that act on demand, one fact should be obvious. No totally infallible method of predicting the future has yet been devised. Forecasting is a special skill rather than a science. The key inputs in science are constant laws of nature, whereas the key inputs in forecasting are informed judgments. A forecaster may use sophisticated mathematics and sci-entific methods in analyzing data to arrive at a forecast, but there are no laws that require future values of the variables to behave as predicted. Most forecasts are subject to error. Yet the effectiveness of a company's plans and decisions often depends on how well the company was able to forecast demand or how well it is able to forecast the conditions that would result from alternative courses of action. Many companies operate with extra resources as a contingency to protect themselves in case of forecast error. Companies face a dilemma in de-termining whether to spend more money to try to improve their forecasting accuracy or to spend more for additional contingency resources.

Measurement of Forecast Accuracy   The accuracy of a forecast is affected by the dynamic nature of the demand pattern that is to be forecast and the forecast method that is used. It is useful to have an estimate of the amount of error that typically occurs when a particular forecast model is used to try to predict a particular pattern. This information is valuable in selecting the most appropriate model to use and it provides some estimate of the extent to which a company should prepare for deviations from the expected demand. We will discuss the mean absolute deviation, MAD, the mean square error, MSE, the mean forecast error, MFE, and the mean absolute percentage error, MAPE, as four measures of forecast error. These measures are best explained by illustrating them with quantitative data, so we will present them when we discuss quantitative forecast models later in the chapter.

Forecast Time Spans and Update Frequencies

The business world is a dynamic place. Since demand is influenced by many factors, the likelihood is great that some of the factors will change within a fairly short time. As more time passes, more and greater changes are likely to occur. Consequently, a short-term forecast is generally more accurate than a long-term forecast. Each day something may occur to change a company's prospects or to change the available information from which it infers its future prospects. At the end of each sales period, the company can tally another measure of its performance. A forecast should be reviewed and revised often if a company is in a dynamic environment.

At designated time periods, usually each month, the new sales records are compiled and actual demand is compared with forecasted demand for that period. This comparison indicates whether the forecasting method is working satisfactorily and helps management decide if any plans need to be revised due to unanticipated levels of demand. Sometimes an evaluation of forecast accuracy is done by a subjective review. Alternatively, an objective calculation such as a tracking signal (to be discussed later) is used. New sales data are periodically used to develop an updated forecast, usually on a monthly or quarterly basis. These frequent forecasts estimate demand, usually for a horizon of up to one year. In addition to frequently developing a one-year forecast, many companies

Table 3.1
TYPES AND CHARACTERISTICS OF FORECASTS

Type of Forecast	Time Span	Use	Characteristics	Methods
Long-range	Generally 5 years or more	Business planning: Product planning Research programming Capital planning Plant location and expansion	Broad, general Often only qualitative	Technological Economic Demographic Marketing studies Judgment
Intermediate-range	Generally 1 season to 2 years	Aggregate planning: Capital and cash budgets Sales planning Production planning Production and inventory budgeting	Numerical Not necessarily at the item level Estimate of reliability needed	Collective opinion Time series Regression Economic index correlation or combination Judgment
Short range	Generally less than 1 season; 1 day to 1 year	Short-run control: Adjustment of production and employment levels Purchasing Job scheduling Project assignment Overtime decisions	May be at item level for planning of activity level Should be at item level for adjustment of purchases and inventory	Trend extrapolation Graphical Explosion of short-term product or product family forecasts Judgment Exponential smoothing

will annually develop a longer-range (often five-year horizon) forecast which is used as the basis for long-range planning.[1] A company might have multiple forecasts, each of which focuses on a different horizon, to facilitate decisions that deal with different lead times. Some of the characteristics of forecasts with different horizons and some decisions that are based on these types of forecasts are shown in Table 3.1. It is important that these decisions and forecasts be consistent. That is, short-range decisions should be leading toward the same objectives as the longer-range decisions.

The time span appropriate for one decision may be inappropriate for another. Forecasting methods therefore vary with the plans to be formulated. Some decisions are primarily oriented toward short time spans. The current

[1] Judy Pan, Donald R. Nichols, and O. Maurice Joy, "Sales Forecasting Practices of Large U.S. Industrial Firms," *Financial Management*, Fall 1977.

level of demand places short-term requirements on the operations function, and on other parts of an organization as well. For example, the current level of demand influences decisions regarding the number of hours to be worked and the use of overtime or part-time work in the operations function. It also influences the activities of procurement, shipping, and receiving subunits.

The trend of demand is equally important. Projection of the trend may stimulate such long-range planning as expansion of capacity, the opening of a new plant, or the closing of an existing facility or its conversion to a new purpose. A new facility may require a rather long planning horizon to allow time to evaluate and select the site, design the facility, raise the necessary capital, construct the building, recruit and train personnel, and purchase the equipment and supplies necessary to begin operation. Construction of a nuclear power plant may require ten years or more from initial plans to actual power production. Obviously a power company must know well in advance that it will need additional generating capacity.

Two General Approaches: Buildup Versus Breakdown

There are two general approaches to forecasting. One is a "buildup" approach, whereby sales forecasts for many individual items are developed and then combined to arrive at some expected total. The other is a "breakdown" approach: a forecast is made for a homogeneous group of items and then the portion of the total forecast that each item is expected to contribute is estimated. Since totals are generally more stable than small units, the breakdown approach probably is a good one to use when it is suitable. If a product line shows a stable relationship among the sales of its components, these items probably may be lumped so that the breakdown approach can be used to forecast the demand for them. The sales of clothes washers and dryers, for example, are probably closely related, so that a gross total can be divided between them, with some usual percentage expected for dryer sales. A company that sells cattle feed and dog food, however, might find that the products have no stable relationship. In such a case, it would be necessary to forecast each item independently. As discussed previously, the purpose of the forecast also will affect the grouping of items.

The Need for Judgment   After the items or groups of items have been determined, a forecaster may consider one or more methods of formulating the forecast. No forecasting method gives highly accurate results in all applications. A sound approach is the use of two or more complementary methods. Managers should not look upon any forecast as a substitute for common sense or judgment. Good forecasting is essentially a blend of information, analysis, experience, and judgment. Several methods of forecasting are discussed briefly in the following paragraphs. The intent is to provide only a general understanding of the method. Further information should be reviewed before any method is selected and used.

QUALITATIVE VERSUS QUANTITATIVE METHODS

Qualitative or Subjective Forecasting Methods

Forecasts can range from spur-of-the-moment hunches to complex mathematical equations. Certainly the simplest and sometimes the fastest methods are those involving only subjective judgment without expressing the forecast in mathematical formulas. Of the many possible subjective methods, we shall consider three. Each method uses a different source for the subjective data.

Field Sales Force   The first subjective forecasting method is that of having each sales representative estimate the sales within his or her territory. The estimates are combined and reviewed at successive levels of the management hierarchy so that the opinions of the district managers and the sales managers are also incorporated.

Forecasts of this nature have several advantages, one of which is that they are easily divided by territory, branch, sales representative, or product. The sales representatives may be more highly motivated when they have a feeling of participating in the planning process. This method provides input from persons in direct contact with the customer. A method such as this is most suitable for a new product.

Since this is a subjective method, it has the disadvantage of being subject to individual biases. Sales representatives may be unduly influenced by recent market responses. If the sales performance goals are based on the forecast, sales representatives may be tempted to underestimate. If the forecast is a basis for the allocation of some scarce products, sales representatives may overestimate.

Jury of Executives   The second subjective forecasting method involves the averaging of independent estimates or a discussion by a group of executives that results in a single estimate. Sometimes one senior officer reviews estimates from sales, production, and finance executives and applies his or her judgment to come to a single estimate.

An advantage of this method is that it can provide a forecast in a relatively short time. It also brings a variety of viewpoints to bear on the subject and can foster a team spirit.

This method, however, requires the time of highly paid executives. It is more difficult to develop breakdowns by territory, district, sales representative, and product. It is also subject to biases due to individual attitudes and situations.

Users' Expectations   A company may seek subjective opinions from people outside the organization. One such method is the users' expectations method. Sales representatives may poll their customers or potential customers about their purchasing plans for the future. Mail questionnaire or telephone surveys may be used to obtain the opinions of existing or potential customers.

An advantage of this method is that it provides the forecaster with an opportunity to learn some of the thinking behind the customer's intentions. The forecaster may obtain the users' views of the product's advantages and weaknesses as well as insight into the reasons some consumers are failing to buy the product. Such information makes this method useful in planning product improvements or product developments.

One potential disadvantage of the users' expectation method is that it may annoy some highly valued customers. This method commands more confidence than it may warrant because customers' buying expectations are based on their forecasts, which are also subject to change and error. This method of forecasting often requires a considerable amount of time and a large staff.

Quantitative or Statistical Forecasting Methods

Quantitative forecasting methods use a mathematical expression or model to show the relationship between demand and some independent variable or variables. There are two major types of quantitative forecasting models: time series models and causal models. Time series models use time as the independent variable and project the "pattern"—that is, the relationship that demand has had with time in the past—to estimate demand in the future. Causal models use some independent variable or variables instead of or in addition to time, with which demand has tended to show a consistent relationship in the past. Values of the independent variable or variables are used in the model to calculate the future value of demand that the model predicts. Of course, for the model to be useful as a forecasting tool, changes in the independent variables must take place with sufficient lead time before the associated changes in demand. (These variables are sometimes called *leading indicators.*)

Use of either of the two types of quantitative models (time series or causal) as a forecasting tool rests on an assumption of continuity. That is, one assumes that the type and degree of relationship between demand and the independent variable(s) that existed in the past will continue in the future. We do not have to understand why the relationship exists, but for the model to work, the relationship must continue to follow the model.

Forecasting by time-series methods can involve the application of either of two types of models. Time series smoothing models or time series decomposition models can be applied, depending on which seems more appropriate for the type of demand pattern that exists and the purpose for which the forecast is to be used. We will discuss time series smoothing models in the next section of the chapter. Later, we will discuss time series decomposition, after presenting material about quantitative measures of forecast error that can be used to compare the accuracy of various forecast methods. Causal models are briefly discussed as the last category of forecast models in the chapter.

TIME SERIES SMOOTHING

A *time series* is a sequence of data points at constant intervals of time. A chain of daily, weekly, or monthly sales data, for example, is a time series. Although at times no immediately discernible pattern can be seen in a time series, the

FIGURE 3.3

A Four-Year Time-Series and Its Components

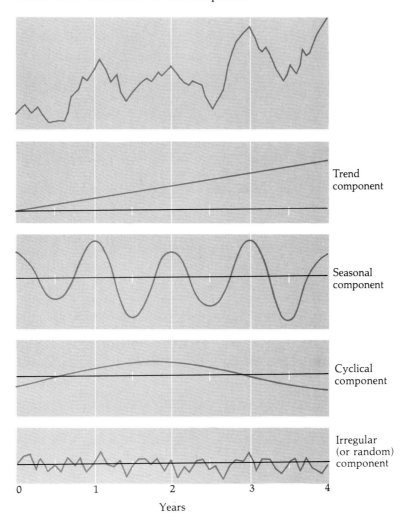

data can contain components that have a pattern. Four commonly recognized components of a time series are its trend, seasonal, cyclical, and irregular components, which are briefly described below and are shown in Figure 3.3.

1. The *trend component* is the general upward or downward movement of the average over time. These movements may require as much as fifteen or twenty years of data to determine and describe them.

2. The *seasonal component* is a recurring fluctuation of demand above and below the trend value that repeats with a usual frequency of one year.

3. The *cyclical component* is a recurrent upward and downward movement that repeats with a frequency that is longer than a year. This movement

is usually attributed to business cycles (inflation, recession, etc.), so it may not have a consistent period of repetition.

4. The *irregular* (or random) *component* is a series of short, erratic movements that follow no discernible pattern.

When the irregular component of a time series has large fluctuations relative to the other components, it is often useful to smooth out the data by averaging several observations together so that the basic nature of the pattern is more apparent. Three averaging techniques—simple moving average, weighted moving average and exponential smoothing—are discussed below. Generally, these techniques are appropriate to produce final forecasts only if there is no trend in the data, that is, if the slope is horizontal. Averaging techniques that determine and project trends are available, but these techniques are not discussed here.[2]

Simple Moving Average

A *simple moving average* is a method of computing the mean of only a specified number of the most recent data values in a series. Assume, for example, that we were keeping records of monthly sales. We might compute, say, a three-month moving average at the end of each month to smooth out random fluctuations and get an estimate of the average sales per month. This number would be useful to see if the average had increased or decreased since some prior period. A moving average is also useful for other reasons. If there is no noticeable trend or seasonality in the data, the moving average gives a forecast of the mean value of sales in future periods. A moving average can be used to average out seasonality if the number of periods included in the average is equal to the amount of time required for the seasonal pattern to start to repeat itself, i.e., 12 months of monthly data or four quarters of quarterly data, etc. if the seasonal pattern repeats each year.

To compute a three-month moving average, at the end of each month we would add sales for the latest three months and divide by three. If we wanted a four-month moving average, at the end of each month we would sum sales for the latest four months and divide by four. At the end of a period, t, the n-period simple moving average, which might be used as a forecast for period $t + 1$ if the data series is stationary, is given by equation 3.1.

$$SMA_{t+1} = \left(\frac{1}{n}\right) \sum_{i=t+1-n}^{t} A_i \qquad (3.1)$$

SMA_{t+1} = the simple moving average at the end of period t (It might be used as a forecast for period $t + 1$.)

A_i = actual demand in period i

n = the number of periods included in each average.

[2]See Spyros G. Makridakis, Steven C. Wheelwright, and Victor E. McGee, *Forecasting Methods and Applications*, 2nd ed. (New York: Wiley, 1983), p. 77.

Table 3.2
EXAMPLE OF 3-MONTH SIMPLE MOVING AVERAGE

Month	Demand for Month (Units)	Total Demand During Past 3 Months (Units)	3 Month Average Demand (Units/Month)
20	120 ⎫		
21	130 ⎬ — — — — — — 360 - — — — — ÷ 3 — — →120		
22	110 ⎭	380	126.67
23	140	360	120
24	110	380	126.67
25	130		

An example of the computations for a three-month simple moving average is shown in Table 3.2. At the end of month 22, the demand for months 20, 21, and 22 are added and divided by 3 to give a value of 120. At the end of month 23, the demand for months 21, 22, and 23 are added and divided by 3 to give a value of 126.67, and so on. If too many periods are included in the moving average, the method suffers a shortcoming. Such a forecast is said to be very "stable," meaning it does not shift quickly with changes in demand. *Stability* refers to the ability of a forecast to maintain consistency in the face of (not to be fooled by) random fluctuations about the true base level of demand.

Responsiveness is the ability of a forecast to adjust quickly to true changes in the base level of demand. Both stability and responsiveness are desirable in a forecast. Unfortunately, these two characteristics are in conflict. Several demand periods are required to determine if the new level of demand is persisting or if a change has been just a random fluctuation. If a forecast is changed in immediate response to each change in actual demand, it will also respond to random fluctuation. If a demand pattern is known to have relatively small random fluctuations about some fairly stable level, then a responsive forecasting method should be used. If a demand pattern is known to have large random fluctuations, then a stable forecasting method should be used. Both responsiveness and stability are difficult to achieve with a forecasting method that looks only at the series of past demands without considering factors that may have caused a change in that pattern. Naive forecasting methods alone do not consider the external causative factors.

The responsiveness of a four-period moving average to a shift in a stable level of demand is illustrated in Figure 3.4. Random variations have been omitted but would be expected to cancel out one another fairly well so that the average would be close to the values depicted in the figure. Notice that the four-period moving average took four periods to adjust to the new level of demand. A ten-period moving average would have required ten periods to adjust. An *n*-period moving average would require *n* periods to adjust. We see

FIGURE 3.4

Responsiveness of a Moving Average to a True Shift in the Average Level of Demand

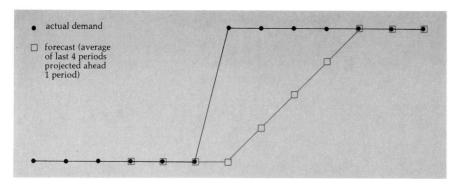

that the responsiveness of a moving average forecast is inversely related to the number of periods included in the average.

Stability is illustrated in Figure 3.5. Notice that a single random fluctuation above the stable average will be reflected in the average, causing it to increase by $1/n$, where n is the number of periods included in the average. This means that the more periods that are included in a moving average, the more stable the forecast will be. Since a moving average is an average of a group of past demand values, it does not anticipate future trends. In the presence of a consistent trend in demand, the simple moving average will lag behind the next value in the series by $(n + 1)/2$ periods. If it were plotted on the time period corresponding to the center of the time periods being averaged, it would be close to the trend line. When it is used as a tool to forecast (meaning to throw ahead), however, the actual demand values will have already moved away from the forecast value. This property of the simple moving average is illustrated in

FIGURE 3.5

Stability of a Moving Average When a Random Pulse or "Spike" Occurs

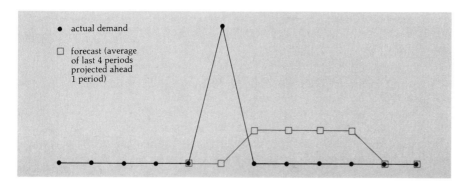

FIGURE 3.6

Reaction of a Moving Average to a Trend

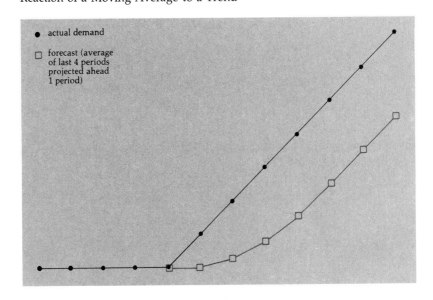

- ● actual demand
- □ forecast (average of last 4 periods projected ahead 1 period)

Figure 3.6. If the up trend continues, the forecast average will always be below the actual values.

Weighted Moving Average

Equal weights were assigned to all periods in the computation of a simple moving average. A *weighted moving average* assigns more weight to some values than to others. Table 3.3 shows the computations for a three-month weighted moving average with a weight of 3 assigned to the most recent demand value, a weight of 2 assigned to the next-most-recent value and a weight of 1 assigned

Table 3.3
EXAMPLE OF A THREE-MONTH WEIGHTED MOVING AVERAGE

| Month | Demand | WEIGHTED VALUES FOR MONTH | | | | Total Weighted Value | Weighted Moving Average (Total ÷ 6) |
		Month 22	Month 23	Month 24	Month 25		
20	120	1 × 120					
21	130	2 × 130	1 × 130				
22	110	3 × 110	2 × 110	1 × 110		710 ⟶ 118.33	
23	140		3 × 140	2 × 140	1 × 140	770 ⟶ 128.33	
24	110			3 × 110	2 × 110	720 ⟶ 120.0	
25	130				3 × 130	750 ⟶ 125.0	

to the oldest of the demand values included in the average. The rationale for varying the weights is usually to allow recent data to influence the forecast more than older data. If there is a long-run trend in demand, a weighted average with heavier emphasis on recent data is an improvement over a simple average, but it will still lag behind demand. We cannot average the past sales values and get a higher value than any past sales value, which is what one desires when one is trying to project the next value in a continuing upward trend. There are methods of adjusting a moving average to compensate for the presence of a trend in demand data, but these will not be discussed here.[3]

Exponential Smoothing

Another form of weighted moving average is an exponentially smoothed average. This method keeps a running average and adjusts it each period in proportion to the difference between the latest actual demand figure and the latest value of the average, as expressed in equation 3.2.

$$SF_{t+1} = \alpha A_t + (1 - \alpha)SF_t \quad \text{or} \quad SF_{t+1} = SF_t + \alpha(A_t - SF_t) \qquad \textbf{(3.2)}$$

where SF_{t+1} = the single smoothed forecast for the time period following period t

SF_t = the value of the smoothed forecast for period t

α = a smoothing constant that determines the weight given to previous data ($0 \le \alpha \le 1$)

A_t = actual demand in period t.

The smoothing constant, α, is a decimal between 0 and 1 and often is set at a value that produces forecasts that fit past data better than forecasts computed with any other value of α. It also influences the stability and responsiveness of the forecast. Examination will show that if α were set to equal 0, the old forecast would not be adjusted in any way, regardless of the actual demand that occurred. This would result in a very stable forecast but it would not respond in any way to changes. If α were set to equal 1, the latest forecast would equal the last actual value—very responsive but not stable if there is any random fluctuation in the data. Values of α between 0.1 and 0.3 are often used. An initial forecast must be obtained by another method (such as simple average or weighted average) to begin a series of exponentially smoothed forecasts.

Exponential smoothing gets its name because it results in a series of weights assigned to past data that decay exponentially as the data get older. Our latest forecast, SF_{t+1}, depends on the latest actual value, A_t, and the previous forecast, SF_t. But SF_t depended on A_{t-1} and SF_{t-1}; SF_{t-1} was determined by A_{t-2} and SF_{t-2}; and so on. One can see that many periods are included in the average even though they do not appear explicitly in equation 3.2. The weights given to data will be a function of α, as shown in Figure 3.7.

[3]See, for example, Makridakis, Wheelwright, and McGee, *Forecasting Methods and Applications*, p. 77.

FIGURE 3.7

Weights Assigned to Past Data by Exponential Smoothing with Various Values of α

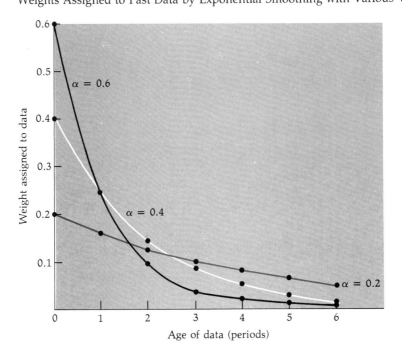

Single smoothed forecasts are a form of moving average, so they also have the limitation of lagging behind a trend in actual demand. Since single smoothed forecasts adjust to deviations by only the fraction α, these forecasts will fall further and further behind as the trend persists. These limitations are illustrated in Figure 3.8. Exponential smoothing is intended to estimate the average of a fairly uniform level of demand by smoothing out the fluctuations. It also smooths out periodic fluctuations in demand due to seasonal variation. The single smoothed forecast lags behind the demand movements and does not swing with so large an amplitude as does the actual demand. This can be seen in Figure 3.8(b).

A trend in the demand pattern can be adjusted for by double exponential smoothing. As the name implies, double exponential smoothing keeps two smoothed averages: one estimates the average level of demand and the second estimates the average trend. The trend can be projected beyond the average to overcome the lag that would occur if only a single smoothed forecast were used. Winters' model for triple exponential smoothing can be used to forecast demand when both trend and seasonal variations occur. It adds a third type of smoothed average to estimate the seasonal coefficient for each period.[4]

---

[4]See Makridakis, Wheelwright and McGee, pp. 103–109, for example.

FIGURE 3.8

Relationship of Single Smoothed Forecast to Actual Data

(a) Trend in data

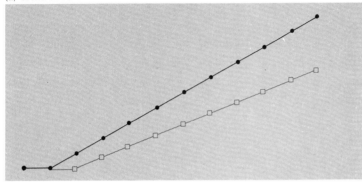

(b) Seasonal data

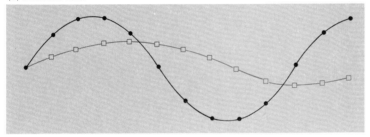

MEASURES OF FORECAST ERROR

It was mentioned earlier that a forecast should not be expected to be right every time. In fact, for many forecast situations, it is rare that the forecast is exactly right in any time period. An unbiased forecasting model should overforecast about as much as it underforecasts, but it will make errors. An error is a deviation, or the difference between the forecast value and the actual value. A calculation of the average error made by a forecast model over time provides a measure of how well the forecast matches the pattern of past data. This measure is often used as an estimate of how well the model will fit the demand pattern one is trying to predict. Such a measure for alternative forecast models provides a basis for comparison to see which model seems to do the best job. Four useful measures of forecast error are discussed below.

The Mean Absolute Deviation (MAD)

A common measure of forecast error is the *mean absolute deviation*, or MAD. The MAD is the mean of the errors made by the forecast model over a series of time

Table 3.4
CALCULATION OF MAD, MSE, AND MAPE

(1) Demand A	(2) Forecast F	(3) Deviation $A - F$	(4) Absolute Deviation $\|A - F\|$	(5) Squared Error $(A - F)^2$	(6) Percentage Error $\left(\dfrac{A - F}{A}\right)100$	(7) Absolute Percentage Error $\left\|\dfrac{A - F}{A}\right\|100$
120	125	−5	5	25	−4.17	4.17
130	125	+5	5	25	3.85	3.85
110	125	−15	15	225	−13.64	13.64
140	125	+15	15	225	10.71	10.71
110	125	−15	15	225	−13.64	13.64
130	125	+5	5	25	3.85	3.85
			60	750		49.86

$$\text{MAD} = \frac{60}{6} = 10$$

$$\text{MSE} = \frac{750}{6} = 125$$

$$\text{MAPE} = \frac{49.86}{6} = 8.31 \text{ percent.}$$

periods, without regard to whether an error was an overestimate or an underestimate. The MAD is sometimes called the mean absolute error, or MAE. To calculate a MAD, one would subtract the forecast value from the actual value for each time period of interest, change all the signs to positive, add them, and divide by the number of values that were used to obtain the sum. The expression for these operations is given in equation 3.3.

$$\text{MAD} = \frac{\sum_{t=1}^{n} |A_t - F_t|}{n} \tag{3.3}$$

where A = actual demand in period t
F = forecast demand in period t
n = the number of periods being used
$|\ |$ means; use the absolute value, i.e., ignore the direction of the deviation
Σ means: sum all the n values

Suppose that a forecast of 125 units had been made for the demand in every period for the data given in Table 3.3. The MAD could then be calculated as shown in Table 3.4.

The MAD is similar to a standard deviation, but it is easier to calculate because it does not require squaring numbers or taking square roots. If the forecast errors are normally distributed, the MAD will be about 0.8 times the standard deviation of the forecast errors. About 58 percent of the errors will be less than one MAD, 89 percent of the forecast errors will be less than two times the MAD, and 98 percent will be less than three times the MAD.

Mean Square Error (MSE)

The *mean square error*, MSE, can also be used as a measure of forecast error. The MSE is found by squaring each of a series of errors made by the forecast model, summing these squared errors, and dividing by the number of errors used in the calculation.

$$\text{MSE} = \frac{\Sigma(A_t - F_t)^2}{n} \tag{3.4}$$

If, for example, we had forecast three periods and the errors were 22.8, −26.2, and 29.3, the MSE would be $\frac{1}{3}(22.8^2 + 26.2^2 + 29.3^2) = 688.3$.

Mean Forecast Error (MFE)

Due to random variations in actual demand, a forecast value will rarely be equal to the actual demand. The average forecast value over several time periods, however, should be very close to the average of the actual values over these same time periods. That is, the forecast model should not be biased—it should not consistently overestimate or underestimate the demand. If the forecast model is unbiased, the *mean forecast error* (MFE) should be very close to zero. The MFE is calculated by summing the forecast errors over a series of periods and dividing this sum by the number of errors used to compute the sum. The equation for the mean forecast error is:

$$\text{MFE} = \sum_{t=1}^{n} \frac{(A_t - F_t)}{n} \tag{3.5}$$

where A = the actual demand in period t
F = the forecast demand in period t
n = the number of forecasts used in the sum

The numerator of the equation is called the running sum of forecast errors (RSFE). The RSFE should be close to zero if the forecast model is unbiased—that is, if the positive errors sum to about the same amount as the negative errors.

The Mean Absolute Percentage Error (MAPE)

Instead of knowing that a forecast model has a mean error of 26.1 or a mean square error of 688.3, it is sometimes more informative to know the relative error. An error of 26.1 in predicting a series that has an average value of about 500 will probably be considered pretty good. An error of 26.1 in predicting a series that averages 50 may be another matter. The relative error that a forecasting model makes can be measured by the *mean absolute percentage error*, or MAPE. Equation 3.6 provides an expression for calculating a MAPE.

$$\text{MAPE} = \left(\frac{100}{n}\right) \sum_{t=1}^{n} \left| \frac{A_t - F_t}{A_t} \right| \tag{3.6}$$

where A_t = the actual value in period t
F_t = the forecast value in period t
n = the number of periods over which the error is being calculated

Calculation of the MAPE is illustrated in columns 6 and 7 of Table 3.4.

APPLICATION

Example of Exponential Smoothing

The regional distribution center for the Komfort King Kompany has been developing models to forecast demand for some replacement parts it stocks. Several sizes of blower motors are used in furnaces, heat pumps, and air conditioners, so the demand is rather uniform throughout all seasons. Single exponential smoothing is considered to be an adequate forecasting method. The company has enough data from past months and wants to select an α that will make the model fit the past data as well as possible. Demands for several early months are averaged (simple mean is used) to get an initial forecast to begin the series. Twenty-four months are forecast in a series beyond the initial value using an α of 0.1, then repeated using an α of 0.2, and so on.

The purpose of these calculations with past data, sometimes called "retrospective testing," is to find the value of α that makes the forecasting model best fit the known demand pattern. Forecast accuracy is measured by calculating the *mean absolute deviation* (MAD) for each model. Komfort King has no reason to believe that new forces are influencing demand, so its forecaster assumes that the value of α that minimized the MAD for the past data would be the best value of α to use in the future. Table 3.5 shows some of the calculations that illustrate a comparison of $\alpha = 0.2$ and $\alpha = 0.3$ using only six months' data. This example shows only a small portion (six months) of the amount of data that would actually be used to compare the accuracy of various forecast models. The table illustrates the type of calculations used to compare the MAD of a model using $\alpha = 0.2$ to the MAD of a model with $\alpha = 0.3$. The actual application would involve perhaps several years' demand history if it were available and several values of α would be compared. There is a risk in using only a few months' data to select a model or a smoothing constant. The calculated forecasts for the first eight or more periods (and hence values of MAD) are influenced by the initial estimate of demand used to start calculating the series of forecasts. Often the values for the first eight or ten periods are omitted in calculating the MADs for each model, so that the MAD is based on forecasts generated by the model after most of the effect of the initial estimate has been removed ("washed out") by the response of the model to actual demand values.

Notice that in Table 3.5 the first two deviations were omitted in this example of calculating a MAD to overcome some of the effect of fixing an initial forecast that was not determined by the model that is being evaluated. In an actual application more values of monthly demand would be available and more of the early deviations would be eliminated so the MADs would be based on more data values that were not influenced by the initial estimate at the start of the series of forecasts.

TABLE 3.5
CALCULATIONS OF EXPONENTIAL SMOOTHED FORECASTS
AND MAD[a]

Trial Month, t	Actual Demand, A_t	$\alpha = 0.2$ Forecast, SF_t	Deviation $A_t - SF_t$	|Deviation| $\|A_t - SF_t\|$	$\alpha = 0.3$ Forecast, SF_t	Deviation $A_t - SF_t$	|Deviation| $\|A_t - SF_t\|$
1	210	196.2[a]	+13.8	—[b]	196.2[a]	13.8	—[b]
2	206	199.0	7.0	—	200.3	5.7	—
3	181	200.4	−19.4	19.4	202.0	−21.0	21.0
4	201	196.5	4.5	4.5	195.7	5.3	5.3
5	192	197.4	−5.4	5.4	197.3	−5.3	5.3
6	186	196.3	−10.3	10.3	195.7	−9.7	9.7
				39.6			41.3

$$MAD(\alpha = 0.2) = \frac{39.6}{4} = 9.9 \qquad MAD(\alpha = 0.3) = \frac{41.3}{4} = 10.3$$

$$SF_{t+1} = SF_t + \alpha(A_t - SF_t)$$
$$SF_2 = 196.2 + .2(210 - 196.2) = 196.2 + 2.8 = 199.0$$
$$SF_3 = 199.0 + .2(206 - 199) = 199.0 + 1.4 = 200.4$$
$$SF_4 = 200.4 + .2(181 - 200.4) = 200.4 - 3.9 = 196.5$$
$$SF_5 = 196.5 + .2(201 - 196.5) = 196.5 + .9 = 197.4$$
$$SF_6 = 197.4 + .2(192 - 197.4) = 197.4 - 1.1 = 196.3$$

[a]Initial mean estimated prior to these calculations = 196.2
[b]Omitted to reduce the effect of the initial mean

The model with $\alpha = 0.2$ has a smaller MAD than the model with $\alpha = 0.3$ so $\alpha = 0.2$ appears preferable on the basis of these data. Other values of α were evaluated in forecasting demand for this blower motor, and the one ($\alpha = 0.2$) with the smallest MAD was selected. Selection of the smoothing constant to use for other products stocked by Komfort King was performed in the same manner. Since other products had different demand patterns, different values of α were best for many of them.

TIME SERIES DECOMPOSITION

Time series decomposition is breaking the overall series into some of its basic components which are more likely to have recognizable and more predictable patterns. These basic components can then be projected into the future and recombined to form a forecast. The four basic components—trend, cyclical, seasonal, and irregular—were defined earlier and were illustrated in Figure 3.3.

It is assumed that these components act independently of one another. If they are projected into the future, it is assumed that the forces that have caused them to occur in the past will continue into the future. In view of the many factors that influence demand, there is some danger in projecting the past too far into the future. Judgment and experience are needed to recognize when a change has occurred in the forces that have acted on demand in the past. These situations are called *turning points.* For example, consider the rate of increase in American automobile sales before the 1973 oil embargo and the rate of decrease in sales immediately afterward and the increase in demand for larger cars 10 years later when gasoline prices were stable and the mileage of these cars had improved. When a forecast model has been used for an extended time, one should consider this question: Have the conditions and forces that act on demand changed significantly since the time that the model was developed?

Multiplicative and Additive Models

There are two general forms of time series models. The most common is the *multiplicative model,* in which the components are ratios that are multiplied together to provide the estimated demand. The second type is an *additive model,* in which the components are added together to provide the estimate. Equations 3.7 and 3.8 are multiplicative and additive models, respectively.

$$TF = T \cdot S \cdot C \cdot I \tag{3.7}$$

$$TF = T + S + C + I \tag{3.8}$$

where T = the trend component
S = a measure of seasonality, either a ratio or an amount to add
C = a measure of the cyclical adjustment, either a ratio or an amount to add
I = the irregular component, which is any variation in demand not explained by the previous factors

Visual inspection of a plotted time series is often helpful to determine the type of model that most appropriately represents the data. The data might appear to fit one of the general patterns presented in Figure 3.9.

The seasonal and irregular components of a time series can often be removed by calculating one-year moving averages, starting with the first year and moving forward through the data. If many years' data are available, the forecaster may use only the most recent several years because they are more likely to reflect current conditions. The averages can be plotted at the center of the time periods used to compute each average. This plot shows how the combined trend and cycle components are moving. If there is no trend or cycle, the moving averages will appear approximately as a straight horizontal line.

It may take fifteen to twenty years of data to define and separate the trend and cycle components. However, very few products remain in stable condition this long—either competitive conditions or the product's life-cycle stage will change well before the end of this period. Decisions cannot be postponed fifteen years while managers wait to see what the trend really is. The trend is sometimes estimated from data from two or more years. Consequently, in practice many planners identify only the seasonal component and a combination trend-cycle component. The irregular component is assumed to be averaged out over multiple observations.

The plotted combination trend-cycle component may appear as a straight

FIGURE 3.9

Some Possible Time Series Patterns

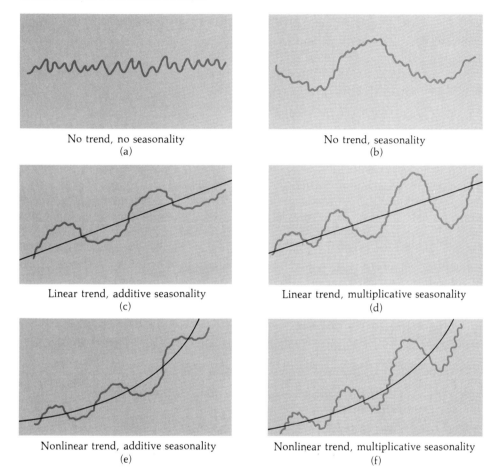

No trend, no seasonality
(a)

No trend, seasonality
(b)

Linear trend, additive seasonality
(c)

Linear trend, multiplicative seasonality
(d)

Nonlinear trend, additive seasonality
(e)

Nonlinear trend, multiplicative seasonality
(f)

line or as some form of curve, after the seasonal and irregular components are averaged out. A least-squares curve fitting program can be run on a computer to determine the equation for a curve. Linear regression (which is presented later with equations 3.9 and 3.10) can be used to find the slope and intercept for a straight line, if the data appear to form a linear function.

The trend-cycle function (which we will call the trend) can be extended into the future by visually extrapolating the plotted values or by calculating future values, if an equation has been determined. Extension of the trend line should be used with caution, particularly for long-range projections, because the trend estimate might be distorted by changes in the cycle component that is mixed with the trend.

Extension of the trend line does not provide a completed forecast for each future period if there is seasonal variation about the trend. The pattern of seasonal variation about the trend line must also be projected into the future to form a forecast for the expected sales in each future period. If the data appear to be following an additive model, one must determine the proper seasonal adjustment (positive or negative) to be made for each time period for which a forecast is to be made. For monthly data, one can compute the average difference between the actual value and the trend value (i.e., the $A - T$ values) for a particular month in each of the past few years. This value, say for January, would tell us by what amount the typical January differs from the trend line value in January. For example, January sales may typically be 86 units above the trend value. We would add 86 units to the trend value to forecast sales for a future January. If the $(A - T)$ values for some other month average -38 (i.e., the actual values are usually 38 units below the trend), we would add -38, which is equivalent to subtracting 38 units from the trend value in that month. This procedure can be repeated to find the seasonal adjustment for February, etc. The additive adjustment for each period is added to the projected trend line value for that period to compute the forecast for the period.

Seasonal adjustments for a multiplicative model are found by computing the average ratio of actual demand to the trend value (i.e., the A/T values) for each period of interest. If data are available for, say, several Octobers, we might average the ratios of A to T that we can compute for each October. The result is a multiplier, or seasonal index, for the typical October. For example, if the A/T ratios for the past three Octobers average to be 1.18, it means that the sales in October typically are about 18 percent above the trend value for that month. We would multiply the projected trend value for a future October by 1.18 to compute the sales forecast for that month. If the ratios for some other month, say June, average to be 0.82, we would multiply the trend value for a future June by 0.82 to obtain the forecast for that month. This type of seasonal adjustment can be used with weekly, quarterly, or other data series.

APPLICATION

Example of Time Series Decomposition

Don McDoe has operated a cafeteria in a resort area for almost three years. He is making a serious reexamination of his business because he has had some trying challenges in staffing his cafeteria and it is now time to renew his lease. Each time that Don has hired a sufficient number of people, either demand has increased so that he has had to add more personnel or demand has decreased so that he has had idle people on his payroll. He believes he could employ college students to work in the resort area where his business is located during the summer, but in the past he has used permanent people because the increase appeared to continue long enough to be a trend. He has renewed the lease each previous summer, just when things were really looking good, then lost money during the winter. Don decided to plot a time series to see how his first three years look as far as volume of business is concerned. He has been able to adjust his prices adquately to compensate for inflation. Sales data are shown in column 2 of Table 3.6.

Don plotted the sales data from column 2 of Table 3.6 (see Figure 3.10). When you examine these data (solid line) you can see why each spring Don thought his business was growing so quickly that he needed more personnel. Week after week demand continued to climb at a rapid rate. You can also see why each winter he thought he was headed for bankruptcy.

Table 3.6
TOTAL AND FOUR-QUARTER MOVING AVERAGE OF MEALS SERVED AT McDOE'S CAFETERIA

Quarter	Meals Served	Total Meals Past 4 Quarters	1-Year (4-Quarter) Moving Average	Centered at Period
1	11,800			
2	10,404	41,729 ÷4 →10,432.3		2.5
3	8,925	42,214	10,553.5	3.5
4	10,600	42,819	10,704.8	4.5
5	12,285	43,107	10,776.8	5.5
6	11,009	43,793	10,948.3	6.5
7	9,213	44,858	11,214.5	7.5
8	11,286	45,119	11,279.8	8.5
9	13,350	46,172	11,543.0	9.5
10	11,270	47,024	11,756.0	10.5
11	10,266			
12	12,138			

A longer-term trend provides a better picture of future prospects for a business. Don computed the one-year moving average for the data (column 4 of Table 3.6) and plotted it, centered on the middle of the period it represented (the black dots in Figure 3.10). This one-year moving average smoothed out the seasonal variation, making the actual trend more apparent. He drew a dashed line through the approximate center of these points and enjoyed a feeling of confidence that his business was prospering on the average, although it was very seasonal.

Don wanted to compute indices to measure the extent of seasonal variation, which would provide him with general guidelines for planning staffing levels and budgets. He did not have enough data to estimate long-term business cycles. Since the seasonal change was not a constant amount, he used a multiplicative model, $TF = T \cdot S$, with the assumption that the irregular component would be averaged out over the three years. Actual demand was very close to the trend value each spring and fall, so Don concluded that the seasonal index for spring was 1.0 and for fall it was also 1.0.

An estimate of the seasonal index for the first summer was 1.16, which was found by dividing the 11,800 actual sales by the 10,200 estimated for this period from the height of the trend line at the middle of this period. For the second summer the ratio was the actual demand of 12,285 ÷ 10,850, estimated for this period from the trend line, or 1.13. The seasonal index for the third summer was the actual demand of 13,350 ÷ 11,400, estimated for this period from the trend line, or 1.17. Don averaged these ratios and concluded that the level of business in the summer averages about 15 percent above the trend line value at the middle of a summer.

Indices of seasonality for the winter quarter were also computed by taking the ratio of actual winter sales to the trend value for that winter. The three winter indices are found to be as follows:

First winter: 8,925/10,500 = 0.85
Second winter: 9,213/11,100 = 0.83
Third winter: 10,266/11,800 = 0.87

The level of business in the winter averages about 85 percent of the overall trend value for the period. To estimate demand during a summer Don can project the trend line to that period and multiply the trend value by 1.15. Don can forecast the level of demand during a winter by projecting the trend line to that winter and multiplying the trend level by 0.85.

Don could see that the swings in the level of demand are fairly predictable. Such patterns are very useful in planning operations. Don could project the expected amount of business for a quarter by extending the trend line and multiplying the trend value by the seasonal index for the period.

He estimated the parameters of an equation for the trend line by the following reasoning. The intercept (height of the line at quarter zero) of the trend line was read directly from the plotted data of Figure 3.10 to be approximately 10,000 meals. The trend line was observed to be at 12,000 meals at quarter 12, so the slope was estimated to be (12,000 − 10,000)/12 or approximately 166.7 meals per quarter. The equation for the trend line therefore is,

FIGURE 3.10

Sales History of McDoe's Cafeteria

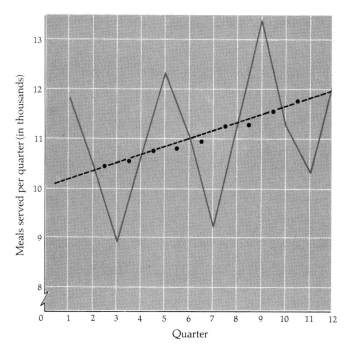

Trend value = 10,000 + 166.7(q) where,
    q = the quarter number as shown on the horizontal
        scale of Figure 3.10

The trend equation and the seasonal indices were combined by the calculations shown in Table 3.7 to provide a forecast for each quarter of the next year.

Table 3.7
CALCULATION OF QUARTERLY FORECASTS
FOR McDOE'S CAFETERIA

(1) Quarter	(2) Quarter Number	(3) Trend Value	(4) Seasonal Index	Forecast (3) × (4)
Summer	13	10,000 + 166.7(13) = 12,167	1.15	13,992
Fall	14	10,000 + 166.7(14) = 12,334	1.00	12,334
Winter	15	10,000 + 166.7(15) = 12,500	0.85	10,625
Spring	16	10,000 + 166.7(16) = 12,667	1.00	12,667

Don then decided to try the same procedure using monthly instead of quarterly data to get more details.

After looking over his figures and admiring the trend, he feels encouraged about the future prospects for his business and has decided to (1) renew his lease, (2) use students as temporary employees in the peak season, and (3) take a vacation (next winter!).

CAUSAL MODELS

The time series analysis method of forecasting and the averaging methods presented previously used time as the only independent variable. However, the use of time alone does not provide a means to identify turning points that are not inherent in past patterns. The time series analysis forecasting method used time as the independent variable (X axis) and demand as the dependent variable (Y axis). Some forecasting methods use other independent variables to assist the forecaster in estimating future demand. Such methods allow forecasters to use some of the factors they probably would consider if they were making subjective forecasts.

Regression Methods

We may want some measure of external conditions, such as an economic indicator, as the variable to explain demand. The Federal Reserve Board, the Department of Commerce, and many other governmental agencies publish values of economic indicators. Trade associations, local planning commissions, licensing agencies, and banks also have information that may be related to a company's sales.

The objective is to find an available indicator that moves before the company's sales change (a *leading indicator*) and that has a sufficiently stable relationship with sales to be useful as a prediction tool. Linear regression is a means of finding and expressing such a relationship. Simple linear regression fits a line to a series of points that indicate past values of one *dependent variable* (sales) and one *independent variable* (the indicator). Often the method of least squares is used to fit the line to the data points so that the sum of all the squared deviations from the points to the line will be minimized.

Probably the use of other variables in addition to an economic indicator (for example, advertising expenditures or the price of the good or service) will better explain sales. Multiple regression involves the establishment of a mathematical relationship between a dependent variable and two or more independent variables. The complexities of multiple regression are beyond the scope of this book, but an example of simple linear regression is presented to provide a general introduction to the concept. The method of least squares is used to fit the line to the data in this example. Remember, the least squares method was also mentioned as a way to estimate the trend line in time series analysis.

APPLICATION

An Example of Simple Linear Regression

The Mover City Transit Authority has been examining the demand for its service. Its managers need to know how many vehicles and employees will be needed in the next year so that they can request an adequate subsidy in the budget for the coming fiscal year. They have found that business has declined during the past several years, but the pattern is not obvious. They know that patterns vary within a year and within each week, but the question at hand is one of capacity for the coming year, so seasonal variations are not examined. One department manager has expressed a belief that the year's business should be related to the percentage

Table 3.8
DEMAND HISTORY FOR MOVER CITY TRANSIT AUTHORITY

Year	Passenger Fares Collected (in Millions)	NOCAR (in Thousands)
1	5.5	77
2	5.1	75
3	4.7	72
4	4.8	73
5	4.6	71

FIGURE 3.11

Demand for Mover City Transit Authority

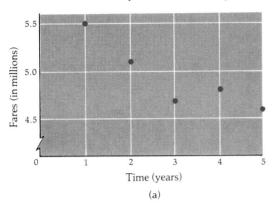

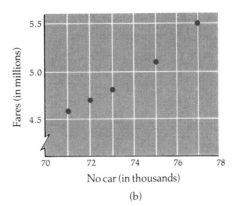

(a)

(b)

of the population without automobiles. He has formed a variable, NOCAR, equal to the city population the previous year minus the number of automobile registrations. Some families own two cars, some people who live outside the city use the transit system, some walk or ride bicycles, and the number of trips per user may vary from year to year, so the variable NOCAR may not be exactly related to use of the system. The data for the past five years are presented in Table 3.8 and are plotted in Figure 3.11.

Simple linear regression solves by the method of least squares to find a line of the form $Y_T = a + bx$, where Y_T is the value of the dependent variable estimated by the fitted trend line. The slope of the trend line (b) can be found by equation 3.9. The intercept (a), or the point where the trend line crosses the vertical axis, can be found by equation 3.10.

$$b = \frac{n\Sigma XY - \Sigma X \Sigma Y}{n\Sigma X^2 - (\Sigma X)^2} \qquad (3.9)$$

$$a = \overline{Y} - b\overline{X} = \frac{\Sigma Y}{n} - b\frac{\Sigma X}{n} = \frac{\Sigma Y - b\Sigma X}{n} \qquad (3.10)$$

where $\overline{Y}$ = the arithmetic mean of the dependent variable (FARES in this example)

$\overline{X}$ = the arithmetic mean of the independent variable (NOCAR in this example)

n = the number of data points or X, Y pairs (number of years in this example)

Σ = a summation sign meaning: add together all of the values of the variable to the right of the symbol

Y = the actual values of the dependent variable

X = the values of the independent variable.

Equation 3.10 makes use of the fact that the point $(\overline{X}, \overline{Y})$ lies on the line fitted by least squares. Moving a point $(\overline{X}, \overline{Y})$ toward the Y axis a distance of $\overline{X}$ positions it on the Y axis. If we wanted this point to be on the trend line, it would have to be moved vertically a distance equal to the X movement times the slope (i.e., b times $- \overline{X}$). These corrections place the point on the line where the line crosses the Y axis, which is the Y intercept, a. The intercept merely specifies a point on the line to distinguish which straight line with slope b will best fit the data points. The intercept by itself is often meaningless and is of interest only in problems where we want to make forecasts of Y when the values of X are near zero.

Solution of the least squares method by the above equations is facilitated by a table such as Table 3.9. The equation for the line that best fits our data is

$$Y_T = -6.10 + 0.15X \tag{3.11}$$

Table 3.9
COMPUTATIONS FOR REGRESSION ANALYSIS OF MOVER CITY TRANSIT DATA

X (NOCAR)	Y (FARES)	X^2	XY
77	5.5	5,929	423.5
75	5.1	5,625	382.5
72	4.7	5,184	338.4
73	4.8	5,329	350.4
71	4.6	5,041	326.6
$\Sigma X = 368$	$\Sigma Y = 24.7$	27,108	1,821.4

$$\overline{X} = \frac{368}{5} = 73.6 \quad \overline{Y} = \frac{24.7}{5} = 4.94$$

$$b = \frac{n\Sigma XY - \Sigma X \Sigma Y}{n\Sigma X^2 - (\Sigma X)^2} = \frac{5(1,821.4) - 368(24.7)}{5(27,108) - 368^2} = \frac{17.4}{116} = 0.15$$

$$a = \overline{Y} - b\overline{X} = 4.94 - 0.15(73.6) = -6.10$$

The negative intercept has no significant meaning, since the model is to be used for values of NOCAR near the range of the original data.

Since the variable NOCAR (the X in equation 3.11) was 71.0 again this year, the transit authority estimates that the number of passenger rides it can expect to provide next year is 4,550,000, as shown below:

$$Y_T = -6.10 + 0.15(71.0)$$
$$= -6.10 + 10.65$$
$$= 4.55$$

Some measure of the closeness of fit between the line and the actual data is necessary if one wishes to compare the indicator in the example (NOCAR) with other variables we may evaluate. The variable that has the best score for fit will be considered a good candidate for a forecasting model. Two common measures are the coefficient of linear correlation and the standard error of the estimate. These measures will be calculated for the Mover City model.

The *coefficient of linear correlation*, often called the *correlation coefficient*, tells how closely a group of points coincides with a straight line. Using the symbols in equation 3.9, we can calculate the correlation coefficient (r):

$$r = \frac{n\Sigma XY - \Sigma X\Sigma Y}{\sqrt{[n\Sigma X^2 - (\Sigma X)^2][n\Sigma Y^2 - (\Sigma Y)^2]}} \tag{3.12}$$

The coefficient can be positive or negative. A positive r means that large values of X generally are associated with large values of Y; that is, as X increases, Y increases. A negative r generally means that Y declines as X increases. The closer the absolute value of r is to 1.0, the better the line fits the points. For the Mover City data the correlation coefficient is $+0.9905$, which indicates that the points lie very near a straight line and that the line has a positive slope.

The *standard error of the estimate, s_y*, is similar to the standard deviation except that it is based on the mean square vertical deviation of the points from the trend line rather than from their mean. The expression for standard error of the estimate is

$$s_y = \sqrt{\frac{\Sigma(Y - Y_T)^2}{n - 2}} \text{ or } \sqrt{\frac{\Sigma Y^2 - a\Sigma Y - b\Sigma XY}{n - 2}} \tag{3.13}$$

The standard error of the estimate for the Mover City Transit Authority data using NOCAR as the independent variable is 0.0577.[5] If the Mover City Transit Authority tries other models, it can compare the standard errors to see which model fits the data best, that is, which has the smallest standard error. Also there should be some logical relationship or explanation for the variables used in regression models. The model that uses NOCAR as an explanatory variable has a logical relationship and fits the data very well.

USING COMPUTERS TO FORECAST

Forecasting often involves manipulation of great amounts of data, particularly when forecasting models are being developed by trying many variables in many

---

[5]The left-hand expression of equation 3.13 was used to calculate s_y. In larger problems, however, the right-hand formulation often is used because it eliminates rounding errors. To use this formula we must calculate Y_T for all the X values used to develop the trend line. A table is helpful in this calculation also:

X	Y	Y_T	$(Y - Y_T)$	$(Y - Y_T)^2$
77	5.50	5.45	0.05	0.0025
75	5.10	5.15	-0.05	0.0025
72	4.70	4.70	0	0
73	4.80	4.85	-0.05	0.0025
71	4.60	4.55	0.05	0.0025
				$\Sigma(Y - Y_T)^2 = 0.0100$

$$s_y = \sqrt{\frac{\Sigma(Y - Y_T)^2}{n - 2}} = \sqrt{\frac{0.0100}{5 - 2}} = \sqrt{0.0033} = 0.0577$$

different combinations and when those models involve complex calculations. Computers can greatly reduce the work and time involved in forecasting. Since commercial companies often keep records of sales or order data, a computer can be programmed to process these data routinely to develop and update company forecasts for products or product groups. Such forecasts can be used for routine needs, such as managing inventory and purchase orders, or for such activities as planning employment levels or aggregate planning.

Computers are almost essential when one desires to try numerous alternative forecast models on a massive data base. Different combinations and transformations of variables in the data base can be tried to determine which provide the best estimate of demand. The ability to perform repetitive calculations with a computer makes it possible to try values of an independent variable one period prior to the demand value, then two periods prior to the demand value, and so on, to find the amount of "lag" that appears to give the best fit with the demand data. Obviously, computers add a lot of power and convenience to the forecaster's job and can improve the quality of the forecast (see box).

OPERATIONS MANAGEMENT IN ACTION

How Personal Computers are Changing the Forecaster's Job

Remember the old story of the compulsive gambler who finds that he must spend the night in a small town? He ends up in the village's only gambling house, and through the night he loses heavily at roulette. One of the townspeople sidles up and whispers, "The wheel is crooked." The gambler nods and answers, "I know, I know—but it's the only wheel in town."

Economists have long been in much the same predicament. Their favorite forecasting tool—the elaborate econometric model—has been coming up with losing numbers for the past several years. Even though these complex mathematical representations of how the economy is supposed to behave have disappointed their users, for many economists they are still the only game in town. "While there are problems with all of the models, they are a good tool to help organize your thinking," says Richard B. Berner, an economist with Morgan Guaranty Trust Co.

But help may be on the way. Model builders are beginning to transfer their abstruse mathematical calculations from the large mainframe computers to the personal computer. And this may change the whole face of economic forecasting. It seems likely that for economists, the personal computer in the second half of the 1980s will be as indispensable as the electronic calculator became in the 1970s and the slide rule in the 1950s.

Side Effects.

The application of the PC to economic forecasting and analysis will have three far-reaching effects. For one thing, it will sharply reduce the costs of forecasting and thus allow corporate economists to rely less on the forecasts and analyses of the large consulting firms. Second, experimentation with models will no longer be largely confined to the econometricians of academia or to the economists of well-heeled corporations, who can tap into their universities' or employers' large computers. Finally, and perhaps most important, the greater flexibility of using the PC for economic models may well improve economists' forecasting ability.

A year ago, Ray C. Fair, professor of economics at Yale University, together with Urban Systems Research & Engineering, of Cambridge, Mass., brought out the FairModel, a PC econometric model of the U.S. economy. Last spring, Laurence H. Meyer, professor of economics at Washington University in St. Louis, founded Laurence H. Meyer & Associates Ltd. and also assembled a PC-run model. Both of these models are making inroads at corporations, government agencies, and universities.

The internal workings of the PC models are much the same as those of the economic consultants' larger models. The LHM&A model is currently forecasting real gross national product growth of 4.8% in the third quarter and 3.5% in the fourth. The FairModel is more optimistic, projecting a gain of 5.9% in the third quarter and 5.2% in the final period. Neither model foresees a recession anytime in 1985. These forecasts are in line with what most other models project. And since the consensus of individual forecasters does not wander far from the average of the econometric models, the PC models are also in tune with individual forecasts.

Good Track Record.

How have these PC models fared so far? While the LHM&A model has only several quarters under its belt, the FairModel has been operating for a year and has already established a good track record. Its projection for 1984 was included in the survey that BUSINESS WEEK conducted for its 1983 yearend investment issue. Fair's forecast for the first half of this year was—like all other forecasts—too modest. Yet in the short time since it entered the lists, it has managed to unhorse most of its better-known rivals. Last fall's forecast for the first half of this year was much better than the average and closer to the mark than any of the 37 individual and 12 other econometric forecasts that were surveyed.

The new PC models will enable business economists to do a better job. Forecasters will not be so closely tied to the policy assumptions that form the basis of macroeconomic models provided by economic consulting services. Because it costs hundreds of dollars to run a single simulation on the consulting companies' computers, and extensive runs rise well into the thousands of dollars, economists are reluctant to test a variety of assumptions. With a PC model, if an economist does not like the assumptions that come from a consulting service, they can be changed—and cheaply. Says Stephen H. Zeller, chief of model simulation at the Congressional Budget Office: "With the PC model, after you buy it, all you do is pay for the electricity." In a few months, notes James F. Hudson, vice-president of Urban Systems, his company will be developing tables to show how different simulations of the FairModel will affect forecasts of production for more than 100 industries.

William C. Melton, vice-president and senior economist at IDS/American Express, Inc., in Minneapolis, says that "it is hard for the judgmental forecaster to make all of the elements balance." Now he can run a simulation at home in 10 minutes without, he adds, "buying a one-way ticket to the poorhouse." The LHM&A model, which requires installation of an arithmetic chip in the computer, can run off the solutions of equations for eight quarters ahead, in rather exquisite detail, in about 52 seconds. That means that an impressive number of simulations using different assumptions can be examined in several hours.

Human Error?

To a large degree, the errors in econometric forecasting stem not from the models' internal structure but from incorrect assumptions. For instance, since monetary influences are so powerful, an incorrect assumption on prospective Federal Reserve policy is almost sure to yield a wrong forecast. The PC appeals to economists not only in the private sector but also in government agencies that need to determine the consequences of various combinations of government actions.

Changing the policy-mix input can lead to some intriguing results when monetarist and supply-side ideas on how to run the economy are applied and tested. For instance, if the money supply is kept growing at a steady rate of 4.5%, as some hardline monetarists recommend, it would hold inflation in check. According to the FairModel, prices would be rising at a rate of only a bit above 5% three years from now. However, the model shows that economic growth would quickly settle into a dull 2% annual rate, unemployment would edge up to 8%, and the budget deficit would rise to more than $200 billion a year. The LHM&A model yields similar results when tight-fisted monetary policy is used as an assumption.

The FairModel also shows that the economy could grow itself out of the deficit, but with a bit more cost in inflation than the supply siders claim. And that can happen, for instance, if—and it is a huge if—the Federal Reserve forces the short-term Treasury bill rate down from its current 10.3% to 8% in the fourth quarter, and then manages to cut the rate another point each year for the next three years. Economic growth under those conditions would remain above its long-term trend for several years, and unemployment would sink to 4.5%. Although the money supply would be rising at a 12.5% rate by late 1987, inflation would not top 8%. And the federal budget deficit would decline from its current $170-plus billion, moving into surplus three years down the road.

Of course these simulations are just that— simulations. The outcomes projected for alternative policies in the final analysis are of value only if the models accurately reflect how the economy really works. Says Fair: "Given the correct policy assumptions, the effectiveness of the models depends on their ability to forecast."

The large time-sharing economic consultants are only beginning to explore ways to use the personal computer to market new services and to offer existing services differently. Wharton Econometrics and Data Resources, Inc., among others, provide for the transfer of their data packages into the memory banks of PC users. Wharton also provides a modified version of its model for simulation by a PC user—but that model must be run on the time-sharing computers of Wharton, not on the vastly cheaper PC.

While the personal computer models yield a distinct advantage to trained economists, they will also greatly improve the teaching of both elementary and advanced economics at universities. Karl E. Case, chairman of the economics department at Wellesley College, says that because the PC makes the interplay of economic relationships easy to observe, the PC "will revolutionize the teaching of macroeconomics."

And just as constant competition in horse racing improves the breed, the linkup between economics and the personal computer opens the way for more competition to produce better economic models and forecasts. Although, as Melton comments, "there will never be any one model that can satisfy more than 8 or 10 economists," the significant increase in research activity will eventually yield better understanding of what makes the economy tick. It will also, says Case, exploit the talents "of a lot of underemployed economists."

Reprinted from the October 1, 1984 issue of Business Week *by special permission,* © *1984 by McGraw-Hill Inc.*

Many commercial software packages for inventory management include forecasting or sales analysis programs. Other forecasting packages are also available for computers. Standard regression programs can be used to develop forecasts. Some packages, such as SIBYL/RUNNER, can be used for instruction or for commercial applications. The Carpenter, Deloria, and Morganstein reference in the chapter bibliography includes information and comparisons of several microcomputer packages that will perform the types of forecasts discussed in this chapter.

MONITORING AND CONTROLLING FORECASTS

Sales patterns are seldom static, and sales forecasts should strive to move with them or even anticipate their movements. New accounts are gained and old ones lost. The level of activity of existing accounts may rise or fall. Sales forecasts should be reviewed and revised periodically. Sometimes the forecasting method may be changed.

Recall from our previous discussion that many companies revise or update their forecasts for every month or every quarter. As new data become available they are incorporated into the forecast because it is usually these recent data that are most relevant, at least in short-range planning. New data can also be compared with the forecast values to permit an evaluation of the forecasting method's performance. Once way of determining whether a forecasting method is performing adequately is, of course, visually comparing new data and forecast values. Another method is the use of a tracking signal.

A *tracking signal* is a ratio of the *running sum of forecast errors* (RSFE) to the mean absolute deviation, MAD.

$$\text{Tracking signal} = \frac{\text{RSFE}}{\text{MAD}} = \frac{\sum_{t=1}^{n} (A_t - F_t)}{\text{MAD}} \qquad (3.14)$$

where A_t = the actual value of demand for period t
F_t = the forecast value of demand for period t.

The tracking signal is recalculated each time the actual demand data for a sales period become available and the forecast is updated. The tracking signal should remain fairly small (near zero) if the forecasting method is performing adequately. Small deviations occur but should balance one another—some deviations will be positive and some negative. If demand departs significantly from the forecast during several periods, the numerator of equation 3.14 will grow, causing the tracking signal to deviate significantly from zero. A graph of a tracking signal indicating poor performance is illustrated in Figure 3.12. When the tracking signal moves outside of some preestablished range it trips a signal, indicating that it is time to reevaluate the demand pattern and the forecasting method. A company might examine its past data to see what tracking-signal limits are appropriate for its needs for forecast accuracy and demand patterns. Limits that permit the tracking signal ratio to be as large as 4 to 8 often are

FIGURE 3.12

A Tracking Signal

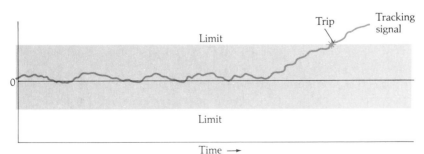

used. The larger limits are used where the penalties for a forecast error are small. The tracking signal is an application of the management-by-exception principle: If things are working all right, don't waste time trying to fix them; spend your time where it's needed.

A method of checking forecasts is particularly useful if forecasting is done by a computer, as it often is when forecasts must be maintained for a great variety of products. The computer may be programmed to print out only the expected demand unless the tracking signal "trips" a limit (see Figure 3.12). If the tracking signal passes a limit, the computer may print a report showing the past history so that one can decide what to do. When a type of exponential smoothing is used, the computer may be programmed to change the value of α (so the forecast will be more responsive) and to continue forecasting. This technique is called *adaptive smoothing* because the exponential smoothing model is being adapted when the situation warrants.

SUMMARY

Forecasting is important in operations management and in other functions within an organization. Long-range, intermediate-range, and short-range decisions must be made, and all require some inferences or assumptions about the future. Forecasting is basic to operations decisions because projections (1) indicate when decisions are needed, (2) determine which alternatives are reasonable, and (3) help to indicate which alternative solution to a problem should be selected.

Demand forecasts are particularly important to operations managers because managers seldom control demand yet have the responsibility of providing the goods and services in response to it. Demand forecasts also are basic inputs to financial plans, personnel plans, facilities plans, and marketing plans. Companies often have short- to intermediate-range forecasts of demand for specific products or product families. These specific forecasts are used to plan production, to procure inputs, and to schedule transformation of those inputs into products or services. Specific forecasts may be updated with a frequency of a week to a month. Longer-range forecasts may be made quarterly or annually to aid in making long-range plans

for facilities, research and development programs, and marketing strategies.

Forecasting methods of several types may be used to estimate future demand. Quantitative or qualitative methods may be used to develop forecasts. Time series data can be used to forecast by simple moving averages, weighted moving averages, exponential smoothing, and decomposition. Causal models that use regression to express the relationship between demand and some economic index or other variable can be used for forecasting.

Moving average and exponential smoothing methods are useful for short-range forecasts and do not require extensive historical data.

Time series analysis and higher-order exponential smoothing are useful when a knowledge of seasonal variations is important to planning. A considerable amount of historical data should be available (three or more years) to provide estimates of the consistency of seasonal indices.

Regression analysis is useful to determine trends in time series analysis, which can be extended for estimates of long-range changes. Regression can be used also to estimate the relationship between sales and some index of economic activity. To be useful as a forecast base, the index should change an adequate lead time before a change in sales occurs. Extrapolation of any pattern always is subject to the danger of a turning point in the pattern.

Some of the forces that have been in effect in the past may change. It is advisable to compare the forecast made by one method with other forecasts and to compare a forecast to what common sense suggests before basing plans on the forecast.

SOLVED PROBLEMS

PROBLEM:

The following are three months of demand data for emergency-room service at a hospital. Using $\alpha = .2$ and an estimate of 706 for the first month, calculate exponentially smoothed forecasts for the demand in months 2 through 4.

Month	Actual
1	721
2	816
3	671

SOLUTION:

For the first month, the forecast was 706 and the actual demand was 721, so the error was $(A - SF) = 721 - 706 = 15$. This information is used to adjust the forecast of 706 upward by 0.2(15) or 3, so the forecast for month 2 is $706 + .2(721 - 706) = 709$.

The forecast for month 3 is

$SF_3 = SF_2 + 0.2(A_2 - SF_2)$ or
$= 709 + 0.2(816 - 709) =$
$\qquad 709 + 21.4 = 730.4$

Since this is an average level of demand, we can keep the decimal. We will carry one decimal place to know whether to round up or down if we want to estimate an integer value for demand.

$SF_4 = SF_3 + 0.2(A_3 - SF_3) =$
$\qquad 730.4 + 0.2(671 - 730.4) =$
$\qquad 730.4 + 0.2(-59.4) =$
$\qquad\qquad 730.4 - 11.9 = 718.5$

Notice that in month 3 the forecast was higher than the actual, resulting in a negative forecast error. This negative error causes the forecast or smoothed average to be reduced, and the forecast for month 4 is 718.5 as an average level of demand.

PROBLEM:

The following are a company's quarterly demand figures for the past two years.

Year 1		Year 2	
Quarter	Demand	Quarter	Demand
1	26,209	1	25,390
2	21,402	2	19,064
3	18,677	3	18,173
4	24,681	4	23,866

(a) Compute one-year moving averages centered at the end of quarters 2.5 through 6.5, respectively, to remove the seasonality. (Assume the demand figures are at the center of the quarters they represent.)

(b) Compute a linear regression equation for the trend through the five moving averages.

(c) Compute an average seasonal index (multiplicative) for each quarter of the year.

(d) Forecast the demand for each quarter of year 3.

SOLUTION:

(a) The first year's moving average would be centered between the second quarter and the third quarter, i.e., at the X-coordinate of 2.5. The X-coordinate for the next moving average will be 3.5, etc.

The four-quarter moving averages and the corresponding X-coordinates are shown below.

Actual Demand	Sum of 4 Quarters	Sum ÷ 4	X-Coordinate
26,209			
21,402			
18,677			
24,681	90,969	22,742.25	2.5
25,390	90,150	22,537.5	3.5
19,064	87,812	21,953	4.5
18,173	87,308	21,827	5.5
23,866	86,493	21,623.25	6.5

(b) We can compute a linear regression equation to show the relationship between the quarter and the trend value of demand.

x	y	x^2	xy
2.5	22,742.25	6.25	56,855.625
3.5	22,537.5	12.25	78,881.25
4.5	21,953	20.25	98,788.5
5.5	21,827	30.25	120,048.5
6.5	21,623.25	42.25	140,551.125
22.5	110,683	111.25	495,125.0

$$b = \frac{n\Sigma XY - \Sigma X \Sigma Y}{n\Sigma X^2 - (\Sigma X)^2} =$$

$$\frac{5(495,125) - 22.5(110,683)}{5(111.25) - 22.5^2} =$$

$$\frac{2,475,625 - 2,490,367.5}{556.25 - 506.25} =$$

$$-\frac{14,742.5}{50} = -294.85$$

$$a = \frac{\Sigma Y - b\Sigma X}{n} =$$

$$\frac{110,683 - (-294.85)(22.5)}{5} =$$

$$\frac{117,317.125}{5} = 23,463.425$$

(c) The time period at which actual demand occurs corresponds to the periods 1, 2, 3, 4 etc. on the time scale. Using these values for X, we can determine the trend value at each of these times so that we can compute seasonal relatives or seasonal indices for a multiplicative model.

Year	Quarter	X-Coordinate	Trend Value	Actual Demand	Actual ÷ Trend
1	1	1	23,168.6	26,209	1.131
1	2	2	22,873.7	21,402	0.936
1	3	3	22,578.9	18,677	0.827
1	4	4	22,284.0	24,681	1.108
2	1	5	21,989.2	25,390	1.155
2	2	6	21,694.3	19,064	0.879
2	3	7	21,399.5	18,173	0.849
2	4	8	21,104.6	23,866	1.131

$$\text{Average index for 1st quarter of year} = \frac{1.131 + 1.155}{2} = 1.143$$

$$\text{2nd quarter} = \frac{0.936 + 0.879}{2} = 0.908$$

$$\text{3rd quarter} = \frac{0.827 + 0.849}{2} = 0.838$$

$$\text{4th quarter} = \frac{1.108 + 1.131}{2} = 1.120$$

(d) The forecast for year 3 is found by projecting the trend to quarters 9 through 12 and multiplying these figures by the appropriate seasonal indices.

Quarter	X-Coordinate	Trend Value	Seasonal Index	Forecast (Trend × Seasonal Index)
1	9	20,809.8	1.143	23,786
2	10	20,514.9	0.908	18,628
3	11	20,220.1	0.838	16,944
4	12	19,925.2	1.120	22,316

DISCUSSION QUESTIONS

1. Why is sales forecasting the key to many other types of forecasts?
2. What is meant by a qualitative or subjective as compared to a quantitative or statistical forecast?
3. Is forecasting a skill or a science? Explain.
4. Why do some investments in forecasting yield a negative net return?
5. Why does the marketing function usually make sales forecasts?
6. When should a quantitative forecast be substituted for judgment?
7. Name three subjective methods of forecasting, and give the origin of the data for each.
8. Name three quantitative or statistical forecasting methods that use time as the basis for changes in demand.

9. What cautions should be observed in checking on statistical forecasts? Why?
10. Why are computers often used in evaluating forecast models to select one that appears to be best suited to a pattern of previous demand and for making routine, repetitive forecasts after a company has selected a model?
11. (a) Discuss a possible reason for using the MAD as a measure with which to compare the accuracy of two forecast models.
    (b) for using the MSE.
    (c) for using the MAPE.
12. Why do forecasting methods need to be monitored or controlled?

PROBLEMS

1. Quarterly demand for a product is shown below.

Quarter	Demand
1	6,228
2	5,067
3	4,629
4	6,018
5	6,525
6	5,090
7	4,810
8	6,388
9	6,535
10	5,762
11	5,175
12	6,223

(a) Compute the four-quarter moving averages for the data.
(b) Plot the actual demand and each four-quarter average, centered between the periods it represents. Does the four-quarter average remove any of the seasonality in the data series?

2. Given below are data on the monthly demand for a product.

(a) Compute the three-month moving average of this demand. Does this series still show seasonal variation?
(b) Compute the twelve-month moving average of this demand. Does this series of averages still show seasonal variation?
(c) Plot the original data and the two moving averages, centered between the periods they represent.

Month	Demand	Month	Demand	Month	Demand
1	487	13	528	25	517
2	602	14	622	26	595
3	551	15	608	27	619
4	587	16	592	28	602
5	509	17	536	29	545
6	457	18	504	30	486
7	349	19	461	31	431
8	386	20	391	32	416
9	490	21	437	33	444
10	507	22	503	34	492
11	516	23	562	35	538
12	573	24	570	36	575

3. Demand for a special model of microchip during the past five months is shown below:

October	1,170
November	1,310
December	1,560
January	920
February	1,235

(a) Compute the forecast demand for each month through March, using single exponential smoothing with $\alpha = 0.2$. Assume that the forecast for October was 1,200.

(b) Compute the MAD for this forecasting model based on the November, December, January, and February data.

4. (a) Repeat problem 3 with $\alpha = 0.4$.

(b) Compute the MAD for this forecast model based on the November, December, January, and February data.

(c) Which appears to be the better value of α, 0.2 or 0.4?

5. Given below is a series of weekly demands for outpatient care at an ambulatory center. Also shown are forecasts of demand calculated by two forecasting methods that are under consideration.

Demand	Forecast Model A	Forecast Model B
566	610	580
620	630	600
584	610	580
652	630	630
748	640	702
703	650	680
670	655	680
625	655	680
572	630	600
618	630	600

(a) Compute the MAD for each forecast model.

(b) Compute the RSFE for each forecast model.

(c) Indicate which model you think is better and why.

6. The Olde Favorite Ice Cream Shoppe has recorded the demand for a particular flavor during the past six weeks as shown below.

Week	Gallons
1st week, May	16
2nd week, May	15
3rd week, May	19
4th week, May	22
1st week, June	26
2nd week, June	29

(a) Calculate a 3-week moving average for the data to forecast demand for the next week. (*Three weeks of data are used for each forecast so you can make only three forecasts for periods where actual data are available*)

(b) Calculate a weighted average forecast for the data using a weight of 0.6 for the most recent data and weights of 0.3 and 0.1 for successively older data.

(c) Compare the forecasts from parts a and b. Which forecast do you think is more appropriate? Why?

(d) Do you feel that a regression trend forecast for this product would be appropriate? Why or why not?

7. A telephone answering service has the following record of the number of calls received per day on a series of days: 610, 570, 700, 570, 530, 530, 510, 530, 590, 520, 680, 550, 510, 600, 660.

(a) Use a simple average of the number of calls for the first 5 days to forecast demand on day 6, then use a single exponential smoothing model with $\alpha = 0.2$ to forecast the number of calls during each of the days 7 through 16.

(b) Find the MAD of the single smoothed forecast based on the data for days 9 through 15. (This permits some of the effect of the initial estimate to be "washed out.")

(c) Find the MAD over the last 7 days if

the average of the first 5 days is used as the forecast for the last seven days.

8. A local supermarket recorded the number of cases of soft drinks sold during 10 weeks. Looking for a way to forecast drink sales, the market manager obtained from the weather bureau the mean noontime temperature for each of these weeks. The data are recorded below.

Week	Average Noon Temperature	Cases of Drinks Sold
1	75	25
2	70	21
3	76	26
4	76	22
5	81	30
6	85	32
7	86	33
8	79	29
9	84	34
10	81	31

(a) Compute the coefficient of correlation between temperature and sales.

(b) Develop a regression equation to predict soft drink sales in relation to mean temperature.

(c) If the mean temperature for next week is predicted to be 82°, how many cases of drinks should the manager expect to sell?

9. The manager of Semolina Supreme Pizza Company has the following record of demand for the company's product:

Year	Demand (Tons)
1	62
2	79
3	86
4	94
5	107
6	120

(a) Develop the linear regression equation that best fits these data.

(b) Use the regression equation to estimate demand in years 7 and 8 so company managers can begin planning requirements for processing capacity and negotiating contracts to obtain the ingredients the company uses.

10. Soft Touch Carpet Installers is trying to select a forecasting model to determine the number of carpet installers the company will require each month. A relationship is thought to exist between the demand for carpet installation and the number of building permits issued some months prior to the demand. Given below are the number of building permits issued in a series of months and the demand for carpet installation in most of these months and in some later months.

Month	Building Permits Issued During Month	Demand for Carpet Installation
1	506	87
2	491	84
3	517	76
4	563	82
5	619	81
6	632	86
7	686	95
8	692	107
9	703	117
10	714	125
11	652	118
12	619	121

(a) Using the first eight months of building permit data, compute the coefficient of linear correlation between demand for carpet installation in a one-month period and the number of building permits issued two months prior to that period (a two-month lag model).

(b) Using the first eight months of building permit data, compute the correlation coefficient for a three-month lag model.

(c) Using the first eight months of building permit data, compute the correlation coefficient for a four-month lag model.

(d) The company is considering the development of a linear regression model to estimate demand on the basis of building permits issued in some prior month. Against which month's building permits should the demand data be regressed to develop the best model?

11. (a) Using the data in problem 10, develop a regression model to express demand for carpet installation as a function of the building permits issued three months prior to the demand. (Use the first eight months of building-permit data.)

(b) Forecast the demand for carpet installation three months following a month in which 693 building permits were issued.

12. The Deadweight Anchor Company has experienced the following demand for a particular model of boat anchor during the past two years:

Month	Year 1	Year 2
January	1,361	1,415
February	1,286	1,325
March	1,230	1,286
April	1,225	1,295
May	1,220	1,275
June	1,250	1,255
July	1,210	1,290
August	1,190	1,240
September	1,240	1,300
October	1,288	1,375
November	1,362	1,422
December	1,438	1,490

(a) Compute and plot the four-month moving averages for these data.

(b) Compute a twelve-month average for the first twelve months and the last twelve months. Plot these points and draw a trend line that represents the trend of these data. What are the intercept and slope of the line?

13. Assume that the trend line equation for the data of problem 12 is $Y = 1,244 +$

4.533X, where X is each month in the series of data beginning with 1, 2, 3, etc.

(a) Compute the average multiplicative seasonal index for each month of the year.

(b) Compute the trend value for each of the next six months and adjust each month's trend value by the seasonal index.

14. The owners of a beer distributorship want to forecast the level of sales for the next two years so they can determine the requirements for resources such as storage space, refrigerated storage, trucks, workers and capital. The quarterly sales for the past two years and the first half of this year are given below.

Quarter	Year Before Last	Last Year	Current Year
1	24,500	26,200	29,200
2	33,200	36,600	38,100
3	36,900	39,700	
4	26,400	28,500	

(a) Average the first year's sales to establish one point on a trend line. Average the second year's sales to determine the second point. Develop an equation for this trend line which expresses sales as a function of the quarter.

(b) Determine the average seasonal index as a ratio of the actual demand to the trend value for each quarter using the data for the first two years.

(c) Do the sales for the first two quarters of the current year appear to be consistent with the model?

(d) Estimate the quarterly sales for the last two quarters of the current year and for next year.

15. A linear equation for the trend in demand data was found to be $Y' = 1724 + 5.21X$ where X is the number of the month as designated in the table below.

Month	YEAR 1 Month Number	YEAR 1 Actual Demand	YEAR 2 Month Number	YEAR 2 Actual Demand
January	1	1619	13	1695
February	2	1541	14	1590
March	3	1440	15	1519
April	4	1553	16	1620
May	5	1637	17	1706
June	6	1747	18	1827
July	7	1887	19	1919
August	8	1955	20	2001
September	9	2062	21	2121
October	10	1982	22	2051
November	11	1870	23	1936
December	12	1776	24	1859

(a) Project the trend values for each month and determine the deviation from the trend for each month.

(b) Does a multiplicative or additive adjustment seem to be more appropriate?

(c) Determine the average additive factor to adjust each month's trend projection for seasonal variation.

16. The Niagra Rainware Company has the following demand pattern for one of its products over the past three years.

DEMAND

Quarter	Year 1	Year 2	Year 3
1	1,683	1,736	1,752
2	1,970	2,055	2,104
3	2,003	2,078	2,122
4	1,702	1,757	1,762

(a) Compute the average demand per quarter for each of the three years, and plot these three data points. (The first year's average corresponds to the end of quarter 2, the second year's corresponds to the end of quarter 6, etc.)

(b) Determine the linear regression equation that best fits this deseasonalized data.

(c) Calculate the average seasonal indices for the four quarters of the year assuming a multiplicative model. (The actual demand will correspond to quarters 0.5, 1.5, 2.5, etc.)

(d) Forecast the demand for the following year under the assumption that the model developed in the previous parts of the problem is valid.

17. The Terrific Tanning Tonic Company produces suntan oil and sunburn cream. Demand is highly seasonal, and the company has some difficulty in planning material purchases, employment needs, and cash requirements. Company managers are interested in forecasting future demand with quarterly seasonal indices. Quarterly sales data for Tanning Tonic over the past three years are shown below:

Year	Quarter	Demand (bottles × 1,000)
1	1	95
	2	200
	3	175
	4	100
2	1	110
	2	210
	3	190
	4	120
3	1	130
	2	235
	3	215
	4	135

(a) Find the trend by visual plotting.

(b) Find the trend line by use of a one-year—i.e., four-quarter—moving average.

(c) Compute an average seasonal index for each quarter of the year by computing the ratio of the actual demand to the approximate trend value.

(d) Project the quarterly sales, with seasonality included, for the next two years.

18. (a) Can you think of any reason why linear regression of the unaveraged demand data in problem 17 might not be appropriate?

(b) Compute the trend by least squares regression of the data without deseasonalizing it, and compare it with the trend indicated by a four-quarter moving average. Why is it different?

19. A bank in a rapidly growing city finds that it is outgrowing its facility. The bank officers feel that the operations (proof, transit, computer, bookkeeping) part of the bank should be moved. They are looking for an existing building to lease or buy or for a site on which to build an operations center. They feel that the current facility will handle a quarterly volume that averages 330,000 checks per day. The lead time to obtain a site and design and construct a new facility is at least two years.

Given below are the quarterly averages of the daily check volume, in thousands:

Quarter	Year 1	Year 2	Year 3	Year 4
1	141	157	181	206
2	132	147	166	193
3	152	168	192	222
4	171	192	221	254

(a) Determine the four-quarter moving averages, and plot them along with the past quarterly values.
(b) By use of the graph, determine the average seasonal adjustment (multiplicative) for the peak quarter of the year.
(c) When should the bank have its new facility available?
(d) What additional information would be helpful in developing this forecast?

*20. Use the thirty-six successive values of demand data given in problem 2 to determine the number of periods to include in a moving average so that the MAD is minimized. You can construct a spreadsheet with columns for month number, demand, sum of n months, forecast, deviation, and absolute deviation. Sum the absolute deviation column for months 13 through 36 to get the numerator for the

MAD. Use 450 for the initial forecast, and use a two-month moving average. Record the MAD, then repeat with a three-month moving average, etc., until you find the number of months in a moving average that minimizes the MAD. Use the prior month (a one-month average) as a forecast. Which forecast model seems to fit the data best? Why?

*21. Given below are thirty-six months of sales data from Redwood Rummage Company. Construct a spreadsheet to calculate exponential smoothing forecasts for each month, using an initial forecast of 450 for the first month. Use a column for each of the following: month number, demand, forecast, error, alpha × error, absolute error, error squared, percentage error, and absolute percentage error. Sum the appropriate columns from month 13 through month 36 to compute the mean absolute deviation (MAD), mean squared error (MSE), and the mean absolute percentage error (MAPE). Perform the first computations with α = 0.1 and record the measures of error for this α. Change α to 0.2 and repeat, then use α of 0.3. When the MAD starts to increase, you have passed the best α (as measured by the MAD). Reduce α by 0.02 (use a two-decimal-place value for α) for a series of trials until you find the value of α that makes the MAD the smallest.

Month	Demand	Month	Demand
1	447	19	411
2	652	20	351
3	501	21	477
4	627	22	553
5	549	23	522
6	407	24	610
7	309	25	567
8	436	26	555
9	450	27	669
10	557	28	552

*These problems require more detailed computation and are intended for programmable assistance such as that provided by a microcomputer.

Month	Demand	Month	Demand
11	466	29	505
12	613	30	436
13	478	31	471
14	662	32	376
15	558	33	394
16	552	34	452
17	586	35	538
18	544	36	575

*22. Repeat problem 21, but select the forecast model that minimizes the mean squared error, MSE. Why might the model (value of α) be different from the one that minimized the MAD?

*23. Use a spreadsheet template to see how long it takes for the effects of an initial forecast to "wash out." You can develop another template or you can use the one developed for problem 21, but you will not need all of the columns. Use an α of 0.3 and an initial forecast of 350 (your instructor may give you different values of the initial forecast). How many months does it take until the forecast with an initial value of 350 rounds to the same integer as the forecast made when an initial forecast of 447 was used?

*24. Repeat problem 23 using an α of 0.5.

BIBLIOGRAPHY

Brown, Robert G. *Smoothing, Forecasting, and Prediction of Discrete Time series.* Englewood Cliffs, N.J.: Prentice-Hall, 1963.

Carpenter, James, Dennis Deloria, and David Morganstein. "Statistical Software for Microcomputers." *Byte,* April 1984, pp. 234–264.

Chambers, John C., Satinder K. Mullick, and Donald D. Smith. "How to Choose the Right Forecasting Technique." *Harvard Business Review,* July–August 1971, pp. 45–74.

Chisholm, Roger K., and Gilbert R. Whitaker, Jr. *Forecasting Methods.* Homewood, Ill.: Irwin, 1971.

Gardner, Everette S., Jr. "The Strange Case of the Lagging Forecasts." *Interfaces,* May–June 1984, pp. 47–50.

Makridakis, Spyros G., Steven C. Wheelwright, and Victor E. McGee. *Forecasting Methods and Applications.* 2nd ed. New York: Wiley, 1983.

Makridakis, Spyros G., and Steven C. Wheelwright. *Interactive Forecasting: Univariate and Multivariate Methods.* San Francisco: Holden-Day, 1978.

Shore, Barry. *Operations Management.* New York: McGraw-Hill, 1973. Chaps. 11 and 12.

Wheelwright, Steven C., and Darrel G. Clarke. "Corporate Forecasting: Promise and Reality." *Harvard Business Review,* November-December 1976.

Wheelwright, Steven C., and Spyros G. Makridakis. *Forecasting Methods for Management.* New York: Wiley, 1973.

*These problems require more detailed computation and are intended for programmable assistance such as that provided by the microcomputer.

PART II
PLANNING AND CONTROLLING OPERATIONS

On the basis of forecasts of demand to which the production function must respond, managers must determine how the production system will be operated within the short- and intermediate-term horizon. Part II consists of eight chapters and three supplements that address the issues, tools, and techniques related to planning and controlling operations activities. (Decisions relating to the design of production systems are discussed in Part III.)

Chapter 4 discusses aggregate capacity planning, that is, planning generally how capacity to meet demand will be made available during the intermediate-term horizon. Supplement E provides a review of linear programming, which is sometimes used in aggregate planning. To carry out the aggregate plan, most production systems (particularly in manufacturing) need supplies or raw materials. Chapter 5 presents an overview of materials management. Chapters 6 and 7 discuss inventory systems and techniques for managing a company's supply of materials.

Effective scheduling ensures that customer demand is served with the correct goods or services at the appropriate time, and that productive resources are wisely utilized.Chapter 8 considers the scheduling and controlling of manufacturing, which must coordinate both capacity and materials availability. Chapter 9 focuses on scheduling in service operations. Supplement F discusses simulation, which is a technique sometimes used to develop schedules or to evaluate scheduling methods. Chapter 10 presents information on scheduling and controlling projects, which are long-duration, special-purpose operations. Supplement G discusses maintenance, which in many respects resembles the managing of projects.

Another aspect of making resources productive is seeing that goods or services of the appropriate quality are provided. Good strategy and good use of resources require that resources be used to furnish customers with goods or services that the customers will find suitable. Thus Part II concludes with Chapter 11, in which issues and methods of quality assurance are reviewed.

Chapter Outline
AGGREGATE CAPACITY PLANNING

THE PLAN DOES NOT ALWAYS EQUAL THE FORECAST

Strategies for Responding to Nonuniform Demand

APPROACHES TO AGGREGATE PLANNING

BOTTOM-UP AGGREGATE PLANNING

Production Planning: Basis for Detailed Scheduling / Resource Requirements Planning

TOP-DOWN AGGREGATE PLANNING

The Trial-and-Error Method / Linear Programming / *Application: Example of the Transportation Method of Linear Programming* / The Linear Decision Rule, LDR / Computer Search Methods of Aggregate Planning / Problems in Disaggregating a Top-Down Aggregate Plan

SELECTING AN AGGREGATE PLANNING HORIZON

ALLOCATION OF INSUFFICIENT CAPACITY

Allocating Limited Resources to Competing Uses / *Application: Example of the Graphical Method of Linear Programming*

Summary / Solved Problems / Discussion Questions / Problems / Bibliography

KEY TERMS

Fixed capacity	Bottom-up (inductive) approach	Master (production) schedule	Rough-cut capacity planning
Adjustable capacity	Top-down (deductive) approach	Bill of labor	Linear decision rule (LDR)
Aggregate planning	Time fence	Pseudoproduct	Search decision rule (SDR)
Load profile	Production plan	Disaggregation	Isoprofit line
Pure strategy		Resource requirements planning	
Mixed strategy			

Chapter 4
AGGREGATE CAPACITY PLANNING

One important function of management is planning. Managers must develop plans that wisely use the company's resources, and they must use their other skills—such as organizing, communicating, coordinating, leading, and motivating—to see that the plans are carried out. However, no matter how effective managers may be, their efforts will not yield the greatest results if the plans themselves are poor or inappropriate. It is important therefore that managers have good planning procedures in effect. In this chapter we discuss intermediate-range planning of production capacity. We will consider the subject primarily from the standpoint of a manufacturing operation and then comment on the ways in which nonmanufacturing operations are similar to or different from this model. Nonmanufacturing operations are considered in greater detail in Chapter 9, where we discuss the scheduling of service operations.

Many of the plans managers make are concerned with how much capacity the company will have, how that capacity will be provided, and how that capacity will be used. Long-range plans address the matter of major capital expenditures, such as new plant and equipment, which determine what is sometimes called *fixed capacity*. This part of the company's capacity cannot be easily changed within the time periods covered by the intermediate-range planning horizon. The fixed capacity (with the possible exception of some subcontracting) represents an upper limit to the firm's production capacity during the intermediate horizon. Within the limit of the fixed capacity, a firm's production capacity can be varied during the intermediate horizon by varying such factors as work force size, work hours per week, number of shifts, and the use of subcontractors. These adjustable factors are considered as *adjustable capacity.* For many companies, the lead time to adjust capacity smoothly is longer than the lead time to obtain materials. The usual approach is first to develop a plan that makes wise use of the company's capacity, then to plan for the materials that are required to implement the plan. Some types of companies must order long-lead-time materials before sufficient information is available for realistic capacity planning, then develop production plans in light of the available materials and adjustable capacity. We will discuss capacity planning in this chapter and materials management in the next three chapters.

Aggregate planning involves planning the best quantity to produce during time periods in the intermediate-range horizon and planning the lowest-cost method of providing the adjustable capacity to accommodate the production requirements. For a manufacturing operation, traditional aggregate planning analysis reported in the literature involved planning work force size, production rate (work hours per week), and inventory levels. But other options for adjusting capacity are possible in trying to deploy the company's resources in the best way.

The objectives of aggregate planning are to develop plans that are:

1. *Feasible:* The plans should provide for that portion of demand that the company intends to serve and should be within the capacity of the firm.
2. *Optimal:* Although this desire is seldom achieved, the company should aim for plans which will ensure that resources are used as wisely as possible and costs kept as low as possible.

Managers want to plan ahead to prevent a situation arising wherein the company enters a period of high demand and finds that if only they had added to the work force and accumulated some inventory, the company would have had a bonanza. They want to avoid making unrealistic sales commitments that result in disappointing or losing customers because the company lacks sufficient production capacity. On the other hand, managers want to avoid allowing the company to enter extended periods of low demand with excessive operating costs for adjustable capacity that cannot be used within some reasonable time.

THE PLAN DOES NOT ALWAYS EQUAL THE FORECAST

A company will develop a production plan or schedule for far enough into the future to permit smooth adjustment of the capacity and provide time to obtain any raw materials that may be required. For many make-to-stock manufacturing companies, the production requirements will occur some time prior to the forecasted demand, to permit time for packaging, shipping to distribution points, unloading, supplying retailers, or performing other steps in the supply chain. Because of this time offset, the production plan may differ from the demand forecast—as is shown in Figure 4.1. However, companies that can hold inven-

FIGURE 4.1

Capacity Requirements Do Not Always Coincide with Demand

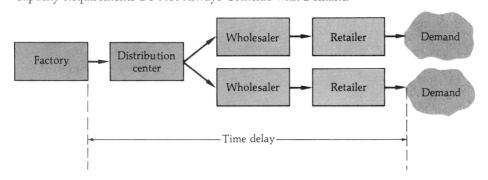

tory—primarily make-to-stock manufacturers—can use inventory to make the production requirements occur prior to the forecasted demand by even more than the time required for products to flow through the distribution channel. A second reason for a possible discrepancy between the demand forecast and the production plan is that in some instances a company may decide not to serve all of the forecasted demand, particularly in situations where demand is highly seasonal. Let's examine some of the ways companies adjust production plans to deal with seasonal demand patterns.

Strategies for Responding to Nonuniform Demand

Competition, product life cycle, seasonal usage, and other factors usually cause demand to change, so that very few companies have uniform demand. The more dynamic the conditions, the more important planning becomes. A non-uniform demand pattern presents a nonuniform *load profile* (i.e., requirement for work per time period throughout some time span). Suppose, for example, that a manufacturing company's demand forecast has been converted into a seasonal load profile such as that pictured in Figure 4.2. Managers facing such a load profile could deploy the company's resources in a variety of ways to serve this demand. If the plant had been built with enough space and equipment to produce at the peak demand rate, management could consider holding the work force at a level sufficient to produce at the peak rate, as shown in Figure 4.2a. But the company would then have idle people and equipment most of the year—unless it overproduced. As an alternative, the company could hold the staffing at a lower level and use overtime during the peak season, so that there would be fewer idle resources during the off-season. The company could elect to hire and lay off workers in accordance with the load profile. Since we assumed that this is a manufacturing company, holding inventory is also a viable option. The company could operate with a lower investment in plant and equipment than is required to produce at the peak demand rate if inventory is held. The company could operate at a level production rate, as shown in Figure 4.2b,

FIGURE 4.2

Seasonal Load Profile Faced by a Manufacturing Company

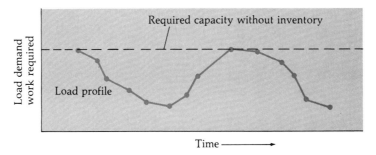

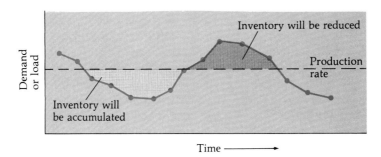

accumulating inventory when demand is lower than this production rate and selling down the inventory when demand is higher than this production rate.

If the company plans to change only one variable—such as work force, production rate (idle time and overtime), or inventory level—it is said to use a *pure strategy*. However, it often is desirable to change a combination of variables, which is termed a *mixed strategy*. Table 4.1 presents some considerations about three major types of strategies that often are used to meet nonuniform demand, each of which stresses a different variable. The three strategies can be combined in an infinite number of ways to arrive at an operating plan that managers feel is feasible and desirable (perhaps optimal but more likely satisficing). Aggregate planning attempts to determine the strategies that should be used. A variety of methods can be used to evaluate and select aggregate plans, several of which are discussed in the remainder of the chapter.

APPROACHES TO AGGREGATE PLANNING

An aggregate plan, as the name implies, is a sum or collection of plans for various products or services that must share resources. There are two basic approaches to aggregating the capacity requirements of a company's assortment of goods or services, a "bottom-up" or inductive approach and a "top-down" or deductive approach.

Table 4.1
SOME STRATEGIES THAT MAY BE USED FOR MEETING NONUNIFORM DEMAND

1. STRATEGY: ABSORB DEMAND FLUCTUATIONS BY VARYING INVENTORY LEVEL, BACK-ORDERING, OR SHIFTING DEMAND

Methods	Costs	Remarks
Produce in earlier period and hold until product is demanded.	Cost of holding inventory.	Service operations cannot hold service inventory. They must staff for peak levels and/or shift demand.
Offer to deliver the product or service later, when capacity is available.	Delay in the receipt of revenue, at the minimum. May result in lost customers.	Manufacturing companies with perishable products often are restrained in the use of this method.
Exert special marketing efforts to shift the demand to slack periods.	Costs of advertising, discounts, or promotional programs.	This is another example of the interrelationship between functions within a business.

2. STRATEGY: CHANGE ONLY THE PRODUCTION RATE IN ACCORDANCE WITH THE NONUNIFORM DEMAND PATTERN

Methods	Costs	Remarks
Work additional hours without changing the work force size.	Overtime premium pay.	Reduces the time available for maintenance work without interrupting production.
Staff for high production levels so that overtime is not required.	Excess personnel wages during periods of slack demand.	Sometimes work force can be utilized for deferred maintenance during periods of low demand.
Subcontract work to other firms.	The company must still pay its own overhead plus the overhead and profit for the subcontractors.	Utilizes the capacity of other firms but provides less control of schedules and quality levels.
Revise make-or-buy decisions to purchase items when capacity is fully loaded.	The company must have skills, tooling, and equipment that will be unutilized in slack periods.	All of these methods require capital investments sufficient for the peak production rate, which will be underutilized in slack periods.

3. STRATEGY: CHANGE THE SIZE OF THE WORK FORCE TO VARY THE PRODUCTION LEVEL IN ACCORDANCE WITH DEMAND

Methods	Costs	Remarks
Hire additional personnel as demand increases.	Employment costs for advertising, travel, interviewing, training, etc. Shift premium costs if an additional shift is added.	Skilled workers might not be available when needed since they are more likely to seek employment elsewhere.
Lay off personnel as demand subsides.	Cost of severance pay and increases in unemployment insurance costs. Loss of efficiency due to decreased morale and due to higher seniority workers being moved into jobs for which they are inexperienced as they move into ("bump") jobs of workers with less seniority.	The company must have adequate capital investment in equipment for the peak work force level.

The *bottom-up approach* has come to be more widely used, as massive computing capability has become more economical and widely available in more companies. This approach starts with plans for major products or product families and sums (i.e., aggregates) the impact that these plans will have on the company's capacity. If the capacity requirements for individual plans appear to sum to a satisfactory overall use of the company's resources, the plans are accepted to be implemented. If the plans add up to be unfeasible or do not make wise use of the company's resources, then some of the individual plans are revised to improve the overall impact of the aggregate plan. Individual plans are revised until a desirable aggregate plan is evolved.

The *top-down approach* is the more traditional and is seen more frequently in the literature on aggregate planning. In the top-down approach, the planner(s) develops an overall or aggregate rate of production, which is then allocated to the individual components (i.e., it is disaggregated). Top-down approaches fall into two major categories, the second of which can be further subdivided—as is shown in the following outline:

1. Methods that rely on subjective judgment to propose alternative mixes of resources and to determine which plan is best
2. Methods that attempt to model mathematically the costs of plans and that systematically seek the best plan
   a. Methods that solve mathematically for the optimal solution to the cost function to find the best plan
   b. Methods that perform a computer search for what appears to be the lowest-cost plan

We will now proceed to discuss some aggregate planning methods, beginning with the bottom-up approach then going on to present several of the methods within the top-down approach.

BOTTOM-UP AGGREGATE PLANNING

Production Planning: Basis for Detailed Scheduling

The bottom-up method of aggregate planning (also called resource requirements planning or rough-cut capacity planning) is usually used in conjunction with *material requirements planning* (MRP), which originally was a computer-based method for managing materials required to carry out a schedule. MRP has been expanded and enhanced to become a method of coordinating requirements for materials, capacity, and perhaps other company resources such as cash. Fully expanded applications of the MRP method are sometimes called manufacturing resources planning or MRP II. Application of MRP concepts is discussed in detail in Chapter 7, where we consider materials management for components and subassemblies used to make products. Here we are concerned with the way in which that capacity is planned in a company that is managed according to MRP concepts. Before going into the details of how this capacity planning is done, we will briefly review the setting in which this technique might be applied. Some of the terminology is more common to MRP, but the challenges of aggregate capacity planning are representative of a broader set of companies.

Consider the planning process in a make-to-stock manufacturing company that uses MRP concepts in managing manufacturing resources. The forecast provides an estimate of the demand to be served through some future horizon. The forecast accuracy will be better for the near portion of the horizon and decline as it estimates more distant periods. We can think of time as extending out ahead of the present and moving toward the present by one day each day. The company must prepare to respond to the forecast demand for a period before that period gets too close. The declining accuracy of the forecast as it extends out into the future is consistent with the need for planning. Plans for more distant periods are only general and will be refined, perhaps revised, before the time arrives to implement them. Plans for near periods must be specific and accurate enough to meet the conditions that are actually materializing. These plans must be finalized before the periods move within a specified horizon called a *time fence*. The time fence for planning should be ahead of the present by at least the amount of time required to purchase the necessary materials and produce the longest lead time product. When a time period moves within the time fence, the planning for that period should be complete and execution activities should begin.

Planning occurs in two stages: (1) a broad, general *production plan* that addresses how much capacity will be available and how it will be allocated and (2) a detailed plan of specific models of what products to produce and when. (This is called a *master schedule* or *master production schedule*.) The production plan is the topic we will consider because it deals with capacity at the aggregate level. This general production plan is developed for a planning horizon that begins near the time fence and extends into the future for maybe a year or two, depending on the needs of the company. For a seasonal business, this plan should definitely extend through the next peak in demand. Production planning is performed each month, with a new month being added to the far end of the horizon as another enters the time fence. Unless a company has only a small number of products, the production plan is made for logical groups of products such as product families or product lines. Major products might be planned separately. A company with a hundred or more products might condense them into ten to twenty-five product families. The production plan is made in terms of the product families that will be produced in each month, so it is a rather general plan. However, before the time period enters the time fence, the general production plan will be converted into a firm master schedule for specific product models that will be produced in each week.

The production planning process develops what can be thought of as the company's overall game plan. It is recommended that this planning be performed by the chief executive officer (CEO) and the top officers in marketing, manufacturing, finance, and engineering, to coordinate the commitment of various resources to serve anticipated demand in what appears to be the best way.

Tough trade-off decisions should be made at this level. The production plan establishes the amount of capacity the company must have, how many employees are required, and how much material must be purchased; it is therefore a major determinant of the company's expenses and its ability to serve its customers. Evaluation of the capacity requirements that result from a particular production plan or a tentative master schedule can be accomplished through a bottom-up summation process called resource requirements planning.

Resource Requirements Planning

Resource requirements planning, also known as *rough-cut capacity planning,* can be used to evaluate the impact that a trial production plan or a trial master schedule will have on the capacity of a company. As an aggregate planning tool, it would be used to sum and evaluate the work load that a production plan imposes either on all work centers or on only selected key work centers where resources are limited, expensive, or difficult to obtain. This planning might include capacity considerations for key subcontractors.

In resource requirements planning, the production committee would develop a trial production plan that expresses the quantities of the company's product families that are planned for production in each month of the planning horizon. The work load that this plan will impose on each key work center for each period of the planning horizon is then calculated by a computer. The load on each work center over time, called a *load profile,* is evaluated subjectively for feasibility and how well it appears to approach optimality. If the trial plan does not appear to be feasible or does not make optimal use of the resources in a work center, the plan may be revised. The capacity requirements of the new plan can then be evaluated to determine the desirability of this plan. Iterations of this process can be continued until the process develops a plan that is considered to be satisfactory. The process does not guarantee a mathematically optimal solution, but it provides disaggregated plans that are feasible when aggregated. This approach to planning requires a great deal of data manipulation for companies with a broad product line or with complex products requiring numerous operations. Rough-cut capacity planning is usually performed by computer to take advantage of its ability to process massive amounts of data rapidly.

An adjustment for the lead time might be made if the work load in a work center occurs significantly in advance of the final products indicated in the production plan. Since aggregate planning requires only an approximate plan for the distant horizon, some companies combine the options mentioned above. For example, they might plan product families to be produced in each month of the distant part of the planning horizon, then fill in the specific products to be produced in specific weeks as that time moves into the nearer part of the horizon.

A company that runs rough-cut capacity planning on its computer must have stored in memory a *bill of labor,* which lists the standard hours of work

Table 4.2
SAMPLE BILL OF LABOR

Product: Product Family 6 Work Center	Standard Hours Required/Unit
04 Shear	0.042
09 Stamping	0.012
14 Brake	0.026
16 Welding	0.051
17 Finishing	0.020

required in each key work center for a unit of each of the products or product families to be produced. A sample bill of labor is shown in Table 4.2. A trial production plan would be prepared showing how many units of each product or product family are to be produced in each period of the planning horizon. The computer would then sum the standard hours required in each work center during each period (perhaps with an adjustment for lead time). The output of the process would be a load profile for each of the work centers for which requirements have been indicated. The format of a load profile might be shown in a table similar to Table 4.3, or it might be shown graphically, as in Figure 4.3.

To use this system as an aggregate planning tool, the committee will go through a series of steps such as those outlined above. If the load profile in one or more work centers is unacceptable, the committee may revise the portion of the production plan that appears to have caused the difficulty. The process continues until a desirable production plan is found, if this appears to be the best way to achieve a match between resources and demand for resources. A flow chart representing this process is presented in Figure 4.4. By this procedure if the load profiles cannot be leveled within the current capacity level, the problem will be brought to management's attention in time for some adjustments to be made. A decision must then be made to do one or more of the following:

1. Miss some potential sales.
2. Work overtime.
3. Subcontract some of the work.
4. Add a shift.
5. Hire more people.
6. Transfer some work to another work center.
7. Transfer personnel into the work center.

Table 4.3
EXAMPLE OF A TABULAR LOAD REPORT

LOAD REPORT								
Work Center: *R 58* Normal Capacity (Hours per Week): *300*								
Week number	8	9	10	11	12	13	14	15	16
Load (hours)	380	275	200	265	225	175	160	140	120

FIGURE 4.3

Example of a Graphical Load Report or Load Profile

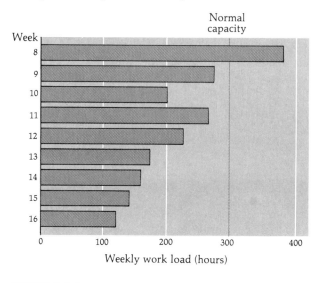

FIGURE 4.4

Flow Chart of Rough-Cut Capacity Planning Process

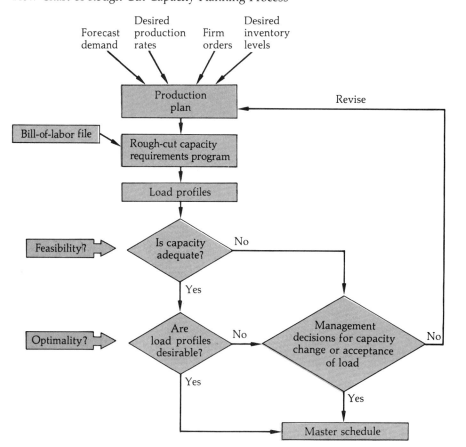

TOP-DOWN AGGREGATE PLANNING

The bottom-up approach to aggregate planning requires a great deal of calculation because the capacity impact is calculated for several work centers and for several product families, and these capacity requirements are then summed to determine their aggregate impact. Some companies, particularly those without either MRP or larger computers, might therefore use a top-down approach as an alternative. With the top-down approach, the desirable overall plan is developed for the periods in the planning horizon, with the plan for the first few periods being fairly firm. The intent is that this overall plan will disaggregate into feasible and desirable individual plans for the various work centers. This approach, then, rests on the assumption that if the proper amount of total capacity is available, the right amount of capacity for all of the parts will be available.

Aggregate planning for a top-down approach is performed in terms of a *pseudoproduct*, which is a fictitious product that represents the average characteristics of the entire product line to be planned. In the case of a paint company, the pseudoproduct might be gallons of paint without regard for the color or composition; for an automobile manufacturer the pseudoproduct might be a three-door model with half an automatic transmission and half a manual transmission. However, difficulties may arise in *disaggregation* if the product mix varies over time and the different products require different production resources. We will now consider the various methods that have been developed to perform top-down aggregate planning, beginning with the trial-and-error method.

The Trial-and-Error Method

Trial and error is probably the most widely used method of aggregate planning. This method simply evaluates the cost of alternative ways of using resources to provide the necessary production capacity. Managers evaluate options until they arrive at the one that seems most desirable. The method does not involve elaborate mathematics to develop the best plan, hence, it is relatively easy to understand and use. The method does, however, involve tedious repetition of simple calculations to evaluate the costs of alternative plans. It is helpful to develop a table to display these calculations. In an actual application, such a table would be developed and the calculations repeated for several trials during each planning session. The planning process would be repeated at each planning session, say every month. This repetition of calculations makes it desirable to develop a computer program or electronic spreadsheet to perform this work. The cost coefficients and relationships between the variables can be stored in the program. The planner has only to change the values of the desired variables and let the program compute the resulting cost. Alternative plans can thus be evaluated easily and quickly with computer assistance.

Let's go through an example of trial-and-error aggregate planning by evaluating some alternative operating strategies for Imperial Sail Company, which experiences seasonal demand for its original equipment and replacement boat sails. The demand forecast has been advanced so that it represents production requirements, which are given in Table 4.4 with other data that are useful for planning. Often a graph is useful to help one visualize the demand pattern and to suggest possible aggregate planning strategies. Figure 4.5 shows the cumulative production requirements versus the cumulative work days in the planning horizon, represented by the black line. Also shown in Figure 4.5 are the alternative strategies we will evaluate. We will first consider varying the work force so that cumulative production matches the cumulative requirements and coincides with the black line in the graph. Next we will consider maintaining a uniform production rate, represented by the blue line in the graph, so that all of the variation in demand is accommodated by inventory that will be accumulated during part of the year. Finally we will consider a mixed strategy. This mixed strategy, represented by the white line in the graph, changes the production rate and accumulates some inventory during the year.

Imperial's management estimates that the typical sail, the pseudoproduct, requires 20 hours to produce. Each employee is estimated to contribute 8 hours per day, and no scrap or rework is assumed for their aggregate planning. Estimates indicate that it costs $300 to hire an employee and $200 to lay off an employee. It has been found that about 1,000 units should be available as work-in-process and safety stock, at least during peak production months, and this amount will be on hand at the start of the planning horizon. It costs $6 per month to hold a unit in inventory.

Table 4.4
PRODUCTION REQUIREMENTS FOR IMPERIAL SAIL CO., BY MONTH

(1) Month	(2) Monthly Forecast Production Requirements (Units)	(3) Cumulative Production Requirements	(4) Normal Production Days in Month	(5) Cumulative Normal Production Days
April	1,600	1,600	21	21
May	1,400	3,000	22	43
June	1,200	4,200	22	65
July	1,000	5,200	21	86
August	1,500	6,700	23	109
September	2,000	8,700	21	130
October	2,500	11,200	21	151
November	2,500	13,700	20	171
December	3,000	16,700	20	191
January	3,000	19,700	20	211
February	2,500	22,200	19	230
March	2,000	24,200	22	252

FIGURE 4.5

Cumulative Production Requirements and Cumulative Production vs. Cumulative Production Days

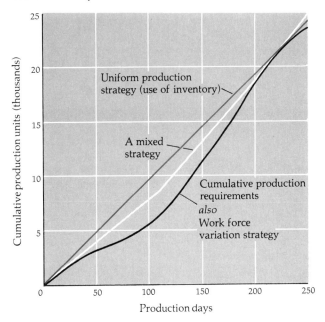

Imperial's management expects the demand pattern in the years preceding and following the planning year to be about the same as the demand pattern for the year we are planning. Therefore, the number of employees at the beginning of the planning year will be set equal to the number of employees at the end of the planning year. This condition is also assumed for all of the alternative strategies that are evaluated in this example.

In actual situations, a company might need to evaluate the cost of changing the work force and inventory levels from their current levels to the levels that are considered for the beginning of the planning year. Also, different demand levels for the year after the planning year might be expected, so the company might want to end the year with work force and inventory levels that differ from the levels at the beginning of the year. The conditions assumed in this example are only that the year start and end with the same work force level and with approximately the same inventory level. These conditions are sufficient to illustrate how the trial-and-error method would be employed to evaluate alternative aggregate plans.

Cost of Varying Only the Work Force   One pure strategy that Imperial might consider is that of changing only the size of the work force. This strategy assumes that persons with the necessary skills can be employed when they are

TABLE 4.5
COST TO VARY WORK FORCE IN ACCORDANCE WITH MONTHLY PRODUCTION REQUIREMENTS[a]

(1) Month	(2) Monthly Production Requirements	(3) Production Hours Needed (20 × col 2)	(4) Production Days in Month	(5) Production Hours Per Employee During Month	(6) Direct Employees Needed During Month, Rounded	(7) Employees Added at Start of Month	(8) Employees Laid Off at Start of Month	(9) Cost of Changing Employment Level ($300 × col 7 or $200 × col 8)
April	1,600	32,000	21	168	190		37	$ 7,400
May	1,400	28,000	22	176	159		31	6,200
June	1,200	24,000	22	176	136		23	4,600
July	1,000	20,000	21	168	119		17	3,400
August	1,500	30,000	23	184	163	44		13,200
September	2,000	40,000	21	168	238	75		22,500
October	2,500	50,000	21	168	298	60		18,000
November	2,500	50,000	20	160	313	15		4,500
December	3,000	60,000	20	160	375	62		18,600
January	3,000	60,000	20	160	375			
February	2,500	50,000	19	152	329		46	9,200
March	2,000	40,000	22	176	227		102	20,400
						256	256	$128,000

[a] It is assumed that the company would have 227 direct employees at the beginning of the planning period if the strategy were used.

Cost of changing employment level = $128,000
Cost of maintaining 1,000 units of inventory = 72,000
Total cost = $200,000

148

needed and that they will be hired or laid off to keep the direct labor hours that are available equal to the demanded production hours. The graph of cumulative production during the year will coincide with the black line representing cumulative production requirements in Figure 4.5. The cost to implement this strategy is developed in Table 4.5 and is estimated to be $200,000.

Cost of Varying Only the Inventory Level   Another strategy to meet the varying demand is to set a uniform production rate that will produce in one year the amount that is forecast to be needed during that year. This strategy is feasible if back-ordering (delivering the product in some period after the one in which it is ordered) is permitted or if inventory is held. The aggregate plan in this example begins with a period after the peak demand. This beginning point makes it more obvious that surplus inventory can be accumulated in some early period, when demand is less than the production rate, to be sold in some later period, when demand is higher than the production rate.

Since the company needs to produce 24,200 units in 252 days, it must produce at an average rate of at least 96.03 units per day. A work force of 241 persons will be required, which will provide a production rate of 96.4 units per day. The cost to hold an item in inventory is $6 per month for the average amount in inventory, including work in process. The monthly inventory levels and the resulting cost of $209,253 are developed in Table 4.6.

Consideration of Other Strategies   Other strategies can be used to meet a nonuniform demand for the outputs of the operation function. For the example being considered, a wide variety of pure and mixed strategies could be used. The company could consider staffing at some intermediate level and using overtime and undertime (idle time). Or perhaps the company could subcontract

Table 4.6
COST TO USE INVENTORY WITH A UNIFORM PRODUCTION RATE

(1) Month	(2) Cumulative Production Days	(3) Cumulative Production (2) × 96.4	(4) Cumulative Forecast Demand	(5) Ending Inventory (3) − (4) + 1,000	(6) Inventory Holding Cost $6 (Beginning + Ending)/2
April	21	2,024	1,600	1,424	$ 7,272
May	43	4,145	3,000	2,145	10,707
June	65	6,266	4,200	3,066	15,633
July	86	8,290	5,200	4,090	21,468
August	109	10,508	6,700	4,808	26,694
September	130	12,532	8,700	4,832	28,920
October	151	14,556	11,200	4,356	27,564
November	171	16,484	13,700	3,784	24,420
December	191	18,412	16,700	2,712	19,488
January	211	20,340	19,700	1,640	13,056
February	230	22,172	22,200	972	7,836
March	252	24,293	24,200	1,093	6,195
					$209,253

some work during the season of peak demand. Mixed strategies might include a combination of subcontracting and overtime, or overtime and inventory, and so on. When you consider the possibility of mixing three or more strategies and the infinite variety of ratios for blending strategies, you see how challenging the problem is.

Consideration of a Mixed Strategy   Let us consider a mixed strategy for the Imperial Sail Company. The company might want to set a relatively low but uniform production rate for the first part of the year and a higher but uniform rate for the latter part of the year. This would reduce the amount of inventory that would be accumulated early in the year, resulting in lower inventory costs than a pure strategy involving only inventory. Since some inventory would be used, the production rate changes would not be as extreme as under a pure strategy of changing only the work force, and the cost of changing the work force would not be so great. We will calculate the cost of one possible mixed strategy of this type.

Through the first month of the planning period, Imperial will need to have produced at least 1,600 units, which would require a minimum production rate of 76 units per day if no inventory were accumulated. If the production rate were set at 80 units per day for the initial part of the planning horizon, it would require (80 units × 20 hours/unit) ÷ 8 hours/person day = 200 persons. At the end of 109 days, the company would have produced 109 × 80 = 8,720 units. (Again, we are not considering absenteeism, scrap, or other matters that might occur in actual situations.) At the end of production day 252, Imperial needs to have a total production of 24,200 units. So the company will need to produce 15,480 units during the last 143 production days of the year, or an average of about 108.3 units per day. The work force required for this production rate is approximately 271 direct employees, which will provide a production rate of 108.4 units per day. Seventy-one persons should be hired at the beginning of September and laid off at the end of the year to achieve these employment levels and to end the year with the same number of employees that were on the payroll at the start of the year.

By using the mixed strategy just analyzed, Imperial Sail Company will accumulate some inventory for part of the year. It is assumed that the average inventory for a month is halfway between the starting and ending inventory for the month and it costs $6 per average unit on hand during the month. The cost of this mixed strategy, which is developed and presented in Table 4.7 is estimated to be $179,275. Notice that the cost of this mixed strategy is lower than the cost of using only inventory changes or only work force changes, which were discussed above.

Lessons from the Imperial Sail Company Example   The Imperial Sail Company example illustrates several points worth elaborating. For one thing, it shows the lengthy calculations necessary to evaluate possible aggregate production plans by the trial-and-error method. (You can see why an electronic spreadsheet or other computer program would be useful in an actual situation.)

Table 4.7
COST OF MIXED STRATEGY—VARYING WORK FORCE AND USING INVENTORY

	(1) Cumulative Days	(2) Production Rate Units/Day	(3) Cumulative Production	(4) Cumulative Demand	(5) Ending Inventory (3) − (4) + 1,000	(6) Inventory Cost $6 (beginning + ending)/2	(7) Cost of Changing Work Force
April	21	80.0	1,680	1,600	1,080	6,240	
May	43	80.0	3,440	3,000	1,440	7,560	
June	65	80.0	5,200	4,200	2,000	10,320	
July	86	80.0	6,880	5,200	2,680	14,040	
August	109	80.0	8,720	6,700	3,020	17,100	
September	130	108.4	10,996	8,700	3,296	18,948	71 × 300 = 21,300
October	151	108.4	13,273	11,200	3,073	19,107	
November	171	108.4	15,441	13,700	2,741	17,442	
December	191	108.4	17,609	16,700	1,909	13,950	
January	211	108.4	19,777	19,700	1,077	8,958	
February	230	108.4	21,836	22,200	636	5,139	
March	252	108.4	24,221	24,200	1,021	4,971	71 × 200 = 14,200
						$143,775	$35,500

Total cost = $143,775 + $35,500 = $179,275

It illustrates also some of the many strategies that may be employed. It makes clear that a combination strategy can be even more economical than a pure strategy. But a pure strategy might be better if the cost of one variable, such as carrying inventory, were much less than the cost of other variables. Notice that we did not find the optimal solution. We would have to try many strategies that seemed reasonable and see which was most economical. The next three methods of aggregate planning that are discussed—linear programming, linear decision rule, and computer search— are all top-down approaches that seek to find an optimal solution to the problem.

Application to Nonmanufacturing Operations   If the operation in question is a nonmanufacturing one, the same type of analysis can be applied. The major difference is that inventory accumulation is not a permissible variable to use in smoothing capacity requirements. Other variables, such as changes in the employment level and use of overtime and idle time, still apply. A cost penalty for delayed delivery of the service to the customer is analogous to a back-order penalty. Back-ordering is delivering the demanded item at a later time. This is what service companies do when they tell you that they can get to your job late next week. There is no significant cost penalty to such a delay unless the customer decides to go elsewhere.

Linear Programming

The objective of aggregate planning is to find a production plan that makes optimal use of the company's resources. Several methods of aggregate planning have been developed to express the cost of the aggregate plan as a mathematical expression and to seek the plan that minimizes this cost. All of these methods are top-down aggregate planning methods. It would be difficult to express mathematically all of the trade-offs that must be made for all of the work centers considered in bottom-up aggregate planning. When the company is working with only one pseudoproduct, the problem is less complex to model mathematically. Linear programming can be used if the costs of various resources are assumed to be linear functions of the amount of those resources used by the aggregate plan.

It can be used to plan production over some horizon for an actual product or for some pseudoproduct. Use of linear programming implies that a linear function adequately fits the variables for the subject company. Edward H. Bowman published an approach to aggregate planning that used the transportation method of linear programming,[2] a method that can be used to analyze the effects of holding inventory, back-ordering, the use of overtime, and the use of subcontracting. When more factors are to be considered, the more versatile simplex method must be used.[3] The simplex formulation can include the cost of hiring and layoff in the model. The mathematics becomes more lengthy when the simplex method is employed, particularly when additional variables are included in the problem.

[2]Edward H. Bowman, "Production Planning by the Transportation Method of Linear Programming," *Journal of the Operations Research Society*, February 1956, pp. 100–103.
[3]Fred Hanssmann and S. W. Hess, "A Linear Programming Approach to Production and Employment Scheduling," *Management Technology*, no. 1 (January 1960), pp. 46–52.

APPLICATION

Example of the Transportation Method of Linear Programming

The Mo-Go Co. sells mowers and go-carts, both products that have a seasonal demand pattern with a peak in the spring. Assume that it is March and we are planning the production rates and inventory levels for the next four months, which will see the company through its peak demand period. (A longer horizon could be used, but it would only make the illustration more lengthy.)

The company does not subcontract, so it will use only regular time and overtime capacity. The company can produce 500 units per month on regular time and 200 on overtime. Overtime production costs $20 more per unit than regular-time production. The company will enter April with an estimated inventory of 200 units and wants to have at least 100 units on hand at the end of the planning horizon. Inventory carrying costs are estimated to be $3 per month for each unit held. The estimated demand for the four months ahead are 600, 700, 800, and 600 units respectively. The transportation method requires that the sum of the supply be equal to the sum of the demand. A dummy demand will be used, since these monthly demands total less than the capacity of the four months plus the beginning inventory.

Figure 4.6 shows the preceding information in a transportation-method for-

FIGURE 4.6

A Transportation-Method Linear Programming Tableau for Mo-Go Co.

Source of product	Period in which product is forecast to be sold				Ending inventory	Dummy demand	Capacity
	1	2	3	4			
Beginning inventory	0 / 200	3	6	9	12	0	200
Regular-time production in period 1	0 / 400	3	6 / 100	9	12	0	500
Overtime production in period 1	20	23	26	29	32	0	200
Regular-time production in period 2		0 / 500	3	6	9	0	500
Overtime production in period 2		20 / 200	23	26	29	0	200
Regular-time production in period 3			0 / 500	3	6	0	500
Overtime production in period 3			20 / 200	23	26	0	200
Regular-time production in period 4				0 / 500	3	0	500
Overtime production in period 4				20 / 100	23 / 100	0	200
Forecast requirements	600	700	800	600	100	200	Total 3,000

mat. The allocation of production shown in the tableau is an optimal assignment of capacity to demand. The Mo-Go Co. decided, on the basis of this solution, to produce 500 units on regular time during April (100 will remain in inventory until June). The company will utilize its full regular-time and overtime capacity during the next three months. The additional cost of this plan above the cost of producing all units with only regular time during the month they are to be sold can be computed easily from Figure 4.6. Simply multiply the amount in each occupied cell by the cost coefficient in the upper right-hand corner of the cell and total the results. I got $12,900—what did you get? This is useful information if a company is considering expansion. It would indicate the maximum amount that could be saved by the elimination of anticipation inventory and overtime work. Naturally, the cost of expanding the capacity of Mo-Go Co. would have to be considered.

The transportation method can be used for consideration of additional variables. If Mo-Go Co. could subcontract some work in each period, an additional row for each period could be added to the tableau of Figure 4.6 to represent this additional source of production. The shaded portion of the matrix in Figure 4.6 would be used if back-ordering were permitted.

Nonmanufacturing Applications The transportation method also can be used for aggregate planning in nonmanufacturing operations. If we have a service operation and inventory cannot be used, the upper right-hand corner of the transportation-method tableau in Figure 4.6 should be shaded in. Back-ordering (delaying the delivery of the service) would be represented by the lower left portion of the matrix. The back-order cost per period would be the cost penalty incurred for each period's delay in providing the service. As cost entries are made in each cell down a column of Figure 4.7, the increase from one period to the next would be the amount of a one-month back-order cost.

If back-ordering is not permitted, then the manager works with regular time and overtime work and perhaps part-time assistance, which is much like subcontracting. Of course, the possibility of actual subcontracting may apply in some service organizations. When back-ordering and inventory are not to be employed as variables in planning production, the manager would gain little if anything from use of a transportation-method tableau. The manager cannot move the performance of work forward or backward in time. (The transportation tableau would be shaded both above and below the diagonal cells.) The system

FIGURE 4.7

A Transportation-Method Linear Programming Tableau When Inventory Is Not Permitted and Back-Ordering Is Permitted

Means by which service is provided	Period in which service is demanded				Service capacity
	1	2	3	4	
Regular-time work in period 1					
Overtime work in period 1					
Regular-time work in period 2					
Overtime work in period 2					
Regular-time work in period 3					
Overtime work in period 3					
Regular-time work in period 4					
Overtime work in period 4					
Total demand per period					

therefore must provide demanded service in the period it is demanded or not at all. The obvious solution to such a situation is to employ optional production methods in order of their increasing cost—regular time to the extent available, then the next most costly method, such as overtime, and so on.

The transportation method of linear programming can be used to arrive at an optimal solution to the problem by working with numbers in a table or by using a computer. As mentioned earlier, the simplex method can deal with more variables. Another mathematical model through which optimal solutions to the problem may be sought is the linear decision rule, which is discussed next.

The Linear Decision Rule (LDR)

The *linear decision rule* is a pair of linear equations that recommend the best production rate and work force size for the upcoming month, based on the forecast demand for the intermediate planning horizon. Holt and other developers studied the costs that resulted from several years' operation of a paint factory.[4] The production level and forecasts were considered in terms of a pseudoproduct—gallons of paint, without regard to their color or type. Actual costs that resulted each month from changes in inventory level, production rate, and work force size were determined. Quadratic equations were fitted to the actual costs, as shown in Figure 4.8.

The relevant costs in a month were the sum of the costs shown in Figure 4.8, with the 360 omitted from the regular payroll cost because it was a constant that would be paid regardless of changes in the decision variables. The expression for the cost in any month is given by equation 4.1.

$$C_t = 340\,W_t + 64.3(W_t - W_{t-1})^2 + 0.20(P_t - 5.67W_t)^2 \tag{4.1}$$
$$+ 51.2\,P_t - 281\,W_t + 0.082(I_t - 320)^2$$

There was a restraint that $I_{t-1} + P_t - O_t = I_t$, where

W_t = size of work force in period t

P_t = production in period t

I_t = net inventory level in period t (net inventory = inventory − back orders)

O_t = order rate (units of product whose shipment was ordered during the month).

The total cost over a planning horizon was the sum of these monthly costs. The total cost for a one-year planning horizon would be twelve times as long as equation 4.1. Equations for the work force size and production rate that minimized the total cost equation were found. The inventory level did not have to be determined because it is automatically the result of the old inventory level plus production minus sales. Equations 4.2 and 4.3 are the expressions for the best production rate and work force level, that is, the linear decision rule. Just

[4]Charles C. Holt, Franco Modigliani, John F. Muth, and Herbert A. Simon, "A Linear Decision Rule for Production and Employment Scheduling," *Management Sciences*, October 1955, pp 1–10.

FIGURE 4.8

Cost Structure and Equations for Cost Components in the Linear Decision Rule

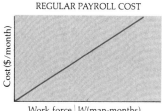

REGULAR PAYROLL COST

Regular payroll cost $= 340W_t + 360$

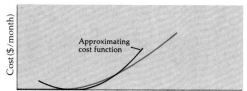

OVERTIME COST WHEN THE WORK FORCE IS
OF THE SIZE W_1 AND RANDOMNESS IS PRESENT

Expected cost of overtime $=$
$0.20\,(P_t\text{-}5.67W_t)^2 + 51.2P_t - 281.0W_t$

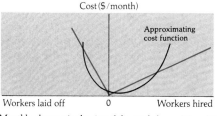

HIRING AND LAYOFF COSTS

Monthly changes in the size of the work force, $W_t - W_{t-1}$

Cost of hiring and layoffs $= 64.3(W_t - W_{t-1})^2$

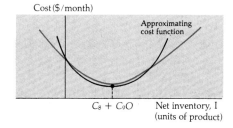

INVENTORY, BACK-ORDER,
AND MACHINE SET UP COSTS

Expected inventory, back-order, and setup costs $=$
$0.082(I - 320)^2$

Source: Charles C. Holt, Franco Modigliani, John F. Muth, and Herbert A. Simon, "Cost Structure and Equations for Cost Components in the Linear Decision Rule," *Management Science,* October 1955, pp. 8, 13.

before each month, equation 4.2 can be used to find the recommended production rate for the month as a function of the forecast orders in future months, the current work force, and inventory. Equation 4.3 gives the recommended work force level as a function of the same variables.

$$P_t = \begin{cases} +0.463\,O_t \\ +0.234\,O_{t+1} \\ +0.111\,O_{t+2} \\ +0.046\,O_{t+3} \\ +0.013\,O_{t+4} \\ -0.002\,O_{t+5} \\ -0.008\,O_{t+6} \\ -0.010\,O_{t+7} \\ -0.009\,O_{t+8} \\ -0.008\,O_{t+9} \\ -0.007\,O_{t+10} \\ -0.005\,O_{t+11} \end{cases} +0.993\,W_{t-1} + 153 - 0.464\,I_{t-1} \qquad \textbf{(4.2)}$$

$$W_t = 0.743\, W_{t-1} + 2.09 - 0.010\, I_{t-1} + \left\{ \begin{array}{l} 0.0101\ O_t \\ 0.0088\ O_{t+1} \\ 0.0071\ O_{t+2} \\ 0.0054\ O_{t+3} \\ 0.0042\ O_{t+4} \\ 0.0031\ O_{t+5} \\ 0.0023\ O_{t+6} \\ 0.0016\ O_{t+7} \\ 0.0012\ O_{t+8} \\ 0.0009\ O_{t+9} \\ 0.0006\ O_{t+10} \\ 0.0005\ O_{t+11} \end{array} \right\} \qquad (4.3)$$

Past data were used to compare actual management decisions to the decisions the LDR would have recommended if a four-month moving average forecast were used. As shown in Table 4.8, the LDR had about an 8 percent advantage. The LDR was a specific model for the particular company that was studied. If another company wanted to use an LDR model, new equations would have to be fitted to the cost of functions of that company. The data used to develop and test the LDR are sometimes used to compare the performance of other approaches to aggregate planning.

Computer Search Methods of Aggregate Planning

Both linear programming and the linear decision rule assume a specific mathematical structure for the functions to be optimized. Each can guarantee an optimal solution to the assumed model. The true cost, however, may not be expressed accurately by linear or quadratic equations. Several other methods of aggregate planning have been developed that do not place these restrictions on the cost equation.

Table 4.8
**COMPARISON OF LINEAR DECISION RULE
RESULTS AND ACTUAL DECISIONS**

Cost Category	COST (THOUSANDS OF DOLLARS)	
	Company Performance	Decision Rule—Moving Average Forecast
Regular payroll	$1,256	$1,149
Overtime	82	95
Inventory	273	298
Back orders	326	246
Hiring and layoff	16	12
Total cost	$1,950	$1,800
Percent	108.5%	100%

The mathematical complexity of the problem increases greatly when step functions and equations of a higher order than quadratic are involved. Large-scale computers have made it possible to apply simulation and search methods to the aggregate planning problem. Rather than develop an analytic solution that can be proved optimal, the computer solves the problem for many possible values of the variables and picks the least costly. Several such models appeared in the literature during the 1960s.

William H. Taubert developed a method called the *search decision rule* (SDR), which did not restrict the mathematical form of the cost equations.[5] A "pattern search" technique was used to find what appeared to be the minimum point on the surface described by the cost equations. The pattern search starts at a base point with a trial set of values for the work force sizes (W_i) and production rates (P_i) for the next ten periods in the planning horizon. The model works with these twenty variables to find the best combination. Small movements are made in a pattern around this base point, and the most promising direction to move is selected. A new trial point is selected by moving in the most promising direction. If this trial point improves the objective function (gives a lower cost), it becomes the base point and a pattern is tried around it. If the trial point does not improve the objective function, the search goes back to the old base point and moves in a different direction. If no improvement can be found, the search terminates and the values for the W_i's and P_i's of the current base point are recommended. A flow chart of the logic used in the SDR is presented in Figure 4.9.

The pattern search method is adaptive and heuristic. If the best direction to move is the one that would be expected from the last move, the search proceeds in larger steps. If something unexpected occurs, a smaller step is taken. After a series of successful moves, the step size may increase to 100 times the distance moved at the start of a series. This adaptive feature reduces the computer time necessary to complete a minimization. The search decision rule method is somewhat like the trial-and-error method except that logic is programmed into the computer to determine which variable should be changed and how much of a change will be tried. The search logic guides the trials to what appears to be a near optimal solution.

Researchers have compared several aggregate planning models. Often the Holt LDR model and the paint factory data are used as standards for comparison. An article by William Lee and Basheer Khumawala[6] reported a comparison of the linear decision rule, the search decision rule, parametric production planning, and the management coefficients model.[7] These researchers reported that

[5]William H. Taubert, Jr., "A Search Decision Rule for the Aggregate Scheduling Problem," *Management Science*, February 1968, pp. 343–359.

[6]W. B. Lee and B. M. Khumawala, "Simulation Testing of Aggregate Production Models in an Implementation Methodology," *Management Science*, February 1974, pp. 903–911.

[7]The adjustment is determined by a regression model based on past responses of managers. See E. H. Bowman, "Consistency and Optimality in Managerial Decision Making," *Management Science*, January 1963, pp. 310–321.

FIGURE 4.9

Descriptive Flow Chart of the SDR Pattern Search Heuristic

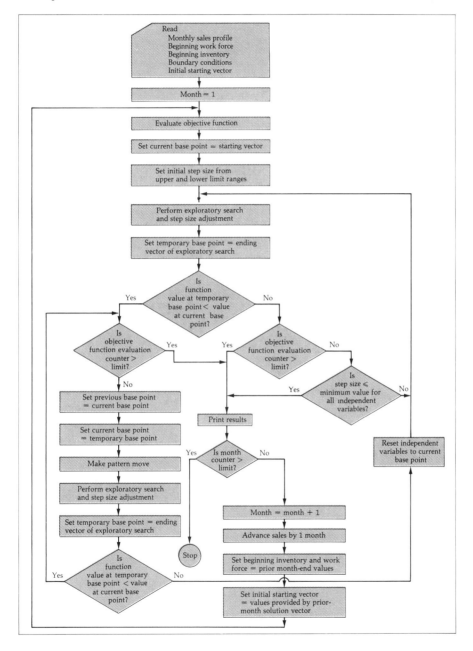

Source: William H. Taubert, Jr., "A Search Decision Rule Approach for the Aggregate Planning Problem," *Management Science*, February 1968, p. B351.

Table 4.9
COMPARATIVE PROFIT PERFORMANCE
OF FIVE AGGREGATE PLANNING METHODS

	Imperfect Forecast	Perfect Forecast
Company decisions	$4,420,000	—
Linear decision rule	$4,821,000	$5,078,000
Management coefficients model	$4,607,000	$5,000,000
Parametric production planning	$4,900,000	$4,989,000
Search decision rule	$5,021,000	$5,140,000

Source: William B. Lee and Basheer M. Khumawala, "Simulation Testing of Aggregate Production Models in an Implementation Methodology," Management Science, *February 1974, p. 906.*

"the Search Decision Rule clearly outperformed the other three models evaluated in the study and seems to offer the most promise for future development." Comparisons of the profit improvement for a set of test data are shown in Table 4.9 and Figure 4.10.

Problems in Disaggregating a Top-Down Aggregate Plan

The aggregate planning models discussed above require that demand be forecast and that inventory be expressed in terms of a common unit or pseudoproduct. The unit of measure could be pounds of detergent, tons of steel, hours of design time, gallons of paint, or some other unit. Companies that produce a variety of products might encounter difficulties when the time comes to coordinate the production of actual products with the capacity allocated by the aggregate plan. Aggregate planning based on a pseudoproduct assumes that the product mix

FIGURE 4.10

Profit Comparison

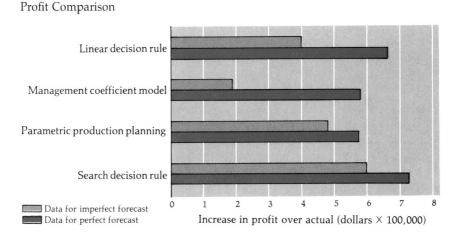

Increase in profit over actual (dollars × 100,000)

will remain in the same proportion as that represented by the pseudoproduct, or that the company's capacity is versatile enough for the product mix to vary. If actual demand causes the product mix to vary, the company may have idle capacity in some work centers and insufficient capacity in others. This problem is more likely to occur when the facilities and equipment required to produce part of the product line are significantly different from those required to produce other products. Consider, for example, a company that produces shoes and kitchen ranges. Production hours and inventory investment can be planned with the use of some average of these two products. Work would go as planned, however, only if the two products were actually produced in the ratio that was the basis for computing the average. The company could have an ideal average amount of work yet it could result from too much required work in the shoe division and too little demand for ranges, or vice versa.

The problem of inconsistency between detailed plans and schedules and the aggregate plan is reduced when widely divergent products (goods or services) are not aggregated. Conglomerates or companies that offer broad lines of products should go through intermediate levels of aggregating. Many broadly diversified companies have divisions responsible for closely related product groups at an intermediate organizational level. Planning within each division can avoid some of the problems that would be entailed by lumping together extremely diverse products and evaluating plans in terms of some hypothetical average product.

SELECTING AN AGGREGATE PLANNING HORIZON

The appropriate forecast horizon (length of time into the future for which the forecast is considered) for aggregate planning depends on the nature of the business for which the aggregate plans are being made and the extent into the future for which a reasonably accurate forecast can be made. It would seem that any company must plan far enough ahead to allow time to recruit and train workers. A make-to-stock company would need to add to this the amount of time required to produce the product. If the demand pattern is highly seasonal, the company might need to plan as far ahead as a year or more to determine how to meet the next demand peak. This is particularly true if the nature of the process is such that production capacity is very expensive and little slack capacity can be afforded. Conversely, a company might not plan very far ahead if slack plant capacity is available and workers with the necessary skills can be employed on relatively short notice.

It was mentioned in the previous chapter that forecasts are less accurate the further into the future they are extended. There is little to be gained by making plans for periods in the distant future if the forecast on which those plans are based is very inaccurate; decisions for those periods can be made later. The company should evaluate the forecast and use it as the basis for plans only as far into the future as it has a significant impact on decisions that are to be

FIGURE 4.11

Percentage Cost Penalty vs. Forecast Horizon

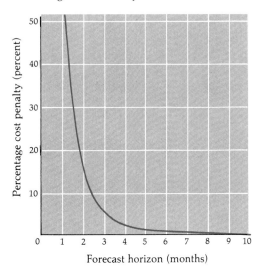

Source: William H. Taubert, Jr., "A Search Decision Rule Approach for the Aggregate Planning Problem," *Management Science*, February 1968, p. B356.

FIGURE 4.12

Computer Time vs. Forecast Horizon

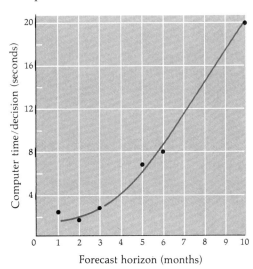

Source: William H. Taubert, Jr., "A Search Decision Rule Approach for the Aggregate Planning Problem," *Management Science*, February 1968, p. B356.

put into effect before the next planning session, say next month. When the next month comes, there will be a new forecast that is probably more accurate for the more distant periods.

In addition to being based on less accurate forecast information, aggregate plans that extend too far into the future are more complex to analyze. Computer processing of data becomes more expensive when a longer horizon is evaluated. These costs increase at a nonlinear rate because as more variables are introduced, the number of interrelationships between the variables increases rapidly.

Taubert used his search decision rule to investigate the effect of forecast horizon on cost for the set of data from the paint factory study by Holt and his associates, discussed earlier. The results are shown in Figure 4.11. Notice that the marginal reduction in cost penalty is much less after the fourth month is added to the forecast. Apparently nine or ten months were sufficient to produce good results for the data that he tested. Figure 4.12 shows the effect that an extension of the planning horizon has on the computer time required for a run. For any company, the incremental cost versus the incremental gain from the use of additional data will result in some maximum desirable planning horizon.

ALLOCATION OF INSUFFICIENT CAPACITY

A company might lack sufficient capacity to meet all of the demand for its goods or services. As in the previous discussions, we shall use the terms *product* and *production* in a broad sense, to refer to manufactured tangible products and to services. A seasonal demand pattern might present a situation of insufficient capacity for some part of each year, particularly if the seasonal peak is so much higher than the average demand that meeting it would require a large investment in facilities that would be used only a small portion of the year. Capacity constraint situations are likely to be considered within the intermediate range of aggregate planning because there is usually insufficient time for major capital investments, such as those for facilities expansion. Facilities expansion is therefore usually excluded as an aggregate planning strategy.

Allocating Limited Resources to Competing Uses

A company may wish to allocate capacity among a variety of products when the demand in each period must be met with the capacity that is available in the same period. In this situation, inventorying or back-ordering is not permitted. Such a situation can occur in service operations (which generally cannot inventory their products) or when a product is perishable, so that carrying it in inventory is impractical. A similar condition, and one to which the same type of analysis can be applied, occurs when demand is consistently above available capacity. When there is no available capacity in some other period to use, inventory and back-ordering are precluded. How should insufficient capacity be allocated between two products when only one time period can be considered?

When certain conditions are met, linear programming can be used to allocate a limited resource to competing uses.[8] There are three general methods of linear programming: the graphical method, the transportation method, and the simplex method. The transportation method was discussed earlier. The graphical method is applicable to this type of problem when only two or three products are competing for available capacity. It is useful primarily to illustrate what takes place in the more powerful mathematical methods. The graphical method is presented here because our purpose is to illustrate the concept. The same problem is solved by the simplex method in Supplement E.

[8]See Supplement E, at the end of this chapter, for an introductory description of the assumptions of linear programming and the ways in which it can be performed.

APPLICATION

Example of the Graphical Method of Linear Programming

Mo-Go Co., you may recall, produces mowers and go-carts. Assume that the company is trying to allocate the regular-time capacity in a month that has sufficient demand so that it can sell any combination of go-carts and mowers that it can produce. When we previously visited Mo-Go Co. to study its aggregate planning, the capacity was 500 units. We must assume that it could sell 500 mowers, 500 go-carts, or any combination of the two totaling 500. Now the question is how it should allocate the capacity between the two products. They require different amounts of resources and contribute different amounts to profit and overhead, so this information should be used. Each mower contributes $80 and each go-cart

Table 4.10
HOURS REQUIRED IN EACH WORK CENTER TO PRODUCE ONE MOWER OR ONE GO-CART, AND TOTAL CAPACITY, MO-GO CO.

Work Center	HOURS REQUIRED FOR PRODUCTION (per unit) Mower	Go-cart	TOTAL CAPACITY (hours)
Machining	6	4	2,400
Welding	2	3	1,500
Assembly	9	3	2,700

contributes $40. Table 4.10 shows the common resources that must be allocated and the amount of each that is required to produce a unit of either product.

Waldo Petroni, the production manager, graphed the problem as shown in Figure 4.13. In order to graph the constraint imposed by machining capacity, he reasoned that the company could machine 2,400/6 = 400 mowers if all machining

FIGURE 4.13

Allocation of Resources to Products of Mo-Go Co.

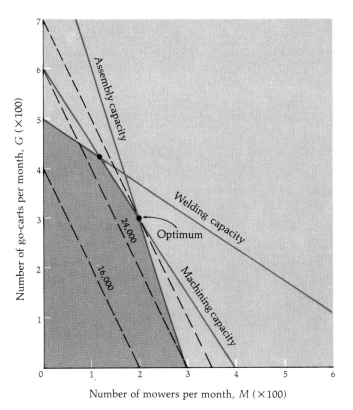

capacity were devoted to mowers, or $2,400/4 = 600$ go-carts if all machining capacity were devoted to go-carts. Since the requirements are linear, a straight line connecting the two intercepts represents the upper limit of product combination that can be machined in a month. Any combination of mowers (M) and go-carts (G) below this line is feasible in the machining department.

The intercepts and constraint lines for the welding department were found in the same way. This procedure was then completed for the assembly department, to provide the three solid lines shown in Figure 4.13. These three lines bound the region of feasible combinations of M and G that could be produced (shown by the shaded portion of the graph). Other constraints (including some maximum amount of M or G that could be sold) could have been plotted if these demand constraints were more restrictive than the production capacity constraints so that the demand constraints would form part of the border of the feasible region.

So far, Petroni had found a polygon of feasible combinations of M and G. An infinite number of combinations that fall within the feasible region could be found. In order to find the optimal solution, Petroni had to plot the objective function. The contribution is expressed by

$$P = \$80M + \$40G$$

This expression has three unknowns, so in order to plot it on the two-dimensional graph Waldo had to assume a value for P. He knew that his fixed costs were about $16,000 per month, so he used this figure for the first line.

$$\$16,000 = \$80M + \$40G$$

If no go-carts are produced, 200 mowers must be produced and sold in order to contribute $16,000. If no mowers are produced, then 400 go-carts will be needed to provide $16,000. The line connecting these two points is an *isoprofit line* (all points on it will provide the same profit contribution). Another line for $P = \$24,000$ was plotted. Notice that it is parallel to the $16,000 line. As long as a mower contributes twice as much as a go-cart, all of the isoprofit lines will be parallel. Petroni knew that he had to find the isoprofit line that represented the greatest contribution and on which at least one point lay within the feasible region. To do so he visualized keeping an isoprofit line parallel to the first line and moving it away from the origin as far as possible while still keeping some part of it within the feasible region. The third dashed line in Figure 4.13 represents the highest isoprofit line that still has a point in the feasible region. The last feasible point an isoprofit line touches before it is completely beyond the feasible region is the point of maximum profit. From this analysis, Waldo Petroni concluded that the best allocation of production capacity would be 200 mowers and 300 go-carts.

A "Logical Misconclusion"   Let me call your attention to an interesting point about Mr. Petroni's problem and its solution. He might have reasoned that since mowers are twice as profitable as go-carts, the company should devote all of its capacity to producing mowers. If no go-carts are produced, the company can produce a maximum of 300 mowers without exceeding the capacity of the assembly department—the most constraining department of the company. Sales of 300 mowers will contribute $300 \times \$80 = \$24,000$.

The optimal solution found by Mr. Petroni indicated that the company should produce only 200 mowers and an additional 300 go-carts. Sales of this product mix would contribute $(200 \times \$80) + (300 \times \$40) = \$28,000$. The reason for an increase in contribution, even though production of the most profitable product is reduced, is simple once you examine it in more detail. The limiting constraint is the assembly department. It takes three times as long to assemble a mower as it does to assemble a go-cart (9 hours versus 3 hours). By giving up production of 100 mowers ($8,000 given up), we free enough capacity to produce 300 go-carts ($12,000 worth gained). The net result is an improvement of $4,000 in the objective function.

Trade-offs between products and resources are made automatically in linear programming, without any need to search for alternatives so they can be identified and evaluated. When a problem is solved graphically and the objective function line is parallel to a constraint line, alternative optimum solutions can be obtained. Any point along the constraint line that is parallel to the objective function (as long as the constraint line is an edge of the feasible region) is an optimum solution.

SUMMARY

This chapter has introduced the concept of aggregate planning within the intermediate-range horizon. Several strategies for adjusting capacity in response to seasonal demand were discussed, as well as several methods of solving the aggregate planning problem. Each method has its advantages and limitations, some of which are summarized in Table 4.11.

The trial-and-error method of aggregate planning is probably the most widely used. The search decision rule appears to offer great promise as a means of finding an almost optimal solution when the objective function is explicitly quantified. Materials requirements planning (MRP) is becoming widely used by manufacturing operations. Since MRP rough-cut capacity planning is often run in conjunction with MRP, it is likely that rough-cut ca-

Table 4.11
SOME ADVANTAGES AND LIMITATIONS OF AGGREGATE PLANNING METHODS

Method	Advantage	Limitation
Resource requirements planning	Can deal with variety of products Can use weekly time blocks	Relies on judgment to determine the most desirable master schedule; i.e., does not guarantee optimum solution
Trial-and-error method	Simple to understand and apply	Approximates with an aggregate product Does not guarantee optimum solution
Linear programming method	Will find optimal solution to stated problem	Approximates with an aggregate product Actual problem may not fit the linear model
Linear decision rule	Will find optimal solution to stated problem	Approximates with an aggregate product Actual problem may not fit the quadratic model
Computer search techniques	Does not constrain mathematical form of problem	Approximates with an aggregate product Search may be tricked into selecting local instead of global minimum

pacity planning is the second most common method. It can provide rapid evaluation of alternatives until a satisficing schedule is found.

Planning may involve some additional analyses when demand exceeds the company's capacity. Linear programming can prove useful in deciding which products to produce and in what quantities. The topic of linear programming was discussed in order to give some insight into the technique and one of its applications in operations. Readers who are not familiar with linear programming may refer to the Supplement E, which follows this chapter.

After aggregate plans have been formulated, a company must make more detailed plans in order to implement the strategy selected. Schedules must be formulated so that the proper work tasks will be performed on all of the parts of a product or a service job. Often work cannot be performed until material inputs have been obtained. Repair service companies must purchase and receive necessary replacement parts before they can make repairs. Other service operations may require operating supplies. Manufacturing operations must have both raw materials and productive capacity available to start production, so plans must consider materials inputs as well as capacity. Chapter 5 discusses materials supplies and materials flow within operations, with primary emphasis on obtaining materials inputs.

SOLVED PROBLEMS

PROBLEM:

The following is a tentative master schedule for four weeks at a small company:

Week	1	2	3	4
Product A	2,000	4,000	1,000	2,000
Product B	3,000	1,000	4,000	3,000

The bill of labor in the key work centers for the company's two major products is as follows:

Department	Product A	B
4	.21	.07
11	.06	.10
14	.11	.08

Determine the load on Department 4 over the next four weeks.

SOLUTION:

The load profile for Department 4 over the next four weeks is found by multiplying the labor requirement in Department 4 for each product by the quantity of that product to be produced in each week and summing the hours required for all products in each week.

Hours required in each week

Week 1

For Product A	.21(2,000) = 420
For Product B	.07(3,000) = 210
Total load for week	630

Week 2

For Product A	.21(4,000) = 840
For Product B	.07(1,000) = 70
Total load for week	910

Week 3

For Product A	.21(1,000) = 210
For Product B	.07(4,000) = 280
Total load for week	490

Week 4

For Product A	.21(2,000) = 420
For Product B	.07(3,000) = 210
Total load for week	630

Notice this load profile is not very uniform, even though 5,000 units of product are produced each week.

PROBLEM:

A manufacturing company has a seasonal demand pattern, with the forecast demand for each month next year equal to 1,300, 1,000, 800, 700, 700, 700, 800, 900, 1,000,

1,200, 1,400, and 1,500 units respectively. The company plans to end the current year with about 800 units in inventory. The company requires a minimum of 500 units in inventory for safety stock and work in process. It costs $1.10 per month to hold a unit in inventory.

The company will end the current year with 40 employees, and it costs $400 to hire an employee and $600 to lay off an employee. It takes an employee 5 hours to make a product. Employees are paid $9.00 an hour for regular-time work or $13.50 for overtime work. For simplified planning, each month is considered to have 20 days. Employees can begin or end employment on any day of the month, so an employee can work fractions of a month.

(a) Compute the cost of a "chase strategy," that is, one in which the number of employees is changed so the monthly production rate is made equal to the monthly demand rate.

Use the following method to find the approximate number of employees to be hired or laid off in each month. Find the unrounded employment level (to two decimal places) needed for each month by dividing the number of units to be produced that month by the number of units an employee can produce in a month. Determine the integer number of employees on the payroll at the end of each month and find the difference between successive values to determine how many employees would be hired or laid off. Estimate the integer employment level at the end of the month as follows: When employment is decreasing, round the approximate employment level down to the next lower integer. Decreasing is when the unrounded employment level before a particular value (or before the series of equal values of which it is part) is higher than it and the value after it (or after the series of equal values of which it is part) is lower.

For increasing employment (the reverse case), round up. When the employment cycle is reversing at a peak or valley, round up if the decimal is greater than .50 and round down if the decimal is less than .50. If one of these values should happen to have a decimal equal to .50, round down if it is at a peak and round up if it is at a valley.

(b) Compute the cost of a pure inventory strategy, with the work force and production rate held constant at the average demand rate and the variation in demand rate accounted for by accumulating and depleting inventory. A part-time employee can be used to provide any fractional employment level to obtain the desired production rate.

SOLUTION:

(a) Since the company will begin the year with 800 units in inventory and needs only 500 in inventory for a chase strategy, the production required in the first month was reduced by 300 units. The production required in each month is shown in column 2 in the first table below.

Each employee contributes 160 hours each month and it takes 5 hours to make a unit, so each employee can produce $160/5 = 32$ units per month. Column 3 in the table shows the demand divided by 32 to show the unrounded number of employees required to make the number of units needed in any month. These numbers must be rounded to determine the number of employees to be hired or laid off in the month. If the company is reducing employment, we will round down to find the number of employees at the end of the month and how many layoffs there would be during the month. If the company is expanding its employment, we would round up. At the lowest level of production, we round up so that the company will have at least the required capacity. Column 4 shows the rounded number of employees. The change in employment level is shown in column 5 if the number of employees is being reduced and in column 6 if the number of employees is being increased. The first number in column 5 is found by subtracting 31 from the number of employees at the end of the prior year (40). The sum of column 5 is multiplied by $600 to get the total layoff cost, and the sum of column 6 is multiplied by $400 to get the total hiring cost. (If you are familiar with a spreadsheet program you can see how the table could easily be developed.)

The company needs a minimum of 500 units in inventory each month. If it is assumed that this inventory will be carried, there is an additional cost of $550 each month to hold this inventory—at $1.10 to hold a unit for a month. The cost to hold this inventory for a year will be $500 \times \$1.10 \times 12 = \$6,600$. The total cost of this strategy will be $\$20,800 + 6,600 = \$27,400$.

(b) Since the total demand for the year is 12,000 units, the company should produce 1,000 units each month to keep the production rate uniform. It will require $1,000/32 = 31.25$ which is rounded to 31, and a part-time employee will be used to provide this production rate. Column 3 shows the change in the inventory level that will occur each month if the demand and production rate occur as planned. Since the minimum inventory must not get below 500 units, the company will need to start the year with 800 units, as is planned.

Chase Strategy Cost for Part (a)

(1)	(2)	(3)	(4)	(5)	(6)
		Unrounded Employment Level			
Month	Required Production	(2)/32	Col (3) Rounded	Layoffs	Hires
1	1,000	31.25	31	9	
2	1,000	31.25	31	0	
3	800	25.00	25	6	
4	700	21.88	22	3	
5	700	21.88	22	0	
6	700	21.88	22	0	
7	800	25.00	25		3
8	900	28.13	29		4
9	1,000	31.25	32		3
10	1,200	37.50	38		6
11	1,400	43.75	44	•	6
12	1,500	46.88	47		3
			Total	18	25
			Cost	$10,800	$10,000

Hiring & Layoff Cost =	$20,800
Inventory Cost	6,600
Total	$27,400

The inventory that will be on hand at the end of each month is shown in column 5. The average inventory during the month, shown in column 6, is found by averaging the ending inventory for the month with the ending inventory for the previous month. The sum of column 6 is the total unit-months of holding inventory. This is multiplied by $1.10 to get the total inventory cost. There is an additional one-time cost to adjust the employment level from 40 employees at the end of the prior year to 31 employees being considered for this strategy. These 9 layoffs will cost 9 × $600 = $5,400. The total cost of this strategy will be $16,500 + $5,400 = $21,900.

Inventory Strategy Cost for Part (b)

(1)	(2)	(3)	(4) Inventory Change	(5) Ending Inventory	(6) Average Inventory
Month	Demand	Production			
1	1,300	1,000	−300	500	650.00
2	1,000	1,000	0	500	500.00
3	800	1,000	200	700	600.00
4	700	1,000	300	1,000	850.00
5	700	1,000	300	1,300	1,150.00
6	700	1,000	300	1,600	1,450.00
7	800	1,000	200	1,800	1,700.00
8	900	1,000	100	1,900	1,850.00
9	1,000	1,000	0	1,900	1,900.00
10	1,200	1,000	−200	1,700	1,800.00
11	1,400	1,000	−400	1,300	1,500.00
12	1,500	1,000	−500	800	1,050.00
				Total Unit-Months	15,000.00

Inventory Cost =	$16,500.00
Layoff cost	5,400.00
Total =	$21,900.00

DISCUSSION QUESTIONS

1. What is aggregate planning?
2. Why should some companies have longer planning horizons than others? What are some of the factors that determine how far ahead a company should plan?
3. What are some methods that nonmanufacturing companies use to smooth the level of demand by removing seasonality and short-term variations in demand?
4. What are some of the dangers of planning production rates and work force sizes on the basis of an aggregate product?
5. Describe in your own words the steps involved in rough-cut capacity planning.
6. Discuss some of the advantages and some of the problems associated with planning overall employment by summing all of the requirements for individual items in the company's product line.
7. Discuss the advantages and disadvantages of various aggregate planning methods.
8. Why is the trial-and-error method of aggregate planning widely used?
9. Discuss some of the advantages and disadvantages of relying on overtime work to meet a significant portion of demand.
10. Discuss some of the advantages and disadvantages of hiring and laying off employees as demand increases and subsides. Should a company employ workers with the intention of laying them off within a few months? Should it just hire tempo-

rary personnel who are not expecting permanent employment?

11. How does detailed scheduling relate to aggregate planning?

PROBLEMS

1. Mr. Baker, the scheduler at Idaho Manufacturing Company, has developed the following tentative master schedule for the next six months and wants to evaluate it.

Month	1	2	3	4	5	6
Product A	171	318	362	547	421	290
B	175	197	216	224	206	190
C	400	400	390	362	325	300
D	400	400	460	500	560	600

The following bill of labor gives the hours required in each of the company's five key work centers to make one unit of the company's products.

BILL OF LABOR

Product	A	B	C	D
Department 2	0.61	0.19	0.22	0.71
3	0.56	0.42	0.68	1.74
4	0.71	0.41	0.59	0.00
6	0.14	0.00	0.24	0.61
8	0.44	0.61	0.28	1.06

Develop the capacity requirements for each of the next six months—that is, the load profile—for Department 2.

2. For the data in problem 1:
   (a) Develop the load profile over the six-month horizon for Department 3.
   (b) For which product or products would you revise the schedule so the company would produce the product early and hold it in inventory until it is needed, resulting in the load requirements in Department 3 being made more uniform?

3. For the data in problem 1, compute for each month the total load in all of the company's key work centers.

4. A manufacturing company produces two products, A and B. The bills of labor for these products are shown below along with a trial master schedule for a six-month horizon. The production cycles for the products are so short that the lag between the loads on the work center and the final production operation shown on the master schedule need not be considered in rough-cut capacity planning.

Bill of labor, product A		Bill of labor, product B	
Work Center	Hours Required	Work Center	Hours Required
16	2.1	10	2.8
19	6.8	18	1.3
25	4.1	19	3.6
41	7.2	35	2.1
52	3.9	52	1.7

TRIAL MASTER SCHEDULE
(UNITS TO BE COMPLETED)

Month	1	2	3	4	5	6
Product A	400	200	250	350	200	100
Product B		300	350	200	300	300

   (a) Determine the load profiles for work centers 19 and 52 caused by the trial master schedule.
   (b) Adjust the trial master schedule so that it provides more uniform load profiles yet meets the following conditions: at least 400 As must be available by the end of the period 1, 750 additional As must be available by the end of period 5, and 1,100 Bs must be made by the end of period 5.

5. The Keep It Trucking (KIT) Company provides routine preventive maintenance and minor repair service at a fixed charge for clients within a 20-mile radius. The company's customers have seasonal businesses and try to postpone some maintenance until their slow seasons. This results in a seasonal demand for KIT services. The number of jobs forecast for the four quarters of next year are 840, 1,060, 940, and

1,180, respectively. The typical service call requires 7.4 hours, including travel and paperwork. Employees are paid $9.20 per hour, and the typical employee provides 490 hours of work per quarter. Employees will be paid for 2,080 regular hours per year plus any overtime they work.

Skilled workers who are reliable enough to make these service calls are scarce, and KIT wants to provide permanent employment to its work force. The company is considering the use of overtime, paid at time and a half, to meet some of the peak demand.

(a) Compute the payroll cost if the company maintains a constant work force of sufficient size so that overtime during the peak demand will be 15 percent of regular-time capacity.
(b) Repeat part (a) allowing 20 percent overtime.
(c) Repeat part (a) allowing 25 percent overtime.

6. Suppose that the KIT Company described in problem 5 can employ temporary employees who are less skilled than its normal work force. These temporary employees work at 85 percent efficiency (i.e., they require 7.4 ÷ 0.85 hours to provide the typical unit of service), yet they are paid $9.20 per hour as are permanent employees. It is estimated to cost $500 to find, hire, and indoctrinate one of these employees and an equal amount when one is terminated.

Compare the cost for hiring-related expenses, labor, and severance pay for two optional strategies. The company will staff with permanent employees with capacity for the average demand of 1,000 calls per quarter and (1) use overtime or (2) use temporary employees for demand above this level. Temporary employees will be paid for the entire quarter (490 hours) that

they are employed, but will not be retained at the end of a quarter if they are not needed in the next quarter.

7. A company has the following demand forecast for the next year, expressed in six bimonthly (i.e., two-month) periods:

Period	Forecast Demand (standard units of work)
1	400
2	380
3	470
4	530
5	610
6	500

(a) Graph the cumulative demand vs. cumulative workdays, assuming that each month has 22 working days.
(b) Assume that an employee contributes 176 regular working hours each month and that each unit requires 20 standard hours to produce. How many employees will be needed during the peak bimonthly period if no overtime production is to be scheduled?
(c) What will be the average labor cost for each unit if the company pays employees $5 per hour and maintains for the entire year a sufficient staff to meet the peak demand without overtime?
(d) What percentage above the standard-hour cost is the company's average labor cost per unit in this year due to excess staffing for all but the peak bimonthly period?

8. Assume that the company in problem 7 can use overtime up to a maximum of 25 percent of regular-time hours. Each overtime hour costs $7.50. What is the average cost per unit produced during this year if the work force is maintained at a level so that overtime can be used to the maximum during the peak period?

9. The company discussed in problems 7 and 8 wants to determine the cost of meeting

the demand for its services through changes in the number of employees and the use of overtime work. To keep from adding too many temporary employees during the peak demand period, the company will use overtime equal to up to 25 percent of the regular-time hours available. As soon as the company believes that 50 percent of a new employee's regular-time capacity could be utilized during the current period and the following period, it will add an employee and will continue to hire up to the maximum employment level. Overtime will be discontinued before employees are laid off during the decline in demand after the seasonal peak. The company wants to end this year with 23 employees. It costs $300 to hire and $400 to lay off an employee. Overtime hours are compensated at $7.50 per hour. Assume all changes in the employment level occur at the end of a bimonthly period and that the company already has the desired number of employees at the start of the year.

(a) Find the employment level for each bimonthly period.
(b) Find the total payroll-related costs for the year.
(c) What cost per unit results from these payroll-related costs?

10. Assume that the company in problem 7 is a manufacturing operation and that its product can be inventoried. Assume that it costs $3 per month ($6 per bimonthly period) to hold an item in inventory. The company plans to maintain a constant production rate, begin and end the year with the same inventory level, and absorb all demand fluctuation by accumulating and depleting inventory. The number of employees will be set at a level so that no overtime will be required. What will be the average cost per unit due to the cost of labor and the additional inventory held during the year?

11. The Decota Manufacturing Company forecasts demand for its product during twelve months (expressed in units needed per month) as 418, 414, 395, 381, 372, 359, 386, 398, 409, 417, 421, 425. The current production work force level is 40 employees, and each employee can produce 10 units per month. An employee can produce 11 units per month by working 10 percent overtime, and 12 units per month by working 20 percent overtime. The cost of hiring an employee is $500 and the cost of laying off an employee is $450. Regular-time pay for the employees is $1,250 per month, and they earn time and one-half pay for overtime. The cost to hold a unit in inventory for a month is $4.00, and the current level of inventory is 800 units, which is the approximate amount of inventory that the company wants to maintain.

(a) Develop a mixed strategy for meeting the forecast demand.
(b) What is the cost of this strategy?
(c) Do not revise the strategy but recommend types of changes that you think would provide a lower cost strategy.

12. The Arizona Chili Company has the following demand for cases of its product in each of the four quarters of next year: 800, 500, 800, and 1,200. Company managers want to begin the year and end the year with 400 cases in inventory. Production capacity in each quarter is 800 cases on regular time and 200 cases on overtime. The cost to produce a case is $20 on regular time and $25 on overtime, and it costs $1.00 per quarter to hold a case in inventory. Develop a transportation method tableau for the problem, and find an optimal production plan for next year.

13. The Mesquite Company produces a patented product with seasonal demand. The following quantities are forecast for the six bimonthly periods of the coming year.

Period	1	2	3	4	5	6
Forecast	60	70	80	90	80	70

It costs $15 to produce a unit by regular time, and the regular-time capacity is 70 units. Overtime production costs $20, and there is capacity to produce 10 units per period on overtime. Inventory cost is $3 per bimonthly period. The company has no initial inventory and does not plan to end the sales period with any inventory. By use of a transportation-method tableau, plan how the company should employ its resources to fulfill the forecasted demand at the lowest cost.

14. The paint company for which the linear decision rule was developed currently has a work force of 95 employees and has 310 gallons of paint in inventory. The demand forecast for the next 12 months in sequence is 500, 550, 600, 650, 700, 750, 800, 800, 750, 700, 650, and 600.
    (a) Use the equations of the linear decision rule to determine the recommended production rate and work force level for the next month.

15. The Colossal Paint Company is much larger than the company for which the linear decision rule was developed. It uses automation to a greater extent, offers lower prices, and is able to sell ten times as much paint. Currently Colossal has a work force of 300 people and has 3,100 gallons of paint in inventory. The demand forecast for the next twelve months is 5,000, 5,500, 6,000, 6,500, 7,000, 7,500, 8,000, 8,000, 7,500, 7,000, 6,500, and 6,000 gallons respectively.
    (a) Use the linear decision rule equations to see what recommendations it suggests for the production rate and the work force.
    (b) Comment on your findings.

16. Carmell Electronics, Inc., produces two models of electronic calculators, the X15 and Y10. The company has been extremely surprised by the demand for its products. Until an expansion program is completed, the company will be able to sell as many of either model as it can produce. Production capacity is limited in three departments: soldering, assembly, and molding. Each month the company has 50,000 minutes of molding capacity. Either model requires 1 minute of molding time, Model X15 requires 5 minutes to assemble; Y10 requires 2.5 minutes. The company has 200,000 minutes of assembly time each month. Soldering operations require 3 minutes on the X15 and 8 minutes on the Y10. The company has 300,000 minutes of soldering time each month. Model X15 contributes $10 to profit and overhead, Y10 $8.
    (a) By graphical linear programming, determine the optimum product mix.
    (b) What is the total contribution for the optimum product mix determined in part (a)?

*17. Construct an electronic spreadsheet to perform aggregate planning by the trial-and-error method. Use the Imperial Sail Company example in the chapter. Enter the beginning inventory, desired ending inventory, regular time production per employee-month, beginning number of employees, cost to hire, cost to lay off, regular-time wage rate, and overtime wage rate in blocks at the top of the template, and refer to these locations. This will allow you to change the problem easily if you want to analyze other problems with this template.

    You may want additional columns, but you will find these helpful: demand

---

*This problem requires more detailed computation and is intended for programmable assistance such as that provided by a microcomputer.

per period, employees needed for chase strategy, employees used (the variable you will change), cumulative demand, cumulative regular-time production, overtime required (if cumulative demand is greater than cumulative production), inventory cost (if cumulative production exceeds cumulative demand), hiring cost (where employees are added), and layoff cost. Accumulate the appropriate columns, and develop the cost of payroll + overtime + hiring and layoff + inventory. Use $8.50 per hour as the regular-time wage rate and $12.75 for overtime.

Use the spreadsheet to compare at least three employment patterns. Compare the total cost of your best plan to the costs and best plans developed by others.

BIBLIOGRAPHY

Buffa, Elwood. *Modern Production Management: Managing the Operations Function.* 7th ed. New York: Wiley, 1983. Chap. 9.

Campbell, Kenneth L. "Rough-Cut Capacity Planning—What It Is and How to Use It." *Conference Proceedings,* American Production and Inventory Control Society, 1982.

Fisk, John C., and J. Peter Seagle. "The Integration of Aggregate Planning with Resource Requiremens Planning." *Production and Inventory Management,* 3d quarter, 1978, pp. 81–91.

Krajewski, Lee, and L. Ritzman. "Disaggregation in Manufacturing and Service Organizations," *Decision Sciences,* Vol. 8, *no. 1,* 1977, pp. 1–18.

Orlicky, Joseph. *Material Requirements Planning.* New York: McGraw-Hill, 1975. Chaps. 7 and 11.

Plossl, George W., and Oliver W. Wight. "Capacity Planning and Control." *Production and Inventory Management,* 3d quarter, 1973, pp. 31–67.

Plossl, George W. *Production and Inventory Control: Applications.* Atlanta: George Plossl Educational Services, 1983.

Sasser, W. Earl. "Match Supply and Demand in Service Industries," *Harvard Business Review,* November–December 1976, pp. 130–140.

Wight, Oliver W. *Production and Inventory Management in the Computer Age.* Boston: Cahners Books International, 1974. Chaps. 5 and 6.

Wight, Oliver W. *MRP II: Unlocking America's Productivity Potential.* Boston: CBI Publishing, 1984.

Supplement E Outline
LINEAR PROGRAMMING

ASPECTS OF LINEAR PROGRAMMING
Applications / Assumptions / Methods / General LP Model

THE GRAPHICAL METHOD

THE SIMPLEX METHOD
Steps in the Simplex Method / Shadow Prices / Degeneracy / Other Constraints and Minimization

THE TRANSPORTATION METHOD
Initial Solution by the Northwest Corner Method / The Stepping-Stone Method / Vogel's Approximation Method / Degeneracy / Maximization Procedure / What If Supply Does Not Equal Demand?

Summary / Discussion Questions / Problems / Bibliography

KEY TERMS

Linearity
Objective function
Constraint equations
Certainty
Divisibility
Nonnegativity
Graphical method
Transportation method
Isoprofit line

Feasible region
Optimum corner
Optimum edge
Isocost line
Simplex method
Slack variable
Artificial variable
In solution
Out of solution

Identity matrix
Key column
Key row
Pivot element
Shadow prices
Ranging (sensitivity analysis or parametric programming)

Degeneracy
Algorithm
Dummy supply or dummy user
Vogel's approximation method (VAM)

Supplement E
LINEAR PROGRAMMING

Linear programming (LP) is the most widely used of a family of mathematical programming methods that have been developed mainly since World War II. It has been applied to a variety of operations management problems, some of which were illustrated in Chapter 4. The format of LP and the solutions to some LP problems were presented, but the way the solutions were developed was not discussed, as the purpose of the chapter was to focus on planning capacity rather than on the mechanics of a mathematical technique. For readers who are not familiar with LP, or as a review for those already familiar with it, this supplement presents some of the mechanics of solving LP problems but does not delve into the theory behind the methods or explain why they work. This summary treatment is adequate for the problems and applications presented in this book; the bibliography contains several references for further study of the subject.

ASPECTS OF LINEAR PROGRAMMING

Applications

The typical linear programming problems involve allocation of some scarce resource among competing alternative uses. This ability to allocate resources may be applied to a wide variety of circumstances: (1) to the allocation of limited production time to competing products that can be produced and sold; (2) to the allocation of component materials so as to minimize the cost of the product when the proportions of its components may vary; (3) to schedule the allocation of resources at one point in time (i.e., productive capacity) to their uses at some other point in time (i.e., demand); (4) to the allocation of products at one location to users at some other location. After the optimal solution has been found, LP can also (5) provide useful information to determine the marginal value of additional resources and the range over which these values are valid.

Assumptions

Four basic assumptions are fundamental to the general linear programming problem:

1. *Linearity:* the *objective function* and the *constraint equations* are assumed to be linear (straight lines).
2. *Certainty:* the method does not have provisions for probability. The stated conditions are assumed to follow precisely the given mathematical expressions.
3. *Divisibility:* the values of the decision variable may take on fractional or integer values (e.g., it is possible to produce 58.61 gallons of a product).
4. *Nonnegativity:* the values of the variables that the method selects (decision variables) must be greater than or equal to zero.

These assumptions may suggest that linear programming applications are limited. Linear functions that are assumed to be continuous, however, may be used to approximate a wide variety of problems. When the problem is not appropriate for the general linear programming technique, perhaps another mathematical programming method is suitable. Table E.1 summarizes some of the characteristics of other mathematical programming methods.

The discussion in this supplement will deal with general linear programming and some of the conditions under which it can be applied when the solution is not restricted to integer values or 0 and 1.

Methods

There are three types or methods of LP. The *graphical method,* which can be used if only two or three variables are involved, was illustrated within the body of Chapter 4. The *simplex method*—much more useful because the number of variables it can analyze is not limited—is discussed in the next section. The *transportation method* frequently is applied to the allocation of products or resources at one location to uses at some other location. The objective is to minimize the transportation costs of the allocation. A simple transportation-method problem is illustrated later in this supplement.

General LP Model

The general model for an LP problem is:

Maximize (or minimize): $F = C_1 X_1 + C_2 X_2 + \cdots + C_N X_N$

Table E.1
CHARACTERISTICS OF SOME MATHEMATICAL PROGRAMMING METHODS

Method	Characteristic
Integer programming	Linear programming with the decision variables restricted to integer values.
0, 1 programming	Linear programming, but the variable must be used entirely or not at all. One is in solution or none is.
Nonlinear programming	Programming in which the objective function and/or constraints are not restricted to straight lines or surfaces.
Dynamic programming	A multistage decision process that considers the effect of a decision at one stage upon the results of other stages and upon the system as a whole.

subject to the constraints: $a_{11}X_1 + a_{12}X_2$
$$+ \cdots + a_{1n}X_n \leq b_1$$
$$a_{21}X_1 + a_{22}X_2 + \cdots$$
$$+ a_{2n}X_n \leq b_2$$
$$\cdots$$
$$\cdots$$
$$a_{m1}X_1 + a_{m2}X_2 + \cdots$$
$$+ a_{mn}X_n \leq b_m$$
$$X_1 \geq 0, X_2 \geq 0, \ldots,$$
$$X_n \geq 0$$

where a_{ij}, b_i, C_j = given constants
X_j = the variable selected by the process (i.e., decision variable)
n = the number of decision variables
m = the number of constraints.

Note: Any row in the constraint expressions, with the exception of the last, can have an equal-to or a greater-than-or-equal-to relationship instead of the less-than-or-equal-to ones indicated. The last row of the constraints is the nonnegativity constraint and always requires the decision variables to be greater than or equal to zero.

It is helpful to express a problem in the general model form if it is to be solved by the graphical method or by the simplex method. The transportation method has its own format, which is illustrated later.

THE GRAPHICAL METHOD

The graphical method of LP was described within the chapter for the Mo-Go Co. allocation of limited production capacity. The problem is restated in the general model format and will be solved graphically below. The Mo-Go-Co. problem is:

$$\text{Maximize } P = 80M + 40G$$
$$6M + 4G \leq 2{,}400$$
$$2M + 3G \leq 1{,}500$$
$$9M + 3G \leq 2{,}700$$
$$M \geq 0, G \geq 0$$

The decision variables are G (how many go-

carts to produce) and M (how many mowers to produce). The last row of constraints says we cannot produce negative units of the product.

The discussion within Chapter 4 shows the optimal solution to this maximization problem. Recall that we found the optimal solution by assuming a value for the contribution and plotting the objective function, an iso-profit line representing product combinations that would contribute some assumed amount of profit. (See Figure E.1) Then the objective function was increased (i.e., moved away from the origin) as far as possible with at least one point of the *isoprofit line* (i.e., a line connecting combinations of M and G that all provide the same profit) falling in the *feasible region*. Obviously, if the line is moved as far as possible from the origin yet has a point on it within the feasible region, that point will be on the border of the feasible region. A corner of the feasible region will be an optimal solution. This fact is fundamental to linear programming. The objective function leads to the *optimum corner* (or *optimum edge*) of the feasible region.

The graphical method can also be used to deal with equality constraints and less-than-or-equal-to constraints. Let us assume a very simple and obvious problem to illustrate minimization when equality constraints and greater-than-or-equal-to constraints are involved. Suppose a company produces a product that has a fixed total weight, say a 10-pound bag of grass seed. The particular product could be a mixture of rye (R) and fescue (F) seeds. Assume that specifications state the product must contain at least 3 pounds of fescue and at least 4 pounds of rye. Our objective is to minimize the total cost of the product when rye seeds cost 60¢ a pound and fescue costs 40¢ a pound. The problem can be stated as follows:

$$\text{Minimize } C = 0.60R + 0.40F$$
subject to
$$R + F = 10$$
$$R \geq 4$$
$$F \geq 3$$
$$R \geq 0, F \geq 0$$

FIGURE E.1

Graphical Solution to the Mo-Go Co. Product Mix Problem

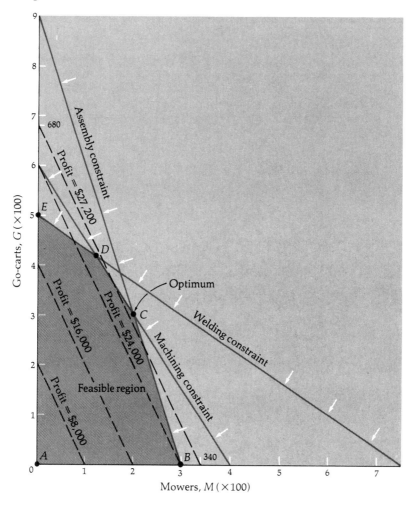

The last row is not needed since it is redundant, but if there were no higher constraints it still would not be possible to have negative pounds of either kind of seed in the product. A graph of these constraints is shown in Figure E.2. The feasible region for the problem is represented by the line segment between B and C.

We need to plot an objective function in order to see which point on line $B-C$ is the optimal mixture of rye and fescue. Let $C = 0.6R + 0.4F = \$6$. This *isocost line* (line of equal cost) would connect $R = 10$ pounds and $F = 15$ pounds and is shown as the dashed line in Figure E.2. Since this is a minimization problem, we should move the dashed line as close to the origin as we can while keeping some point on the dashed line on line $B-C$. Point C is the optimal combination of F and R. This solution says that we should use the smallest

FIGURE E.2

Graph of Minimization Problem

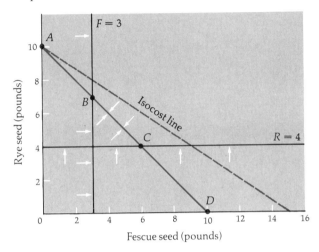

possible amount of rye seeds, 4 pounds; the remaining 6 pounds should be fescue. This result is as one would expect. We minimize cost by minimizing the amount of the costly ingredient. When several ingredients are involved, the solution is not so obvious.

The above illustrations have presented both maximization and minimization of the objective function. All three forms of constraints ($\geq$, $=$, $\leq$) have also been included.

THE SIMPLEX METHOD

We saw from the graphical solution method that some corner of the feasible space will be an optimal solution to a linear programming problem. In order to find an optimal solution, we could evaluate all of the corner points of the feasible polygon and see which corner gave the best value of the objective function. This procedure might take a great deal of time, however, and it would be difficult to visualize and solve all of the possible solutions unless we had a systematic method to follow. The

simplex method is a systematic method of examining the corner points of the feasible space. Further, it has the advantage of not forcing us to examine all of the corners to be assured that we have found a corner that is as good as or better than any other so far as the objective function is concerned.

The simplex method is an iterative computational routine. An initial solution, represented by the origin if the problem is graphed, is formulated. Each iteration moves the solution to some feasible corner that represents an improvement over the previous solution. The format for working simplex problems displays information about the solution at each iteration. The method tells us what combination of the decision variables represents the solution (i.e., is "in solution"), the value of the objective function for this solution, and the change that should be made in the decision variable combination (i.e., the variable that should be "brought into the solution") to achieve a better solution. If no change will improve the value of the objective function, then the optimum has been found and no further iterations are required. Once the optimal solution has been found, we can obtain additional information about shadow prices.

The simplex method will be applied to the Mo-Go Co. capacity allocation problem worked earlier by the graphical method. This procedure will enable us to compare each iteration of the simplex method to the graphical problem (Figure E.1) so that we can visualize the way the simplex method is used to solve the problem.

Suppose that Mr. Petroni had wished to allocate capacity by the simplex method. We will divide the problem into a series of steps and illustrate each step with the Mo-Go Co. problem.

Steps in the Simplex Method

STEP 1. Make equations from the constraints such that each of the equations contains a positive 1 times one of the decision variables so that no other equation has this variable in it. The coefficients for this variable in all of the other equations will be zero. Usually a slack or an artificial variable must be introduced for each row in addition to the original variables of the problem to convert the relationship to an equation.[1] These expressions form the initial solution. The nonnegativity constraints are always a part of a linear programming problem, so they can

---

[1] A *slack variable* represents the difference between the value of a variable and the limiting value it can take on. For example, if X must be ≤ 5, we could state $X + S = 5$, where S is a slack variable. If $X = 0$, then $S = 5$. If $X = 1$, then $S = 4$, and so on. An *artificial variable* is one that is not a part of the original problem but is introduced to make an equation. The artificial variable is assigned a very large cost so that it will automatically be removed from the problem as the simplex method minimizes cost or maximizes profit. If the solution were to be restricted to the line $Y = 10$, this constraint would be stated as $Y + A = 10$, where A is an artificial variable. A would be equal to zero in the final solution so that the solution value of Y would be 10.

be disregarded in formulating the problem.

The problem is to maximize $80M + 40G$ subject to the following three constraints:

$6M + 4G \leq 2,400$ machining time constraint
$2M + 3G \leq 1,500$ welding time constraint
$9M + 3G \leq 2,700$ assembly time constraint.

In order to make equations from these inequations we must add S_M (slack machining time) to the first, S_W (slack welding time) to the second, and S_A (slack assembly time) to the last.

$$6M + 4G + S_M = 2,400$$
$$2M + 3G + S_W = 1,500$$
$$9M + 3G + S_A = 2,700$$

We now have equations; however we have only three equations in five unknowns. Determining five variables by simultaneous solution of equations would require five equations, yet there are only three. If we set two variables equal to zero, we can solve for the other three variables. Always having two variables equal to zero will restrict the solution to the edge of the feasible region, which is the only part of it that can contain an optimal solution. The general linear programming problem will have m equations in n unknowns, so $n - m$ of the variables must always be equal to zero. The other m variables will be determined by the amount of the limited resources to be divided among the variables and are automatically found by the procedure. The simplex procedure guides the selection of the variables that are not equal to zero (these variables are said to be *in solution*) and the variables that are equal to zero (*out of solution*).

STEP 2. Enter the constraint equations and the objective functions into the simplex tableau format, illustrated by Table E.2.

Several formats for the simplex tableau exist. The reader may see some that differ from the one used here.

Table E.2
SIMPLEX TABLEAU FORMAT

C_j		80	40	0	0	0	
			DECISION				
	Solution		**VARIABLES**				Solution
	Variable	M	G	S_M	S_W	S_A	Quantity
0	S_M	6	4	1	0	0	2,400
0	S_W	2	3	0	1	0	1,500
0	S_A	9	3	0	0	1	2,700
	Z_j	0	0	0	0	0	0
	$C_j - Z_j$	80	40	0	0	0	

The M, G, S_M, S_W, and S_A column headings indicate the decision variable that is represented by each column. The "Quantity" column indicates the right-hand side of the equations that are represented by rows within the body (between the solid lines) of the tableau. The "Solution Variable" column indicates the variables that are in solution. The number of variables in solution at any time will be equal to the number of rows between the two solid horizontal lines. The C_j at the upper left-hand corner of the tableau is both a column heading and a row heading. Each C_j stands for the contribution to the objective function by a unit of the variable in the jth column. The contribution for each variable is shown in the top row of the tableau above the symbol for the variable. The contribution for each variable that is in solution is repeated in the left-hand column of the tableau.

The numbers within the body of the tableau represent rates of substitution. Look at the M column, for example. The 6 indicates that 6 units of S_M must be given up if one unit of M is added to the current solution; the 2 indicates that 2 units of S_W must be given up for each unit of M added to the solution; and so on. Recall that production of a mower requires six hours of machining time. The simplex method will cause all of these numbers to change so that at each solution they still rep-

resent the rates of substitution. In general, a number in the body of the table indicates the number of units of the variable represented by the row that will be given up for each unit of the variable represented by the column that is brought into the solution.

Each entry in the Z_j row (just below the bottom solid line in the tableau) represents an opportunity cost per unit for the variable represented by the column. Each Z_j indicates the contribution that will be given up for each unit of the variable (indicated at the top of the column) that is added to the current solutions. A Z_j value for the jth column is found by multiplying each entry in the column by the C_j value at the far left of the same row and summing the products for every row.

$$Z_j = \sum_{i=1}^{m} a_{ij} \cdot C_j$$

where a_{ij} = a coefficient in the ith row and the jth column within the body of the tableau

C_j = the coefficient at the left end of the ith row

m = the number of rows in the body of the table between the solid horizontal lines.

For example, the Z_j for the column headed M is $(6 \times 0) + (2 \times 0) + (9 \times 0) = 0$. Similar calculations are repeated for each column. The Z_j for the "Solution Quantity" column represents the contribution obtained with the current solution shown in the tableau.

The numbers in the bottom row of the tableau are found by subtracting the Z_j at the bottom of each column from the C_j at the top. These numbers are the contribution minus the opportunity cost, which is the net contribution for a unit of the variable that the column represents. The $C_j - Z_j$ values represent the net change in the objective function that will result from the addition of one unit of the variable represented in the column.

Notice that the last three variable columns contain an *identity matrix* (1's along the diagonal and 0's everywhere else). A column that has a $+1$ in it with 0's everywhere else represents a variable that is in solution. The value of the variable can be read from the right-hand column of the tableau in the row that contains the 1. The "Solution Variable" column is not necessary but is used to show which variables are in solution and which row expresses the value of the variable. Any variable that is not represented by a column with a 1 in one row and 0's in all the other rows is defined as not in solution and equal to zero.

Notice that M and G are not in solution and therefore are equal to zero in the initial solution. This corresponds to the origin of the graph in Figure E.1. Since no product is being produced, S_M = the full 2,400 hours available, S_W = the full 1,500 hours available, and S_A = the full 2,700 hours available. The lower right-hand corner of the tableau indicates that the value of the objective function is zero. This is the amount of profit we would expect, since we are producing no mowers or go-carts in this initial solution.

STEP 3. Find the *key column*, which represents the variables that should be entered into solution on this iteration. This is the column with the largest positive

coefficient in the bottom row if we are maximizing. (The most negative element would indicate the key column if we were minimizing.) If there are not elements with the sign we seek, the objective function cannot be improved further and this is an optimum solution.

In our problem the M column is the key column.

STEP 4. (a) Find the *key row* by computing θ for each row and selecting the row with the smallest positive θ. θ for a row is the quotient of the number in the "Quantity" column divided by the number in the key column for the row. (b) Find the *pivot element*, the intersection of the key row and the key column. (See Table E.3.)

The key column tells us that the objective function will be improved most per unit of variable added if we bring M into solution. This means we will move along the M axis of the graph in Figure E.1. The θ values tell us how far the available resources will let us move. There are 2,400 hours of machining time and each unit of M consumes 6 hours, so we can

Table E.3
SIMPLEX TABLEAU INDICATING KEY COLUMN, KEY ROW, AND PIVOT ELEMENT

C_j		80	40	0	0	0		
	Solution Variable	DECISION VARIABLES					Solution	
		M	G	S_M	S_W	S_A	Quantity	θ
0	S_M	6	4	1	0	0	2,400	$2,400/6 = 400$
0	S_W	2	3	0	1	0	1,500	$1,500/2 = 750$
0	S_A	⑨	3	0	0	1	2,700	$2,700/9 = \boxed{300}$ ←Key row
	Z_j	0	0	0	0	0	0	
	$C_j - Z_j$	$\boxed{80}$	40	0	0	0	0	

Pivot element   Key column

increase M by $^{2,400}\!/_6 = 400$ units with regard to the row representing S_M. The 300 value of θ for the third row is the smallest, so this constraint will stop us from increasing M beyond 300 units. Since the third row is the one we must comply with, it is the key row. The 9 in the third row and the M column is the pivot element.

STEP 5. Generate the next tableau by the following procedure. The pivot row in the new tableau is found by dividing the key row in the old tableau by the pivot element so that the pivot element is replaced by a 1. Write this row in the new tableau. We will call it the pivot row. Generate the other rows so that the elements in the key column will become 0. You can do this by multiplying the pivot row in the new tableau by -1 times the number in the key column of the row in the old tableau that is to be replaced and adding this expression to the row in the old tableau. The sum of these two equations is still a valid equation, but the new expression will have a 0 where you want it. This expression should be entered into the new tableau in the row that you are replacing. After this procedure is completed for each row, you have a new tableau with the key column replaced by a column of an identity matrix (a 1 where the pivot

element was in the previous tableau and 0's in the remainder of the column). Return to step 3.

The objective of this step is to make the key column of the old tableau into a column of the identity matrix by performing row operations upon the matrix. We want a 1 where the pivot element was, and we obtain it by dividing the key row of the old matrix by the pivot element. If we divide an equation by a constant it is still a valid equation, so this step does not change the nature of the problem. The third row of the new tableau is shown in Table E.4.

Table E.4
THIRD ROW IN NEW SIMPLEX TABLEAU

Solution Variables	M	G	S_M	S_W	S_A	Solution Quantity
M	1	$^1\!/_3$	0	0	$^1\!/_9$	300

Now let's perform the necessary operations to obtain the new first row. We want a 0 in the M column where the 6 is, so we would like another equation with -6 in the M column to add to this row. We obtain the necessary value by multiplying the new pivot row by -6. For each column of the first row we will obtain the coefficients shown in Table E.5.

Table E.5
OPERATIONS TO OBTAIN THE COEFFICIENTS OF THE FIRST ROW OF THE SIMPLEX TABLEAU

Column	M	G	S_M	S_W	S_A	Solution Quantity
a. coefficient is in old 1st row	6	4	1	0	0	2,400
b. Multiplier times element in pivot row	$-6(1)$	$-6(^1\!/_3)$	$-6(0)$	$-6(0)$	$-6(^1\!/_9)$	$-6(300)$
New 1st row element (sum of a and b)	0	2	1	0	$-^2\!/_3$	600

Table E.6
NEW SIMPLEX TABLEAU

C_j		80	40	0	0	0		
	Solution	DECISION VARIABLES					Solution	
	Variables	M	G	S_M	S_W	S_A	Quantity	θ
0	S_M	0	→②	1	0	$-\tfrac{2}{3}$	600	300 ←Key row
0	S_W	0	$\tfrac{7}{3}$	0	1	$-\tfrac{2}{9}$	900	$385\tfrac{7}{8}$
80	M	1	$\tfrac{1}{3}$	0	0	$\tfrac{1}{9}$	300	900
	Z_j	80	$\tfrac{80}{3}$	0	0	$\tfrac{80}{9}$	24,000	
	$C_j - Z_j$	0	$\tfrac{40}{3}$	0	0	$-\tfrac{80}{9}$		

Pivot element   Key column

The first row of the new tableau can be read from the bottom row of Table E.5. The second row of the new tableau can be found by the same procedure with the use of a multiplier of -2. It is not necessary to make a table such as Table E.5 because the operations can be performed mentally, by working across a row one column at a time, and the coefficients written in the new tableau as they are obtained. The Z_j and $C_j - Z_j$ rows are developed by the procedure described in step 2.

The completed new tableau is shown in Table E.6. This solution says that $M = 300$ and $G = 0$, since it is not in solution. Available machining time, S_M, is 600 hours, and available welding time, S_W, is 900 hours. Notice that the slack assembly time equals zero, since it is

no longer in solution (i.e., it is no longer a column of an identity matrix). This solution corresponds to the lower right-hand corner of the feasible region shown in Figure E.1. The value of the objective function can be read from the right-hand side of the bottom row: $24,000.

Returning to step 3 of the solution procedure, we see that this is not the optimal solution because there is still a positive number in the bottom row. The key column is that representing G, and the first row is the key row. Repeating the remaining steps of the solution procedure produced the tableau shown in Table E.7.

This is an optimal solution, since there are no positive numbers in the bottom row. It says that optimal product mix is $G = 300$ and

Table E.7
SIMPLEX TABLEAU SHOWING OPTIMAL SOLUTION

C_j		80	40	0	0	0	
	Solution	DECISION VARIABLES					Solution
	Variables	M	G	S_M	S_W	S_A	Quantity
40	G	0	1	$\tfrac{1}{2}$	0	$-\tfrac{1}{3}$	300
0	S_W	0	0	$-\tfrac{7}{6}$	1	$\tfrac{5}{9}$	200
80	M	1	0	$-\tfrac{1}{6}$	0	$\tfrac{2}{9}$	200
	Z_j	80	40	$\tfrac{20}{3}$	0	$\tfrac{40}{9}$	28,000
	$C_j - Z_j$	0	0	$-\tfrac{20}{3}$	0	$-\tfrac{40}{9}$	

$M = 200$. Mo-Go Co. would have 200 hours of slack in the welding department if it produced the product mix. The contribution from this solution is $28,000. The solution corresponds to the same corner of the feasible region that was found to be optimal by the graphical method.

Shadow Prices

Shadow prices are useful in capacity planning situations such as the one above. They are the marginal change in the objective function caused by a unit of a designated resource. Shadow prices can be read directly from the bottom row of the simplex tableau in the column representing the resource in question, only the sign must be reversed. For example, another hour of machining capacity would be worth $20/3$ dollars to Mo-Go Co. The zero at the bottom of the S_W column indicates that another hour of welding capacity would be worth nothing. This value is logical because the company already has 200 hours of welding capacity that it is unable to use. The value of another hour of assembly time is $40/9$ dollars.

Operations managers can compare the cost of additional units of capacity to the shadow price for the capacity and see if it is worthwhile to work overtime, to subcontract, or to use another method to expand capacity in a department.

Ranging for Shadow Prices   Shadow prices indicate the value of one more unit of a resource; yet it would hardly be worthwhile to add just one more hour of a capacity. Resources usually come in larger blocks, and we may want to know how many units can be added at the marginal value indicated by the shadow price. *Ranging, sensitivity analysis,* and *parametric programming* are terms that refer to the process of finding the range over which the variables shown to be in solution will remain in solution. Ranging tells us how far we can increase capacity and still gain the amount

indicated by the shadow price for each unit we add.

Ranging is accomplished by the process of dividing the number in the right-hand column by -1 times the number in the column representing the resource in which we are interested. This procedure is analogous to finding θ during the solution of a linear programming problem. (Rather than being a part of the usual solution technique, however, ranging is a form of postoptimality analysis.) The smallest positive quotient tells how many units of the resource can be added before the solution mix will be changed. A change in solution mix means that the line (plane or hyperplane) representing the constraint we are moving has reached an intersection of other lines. At this point the shadow prices can change.

Let us examine how far the capacity can be increased in the machining and assembly departments. These two departments are the only ones with shadow prices. Calculating the ratios of the "Quantity" column to the S_M column with the signs reversed gives $300 \div (-\frac{1}{2}) = -600$, then $200 \div (\frac{7}{6}) = 1,200/7$, and $200 \div (\frac{1}{6}) = 1,200$. The smallest positive value is $1,200/7$, so the machining capacity can be increased $1,200/7$ hours before the shadow price is changed. Calculating the ratios of the "Quantity" column to the S_A column with the signs reversed gives $300 \div (\frac{1}{3}) = 900$, then $200 \div (-\frac{5}{9}) = -360$, and $200 \div (-\frac{2}{9}) = -900$. The capacity of the assembly department can be increased by 900 hours before the shadow price changes.

Degeneracy

Occasionally the simplex procedure will encounter a minor difficulty called *degeneracy*. Degeneracy is indicated when the θ column has two or more values that tie as the smallest nonnegative number. Selection of the key row can be made arbitrarily and the simplex procedure continued. Degeneracy will be indicated if the variable that should be brought into solution is one that recently was removed from solution. If the problem is degenerate, return to the solution that had the tied θ's and select another of the smallest θ values for the key row.[2]

It is possible to prevent the additional work of performing iterations that may not lead to a solution by the following procedure. When an iteration occurs where the θ values are tied for the smallest value, divide each tied row by the number in the key column of that row. Then compare the numbers in the tied rows, starting at leftmost slack column and moving to the right. The first row with the smaller coefficient should be used as the key row.

Other Constraints and Minimization

In order to illustrate the formulation of greater-than-or-equal-to constraints and equal-to constraints, let us now look at the seed-blending problem that was solved earlier by the graphical method. This problem is used to illustrate how the other types of constraints are formulated into the simplex tableau. It also serves to illustrate a minimization problem. The problem, as you may recall, was:

$$\begin{aligned} \text{Minimize } C &= 0.60R + 0.40F \\ \text{subject to} \quad R + F &= 10 \\ R &\geq 4 \\ F &\geq 3 \end{aligned}$$

According to step 1 of the simplex procedure, each row must have a positive 1 in it in a column that has 0's in the remainder. The first constraint is already an equation with one R and one F in it, but there will be other rows that contain R and F. An artificial variable, A, is introduced when a row of a simplex tableau is being developed to represent an equality constraint. This variable should not be used in any other constraint so that it will have 0's in

[2]Harold Bierman, Jr., Charles P. Bonini, and Warren H. Hausman, *Quantitative Analysis for Business Decisions*, 6th ed. (Homewood, Ill.: Irwin, 1981), p. 288.

the remainder of its column. This format will result in one column of the identity matrix. Since A is not a part of the problem that we wish to solve, it must be taken out of solution by the simplex procedure. We assign each artificial variable an extremely large cost, M, to ensure that it will be driven out of the solution by the minimization process. M is like ∞, it is larger than any other number that occurs in the problem.

A $\geq$ constraint, as you would assume, can be made into an equation by subtraction of a slack variable from the left-hand side of the original constraint. This would result in a -1 in the column for the slack variable so that it could not be a part of the identity matrix. Therefore -1 times a slack variable and $+1$ times another artificial variable must be added to form a row of the simplex tableau that represents a $\geq$ constraint in the problem. The slack variable has a cost of zero and the artificial variable is assigned a large cost, M, to ensure that it will not be in the final solution.

The simplex tableau for the initial solution of the grass-seed problem is shown in Table E.8. Notice that there are three equations in seven variables, so $7 - 3 = 4$ of these variables will be $= 0$ at any solution. The initial solution represented by Table E.8 shows all three artificial variables in solution. Both R and $F = 0$, so the solution represents the origin of the graph in Figure E.2, which is outside of the feasible region. The artificial variable represents the amount by which the solution lies outside the feasible region. As the artificial variables are driven out of the solution, the solution will be moved to the feasible region. We then continue the optimization process by working with only the real variables involved.

This problem was solved by the simplex procedure as presented before, except that the variable with the most negative value in the bottom row was chosen as the key column at each iteration. The final tableau for the problem is presented in Table E.9. It shows that the

Table E.8
INITIAL SOLUTION FOR THE GRASS SEED BLENDING PROBLEM

C_j		0.6	0.4	M	0	M	0	M	Solution
	Solution			DECISION VARIABLES					Solution
	Variables	R	F	A_1	S_R	A_2	S_F	A_3	Quantity
M	A_1	1	1	1	0	0	0	0	10
M	A_2	1	0	0	−1	1	0	0	4
M	A_3	0	1	0	0	0	−1	1	3 ←Key row
	Z_j	2M	2M	M	−M	M	−M	M	17M
	$C_j - Z_j$	0.6 − 2M	0.4 − 2M	0	M	0	M	0	

↑
Key column

optimum mixture is 4 pounds of rye seed and 6 pounds of fescue seed with a cost of $4.80.

THE TRANSPORTATION METHOD

Sometimes, allocation of a limited resource involves the distribution of resources at several locations to some other set of locations where the resource is to be used, stored, sold, or employed in some manner. When the cost of moving the resource from one location to another is a linear function of the number of units moved, we have a special type of linear programming problem.

The objective of the typical problem of this type is to minimize the cost of moving the resource, hence this type of problem often is called a transportation problem. The simplex method can be used to solve this type of problem, although it is not the easiest method to use. A special *algorithm* (a computational procedure) called the transportation method, or distribution method, is available for solving transportation problems. The transportation method greatly simplifies the computation for a problem that can be expressed in the transportation-method format. In fact, the transportation method allows us to solve manually a problem that would require very lengthy calculations or a computer to solve by the simplex method.

The transportation method is an iterative process. It begins with a feasible solution, then

Table E.9
FINAL SOLUTION FOR THE GRASS SEED BLENDING PROBLEM

C_j		0.6	0.4	M	0	M	0	M	Solution
	Solution			DECISION VARIABLES					Solution
	Variables	R	F	A_1	S_R	A_2	S_F	A_3	Quantity
0	S_F	0	0	1	1	−1	1	−1	3
0.6	R	1	0	0	−1	1	0	0	4
0.4	F	0	1	1	1	−1	0	0	6
	Z_j	0.6	0.4	0.4	−0.2	0.2	0	0	4.8
	$C_j - Z_j$	0	0	M − 0.4	0.2	M − 0.2	0	M	

improves it at every iteration until it can be improved no further. The objective function for a transportation problem can be expressed in terms of cost or profit, and the algorithm can be worked to reduce costs to a minimum value or to increase profit to a maximum. The costs considered in a minimization problem are not limited to transportation costs, so the method has more versatility than the name implies. For example, the costs used in a problem can represent production cost at each factory plus transportation costs to each location that each factory may supply.

In some instances, the transportation method can be used to allocate a resource that actually is not to be physically moved. The method has been employed in production scheduling and aggregate planning to allocate production capacity during some time period (the resource) to competing uses of that capacity (demand) during a series of time periods. This application was illustrated in Chapter 4. Further, it was shown that the production capacity can be subdivided to represent such possible production options as regular-time production, overtime production, and production by a subcontractor. An application of the transportation method to problems of selecting facility locations is discussed in Chapter 12. The discussion in this supplement deals with the typical problem of distributing a product

at several locations to several other locations so as to minimize the total transportation costs.

Suppose that the Jonah Ander Fish Food Company has three fish food factories that supply four regional warehouses. Mr. Ander would like to determine the shipping schedule that will minimize the total transportation cost for distributing the product from the factories to the warehouses.

The monthly production capacity at the factories and the monthly demand at each warehouse are shown in Table E.10. The shipping costs between each possible source and combination of destinations are shown in Table E.11. The production cost is the same at all of the factories and the product sells for the same amount at all locations, so minimizing transportation costs will maximize the profit on the product.

Mr. Ander suspects that he may have oversimplified the problem and overlooked something in previous intuitive solutions, so he has decided to try the transportation method to solve his problem.

In the past, Mr. Ander has distributed the product by the following logic. The lowest cost shipping routes are from factory A to warehouse 3 and from factory C to warehouse 2. The capacity at each of these factories matches the requirements at the corresponding warehouse. Therefore, factory A supplied ware-

Table E.10
MONTHLY PRODUCTION CAPACITIES AND WAREHOUSE DEMANDS, ANDER FISH FOOD COMPANY

Source	Production Capacity (cases)	Destination	Requirements (cases)
Factory A	300	Warehouse 1	200
Factory B	300	Warehouse 2	200
Factory C	200	Warehouse 3	300
		Warehouse 4	100
Total Capacity	800	Total demand	800

Table E.11
SHIPPING COST FROM FACTORY TO WAREHOUSE,
ANDER FISH FOOD COMPANY

Source	DESTINATION			
	Warehouse 1	Warehouse 2	Warehouse 3	Warehouse 4
Factory A	$2	$4	$1	$3
Factory B	8	2	6	5
Factory C	6	1	4	2

house 3 and factory C supplied warehouse 2. The capacity of factory B was used to supply 200 cases to warehouse 1 and 100 cases to warehouse 4. The total cost of the shipping schedule was $2,600 each month.

Now let's develop a solution to the problem by the transportation method. The first step is to enter the problem into a transportation-method tableau, as shown in Figure E.3. The cost for each shipping route is shown in the small block in the upper corner of each cell. Notice that the sum of the requirements is equal to the sum of the available resources to be allocated. This equality is a requirement of the transportation method. If the two quantities are not equal, a *dummy supply* or a *dummy user* must be added to make the total resources available equal to the total resources needed.

The shipping cost for the dummy units is equal to zero, whether it is from a dummy source or to a dummy user.

The second step is to arrive at an initial solution by placing quantities into the cells so that all of the rim requirements are satisfied. The rim requirements are the four warehouse requirements for the columns and the three factory capacities for the rows. Our objective is to find the best cells to use and to place as large a quantity in these cells as possible without violating a constraint of a row or column. This effort corresponds to the comparisons to find the best variable to bring into solution in a simplex problem and to put as much as possible of that variable into solution so that the minimum θ (i.e., most restrictive constraint) is not violated. Solution by the graphical method

FIGURE E.3

Transportation Tableau for Ander Problem

Source	Destination				Resources available
	W_1	W_2	W_3	W_4	
F_A	2	4	1	3	300
F_B	8	2	6	5	300
F_C	6	1	4	2	200
Requirements	200	200	300	100	Total 800

is similar. One finds the best direction to move within the feasible region to increase or decrease the objective function, then moves as far as possible in that direction. When the transportation method is used, one determines the best cell to use and adds the greatest quantity to that cell without violating a rim requirement. If we have used the correct set of cells, we have an optimal solution, because we can put no more into those cells. If there is a better cell to use, then the solution can be improved. The test for optimality in the transportation method is to evaluate the unoccupied cells after each solution to see if using any of them would improve the solution.

Initial Solution by the Northwest Corner Method

There are several ways to arrive at an initial solution to a transportation-method problem. One method is to use inspection to arrive at a judgmental solution initially. Another is Vogel's approximation method (VAM), which will be discussed later in the supplement. First we shall discuss and illustrate the northwest corner method, which assigns the initial solution in a completely arbitrary manner. If the tableau were a map, the northwest corner would be at the upper left, hence the name. Starting at the upper left corner, place a quantity into the cell equal to the smaller of the first row constraint or the first column constraint. Move to the next cell in the direction of the unsatisfied constraint and place as large a number in it as possible until either the row or column constraint is satisfied. Repeat this step, moving one cell in the direction of the unsatisfied constraint and placing as large a number in that cell as possible until you reach the lower right corner of the tableau. If both the row and column constraints become satisfied at some cell before you have reached the lower right cell, move to the right one column and down one row and continue the above procedure. The results will be a set of occupied cells that resemble a set of stairsteps from the upper left cell to the lower right cell, as you can see in Figure E.4. This is a feasible initial solution. We can find the cost of the transportation schedule represented by any tableau by summing the products we get when we multiply the quantity in each occupied cell by the cost coefficient in the upper right corner of the cell. For this solution the cost is $200(2) + 100(4) + 100(2) + 200(6) + 100(4) + 100(2) = \$2,800$.

The next step is to determine if this feasible solution is optimal. We test for optimality

FIGURE E.4

Initial Solution by the Northwest Corner Method

Source	Destination				Resources available
	W_1	W_2	W_3	W_4	
F_A	200 \ 2	100 \ 4	\ 1	\ 3	300
F_B	\ 8	100 \ 2	200 \ 6	\ 5	300
F_C	\ 6	\ 1	100 \ 4	100 \ 2	200
Requirements	200	200	300	100	Total 800

by evaluating all unoccupied cells to see if any of them would cost less per unit if material were placed in it instead of in some currently occupied cell.

The Stepping-Stone Method

Every unoccupied cell must be evaluated after each iteration to see if it represents a potential improvement in the solution. We shall use what is referred to as the stepping-stone method to evaluate the unoccupied cells in each tableau. First, count the occupied cells to see if material is allocated to $R + C - 1$ cells, where R = the number of rows and C = the number of columns in the tableau. Our solution had six occupied cells, which is the required number. If a solution does not have $R + C - 1$ occupied cells, it is said to be a degenerate solution, and we would have to employ a slight modification of the method to evaluate the unoccupied cells. Degeneracy is discussed below, following completion of this nondegenerate problem.

If there are $R + C - 1$ occupied cells, then it is possible to evaluate each unoccupied cell to determine if it is a better cell to use in the solution. We evaluate a cell by summing the changes in cost that would occur if a unit

of the product were placed in the cell. We find the cost change for a cell by drawing a closed path that leaves the cell and moves only vertically or horizontally and turns corners (always 90 degrees) only on occupied cells (i.e., the stepping-stones). The path can cross both occupied and unoccupied cells and can cross itself, but it cannot move along a diagonal or turn on an unoccupied cell. Some closed paths are shown in Figure E.5. The empty cell to be evaluated, which is one corner of the closed path, and alternate corners of the path are assigned a plus sign. The remaining corners, between those with plus signs, are assigned a minus sign. Add the cost coefficients in the corners with plus signs and subtract from this amount the sum of the cost coefficients in the corners with minus signs along the path. The result is the signed amount that the objective function will be changed for each unit placed in the unoccupied cell associated with the path. If an unoccupied cell has a negative evaluation, then a minimization problem is not optimal because some material can be moved to a better cell. We would assign the greatest amount possible to the most negative cell on the next iteration, then evaluate the new set of unoccupied cells by the use of the new set

FIGURE E.5

Examples of Closed Paths for Evaluation of Unoccupied Cells by the Stepping-Stone Method

Source	Destination				Resources available
	W_1	W_2	W_3	W_4	
F_A	200 ⟍2	100 ⟍4	⟍1	? ⟍3	300
F_B	? ⟍8	100 ⟍2	200 ⟍6	⟍5	300
F_C	⟍6	⟍1	100 ⟍4	100 ⟍2	200
Requirements	200	200	300	100	Total 800

of stepping-stones. (Maximization problems will be discussed later in the supplement.)

The reasoning behind the change in signs at every corner of the closed path is as follows: For every unit we assign to the unoccupied cell being evaluated (a plus cell), we must remove a unit from a cell in the same row (the minus cell at the other end of the horizontal line from the unoccupied cell); otherwise the row constraint will no longer be satisfied. But if we remove some material from the minus cell, we must add the same amount to the plus cell in its column so that the constraint for that column will remain satisfied. You can see that this reasoning applies all the way around the path until we return to the cell we are evaluating.

The number that results from evaluating a cell by a closed path can be thought of as the change in cost that would occur if one unit were pushed along each straight-line segment of the path from the minus cell to the plus cell. We do not want to push just one unit around the segments of the path, however. If the cell will reduce cost, we want to move the greatest amount possible into it. The most we can move along the path is the smallest amount in a minus corner of the path. Just as in the graphical and simplex methods, the most restrictive constraint or smallest amount is the one that stops further change.

As a first example, let us evaluate the unoccupied cell that represents shipping the product from factory B to warehouse 1. (We will shorten the expression by calling this cell B1, etc.) If we were to add a unit to cell B1, we would have to remove a unit from cell A1, add a unit to cell A2, and remove a unit from cell B2, so that the rim requirements would remain balanced. We find the change in cost that would result from shifting one unit through these steps by summing the cost coefficients for the corner cells with plus signs if material is to be added to the cell and for those with minus signs if

material is to be removed from the cell. The results for cell B1 are:

$$
\begin{array}{l}
+8 \text{ for cell B1} \\
-2 \text{ for cell A1} \\
+4 \text{ for cell A2} \\
\underline{-2 \text{ for cell B2}} \\
+8
\end{array}
$$

The objective function will increase by $8 for every unit added to cell B1. Obviously this is not a desirable cell to use, since we wish to reduce the objective function, that is, total transportation cost.

Now examine cell A4. Evaluation of the closed path corresponding to this unoccupied cell shows the following:

$$
\begin{array}{l}
+3 \text{ for cell A4} \\
-2 \text{ for cell C4} \\
+4 \text{ for cell C3} \\
-6 \text{ for cell B3} \\
+2 \text{ for cell B2} \\
\underline{-4 \text{ for cell A2}} \\
-3
\end{array}
$$

The objective function will be decreased by $3 for every unit we can put in cell A4. At this stage we know that the current solution is not optimal and at least one more solution must be developed. But before we develop the next solution, all unoccupied cells should be evaluated and the most negative cell selected to be brought into the solution (i.e., have material put into it). Evaluations of the unoccupied cells yield the following:

Cell	Evaluation	Cell	Evaluation
B1	+8	A3	−7
C1	+8	A4	−3
C2	+1	B4	+1

Cell A3 is the most negative cell and will save $7 for each unit that can be shifted into it. We should like to shift as much material as possible into cell A3. Examining the negative corners of the path used to evaluate this cell shows one minus cell with 100 units that could be shifted around the path and another with 200 units that could be shifted. Since the same amount must be shifted around the entire path, we are limited to 100 units at the next iteration. The 100 units in cell A2 will be shifted to cell A3 and 100 of the 200 units in cell B3 will be shifted to cell B2. The next solution, shown in Figure E.6. reflects this shift of material into cell A3 and around the closed path that was used to evaluate this cell.

Notice that no material was shifted into cell A4. Only one shift around one closed path should be made per iteration. And notice that there are still $R + C - 1$ occupied cells, so each unoccupied cell will have a unique path for its evaluation. Since a different set of cells is occupied, different paths will be used to evaluate some of the cells and different answers may be obtained. Evaluation of the unoccupied cells reveals the following results:

Cell	Evaluation	Cell	Evaluation
B1	+1	C2	+1
C1	+1	A4	+4
A2	+7	B4	+1

Since all of these values are positive, this is an optimal solution. If we use any cells other than the ones we have used, cost will be increased,

so we know that the best possible cells are in solution. Also we have used the occupied cells to the greatest extent possible, so the solution cannot be improved in any way (i.e., it is optimal). Notice that cell A4 has changed from a -3 to a $+4$ with this iteration. We saved $7 per unit on the iteration, whereas cell A4 could have saved $3 per unit. Now if we regressed from the optimal solution by using cell A4, we would increase cost by $4 per unit.

The cost of the final solution is 200(2) + 200(2) + 100(1) + 100(6) + 100(4) + 100(2) = $2,100, which is $700 less than the previous solution. This is what we would expect, because we moved 100 units into a cell that would save $7 per unit.

Mr. Ander examined the results provided by the transportation method and was surprised to see that it did not use cell C2, which is one of the lowest cost cells. Also, only 100 units were in cell A3, which is another of the lowest cost cells. His solution had been to spring for these low-cost cells, putting 300 units in cell A3, 200 units in cell C2, 100 units in cell B4, and then filling the requirements for W1 by putting 200 units in cell B1. He concluded that sometimes we have to pass up some of the lowest cost cells in order to keep from being forced into other cells that have penalties higher

FIGURE E.6

Second Solution to the Ander Fish Food Distribution Problem

Source	Destination				Resources available
	W_1	W_2	W_3	W_4	
F_A	200 ^{2}	^{4}	100 ^{1}	^{3}	300
F_B	^{8}	200 ^{2}	100 ^{6}	^{5}	300
F_C	^{6}	^{1}	100 ^{4}	100 ^{2}	200
Requirements	200	200	300	100	Total 800

than savings we would get from the low-cost cells. The transportation method makes these comparisons automatically as one proceeds through the algorithm.

Vogel's Approximation Method

The initial solution to the previous example was made by a rather arbitrary method so that the methods of evaluating and improving a nonoptimal solution could be illustrated. A more logical selection of the initial solution can often reduce the amount of work required to reach an optimal solution. *Vogel's approximation method* (VAM) will frequently lead to an optimal or nearly optimal solution on the initial assignment. In general terms, VAM develops for each row and column a minimum penalty that will be incurred if an assignment is not made to the lowest cost cell in that row or column. The maximum amount possible (within the rim constraints) is then assigned to the lowest-cost cell in the row or column with the greatest penalty. After material is assigned to some cell, the penalties are recalculated to determine where the next assignment should be made.

The steps involved in VAM for a minimization problem are as follows:

1. Determine the difference between the lowest-cost cell and the next-to-lowest-cost cell in each row, including dummy rows, if any. Repeat for all columns. (This step determines the minimum penalty that will be incurred if the best cell in the row or column is not used.)

2. Choose the row or column that has the largest penalty and assign the maximum permissible amount to the lowest-cost cell in this row or column. (If two or more rows or columns have equally large penalties, pick the one with the lowest-cost cell. If more than one cell has the same lowest cost, pick the one into which more material can be assigned. If a tie still exists, pick either tied cell, because one is as good as the other.)

3. Eliminate the row or column in which the

rim requirement was satisfied in the previous step.

4. Return to step 1 and repeat the process on the remaining rows and columns to make an assignment to another cell until all rim requirements are satisfied.

The VAM procedure is used to make the initial assignment for the Jonah Anders Fish Food problem in Figures E.7 through E.11.[3] The penalty for column 1 in Figure E.7 is $6 - 2 = 4$, for the last row it is $2 - 1 = 1$, and so on. The largest penalty (circled) is for column 1, so 200 units are assigned to the A1 cell, because it is the lowest-cost cell in column 1. Column 1 is eliminated from further consideration, as shown in Figure E.8.

Column 3 and row B of Figure E.8 are tied with penalty values of 3. Column 3 is selected because it contains a cell with a cost of 1 while the lowest-cost cell in row B has a cost of 2. One hundred units can be assigned to cell A3 without violating the rim requirement for row A. Row A is eliminated (Figure E.9), as it now is satisfied.

Row B and column 4 are tied with a penalty of 3. The lowest-cost cell in row B has a cost of 2, which is equal to the cost of the best cell in column 4, so the tie still exists. But we can place 200 units in the lowest-cost cell of row B and only 100 units in column 4. The tie has been broken because row B permits more units in its low-cost cell. The rim requirement for column 2 is satisfied, so this column is eliminated (Figure E.10).

Column 4 has the greatest penalty, so material should be assigned to the lowest cost in this column, cell C4. The maximum that can be placed in this cell without violating a rim constraint is 100 units. When this cell is filled, the remaining assignments also are established by the rim requirements. The initial assignment by VAM is shown in Figure E.11. This is

---

[3]James L. Riggs, *Production Systems: Planning Analysis and Control* (New York: John Wiley, 1976), p. 167.

FIGURE E.7

First Step in an Initial Assigment by VAM

Source	Destination				Capacity	Penalty
	W_1	W_2	W_3	W_4		
F_A	2	4	1	3	300	1
F_B	8	2	6	5	300	3
F_C	6	1	4	2	200	1
Requirements	200	200	300	100	Total 800	
Penalty	(4)	1	3	1		

the optimal solution developed when the problem was solved earlier. The initial assignment developed in the earlier solution, however, required a further iteration by the stepping-stone method.

The VAM procedure can reduce the number of iterations required to move from the initial assignment to the optimal solution. The VAM procedure often provides an improved initial solution, but the solution still must be checked to see if it is optimal. In this case just illustrated, the initial solution *was* optimal, so no further work was required. Several tableaus were used to illustrate VAM, but the procedure actually requires only one, since the body of the tableau remains the same while assigned amounts are entered into the cells as the solution is developed. Extra columns can be added to the right of the table and extra rows to the bottom. One row and one column could then be used to record the current value of the penalties prior to each assignment step.

FIGURE E.8

Second Step in an Initial Assignment by VAM

Source	Destination				Capacity	Penalty
	W_1	W_2	W_3	W_4		
F_A	200	4	1	3	300	2
F_B		2	6	5	300	(3)
F_C		1	4	2	200	1
Requirements	200	200	300	100	Total 800	
Penalty	X	1	(3)	1		

FIGURE E.9

Third Step in an Initial Assignment by VAM

Source	Destination				Capacity	Penalty
	W_1	W_2	W_3	W_4		
F_A	200		100		300	X
F_B		2	6	5	300	③
F_C		1	4	2	200	1
Requirements	200	200	300	100	Total 800	
Penalty	X	1	2	③		

Degeneracy

Degeneracy in a transportation problem occurs when any solution has a number of occupied cells that is less than the number of rows plus the number of columns minus one, $R + C - 1$. It will occur on any iteration in which an entry in some cell satisfies the requirements of both a row and a column. The result is that there are not enough stepping-stones to form closed paths so that all of the unoccupied cells can be evaluated.

When degeneracy exists, a very simple "patch-up" will enable the transportation algorithm to proceed. We simply place ϵ (epsilon), an exceedingly small amount of material, in some cells until $R + C - 1$ cells have some amount in them. The cells with ϵ in them can be used as stepping-stones but have no effect on the cost of a solution, so if ϵ is still in the final solution, it can be ignored.

The initial placement of an ϵ is arbitrary, so it is wise to select a location that will simplify the construction of closed paths. Once

FIGURE E.10

Fourth Step in an Initial Assignment by VAM

Source	Destination				Capacity	Penalty
	W_1	W_2	W_3	W_4		
F_A	200		100		300	X
F_B		200	6	5	300	1
F_C			4	2	200	2
Requirements	200	200	300	100	Total 800	
Penalty	X	X	2	③		

FIGURE E.11

Initial Assignment by VAM

Source	Destination				Capacity
	W_1	W_2	W_3	W_4	
F_A	200		100		300
F_B		200	100		300
F_C			100	100	200
Requirements	200	200	300	100	Total 800

the ϵ is inserted into a tableau, it is treated like another number. If it is in a negative corner of a path, it will be the limiting amount that can be shifted along the path. The result is that such numbers as $20 - \epsilon$ or $100 + \epsilon$ may appear in some of the cells. These ϵ's remain in the iteration unless they are removed by subtraction of an ϵ from an ϵ. When the final solution is achieved, the ϵ's can be ignored or assumed to be zero.

Maximization Procedure

Suppose that the objective function of a transportation-method problem were written in terms of profit rather than cost. Optimization of such a problem would require the maximization of the objective function. The only change in the transportation algorithm is to move material into the unoccupied cell with the largest positive value on each iteration. Cells in a dummy row or column represent material that actually will not be shipped or sold, so they still contribute zero to the objective function and should have 0's in their upper corner blocks.

Nothing else should be changed in the procedure that was outlined previously. A closed path is evaluated with a plus sign in the unoccupied cell where the path begins, just as

before. The amount that should be shifted in a path is still the smallest amount in the negative corners of the path.

What If Supply Does Not Equal Demand?

Supply (i.e., capacity) and demand may differ in amount. Probably the most usual circumstance is for the available capacity to exceed demand. Many companies try to maintain extra inventory or service capacity to ensure flexibility and prompt response to demand. Usually the choice of the supply location to be underutilized in such circumstances is an issue that affects only the operations function. Operations managers can obtain useful guidance in reaching capacity underutilization decisions by use of the transportation method.

Response to an undersupply situation has serious implications for customer relations and future business transactions. The typical transportation-method solution minimizes transportation costs and does not address the issue of ill will and lost sales. The model could be applied in a situation of supply shortage if the cost for the dummy supply were the cost of the lost sales rather than being set at zero. Another approach is to consult with the marketing function and determine where the short-

FIGURE E.12

Initial Solution with Oversupply and Degeneracy

Source	Destination					Available supply
	W_1	W_2	W_3	W_4	W_5 Dummy	
F_A	200 [2]	200 [4]	[1]	[3]	[0]	400
F_B	[8]	[2]	200 [6]	100 [5]	[0]	300
F_C	[6]	[1]	[4]	100 [2]	100 [0]	200
Requirements	200	200	200	200	100	Total 900

ages can be tolerated with the least harm. The amount of capacity shortage can then be subtracted from the requirements in these locations so that the supply and remaining requirements are equal. The transportation method then may be used to minimize the transportation costs (or production costs plus transportation costs) to meet the portion of the total demand that the company intends to satisfy.

Suppose that the capacity of factory A had been 400 units per month and that each warehouse required 200 units per month. The initial solution by the northwest corner method is shown in Figure E.12. Two points about this solution should be recognized. First, since there

is an excess of capacity, a dummy warehouse has been added to make the sum of the supply equal to the sum of the demand. The cost of shipping from any factory to this dummy warehouse is zero because these goods will not actually be shipped. The factory or factories that are selected to supply the dummy warehouse will have their capacity underutilized. The second point to be noticed is that this is a degenerate solution. Only six cells are occupied, and there should be $3 + 5 - 1 = 7$ occupied cells if we are to have enough paths to evaluate all of the unoccupied cells.

An artificial amount, ϵ, must be added to some cell in the tableau in Figure E.12 so that there will be a unique closed path for each un-

FIGURE E.13

Initial Solution Repeated, Showing Cell Evaluations and Some Paths

Source	Destination					Available supply
	W_1	W_2	W_3	W_4	W_5 Dummy	
F_A	200 [2]	200 [4]	(−7) [1]	(−4) [3]	(−5) [0]	400
F_B	(+8) [8]	ϵ [2]	200 [6]	100 [5]	(−3) [0]	300
F_C	(+9) [6]	(+2) [1]	(+1) [4]	100 [2]	100 [0]	200
Requirements	200	200	200	200	100	Total 900

FIGURE E.14

Second Solution to Oversupply Problem

Source	Destination					Available supply
	W_1	W_2	W_3	W_4	W_5 Dummy	
F_A	2 200	4 (+7)	1 200	3 (+3)	0 (+2)	400
F_B	8 (+1)	2 200 + ε	6 ε	5 100	0 (−3)	300
F_C	6 (+2)	1 (+2)	4 (+1)	2 100	0 100	200
Requirements	200	200	200	200	100	Total 900

occupied cell. Although the placement of ε is arbitrary, it is placed in cell B2 so that every row overlaps another, a device that often makes finding paths a little easier. Evaluation of the unoccupied cells proceeds just as though ε were another number. The cell evaluations (in circles) and the paths used to evaluate some of the unoccupied cells for the initial solution are shown in Figure E.13.

The tableau shown in Figure E.13 indicates that material should be moved into cell A3. Both negative corners of the square path used to evaluate this cell contain 200 units, so 200 units can be moved along the path. This shift of material is reflected in Figure E.14.

Figure E.14 has only six occupied cells

after material is shifted out of cells A2 and B3. The artificial amount, ε, is added again, this time to cell B3, which has just had material shifted out of it. If, by use of ε, we should arbitrarily occupy a cell that would be negative when evaluated, we would not find the best solution. The cell with ε in it would not be evaluated because it would be occupied. Placing ε in a cell that has been vacated by an improved solution prevents this possibility. The cell evaluations for the second solution are also shown in Figure E.14. Notice that 100 units should be shifted into cell B5. This shift is made, and the third solution is presented in Figure E.15. Since all of the cell evaluations are positive, this is the optimal solution.

FIGURE E.15

Final Solution to Oversupply Problem

Source	Destination					Available supply
	W_1	W_2	W_3	W_4	W_5 Dummy	
F_A	2 200	4 (+7)	1 200	3 (+3)	0 (+5)	400
F_B	8 (+1)	2 200 + ε	6 ε	5 ε	0 100	300
F_C	6 (+2)	2 (+2)	1 (+1)	4 200	0 (+3)	200
Requirements	200	200	200	200	100	Total 900

SUMMARY

This supplement has presented a summary of linear programming by use of the graphical, simplex, and transportation methods of linear programming. Examples of maximization and minimization by all of these methods have been presented, with the exception of maximization by means of the transportation method. Degeneracy was discussed for both the simplex method and the transportation method and was illustrated for the transportation method.

DISCUSSION QUESTIONS

1. To what types of problems may linear programming be applied in operations management?
2. Explain the concept of a slack variable.
3. What is an objective function and why is it required?
4. Why is a large cost, M, assigned to artificial variables?

PROBLEMS

1. Solve the following linear programming problem by the graphical method.

$$\text{Maximize } 3X + 4Y = P$$
$$\text{subject to } \quad X + Y \leq 7{,}000$$
$$3X + 7Y \leq 42{,}000$$
$$5X + 3Y \leq 30{,}000$$
$$X \geq 0, Y \geq 0$$

2. Solve the following linear programming problem by the graphical method.

$$\text{Minimize } C = 4X + 5Y$$
$$\text{subject to } \quad X \geq 600$$
$$Y \geq 300$$
$$3X + 5Y \geq 4{,}000$$

3. Solve problem 1 by the simplex method.
4. Solve problem 2 by the simplex method.
5. Carmell Electronics, discussed in problem 16 at the end of Chapter 4, has added a third calculator, model Z28, to its product line, yet it still has the capacity stated in the problem. The Z28 requires 1 minute to mold, 4 minutes to solder, and 5 minutes to assemble. The profit contribution from each Z28 is $12.50.
   (a) Use the simplex method to find the most profitable product mix.
   (b) How much profit will the company make with this mixture?
6. (a) If Carmell Electronics can expand only one department, which should it expand?
   (b) How much capacity can be added before some other constraints are encountered?
   (c) How much profit will be made if the company adds the amount of capacity determined in part b?
7. The Johnson Seating Company produces two types of chairs. The profit from chair A is $13.00 and the profit from chair B is $10.00. Chair A requires 1 hour of manufacturing time and 1.5 hours for assembly. Chair B requires 2 hours of manufacturing and 2 hours for assembly. Demand in the market will consume all of the chair A's the company can produce up to 120. Up to 60 chair B's can be sold in addition. The company has 160 hours of manufacturing capacity and 210 hours of assembly capacity.
   (a) Find the optimal product mix, considering both the company's capacity limits

and the demand limits (graphical method or simplex method).

(b) What profit can the company expect to earn with this mixture?

8. Minimize the total transportation cost to distribute the resource from the factories to the warehouses, as shown in the figure below.

Source	Destination			Supply
	W_1	W_2	W_3	
F_A	16	30	6	3,000
F_B	10	20	18	1,500
F_C	12	24	20	1,500
Demand	2,400	1,600	1,600	6,000 / 5,600

BIBLIOGRAPHY

Bierman, Harold, Jr., Charles P. Bonini, and Warren H. Hausman. *Quantitative Analysis for Business Decisions.* 6th ed. Homewood, Ill.: Irwin, 1981.

Bowman, Edward H., and Robert B. Fetter. *Analysis for Production and Operations Management.* Homewood, Ill.: Irwin, 1967. Chaps. 3 and 4.

Cabot, A. Victor, and Donald L. Harnett. *An Introduction to Management Science.* Reading, Mass.: Addison-Wesley, 1977, Chaps. 2–4.

Levin, Richard I., and Charles A. Kirkpatrick. *Quantitative Approaches to Management.* 3d ed. New York: McGraw-Hill, 1975. Chaps. 9–11.

Siemens, Nicolai, C. H. Marting, and Frank Greenwood. *Operations Research: Planning, Operating, and Information Systems.* New York: Free Press, Macmillan, 1973. Chap. 5.

Chapter Outline
OVERVIEW OF MATERIALS MANAGEMENT ACTIVITIES

MATERIALS FLOW
Materials Flow in Manufacturing Operations / Materials Flow in Nonmanufacturing Operations

FUNCTIONS WITHIN MATERIALS MANAGEMENT
Production Control / Traffic / Receiving / Shipping

PURCHASING
Categories of Purchasing Needs / Objectives and Responsibilities / Purchasing Steps / Value Analysis / Make-or-Buy Analysis / Vendor Relations

INVENTORY
Reasons for Inventory / Movement Inventory / The Trend Toward Operating with Less Inventory

SINGLE-PERIOD AND MULTIPLE-PERIOD INVENTORIES
Marginal Analysis for Single-Period Inventories / *Application: Example of Marginal Analysis to Determine the Amount of Single-Period Inventory to Stock* / Multiple-Period Inventory Systems / Inventory Systems for Independent-Demand Items / ABC Classification / *Application: Example of ABC Classification* / Management of Dependent-Demand Inventories

JUST-IN-TIME PRODUCTION
Operations Management in Action: JUST-IN-TIME PURCHASING AT STANLEY-VIDMAR, INC.

Summary / Solved Problem / Discussion Questions / Problems / Bibliography

KEY TERMS

Materials management
Logistics Management
Physical distribution
   management
Production control
Receiving department
Shipping department
Purchasing department
Value analysis
Make-or-buy decision
Raw materials

Finished goods
   inventories
In-process inventories
Movement inventory
Single-period inventory
Multiple-period
   inventory
Critical probability
Independent demand
Dependent demand

Fixed-quantity
   inventory system
Reorder level
Two-bin system
Fixed-interval inventory
   system
Joint-replenishment
   items
Minimum-maximum
   inventory system
Budget allocation
   inventory system

ABC classification or
   distribution by value
Annual dollar usage
Material requirements
   planning (MRP)
Just-in-time (JIT)
   production
Zero inventories
Stockless production
Kanban system

Chapter 5

OVERVIEW OF MATERIALS MANAGEMENT ACTIVITIES

Aggregate planning, discussed in the previous chapter, assists operations managers to develop plans for the efficient utilization of resources to provide goods and services in accordance with the corporate strategy. The discussion of aggregate planning focused primarily on capacity—how much to have and the most economical way to utilize that capacity to serve demand. Aggregate plans determine to a general degree the production rate and the amount of inventory of the production system's output that will be maintained over time. Many subsequent details must be decided to implement the general plan efficiently. When will each type of product be produced? At what production rates for each product? In what quantities? Which finished goods will be held in inventory? To achieve the planned production rate, adequate quantities of all of the necessary inputs must be obtained at the proper time and must be of acceptable quality. The transformation and throughput of all components must be coordinated through what is sometimes a complex web of organizational units.

Materials-related decisions and capacity-related decisions must be coordinated to make efficient use of resources. Both the necessary material inputs and the necessary capacity must be available before transformations can be performed to provide goods or services. An organization needs to know when materials will be available before it can accurately schedule use of capacity. It has to have some idea when capacity will be available before it can know when materials will be needed. Sizable companies that buy large quantities of items over extended periods can sometimes exert enough pressure on suppliers to obtain materials almost when they want them. Companies that do not make large purchases may have to fit their schedules to the dates on which materials can be obtained, or purchase with sufficient lead time so that materials will be available when the company needs them.

The objective in materials management is not simply to make sure that plenty of raw materials and supplies are available for input and plenty of finished goods are available as output. The objective is rather to have little, if any, more than will be efficient and to obtain or produce this amount at the proper time. The efficient amount and the proper time, however, will be affected by such factors as rising prices, possible work stoppages, and a host of other factors. A firm must be careful not to overinvest in inventories that tie up capital and may become obsolete, yet it must take the proper care not to run out of supplies (thus idling people and equipment) or products (thus losing sales and customers).

This chapter introduces some of the organizational functions that must be performed to manage materials in both manufacturing and nonmanufacturing operations. The concepts of independent and dependent demand are discussed, as are four systems for managing independent-demand inventory. Then materials requirements planning, or MRP, is introduced as an inventory system for managing dependent-demand items—components or raw materials that are subsequently assembled into other items. The two chapters following examine in greater detail the management of independent- and dependent-demand materials.

MATERIALS FLOW

Materials Flow in Manufacturing Operations

The introductory description of an operations system as a collection of inputs, transformations, and outputs is most clearly applicable to manufacturing operations producing tangible items. One of the most apparent features of large factories is *movement*. A factory is a dynamic, vibrant center of activity. Trucks, barges, railroad cars, or other vehicles arrive with supplies and leave with completed or partially completed products. Large numbers of people and a wide variety of equipment may be involved in materials handling within the factory. Materials are moved from one operation to another as the inputs are transformed into outputs by the manufacturing process. Of course, the purpose of the factory's existence is to make the utility and value of the outputs greater than those of the inputs.

Movement of some of the tangible inputs and outputs into, through, and out of a manufacturing operation is summarized in Figure 5.1. The input portion of materials flow involves such activities as purchasing, traffic control, and receiving. Activities associated with materials and their flow within the factory may include production control, inventory control, and materials handling.

FIGURE 5.1

Materials Flow Through a Manufacturing Company

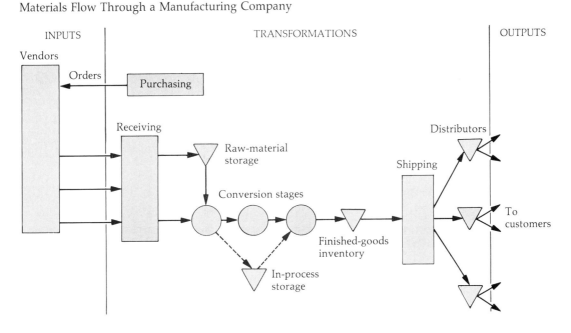

Output-related activities may include packaging, shipping, and warehousing. Some companies have attempted to improve the coordination of materials-related activities by including several, perhaps all, of these activities in one unified organization.

The term *materials management* is sometimes used to refer to a broad organizational unit that oversees purchasing, production control, and physical distribution of materials. Robert Ballot defines *materials management* as the "coordinated function responsible to plan for, acquire, store, move, and control materials and final products to optimize usage of facilities, personnel, capital funds, and to provide customer service in line with corporate goals."[1] But there is no universal agreement about the activities that are included in materials management. Sometimes the term is used to refer to only those activities related to input materials: purchasing, traffic control, and inventory control. The terms *logistics management* and *physical distribution management* sometimes are used to refer to shipping, transportation, and warehousing activities associated with getting adequate quantities of the finished product to the proper place to ensure customer service.

Whether the persons who engage in these activities report to a single manager or to several managers, materials-related activities must be coordinated

[1]Robert B. Ballot, *Materials Management: A Results Approach* (New York: American Management Association, 1971), p. 6.

if the company is to be successful. The major concept to keep in mind is that all of the materials-related suborganizations shown in Figure 5.1 make up a system of interrelated components. Unifying some or all of them under a single manager constitutes an attempt to make the coordination more effective. We shall use the term *materials management* to refer to this broad group of activities even though the responsibility may be divided among many organizations.

Materials management is becoming increasingly important. Faster transportation and multinational marketing have expanded competition for consumers' business. This intensified competition exerts pressure to reduce costs and to improve the availability of products. Automation and large capital investment often are used to raise production efficiency and to reduce costs. But improved production technology will reduce cost only if it can be kept running. Insufficient quantity or quality materials can idle expensive equipment and skilled personnel. To protect against materials shortages, a company can hold inventories of necessary materials, yet inflation and scarcities have made this an expensive option. Companies are under pressure to use new materials management techniques, perhaps employing the computer and rapid communications to manage efficiently their material inputs, throughputs, and outputs.

Materials Flow in Nonmanufacturing Operations

Materials functions exist in many nonmanufacturing operations as well as in manufacturing operations. Since we are dealing here with materials and inventory, however, we shall confine our discussion to operations that deal with tangible items, even though some of the organizations may not perform manufacturing operations. Service operations that provide advice or counseling have no tangible item to purchase or inventory other than a few office supplies, so that materials are a very minor consideration.

Operations that provide repair services, such as automotive and appliance repair centers, may require sizable inventories of replacement parts and supplies. A hospital, which is a type of repair operation, needs inputs of food, linens, drugs, and medical supplies, many of which are inventoried.[2] The transportation and output are not so obvious in some nonmanufacturing systems as they are in manufacturing operations. An airline, for example, purchases fuel as an input, but it does not become a desirable output. The fuel is consumed (or converted to less desirable by-products) by the aircraft as it provides its service. The intended output is the transfer of passengers and/or cargo to a new location that represents a higher utility to the people who pay the bill. Materials management in this type of operation primarily is concerned with the input side of Figure 5.1.

Materials management in other types of operations is concerned primarily with activities relating to the output side of the materials-flow chain. Whole-

---

[2]Dean S. Ammer, *Purchasing and Materials Management for Health Care Institutions* (Lexington, Mass.: D. C. Heath, 1975).

salers, retailers, and military supply organizations perform little or no manufacturing, and therefore are concerned with obtaining finished goods and distributing them through a logistics system so that their ultimate use is facilitated. The primary operation within these systems is a change of location or transfer of ownership. Since these organizations do not perform manufacturing processes, they are not involved with the control of production or of raw material or in-processs inventories.

FUNCTIONS WITHIN MATERIALS MANAGEMENT

Continuous manufacturing operations usually involve all aspects of materials management. Regardless of the way a company may be organized, several materials-related functions probably are performed by some organizational unit. A study reported by *Purchasing* magazine in 1976 asked companies to indicate the functions that were included in their formal materials management systems. The resulting percentages are indicated in Table 5.1. You can see that inspection of materials is seldom controlled by a materials manager. This function usually is the responsibility of quality control (discussed in Chapter 11).

Some of the activities shown in Table 5.1 are often performed by personnel under the direction of the operations manager. The organizational structure of a company and assignment of responsibilities depend on the capabilities of employees and the needs of the organization as perceived by its decision makers. The complexity of the company's materials activities and their effectiveness under any other organizational form will certainly affect the desire to combine

Table 5.1
COMPOSITION OF FORMAL MATERIALS MANAGEMENT SYSTEMS

Function	Approximate Percentage of Respondent Companies with Formal MM Systems that Include the Function
Purchasing	100
Inventory control	90
Production control	85
Inbound traffic	74
Receiving	74
In-plant storage	74
Outbound traffic	65
Materials handling	60
Outside warehousing	55
Distribution	30
Incoming inspection	10
Outgoing inspection	5

Source: Somerby Dowst, "Stormy Economy Brings Payoffs for MM Systems," Purchasing, February 24, 1976, pp. 59–61.

any of these responsibilities. Whether the people responsible for the functions report to a materials manager, a purchasing manager, or an operations manager, these functions must be performed and coordinated to ensure efficient operations. An operations manager must know how these functions are linked in the organization so that the company can perform effectively.

Companies organize in a variety of ways, so it is impossible to name specific department titles and the exact responsibilities such departments will have. We shall discuss materials-related activities in production control, traffic, receiving, shipping, purchasing, and inventory control. The first four are most likely to occur only in manufacturing operations and will be briefly discussed in that context. Purchasing and inventory control occur in both manufacturing and nonmanufacturing operations. Since these activities are almost universal, they will be discussed in greater detail after the first four topics have been outlined.

Production Control

Production control develops short-range operations plans and schedules from longer-term plans. In doing so it performs the following functions:

1. Scheduling production operations in accordance with the scheduled availability of materials, the anticipated backlog of work, the criticality of need for the product, and the lead time for production.
2. Dispatching or directing the production departments and materials control to perform the necessary operations to meet the production schedule.
3. Issuing materials to operating departments, when this function is not performed by a materials control department.
4. Monitoring the progress of work in operating departments, expediting the work of those that are behind schedule, and deexpediting the work of some departments when schedules are changed.

Traffic

The cost of transportation and the time it takes to receive their inputs or deliver their outputs are important to both manufacturing and nonmanufacturing firms. Selection of locations for a firm's facilities (discussed in Chapter 12) is inherently related to these costs and lead times. After the location for a facility has been selected, the cost and transportation time for its inbound and outbound shipments can be controlled to some extent by the firm's traffic department.

The traffic department is responsible for selecting and contracting with carriers to transport incoming and outgoing shipments. This responsibility may include:

1. Selecting the transportation mode: parcel post, bus service, air freight, rail freight in full carloads (CL) or less than full carloads (LCL), motor freight in full truckloads (TL) or less than full truckloads (LTL), freight forwarder, water freight, the company's own fleet, or other means of transportation.

2. Arranging shipping terms, such as FOB (free on board) the seller's plant or FOB the buyer's plant. FOB the seller's plant means the seller loads the goods and the buyer pays all other transportation costs. FOB the buyer's plant means the seller pays the cost of shipping the goods there.
3. Maintaining familiarity with regulations of the Interstate Commerce Commission or other agencies and with freight rates between various points for the commodity classifications of interest, so that the best routing and mode may be selected consistent with the cost and criticality of need for the item.
4. Auditing of freight bills to see that billing is proper.
5. Coordinating arrivals and departures of shipments so that demurrage costs—charges for delay of rail cars beyond some normal time allowed for unloading—are reasonable.

Receiving

Some subunit of the organization—usually a *receiving department*—must be responsible for receiving shipments of incoming materials and for maintenance, repair, and operating (MRO) supplies. The receiving department is responsible for:

1. Unloading and identifying incoming shipments.
2. Preparing a receiving report.
3. Dispatching the items to the point where they are to be inspected, stored, or used. (Sometimes materials handling is reduced by performing inspection of purchased goods in the receiving department or at the point where the items are to be used.)

Shipping

The responsibilities of the *shipping department* may include:

1. Selecting from inventory those items to be shipped to the customer ("order picking").
2. Packaging and labeling the shipment.
3. Loading shipments onto vehicles.
4. Managing the company's fleet of vehicles.

PURCHASING

The *purchasing department* spends most of the money in the typical large manufacturing company. Procurement of goods and services accounts for more than half of these companies' expenditures, as depicted in Figure 5.2. For this reason, purchasing is usually placed high in a company's organization so that it has direct communication with top management. In a survey conducted in 1971 by *Purchasing* magazine, 500 purchasing executives were asked to whom they reported. The results, shown in Table 5.2, indicate that 72 percent report to a vice-president or the president of the firm. Obviously the acquisition of materials and supplies is important to many firms.

FIGURE 5.2

Distribution of Revenue Dollars in Large
Manufacturing Firms

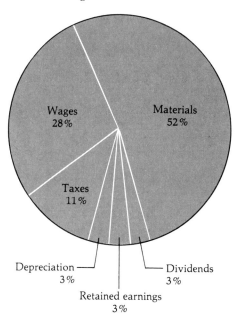

Source: William R. Stelzer, Jr., *Materials Management*,
p. 23. © 1970 by Prentice-Hall, Inc. Published by Prentice-
Hall, Inc., Englewood Cliffs, N.J. 07632.

Table 5.2
PURCHASING EXECUTIVES RESPONSES TO QUESTION: "TO WHOM DO YOU REPORT?"

Officer to Whom Survey Respondent Reported	Percentage of Respondents
President	26
Manufacturing VP	22
Executive VP	13
Materials manager	9
Procurement VP	7
Financial VP	4
Other (includes general manager or administrative services manager)	19

Source: Purchasing, *December 9, 1971, p. 59.*

Categories of Purchasing Needs

Not all purchases need to be handled by a member of the purchasing department. Purchases can be made under many circumstances. Three general categories of purchases are:

1. Low-quantity or small, infrequent purchases that are of small monetary value.
2. One-time or infrequent purchases of significant monetary value.
3. High-volume purchases that may be used over time or in multiple locations.

The cost of processing a purchase order may sometimes be more than the cost of the item to be purchased. A company may establish a policy of permitting its personnel to purchase category 1 items directly for themselves. For example, suppliers may invoice the company for items costing less than $15 just by enclosing a receipt showing that an authorized company employee has received the item. No purchase order is necessary.

Items in categories 2 and 3 represent sizable expenditures, and it usually is recommended that they be purchased for the company only by authorized purchasing agents or buyers. Purchasing agents' or buyers' jobs permit them time to find potential vendors and negotiate with them. Also, purchasing personnel are familiar with the legal ramifications of contracting for goods or services.

Items that are purchased in large quantities—category 3 items—might be purchased on blanket purchase orders. A blanket purchase order specifies some total amount to be purchased over some stated time, from several months to several years. It does not necessarily specify when the items are to be delivered. Purchases of this type allow the buyer to use the purchasing power of large quantities to obtain discounts. They also give suppliers assurance of some future business that can be used to fill in low portions of the demand forecast. Suppliers can be assured of a volume of business that may change the types of tooling they plan to use or the aggregate plans they make. For example, they can decide whether to produce ahead of schedule items that will be demanded sometime in the future instead of reducing the work force.

Objectives and Responsibilities

Some of the objectives and responsibilities of the purchasing department are:

1. To locate, evaluate, and develop sources of the materials, supplies, and services that the company needs.
2. To ensure good working relations with these sources in such matters as quality, delivery, payments, and exchanges or returns.
3. To seek out new materials and products and new sources of better products and materials so that they can be evaluated for possible use by the company.
4. To purchase wisely the items that the company needs at the best price consistent with quality requirements and to handle the necessary negotiations to carry out this activity. The best value does not always represent

the lowest initial cost, so products should also be evaluated for their expected lifetime, serviceability, and maintenance cost.

5. To initiate if necessary and to cooperate in cost-reduction programs, value analyses, make-or-buy studies, market analyses, and long-range planning. Purchasing should keep abreast of trends and projections in prices and availability of the inputs that a company must have.

6. To work to maintain an effective communication linkage between departments within the company and between the company and its suppliers or potential suppliers.

7. To keep top management aware of costs involved in the company's procurements and any market changes that could affect the company's profits or growth potential.

Purchasing Steps

Some of the steps that may be followed in the procurement process are:

1. Receive requisitions from other functional departments or inventory planners.
2. Define product specifications or commercial grade that must be met.
3. Group like items or items that can be supplied by the same vendor.
4. Ask for bids on the specified materials.
5. Evaluate bids in terms of quality, price, and likelihood of delivery.
6. Select supplier(s).
7. Follow up with the vendor to see if the order will arrive on time.
8. Follow up internally to see that the order has arrived and is of specified quality.
9. Keep records on punctuality, price, and quality for vendor evaluations.

Before consummating contracts for the purchase of large volumes of identical items, perhaps in consultation with other functional areas, the buyer should decide whether to use a single source for the product or more than one source. Some factors to be taken into consideration are listed in Table 5.3.

Table 5.3
ADVANTAGES OF PURCHASING FROM SINGLE SOURCE VS. MULTIPLE SOURCES

Single Source	Multiple Sources
Bargaining power and likelihood of quantity discounts are increased	Risk of interruption in supply is reduced
Paperwork and coordination effort are reduced	Competition for future business is stimulated (a single supplier may develop a monopoly)
Supplier is more likely to regard himself as a partner.	
The number of sets of special tooling required for production is reduced	New supplier can be evaluated and may become a superior source, perhaps a new sole source

Source: Adapted from Dean S. Ammer, Materials Management, *4th ed. (Homewood, Ill.: Richard D. Irwin, 1980), p. 415–417.*

Purchasing activities naturally involve other departments, in efforts to reduce the cost of materials and supplies. Two of these activities are value analysis and make-or-buy decisions.

Value Analysis

Value analysis is an organized effort to reduce the costs of purchased parts and materials. It involves a study of items or services that are to be purchased in sufficient quantities to justify study. Value analysis seeks to answer such questions as: What is the function of the item? Is the function necessary? Are all of its features necessary? Can a standard part that will serve the function be found? What does the item cost? What else will perform the equivalent function? What does this substitute cost? The concept sometimes is applied by a team or task force that may involve engineering, production, and purchasing in a review of existing and new products to ensure that expenditures result in the receipt of appropriate value.

Make-or-Buy Analysis

An important issue that must be addressed is the *make-or-buy decision*. A company must decide if it is going to perform the actual manufacturing operations or if it is going to contract with another company to be a supplier. If the company uses only a few units of a particular item and special equipment is needed to produce it, the company probably will look for a vendor. If several companies purchase the item from the same vendor, the volume of demand may be great enough so that the vendor can sell it at a lower cost than the purchasing company would have to pay to produce it. A small volume of demand for a product that no other companies are buying, however, may not be attractive enough to induce a vendor to produce it. Some companies both make and buy to ensure that they will have a source of supply if the vendor has a strike or fire or goes out of business. Several factors are involved in the make-or-buy decision. Some of those that may lead a company to make a product or component internally instead of purchasing it are:

1. Lower cost, because the company does not have to pay the vendor's overhead and profit.
2. Assurance of availability.
3. Opportunity to control quality.
4. Availability of equipment and expertise.
5. Desire to preserve confidentiality.
6. Savings on transportation costs.

The decision to obtain supplies and components from outside, either by subcontracting or by purchasing components from vendors, enables a company to utilize its own capacity for other purposes. (The subcontracting of work to other firms as a means of varying capacity was discussed in the previous chapter, on aggregate planning.) On the other hand, it also makes a company dependent on the vendor's effectiveness in such activities as scheduling and quality control.

Vendor Relations

The twentieth century has brought with it complex business relationships in which one company is dependent on many other companies for goods and services. Many raw materials and components that are part of a company's product are supplied by other companies that may be remote, even located in other countries. Many companies are retailers or wholesalers that have no production operations as such. Some companies only assemble components fabricated by vendors. Service companies may use supplies that are purchased from other companies. Vendor relations are important in nearly all types of operations.

It is important that the purchasing department work to ensure that specifications are sufficiently clear and detailed, so that the desired performance is obtained from vendors without lost time and so that good working relations are maintained. The company should review the performance of vendors through some type of vendor rating plan. Designs, specifications, and deviations from quality standards should be rapidly and accurately communicated. A company can help itself and its vendors by passing along helpful information about product quality, standard practices, and useful tricks of the trade. A company must consider factors such as those listed in Table 5.3 when deciding whether to deal with multiple vendors or only one vendor for a particular item. Some companies are adopting the approach of using long-term agreements with only one supplier for some items and working closely with that vendor by supplying long range production planning information and perhaps technical assistance. This arrangement is often used as part of a "just-in-time" production program, which is discussed later in this chapter and in Chapter 8.

INVENTORY

Whether a company buys components and products or produces them, it will be faced with decisions about inventory. Inventory is any idle resource held for future use. Whenever the inputs and outputs of a company are not used as soon as they become available, inventory is present. Service operations and job shops tend to have small investments in inventory. For many companies, however, inventory accounts for a large percentage of assets. Wholesale distributors and retail companies may own little more than inventory, particularly if they lease their buildings.

Each unique entity—such as a part, subassembly, or type of raw material—that a company identifies for purposes of control may be called a "stockkeeping item," simply an "item," or sometimes a "stockkeeping unit." The first two terms are preferred. The latter term can cause some confusion, because the word "units" is used to express the quantity of a particular stockkeeping item.

We shall use the term "units" to refer to an amount or quantity of an item. The term "item" will be used to refer to a unique type of material that is inventoried.

Large manufacturing companies may have 100,000 or more different items to maintain in inventory and control. This number alone is large, but when it is multiplied by the number of units of each item that may be on hand, it can be seen that the number of units and the investment in inventory of such a company is tremendous.

The value of inventory in the average manufacturing company is equivalent to about 1.6 months' sales or 13 percent of annual sales; in a retail company it is equivalent to about 1.4 months' sales or 12 percent of annual sales; in a wholesale company it is equivalent to about 1.2 months' sales or 10 percent of annual sales.[3] During the five years 1979 through 1983 the after-tax profits for manufacturing companies averaged 4.7 percent of sales. This figure indicates that they had more than 2.8 years' profits invested in inventory.[4] Why do companies invest so heavily in idle resources?

Reasons for Inventory

We have seen from our study of aggregate planning that a company's intermediate-range strategy may involve the intentional use of extensive amounts of inventory to make capacity utilization more uniform. Inventory can also be valuable for a variety of other reasons.

Reduction in Lead Time   Inventory enables a company to reduce lead time in meeting demand. A customer who requests a product and is told that it will be ordered and should be available in about a month is likely to go to another source. The company may miss sales if it does not maintain finished goods ready for purchase or maintain an inventory of components that can be used to reduce the time required to meet demand.

Spreading of Fixed Costs   Inventory enables a company to purchase or produce items in economic quantities. If there is a fixed charge for delivering materials or if there is a fixed cost to set up production equipment, a company may wish to spread the fixed cost over enough units so that the unit cost is reduced. If quantity discounts are available, a company may purchase in quantities that minimize the total cost of purchasing and holding the material until it is used. If the price of an item is increasing or will soon increase, a company may wish to purchase large quantities in order to take advantage of the lower price.

Stabilization   Inventory can be used to stabilize production and employment rates when demand is not uniform. The discussion of aggregate planning in

[3]U.S. Department of Commerce, Bureau of Economic Analysis, *Survey of Current Business. 62 no. 1* (Jan. 1982), Table S–3; 62, *no.* 6 (June 1982) Table S–3; 64 *no.* 5 (May 1984) Table 5–3.
[4]U.S. Department of Commerce, Bureau of Economic Analysis, *Survey of Current Business*, 62, *no. 1* (January 1982), Table S–15; 62, *no. 6* (June 1982), Table S–15; and 64, *no. 5* (May 1984), Table S–15.

the previous chapter illustrated the economies afforded by the accumulation of inventory when demand is low but will increase.

Protection Against Underestimates of Demand   Inventory can be used as protection from unexpected surges in demand. In Chapter 3 we saw that forecasting is not an exact science. Inventory serves as insurance in case demand is greater than expected in some period. If demand is less than expected in some period, we will bear the expense of holding the product until some later period. Of course, there is also some risk that demand will not arise even in later periods, and we will be left with our warehouses full of obsolete products.

Protection Against Strikes and Shortages   Inventory can also serve as protection against temporary shortages of supply. Having *raw materials* or supplies on hand allows time to find new sources of supply or to reinstate old sources in case of a strike, flood, or fire, or if for other reasons we are not able to (or do not desire to) obtain a product from the usual source.

Flexibility in Production Rates   Inventory can be used to decouple various stages of production, just as it can be used to allow the production rate to differ from the demand rate. One production operation might run at a much more rapid rate than the next stage. Accumulating in-process inventory between the two stages allows both processes to run at their full capabilities. The faster process will not be run for the same amount of time, so it will be available for work on other products.

Many of the reasons for carrying inventory can be related to materials flow in manufacturing, discussed earlier and depicted by Figure 5.1. *Finished-goods inventories* (outputs) can be used to divorce the operations system from variations in demand so that the system can operate more economically and with greater stability. They also shorten lead times to achieve more rapid response to demand and protect against forecast errors. *In-process inventories* are items held in some intermediate stage of conversion from raw material (input) to the final form in which material leaves the transformation system. In-process inventories help decouple steps in the transformation process so that production rates and volumes can vary at the various steps. In-process inventories can also be held for components and completed subassemblies so that a wide variety of finished products may be assembled from a relatively small supply of optional components. For example, an automobile manufacturer can assemble the combination of body, engine, air conditioner, radio, and other accessories that a customer wants from inventories of these subassemblies. The customer does not have to wait for raw materials (steel, glass, wire, cloth, and so on) to be converted into an automobile. Yet the manufacturing company does not have to maintain an inventory of automobiles with every possible combination of components, some of which may never be sold. Raw materials and purchased-component inventories (inputs) help to ensure a supply of inputs and enable a company to purchase in economic quantities.

Movement Inventory

Some inventory is not readily apparent because it is not intentionally being held in a warehouse, but still it represents goods that are owned and not being used. If a company moves goods between several stock locations or if transportation times are long, the company may have sizable amounts of goods in transit—or "pipeline inventory." Suppose that before its goods are actually sold a company moves them from the factory to a central warehouse, then to a regional warehouse and eventually to the customer. If the average transportation time required for all these moves is eight days and the company sells an average of 1,000 units per day, there will be an average of 8,000 units in transit. A company might try to ship by a faster mode of transportation or reduce the number of shipment steps to reduce the costs of its *movement inventory.*

The Trend Toward Operating with Less Inventory

Even though there are reasons that a company might want to have some inventory, it must be on guard to see that it does not accumulate a great investment in inventory that is expensive to maintain. As a company tries to use its resources wisely, it should explore alternatives that reduce some of the reasons for holding inventory, rather than simply holding more inventory "just in case." A trend in the past several years has been for companies to try to hold less inventory than they previously did. Companies have found that they can sometimes reduce the lead times required to obtain materials and to produce products, so that they can operate with less inventory and still serve their customers effectively. Sometimes companies can reduce their setup or procurement costs so that they can economically operate with more numerous but smaller lots, thus keeping inventory low. Many companies have worked with their suppliers to build more reliable sources of quality materials so that it is not necessary to keep so much inventory to protect from supply shortages or scrap losses. For example, General Motors reduced the amount of steel in its stamping plants from 21 days' supply down to 2.5 days' supply. Overall, the company reduced its worldwide inventories from a staggering $9.7 billion in 1981 to $7.5 billion in 1983.[5]

Inventories that are to be held might not all be managed in the same way. Selection of an inventory control method depends on a number of things: the length of time the company intends to maintain the inventory, the type of demand it is to serve, the cost of the item, the degree of control desired, and so on.

SINGLE-PERIOD AND MULTIPLE-PERIOD INVENTORIES

Single-period inventory involves items that will be stocked only once, with no intention of restocking them after they are consumed. *Multiple-period inventory*

---

[5]"Detroit's Merry-Go-Round," *Business Week*, September 12, 1983, p. 75.

involves items that will be maintained in inventory long enough so that units that have been consumed may be replenished. The amount and timing of future replenishments can be varied to adjust the inventory level in response to demand. Multiple-period inventories are kept for most finished products and their components, and are much more common than single-period inventories.

Marginal Analysis for Single-Period Inventories

Consider a business that is to select the quantity of an item to buy when there is only one period in which demand for the item can occur and the level of that demand is not known. Assume, however, that a probability distribution for the various levels of demand that might occur is available or can be estimated. Assume also that the company will not be able to purchase additional quantities of the item if it does not buy enough the first time. If a unit of the product is not sold, there will be a cost to the company of C_o for overstocking. This cost is the amount spent for the unit less any salvage value. The company will suffer an opportunity cost of C_u per unit for understocking. C_u is the contribution to profit from a unit. The company should add units to the order quantity so long as the expected cost of adding the last unit is less than expected gain. That is, the order should be increased so long as the expected cost of overstocking is less than the expected cost of understocking. These two costs are equal when the last unit added to the order is the unit of indifference. The company should increase the order size up to but not beyond this unit. The objective, then, is to find which unit is the last that the company should add to the order.

Let $P(D)$ be the probability that the level of demand will be greater than or equal to a particular number of units, D. $P(D)$ then is a value from a cumulative probability distribution with cumulation beginning at the right-hand tail or highest possible level of demand. The company should add the Dth unit if the expected cost of understocking for this unit is greater than the expected cost of overstocking for it. That is,

$$P(D) \cdot C_u > [1 - P(D)]C_o \tag{5.1}$$

$P(D)$ will decrease as the order size is increased from the minimum possible level of demand until, at some point, the two sides of expression 5.1 become equal. The optimum order size is associated with the $P(D)$ that makes the two expected costs equal. Let us identify the *critical probability* that makes the two costs equal as $P(D)^*$. $P(D)^*$ can be found by expression 5.2:

$$P(D)^*C_u = [1 - P(D)^*]C_o$$
$$P(D)^*C_u = C_o - C_oP(D)^* \tag{5.2}$$
$$P(D)^*(C_u + C_o) = C_o$$

$$P(D)^* = \frac{C_o}{C_u + C_o}$$

The best quantity to stock is the highest possible quantity that has a cumulative probability of demand that is greater than or equal to the critical probability.

APPLICATION

Example of Marginal Analysis to Determine the Amount of Single-Period Inventory to Stock

The Lake Nocee Department Store has an opportunity to purchase a special shipment of tableware at $28 a set. These sets of tableware are to be sold for $35 as a special promotion during the store's thirty-fifth anniversary sale. Nocee must purchase the item in units of a dozen sets. Tableware is not part of the store's normal product line, so if the items are not sold during the anniversary sale they will be sold to The Bargain Basement for $22.50 per set. Caleb McKinney, a buyer for the store, has estimated the probability distribution for demand for the item, as shown in Table 5.4. McKinney solved for:

$$C_o = \$28 - \$22.50 = \$5.50$$
$$C_u = \$35 - \$28 = \$7.00$$

Then

$$P(D)^* = \frac{C_o}{C_u + C_o} = \frac{\$5.50}{\$7.00 + \$5.50} = 0.44$$

By referring to the cumulative probability column in Table 5.4, McKinney found the largest quantity with $P(D) \geq 0.44$ was 8, so he ordered 8 dozen sets of tableware.

Table 5.4
PROBABILITY OF DEMAND FOR TABLEWARE, LAKE NOCEE DEPARTMENT STORE

Demand (D) (dozens)	Probability of Demand [P(D)] (i.e., probability demand will be at this level)	Cumulative Probability of Demand [P(D)] (i.e., probability demand will be at least this amount)
4 or fewer	0	1.00
5	0.10	1.00
6	0.15	0.90
7	0.25	0.75
8	0.20	0.50 ←
9	0.15	0.30
10	0.10	0.15
11	0.05	0.05
12 or more	0	0

Multiple-Period Inventory Systems

Many continuous manufacturing operations and other companies have standardized products that are sold for many sales periods. Some job shops have repeat orders for the same or similar items so that they have fairly stable utilization of certain raw materials and components. Single-period analysis is not appropriate for such situations, so other models and inventory systems have been developed to assist in the management of inventories of such items. The type of demand that is to be supplied from inventory determines the type of inventory system that is appropriate. Multiple-period inventories can be classified according to whether they are primarily intended to serve independent demand or dependent demand. This distinction has become increasingly important in the past decade because advances in electronic data processing equipment and software have made it possible for large, complex companies to take dependencies of demand into account.

Independent Demand   *Independent demand* is demand for an item in its current form (rather than for a kit or assembly of which the item becomes a part) from some user outside the organization that has the inventory. The item may be a finished good, sold for use as is; a repair or service part; or a subassembly that some other organization will further transform into a final product. Independent demand is the demand for outputs of the operations system, shown in Figure 5.1 as arrows leaving the transformation block. Since the demand rate is determined by some entity outside the producing organization, demand is not known for certain and must be forecast. Independent demand forecasting was the primary topic in Chapter 3.

Dependent Demand   *Dependent demand,* as the name implies, is directly related to the demand for another item or other items. It is the requirement for any of the parts or materials necessary to make some other item. Therefore, instead of requiring forecasts, dependent demand for an item can be derived or calculated from the demand for the assembly or assemblies of which it becomes a part. Dependent demands are shown in Figure 5.1 as input arrows and arrows connecting processing stages or in-process inventories within the transformation block. Most usage rates other than the rate of final output from the operations system are dependent on other usage rates (i.e., dependent demands).

Differences Between Independent and Dependent Inventory Systems   Independent-demand systems supply demand outside the organization; dependent-demand systems supply requirements inside the organization. Consequently the need for independent-demand items must be estimated. A large percentage of many independent-demand inventories may therefore consist of items accumulated to provide protection from uncertainty. Independent-demand inventories enable the organization to supply an external user—to make a sale. Lack of sufficient available products may result in significant loss of profit from the direct sale and future sales that may be lost as a result of customer ill will. Since companies don't know exactly when a customer will want a product, independent-demand systems are designed to keep material available almost all of the time. About the only time material is not available is when sales are greater than anticipated and a stockout occurs.

Most dependent-demand items are used to produce independent-demand items. Since dependent-demand inventories supply requirements within the organization, there is less uncertainty about the amount that is required. The requirements for dependent items occur only when the company produces salable products or subassemblies that go into salable products. The number of dependent items required is directly related to the number of higher-level assemblies the company intends to make (plus allowances for scrap and other losses). The company may forecast inaccurately the number of salable products that should be made. But once a company decides how many finished products it will make, it can determine fairly accurately the number of dependent items it needs.

Some items are demanded both independently and dependently. That is, some items are used within the organization and some are sold externally. Some items may be used in a variety of products, so that the demand for them is fairly uniform over time. These items often are managed as independent items even though all or part of their use is dependent. We will describe and compare some of the general features of independent-demand inventory systems and then briefly discuss material requirements planning (MRP), the system for managing dependent-demand items.

Inventory Systems for Independent-Demand Items

An inventory system is a set of procedures that indicate how much material should be added to inventory at what time, and the necessary personnel and equipment to carry out the procedures effectively. Sometimes mathematical models are used to determine the most economical amounts to add to inventory and when they should be added. Mathematical models to help manage independent-demand inventory items have been used since approximately 1915. Since then, many complex and sophisticated models have been developed and proposed for use. Complex models, however, often apply to a rather specialized, restrictive set of conditions. We shall discuss only the more general characteristics of basic models and the types of systems that employ them.

Some companies must have available the exact item that the customer calls for or the exact item that is used at some stage in the company's processing. They cannot select something that is somewhat related. For example, if a man needs a picture tube for a nineteen-inch Brand X color television, he cannot substitute a twenty-one-inch replacement tube.

Since companies may stock thousands of different items, they need some fairly simple and reliable way to indicate when each item should be purchased and in what quantity. Remember that the usual objective of systems to control independent-demand items is to make the item available most of the time.

Fixed-Quantity System   A *fixed-quantity inventory system* adds the same pre-established amount to the inventory of an item each time it is replenished. Chapter 6 discusses in detail how the lowest-cost replacement quantity—that is, the economic order quantity or EOQ—is determined. Orders are placed when the inventory on hand and already on order is reduced to an amount called the *reorder level.* A graph of the inventory level over time in a fixed-quantity system

FIGURE 5.3

Inventory Level in a Fixed-Quantity System

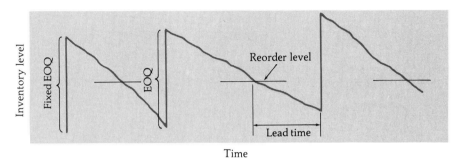

is shown in Figure 5.3. The amount on hand and on order should be considered if the replenishment lead time is long enough so that the time to place another order may occur before some previous order has arrived. Notice that the same amount is added to inventory level at each replenishment cycle. The time between replenishments varies in accordance with the rate of use between orders. The reorder level normally is set high enough so that the system does not run out of stock unless the use rate during the reorder lead time (i.e., the time between placing an order and the time it arrives) is much greater than expected.

The fixed-quantity system is appropriate for many items that have relatively constant use rates. This type of system requires some means of determining when the reorder level has been reached. When the item is expensive enough to justify the expense of reporting each inventory transaction (i.e., additions and withdrawals), a running balance may be maintained. These perpetual inventory records may be kept by manual methods or by computer systems. A punched card or other data entry method can be used to report the part number and the amount withdrawn or added. When the inventory balance reaches the reorder level, the computer may print out a purchase order.

Sometimes other methods are used to signal when the reorder level has been reached. A ring may be painted at a certain height in the storage bin or a colored paper may be placed at the appropriate level in a stack of material, or some other method may be used to reduce the paperwork required to maintain inventory.

One inventory system with a very simple way to signal that more material should be ordered is the *two-bin system*. This system is useful for inexpensive items that cost more to count and monitor than it costs simply to use some approximate reorder level. A two-bin system has a designated location such as a physically separate bin, a hold area with a painted outline on the floor, or a portion of the larger bin below a painted line, to hold stock for use during the reorder lead time. The reorder level is signaled and a replenishment order is placed when the normal working stock is exhausted and the company begins using stock from this "second bin." When the order arrives, the second bin is refilled and the remainder of the order is placed in working stock.

Fixed-Interval System   Replenishment of inventory can be triggered by the passage of a given amount of time rather than by inventory level. In a *fixed-interval inventory system*, the inventory level is checked on a uniform time frequency, say every two weeks. The quantity ordered each period is the amount necessary to bring the inventory level up to some maximum target level. A graph of the inventory level over time for a fixed-interval system is shown in Figure 5.4. Notice that the order size varies with the number of units used since the last order.

This type of system is best suited for *joint-replenishment items,* that is, items that are purchased at the same time from the same source. The frequency of orders for each item can be established so that the average order for the item or for a group of jointly ordered items is for some economical amount. Ordering groups of items at the same time reduces the ordering cost per item, may reduce the shipping cost per item, and may increase the value of each purchase sufficiently to qualify for price discounts. Perpetual monitoring of inventory is not necessary with the fixed-interval system, since the inventory clerk merely has to count the stock on hand each time the ordering date occurs. Ordering dates for various items can be spaced at particular intervals to smooth the work load for the inventory clerks and buyers.

Minimum-Maximum System   The fixed-interval system can sometimes result in the placing of very small orders. A *minimum-maximum inventory system* (sometimes called an *S,s* system) eliminates the handling of quantities that are considered too small to be economical. This system combines some of the features of the fixed-quantity and fixed-interval systems. A maximum target level (*S*) and a minimum target level (*s*) are established. The inventory is reviewed at fixed intervals (*t*), and an order is placed only if the inventory is found to be below the minimum level. If it is not below the minimum level, no material is ordered because the quantity on hand is probably sufficient for the next review period and the quantity ordered would be small.

FIGURE 5.4

Inventory Level in a Fixed-Interval System

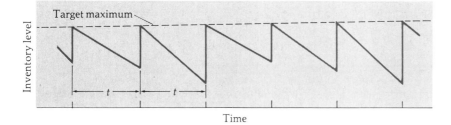

FIGURE 5.5

Inventory Level in a Minimum-Maximum Inventory System

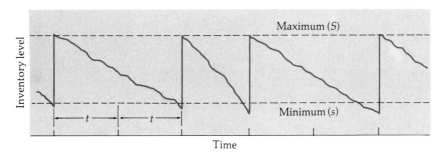

A graph of the inventory level for a minimum-maximum system is shown in Figure 5.5. This type of system is suitable for items that are not expensive, so that holding sizable inventory levels is less costly than keeping track of just how many are on hand and spending more to place frequent orders for small amounts.

Budget Allocation   The *budget allocation inventory system* is more of a general guideline than a precise set of operating rules. Systems of this general nature are used to control inventories in retail establishments—gift shops, furniture stores, department stores, and the like. The budget allocation method relies on the discretion of a buyer or department manager to determine how many of which items should be in stock. General allocations of a total budget to various categories of merchandise may be made to keep a balanced selection available to customers. Within these allowable investment amounts, the company's buyers observe what is selling and order replenishments from vendors. Buyers also may make decisions to purchase items that currently are not stocked if they believe the products will sell. Some companies have agreements with suppliers whereby the supplier's representatives periodically visit the store, check the inventory on hand, and replenish the stock to some target level. Budget allocation methods are useful when customers have some latitude in selecting products.

ABC Classification

We have seen that there are a variety of types of inventory systems that a company might use to manage its inventories of independent-demand items. More than one type of system might be used within the same company—a fixed-quantity system for some items, a fixed-interval system for others. The interval between orders might be relatively short for some items and much longer for others. Selection of the type of independent-demand inventory system to use might be influenced by several factors, such as the variability of demand, the cost of operating the inventory system, the unit cost of the item, or the seriousness of the problem if the item is not available.

Some companies have 100,000 or more inventory items, so it would be very time-consuming to examine thoroughly the characteristics of each item and select an appropriate inventory system for it. Often *ABC classification*, or *distribution by value*, is used to provide an initial sorting of items into groups according to the annual expenditures they cause. Items that represent the highest inventory expenditures are identified through this procedure so they can be given the greatest amount of attention, and so on. Some items may warrant the expense of perpetual inventory records to ensure that they are being carefully controlled because even one extra month's supply of these particular items is very costly. For other items, it may be less expensive to keep an extra three months' supply than to pay for operating an inventory system that would carefully control the amount on hand. Items with a very low cost and a small usage rate would fall into this latter category.

The following procedure is one approach to *ABC* classification:

1. Multiply the cost of each item by forecast usages of the item for the coming year to get the *annual dollar usage* (annual expenditure) for each item.
2. List all of the items in descending order of annual dollar usage, keeping their identity.
3. Number the items from top to bottom of the list, and determine the cumulative percentage of the items at and above each item on the list. For example, the 280th item in a list of 1,000 would represent 28 cumulative percent of the items.
4. Starting at the top and moving item by item down the list, compute the cumulative total annual dollar usage represented by the item and all the items above it.
5. Determine the percentage that each item's cumulative annual dollar usage represents out of the entire annual dollar usage for all items (i.e., the cumulative annual dollar usage for the last item on the list).

The distribution by value can be visualized if the cumulative percentage of annual dollar usage is plotted against the cumulative percentage of the items. A relationship similar to that shown in Figure 5.6 is usually obtained when these data are plotted. As little as 10 to 20 percent of the items might account for 60 to 80 percent of the annual dollar usage. In a wholesale or technical industry (such as a distributor of electronic components) where the product line includes both major products and minor replacement parts, 10 percent of the products might account for 80 or 90 percent of the annual dollar usage. Although it would be rare, a company could handle a product line with each item having about the same annual dollar volume.

The items with the highest annual dollar usage are called *A* items. Buying a few months' extra supply of these items means that many unnecessary dollars will be invested in inventory. Even keeping just one or two extra units in inventory may be very expensive. *A* items should be controlled closely. They often justify perpetual inventory records in a fixed-quantity system or frequent review in a fixed-interval system.

B items, those with the second-highest annual dollar usage, may represent 20 to 30 percent of the items a company keeps and may account for about the

FIGURE 5.6

Relative Value of Items vs. Relative Percentage of Items

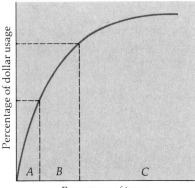

same percentage of annual cost of use. These items would be reviewed less frequently than *A* items if a fixed-interval system were used. A minimum-maximum system could be used.

C items represent a large percentage of the items a company may keep in inventory—perhaps half of them but usually less than one-fourth of the annual dollar volume. Very simple, approximate inventory control methods may be used to control *C* items. A company may have a crude minimum-maximum system whereby, whenever the inventory gets down to two months' supply, an additional six months' supply is ordered. Frequently, it is less expensive to have extra inventory of *C* items than to keep track of the inventory balance and purchase frequently.

It is important to recognize that the cost of use is the basis for only a first approximation to classification of items. An item may be an essential part of a company's product, even though it does not cost much. The list of *C* items should be reviewed to see if any of these items should be moved to a higher classification.

APPLICATION

Example of ABC Classification

Since she was a young child, Stephanie Stanton has enjoyed working with boats and being near the water. She is working with her father and will eventually take over operation of the family's wholesale boat and trailer parts business, Stanton Equipment Company. The company's inventory consists of about 12,000 different items that are sold to boat manufacturers, dealers, and hardware stores in the region. Several groups of items are produced by the same manufacturer, so the company controls its inventory with a fixed-interval inventory system. This system permits counting on a particular day the group of items that come from a common supplier and purchasing them all on the same order. This joint replenishment has worked well to help Stanton receive quantity discounts for large purchases and economies on shipping costs.

The business has grown to the extent that the stock clerks who keep track of the inventory are working excessive overtime to count inventory and order items. They do not have time to store items properly and keep accurate records. The usual procedure has been to count all items once a week. Stephanie has found that many of the items that are counted do not need to be ordered because no sales of these items were made during the week, yet very large orders are made for some items. Stephanie has recommended that she and her father determine the "moderate movers," which could be counted, say, every other week, and the "slow movers," which could be counted less often, say every third week. This practice would reduce the stock clerks' work load so they could work more accurately, and it would reduce overtime costs.

Stephanie obtained an ABC analysis program that would run on the company's computer. The program accessed the company's purchasing files to obtain the latest average usage rate (col. 2, Table 5.5) and the average price paid (col. 3) for each item on the last three buys. The purpose of running the program was to determine which items were A items (those that should be counted each week), which were B items (those that could be counted maybe every other week), and which items were C items (those that could be counted less often). Table 5.5 shows a small sample (one thousandth of the file), for which the usage was multiplied by the cost of the item. The program then sorted the list in the "Annual use in dollars" column to arrange the list in descending order of that variable. The results of the sort are shown in Table 5.6. Stephanie and her father discussed the list and determined that the first two items in Table 5.6 definitely were A items. The next three were considered to be B items, and the remainder were considered C items. They concluded that all items did not have to be controlled by the same procedure and that they would try to develop new inventory levels and ordering frequencies for the B and C items so the company could make better use of its resources.

Table 5.5
CALCULATION OF USAGE IN DOLLARS, STANTON EQUIPMENT

(1) Item Number	(2) Annual Usage Rate	(3) Average Cost/Unit in $	(4) Annual Use in $
4837	6,850	$ 1.20	$ 8,220.00
9261	371	8.60	3,190.60
4395	1,292	13.18	17,028.56
3521	62	91.80	5,691.60
5223	12,667	3.20	40,566.40
5294	9,625	10.18	97,982.50
6081	7,010	1.27	8,902.70
4321	5,100	0.88	4,488.00
8046	258	62.25	16,060.50
9555	862	18.10	15,602.20
2926	1,940	0.38	737.20
1293	967	2.20	2,127.40
		Sum	$220,597.66

Table 5.6
LISTING IN DESCENDING ORDER OF ANNUAL DOLLAR USE, STANTON EQUIPMENT

Item Number	Annual Usage in $	Percentage of Sum	Cumulative Percentage
5294	$ 97,982.50	44.42	44.42
5223	40,566.40	18.39	62.81
4395	17,028.56	7.72	70.53
8046	16,060.50	7.28	77.81
9555	15,602.20	7.07	84.88
6081	8,902.70	4.04	88.91
4837	8,220.00	3.73	92.64
3521	5,691.60	2.58	95.22
4321	4,488.00	2.03	97.26
9261	3,190.60	1.45	98.70
1293	2,127.40	0.96	99.67
2926	737.20	0.33	100.00
	Sum $220,597.66		

Management of Dependent-Demand Inventories

Consider an independent-demand manufactured product that is controlled by a fixed-quantity, fixed-interval, or minimum-maximum system. Assume that the demand for this product is fairly uniform (perhaps the result of many consumers' making fairly small purchases). Components of the final assembly (dependent demand) will be required only when the inventory of the final assembly reaches its reorder level. Consequently, requirements for a component will be zero for each week between reorders, then it will be equal to the number of components required for the number of assemblies that the company plans to produce. This "lumpy" demand for the component is much different from the pattern of demand for the finished product.

Material Requirements Planning   Remember that independent-demand inventory systems keep items on hand almost constantly because demand might occur at any time. Dependent demand for components of a product occurs only when the company is in the process of assembling the product. It is less expensive to have these items available only when they are needed, instead of stocking them constantly. The company schedules when assemblies are to be produced and, therefore, controls when dependent components will be needed. It is possible to schedule backward from the date at which the assembly will be completed to determine when each component will be needed and should be available. A great amount of data must be processed if the company produces a broad line of products with many components. *Material requirements planning (MRP)* is a technique to perform these calculations taking dependent-demand relationships into account. MRP, which is discussed in Chapter 7, can be used to schedule purchases of components or to schedule various levels of fabrication or assembly in the production of products.

JUST-IN-TIME PRODUCTION

Japanese repetitive manufacturers have become very effective at operating with very small inventories through an approach called *just-in-time (JIT) production, zero inventories,* or *stockless production.* This approach to production is now used in many countries. Just-in-time production involves purchasing or producing exactly what is needed at the precise time it is to be used and conveying it directly to the point that it is needed (see box). When a company has no standard product or when its products are demanded spasmodically in large quantities, there is little or no way to prevent lumpy demand for component parts. Lumpy demand and irregular flow of materials are likely to cause accumulations of inventory, unless production is carefully timed by some method such as MRP to occur precisely when materials are needed.

Repetitive manufacturing companies, which have a high demand for a standard product, can prevent lumpy demand for components by producing or ordering the products in numerous small lots instead of in larger, infrequent lots. The result is a smooth, uniform flow of small amounts of the appropriate components to the assembly department and a smooth flow of products from the assembly department, with the accumulation of very little inventory at any stage of production. Coordination of production activities in these companies is often achieved through the use of a card system called a *kanban system.* Just-in-time production and the kanban system are discussed under "Production Control for Repetitive Manufacturing" in Chapter 8.

OPERATIONS MANAGEMENT IN ACTION

Just-In-Time Purchasing at Stanley-Vidmar Inc.

The practice of maintaining large raw material inventories is now, more than ever before, being affected by the need for cost-cutting measures. Because of escalating costs for new construction, higher interest rates on money, and rising rent rates, many manufacturers are now looking more closely at inventory cost or "cost of possession."

Companies are increasingly making do with existing space. They are looking for ways to better utilize the space they have for procedures which reduce or eliminate large storage areas. Many U.S. manufacturers are adopting variations of the Japanese Just-in-Time method of inventory management, whereby raw material stocks are kept low and supplies move quickly and smoothly into the plant to meet production schedules.

Manufacturers in Japan usually rely on one supplier for a product or specific raw material and buy directly from the original or primary source. In Japan, suppliers are typically within a 50-mile radius of a manufacturing facility, or even on the premises. Often, suppliers are actually part of the parent corporation, thereby assuring continuity and control of manufacturing.

In the U.S. however, most manufacturers do not have the luxury of having suppliers within a 50-mile radius, so many companies work with more than one supplier. And rather than buying directly from primary-source suppliers, they deal with secondary suppliers or service centers. Here, too, they don't usually work with just one service center, but several.

The Middlemen

Service centers act as middlemen for the distribution of raw materials to a manufacturer. And just as manufacturers deal with more than one service center, service centers deal with more than one primary source.

In the early 1970s, Stanley-Vidmar Inc., a modular storage systems manufacturer, was purchasing steel directly from mills and from service centers alike. At that time, we started modernizing our tooling and manufacturing operations, and decided to make a fundamental transition from using sheet steel to coil steel. Our new manufacturing requirements called for the purchase of coil steel in various widths, not just standard 36-to-48-inch coil widths supplied by the mills. Since the mills could not supply us with coils in varying widths, and since we had no intention of going into the steel business ourselves, we began to shift our purchasing more heavily toward service centers, which were tooled to supply this specialized need.

Service centers took on the responsibility of working directly with the mills, providing us with the assurance that we would not be caught waiting for materials, and agreeing to meet delivery schedules based on our manufacturing operations. So, by 1975 we were dealing solely with service centers for our raw material needs.

There were other factors which affected our decision to make the transition from mills to service centers. First, service centers are set up to handle and maintain buffer stocks in order to keep materials moving smoothly and on time to a manufacturer. Raw material inventory is stocked by the service center, not the manufacturer, freeing up valuable warehouse space for the manufacturer.

Cost Reductions

Second, because mills compete for business from the service centers, the initial cost of raw materials is reduced. Third, manufacturers can negotiate long-term contracts with service centers, thereby obtaining firm commitments to lower prices. These contracts often enable service centers to offset price increases from the mills.

These long-term commitments can also help the service centers. Since the service centers know a manufacturer's needs and production schedule, and since they also know the production capabilities and quality levels of the mills with whom they work, they can buy more

intelligently, fill voids in production schedules more easily, and better utilize their own equipment and resources.

Generally speaking, there seems to be a much more concerned response from the service centers, and we have developed much closer relationships with them than we had with the mills. The service centers have also established a reputation for significantly higher product quality.

Service centers often have a high rejection rate back to the mills. In 1981–82 and back in 1973–74, rejection rates back to the mills were sometimes as high as 50 percent. As a result, the quality of product coming to the manufacturer is much higher—owing to quality control procedures established by the service centers. The rejection rate from manufacturers back to service centers now averages only about eight percent nationally, and because of the close relationships we have developed with our service centers, Stanley-Vidmar's rejection rate is about half of the national average.

Fewer Inspections

Moreover, since rejection rates to the service centers are so low, manufacturers need only to perform periodic quality control checks. Raw materials now come into a plant and go directly to production staging areas and then into processing. All of this saves time, labor and space.

The diversity of their customer base enables service centers to provide a high level of service and quality. They work with many different mills until they find those that provide the most consistent service and the best product. They also work with "sister" service centers which broadens their purchasing base even more and enhances their ability to provide a quality product and on-time delivery.

The Just-in-Time approach of maintaining smaller inventories and working closely with service centers for the purchase of raw materials has many advantages over the traditional method of keeping large inventories and buying directly from the primary source suppliers.

Valuable floor space, previously used for maintaining large stocks, is freed for use in manufacturing and other areas. Capital, previously tied up in large inventories, also becomes available for other expenditures and investments. The "cost of possession" is radically reduced because the amount of inventory on hand at any given time is so much smaller. Also, a company's cash flow is significantly improved, thereby permitting greater flexibility of operation.

The potential disadvantages of the Just-in-Time method include the failure of primary source suppliers and/or service centers to maintain delivery and quality standards, and the possibility of strikes or other unforeseen interruptions in service. These potential problems can be avoided simply by dealing with several service centers who, in turn, work with a variety of mills and "sister" service centers.

From the 10 years of experience that Stanley-Vidmar has had with Just-in-Time techniques, we have found that there are certain key elements necessary for successful purchasing and inventory management. Of primary importance is the selection of reliable, financially stable, quality-oriented service cen-

ters and the formation of close, long-term relationships with them. Secondly, the operation, efficiency and quality of service centers and mills should be monitored closely by the manufacturer's purchasing department. Finally, the knowledge and expertise of service center personnel is helpful in obtaining timely information and innovative ideas for producing an even better product at lower cost.

This method of purchasing and inventory management, if properly planned and carefully executed, can yield tremendous savings in space, time and labor, and at the same time increase the operating efficiency of many manufacturing companies. However, it takes time, careful planning and close supervision by an experienced purchasing department to keep the program running efficiently. It took Stanley-Vidmar a number of years to smooth out the rough spots, but in the 10 years since Just-in-Time was instituted, this purchasing method has saved the company just under $1 million.

Source: William Devaney, P&IM Review and APICS News, October 1984, p. 72–73, 87. Reprinted with permission from P&IM Review. Copyright 1984 by T.D.A. Publications, Inc.

SUMMARY

This chapter provides an overview of materials flow and some of the organizational units that are involved with materials. A variety of organizational schemes can be used to direct materials-related activities, depending on the type of company, the talents and ambitions of the available personnel, the objectives of managers, and other factors. The various activities involved in materials handling in manufacturing companies may account for a significant portion of the total manufacturing cost. Purchasing activities might involve the buying of raw materials and components, which in turn would involve vendor relations. The traffic department controls incoming shipments. The receiving department unloads and the inspection department checks the quality of materials that are received. In addition, materials han-

dling involves moving the shipment to inventory control or to a stores department. The materials are then moved through various stages of processing, as capacity is available; usually there are some quality inspections between some operations. The transformed materials then go through final assembly and the finished goods are sent by the shipping department to a distribution center. From there they move to a sales center and on to the customer.

Two of the activities mentioned above, purchasing and inventory, were discussed in greater detail than the other activities. Purchasing is responsible for most of the expenditures in many manufacturing companies, and inventory control is responsible for controlling much of the companies' assets. Buying and maintaining supplies are also important activities in many nonmanufacturing operations, such as repair service companies. Wholesale and retail organizations are greatly dependent on their wisdom in procuring and holding the proper items in inventory. For some operations, such as the postal system or transport companies, materials handling is the primary service.

Inventory items can be classified as single-period or multiple-period inventory. The latter, those that are replenished from time to time, are further classified as either independent-demand items or dependent-demand items. Independent items supply demand outside the organization. They can be managed by fixed-quantity, fixed-interval, minimum-maximum, or budget allocation inventory control systems. Dependent-demand items supply requirements inside the organization. They subsequently become part of an assembly or kit, so that their rate of use is dependent on the production schedule and the rate of use of other items. Dependent-demand items often are managed by material requirements planning, MRP. Some companies use the just-in-time approach to keep inventories as low as possible. The following two chapters examine some details of managing independent-demand inventory and dependent-demand inventory.

SOLVED PROBLEM

PROBLEM:

A style product must be ordered by a store several months before the season and can be purchased at $16.25 per unit. The retail price for the item will be $26.95 during the season. No "fill-in" stock can be ordered during the season if the store runs out of stock of the item. Any excess stock left at the end of the season will be sold for $14.95. The buyer estimates the following probability distribution for selling various numbers of the product. Determine the number of dozen to order that will maximize the store's expected profit.

Number that Might Be Demanded (dozen)	Probability of Demand Being This Number
6	.03
7	.05
8	.07
9	.15
10	.20
11	.20
12	.15
13	.07
14	.05
15	.03

SOLUTION:

If the store overstocks, the loss per unit for every excess unit at the end of the season will be $16.25 − 14.95 = $1.30, that is, C_o = $1.30. If the store understocks, the opportunity cost for every unit the company could sell but did not stock, will be $26.95 − 16.25 = $10.70, that is, C_u = $10.70. The critical probability is found by equation 5.2.

$$P(D)^* = \frac{C_o}{C_u + C_o} = \frac{1.30}{10.70 + 1.30} = 0.108$$

The level of stock that will maximize expected profit is the highest level of stock that has a probability greater than or equal to 0.108 that it will be sold. We begin at the upper end of the probability distribution to develop the cumulative probabilities that demand will be greater than or equal to each level, so we can see what level of demand has a probability greater than or equal to .108 that it will sell. If the store stocks 15 dozen, the probability of selling that amount is only .03, which is less than the critical probability. If 14 dozen are stocked, the probability of selling that amount is .03 + .05 = .08 which still is less than the critical probability. If 13 dozen are stocked, the probability of selling that amount is .08 + .07 = .15 which is greater than the critical probability, so 13 dozen should be stocked. (Often it is useful to construct the greater-than-or-equal-to cumulative probability distribution and examine it to find the highest level that has a cumulative probability equal to or greater than the critical probability.) You can see that 13 is the highest level with a probability greater than .108.

Level that Might Be Stocked	Probability that Demand Will Be at Least This Level
6	1.00
7	.97
8	.92
9	.85
10	.70
11	.50
12	.30
13	.15 ← 0.108
14	.08
15	.03

DISCUSSION QUESTIONS

1. What is materials management? How does materials management in a manufacturing operation differ from that in a nonmanufacturing operation?
2. Obtain information from a nearby company, or one with which you are familiar, about how materials management activities are organized. Present your findings in class, and compare the organization you surveyed to the organizations surveyed by others in the class.
3. Why is purchasing such an important part of materials management?
4. (a) List some reasons for having inventory.
   (b) Why might companies in some industries have more than one year's sales in inventory, while companies in other types of business keep only a few weeks' sales or less in inventory?
5. Discuss some examples of single-period inventories.
6. State two general differences between independent and dependent demand.
7. What is an inventory control system?
8. Briefly describe four systems for controlling independent-demand inventory items.
9. Why are dependent-demand items often managed by a different type of inventory system from that used for independent-demand items?
10. (a) Describe three categories of purchases that a company may make.
    (b) Why should some be made by the purchasing department and some not?
11. Why would the purchasing department be involved in value analysis?
12. What are some changes a company might make in the way it operates so that it will require less inventory?

PROBLEMS

1. The Lob Sport Shop has an opportunity to purchase tennis rackets from the bankrupt Foot Fault Manufacturing Co. However, Foot Fault produced the rackets with a very poor quality of strings, so that they will need new strings by the next season. The rackets can be purchased for $16, and Lob plans to sell them for $30 as a special promotion (with the hope of selling the restring jobs in the near future). If the rack-

ets are not sold this season, Lob must restring them before selling them next season. But the price next year cannot be greater than $20 because customers will know that this was the price previously—and because the Foot Fault rackets will be known as having poor-quality strings even though this will not be true of the rackets Lob tries to sell next year. Lob figures it will lose $6 per racket that is not sold this season.

The probability of selling various quantities of rackets this season has been estimated and is shown below. How many rackets should Lob buy?

Number of Rackets Sold	Probability of Selling Exactly This Number
30	0.05
40	0.10
50	0.15
60	0.20
70	0.15
80	0.15
90	0.10
100	0.05
110	0.05

2. Don's Men's Wear can purchase a special shipment of men's wool caps for $25 a dozen. The caps can be sold for $3.50 during the fall season, but any that have not been sold by Christmas will be reduced to $1.95. The following probability distribution has been estimated for demand for these caps.

Demand (D) (dozen)	Probability That Demand Will Equal This Number [p(D)]	Probability That Demand Will Be Greater Than or Equal to This Level [P(D)]
5	0.15	1.00
6	0.20	0.85
7	0.25	0.65
8	0.20	0.40
9	0.15	0.20
10	0.05	0.05

How many caps should Don purchase?

3. Delish Deli stocks fresh baked bread that costs the store 54¢ per loaf. The bread is sold for $1.25 a loaf on the day it is baked, and for 39¢ a loaf if it remains at the end of that day. All of the old bread can be sold at the discount price. The probabilities of various levels of daily demand for fresh bread are given below. How many loaves of bread should Delish Deli stock?

Level of Demand (dozens of loaves)	Probability of Level
10	.03
11	.09
12	.16
13	.24
14	.18
15	.12
16	.09
17	.06
18	.03

4. The Great News Stand stocks copies of the Sunday newspaper published in a larger city in the region. The papers cost the newsstand 40¢ each and are sold for $1.00. If they are not sold during the week, the papers are sold as scrap paper for approximately 3¢ each. Demand for the paper is distributed according to a normal distribution with a mean of 45 and a standard deviation of 10. How many papers should the newsstand stock?

5. A style item can be purchased for $26.50 a unit before the season and no additional units can be ordered. The product will sell for $64.95 during the season, and any units left at the end of the season will be sold for $24.95. The probability distribution of demand during the season is estimated to be normally distributed with a mean of 100 and a standard deviation of 22. Determine the amount of stock to order that will give the maximum expected profit.

6. For the data in problem 5, determine the amount to order if the company decides to use a selling price during the season of $59.95 and all other factors remain the same.

7. Bonito's Seafood sells fresh snapper received each morning from the coast for $4.49 per pound. If the fish is kept overnight it will be priced at $3.95 per pound the second day. All of the snapper that remains at the end of the second day is sold for cat food at 25¢ per pound. About 82 percent of the snapper that is not sold the first day will be sold the second day. Snapper costs Bonito's $3.60 per pound delivered to the store. Demand for fresh snapper during its first day in the store is normally distributed with a mean of 32 pounds and a standard deviation of 6 pounds. How much snapper should Mr. Bonito order each day?

8. A company uses a very small number of items in its business. The items are listed in the table below, as are their cost and annual usage in units.

Part Number	Annual Usage (units)	Cost/Unit
M 602	31,000	$ 0.10
W 101	5,200	10.00
F 310	1,500	0.65
H 884	100,000	0.14
F 400	60	255.00
D 277	400	3.35
R 802	800	2.40
D 780	600	0.36
M 029	30,000	1.18
B 150	60,000	0.25

(a) Determine the annual dollar usage, and determine which appear to be the A, B, and C items.
(b) Arrange the list in descending order of annual dollar usage, then plot the cumulative percentage of annual dollar usage versus the cumulative percentage of items.

9. A random sample of 10 items was selected from the 10,000-item inventory in the Sahara Marine Manufacturing Company. The following data were obtained.

Part Number	Annual Usage (Units)	Cost/Unit
Q 10	10,000	$13
R 20	5,000	5
S 30	1,000	6
T 40	2,000	18
U 50	100	55
V 60	5,000	7.50
W 70	200	2
X 80	2,000	12
Y 90	25,000	10
Z 100	500	4

(a) Group the data in order of descending annual dollar usage.
(b) Select A items, B items, C items.

10. Apollo Distributors handles only 10 items in its inventory. The annual usage and cost of these items are listed below.

Part Number	Annual Usage (units)	Cost/Unit
095	5,000	$ 17
186	17,000	51
277	6,000	17
368	4,000	75
459	11,000	200
579	60,000	9
631	12,000	60
722	28,000	50
813	4,000	18
904	3,000	25

(a) Calculate the annual dollar usage of each item, and arrange the list in the order of descending annual dollar usage.
(b) Plot the cumulative percentage of annual dollar usage against the cumulative percentage of items.
(c) Select the A, B, and C items.

BIBLIOGRAPHY

Ammer, Dean S. *Purchasing and Materials Management for Health Care Institutions.* Lexington, Mass.: Heath, 1975.

———. *Materials Management.* 4th ed. Homewood, Ill: Irwin, 1980.

Ballou, Ronald H. *Business Logistics Management.* Englewood Cliffs, N.J.: Prentice-Hall, 1973.

Bowersox, Donald J. *Logistical Management: A System Integration of Physical Distribution Management, Material Management, and Logistical Coordination.* New York: Macmillan, 1974.

Buffa, Elwood S., and Jeffrey G. Miller. *Production-Inventory Systems: Planning and Control.* 3rd ed. Homewood, Ill.: Irwin, 1979.

Ericsson, Dag. *Materials Administration.* Trans. A. Franklin Colborn. New York: McGraw-Hill, 1974.

Glaskowsky, Nicholas A., James L. Heskett, and Robert M. Ivie. *Business Logistics.* 2d ed. New York: Ronald Press, 1973.

Hall, Robert W. *Zero Inventories.* Homewood, Ill.: Dow Jones-Irwin, 1983.

Lambert, Douglas M., and James R. Stock. *Strategic Physical Distribution Management.* Homewood, Ill.: Irwin, 1982.

Miller, Jeffrey G., and Peter Gilmour. "Materials Managers: Who Needs Them?" *Harvard Business Review,* July-August 1979, pp. 143–153.

Orlicky, Joseph A. *Material Requirements Planning: The New Way of Life in Production and Inventory Management.* New York: McGraw-Hill, 1974.

Schonberger, Richard J. *Japanese Manufacturing Techniques: Nine Hidden Lessons in Simplicity.* New York: Free Press, 1982.

Tersine, Richard J. *Principles of Inventory and Materials Management.* 2d ed. New York: Elsevier-North Holland, 1976.

Wight, Oliver W. *Production and Inventory Management in the Computer Age.* Boston: Cahners, 1974.

Chapter Outline
MANAGING INDEPENDENT-DEMAND INVENTORY

HOW MUCH INVENTORY IS ENOUGH?

RELEVANT INVENTORY COSTS
Some Costs Increase with Inventory / Some Costs Decrease with Increased Inventory

DETERMINING THE ECONOMIC ORDER SIZE
Total Relevant Inventory Cost / Ordering Costs Equal Holding Costs at the EOQ / Marginal Costs / Application: *Example of Order-quantity Determination*

DETERMINING THE PRODUCTION LOT SIZE
Application: *Example of Production Lot Size Model*

EVALUATING QUANTITY-DISCOUNT OPPORTUNITIES
Application: *Example of Price-break Order Quantity*

DETERMINING THE REORDER LEVEL

SAFETY STOCK
Factors Affecting Safety Stock Level /

Methods of Determining the Safety Stock Level / Application: *Example of Setting a Reorder Level on the Basis of an Empirical Probability Distribution* / Application: *Establishing a Safety Stock Level (Reorder Level) with Explicit Stock-Out Cost*

USING COMPUTERS TO MANAGE INDEPENDENT INVENTORY
Summary / Solved Problems / Discussion Questions / Problems / Bibliography

KEY TERMS

Transaction reporting	Setup costs	Quantity discounts	Service level
Stockout	Stockout costs	Price breaks	Lead-time demand
Reorder level	Economic order	Cycle stock	(LTD)
Reorder point	quantity (EOQ)	Safety stock (buffer	Mean absolute
Order quantity	Holding costs	stock)	deviation (MAD)
Joint orders	Economic production		
Inventory turnover	lot (EPL)		
Relevant costs			

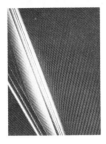

Chapter 6

MANAGING INDEPENDENT-DEMAND INVENTORY

Inventory is very important to many companies because it helps the company respond quickly to customer demand, which is an important element of competitive strategy. Inventories of raw materials or partially processed goods can help a company complete the production cycle in a much shorter time than would otherwise be possible. Inventories of finished goods (i.e., independent-demand inventories) of the correct items, within a reasonable distance of points of demand, play an important role in a company's ability to compete in a market for standardized products. A second reason for the importance of inventory is that it represents one of the largest controllable resources in many companies. For some companies, such as wholesalers or retailers, particularly if they operate in leased facilities, inventory may be the primary asset. Capital investments in such assets as facilities or equipment are relatively fixed in comparison to investments in inventory. A company normally cannot add units of facilities and sell them as easily or as profitably as it can build up and reduce its inventory. The more effective a company's inventory systems, the better able it is to manage its resources and to compete effectively.

An inventory system may be a collection of people, equipment, and procedures that function to keep an account of the quantity of each item that is in inventory and to determine which items to buy or produce in what quantities and at what times. Even very simple methods that accomplish these functions cost money to operate. Some inventory systems require *transaction reporting* to keep track of every occasion when units are added to or taken from the existing inventory. These perpetual inventory records are expensive, but the additional expense can be justified for products that are relatively expensive to hold in inventory. The extent of customer service (i.e., protection from *stockout*) provided by an inventory system depends on how high the inventory level is when replenishment action is started. This level of inventory is called the *reorder level* or *reorder point*. The average amount of resources a company commits to inventory is related to the reorder level and also to the *order quantity,* which is the amount added when replenishment occurs.

This chapter presents models that can be used to determine the order quantity that is most economical to obtain when an item is purchased from a vendor or produced internally. The lot size affects only a part of the inventory a company carries. Additional inventory might be carried as safety stock to protect from uncertainty of the demand. The amount of safety stock a company should carry depends on several factors that will be discussed in this chapter, and on forecast accuracy, which was discussed in Chapter 3.

Economic order quantity development and safety stock determination are discussed in the chapter in the context of a fixed-quantity type of inventory system. Order quantity determination, however, can be applied to other inventory systems also. The difference between the minimum and maximum inventory levels in a minimum-maximum system can be set equal to the economic order quantity so that orders will average approximately the economic amount. Target inventory levels and reorder intervals also must be determined for fixed-period systems. If the item is to be controlled independently of others, the frequency of reorders can be set so that, on the average, an economic quantity would be ordered each time. The target inventory level would be set so that the inventory level would be at the best reorder point when the reorder time occurs. It is more difficult to develop a general model for a situation in which several items are ordered jointly. The best policy for *joint orders* depends on the number of items that are purchased from the same source, the shipping costs, and any applicable discounts. Each company's set of inventory items offers many possible combinations of items that it might be wise to control jointly or order with the same frequency. This chapter will not discuss a general model for this type of situation.

HOW MUCH INVENTORY IS ENOUGH?

Inventory is necessary and desirable for a variety of reasons, mentioned in Chapter 5. For instance, inventory can be used to reduce lead time, to smooth out the production rate when demand fluctuates, and to protect a company from underestimates of demand or shortages of supply. But how much is enough?

Different companies have different answers to this question. Some Japanese manufacturers, Toyota for example, have become noted for their ability to operate with low inventories and to achieve a high inventory turnover. (*Inventory turnover* is basically the ratio of sales to the average inventory level, both measured at cost or retail price.) The Japanese approach is to keep in-process inventory low and to achieve quick flow of the product through the production cycle. Being able to respond quickly to demand, companies can work from a shorter-range forecast, which is more accurate, so they need less safety stock—that is, less inventory to protect from uncertainty. Numerous companies in the United States and other nations are working to become more competitive by keeping their inventories low.

Even within a company there may be differing views on the amount of inventory that is appropriate. Marketing people might like to have a very large inventory of every item so that they would immediately be able to ship any size order. Finance people might like to have low inventories and a flexible production system so that the company would still be able to respond but with a lower investment in idle resources. Production people might like to have long runs of those products that would provide the best utilization of people and equipment; but this could result in high inventories of some products and none of other products. The inventory models discussed in this chapter attempt to balance some of these views by trading off the costs associated with inventory.

RELEVANT INVENTORY COSTS

Having inventory costs money. But not having at least a certain amount of inventory also costs money. As a company increases the amount of inventory it maintains, some costs increase, some costs decrease, and some costs are not affected. Those costs that are not affected by the decision at hand can be ignored in the analysis. The costs that are affected by the decision are called *relevant costs* and definitely should be considered in reaching a decision if the amounts are not trivial.

It is important to keep all costs of operations at the lowest practicable levels. Inventory-related costs are certainly no exception to this objective. With diligent work, companies can sometimes achieve double savings by reducing the conditions that encourage keeping excessive inventories. For example, a company might implement a more effective preventive maintenance program and achieve a reduction in the cost of expensive machine down-time and in the cost of holding inventory to be used in case of a machine breakdown. Extra inventory held because a portion of the stock might be defective can be reduced if the waste that results from producing defective items can also be eliminated. The cost of conditions that encourage keeping inventory should not be accepted as fixed so the company just accepts these costs and protects itself with inventory. Some inventory-related costs are discussed below.

Some Costs Increase with Inventory

Cost of Capital   A company pays for the funds it has available to use. It may pay interest to a bank or other lending institution, to bondholders, or to other creditors, or it may pay dividends to its stockholders. No matter where those funds are invested, any investment should "earn" or be charged a sufficient amount to pay the "rent" on the funds it uses. An investment in inventory is like an investment in a more obvious project such as a new machine or truck. Most companies have limited funds, so that an investment in inventory may preclude investment in some profitable project. The rate of return of the most profitable projects that must be foregone is considered an opportunity cost of capital. Both out-of-pocket and opportunity costs should be considered in making investment decisions. When a company increases the funds invested in inventory, it increases the cost of operation.

Cost of Storage Space   Another cost of holding inventory is the cost of a warehouse or other facility used for storage. If a building is constructed, its cost must be recovered over its useful life. It also costs money to heat, cool, light, clean, repair, and otherwise maintain the facility. There will be other costs too, such as the cost of stock clerks, materials handlers, and materials-handling equipment.

Taxes and Insurance   Many state and local governments collect ad valorem taxes, or taxes on assets. Inventory is one of a company's assets, and the more inventory it has, the more tax it will pay. Taxes on assets are therefore a relevant cost in some inventory decisions. So is insurance. When a company increases its insurance to cover an increase in the value of its inventory, the premiums rise.

Deterioration and Obsolescence   Items held in storage may deteriorate, some more rapidly than others. Many food items, such as produce, have rather short storage lives. Drugs are assigned dates after which their potency or purity is considered inadequate to allow their sale. Other products may become rusty, musty, or dusty, or the paint may fade. They may mildew or become chipped or dented in handling. Pilferage may also decrease the value of the stock of some products.

A stock of goods may become obsolete as time passes. If a new, better product or the fickleness of consumers causes demand for a product to diminish, its value will also diminish. If it deteriorates or becomes obsolete, the company will probably lose money. The greater the inventory, the longer it takes to sell and the greater the likelihood of deterioration or obsolescence.

Some Costs Decrease with Increased Inventory

Order Cost   Some costs are incurred each time a company places an order and receives the resulting shipment of goods. It costs money to solicit and evaluate bids, negotiate prices, prepare purchase orders, and expedite or follow up to ensure that the shipment will arrive on time. Delivery costs may be paid by the purchaser and very likely will have economies of scale. When the purchase is received it must be uncrated, inspected, and moved into storage. Generally, on an annual basis, all these costs will vary inversely with order size. If procurement lot sizes are increased, fewer orders must be processed and received. Fewer procurement people will be required, fewer telephone calls will need to be made, and fewer orders will need to be inspected.

Item Cost   Prices for some purchased items may be reduced as order size is increased. Item cost becomes a relevant cost factor if quantity discounts are available. However, if the cost of each unit remains constant regardless of the size of an order, the item cost can be disregarded in determining lot sizes.

Setup Costs   Manufacturing companies incur certain *setup costs* each time they begin a production run. The equipment on which the parts of the product are to be produced must be prepared. The machines are idle during this period, and additional costs are incurred for the setup workers who install and adjust the necessary attachments. Sometimes trial products are produced, adding the cost of additional labor, additional nonproductive machine time, and the materials turned into defective parts.

If a company produces a greater quantity of the product each time it initiates production (i.e., if it increases the lot size), fewer setups will be needed per year to provide the year's required production. The cost of each setup will be spread over more units, thus reducing the unit cost of the items.

Many companies have in the past tended to treat setup cost as a fixed quantity and have adjusted the lot size to be the best to go with that setup cost. More recently, particularly with Japanese companies, the approach has been to try to make lot sizes small and to work on reducing the setup cost so that it is appropriate for small lots. Remarkable reductions in setup costs have been achieved and have been used with just-in-time production (discussed in Chapter 8) to keep lot sizes and inventories very low. It is important that all inventory-related costs be kept as low as practicable, instead of more inventory being kept just to make the setup cost per unit low.

Production Control Costs   Internal production also results in production control costs. Each production lot must be scheduled, production instructions must be prepared, and the materials must be monitored as they progress through the plant. Larger production lots reduce these costs, since fewer lots must be processed to achieve the same total production, requiring fewer production-control transactions.

Cost of Missed Sales   Availability of inventory can eliminate delays in supplying customers. Forecasts are seldom fully accurate, so extra inventory helps a company to meet unanticipated demand. Customers do not like to wait for a product to be back-ordered, and often they will not tolerate a delay. They may revise their requirements or acquire the item from a competitor if it is not available in stock (i.e., if a stockout occurs). The result is that the company misses a sale and loses the profit it would have made. Sometimes customers become so dissatisfied as a result of missed shipments that they take all future business elsewhere. The cost of missed future business (the cost of ill will) may be considerable. These *stockout costs* are difficult to estimate because of the uncertainty involved in estimating the cost of ill will.

DETERMINING THE ECONOMIC ORDER SIZE

Since some costs increase as inventory increases and others decrease, there is no clearly preferable decision as to the size of an order. The best lot size will result in adequate inventory to reduce some costs, yet will not be so large that it results in needless expenses for holding inventory. A compromise must be made between conflicting costs. The *economic order quantity* (EOQ) model provides assistance in reaching a decision when the conditions are appropriate for its use.

The basic EOQ model is applicable to a procurement situation in which an item is purchased from another company. This basic EOQ model is based on several conditions or assumptions:

1. The usage rate is uniform and known (i.e., constant demand).
2. Item cost does not vary with order size (i.e., no quantity discounts).
3. All of the order is delivered at the same time (i.e., no back-order conditions).
4. The lead time is known well enough so that an order can be timed to arrive when inventory is exhausted (i.e., minimum inventory is zero but no stockouts occur).
5. The cost to place and receive an order is the same regardless of the amount ordered.
6. The cost of holding inventory is a linear function of the number of items held (i.e., no economies of scale in holding cost).

The problem is deterministic—that is, there is no uncertainty or probability to consider—when these conditions are met. Some of these assumptions differ from the typical real-world situation. Recall from our discussion of decision making in Supplement D that the modeling process involves simplifying actual situations so long as the essential characteristics are included. The basic EOQ model is oversimplified for some situations, but it is used successfully by many firms with only a few embellishments, which will be discussed later. First we shall develop the basic formula.

The basic EOQ model is a mathematical model that uses symbols to represent relevant variables. These symbols and others are presented in Table 6.1.

Total Relevant Inventory Cost

The objective of the EOQ is to minimize the total annual cost of inventory factors for the item under consideration. These costs can be clarified by a graphical

Table 6.1
**SYMBOLS USED FOR RELEVANT VARIABLES
IN INVENTORY MODELS**

Variable	Symbol	Description or Unit of Measure
Lot size or order quantity	Q	Units per order or dollar value per order, depending on the units used to measure demand
Economic order quantity	EOQ	The quantity to purchase that minimizes total relevant cost
Economic production lot	EPL	The quantity to produce that minimizes total relevant cost
Annual usage	D_a	The number of units of an item to be used or sold during a year
Usage rate	d	The number of units used or sold per unit of time less than a year, such as per day, per week, or per month
Mean usage rate	$\bar{d}$	The mean value of d when it is a random variable
Item cost	C	Cost of a unit in dollars
Holding cost	H	Dollars per year to hold one unit (the sum of all the costs that increase as inventory is increased)
Fractional holding cost	h	Annual holding cost as a decimal fraction of item cost; therefore $H = C \cdot h$
Order cost or setup cost	S	Dollars per order initiated, whether ordered from an external supplier or from the production department within the ordering company (the sum of all order-related costs)
Production rate	p	Units produced per time period
Annual production rate	P	The number of units that would be produced if the production process were run continually for a year
Reorder level	RL	The level of inventory that signals that an order should be placed (number of units on hand and on order)
Lead time	LT	The time between recognition that an order should be placed and the time it arrives
Lead-time usage or demand	D_L	The number of units demanded during the replenishment lead time
Mean lead-time usage	$\bar{D}_L$	The expected value of D_L: $\bar{D}_L = \bar{d} \cdot LT$
Probability of lead-time demand	$P(D_L)$	Probability that variable demand will be greater than a specified amount during the lead time
Stockout cost	C_S	Cost per unit demanded but not available

model of inventory levels over time, as in Figure 6.1. Notice that every triangle is the same shape. The diagonal lines all have the same slope because the usage rate is considered to be the same over time. The inventory level goes to zero at the end of each cycle because of the assumption that shipments can be timed to arrive at just this moment. An order will be placed when the inventory level reaches the reorder level (RL), so that the inventory will be exhausted at the end of the lead time (LT). The reorder level for this problem is the usage rate

FIGURE 6.1

Inventory Level in an Ideal Procurement Situation

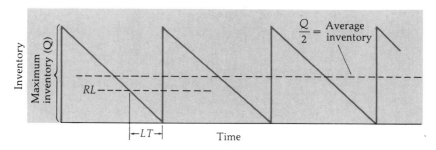

times the lead time, expressed as a fraction of a year (the unit of time being used). The heights of all triangles are the same because the orders that arrive should all be the same size, since the entire shipment arrives each time and all other conditions are assumed to be the same throughout all the cycles. Figure 6.1 illustrates a fixed-quantity inventory system, so called because the same amount is ordered each time. It also represents a fixed-interval system; because the demand is the same each cycle, orders will be needed at the same intervals.

Knowing how order size affects inventory level enables us to write an equation for inventory costs in terms of the order size, Q. Some time base must be established over which we wish to consider cost, so we shall consider the costs per year. If we minimize the average inventory costs for the typical year, we shall have minimized inventory costs. The average inventory will be the average height of a triangle, or one-half its total height. Average inventory for this case is $Q/2$. The cost to hold inventory for a year will be the average number of items held times the cost to hold an item for a year, or $Q/2 \times H$. The average ordering costs will be the number of cycles per year times the cost incurred for each order. If we must buy D_a units during the year and Q units each time we buy, then we will have to place D_a/Q orders and the annual order cost will be $D_a/Q \times S$. The cost of the items is assumed to be constant regardless of the amount we purchase each time we order, so it can be excluded from consideration. Costs that are affected by the lot-size decisions, the relevant costs, are the order-related and *holding costs*. The total annual relevant costs, TC, are determined by equation 6.1:

$$TC = \frac{Q}{2} \cdot H + \frac{D_a}{Q} \cdot S \tag{6.1}$$

or total annual relevant costs equal the average annual inventory times the marginal cost to hold an item for a year plus the number of orders placed per year times the marginal cost to place and receive an order. This equation shows how inventory costs are related to order size. The total cost and its two major components are shown graphically in Figure 6.2. Our objective is to find the

EOQ, that order quantity that will result in a minimum total annual relevant cost, *TC.*

Consider a marginal approach to the problem. Assume that we are considering adding to the order quantity at some point to the left of the minimum cost shown in Figure 6.2. If we increase the order quantity, say from A_1 to A_2, the holding cost will increase by ΔH_A and the order cost will decrease by ΔO_A. The decrease in order costs is greater than the increase in the holding cost, so there is a net reduction in *TC.*

If the order quantity were to the right of the *EOQ,* say at B_1, we might consider increasing it to B_2. The result would be an increase in holding costs larger than the decrease in order cost, or a net increase in costs. Somewhere between points A_1 and B_1 is the ideal order quantity. Moving from A_1 to the right reduced cost. We should continue increasing Q from A_1 as long as costs are reduced but stop before we get to the place where they increase. Costs will then be reduced to their minimum. The minimum is reached when the slope of the *TC* line is horizontal—when it has stopped coming down but has not yet begun to increase. By calculus we can find the expression for the slope of the *TC* line. If we set the slope equal to zero (a horizontal line has a slope of zero) and solve for Q, we will find the Q that makes costs minimum, that is, *EOQ.*

$$TC = \frac{Q}{2}H + \frac{D_a}{Q}S \quad \text{or} \quad \frac{H}{2}Q + D_aSQ^{-1}$$

FIGURE 6.2

Inventory Costs vs. Order Quantity

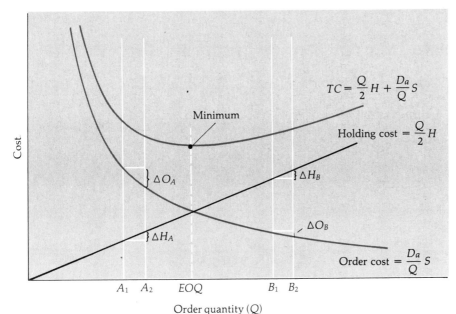

Taking the derivative with respect to Q yields

$$\text{slope} = \frac{dTC}{dQ} = \frac{H}{2}Q^0 - 1(D_aS)Q^{-2} \quad \text{or} \quad \frac{H}{2} - \frac{D_aS}{Q^2}$$

Setting the slope equal to zero and solving for Q yields

$$\frac{H}{2} - \frac{D_aS}{Q^2} = 0 \quad \text{or} \quad \frac{H}{2} = \frac{D_aS}{Q^2}$$

$$Q^2H = 2D_aS \quad \text{so} \quad Q^2 = \frac{2D_aS}{H}$$

$$\text{therefore } Q = \sqrt{\frac{2D_aS}{H}}$$

This is the expression for the Q that will result in a minimum cost. In other words, this is the economic order quantity, EOQ, as shown in equation 6.2. It provides an expression for the amount of an item one should order each time if the assumptions mentioned above are approximately true.

$$EOQ = \sqrt{\frac{2D_aS}{H}} \quad \text{or} \quad \sqrt{\frac{2D_aS}{C \cdot h}} \qquad \text{(6.2)}$$

Notice that under the radical is two times the *annual* demand times the order cost divided by the *annual* holding cost. Demand and holding cost must be expressed for *identical time* bases. Monthly demand over annual holding cost, for example, will give the wrong answer. Monthly demand over monthly holding cost would be correct.

Ordering Costs Equal Holding Costs at the EOQ

The economic order quantity occurs at the minimum of the TC line, where the slope is horizontal. The slope is not changing at this point because the increasing costs (holding costs) are increasing just as fast as the other costs are decreasing; the changes cancel each other, resulting in no net change in total cost. This means the upward slope of the holding-cost line is equal to the downward slope of the order-cost line—the expression

$$\frac{H}{2} = \frac{D_aS}{Q^2}$$

in the calculus derivation. It happens to be true that for the cost functions assumed for the basic EOQ model, the slopes of these lines offset each other where the heights are equal (i.e., where the lines cross). Ordering costs and holding costs will be equal at the EOQ. This relationship provides a means of checking calculations if one is solving a basic EOQ problem. The important point of the derivation, however, is not that we are spending just as much to hold inventory as we spend in ordering it. The important thing is that the costs we are decreasing by adding to the lot size have ceased to overcome the costs we are causing to increase—the point of diminishing returns. In other words, the *rate of increase* of holding costs equals the *rate of decrease* of ordering costs at the EOQ.

Marginal Costs

To solve the EOQ formula one must obtain estimates for annual usage, the marginal cost to place an order, and the marginal cost to hold an item for a year. Marginal costs are the variable costs incurred if one more order is placed or one more unit is held in inventory. The fixed portion of procurement and storage costs are excluded because, being fixed, they will be paid regardless of order size. As was mentioned earlier, costs not affected by a decision are excluded because they are not relevant. If the fixed portions of order and storage are included—that is, if we use average costs rather than variable costs—some error probably will be introduced.

APPLICATION

Example of Order-Quantity Determination

Veneer Furniture Company handles several lines of furniture, one of which is the popular Layback Model T chair, which the company purchases from a plant only ten miles from the store. Since the source is so near, Veneer has not bothered to stock a large number of the chairs in its warehouse. Instead, it sends its truck to "pick up a few" when there are none on the showroom floor. Slim Veneer, the owner, has observed that many times when he needs his truck to make a delivery it is tied up making trips to the Layback plant, and he suspects his ordering practices may not be optimal. He has decided to determine by use of the EOQ model the best quantity to obtain in each order.

    Mr. Veneer has determined from past invoices that he has sold about 200 chairs during each of the past two years at a fairly uniform rate, and he expects to continue at that rate. He has estimated that preparing an order, paying for the driver and truck and the invoice, and other variable costs associated with each order are about $10, and that it costs him about 1.5 percent per month, or 18 percent per year, to hold items in stock. His cost for the chair is $87.00, so it costs him $0.18 \times \$87 = \$15.66$ to hold a chair for one year. (Of course, a chair does not stay in stock that long, but Slim uses annual usage rates, and the holding cost must be based on the same unit of time as the usage rate. He could use the monthly usage rate and the cost to hold a chair for a month. Any other time base could be used, so long as it was used for both usage rate and the cost to hold an item.) Veneer's calculations show that

$$EOQ = \sqrt{\frac{2D_aS}{H}} = \sqrt{\frac{2(200)(10)}{15.66}} = \sqrt{255.43} = 15.98 \text{ units}$$

    He has therefore told the buyer that each time she orders Layback chairs she should order sixteen of them.

DETERMINING THE PRODUCTION LOT SIZE

The assumptions used to develop the basic EOQ formula do not apply to every situation. Some of these assumptions will be changed in the remainder of the chapter and ways of dealing with the new situations will be discussed. The first change will be to relax the assumption that the entire order arrives at one time. Instead assume that the order is produced internally or will be supplied at some uniform rate, p. Naturally, the production rate, p, must be greater than the demand rate, d, or no inventory will be accumulated. For the production situation, the graphical model of inventory level versus time also is a series of triangles, but the inventory replenishment portion of a cycle is not vertical (see Figure 6.3). Instead of building up instantaneously, inventory builds at the production rate minus the usage rate $(p - d)$. If the company produces at a rate of 100 units each day and sells at a rate of 20 units per day, there will be $100 - 20 = 80$ units per day remaining to accumulate in inventory. To maintain consistent units of measure, the production rate and the usage rate must be expressed as units per the same time period. The production rate and usage rate can be expressed as units per year, even though the production process would rarely be run continuously for a year.

The length of time the process must run to produce Q units is Q/p. For example, to produce 500 units at a rate of 100 per day the process would be run $500/100 = 5$ days. Alternatively, using years as the measure of time, assume the production rate is 25,000 units per year (250 production days per year $\times$ 100 units per day). It would require $500/25,000 = 0.02$ year to produce 500 units at that rate. The production time is the same amount, 0.02 year $\times$ 250 workdays per year $= 5$ workdays.

The production process can be run for Q/p year to replenish inventory of one item, then the production equipment can be set up and run for some other product or products while the inventory of the first item is being depleted. In this way, the same equipment is used to produce several products. Our objective is to find the best quantity of a product to produce each time the setup cost

FIGURE 6.3

Inventory Level vs. Time for the Production Situation

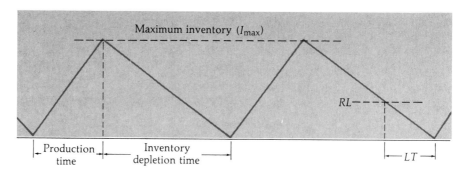

FIGURE 6.4

One Cycle of Inventory Replenishment and Depletion

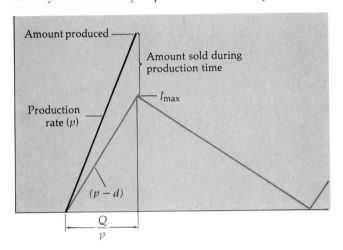

is incurred. Each product probably will have a different setup cost and production rate, and thus its own economic production quantity.

Examining one cycle of inventory replenishment and depletion (Figure 6.4), we see that the maximum inventory, I_{MAX}, occurs at a time, Q/p, after inventory begins to accumulate. We find the maximum inventory by multiplying the inventory accumulation rate by the time inventory is accumulated:

$$I_{MAX} = Q/p(p - d) = Q(1 - d/p) \qquad (6.3)$$

The maximum inventory will be the production lot, Q, times the fraction $(1 - d/p)$ that represents production not sold. d/p is the fraction of production that is sold, so $1 - d/p$ must be stored. Since only the fraction $1 - d/p$ of the production lot must be stored, the holding cost will be $Q(1 - d/p)/2 \cdot H$. The total relevant cost equation for the production situation is like equation 6.1 except that the first Q is multiplied by $(1 - d/p)$.

$$TC = \frac{Q(1 - d/p)}{2} H + \frac{D_a}{Q} S \qquad (6.4)$$

where S = the costs incurred to initiate a production order (setup, production control, and others).

Calculus can be used to derive an expression for the *economic production lot (EPL)*, resulting in equation 6.5. This expression is sometimes called the economic production quantity.

$$EPL = \sqrt{\frac{2D_a S}{H(1 - d/p)}} \quad \text{or} \quad \sqrt{\frac{2D_a S}{H(1 - D_a/P)}} \qquad (6.5)$$

where P is the production rate expressed as units per year.

APPLICATION

Example of Production Lot Size Model

The Layback Chair Company sells to Veneer Furniture and many other retailers. The demand for the Layback Model T chair is relatively uniform at 15,000 per year. The company estimates that it costs $200 to set up all of the equipment and paperwork for production of this chair. When the production facility is running the Model T, the production rate is 150 per day. Each chair costs the company $48.62 to produce and the holding cost is estimated to be 24 percent per year, so $H = $48.62 \times 0.24 = 11.67 to hold a chair in inventory for a year.

The production rate and the demand rate must be expressed on a common time base. Since the demand rate is already on an annual base, the production rate was converted to an annual base. The plant works 5 days a week for 50 weeks a year so there are 250 workdays in its production year. The production in a year, if the process were run that long, would be 150 units per workday × 250 workdays per year or 37,500 units per year. Use of equation 6.5 shows that

$$EPL = \sqrt{\frac{2D_aS}{H(1 - D_a/P)}} = \sqrt{\frac{2(15,000(200))}{11.67(1 - 15,000/37,500)}}$$

$$= \sqrt{856,898} = 925.69 \text{ units}$$

The company should produce about 926 units each time it begins production of the Layback Model T. A production run will require $926/37,500 = 0.0247$ year to produce (0.0247×250 workdays $= 6.17$ days). During the production run, 15,000/37,500 or 0.4 of the units produced will be sold and 0.6 will be held in inventory. The maximum inventory will be 926(0.6) or 556 units, and the annual holding cost will be 556/2($11.67) or $3,244.26. The annual setup cost will be (15,000/926)($200) = $3,239.74. Notice these two costs are approximately equal, as in the case of the economic order quantity determination.

Alternatively, one could reason that since some material is being sold while the lot is being produced, the holding costs will be reduced. Only the faction $1 - d/p$ must be held, so the holding cost can be multiplied by $1 - d/p$. Notice that equation 6.5 is identical to equation 6.2 except that the holding cost is multiplied by $1 - d/p$ or $1 - D_a/P$.

The point was made in our earlier discussion that if the EOQ is used in purchasing situations, the ordering costs will equal the holding costs. This condition is also true for production situations. The annual holding costs will equal the annual setup costs if the economic production lot is produced at each setup. Therefore, efforts to reduce the cost per setup can pay off doubly. If a company reduces the cost per setup and operates with the appropriate production quantity for the reduced setup cost, it will also reduce the cost of its inventory.

EVALUATING QUANTITY-DISCOUNT OPPORTUNITIES

One assumption of the most basic version of the EOQ model was that the cost of the item was not affected by the order size. *Quantity discounts* often are offered for externally purchased items. In addition, economies of scale may result in

Table 6.2
A PRICE DISCOUNT SCHEDULE

Quantity	Price/Unit
Less than Q_1	C_1
Q_1 and up to Q_2	C_2
Q_2 and above	C_3

different unit costs for different production-lot sizes when items are produced internally. This section discusses selection of the economic order size when discounts (as in Table 6.2) are available.

A discount schedule that has *price breaks* at specified quantities results in steps in the total cost curve. The total annual relevant cost equation for this case includes the item costs and is presented in equation 6.6.

$$TC = \frac{Q}{2} H + \frac{D_a}{Q} S + D_a C_i \tag{6.6}$$

Calculus cannot be used to find the slope of a discontinuous curve, so we cannot obtain one equation that will always specify minimum cost. To be sure that the minimum total cost has been found, it may be necessary to solve the TC equation several times, perhaps once for each possible item cost.

The ordering-cost part of equation 6.6 is the same as was developed previously for the first EOQ model. Since the holding cost is a percentage of the item cost, it will also be discontinuous. A graph of the relevant inventory cost as a function of order quantity is presented in Figure 6.5.

The total cost curve of Figure 6.5 is made by connecting portions of three different continuous curves. Each of these continuous curves (shown by a dashed line and the solid portion of the TC curve) is the TC curve that would result if the item cost remained constant over all quantities. The top line would result if all units cost C_1, the middle line if all units cost C_2, and so on. If we solved equation 6.2, the procurement EOQ model, using one cost, we would find the quantity that would result in the minimum holding cost plus ordering cost at this price. There are two problems with this quantity:

1. The resulting quantity might not be feasible; that is, we might not be permitted to purchase that quantity at the price used.
2. Even for a feasible minimum point on the curve, it might be more economical to purchase several more units and obtain a quantity discount. The savings in item cost achieved by purchasing a few more units and receiving a price break might more than offset the additional holding cost for a few extra units.

The procedure for finding the best order quantity in this type of situation is outlined in the following steps:

1. Consider the lowest price and solve the basic EOQ formula (equation 6.2) for the EOQ at this price. If the EOQ is feasible, this is the best quantity, so stop; otherwise go to step 2.

FIGURE 6.5

Relevant Costs vs. Order Quantity with Price Breaks

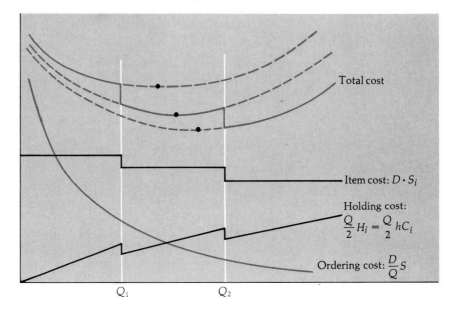

Total cost

Item cost: $D \cdot S_i$

Holding cost:
$$\frac{Q}{2} H_i = \frac{Q}{2} hC_i$$

Ordering cost: $\frac{D}{Q} S$

Q_1 Q_2

2. Solve for the EOQ for the next higher price. If this EOQ is feasible, compute the *TC* (equation 6.6) for this quantity and for all greater quantities where the price breaks occur. Select the quantity with the lowest *TC*.
3. If the EOQ is not feasible, repeat step 2 until a feasible EOQ is found.

Figure 6.6 illustrates the possible relationships that may exist between the total cost where the slope is horizontal and where price breaks occur. The price break quantity is indicated by the vertical dashed line.

Figure 6.6(a) shows the EOQ determined by use of the lowest item cost. Since this EOQ is feasible, it is the lowest total cost, because all points on the *TC* curve for the next higher item cost will be higher.

Figures 6.6(b) and (c) show two relationships that can exist when some cost other than the lowest one is being considered. In Figure 6.6(b), the reduction in total cost due to purchasing at the next higher price break is not sufficient to overcome the holding costs that are increased because more inventory is purchased. Figure 6.6(c) shows a case in which purchasing more will achieve a quantity discount that reduces the item cost more than the increase in the holding cost. Any price-break quantities beyond the next higher one should be evaluated. The same type of analysis can be applied when items are produced internally over time instead of being purchased, and the process used to produce larger lots results in a lower item cost than the process used to produce smaller quantities. For this type of analysis the first Q in equation 6.6 should be multiplied by $(1 - d/p)$ and the *EPL* formula would be used to determine alternative production quantities.

FIGURE 6.6

Possible Total Cost Curve Relationships When Price Breaks Are Available

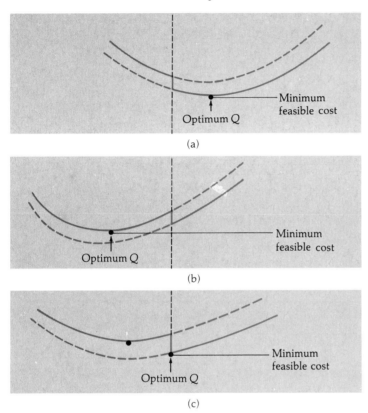

(a)

(b)

(c)

APPLICATION

Example of Price-Break Order Quantity

The Eagle Mountain Hospital uses disposable surgical packages for many routine operations rather than sterilizing and packaging the necessary bandages and instruments. It uses approximately 100 Surg Pac units each month. Elective surgery is scheduled for times when the schedule for other surgery is low, so that demand for Surg Pacs is fairly uniform. Each Surg Pac costs $35 in quantities of less than 75 and $32.50 if purchased in quantities of 75 or more. The hospital controller estimates that it costs $8 to process and receive an order. The cost of holding inventory is estimated to be 12 percent of the purchase price per year.

Karla Karmikel, the purchasing agent, examined the price schedule and performed the following analysis:

Step 1. If Surg Pacs are purchased at the lowest price, $32.50, the holding cost per unit-year, H, will be $0.12 \times \$32.50 = \$3.90$, so for this price:

$$EOQ(\$32.50) = \sqrt{\frac{2D_aS}{H}} = \sqrt{\frac{2(1,200)(8)}{3.90}} = \sqrt{4,923.08} = 70.16 \text{ or } 70.$$

This quantity is unfeasible. The hospital would not receive the lowest price if it purchased 70 packs each time.

Step 2. If Surg Pacs are purchased at $35.00 each, the holding cost will be $0.12 \times \$35 = \$4.20$ per unit year.

$$EOQ(\$35) = \sqrt{\frac{2D_aS}{H}} = \sqrt{\frac{2(1,200)(8)}{4.20}} = \sqrt{4,571.43} = 67.61 \text{ or } 68.$$

This is a feasible order quantity, but another step must be performed to see if it is the best order quantity. The hospital will achieve a sizable saving on the item cost if it purchases 75 units in each order.

Ms. Karmikel used the TC equation (equation 6.6) to evaluate this possibility and found the following total annual cost if 68 were used as the order quantity.

$$TC_{68} = \frac{68}{2}(\$4.20) + \frac{1,200}{68}(\$8.00) + 1,200(\$35) = \$42,283.98$$

If the hospital buys the Surg Pacs in quantities of 75, the total annual cost will be:

$$TC_{75} = \frac{75}{2}(\$3.90) + \frac{1,200}{75}(\$8.00) + 1,200(\$32.50) = \$39,274.25$$

This price-break example for Surg Pacs was like the one illustrated in Figure 6.6(c). It is more economical to purchase an amount above the point on the solid TC line where the slope is horizontal. Ms. Karmikel made a notation on the Surg Pac inventory record card that the proper order quantity was 75.

DETERMINING THE REORDER LEVEL

The previous models have been developed under the assumption of a deterministic usage rate. That assumption was stated, and the illustrations showed that the reorder level was established so that the inventory level would reach zero just as the new material began to arrive. With a known usage rate and lead time, the reorder level would be set equal to the usage rate, d (in units per time period) times LT, the number of these time periods in the lead time.

$$RL = d \cdot LT \tag{6.7}$$

For example, if a company uses exactly 20 units of a particular component each day and the replenishment lead time is known to be 3 days, the RL for this component would be $20 \cdot 3 = 60$ units.

The reorder level refers to the number of units on hand and on order, rather than to just the amount of inventory on hand. In many instances no orders are outstanding when the reorder level is reached, so the reorder level is often thought of as referring only to the number of units on hand. This misconception may cause no problem; but in some instances, the reorder level may be greater than the maximum inventory, and this could cause some confusion. For example, the lead time could be long—causing the reorder level to be very high. Also, the order cost may be low in comparison to the holding cost—causing the order quantity to be small. In instances where one or more orders are outstanding when the reorder level is reached, it is important to remember that the reorder level refers to the number of units on hand plus those on order.

In the following section we deal with probabilistic demand. When we do not know the exact demand rate and lead time, there is a chance that the amount demanded during the lead time will be greater than the reorder level unless we increase the reorder level beyond the amount expressed by equation 6.7. The additional amount added to the reorder level is sometimes referred to as safety stock.

SAFETY STOCK

One reason for inventory is to allow production or procurement in economic lot sizes. Previous discussions in this chapter have dealt with lot sizing under a variety of conditions. The lot size, in effect, determines the *cycle stock*, or stock that is intended to be depleted and replenished, then depleted and replenished again through many cycles.

Another reason for inventory is to protect against uncertainty of demand. In previous inventory discussions, we assumed that demand and lead times were known (deterministic) and that reorders were timed so that replenishment stock arrived just as the previous order was exhausted. Usually one does not know precisely the number of units that will be demanded each day during the lead time. Also the duration of lead times may have unexplained or unexpected variation.

Demand can be thought of as a probabilistic variable with some expected amount of demand during a period of time and unexplained variation about the expected value. If we could replenish inventory on a moment's notice, there would be no reason to be concerned about demand uncertainty. Whenever inventory reached zero, we would restock. With some lead time between the placement of an order and its arrival, however, there is a chance that demand will be greater than we expected and we will incur a loss due to stockout. When stockout costs are high and demand is very unpredictable, the financial risk is sizable. *Safety stock* (or *buffer stock*) is a means of protection against this risk.

Safety stock is the average amount on hand when replenishment orders arrive. Sometimes demand during lead time is less than expected and extra stock is on hand. Sometimes demand is greater than expected and some of the safety stock is used. Safety stock can be thought of as remaining in inventory all year, on the average. Figure 6.7 illustrates inventory level over time when safety stock is present.

Safety stock (SS) is established simply by raising the reorder level above the expected lead-time demand. For probabilistic demand during lead time, the reorder level (RL) is given by equation 6.8, where $\bar{d}$ represents the mean demand per unit of time (the time units are consistent with the units for lead time, LT).

$$RL = (\bar{d} \cdot LT) + SS \qquad \text{(6.8)}$$

FIGURE 6.7

Inventory Level When Safety Stock Is Present

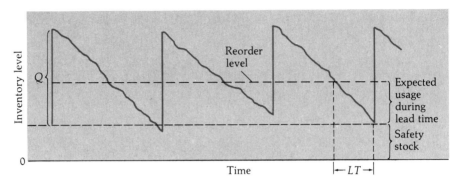

For example, an office supply company may try to maintain a safety stock or minimum inventory of 25 reams of 25 percent-cotton, cream stationery. Suppose that demand for this product averages 5 reams per day and the usual replenishment lead time is 6 business days. In these circumstances RL = (5 reams/day $\times$ 6 days) + 25 reams = 55 reams.

Factors Affecting Safety Stock Level

The most advantageous amount of safety stock to carry depends on the situation, because the cost of carrying safety stock should be compared to the benefits it provides. All other things being equal, the following conditions tend to encourage higher levels of safety stock.

1. *The cost or loss due to stockout may be high.* If an item is inventoried as raw material to supply some production process, a stockout may stop production, idling expensive labor and facilities and resulting in many lost sales. Stockout of some finished goods may merely delay delivery of a product to some patient customer. When stockouts are expensive, it is wise to pay the cost of carrying adequate safety stock.
2. *The cost of carrying safety stock may be low.* If a company has adequate storage space and funds are available, the cost to hold stock may not be great. When this is the case, extensive protection from stockout may be a wise use of funds.
3. *The variability or uncertainty of demand may increase.* This condition indicates a relationship between inventory levels and forecasting accuracy. If forecasts are improved, then less safety stock is needed, and vice versa. Sometimes it is more economical to carry inventory instead of spending to improve forecasting methods.
4. *The number of annual exposures to the risk of stockout may increase.* This factor refers to the interrelationship between order quantity and the risk of stockout. The only time a company is exposed to the risk of stockout is at the end of a replenishment cycle. If a year's supply is purchased each time, stockout can occur only once a year. Holding costs, however, may be

extremely high. Frequent procurement of small orders leads to frequent exposure to stockout, possibly resulting in excessive stockout cost.

A rigorous analysis of inventory costs would include consideration of the interrelationship of order quantity and stockout, solving simultaneous equations to obtain the optimum value for order quantity and safety stock. Several texts and many actual applications ignore the interrelation, and so shall we. We shall determine the EOQ by use of the equations previously developed and then determine the best safety stock level, given the order quantity we have determined.

Methods of Determining the Safety Stock Level

The previous subsection recognized in a general way factors that determine the risk a company is exposed to by varying the level of safety stock it maintains. In this subsection we shall explore the ways in which companies may take such factors into account when they establish the reorder level for an item. Three methods will be discussed: an intuitive rule-of-thumb method, a service-level policy method, and a minimum-expected-cost method that explicitly considers stockout cost.

When demand is probabilistic, inventory may reach its reorder level sooner or later than expected. The cycle time between replenishments will no longer be constant. There is no stockout risk involved with demand fluctuations between the time of maximum inventory and the time the inventory balance reaches the reorder level. The risk occurs after the reorder level has been reached. Demand during the lead time may turn out to be less than, equal to, or greater than the reorder level. These conditions are illustrated in Figure 6.8.

The objective of all three methods of establishing safety stock is to define a reasonable maximum demand during lead time.

FIGURE 6.8

Probabilistic Demand After Reorder Is Placed

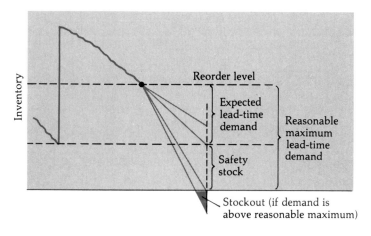

Intuitive Rule of Thumb   Sometimes inventory managers or higher level managers arbitrarily set ratios to guide the establishment of reorder points and safety stocks. They may order whenever the on-hand quantity is twice (or 1.5 times, 1.2 times, or some such amount) the projected usage during a lead time. This method recognizes that lead time may be longer than expected, demand may be higher than expected, or both. The method does not, however, formally consider probabilities of stockout, cost of inventory, or cost of stockout. Examination of past back orders or canceled orders as a percentage of mean lead-time demand gives some indication of demand variation or risk of stockout for various reorder levels. The objective is to establish a reorder level at some "reasonable maximum" level of lead-time demand without identifying probability or stockout costs.

Service Level vs. Holding Cost   *Service level* relates to the percentage of demand that is supplied from inventory. It may be defined in several ways, some of which are listed below.

1. The number of units supplied from stock as a percentage of units demanded during the total cycle.
2. The number of units supplied from stock during a lead time as a percentage of the number of units demanded during lead time.
3. The percentage of customer orders that were completely filled from stock.
4. The percentage of lead times when stockout did not occur.
5. The percentage of a time base longer than just the lead time, such as the percentage of the year during which there is stock on hand—that is, the ability to meet at least a part of demand if it occurs.

A manager should specify which definition is to be used in order to establish a policy or target for service levels. All of these measures can be related to probability of meeting demand, whether it be demand at any time or demand during lead time. We shall use the second definition above.

In order to implement a policy specifying some service level, one must have information concerning the probability of various levels of demand during lead time. Often the quantity of an item demanded during the lead time varies from its expected value. Some of this variation may be caused by fluctuations in the length of the lead time and some by variation of the demand rate about its mean. Records from a number of previous reorder cycles can be examined to determine the number of units demanded between the time a replenishment order was placed and the time that material arrived. Let us call this variable *lead-time demand* (D_L). A frequency or probability distribution for lead-time demand can be constructed as in Figure 6.9. Lead-time demand may occur in discrete or continuous units, but Figure 6.9 illustrates a discrete distribution, and the relationships between safety stock, reorder level, and the probability of stockout are shown.

In setting service levels, however, we are not really interested in the probability that a particular value of lead-time demand will occur. Rather, we are interested in the probability that lead-time demand will be greater than some

FIGURE 6.9

A Probability Distribution for Demand During Lead Time

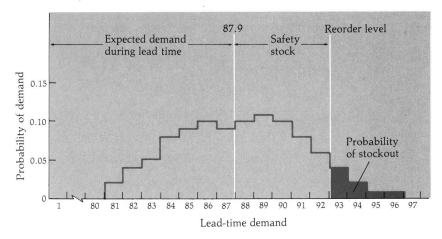

Lead-time demand

particular level, that is, the probability of a stockout for a given reorder level. A "greater-than" cumulative probability distribution can be constructed by adding the probabilities in the right tail of the distribution to determine the service level that would result from possible reorder levels.

The shaded area in the right tail of Figure 6.9 can be computed for various reorder levels and plotted as a "greater-than" cumulative probability distribution. Figure 6.10 shows this type of distribution as a smooth curve, which would result from a continuous variable or from drawing a smooth curve through midpoints of the steps in a discrete cumulative distribution. The ordinate of Figure 6.10 has been provided with two scales: one showing the probability of stockout and one showing service level. Notice that the probability of stockout declines very rapidly near the middle. The service level can be increased from 0.70 to 0.80 by adding only 25 units to the reorder level. But an additional 55 units are necessary to increase the service level by another 0.10 to 0.90. Greater increments in the reorder level, causing greater increases in inventory holding costs, are required for each increment of increase to the service level at the right end of the distribution.

The total cost of holding inventory can be plotted as a function of the service level a company intends to provide. An example of this type of graph is shown in Figure 6.11. Managers may find a graphical presentation such as Figure 6.11 very helpful in establishing a service-level policy. They may be willing to hold a large inventory and provide a high service level if funds are rather plentiful and competition is aggressive. They may elect to reduce service levels if competitive pressures permit and if funds are needed for other purposes. The service-level policy compares the percentage of demand that is met from inventory with the cost of holding inventory. It does not explicitly consider the cost of stockout. Some implicit value of stockout, however, can be inferred from the holding cost a company is willing to pay to prevent stockout.

FIGURE 6.10

A "Greater-Than" Cumulative Probability Distribution of Lead-Time Demand

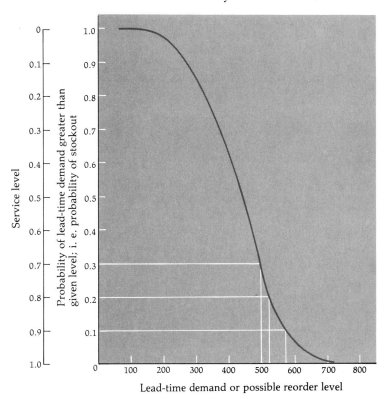

FIGURE 6.11

Holding Cost vs. Service Level

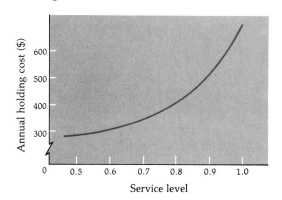

APPLICATION

Example of Setting a Reorder Level on the Basis of an Empirical Probability Distribution

Earlier we saw how Karla Karmikel at Eagle Mountain Hospital determined the most economical number of disposable surgical packs to buy in each order. Now suppose that Ms. Karmikel wishes to determine the appropriate reorder level when there is variation in the number of units required during a lead time. Ordinarily the lead time is four days, but it has varied from two to seven days, and usage per day has varied from zero to ten units. Ms. Karmikel has reviewed data for the past twenty-five orders and has found considerable variation in the number of Surg Pac units that were used between the time the order was placed and the time it was received (i.e., the lead-time demand).

A frequency count for lead-time demand for Surg Pacs is shown in Table 6.3. These data are plotted in a combined frequency distribution and probability

Table 6.3
LEAD-TIME DEMAND FOR SURG PACS
AT EAGLE MOUNTAIN HOSPITAL

Possible Levels of Demand (K)	Frequency of Occurrence	Probability	Cumulative Probability $P(D > K)$
6		0.00	1.00
7	1	0.04	0.96
8		0.00	0.96
9	1	0.04	0.92
10	11	0.08	0.84
11		0.00	0.84
12	1	0.04	0.80
13		0.00	0.80
14	11	0.08	0.72
15	111	0.12	0.60
16	1111	0.16	0.44
17	111	0.12	0.32
18	11	0.08	0.24
19	1	0.04	0.20
20		0.00	0.20
21		0.00	0.20
22	1	0.04	0.16
23	1	0.04	0.12
24		0.00	0.12
25		0.00	0.12
26	1	0.04	0.08
27		0.00	0.08
28		0.00	0.08
29		0.00	0.08
30	1	0.04	0.04
31		0.00	0.04
32	1	0.04	0.00
33		0.00	0.00
	25	1.00	

FIGURE 6.12

Frequency Distribution for Surg Pacs Used During Lead Time

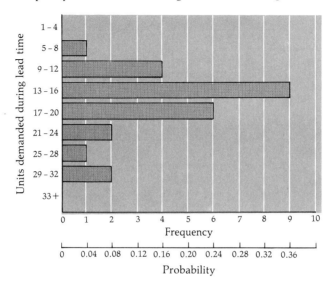

distribution, shown in Figure 6.12. The variable of primary interest is the probability that the number of Surg Pacs required during the lead time will be greater than some specified quantity. This probability will indicate the likelihood that the lead-time demand will be greater than each reorder level that may be selected. The desired probabilities are provided by a "greater than" cumulative probability distribution such as that shown in Figure 6.13. These probabilities are found by accumulating probabilities beginning at the right tail of the probability distribution for demand during lead time (from the right-hand column of Table 6.3).

It has been agreed at meetings between the director of pharmacy, the director of materials, and the medical staff that a 95 percent service level is adequate for disposable Surg Pacs. The operating room staff can prepare nondisposable kits in the event of a stockout. Therefore, Ms. Karmikel has selected 30 units as the reorder

Explicit Tradeoff of Stockout Cost   We have seen that holding costs climb at ever increasing rates as the service level is increased (see Figure 6.11). Attempting to cover all possible levels of lead-time demand can be a very expensive objective. At some point (the reasonable maximum demand) it may be less expensive to allow some stockouts to occur, at least for most products. A rational business executive will raise the safety stock level so long as the expected cost of carrying safety stock is less than the expected opportunity cost of stockout. The problem becomes one of determining the safety stock level that balances the expected cost of carrying safety stock with the expected cost of not having enough stock (Figure 6.14).

FIGURE 6.13

Cumulative Distribution for Probability That Demand for Surg Pacs Will Be Greater Than a Specified Amount

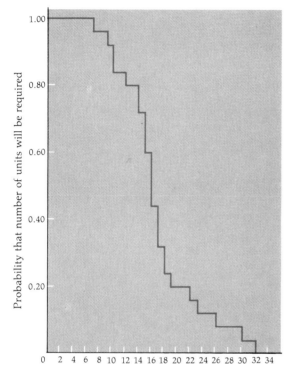

level that appears to be sufficient to cover 95 percent of the units demanded during lead time. The expected demand during lead time is 17 units, so the safety stock for this kit is 30 − 17 = 13 units.

We can find the reorder level at which these costs are in balance by marginal analysis. The marginal cost of adding another unit to safety stock is H, a constant because of the original assumption that holding cost is a linear function of the average amount held. The marginal gain from adding safety stock—that is, the expected reduction in stockout cost—is a variable we can change by varying the reorder level. As the reorder level is raised, the probability of stockout, and hence its expected cost, is reduced.

The expected cost of stockout in a year requires some explanation. A stockout will occur if demand is any value greater than the value of the last unit added to the reorder level. In one lead time the probability of a stockout is

FIGURE 6.14

Balancing Costs of Safety Stock and Stockout

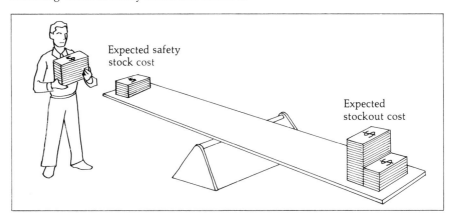

$P(D_L)$, the probability that demand will be greater than the reorder level. This probability can be obtained from a cumulative probability distribution of lead-time demand, as was shown in Figure 6.10. Each time a stockout occurs we shall suffer a loss of C_S, so the expected stockout cost per cycle is $P(D_L) \cdot C_S$. Since there are D_a/Q cycles per year, we must multiply the expected cost per cycle by D_a/Q to get the expected annual stockout cost.

The expected annual stockout cost for a given reorder level, $P(D_L) \cdot C_S \cdot D_a/Q$, declines as the reorder level is increased, because $P(D_L)$, the probability of stockout, is reduced as we add safety stock. Safety stock should be added (i.e., the reorder point should be raised) until the holding cost from adding the last unit of safety stock is equal to the expected gain from adding the last unit. These cost relationships are illustrated in Figure 6.15.

FIGURE 6.15

Cost Relevant to Safety Stock

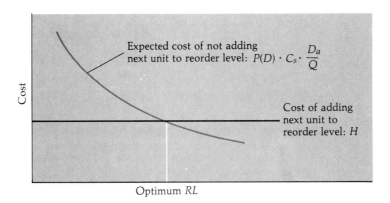

The two costs are equal when

$$H = P(D_L)C_S \cdot D_a/Q$$

Solving this expression for $P(D_L)$, we find $P(D_L)^*$, the probability of stockout at the "optimal" reorder level.

$$P(D_L)^* = \frac{H}{C_S} \cdot \frac{Q}{D_a} \qquad\qquad \text{(6.9)}$$

Equation 6.9 gives the probability of stockout for the optimal reorder level, given the order quantity Q.[1] One can then read the optimal reorder level from an empirical probability distribution for lead-time demand, such as Figure 6.10, if an empirical distribution is appropriate and has been developed.

If the lead-time demand fits a known probability distribution, the reorder level can be found with the aid of probability tables for the appropriate distribution. For example, assume that lead-time demand is normally distributed with a mean of 300 and a standard deviation of 100. Assume the optimal $P(D_L)$ were found to be 0.05, that is, we desire a 95 percent service level. A table giving the area under a standardized normal distribution (i.e., a "Z distribution") can be used to determine the appropriate reorder level. Reference to Table 6.4 reveals that 0.95 of the area under the curve lies to the left of $Z = +1.645$. That is, we must add 1.645σ to the mean of a normal distribution. So for our problem the reorder level we seek is $RL = 300 + 1.645(100) = 465$ units. In general, if lead-time demand is normally distributed, the reorder level can be found by

$$RL = \overline{D}_L + Z\sigma_L \qquad\qquad \text{(6.10)}$$
where $\overline{D}_L$ = average lead-time demand   or $\overline{d} \cdot LT$
$\quad\quad Z$ = the standardized normal deviate
$\quad\quad \sigma_L$ = the standard deviation of lead-time demand. (This must be appropriate for the length of the lead time.)

The expected usage during the lead time is $\overline{D}_L$, so $Z\sigma_L$ is the safety stock. The standard deviation of lead-time demand must be measured over the lead time or adjusted to its length. If it is assumed that the demand in one period is independent of demand in the other periods, then

$$\sigma_L = \sqrt{LT \cdot \sigma_p^2} \qquad\qquad \text{(6.11)}$$
where LT = the number of periods in the lead time
$\quad\quad \sigma_p$ = the standard deviation of demand per period.

---

[1]The order quantity and reorder level are interrelated. A large order quantity causes fewer replenishment cycles with fewer exposures to stockout, so the reorder level can be reduced, and vice versa. Theoretically, we would have to find simultaneous solutions to equations for Q and RL to find their optimal values. The values of D_a, S, and H are only estimates, and the value of the EOQ will be approximate whether or not an adjustment is made for the expected stockout cost. Consequently, as often is done, we shall disregard the interrelationship between Q and RL. We shall solve for the EOQ ignoring its effect on stockout cost and then find the best reorder level for this value of Q.

Table 6.4
SAFETY FACTORS FOR NORMAL DISTRIBUTION
(PLUS DEVIATIONS ONLY)

Service Level (% of order cycles w/o stockout)	SAFETY FACTOR USING:	
	Standard Deviation	Mean Absolute Deviation
50.00	0.00	0.00
75.00	0.67	0.84
80.00	0.84	1.05
84.13	1.00	1.25
85.00	1.04	1.30
89.44	1.25	1.56
90.00	1.28	1.60
93.32	1.50	1.88
94.00	1.56	1.95
94.52	1.60	2.00
95.00	1.65	2.06
96.00	1.75	2.19
97.00	1.88	2.35
97.72	2.00	2.50
98.00	2.05	2.56
98.61	2.20	2.75
99.00	2.33	2.91
99.18	2.40	3.00
99.38	2.50	3.13
99.50	2.57	3.20
99.60	2.65	3.31
99.70	2.75	3.44
99.80	2.88	3.60
99.86	3.00	3.75
99.90	3.09	3.85
99.93	3.20	4.00
99.99	4.00	5.00

Source: George W. Plossl and Oliver W. Wight, Production and Inventory Control (Englewood Cliffs, N.J.: Prentice-Hall, 1967), p. 108. © 1967 Reprinted by permission of Prentice-Hall, Inc.

Suppose that demand averaged 40 units per week with a standard deviation, measured on a weekly basis, of 10 units. If the lead time were constant at three weeks, then σ_L would be found by equation 6.11:

$$\sigma_L = \sqrt{3(10^2)} = \sqrt{300} = 17.32$$
$$\text{and } \overline{D}_L = 3(40) = 120$$

so for a 0.98 service level $Z = 2.05$ and $RL = \overline{D}_L + Z\sigma_L = 120 + 2.05(17.32) = 156$ units.

Sometimes the variability of lead-time demand is measured in *mean absolute deviations* (MADs). An MAD is approximately equal to 0.8σ, so this relationship can be used to establish the required reorder level for a given service level.

Table 6.4 shows the number of MADs or standard deviations required to provide various service levels. In case the MAD is computed for some time period other than the length of the lead time, the MAD for n periods can be found by

$$MAD_n = \sqrt{n}\, MAD_1$$

where MAD_n = the MAD for n periods

MAD_1 = the MAD computed on the basis of one time period.

APPLICATION

Establishing a Safety Stock Level (Reorder Level) with Explicit Stockout Cost

The Celestial Grocery Coop distributes Jolly Red Giant red beans and wishes to establish a fixed-quantity inventory system for the product. Lead time to obtain these red beans from the Red Giant Company averages one week. Examination of past orders shows that demand has been fairly uniform and that lead-time demand has been normally distributed, with a mean of 320 cases and a standard deviation of 40 cases. Since demand averages 320 every week, annual demand is 16,640 cases. The company estimates that order cost is $14.00, holding cost is $1.68 per year per case, and stockout cost is $2.00 per case.

The order quantity is

$$EOQ = \sqrt{\frac{2D_a S}{H}} = \sqrt{\frac{2(16,640)(14)}{1.68}} = \sqrt{27,733.33} = 526.62$$

The company should order 527 cases each time, a quantity that would result in 31.6 cycles per year (16,640/527 = 31.6).

The remaining question is the level of inventory that should be on hand when the order is placed. The optimum probability of stockout in a reorder cycle can be found from equation 6.9.

$$P(D_L)^* = \frac{H}{C_s} \cdot \frac{Q}{D_a} = \frac{1.68}{2} \cdot \frac{527}{16,640} = 0.0266$$

A reasonable maximum demand is one that will be exceeded only 2.66 percent of the time. Referring to a normal probability table, we find that 97.34 percent of the area under the curve lies below a Z of 1.93. Therefore, the optimum reorder level is

$$RL = \overline{D}_L + Z\sigma_L = 320 + 1.93(40) = 397$$

The safety stock provided by this reorder level is 397 − 320 = 77 cases. As a result of these calculations, Celestial has established the following as its inventory policy for Red Giant beans: Order 527 cases every time the inventory level reaches 397 cases.

We can approximate the annual holding cost by assuming that the average inventory will include all of the safety stock and half of the cycle stock. The annual holding cost will be ($1.68 per case) × [77 + (527/2)] = 1.68(340.5) = $572.04. This amount will not be equal to the annual ordering cost because it includes the cost of holding safety stock. The order quantity formula makes the ordering cost equal to the cost of holding only the average cycle stock. The annual ordering cost will be ($14 per order) × (31.6 orders per year) = $442.40.

USING COMPUTERS TO MANAGE INDEPENDENT INVENTORY

You probably have noticed that in some grocery or department stores part of the labeling on products is scanned by some type of bar code reader at the checkout counter. Data indicating the item identification and quantity sold are recorded by this procedure and stored in an electronic memory. These data can be fed to a computer system to update the stock level and usage rate for the

FIGURE 6.16

Flow Chart of a Computerized Inventory System

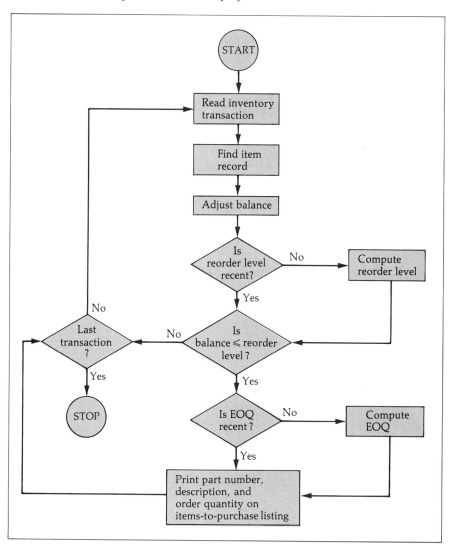

item. In other stores, when an item is sold the clerk removes the part of the price tag that contains the item identification. These tags are later read and the data are fed to a computer. In yet other companies, the item identification and quantity sold are read from sales slips and keyed into the computer. In a factory or warehouse, shipping reports or inventory removal cards may be used as the source of data on stock removal. Receiving reports will indicate additions to the inventory by suppliers, and completed production orders will indicate additions to the inventory by production within the factory. You can see, then, that there are numerous ways to report data on inventory additions or withdrawals and to supply these data to a computer.

Computers can use data on receipts and withdrawals to maintain the amount of stock on hand for all of the inventory items controlled by the computer system. Computer companies and commercial software companies offer software packages that will keep track of the on-hand balance and perform other functions—such as reporting items that are below their reorder levels and recommending the economic quantity to buy or produce. The computer may print a list each day showing the items that need to be replenished. Sometimes a preferred vendor identification for each item is stored in the data base, so the computer can automatically prepare the purchase orders if instructed to do so.

Some software packages for managing independent-demand inventory use the basic theory presented in this chapter and are appropriate for items that have a relatively uniform demand rate. Figure 6.16 shows a simplified flow chart for an independent-demand inventory system to provide an overview of the decisions and calculations that might be made in such a system. Usage history can be used to calculate a forecast of the expected annual demand. Estimates of the holding cost, setup cost, or order cost for each item can be stored in the data base, from which order quantity recommendations can be calculated. The reorder level for each item can be stored in the data base, but often only the lead time and desired service level are stored. The program can compute the reorder level on the basis of the current estimates of the average usage rate and a calculated standard deviation or MAD. This type of system maintains a great amount of data and performs numerous calculations to assist inventory managers. Of course, the system only makes recommendations, which can be overridden or implemented according to the decisions of the appropriate person.

SUMMARY

Inventory can be an important resource to assist a company in its competitive strategy by enabling the company to serve its customers more quickly. Inventory can also help protect a company from unpredicted surges in demand. Running large lots can spread the fixed costs associated with a lot over more units and thus reduce the cost per unit. Large lots, however, can result in large inventories and significant costs to hold them. Since inventory can have advantages and will protect a company from its mistakes or from uncertainty, there has been a tendency for many companies to hold more inventory than they need. Instead of doing the hard work of solving problems, some companies just held extra inventory to protect themselves from error. Recession and tough competition have caused many of these companies to reconsider the question of how much inventory is needed.

Companies have worked to reduce setup costs and to build relationships with their suppliers so that the company can depend on faster resupply of acceptable materials. The result has been significant in many instances. Companies have had to improve their quality because they did not have excess material available just in case. Companies are working to be more flexible so that they can respond to demand without holding as much inventory. It is important to reduce the reasons for having inventory in addition to managing inventory wisely.

The basic EOQ model $\left(\text{i.e., } \sqrt{\dfrac{2D_aS}{H}} \right)$ assumes uniform usage, a fixed cost to process each order, no quantity discounts, the entire order arriving at just the right time to prevent stockout, and a fixed cost per period to hold a unit of an item. Adjustments to deal with quantity discounts and production over time (instead of procurement) were discussed. Increasing the reorder level above the expected demand during lead time will provide some safety stock for protection from variability in demand (i.e., $RL = d \cdot LT + SS$). If demand during lead time fits a known probability distribution, we can use a table of probabilities for that distribution to determine the probabilities of serving demand during lead time from stock for alternative reorder levels. This approach provides a way of setting reorder levels. An arbitrary ratio or explicit modeling with stockout costs taken into account are two other approaches to determining reorder levels.

The models presented in this chapter are very basic but still appropriate where the assumptions are satisfied. These models, together with the ideas on dependent-demand inventory presented in the next chapter, are used by many companies to manage inventories. Some companies are moving to an approach to inventory called "just-in-time" production so that goods do not sit in inventory very long. Just-in-time is discussed in connection with scheduling in Chapter 8.

SOLVED PROBLEMS

PROBLEM:

Battery Wholesale, Inc., purchases batteries for $14 each, and the ordering cost is $11 to process an order. The company sells about 12,000 of a particular type of battery a year at a uniform rate. The company is open five days a week for 52 weeks a year with the exception of six holidays a year. The order lead time is three days, and the company wants to have an average of two days' sales on hand as safety stock when a new order is scheduled to arrive. Holding cost is estimated to be 24 percent of the item cost per year.

(a) Determine the EOQ.
(b) Determine the average level of the maximum inventory.
(c) Determine the reorder level.
(d) Determine the average inventory level.
(e) Determine the average annual cost to hold inventory.

SOLUTION:

(a)

$$EOQ = \sqrt{\frac{2D_aS}{H}} = \sqrt{\frac{2(12,000)(\$11)}{.24(\$14)}}$$

$$= 280.3 \text{ or } 280$$

(b) The average sales per day is 12,000/[(52 × 5) − 6] = 47.24.

The company wants an average of two days' sales or 94.48 units in safety stock when an order arrives, so the maximum inventory should average 280 + 94.48 = 374.48 or 374.

(c) Using equation 6.8:

$RL = (d \times LT) + SS = (3 \times 47.24) + 94.48$
$= 236.2$ or 236.

(d) The average inventory level will be ½ (maximum + minimum) = ½ (374 + 94) = 234. Another way to find the average inventory is ½ (cycle stock) + safety stock = ½ (280) + 94 = 140 + 94 = 234.

(e) The annual cost to hold inventory will be the annual holding cost times the average inventory level, or .24 ($14)(234 units) = $786.24.

PROBLEM:

Postal Posts, Inc., produces and sells cedar mailbox posts to a broad market in the western states. Demand is fairly uniform at 10,000 posts per year. The company can produce 75 posts per day and there are 242 production days in a year. The setup cost for the production equipment is $100 and the holding cost for a post is $2 per year.

(a) How many posts should be produced in each production run?

(b) What will be the maximum inventory level if the company tries to have a minimum of 300 posts in inventory?

SOLUTION:

(a)

$$EPL = \sqrt{\frac{2D_aS}{H(1 - D_a/P)}} = \sqrt{\frac{2(10,000)(100)}{2\left[1 - \frac{10,000}{242(75)}\right]}}$$

$= \sqrt{2,226,993.9}$
$= 1,492$

(b) Production of this amount will take 1,492 ÷ 75 = 19.89 days. During this time the company will sell 19.89 (10,000 ÷ 242) = 822 posts, so the inventory will build up by 1,492 − 822 = 670. If the inventory is 300 when production is initiated, the inventory level will reach a maximum of 970.

DISCUSSION QUESTIONS

1. What are some of the costs that increase with the size of inventory?
2. What are some of the costs that may decrease as inventory is increased?
3. What basic assumptions underlie development of the most basic (procurement version) EOQ model?
4. Which of these assumptions is changed if the item is produced internally?
5. Why is it important to analyze setup procedures and costs to seek all reasonable ways to keep setup costs low?
6. How is the most basic model adapted when demand is not deterministic?
7. Why can fixed cost be ignored in developing the EOQ?
8. Changes in what four general conditions might cause a company to increase its safety stock?
9. Describe briefly three methods that may be used to establish the amount of safety stock a company carries.
10. What is a service level?
11. Why is it difficult to determine an accurate estimate of stockout cost?
12. What is the relationship between MAD and σ?

PROBLEMS

1. Extended Play Stereo, Inc., sells 450 Super Power amplifiers per year and expects sales to continue at that rate. Holding cost is 20 percent of unit cost per year, and the amplifiers cost $180 each. The cost to process a purchase order is $16.
   (a) What is the EOQ?
   (b) How much will the company spend each year to order and hold Super Power amplifiers?

2. Suppose that Extended Play Stereo opens a second outlet but continues to use one central purchasing location. The holding cost, order cost, and item cost remain the same as in problem 1 but the annual demand doubles to 900 units per year.
   (a) What will be the new EOQ? How much has it increased from the EOQ of problem 1?
   (b) How much will the company spend each year to order and hold this model of amplifier with the higher level of demand?
   (c) Do "economies of scale" apply to inventory under some conditions?

3. Each year the Irish Guard Company purchases 14,000 of an item that costs $16 per unit. The cost of placing an order is $12, and the cost to hold the item for a year is 30 percent of the unit cost.
   (a) Determine the economic order quantity.
   (b) Compute the average inventory level, assuming that the minimum inventory level is zero.
   (c) Determine the total annual ordering and holding costs for the item if the EOQ is used.

4. Suppose the Irish Guard Company discussed in problem 3 uses an order quantity of 300 units and maintains a minimum inventory of 50 units.

   (a) Determine the average inventory level.
   (b) Determine the total annual ordering and holding cost for the item if the order quantity is 300 and the minimum inventory is 50 units.
   (c) How much of the difference in total cost is caused by changing from the EOQ found in problem 3 to the order quantity of 300?

5. The Twin Rivers Driving Range has a fairly uniform business all year. About 20 dozen golf balls are lost, stolen, or damaged beyond use each week with almost no variations. The balls cost $5 a dozen to purchase. The cost to hold inventory is 1.5 percent per month, and the cost to place a purchase order is $7. The driving range needs a minimum of 200 dozen balls in inventory, and the lead time to order balls is 3 weeks.
   (a) How many balls should this organization buy each time it buys?
   (b) What is the reorder level for balls?
   (c) Discuss methods of determining when the reorder level is reached. It costs about $12 to count the balls on hand— a job that must be done when the range is not in operation. What methods could be used to manage the inventory?

6. The Domino Taxi company uses 200,000 gallons of gasoline per year at a consistent rate. It costs $40 to have the truck come to the garage and deliver gasoline and to process the orders, invoices, and checks associated with each delivery. Evaporation losses and other storage costs are $0.015 per gallon per month.
   (a) How much gasoline should the company purchase with each order?
   (b) What is the penalty if the company's tank will hold only 8,000 gallons, so that the company can purchase only 7,500 gallons at each order?

(c) Should the company spend $3,000 to have an additional storage tank installed?

7. The Morro Mower Company produces assorted lawn implements. Storage of a stack of housings for 20-inch lawn mowers requires 4 square feet of floor space in the warehouse, but they can be stacked 45 to a stack. The cost of warehouse space including operating expenses is estimated to be $5.40 per square foot per year. The insurance on the materials in the warehouse costs 0.80 percent of the average inventory value, and taxes are 2 percent of the average annual value in inventory. The cost of working capital invested in inventory is 20 percent per year. Each mower housing costs approximately $4.27 to produce. The usage rate for the housings is 36,000 per year. The production rate is 5,000 per month with a setup cost of $80. The company maintains a safety stock of one-half month's usage.
   (a) Find the economic production quantity for 20-inch mower housings.
   (b) Find the average inventory level.
   (c) What is the total inventory-related cost per year for this item?

8. Kincaid Memorial Hospital uses 100 syringes of a particular style each day, 365 days of the year. The distributor of this product offers the following price schedule.

Quantity	Price/Unit
0–999	$1.00
1,000–2,499	$0.80
2,500 or more	$0.70

The cost to hold an item in inventory for a year is estimated to be 30 percent of its cost, and the order cost for this item is estimated to be $15 per order. Determine the most economical quantity to buy each time this syringe is purchased. Assume the minimum inventory is zero.

9. The Williams Manufacturing Company uses an average of 250 Model 178A relays per week at an approximately uniform rate throughout all 52 weeks of the year. The average cost of processing a purchase order is $25. The holding cost for a Model 178A relay is approximately $0.10 per week. The supplier has offered two types of delivery plans to Williams: (a) he will deliver all of an order in one shipment or (b) for an additional $75 per order, he will deliver the order at a rate of 300 per week until the order quantity is completed. Under plan (b), the order quantity must be an even multiple of 300. Determine the most economical procurement option and the quantity that should be ordered. What is the total annual cost for each plan?

10. Cumberland Textile Mills produces a special weave of cloth for pajamas, which is demanded at a relatively uniform rate of 200,000 yards per year (250 days). The production process can be set up at a cost of $175 and produces the cloth at a rate of 2,500 yards per day. The holding cost for a yard of this cloth is estimated to be $0.25 per year.
   (a) Compute the economic production lot.
   (b) How long must the process run to produce this quantity?
   (c) What will the maximum inventory level be, assuming that the inventory reaches zero when the process is initiated?

11. The Whacko Brass Company produces brass door knockers, among other things. The company expects next year's demand for door knockers to be 20,000 units at a uniform rate. It costs $125 to set up the equipment to produce the door knockers, and the production rate is 5,000 per month. The company's accountant estimates that it costs $0.40 per year to hold a door knocker in inventory.
   (a) How many knockers should the com-

pany produce each time it initiates production of the product?

(b) It takes three weeks from the time the warehouse orders more knockers until finished knockers begin to arrive. At what inventory level should the company release production orders if it desires 1.5 times the average lead-time usage to be designated as safety stock?

12. Not Knots, Inc., produces a variety of wood furniture. The production rate for one model of bookcase is 20 units per day. The sales rate for this case is 5 units per day. The setup cost for the equipment used to make the case is $72, and the cost to hold a case for a year is $18.

(a) Determine the economic production lot.

(b) Estimate to the nearest integer the average level of the maximum inventory if the company tries to have 8 units on hand when the first units in a new production run begin to be completed.

13. Super Sport Shoes, Inc., sells a special shoestring at a uniform rate of 2,400 pairs per year. The order cost is $10 and the holding cost is 20 percent of the unit cost. Up to 1,000 pairs, each pair of strings costs $0.22; from 1,000 to 1,500 pairs, each pair costs $0.20; above 1,500 pairs, the cost is $0.18 per pair. What is the EOQ for this item?

14. Gemtronics Corporation produces electrical components for appliance and automotive industries. Previous daily demand for part XK202 has shown little seasonal variation, but has been normally distributed with a mean of 700 per day and a standard deviation of 100. The company works 250 days per year. Ten days' lead time are required to schedule, wait for an available machine, and set up for a production run. The cost to initiate a production run is approximately $200, and the production rate for part XK202 is 4,000 per

day. The holding cost for each unit of this product is $0.25 per year.

(a) Compute the optimal production quantity for this item.

(b) Compute a reorder level that will provide a 0.96 probability of meeting customer demand during the lead time.

15. Alien Auto Co. distributes parts for foreign cars in a large midwestern city. Demand for a particular size of oil filter has been uniform. The lead time to obtain the filters is one month, and the average use rate is 525 per month. The lead-time use is normally distributed with a standard deviation of 50 units. Order cost is $12 and holding cost $0.40 a year per filter. The estimated cost of a stockout is $1.50 per filter.

(a) What is the EOQ?

(b) How many orders per year will be placed at this EOQ?

(c) What is the optimum probability of a stockout?

(d) What is the optimum reorder level?

(e) How much will Alien Auto spend per year to hold inventory on this filter if it implements the values you determined above?

16. (a) How much would Alien Auto spend each year to hold inventory if it tried to stock enough oil filters to give a 90 percent service level? 95 percent? 97 percent? 99 percent? 99.9 percent?

(b) Draw a graph of service level versus annual inventory cost.

(c) Where would you set the level? Discuss your reason.

17. Eleanor's Bike Shop sells an average of 10 bikes per week of a particular model. The weekly demand for this bike is normally distributed with a standard deviation of 3. The cost to process an order is $20, and the cost to hold a bike of this model in stock for a year is $25. In approximately 50

percent of the cases that the company is out of stock and demand occurs, the sale will be lost. The average profit on a sale of this model is $60 per unit. The lead time to obtain this bicycle is three weeks.

(a) Find the economic order quantity.

(b) Find the optimal probability of stock-out during the lead time.
(c) Find the optimal reorder level.
(d) Explain why the reorder level is greater than the order quantity.

BIBLIOGRAPHY

Ammer, Dean S. *Materials Management.* 4th ed. Homewood, Ill.: Irwin, 1980. Chaps. 8–10.

————. *Purchasing and Materials Management for Health Care Insitutions.* Lexington, Mass.: Heath, 1975.

Bierman, Harold, Jr., Charles P. Bonini, and Warren H. Hausman. *Quantitative Analysis for Business Decisions.* 6th ed. Homewood, Ill.: Irwin, 1981.

Buffa, Elwood S., and Jeffrey G. Miller. *Production-Inventory Systems: Planning and Control.* 3rd ed. Homewood, Ill.: Irwin, 1979.

IBM. *Basic Principles of Wholesale IMPACT—Inventory Management Program and Control Techniques.* 2d ed. White Plains, N.Y.: IBM, 1972.

Mize, Joe H., Charles R. White, and George H. Brooks. *Operations Planning and Control.* Englewood Cliffs, N.J.: Prentice-Hall, 1971. Chap. 5

Schonberger, Richard J., and Marc J. Schniederjans. "Reinventing Inventory Control." *Interfaces,* 14 *no. 3,* (May-June 1984) pp. 76–83.

Tersine, Richard J. *Principles of Inventory and Materials Management.* 2d ed. New York: Elsevier North-Holland, 1982.

Chapter Outline
MANAGING DEPENDENT-DEMAND INVENTORY AND CAPACITY

MATERIAL REQUIREMENTS PLANNING

The MRP Technique—A Requirements Calculator / MRP—A Manufacturing Planning and Control System / MRP II—A Broader Resource Coordination System / The Focus Is Manufacturing Planning and Control

A GENERAL OVERVIEW OF MRP

INPUTS AND OUTPUTS OF MRP

The Master Production Schedule / Bill-of-Materials File / Inventory Status File / Outputs of MRP

SOME ADAPTATIONS IN USING MRP

Master Scheduling at a Level Below Finished Product / Regenerative or Net Change MRP? / Scrap Allowances / Safety Stock / Lot Sizing / *Application: Using the Part-Period Algorithm*

CAPACITY REQUIREMENTS PLANNING

POTENTIAL BENEFITS FROM THE USE OF MRP

Operations Management in Action: MOVE TO MRP SYSTEM HELPED STEELCASE BOOM

IMPLEMENTATION OF MRP

Management Commitment / User Involvement / Education and Training / Selection of Packages / Data Accuracy / Realistic Master Scheduling

Summary / Solved Problems / Discussion Questions / Problems / Bibliography

KEY TERMS

Independent-demand inventories
Dependent-demand inventories
Components
Parent item
End item
Lumpy demand
Start dates
Need dates
Production activity control

Shop floor control
Closed-loop MRP
Manufacturing resource planning (MRP II)
Master production schedule
Time "buckets"
Minimum planning horizon
Time fence
Exploding
Where-used listing

Product structure tree
Single-level bills of materials
Gross requirements
Scheduled receipts
Open orders
On hand
Coverage
Net requirement
Offsetting
Low-level code

Modular bills of materials
Regenerative MRP
Net change MRP
Lot-for-lot ordering
Part-period algorithm (PPA)
Capacity requirements planning (CRP)
Production standards
Pegging

Chapter 7

MANAGING DEPENDENT-DEMAND INVENTORY AND CAPACITY

The previous chapter focused on *independent-demand inventories*, which enable a company to respond to demand from outside the production system more quickly than it could if it had to purchase or produce an item between the time it is ordered and the time it is sold. The extent of outside demand is usually not known ahead of time; it must be forecast, and some uncertainty is inherent in these forecasts. Sometimes large amounts of safety stocks of independent-demand items are maintained to ensure that sufficient quantities of these items will be available when and if customer demand occurs. Many kinds of organizations maintain such independent-demand inventories. Make-to-stock manufacturers, hospitals, wholesale distributors, and retail businesses are some of the organizations that must keep independent-demand items on hand.

Manufacturing companies and other companies that use input supplies to perform their activities must have a method to coordinate obtaining the necessary input items with the plans for producing their output, if they are to manage their resources efficiently. That is, they must have a method for managing their *dependent-demand inventories*. Dependent-demand items, you recall, are those *components* that are assembled to become part of some *parent item* or in some similar way become part of a set of components. Dependent-demand items usually are consumed within the production system, not by some external demand. Because of the different demand characteristics, different features are desirable in the methods and techniques used to manage inventories of these two types of items.

The number of dependent items used is directly related to the number of parent items produced. A manufacturing company establishes a master production schedule (i.e., master schedule), which is a basis for further planning. The master schedule states how many of each *end item* will be produced in each time period of some planning horizon, usually twelve months. Once a company has established how many assemblies it will make, the number of dependent components that will be needed can be calculated. This removes the uncertainty about the extent of dependent demand. (Some of the components may also be subject to uncertain external demand as replacement parts, but the amount of dependent demand for them is known.) If a company intends to produce 100 bicycles of a particular model, then the company will need 100 frames, 100 handlebars, 200 handlebar grips, and 200 tires of the type required to make this model of bicycle.

If a company can accurately determine how many of the items are needed and when, the items need not be maintained in stock at all times. Instead, a dependent-demand system can plan to have an item arrive from a vendor or to have it produced just before it is to be used. Thus the average inventory level for a dependent item can be kept much lower and the service level much higher than it would be if the item were managed by an independent-demand inventory system.

Independent-demand inventory usually supplies a demand process that is the result of numerous purchases in rather small quantities, resulting in a fairly uniform usage rate for the item. In fact, a uniform usage rate was one of the conditions assumed for the development of the EOQ formula in Chapter 6. A manufacturer experiencing this type of independent demand for an item will usually produce the item in a specified quantity, either at a fixed interval or whenever the inventory drops below a specific reorder level. Therefore, the components of this item will be needed sporadically. This *lumpy demand* (i.e., nonuniform demand) for the components required to produce the end item does not satisfy the assumed conditions for the EOQ model discussed in the previous chapter.

Consider an independent item demanded at a uniform rate of 12,000 units per year. If the EOQ were 1,000, then production of the item would be scheduled once each month. The components to make this item would therefore be needed only once per month. If 250 of the item could be assembled each day, components would be needed for only four days, so component demand would drop to zero for the remainder of the month—assuming that the components were not used in other products and were not purchased as replacement parts from outside the company.

There is still another reason for using a special system for managing dependent-demand items. An independent-demand inventory system might not be a reliable way to supply dependent components unless huge amounts of safety stock were maintained to make the service level of each component very high. Consider a product with only ten components managed by independent-demand inventory systems that provide a 95 percent chance that each item will be available when it is needed. If we assume that the demands are independent, then the probability that all items will be available when needed is $0.95^{10} = 0.60$. A company that has only a 60 percent chance of meeting its production schedule obviously has serious problems. When the components required to make a product are used only in that one product and are not subject to independent demand as repair parts, a company either needs them all or needs none of them. If some of the components required to produce a product are unavailable, the company will have to pay the cost of keeping inventory of the rest of the components, yet it will not be able to complete the parent product and sell it. High inventories and no sales can quickly lead to the downfall of a business. Naturally, a company would prefer to manage its inventory so that all the components of a product will be available when needed but the inventory of these components will remain low when they are not needed.

For these reasons managers have sought a method of managing dependent items, which often have lumpy demand, that would enable them to maintain a minimum inventory yet provide assurance that production schedules for the parent items can be met. Material requirements planning, MRP, is the result of efforts to develop an inventory system with these highly desirable features. In the early part of this chapter we will primarily discuss MRP and the planning of requirements for dependent-demand components. In the latter part of the chapter we will discuss capacity requirements planning, which MRP makes possible. The use of MRP in scheduling is deferred until the next chapter, where we discuss scheduling and controlling of manufacturing operations.

MATERIAL REQUIREMENTS PLANNING

The term *material requirements planning (MRP)* is used to refer to a range of entities—from a very basic technique to a very broad, integrated information system that has the MRP technique as just one component. Before we proceed let's consider three levels of computer applications that often are labeled MRP or MRP II.

The MRP Technique—A Requirements Calculator

Early in its history, the MRP technique was used for its most limited capability. In its most basic form, MRP is a technique of working backwards from the scheduled quantities and need dates for end items specified in a master production schedule to determine the requirements for components needed to meet the master production schedule. The technique determines what components are needed, how many are needed, and when they are needed, and when they should be ordered so that they are likely to be available when needed. If a company has several products made of numerous components, the amount of data and the number of calculations that must be performed to use the technique become unwieldy without a computer. MRP usually is a computer system that, as the name implies, plans when materials (and other components) will be required. MRP was originally perceived primarily as an inventory control tool, providing reports that specify how many components should be ordered, when they should be ordered, and when they should be completed. When referring in this book to the technique of calculating the requirements for components from plans to make the parent items, the terms *MRP technique* or *requirements calculation* will be used. This limited use of the term *MRP technique*—which is sometimes referred to as an "order launch and hope" approach to managing inventory—does not include the use of feedback for tracking the actual progress of orders, nor for the readjustment of orders in response to actual performance.

MRP—A Manufacturing Planning and Control System

The logic of the MRP technique has made possible expanded computer systems that provide information for planning and controlling both the materials and the capacity required to manufacture products. The MRP logic has been extended, and it now serves as the key component in an information system for planning and controlling production operations and purchasing. Managers have found that the information provided by MRP is highly useful in scheduling because it indicates the relative priorities of shop orders and purchase orders. The system uses lead-time estimates to determine the dates on which each level of assembly should be started in order to meet the scheduled completion date for the end product. *Start dates* are the time that an order for the item should be released to the internal production shop or to some external vendor. The start date for one level of assembly is also the *need date* for all components of this assembly. A schedule is valid if the stated date on which the items are actually to be completed coincides with the need dates for all of the items. When MRP is updated to show the delivery dates quoted by vendors, it shows if production operations can be performed as scheduled. Schedulers can use this information to expedite orders to keep parts on schedule. MRP is the basic foundation for *production activity control* or *shop floor control*, for vendor follow-up systems mentioned earlier, and for detailed capacity requirements planning, which is discussed later in this chapter. When MRP is extended to include feedback from and control of vendor orders and production operations, it is called *closed-loop MRP*. Properly used, it is an effective basis for manufacturing control.[1]

MRP II—A Broader Resource Coordination System

The information available from closed-loop MRP helps companies develop realistic plans and improves their performance in achieving those plans. When there appears to be a good likelihood that a company will accomplish its production

[1]George W. Plossl, *Manufacturing Control: The Last Frontier for Profits* (Reston, Va.: Reston, 1973), Chap. 2.

plan, the production plan and the information that is available from a closed-loop MRP system can be used to plan and coordinate resources other than materials and capacity. With valid projections of what materials and components will be purchased and when, the company can develop its purchasing commitments and a projected purchasing budget. The labor hours projected in the capacity plan for each work center can be summed to develop personnel needs and labor budgets. And the projected on-hand balances of materials can be multiplied by costs to develop inventory budgets.

When the capabilities of closed-loop MRP are extended to provide information on financial resources in a manufacturing company the system is sometimes called *manufacturing resource planning,* or MRP II. Manufacturing resource planning provides a means of simulating to provide information on the use of resources for various assumed plans. Information about inventory investment levels, plant expansion needs, and work force requirements is useful for coordinating marketing, finance, engineering, and manufacturing efforts to achieve the company's overall business plan.

The Focus Is Manufacturing Planning and Control

The major consideration of this chapter is planning and controlling the purchase and production of dependent-demand items. Consequently, the broader use of the MRP technique, such as in MRP or MRP II, is discussed from the standpoint of its capabilities as a manufacturing planning and control system. The basic MRP technique is reviewed to explain how it calculates component requirements. Also discussed is how this information is used in managing the inventory of dependent items and in managing the capacity needed to produce these items. With this focus only a few issues relating to resources outside of the manufacturing function are considered. It is important, however, to recognize that information from MRP can be integrated with additional modules to help coordinate the activities in manufacturing with activities of some other parts of the company.

A GENERAL OVERVIEW OF MRP

MRP is a set of computer programs that are run periodically, usually once a week, to incorporate the latest schedule of production requirements, new information about current conditions, and updated schedules for component receipts. The programs must be supported by accurate data in the numerous files if MRP is to operate correctly. Various types of information can be supplied by an MRP run. But basically, MRP performs three important functions:

1. Order planning and control: When to release orders and for what quantity.
2. Priority planning and control: How the expected date of availability compares to the need date for each item.
3. Provision of a basis for planning capacity requirements and development of broad business plans.

Although MRP can be used in a variety of settings, such as distribution operations, job shops, and process industries, it is primarily applicable to companies that perform fabrication and assembly of standard products. Most companies that are using MRP have been doing so for less than ten years, and many other companies have yet to try it.

Figure 7.1 is a flow chart that provides a general overview of MRP as a means of coordinating and controlling purchasing activities to support manufacturing as well as the material requirements and capacity requirements within manufacturing. The MRP program that performs the requirements calculations of the MRP technique is the central focus of the initial input plans and the feedback loops. The flow chart also shows the types of information that are developed from these calculations and some of the files that must be accurately maintained to make the system work properly.

Top-level executives develop the business plan, which considers the coordinated overall operation of all functions in the company. The production plan represents manufacturing's responsibility in carrying out the business plan and states the number of units of each product family that are to be produced during each general time block, often a month, throughout the planning horizon. Development of an appropriate production plan, or aggregate plan, was discussed in Chapter 4. Notice that the plan is checked for its impact on capacity to ensure that the plan makes reasonable use of capacity.

Schedulers under the direction of middle managers develop a more detailed plan by converting the production plan into a master schedule that states the specific products that will be produced in more specific time periods, such as each week, for a horizon that typically extends for a year or more. The master schedule is the basic input that drives the rest of the system. The MRP program develops even more detailed plans by determining which specific components of all products in the master schedule will have to be purchased or produced and when the orders to initiate these activities should be released. Planning of the material requirements by the program follows the logic represented by the questions in Table 7.1.

When purchase orders are released to vendors, a delivery date is established. This information and information from follow-up contacts to vendors is fed back to provide the projected inventory status for these items. Similarly, information is fed back on the status or actual completion of orders for items that are to be produced internally. New plans are, therefore, based on updated information of actual conditions and the latest projection of future conditions. Such plans are likely to be more accurate than are plans made without feedback information on actual conditions. The kinds of information obtained from an MRP run are:

Error messages.

What orders should be placed.

What open orders should be expedited or deexpedited (indicates priorities).

FIGURE 7.1

Information Flow for Planning and Control with MRP

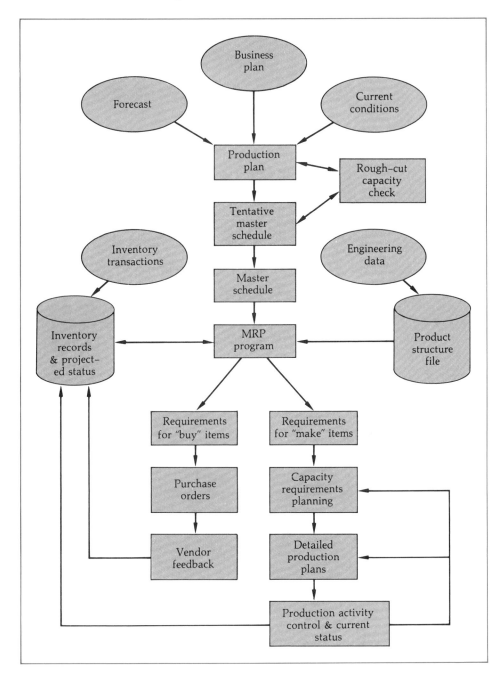

Table 7.1
QUESTIONS ADDRESSED IN MRP PROCESSING

Questions	Remarks
A. What do we want to produce and when?	Input to the MRP program through the master schedule
B. What components are required to make it, and how many does it take?	Provided by the bill of materials
C. How many are already scheduled to be available in each future period?	Obtained from the inventory status file
D. How many more do we need to obtain for each future period?	Subtract C from B, if B is larger
E. When do we need to order these amounts so that they will be available when needed (not too early or too late)?	Move earlier in time by the production or procurement lead time for each item

What open orders should be canceled or suspended.

What order releases are planned for the future.

Information for load reports (capacity requirements planning).

It is apparent from this overview that MRP is useful in coordinating the numerous components that must be obtained and the numerous activities that must be performed to keep a manufacturing operation running efficiently. Let's now examine in greater detail how the MRP program develops its information and the files that are required to support this program. Later in the chapter we will consider some variations from the basic presentation. We will also see how MRP information is used to coordinate requirements for materials with requirements for production capacity.

INPUTS AND OUTPUTS OF MRP

In the following section we will discuss in more detail the master production schedule that drives the MRP program and the two files that are needed to support MRP. We will also describe the processing performed by an MRP program to update the inventory status file and to determine what orders for components should be planned.

The Master Production Schedule

Development of a good master schedule is a key ingredient in the process of manufacturing planning and control. Both productive *capacity* and *materials* must be available before the production process can begin. And companies must make efficient use of both of these valuable resources. The objective of aggregate planning or rough-cut capacity evaluation is to ensure that the company has developed a master schedule that efficiently utilizes the company's capacity, yet one that can be realistically achieved within the capacity limitations of the company and its vendors. After a good master schedule is developed, MRP can be used to ensure that all of the necessary materials will be available so that the master schedule can be achieved. The master schedule is the driving input to MRP that tells the program what the company intends to produce.

The *master production schedule* is a series of time-phased numbers beside each item a company produces, indicating how many of them are to be produced and when they are to be produced. The time period in which the quantity of an item appears can mean that this quantity is to be completed during the indicated period or that this quantity is to be started into the final production operation during the indicated period. We will use the first convention, which means that the master schedule indicates the products that must be completed through the final operation in a particular period. Figure 7.2 shows a portion of the master schedule for the Stowell Company, a manufacturer of office furniture and equipment. This master schedule shows plans based on time blocks, or *time "buckets,"* equal to one week. It indicates, for example, that the company plans to complete final assembly of 100 three-drawer files in week 7, 100 in week 10, and 100 in week 12. These quantities must be moved earlier (i.e., offset) by the lead time to determine when the next-lower-level components are required so the assembly operation can begin. Offsetting is discussed again later in the chapter and is further illustrated at the top of Figure 7.8.

The information contained in a master schedule may include both plans to produce items that have already been ordered by customers and plans to produce items for forecasted sales. Usually the sold orders are in the near portion of the planning horizon, as illustrated in Figure 7.3. The company must forecast probable sales so that future plans can be made. As actual orders arrive they replace some of the forecasted sales. If actual orders exceed the forecasted level of sales, these orders must be delayed or capacity adjustments must be made by some means, such as working overtime or subcontracting some of the work.

A company has more flexibility in planning the portion of the master schedule that lies beyond some minimum planning horizon. The *minimum planning horizon* for each product must usually be greater than the cumulative time

FIGURE 7.2

Portion of the Master Schedule for Stowell Company

Item	Week number											
	1	2	3	4	5	6	7	8	9	10	11	12
001 3-drawer file							100			100		100
005 4-drawer file				60			60	120		60		
007 desk						150			150		90	

FIGURE 7.3

Mixture of Orders and Forecast Demand in a Master Schedule

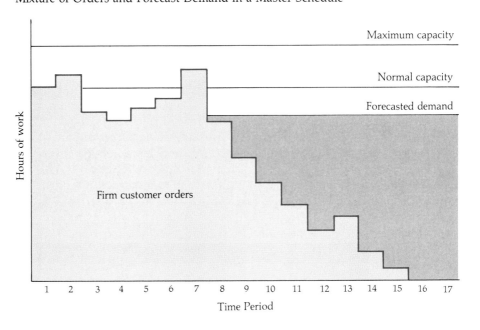

required for procurement of raw materials or other components and for performance of all of the necessary production operations, as illustrated in Figure 7.4. This minimum horizon may be considered a *time fence* within which changes to the schedule are not permitted except in extreme situations (e.g., a customer's order is cancelled).

FIGURE 7.4

The Minimum Planning Horizon for a Product Must Be Longer Than Cumulative Procurement-Production Time

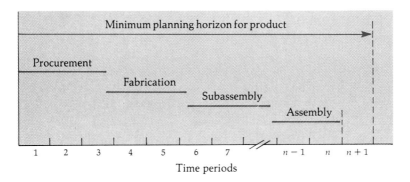

The maximum length of time that is planned in a master schedule will depend on the company's ability to forecast demand and its requirements, but a one-year span is fairly common. The amount of time represented by one block (time bucket) in the schedule does not have to remain the same throughout the entire horizon. For example, a one-year span could consist of 13 weekly time buckets, followed by three monthly buckets and two quarterly buckets. This arrangement provides more-detailed plans in the nearer portion of the horizon, where production plans must be specific. Plans for the later portion of the schedule are likely to be revised, so great detail is unnecessary. The numbers in the distant portion of the horizon are primarily used for general planning. Plans in the distant part of the horizon can also be expressed in terms of product families for general planning of capacity, employment levels, budgets, and so on. The near portion of a master schedule, just before it enters the time fence, must be stated in terms of specific part numbers that the company intends to produce so that MRP can recommend orders for the specific components that must be obtained. The master schedule as described serves as a type of aggregate plan for distant time buckets in the planning horizon. It is disaggregated into specific products for the near portion of the planning horizon before those time buckets enter the time fence. The MRP program obtains information about which components are needed to make an item from the bill-of-materials file, which is discussed in the following section.

Bill-of-Materials File

The bill-of-materials file, also called the product structure file, must contain information that identifies all components required to make one of any end item or component that will be planned through use of the MRP program. A bill of materials for MRP processing must be more than just a listing of all of the required parts; it must be structured to reflect the sequence of steps necessary to produce the product. The bill of materials can be viewed as having a series of levels, each of which represents a stage in the manufacture of the end item. The highest level, or zero level, of the bill represents the final assembly or end product. The next level down might represent the subassemblies that are combined to make the final assembly. The level below it might represent the parts needed to make the subassemblies, and the bottom level might represent raw materials from which the parts are made.

To facilitate MRP processing, each component at any level of the bill of materials must have a unique part number for its identification, even if the item is not held in inventory at this stage of assembly. The separate identifications enable the computer to find any parent item and to determine all of the components needed to make it. Determining all of the lower-level components needed to make a parent is called *exploding* the requirement by the bill of materials. The process can be reversed by imploding the bill to develop a *where-used listing*. A where-used list can be used to determine what products and orders cannot be made if some component is scrapped or will not be available on time.

FIGURE 7.5

Stowell Three-Drawer File Cabinet

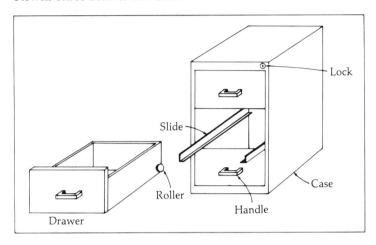

Let us go through a product-structure breakdown for a relatively simple product, a three-drawer file cabinet produced by the Stowell Company, as shown in Figure 7.5. The *product structure tree* for the Stowell three-drawer file cabinet, without screws or other fasteners, is shown in Figure 7.6. The bill of materials for this product, stating the components necessary to produce each level of the product, would be stored in the bill-of-materials file by the part numbers of the components, which are shown in each of the blocks in Figure 7.6.

Product structure data are stored as numerical data so they can be processed easily by a computer. Usually the product structure is stored in a series of *single-level bills of materials,* each of which contains a component's part number and a list of the part numbers and quantities of the components at the next-lower level. The computer must trace through a series of these single-level bills of materials to obtain the total list of components for a product that has several levels. The file may contain pointers to indicate the storage location of the bill for each component in order to link, or chain, the records and facilitate retrieval of a full bill of materials.

The series of single-level bills of materials for the three-drawer cabinet would contain the following data:

Numerical Listing	Description (not a part of the MRP processing)
0001	file cabinet
1001(1)	case assembly
1002(1)	lock
1003(3)	drawer assembly
1001	case assembly
2001(6)	drawer slides
2002(1)	formed case

FIGURE 7.6

Product Structure Tree for Three-Drawer File Cabinet

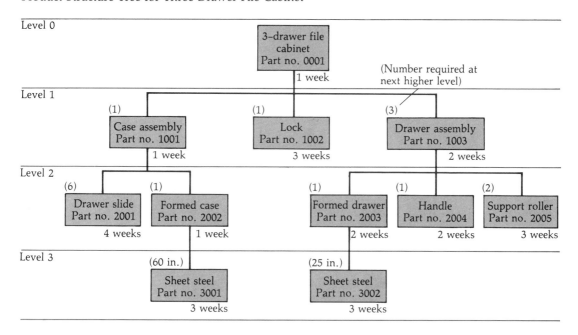

```
1003 . . . . . . . . . . . . . .   drawer assembly
   2003(1) . . . . . . . . .   formed drawer
   2004(1) . . . . . . . . .   handle
   2005(1) . . . . . . . . .   support rollers
2002 . . . . . . . . . . . . . .   formed case
   3001(1) . . . . . . . . .   sheet steel
2003 . . . . . . . . . . . . . .   formed drawer
   3002(1) . . . . . . . . .   sheet steel
```

These figures indicate that the completed file cabinet contains one case assembly, one lock, and three drawer assemblies. They also show that the cabinet case assembly contains six slide runners and one formed case. The lock has no lower-level components because it is a purchased component. A drawer assembly consists of a formed drawer, one handle, and two support rollers. The sheet steel from which the drawers and the case are formed would have the same part number if the same alloys of equal thickness, temper, and so on were used. The units of issue (such as square feet) would have to show the amounts of sheet steel required for each product made from it. Obviously, much work is required to develop the bill-of-materials file and accurately maintain all of the records; moreover, the initial programming of this type of system is very demanding. The bill-of-materials file is updated when new products are added to the line, a product is redesigned, or a new production sequence is established.

The file simply supplies information to the MRP program, and processing of the MRP program does not change it.

Inventory Status File

In contrast to the bill-of-materials file, the inventory status file is dynamic, with contents that can change greatly each time the MRP program is run. Much of the important information provided by MRP about what items should be ordered, how many should be ordered, and when orders should be released is developed in the inventory status file. The contents of this file are changed as the MRP program is run; consequently, we will be discussing the processing logic of MRP as we discuss this file.

A brief overview will show where the inventory status file fits in MRP processing. The master schedule tells the MRP program what end items the company plans to make. The program then accesses the bill of materials to explode each item in each time period to see what components will be needed to produce this parent item. For every component needed in any time bucket, the MRP program must determine which of the following options exists:

1. The inventory on hand plus previously released orders will make a sufficient quantity of the item available when needed, so there is no need to produce it, or
2. The inventory projected to be available will not be sufficient to cover the quantity required in some period, so an order should be released one lead time prior to this period.

Basically, the job of the inventory status file is to keep data about the projected usage and receipts of each item and to determine the amount of inventory that will be available in each time bucket. If the projected available inventory is not adequate to meet the requirement in a period, the MRP program will recommend that the item be ordered.

The inventory status file should contain a record for every item to be controlled by the MRP system. The header, or item master, segment of each record will contain the part identification number, lead time, and perhaps other information such as an item description, list of vendors, and lot size. The inventory status segment of the record shows time-phased data indicating the planned inventory status in each time period throughout the planning horizon. Other data such as usage-to-date, vendor delivery performance, and scrap rates may be stored in a third, subsidiary segment of the record.[2]

Only the item master segment and the inventory status segment of the inventory status file are needed for MRP processing. Figure 7.7 shows a representative format for a printout of an inventory status record. The data in this example show the requirements and inventory plans for the drawer assembly used in the Stowell Company three-drawer file cabinet.

---

[2]Joseph Orlicky, *Material Requirements Planning: A New Way of Life in Production and Inventory Management* (New York: McGraw-Hill, 1975), pp. 181–183.

FIGURE 7.7

Inventory Record for the Drawer Assembly for File Cabinets

Item: 1003 LT: 2 weeks Drawer assembly– file cabinet		Week										
		1	2	3	4	5	6	7	8	9	10	11
Gross requirements							300			300		300
Scheduled receipts			400									
On hand	20	20	420	420	420	420	120	120	120	−180	−180	−480
Net requirements										180		300
Planned order releases								180		300		

Figure 7.7 illustrates the type of data that must be maintained for every item so that the MRP program can plan how much of the item should be ordered and when the order should be released to the vendor or to the production department. In this case weekly time buckets are used, as is usual for at least the early part of the planning horizon. Larger time blocks may be used in the later part of the horizon if the master schedule is constructed in that way. The actual record will usually show calendar dates rather than week numbers for the time periods.

Numbers in the *Gross Requirements* row project usage of the item in parent assemblies. In this case the company needs 300 drawers in week 6 to make the 100 three-drawer cabinets that are to be started in week 6 so they will be completed in week 7, as specified in the master schedule (Figure 7.2). An additional 300 drawers are to be started into assembly in week 9. Some convention must be used to specify when the requirements are withdrawn from inventory. We will assume that the requirements occur in the middle of the week.

Numbers in the *Scheduled Receipts* row indicate when any previously released orders (*open orders*) are scheduled to be received and available for use. An order for 400 drawers is scheduled to be completed in week 2. We will assume that receipt of the item occurs by the middle of the week so that it is available in time to satisfy requirements.

Numbers in the *On Hand* row indicate the number of units projected to be available at the end of each time period. The 20 at the beginning of this row indicates the current inventory of the item. At the end of week zero, which is the beginning of week 1, the company has 20 drawers. The number in any block of the On Hand row represents the number on hand at the end of that period. It is found by adding receipts for the period and subtracting requirements for the period from the amount on hand at the end of the previous period. As long as the quantity on hand is positive, the company is said to have *coverage* for its requirements.

Any period in which there is insufficient coverage for the gross requirement is said to have a *net requirement* for the amount of the shortage. The printout format is usually set up so that in moving from left to right across the On Hand row, the beginning inventory and scheduled receipts will be totally consumed by the gross requirements, and net requirements will begin to occur. The amount of the net requirement in any period can be calculated by subtracting from the gross requirement any scheduled receipts and any positive quantity in the On Hand block for this period. (If the On Hand figure is negative, leave this number out of the calculation.) If the result is positive, this is the amount of the net requirement. If the result is negative, the net requirement is zero. A net requirement of 180 drawers is shown in period 9 of Figure 7.7. The figure 180 is found by the following calculation:

$$
\begin{array}{rl}
300 & \text{gross requirement} \\
-\quad 0 & \text{scheduled receipt} \\
\underline{-120} & \text{on hand} \\
180 & \text{net requirement}
\end{array}
$$

Numbers in the Planned Order Releases row indicate when orders should be placed to maintain coverage of the requirements for the item. The time when the first order should be released is found by moving one lead time earlier than the earliest net requirement. (This procedure is called *"offsetting* by the lead time.") The earliest order must be large enough to cover the earliest net requirement. It may include enough of the item to cover net requirements in subsequent periods, or those net requirements may be covered by releasing separate orders. For now, we will consider that one order is planned for each period in which there is a net requirement. Lot sizing is discussed later in the chapter. The lead time to produce a drawer assembly is two weeks, so the order for the 180 drawer assemblies needed in week 9 should be planned for release in week 7, and the order for the 300 drawer assemblies needed in week 11 should be planned for release in week 9. Orders are usually placed at the first of the week in which they are to occur so that, assuming an accurate lead time estimate has been used, they will be received and available for use before the gross requirement occurs, in midweek.

The inventory status file must be kept current for each run of the MRP program by posting all inventory transactions (receipts and withdrawals) against the inventory file for the appropriate item. The delivery dates and amounts actually stated by vendors in response to released purchase orders should be shown in the Scheduled Receipts row the next time the program is run. File maintenance entries should also be made to keep the lead time, scrap allowances, and other information accurate. It should be emphasized that MRP cannot develop correct data unless it receives correct information from the files and from its other inputs. MRP is a technique of coordinating the plans for all components with the plans to produce end items.

As it develops the projected inventory status of all items, the MRP program works level by level down through all products. The program must add all of the gross requirements for an item within a time bucket before it subtracts to determine the projected quantity on hand or the net requirement for that time bucket. A common component can be used at different levels within the same end item or in multiple end items. A *low-level code* is sometimes stored in the inventory record of an item to indicate the lowest level at which the item is used. This code signals the computer to continue accumulating gross requirements until it reaches the lowest level at which the item appears in any product. When the program has accumulated all of the gross requirements for a period, it then can compute the balance on hand or the net requirement for that period.

A linkage is made between the parent item and its next-lower-level components as the program moves from one level to another. The planned order release date for the parent item tells when all components for the next lower level are needed, thus establishing the time bucket in which their gross requirements occur. The quantity of this gross requirement is determined by exploding the number of parent items to be ordered according to the bill of materials. Figure 7.8 shows the linkage between the master schedule and the inventory record for a parent item, and the linkage between the inventory record for the parent item and one of its components. Notice that the gross requirement for drawer assemblies comes from two sources in the master schedule: plans to begin production of three-drawer file cabinets in period 6 and plans to begin production of four-drawer file cabinets in period 6.

MRP continues to link the planned order release at one level to the gross requirements at the next-lower level until it has worked through all levels of the product's structure. Since it offsets by the planned lead time for each level, MRP develops a schedule of when to release orders for production or procurement of each component. Thus MRP provides valuable scheduling information. The type of schedule developed by MRP can be visualized by turning the product structure on its side and plotting the lead time for each level on a time scale. Figure 7.9 displays an example of this type of information for the Stowell three-drawer file cabinet.

Outputs of MRP

A variety of reports can be constructed from the information made available by an MRP program. The primary information can be grouped into five general categories:

1. Order release notices indicating the quantity of each item to order in the current time period.
2. Planned orders (shown by the inventory status record for each item) indicating the quantity and timing of orders to be released in future time periods if the current master schedule is to be achieved.
3. Revision notices indicating changes in quantity that should be made on open orders.
4. Reschedule notices indicating which order due dates need to be changed and the dates to which they should be changed.
5. Notices indicating any open orders that should be canceled or suspended because there is no longer a net requirement within the planning horizon.

FIGURE 7.8

Linkage from Inventory Record to Master Schedule and to Another Inventory Record

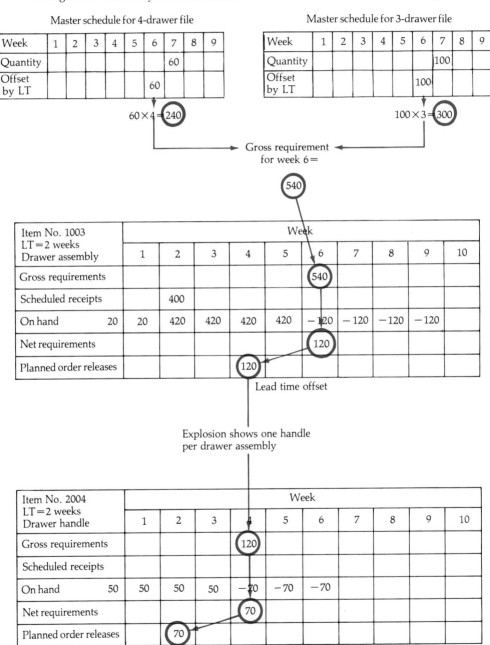

Master schedule for 4-drawer file

Week	1	2	3	4	5	6	7	8	9
Quantity							60		
Offset by LT						60			

$60 \times 4 = 240$

Master schedule for 3-drawer file

Week	1	2	3	4	5	6	7	8	9
Quantity							100		
Offset by LT						100			

$100 \times 3 = 300$

Gross requirement for week 6 =

540

Item No. 1003 LT = 2 weeks Drawer assembly	Week									
	1	2	3	4	5	6	7	8	9	10
Gross requirements						540				
Scheduled receipts		400								
On hand 20	20	420	420	420	420	−120	−120	−120	−120	
Net requirements						120				
Planned order releases				120						

Lead time offset

Explosion shows one handle per drawer assembly

Item No. 2004 LT = 2 weeks Drawer handle	Week									
	1	2	3	4	5	6	7	8	9	10
Gross requirements				120						
Scheduled receipts										
On hand 50	50	50	50	−70	−70	−70				
Net requirements				70						
Planned order releases		70								

If master schedule remains unchanged, an order for 70 handles (or some minimum order size) should be released next week.

FIGURE 7.9

Time-Scaled Assembly Chart Showing Material Order Dates for Three-Drawer File Cabinets

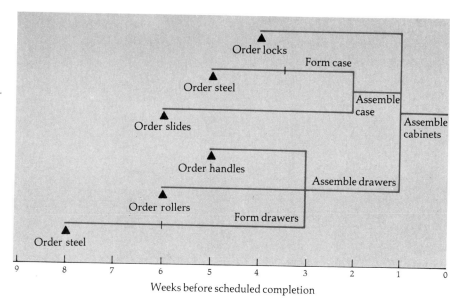

MRP can also provide reports that can be used to determine feasible delivery dates for customer orders. When a potential customer order is entered into the master schedule for evaluation, the system backs up by the lead times and checks inventory availability at each level of the production process to see if sufficient lead time and materials are available to fill the order on time. When augmented by capacity requirements planning, the system will provide additional evaluation of whether the customer's requested delivery date is feasible. The company can evaluate alternative delivery dates, then select a reasonable date to quote to the potential customer.

Other by-product information can be obtained from data developed through MRP. Planned purchasing expenditures and inventory budgets can be developed by multiplying the projected balances on hand by the appropriate item value and summing by period. Pegging reports, to be discussed later in this chapter, can be obtained to trace requirements for components to the end items of which they are a part.

Secondary reports can be obtained from the system to indicate errors. Such messages indicate a wide variety of conditions such as alphabetic information in a numeric field, nonexistent part numbers or transaction codes, a number of digits too great for a field size, or indicated date for a requirement that is outside the planning horizon. This type of information is helpful in guarding against erroneous input that would degrade the data base stored in the supporting files and provide incorrect information to the organization.

SOME ADAPTATIONS IN USING MRP

The preceding discussion presented the basic concepts of MRP and showed how it converts the master schedule to net requirements and planned releases for components. The example we used illustrated a master schedule for production of a finished product. Master schedules can also be developed at a level in the bill of materials below the finished product. Several other adaptations of the general approach to MRP presented thus far have been proposed and are in use. We will now examine some of these deviations from the method we have described.

Master Scheduling at a Level Below Finished Product

Some companies make their products available in a wide variety of options—actually highly variable combinations of a few standard modules. An automobile manufacturer, for example, may have a limited product line: a four-door or a two-door body design. The car, however, can be purchased with a four-cylinder, six-cylinder, or V-6 engine; with no air conditioner, a standard air conditioner, or a deluxe air conditioner; with black bias-belted tires, white-bias belted tires, black radial tires, or white radial tires; with a four-speed or five-speed manual transmission or an automatic transmission; and any of ten different colors. This company would have two body styles times three engine options times three air conditioner options times four tire options times three transmission options times ten colors—or 2,160 unique combinations of its two basic cars. Think of how large this number would be in a more realistic situation where options include include hubcaps, chrome trim, interior, radio, stereo, tape deck, and so on.

To run MRP as we discussed it previously, this company would need to store and maintain 2,160 bills of materials, many of which are identical except for the color of the paint applied to the car. The company would have 2,160 finished products to forecast and would have a master schedule for this number of products. It would be almost impossible to know just how many red two-door cars with four-speed transmission and white radials the company will sell during a particular time period—say, the period one procurement-plus-production lead time into the future. Actually, the company does not need to know that far ahead the exact combination in which its materials will be sold. It only needs to order the proper amounts of materials now. When these materials arrive, they must be processed into the proper number of optional modules—four-cylinder engines, six-cylinder engines, and so on. Production schedulers need to know only a few days in advance which combination of these options should be assembled to provide the finished product that the customer wants. The assembly of modules into finished products can be scheduled on a much shorter lead time than that required for the total sequence of procurement and production operations.

The auto company in our example could work with *modular bills of materials;* that is, it could maintain a bill of material for each optional module and develop its master schedule in terms of modules. The number of bills of materials would be only 2 + 3 + 3 + 4 + 3 + 10, or 25 instead of 2,160. With this approach the company would forecast the number of cars it will sell, then break this total into the appropriate mix of options that its sales are expected to represent. The company would probably maintain an inventory of options to feed the production process, with some safety stock in case actual demand patterns were to differ from its forecasts.

To put this concept in simple terms, the company would not try to forecast the specific number of red cars that will be demanded and then maintain an inventory of these finished products. Rather it would purchase an inventory of red paint and use it on the appropriate cars as orders arrived or in accordance with a very short-horizon forecast.

Regenerative MRP or Net Change MRP?

The previous discussion was written as though regenerative MRP was used. A *regenerative MRP* program constructs new data each time (usually each week) that MRP is run. Alternatively, a company might elect to use *net change MRP*. A net change MRP program revises only the data that are affected by the transactions that are put into it or by a new master schedule. Transactions may be entered into a net change MRP program frequently to reflect conditions as they change.

Scrap Allowances

Suppose that the scrap rate at a particular starting operation averages about 5 percent of the units produced and that MRP processing shows that 100 of a particular component should be completed in a particular time bucket. It seems logical that 105 or more pieces of the raw material should be started into this operation to end up with the desired 100 components. Therefore, the bill of materials explosion could include multiplying by a factor such as 1/0.95 to make an allowance for the usual scrap loss. Where scrap history for a particular operation is available, some MRP systems include a provision for scrap shrinkage so that the user can elect to use this option.

Safety Stock

Safety stock is normally maintained for end items because they experience independent demand, which is subject to uncertainties. Similarly, a safety stock of components that experience both independent and dependent demand may also be maintained. Even for components that have only dependent demand, there may be some uncertainty about how many will be used and when they will be supplied. Shipments of orders for purchased components and raw materials can occasionally arrive late. Scrap rates can be higher or lower than the average value used in planning. Other problems such as absenteeism, rework, or machine breakdown may cause lead times to vary from the planned figure.

These uncertainties raise the question of whether to keep a safety stock of the components that experience only dependent demand.

Maintaining safety stocks for items that have only dependent demand is usually not recommended unless the components are near the lowest level in the bill of materials. Safety stock at this level will help compensate for uncertain supply that is beyond the company's control. Several knowledgeable professionals say that intermediate-level items, if properly managed, do not need safety stock. MRP identifies the priorities and due dates for components. Scheduling these intermediate-level components in accordance with their priorities should make them available at the correct time. Naturally, the company must not plan more work than it has capacity to handle. Even with sufficient capacity there is some chance of excessive scrap or machine breakdowns, but these are ever-present dangers in production. Sometimes components are delayed in spite of realistic capacity plans and good schedules. For a make-to-stock company, safety stock of the end item should provide protection from stockout until components become available if the company happens to get off schedule. Make-to-order companies would not be able to have safety stocks of components since they do not know what end items they will be producing or which components they will require. The presence of safety stock in the on-hand balance will distort the true priorities and degrade the value of the information that MRP provides.

Lot Sizing

As it processes each level of components in a product, MRP develops a series of planned orders for procurement or production. Some of these order quantities may be so small that the setup or order cost will be spread over very few items, perhaps resulting in a sizable increase in the cost per unit. A question that should be examined is whether there is some economic lot size that should be purchased or produced. In production a minimum lot size is sometimes established, so that if a setup is made, at least a certain number of units will be produced. A minimum lot size can result in bringing in a sizable inventory for a small requirement in some period just prior to a series of periods with no requirements—which is counter to one benefit of MRP. Lot sizing at upper levels of the product structure can cause very drastic changes (nervousness) in the order sizes for lower-level components, particularly if the product is a complex one with several levels in its structure. Generally, recommendations in the literature caution against dynamic lot sizing for components at the upper level in the product structure. A company might evaluate its particular situation to compare the cost of nervousness to the cost of excessive orders. A company with a very stable master schedule over a reasonable horizon would have little impact from nervousness.

Lot sizing can be performed by a variety of methods. Four possibilities are:

1. A company may decide not to batch requirements but to release a separate order for each period's net requirement. This is called *lot-for-lot ordering*.

2. Requirements may be batched until they reach some arbitrary or theoretically developed minimum order size. If a requirement exceeds this minimum, the requirement will determine the order size.
3. The Wagner-Whitin algorithm can be used. This is a dynamic programming method that develops the optimal order pattern to minimize the sum of the ordering and holding costs, subject to certain assumptions.
4. The part-period algorithm can be used.

Lot Sizing by the Part-Period Algorithm   The *part-period algorithm, PPA,* is a relatively simple approach to lot size selection when a series of requirements, which are not necessarily uniform, are to be batched into orders so that the total cost will be near the minimum. The PPA does not guarantee the exact optimal solution, but it can be embellished so that it performs almost as well as the Wagner-Whitin algorithm (which does optimize), and it is much easier to understand and perform. The PPA is like the EOQ model in that it attempts to make the holding cost for a lot equal to the ordering cost for the lot, without dividing the amount required within a period into more than one shipment.

Unlike the EOQ model, the PPA may select a different quantity to be ordered each time an order is to be placed, since the requirements it batches are not uniform. Comparison of holding cost and order cost are simplified by expressing both in a unit of measure called part-periods, that is, the cost to hold one part for one time period. This unit of measure is arrived at by multiplying the number of parts on hand by the number of periods they must be held. It is assumed that there is no holding cost for the amount that is used in the period that an order arrives. Each unit used in the next period must be held one part-period, and so on. The order cost is also expressed in part-periods to facilitate its comparison to the holding cost. The expression for the order cost in part-periods is arrived at by dividing the order cost by the cost to hold one part for one period.

The PPA assumes that an order will be scheduled in the first period in which there is a net requirement. The requirement for the next period is added into the order if the cost of holding these units until they are used is less than the cost of receiving them as a separate order. After the requirement for one period is added to the lot, the requirement for the period beyond it is considered. Requirements for future periods continue to be added to the lot until the total holding cost for the lot comes as close as possible to the order cost without dividing a period's requirement. A requirement is never divided; it is either batched into an order for some previous period or it causes a new order to be received in its time period.

You can see that the orders are for different quantities and will provide materials for different spans of time. The lot sizes change with varying requirements and depend on the demand patterns, unlike the equal lot sizes that result when the usage rate is assumed to be the same during each period, as was discussed in Chapter 6.

The part-period algorithm does not consider all possible groupings of requirements into lots and therefore does not always give the theoretical mini-

APPLICATION

Using the Part-Period Algorithm

It is one lead time (three weeks) before a net requirement for rollers at the Stowell Company, and Bill Bearson, an inventory planner, is using the PPA to determine order quantities. For budgeting purposes, Bill has determined the orders that should be received during the next two months, assuming that the master schedule remains approximately the same. That is, Bill used the PPA to compute several future orders. Bill's calculations are shown in Table 7.2.

The calculations in Table 7.2 are identified by steps. Each step works from left to right to develop the cumulative holding cost for an order (lot). The first order must be received in period 4 because there is a net requirement in that period.

Bill added requirements for future periods to this order until the cumulative holding cost exceeded the 300 part-period order cost. He then decided to end the horizon for the first order with the requirement for period 5. This causes the holding cost for the order (225 part-periods) to be nearer 300 than it would be if

Table 7.2
LOT-SIZE CALCULATION WITH PART-PERIOD ALGORITHM

Holding Cost = $0.10 per period   Order Cost = $30 or 30/0.10 = 300 part-periods

Week	4	5	6	7	8	9	10	11
Requirement	100	225	250	125	100	140	60	400

Step 1 Develop → 1st Lot

Holding Cost for Requirement since Order Received (Part-Periods)	100×0	225×1	250×2					
Cumulative Holding Cost for Order	0	225	725					

Step 2 Develop ⟶ 2nd Lot

Holding Cost for Requirement since Order Received (Part-Periods)			250×0	125×1	100×2			
Cumulative Holding Cost for Order			0	125	325			

Step 3 Develop ⟶ 3rd Lot

Holding Cost for Requirement since Order Received (Part-Periods)						140×0	60×1	400×2
Cumulative Holding Cost for Order						0	60	860

Period in Which Order Should Be Received	4		6			9		11
Order Quantity	325		475			200		?

another period's requirements were included in the order. (The holding cost would be 725 part-periods if the period 6 requirement was included.) Bill then started a new order horizon at period 6 and repeated this process. If the second order horizon is extended through period 8, the holding cost of 325 is closer to the 300 part-period order cost than the 125 holding that would result if the horizon were ended with period 7.

mum-cost lot sizes. However it is considered to be less expensive in terms of computer time when a large number of time periods (as are normally required to run MRP) are involved. An adjustment to the part-period algorithm has been developed that brings its results closer to those of the Wagner-Whitin model without the extensive computation that model requires. This refinement is called a look-ahead–look-back test. Basically, it considers improvements that can be made to the basic part-period solution by changing the beginning or ending of the time span covered by an order.

CAPACITY REQUIREMENTS PLANNING

Managers' responsibilities include planning what is to be done, then organizing, directing, and controlling the execution of the plan. Managers often expend great amounts of time in planning, or they delegate planning activities to capable staff members. Time spent on planning can pay great dividends, since hundreds of people and vast sums of money may be involved in executing the plan. Good execution of a poor plan can lead to disaster, but even moderate execution of a good plan can bring success. The point is that if a company starts out with a poor plan, it expends resources doing the wrong thing, and it must then expend extra resources to try to correct its errors or it can never achieve goals that should have been within reach.

Planning and controlling a company's productive capacity (plant, equipment, and people) is a vital responsibility of management. Capacity is a major expense in most manufacturing companies. Operations managers must prudently plan and control the available capacity and its utilization if they are to help achieve the company's objectives for profitability and return on investment. If too much capacity is available, the company has heavy capital and operating expenses. If too little productive capacity is available, or if the proper amount is available but poorly utilized, a company cannot meet the level of demand that could be possible. In either case profitability will suffer.

Capacity requirements planning (CRP) is the effort to develop a match between the production plan (as expressed by the master schedule) and the production capacity of a company. Capacity is the highest sustainable output rate of a unit, given a particular product mix and a level of equipment and labor, working under a normal work schedule. Determination of the capacity of its work centers and the capacity requirements imposed on those work centers by a particular product mix enables a company to know what level of sales its production system can support. Thus the company is less likely to make sales commitments that are unrealistic or overly expensive to achieve. Capacity planning helps to avoid underutilization of capacity, which would prevent the company from achieving the highest return available from its investment in capacity. Capacity requirements planning also enables a company to anticipate production bottlenecks in some work centers in time to take corrective action.

To be accurate and effective, capacity requirements planning must be coordinated with material requirements planning. If materials are available but the capacity is inadequate, the schedule cannot be met and the company must pay to hold materials. If capacity is available but materials have not been obtained, the schedule cannot be met, and the company is paying for unused capacity. A computer program that performs CRP can be run in conjunction with MRP. Working together, the MRP and CRP programs translate the master schedule into requirements for components and capacity, simulating the impact of the master schedule that provided the input for the MRP program. Until a reasonable master production schedule is developed through rough-cut capacity planning (discussed in Chapter 4), the expense of running MRP and CRP is not justified. CRP can be used to refine the master production schedule further after MRP has been run.

The output of MRP tells when planned orders should be released for every component and the quantity needed to support the master schedule. It also tells when open (already released) orders need to be completed to support the master schedule. This information is fed into a CRP module. The CRP module also requires a routing file, stating the sequence of operations that must be performed on each component to convert it into the next-higher-level item, and the work center that is to perform each of these operations. The routing file, or a separate standard-time file, contains information about *production standards*— that is, the time required to perform each operation. The CRP module can then sum the amount of production time required in each work center during each time period covered by the master schedule. This flow of information is shown in Figure 7.10. The output of CRP is a load profile for each work center, similar to the load profiles developed by rough-cut capacity planning. Load profiles based on the output of MRP and CRP, however, are more accurate than the profiles provided by rough-cut capacity planning. CRP considers all affected work centers, whereas rough-cut planning might consider only a few key centers. MRP subtracts available inventory to determine the actual net requirements, it takes into account the sizes of the lots that will be produced, and it adjusts for the lead times at each production stage. Thus by working with the output of MRP, CRP processes data that more accurately represent actual work requirements.

The load profiles produced by detailed CRP can then be used to refine the planning process to develop an improved master schedule or change the capacity that is made available. Management analysis of the load profiles might indicate any of a variety of conditions: (1) The capacity of the major work centers is effectively utilized and no overloads exist. In this case no revisions to the

FIGURE 7.10

Flow of Information in Capacity Requirements Planning

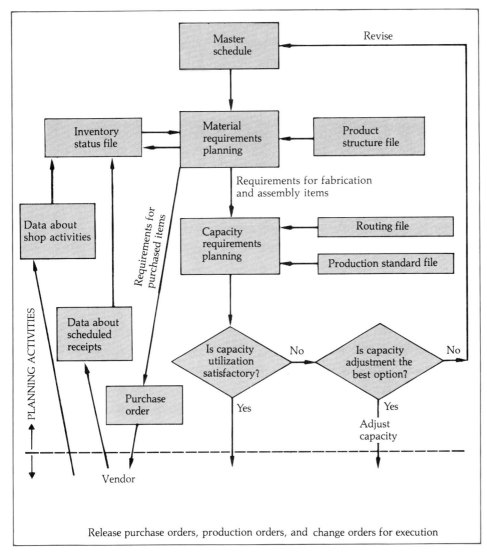

plan are necessary. (2) Capacity is not sufficiently utilized in some work centers. Under this circumstance, managers may elect to revise the master schedule and "pull ahead" some work that was scheduled to be performed further into the future. Alternatively, they may elect to reduce capacity in these work centers. (3) Bottlenecks and overloads may exist in some work centers. Management can revise the master schedule to perform the work in later time periods if capacity will then be available, or they may expand capacity through overtime, additional personnel and equipment, subcontracting, and so on. (4) Some work centers are overloaded and some are underloaded. Under these conditions managers might consider such options as shifting the routing on items where it is feasible so that these items will be worked on in the underloaded rather than in the overloaded work centers. Perhaps personnel can be transferred between work centers to adjust capacity to the anticipated load in those work centers. Alternatively, the master schedule can be revised so that portions of the schedule that cause overloads are planned to occur at other times. It should also be recognized that work that is not in the master schedule will sometimes occur due to factors such as replacement of scrap, rework, new products, or special operations requested by customers.

A technique known as *pegging* enables a planner to trace from a work load in a work center back through its higher-level assemblies to determine what end item in the master schedule caused the load. Often single-level pegging is used, which simply tells the immediately higher-level parent of a component. A series of single-level peg inquiries are required to trace work requirements to the production schedule for end items.

Use of the output from MRP to run CRP, which provides data that are fed back to refine the master schedule, creates a closed loop in the information flow for planning. The flow of feedback information from capacity requirements planning to the master production schedule is shown in Figure 7.10. Also shown is a path depicting the feedback of actual due dates for vendor orders; this tells the time bucket in which scheduled receipts will fall. CRP is a valuable step in establishing manufacturing control. It provides the information needed to adjust plans according to conditions within the production system. The feedback from CRP is based on anticipated conditions that are likely to occur as a result of the plan. Feedback from the other sources can be obtained during the execution phase of the production cycle, allowing the company to revise and refine plans further in response to current conditions. Control, as we have said, involves feedback about actual progress, detection of significant deviations from planned results, and corrective action when it appears to be desirable. The process of using feedback from actual results to revise the plans that are fed into MRP is called closed-loop MRP, a process mentioned early in this chapter. The use of MRP to assist in controlling progress during production is further discussed in a section of the next chapter, which deals with scheduling and controlling manufacturing operations.

POTENTIAL BENEFITS FROM THE USE OF MRP

It has been said that MRP is a new way of managing a manufacturing operation. It has become more than just a way of calculating how much material to order and when. The technology involved in getting the program to run on a computer is only a part of the challenge; it only makes possible the potential benefits of MRP. MRP can, in addition, lead to significant changes in the way that many parts of the company operate.

MRP is not an automatic decision system; it is a decision support system or management information system. It provides timely and valuable information to *people* who make the decisions and who make a company run. We have seen many of the details of how basic MRP works. There are no complex and so-phisticated mathematical models. The contribution of MRP is that it can perform the massive data processing required to plan every component in hundreds of products to be produced over a lengthy horizon. The availability of this infor-mation enables the many diverse elements of an organization to plan and op-erate with greater coordination and effectiveness. People who use MRP must fully understand it and the meaning of the data it provides before they can realize its full potential.

When it is properly developed and is implemented in an appropriate set-ting, MRP can provide numerous benefits to several parts of a company (see box). Some of these benefits are listed below, with the part of a company that might most directly profit identified in each case. Most of these elements of the organization also must provide accurate information to the system to keep MRP operating properly.

1. *Inventory:* MRP provides information to better coordinate orders for com-ponents with the plans for parent items so that the average amount of inventory for dependent-demand items (work-in-process and raw mate-rials) can be reduced. The company can have only what is needed instead of having plenty of everything.

2. *Production:* Human and capital resources (capacity) can be better utilized, because information from MRP will show the need to delay on some components if other necessary components are not available. Better de-livery performance is possible because of more accurate priority infor-mation. MRP can also improve work flow, resulting in reduced elapsed time between the start and finish of jobs.

3. *Sales:* MRP tells ahead of time if desired delivery dates appear achievable. It improves the company's ability to react to changes in customer orders, improves customer service by helping production meet assembly dates (keeping components on schedule and minimizing parts shortages), and helps cut delivery lead times.

4. *Engineering:* MRP helps plan the timing of design releases and changes and aids in their implementation.

5. *Planning:* MRP can simulate changes in the master schedule for evaluation, and it facilitates systems that provide a picture of equipment and facility requirements, work force planning, and procurement expenditures, based on a proposed master schedule.

6. *Purchasing:* MRP recommends changes (to expedite or deexpedite) in due dates for orders. The company can improve vendor relations because it knows the real priorities.

7. *Scheduling:* MRP allows better scheduling through better knowledge of priorities.

8. *Finance:* MRP can facilitate better planning of cash flow requirements. It can lead to identification of true capacity constraints, resulting in better capital investment decisions.

OPERATIONS MANAGEMENT IN ACTION

Move to MRP System Helped Steelcase Boom

Twelve years ago Steelcase, Inc., was the third largest custom office furniture manufacturer in the country. Today, the company is bigger than its next three competitors combined, and it has an excellent reputation for on-time delivery.

At the heart of Steelcase's dramatic success: a materials management program that makes the supplier a central element in the company's scheduling and procurement team. In just the past few years, results like these have become almost routine:

- Over 95% of all customer orders are shipped on time;
- Less than 0.2% of materials orders, on the average, are past due;
- Even during the shortages, maximum materials leadtimes at Steelcase were about six weeks;
- Inventory rose only 12% while sales climbed over 59% between 1973 and 1975;
- Inventory turnaround averages 11 times a year, compared to three or four times a year for most manufacturers.

Just as important, says purchasing's director, John Schorr, there's a healthy sense of professionalism around Steelcase these days: "Purchasing people are no longer regarded as highly paid expediters, shuffling papers from one location to another."

Furthermore, Schorr adds, there are no more of the old arguments about who's responsible for materials shortages and missed schedules. The purchasing department, equipped with a modern, flexible planning tool, takes full responsibility for inventory control, scheduling, and procurement.

Early Beginnings.

While many companies were introduced—sometimes involuntarily—to MM during the shortages of '73–'74, the Steelcase system was laid out back in 1969 in response to a growing number of scheduling and production problems.

One big headache: the sheer volume of products coming out of Steelcase. In a typical week, the Grand Rapids plant alone (there are three others in the U.S.) manufactures and ships about 36,000 chairs, desks, files, and movable walls. By mixing styles, fabrics, colors, finishes, materials, etc., it's possible to come up with about a million different files, 400,000 different chairs, and well over a million different desks.

Like many other companies, Steelcase often found its production and inventory planning functions unable to cope. Bills of materials were frequently faulty, with incomplete or incorrect data. Poor communications between departments resulted in duplication of effort and confusion about responsibilities.

In 1969 and 1970, Steelcase, at the direction of its top management, began working on a prototype materials planning system, starting with IBM's "RPS" software. By mid-1971, a full-time crew had been assembled to iron out the procedures, using four computer programmers, an IBM consultant, a systems analyst, and four other systems planners.

According to Schorr, "The primary question was, and still is, How can we best schedule our operations and those of our suppliers? Materials management is, after all, the most efficient way of helping your vendor act at *his* highest efficiency level. When you look at it that way, MM is a practical system, not theoretical."

Steelcase selected a single supplier from its roster in May, 1973, to be incorporated into the program. Over a period of four months, the supplier was persuaded, on a one-to-one basis, that the company was indeed committing itself to a long-range supply program, and that it was in his own best interests to tag along. By October of 1974, 75 vendors had been brought into the system; by December, the Steelcase plan covered some 80% of all purchased items, excluding paint, steel, and cartons.

How It Works.

Basically, explains Schorr, the Steelcase Materials Requirements Planning system (MRP) is comprised of individual parts forecasts based on historical requirements. That is, the demand for purchased components and materials are computer-tracked over 13-week periods, under the auspices of a buyer-planner.

The buyer-planner, by the way, is fully responsible for both inventory control and purchasing, within a particular product class (MRO items, for example). "With this kind of structure," says Schorr, "the buyer-planner is no longer a 'fire-fighter.' He's actively involved in both scheduling and in getting the materials in the door on time."

Buyers are thus more professionally oriented. Rather than being caught up in a constant maze of paperwork, they can dedicate their time to alternate sourcing, vendor analysis, and negotiations.

"Now the buyers are doing what they're paid to do: 'spend money well.' They have to think of themselves as salesmen of Steelcase's money. And they have to think in terms of what they're getting in return."

A Master Schedule is computer-run every Wednesday. Included on the Master Schedule: shop date of demand, historical forecast, and actual (customer order) demand taken from the open order file. The computer automatically selects the higher of these two numbers as the actual factory demand for each date under consideration.

Suppose a particular item has had an inflated demand during the past few weeks? Suppose, for example, that only 5,000 of some component are used every year, and that they're all bought at once—say, around the beginning of June?

Schorr explains that in such cases, the computer sees an extraordinarily large gap between forecast demand and actual customer demand, and generates a message to alert the buyer-planner that a discrepancy exists.

"That's what we mean when we say that MM is 'management by exception.' The computer handles routine matters, and lets us take care of the unusual."

On Thursday and Friday, Steelcase buyers meet with vendors to discuss projected needs, shipping schedules, and possible hangups. Also studied: previous week's receipts, current and past due receipts, and any necessary re-scheduling. Friday evening the MRP Planning Generation is run, incorporating all changes, deletions, and up-dating.

By Monday morning, says Schorr, purchasing receives the next week's MRP Planning Generation, a sort of Super Master Schedule. Included in the Generation are data on how many of each part will be needed, how many are in stock, planned receipts, leadtimes, dates for ordering parts and materials, minimum order quantities, and the necessary "safety stock."

"And it's all *real*," Schorr emphasizes. "The Planning Generation tells us exactly what we have and what we need for the next several weeks."

Results: Steelcase not only meets 95% of its delivery schedules on time, but the remaining 5% are less than one week late.

"A few years ago, we contracted to supply office furniture to the Sears Tower in Chicago," Schorr recalls. "We shipped five truckloads a day, five days a week, for twenty weeks. Every truck—without a single exception—arrived within a few minutes of schedule."

No Purchase Orders.

Every Wednesday morning, duplicate copies of the vendor orders for the coming week—taken from the Generation—are passed on to the buyer-planners. Here's where the Steelcase system departs from more traditional procedures.

A copy of each vendor order (a computer print-out, actually) is passed on to the vendor, and this alone constitutes his Purchase Order.

"This was a hang-up for awhile," Schorr admits. "Purchasing people find it difficult to deal with print-outs; they long for their old 'security blanket,' the PO."

The reasoning behind the system is this:

"The vendor is fully aware of what's expected of him. We set it all out in the beginning. Why do we have to keep stating the delivery terms over and over again?"

As a result, only about 30 POs a week come out of Steelcase, for occasional special items and materials. Some 30,000 other items a week are covered by the MRP Planning Generation.

An example of how materials management works was provided when Steelcase was arranging for a regular supply of a certain type of fabric. The supplier argued that he needed a leadtime of eight or ten weeks to allow him to buy, weave, cut, and dye to Steelcase's specs.

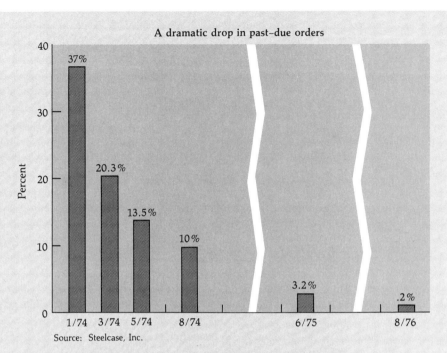

A dramatic drop in past–due orders

MRP system made heroes *out of Steelcase's purchasing team and their chosen suppliers when past-due orders plummeted. This success also cut out much week-end and overtime work by beleaguered buyers.*

But, says Schorr, the supplier's real leadtime was actually much less:

"He has a 13-week notice on all orders. All he has to do is make sure he has the undyed fabric on hand when we specify color. How long does it take to dye the fabric for us? Only about two weeks. So *that's* his leadtime, and that's what we have on the computer."

Another example of the unusual "teamwork" attitude shared by Steelcase and its vendors: a supplier of steel wire, temporarily on hard times, needed $50,000 for raw materials. "That supplier was important to us," says Schorr. "We loaned him the money, interest-free. Now he was able to meet his schedule, and we could meet ours."

Special System for Steel.

Since steel is fundamental to operations at Steelcase, it warrants its very own MRP General-

eration. Implemented in early 1975, the program keeps tabs on the massive quantities of steel which roll through the plant every month. (Steelcase won't say how much steel they buy, but senior buyer Terry Charon says that they're equipped to cut up to 300 tons a day from the giant coils for forming operations.)

"When MRP was first getting under way," recalls Charon, "we found that it really wasn't working as well in Steel Stores as it was in other areas. There were poor communications, misplaced stocks, faulty bills of materials—a general tendency to keep doing things the old way."

Charon helped put together a special "task force" to shape up the steel handling operations, going through 13,000 old bills of materials to find recurring problems and opportunities for streamlining. After six months, a steel "locator" file was developed. All incoming coils are immediately ticketed with a locator number which describes the physical parameters of the coil, the supplier, and its location in the plant. A portion of the ticket is physically entered into the manual locator file on the floor, and the data plugged into the steel MRP program.

"Now we can tell in just a few minutes," says Charon, "what kind of steel we have, where it's located, and how it's scheduled to be used." Besides convincing Steelcase production workers of MRP's value, the locator system has smoothed the daily relationships with suppliers by allowing them to plan their production and shipments more efficiently.

"Once we were rolling," Charon continues, "the benefits were obvious. In late 1975, we completed a period of 13 consecutive weeks with 100% schedule completion—a new record. And that was accompanied by a rise in production volume, too."

Another advantage: while the company still works with the same basic nucleus of steel suppliers, MM has virtually eliminated the need for double-sourcing. Accordingly, Steelcase has been able to cut down on the number of suppliers.

To make things even simpler, Charon says that the steel locator system is now in the process of being converted from a combined manual and computerized program to a cathode ray tube (CRT) operation. The conversion should be completed in early 1977, and will substantially cut costs and processing time.

What kinds of problems has Steelcase encountered with its MRP system? Says Schorr, "The biggest expense in putting a program like this on-stream, in our experience, is getting the EDP together. And there's bound to be some bugs first, of course. But if we were starting the system up today, knowing what we know now, I doubt that we'd change anything."

Adds Charon: "Anytime you make these kinds of changes, there's going to be some resistance, at least subconsciously. There's the tendency to continue doing things like they've always been done, but at Steelcase that was a very minor problem. Once the system had proved itself, the support was total. Everyone in the company could see the benefits."

The most crucial prerequisite, says Charon: the support of top management. "Without that, I doubt that we could ever have gotten MRP off the ground."

IMPLEMENTATION OF MRP

After reading about the potential benefits that can be achieved from MRP, you may wonder why not every manufacturing company is using it. It is important to remember the benefits discussed are only *potential* benefits that can be gained from a *good* manufacturing control system that is *properly* installed and utilized. A basic MRP program does not provide all of the benefits mentioned, such as capacity planning or production scheduling. It is expensive to develop, apply, and maintain an information system that would enable a company to reap all of the potential benefits of MRP.

Moreover, not all installations are successful. The degree of potential improvement that can be realized from implementing MRP depends on the lack of effectiveness in planning and controlling production and inventory activities prior to using MRP. Ironically, many companies that could achieve great improvements through use of MRP have had poorly run operations prior to MRP and consequently are less likely to have the commitment, teamwork, and discipline necessary to achieve the full potential of MRP. Companies that do not carefully plan and administer the implementation of MRP might conclude that the system does not work. The MRP package does nothing more than process the data provided by the organization and provide further information to the organization. The people within an organization must maintain accurate data and must use the output of the system effectively if MRP is to be successful. Just the fact that the computer processes the input data does not assure that the MRP approach to managing production operations is being fully achieved.

Several suggestions for successful MRP implementation appear in the literature. Some of these are discussed below.

Management Commitment

Top-level managers and managers in all parts of the organization that will be affected by MRP must clearly recognize all of the efforts needed to achieve this new way of managing their activities. These managers must fully support all of the changes and must remain supportive of the new system.

User Involvement

A team of people will be responsible for the development and implementation of MRP. This team should include people from all those parts of the company that will use the MRP system so that the system will reflect the particular needs of the system's users. The participation of users of the system in its development will make these people more familiar with the system, so they will know better how to use it effectively. Further, they are likely to become more committed as a result of being involved in the system's development.

Education and Training

In order for a system to work, all of the people who work with it must understand it and know how to use it—what information to provide and how to provide it; what information to ask for and how to obtain it. Beyond this, people must know what conditions in the operation are indicated by the messages provided by the system. Always, there is a need for good judgment and initiative to take the proper action to correct those things that need correcting and to leave alone those things that do not need to be changed.

Selection of Packages

The potential user must decide whether to use net change or regenerative MRP. A regenerative system constructs new data each time (usually each week) that MRP is run. A net change system revises only the data affected by the transactions or schedules that are fed into it, which occurs as frequently as is needed to reflect conditions as they change—perhaps daily or more often.

Several companies offer software packages that perform MRP. A company that is considering the use of MRP must decide whether to develop its own programs or to purchase and adapt some available package. Companies often opt to buy software because a great deal of time is required to develop these programs, and there is the possibility of making mistakes that will probably already have been corrected in a commercial package. It is likely that the company will have some existing systems or elements that it does not intend to change and that must interface with MRP. For example, the software package might need to be compatible with the company's computer, operating system, order entry system, inventory system, purchasing records, labor reporting, cost accounting, bill of material processor, and master scheduling system.

Data Accuracy

For MRP to operate effectively, the company must have accurate records in the supporting files. All of the bills of materials must be reviewed, updated, and structured so that they provide the data needed by MRP. Inventory records also must be reviewed, corrected, and entered into a computer file for access by MRP. After a system is installed, careful attention and discipline must always be exercised to ensure that all data used by the system are accurate. For example, if a clerk is supposed to enter a code 3, indicating that the item is purchased in hundreds, but instead enters a code 2, indicating that it is purchased in dozens, serious errors and material shortages are likely to occur. If a system gives erroneous data at times, people may develop informal methods of getting the data they need and no longer bother to update their input into the formal system, since they no longer use it. The system could then become even less reliable and be a burden rather than a benefit. This is one of the reasons managers must remain supportive of the system and must apply the necessary effort to see that accurate and timely data are supplied to it.

Realistic Master Scheduling

A plan must be realistic if a company is to achieve it—whether the company uses MRP or any other system. The master schedule must not be management fantasy about what the scheduler would like to achieve. If the master schedule overloads the capacity of a plant, MRP will not save the day. MRP can, however, be used to find the relative priorities of components so that the capacity can be most effectively utilized by signaling the proper jobs to be worked on.

Capacity requirements planning used in conjunction with MRP provides great potential. The company can develop plans (master schedules) that effectively utilize its capacity without bottlenecks or overloads. Thus MRP helps to achieve the plan as stated in the master schedule, through procurement and production of the proper components at the proper time. This is a great deal of what good production and inventory management is all about—planning and controlling to achieve the wise use of resources.

SUMMARY

Demand for components that are used only to feed the production process—that is, dependent-demand items—occurs only when production of the parent assembly is performed. In many instances dependent demand is not uniform. Independent-demand inventory models are not appropriate for this "lumpy" demand. Requirements for such dependent items as intermediate-level assemblies, purchased components, and raw materials should not be forecast individually. Requirements should be determined from the master production schedule through material requirements planning, MRP. MRP calculates the requirements for dependent components by multiplying the number of parent items to be produced by the number of components per unit as specified in the bill of materials for the parent item. Timing of each requirement is determined by offsetting—that is, backing up in time from the scheduled completion for each stage of production by the amount of time required to perform that production step.

MRP is usually run weekly but may be run more often, even daily. The output of an MRP run can provide useful information for planning and controlling orders to vendors or orders to the production floor. Information obtained from MRP is also useful in determining capacity requirements and in making plans for effective utilization of capacity.

Production of an item requires not only the availability of the necessary components but also the availability of adequate production capacity to perform the production operations. Thus capacity requirements must be planned in coordination with material requirements. Capacity requirements planning, CRP, attempts to match the production plan and the production capacity of a company. A computer program for CRP uses the output of MRP to make detailed projections of the load imposed on the production system so that overloads, underloads, or bottlenecks can be identified in time to take corrective action. CRP enables a company to plan for the efficient utilization of production capacity, and MRP enables it to execute those plans efficiently. These two packages (MRP and CRP) are valuable assets in achieving efficient use of resources and profitability in production operations.

MRP is a program that evaluates a master production schedule. In addition, it provides recommendations on when to release orders, tells when orders are really needed, and provides data for capacity requirements planning.

MRP requires accurate inventory status records for every component and an accurate bill of materials for every level of component, from the basic raw material through the end item. Implementation of MRP also requires commitment and continuous support from management, proper hardware and software packages, and full training of users and support personnel.

SOLVED PROBLEMS

PROBLEM:

The Kangaroo Special BMX dirt bike is composed of nine major subassemblies: frame, seat assembly, rear wheel assembly, chain, front wheel assembly, fork, brake assembly, handlebar assembly, and pedal-crank assembly. The handlebar assembly consists of the handlebar, post, and two handlebar grips. The front wheel assembly consists of a tire, a tube, a rim, 36 spokes (20 mm), and a front hub assembly. The front hub assembly is composed of the front hub, two bearings, two bearing retainers, an axle, and four axle nuts. The pedal-crank assembly is composed of a crank, a sprocket, two bearings, a bearing retainer, a nut, and two pedals.

Construct a product-structure tree showing the entire composition of a Kangaroo Special one level below the end product, and extend the composition of the front wheel assembly as far as possible.

spokes are not used anywhere else in the company's product line. The following information indicates the current status and open orders that will affect the inventory of these components. Assume the company uses lot-for-lot ordering.

	Wheel Assembly	20 mm Spokes
On-hand balance	10	200
Scheduled receipts	50 in week 1	1,000 in week 2

SOLUTION:

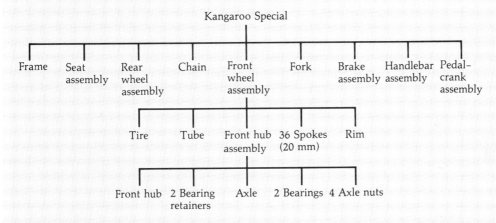

PROBLEM:

Colonel Kangaroo, owner of the Kangaroo Bike Factory, plans to complete assembly of 50 Kangaroo Special BMX bikes in week 3 and 50 in week 5. The lead time to assemble this bike is one week. The lead time to make a front wheel assembly from its components is one week, and the lead time to purchase the 20 mm spokes is two weeks. The front wheel assembly and the 20 mm

Construct time-phased inventory records for front wheel assemblies and for 20 mm spokes.

SOLUTION:

Since the bikes are to be completed in weeks 3 and 5 and the assembly takes one week, the components at the immediately lower level will have to be available in weeks 2 and 4. The gross requirements for front wheel assemblies occur in these weeks.

Front wheel assembly
Kangaroo Special

LT = 1		1	2	Week 3	4	5
Gross requirement			50		50	
Scheduled receipts		50				
On hand	10	60	10	10	−40	−40
Net requirement					40	
Planned order release				(40)		

×36

20 mm spokes

LT = 2		1	2	Week 3	4	5
Gross requirement				1440		
Scheduled receipts			1,000			
On hand	200	200	1,200	−240	−240	−240
Net requirement				240		
Planned order release		240				

The planned order release in week 1 indicates a need to order at least 240 of the 20 mm spokes this week. Since the company uses lot-for-lot ordering, this is the amount that would be ordered—unless the spoke factory sells them only in quantities of, say, 1,000.

DISCUSSION QUESTIONS

1. Why are dependent-demand items often managed by inventory systems that are different from those studied in Chapter 6?
2. What is the basic core of material requirements planning (MRP)?
3. What, if any, applications does MRP have beyond basic inventory control?
4. What is a master production schedule? How does it differ from a forecast? What is lead time offsetting?
5. What basic information must be in the inventory status file? What additional information might a company want to maintain in this file?
6. Discuss some of the fears that people might have about setting a planned lead time and not using safety stock in an MRP system.
7. Briefly describe the steps that MRP goes through in processing a master production schedule to obtain material requirements.
8. Why is data accuracy important for MRP?
9. Why do some companies develop their master schedule for items below the end-item level in the product structure?
10. Distinguish between planned orders and open orders.
11. Is capacity requirements planning important? Give some reasons for your response.
12. What are pegged requirements?
13. Distinguish between net change and regenerative MRP systems.

PROBLEMS

1. A Double Pleasure popsicle is pictured below. Construct a product structure tree for a carton of 12 orange-flavored popsicles.

2. The Easy Roller Skate kit consists of the following: box, warranty, key, left skate, right skate. A skate consists of a strap, a heel plate assembly, and a left or right sole plate assembly. A heel plate assembly consists of the heel plate and a truck assembly. A truck assembly consists of 2 wheels and an axle assembly. An axle assembly consists of a fork, an axle, and 2 nuts. A sole plate assembly consists of a sole plate, 2 toe retainer clamps, a toe retainer adjustment bolt and a truck assembly.

(a) Draw a product-structure tree for the Easy Roller Skate kit.

(b) Construct a single-level bill of materials for the kit and each of its components.

3. The gross requirements, on-hand inventory, and scheduled receipts for steel tubing at the Kangaroo Bike Factory are indicated in the time-phased inventory status record below. Its lead time is 4 weeks. Complete the inventory status records, showing when planning orders should be placed. The company uses lot-for-lot ordering.

4. The current on-hand balance, the gross requirements, and the scheduled receipts for part number X5753 are indicated in the inventory status record shown below. Complete the time-phased inventory record. The company uses lot-for-lot ordering.

5. Given the product structure shown at the top of p. 320, determine the quantity of each component that must be purchased or produced if there is no inventory of any

Steel Tubing:
LT = 4 Weeks

Week		1	2	3	4	5	6	7	8	9	10
Gross requirements		100	300	50	150	150	100	300	400	50	150
Scheduled receipts			600		200						
On hand	100										
Net requirements											
Planned order releases											

Item Number
X5753: LT = 3

Week		1	2	3	4	5	6	7	8	9	10
Gross requirements		10	55	90		50		65			
Scheduled receipts			200								
On hand	60										
Net requirements											
Planned order releases											

component at present and the company has scheduled production of 45 units of product A.

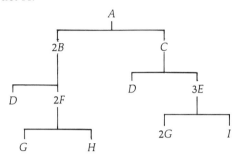

6. The product structure trees for Products A and F are shown below. Part of the master schedule showing when the company will complete production operations for quantities of these products is shown at the top of the next column. Find the gross requirements for item B throughout the first twelve weeks of the master schedule.

Master Schedule					
Week	1	2	3	4	5
Product A			200	150	200
Product F			90	200	150
Week	6	7	8	9	10
Product A	150	250	300	300	300
Product F	200	210	100	180	150
Week	11	12	13		
Product A	200	100	150		
Product F	250	200	250		

7. The Regular Regulator Company produces pressure regulators that are composed of two pan assemblies, a diaphragm, and six bolts. A pan assembly consists of a pan and two half collars. One sheet of rubber provides enough material for three diaphragms. One sheet of 0.100-in. thick steel is required for each ten pans. One sheet of 0.200-in. thick steel is required for each 50 half collars. The product structure tree for

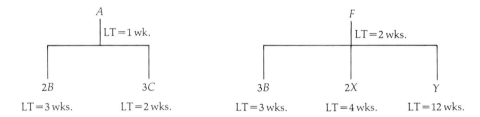

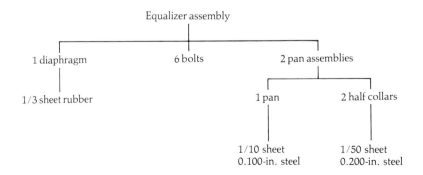

the 16-mm equalizer is shown at the bottom of p. 320. The company plans to make 300 of the 16-mm equalizers in a scheduled production run. How many of each component must be obtained if no inventory is available and no open orders are outstanding?

8. The lead time required to purchase or produce (from its immediately lower components) each component of the 16-mm equalizer is shown in parentheses below the component on the product structure tree below. How many components should be ordered, and when should they be ordered or started into each production operation, so that the company will complete 400 equalizers in week 10 (ten weeks in the future)? Disregard scrap allowances or any equalizers or components that are already on hand.

production lot for 500 equalizers to be started in week 9. These 500 units are to be produced in addition to any inventory of the end item that may be available. Show the time-phased inventory status records for the pan assembly, pan, and 0.100-in. steel for the next 8 weeks to support the production quantities in the master production schedule.

Item	On Hand	Scheduled Receipts of Open Orders
Pan assembly	0	
Equalizer	250	
Diaphragm	1,600	200, week 8
Rubber sheet	400	
Pan	200	
0.100-in. steel	10	60, week 5
Half collar	500	
0.200-in. steel	700	100, week 4
Bolts	3,200	

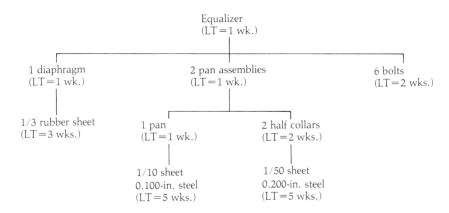

9. The Regular Regulator Company has on-hand inventory of some components for the equalizer shown in problem 8. The inventory levels and open orders for components of this equalizer are indicated below. The master schedule shows only one

10. The structure of a product is shown in the tree diagram at the top of p. 322, with the lead times in weeks indicated in parentheses. The company plans to <u>begin</u> production of 200 A's in week 8, 300 in week 9, and 100 in week 10.

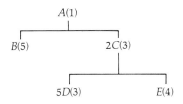

The company has the quantities of the items on hand and on open orders as indicated in the table below.

Item	On Hand	Orders Scheduled to Arrive
B	500	500 in week 4
C	500	
D	2,200	1,000 in week 2
E	1,000	

Show the material requirements plans for items C and D in the format of time-phased inventory status records for the next ten weeks.

11. Refer to the product structures for products A and F that were presented in problem 6. The company has 500 units of B on hand and 1,000 units are scheduled to be received in week 3. The master schedule shows that the company will complete the indicated quantities of end products during the scheduled weeks.

	Master Schedule				
Week	1	2	3	4	5
Product A					
Product F					
Week	6	7	8	9	10
Product A			100	150	80
Product B		225	225	170	

Using the time-phased inventory record show the gross requirements, net requirements, on-hand balance, scheduled receipts, and planned order releases for component B.

12. The Crime Stopper Alarm Company produces two models, A and T, for which the product structures are shown below. The lead time in weeks for each procurement or production stage is indicated in parentheses on each diagram.

The company has on-hand balances and scheduled receipts as indicated in the table below.

Item	On Hand	Scheduled Receipts
C	50	300 in week 2
D	2,000	
F	1,000	5,000 in week 2
G	500	
L	125	

A master schedule, indicating when final assembly of models A and T will begin, is shown below. Construct material requirement plans in the format of a time-phased inventory status record for components C, L, D, and F.

	Master Schedule					
Week	1	2	3	4	5	6
Model A						
Model T						
Week	7	8	9	10	11	
Model A		100	200	150	100	
Model T		225	180	210	250	

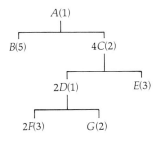

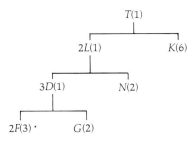

13. The net requirements for an item through a series of time periods are shown below. The setup cost for the item is $100 per order, and the holding cost is $0.25 per unit per period. Use the part-period algorithm to determine the orders into which these requirements should be batched.

Period	1	2	3	4	5	6	7	8	9	10
Requirement	200	150	300	300	250	200	100	100	150	200

14. Net requirements for item R557 during a series of time periods are shown below. The order cost for this item is $30 per order and the holding cost is $0.10 per unit per period.

Period	1	2	3	4	5	6	7	8	9
Requirement	50	200	50	250	0	0	100	100	300

Using the part-period algorithm determine the timing and size of the orders that should be received.

15. Calculate the mean weekly requirement for the data in problem 14, and round it to the nearest integer. Use this number as a uniform weekly requirement and use the order cost and holding cost given in problem 14.

   (a) Use the EOQ formula to determine the optimal order size for the item.

   (b) Using the part-period algorithm compute the sizes of the orders that should be received with the same series of uniform requirements.

   (c) Compare the results you obtained in the solutions to parts (a) and (b) of this problem and explain any differences.

   (d) The average requirement per period in problem 14 also is 117 units. Compare the number of periods that an order covers in the solution to problem 14 to the number in the solution to part (b) of this problem.

BIBLIOGRAPHY

Gallagher, Gerald R. "How to Develop a Realistic Master Schedule." *Management Review,* April 1980, pp. 19–25.

Mather, Hal F. "Reschedule the Reschedules You Just Rescheduled—Way of Life for MRP?" *Production and Inventory Management,* Vol. 18, *No. 1,* First Quarter 1977, pp. 60–79.

Miller, Jeffrey G., and Linda G. Sprague. "Behind the Growth in Material Requirements Planning." *Harvard Business Review,* Vol. 53, *No. 5.* September–October 1975, pp. 83–91.

Orlicky, Joseph. *Material Requirements Planning.* New York: McGraw-Hill, 1975.

Plossl, George W. *Manufacturing Control: The Last Frontier for Profits.* Reston, Va.: Reston, 1973.

———. *Production and Inventory Control: Applications.* Atlanta: George Plossl Educational Services, 1983.

———, **and Oliver W. Wight.** *Material Requirements Planning by Computer.* Washington, D.C.: American Production and Inventory Control Society, 1971.

Wight, Oliver W. *Production and Inventory Management in the Computer Age.* Boston: Cahners, 1974.

———. *MRP II: Unlocking America's Productivity Potential.* Boston: CBI Publishing, 1984.

Chapter Outline
SCHEDULING AND CONTROLLING MANUFACTURING OPERATIONS

MOVING FROM PLANS TO REALITY

THE NATURE OF JOB SHOP MANUFACTURING
Estimation and Precontract Planning

JOB SHOP SCHEDULING AND PRODUCTION CONTROL
The Production Control Department / Scheduling and Controlling Contracts / *Application: Job Sequencing by Johnson's Rule* / The Gantt Chart for Tracking Job Progress

PRODUCTION CONTROL FOR INTERMEDIATE QUANTITIES

PRODUCTION ACTIVITY CONTROL WITH MRP
Input-Output Control / Planning and Controlling Priorities with MRP

PRODUCTION CONTROL FOR REPETITIVE MANUFACTURING

JUST-IN-TIME PRODUCTION
Uniform Production Rate / Pull Versus Push Method of Coordinating Work Centers / The Kanban System / Small Lot Size / Quick, Inexpensive Setups / Multiskilled Workers and Flexible Facilities / High Quality Levels / Effective Preventive Maintenance / Working to Improve the System / *Operations Management in Action:* KAN BAN? CAN DO!

LINE BALANCING
Example of Line Balancing / Other Considerations / Potential for Increases in Production Rate

LEARNING CURVES

Summary / Solved Problems / Discussion Questions / Problems / Bibliography

KEY TERMS

Order control	Backward scheduling	Shop floor control	Kanban system
Flow control	Forward scheduling	Input-output control	Synchronized flow
Routing	Backlog report or load	Priority control	Group technology
Scheduling	report	Overlapping or	Line balancing
Dispatching	Traveler package	telescoping	Cycle time
Controlling	Loading	Dispatch list	Bottleneck
Expediting	Job sequencing	Production line or	Heuristic method
Bill of materials	Dispatching rules	assembly line	Available list
Parts list	Gantt schedule chart	Just-in-time production,	Learning curve
Route sheet	Production activity	zero inventories, or	Rate of improvement
	control	stockless production	

Chapter 8

SCHEDULING AND CONTROLLING MANUFACTURING OPERATIONS

Production capacity is one of the resources that operations managers must utilize wisely to make a company's strategy successful. In this chapter we will confine our attention to scheduling and controlling the use of production capacity in manufacturing operations. The point has been made previously that both capacity and materials must be simultaneously available for manufacturing production to occur. Material is not needed and cannot be transformed if production capacity is not available, and capacity cannot be effectively utilized if materials are not available. The integration of capacity planning and material requirements planning (discussed in Chapter 7) addressed the need for this coordination to achieve production schedules that are realistic. A realistic or valid master schedule is one that can be achieved with wise use of the company's resources.

Scheduling and controlling are concerned with efforts to see that the company's resources are utilized so that actual production activities are within reasonable accord with the current plan. There are two alternative approaches to control—*order control* and *flow control*. Order control is more appropriate for job shops and for operations that intermittently produce small batches of relatively standard products. The parts of custom jobs are unique, so they cannot be used elsewhere and they must all be present to complete the job. All of the parts should be completed at about the same time so they can be assembled. With order control, each job, product, or customer order is assigned a number and tracked as it progresses through each stage of fabrication and assembly.

Flow control is more suited to continuous production operations such as repetitive manufacturing or process industries. Flow control does not track each specific unit but is concerned primarily with the rates at which each standard component of a product is being produced. Both of these methods are discussed in the chapter. First there is a brief discussion of the relationship that planning has to the activities of scheduling and controlling operations. Then there is a detailed discussion of job shop scheduling and control, providing some understanding of the complexities that can occur. Finally, material related to repetitive manufacturing is presented, including line balancing and improvement curves.

MOVING FROM PLANS TO REALITY

Plans and schedules for a company occur in a related series ranging from long-range generalities to short-range specifics, ultimately resulting in actual activities. The appropriateness of the activities is determined to a great extent by the quality of the planning and scheduling that occurred perhaps a long time earlier. Long-range plans might be based on general forecasts of the expected level of business in terms of dollar amounts. These plans affect the kinds of product lines that a company has and the number, size, and location of its plants. Intermediate-range plans, such as aggregate plans, deal with establishing the size of the work force and the number of shifts, and they might include some changes in the amount of equipment available in each plant. These types of plans and decisions, made in past periods, result in the amount of production capacity that is available in a company for the near term. Effective control of production activities determines how wisely this capacity is utilized.

Additional, very specific planning must be done for every type of job a company performs or every type of product it produces. Each order must be broken down into its component parts, and the sequence of operations required to make the part must be recorded as a *routing* of the part through the facility. For repetitive manufacturers, this step may involve extensive process engineering, tooling design, and facility rearrangement—but by the nature of such operations the need for these activities seldom arises—that is, new products do not occur very often. For a job shop, in contrast, job planning is a continuing activity.

Scheduling involves developing and assigning specific dates for the start or completion of the necessary work tasks. The term *dispatching* refers to the act of assigning specific tasks to a specific work center to be performed in a specific sequence. In a job shop, where many different jobs share the same facilities, dispatching requires a careful overview of plans for other jobs and work centers. *Controlling* production activities involves collecting and analyzing the data necessary to measure the actual progress of jobs and compare it to the plan, then initiating corrective action if progress is not reasonably close to the schedule. This corrective action is often called *expediting* if it involves personal attention to improve the progress of specific jobs. Control may also involve revising plans and schedules from time to time to accommodate the changing circumstances with which most organizations must contend.

THE NATURE OF JOB SHOP MANUFACTURING

A job shop has an ever-changing variety of products. Consequently, planning and scheduling the tasks to be performed on every job order requires extensive effort. All of the components for a job must be scheduled to be completed at approximately the same time so that the final product can be assembled. Because scheduling and controlling operations in a job shop involve the dynamic interaction of a constantly changing variety of jobs, often competing for use of the same resources, the job shop provides valuable insight into the complexities of scheduling and controlling operations.

Consider the following factors:

1. The job may never have been performed before, so the time required for each element must be estimated.
2. Even if the expected times are known, there can be random variations about these times because of differences in skills and attitudes of workers, absenteeism, machine breakdowns, variations in materials, and so on.
3. Many jobs can be processed in various sequences of tasks (e.g., a hole can be drilled in one end of a piece of metal before or after a bracket is welded to the other end). The result is an immense number of permutations that have to be evaluated to guarantee that the one with the best expected results has been found.
4. The dynamic nature of business makes the scheduling and controlling of a job shop a difficult and inexact science. Even if all jobs currently on contract are optimally scheduled, by the next day conditions may change. New jobs may arrive to compete for the productive capacity, and some orders may be changed or canceled. Employees may become ill, resign, or be absent for some other reason. Materials may arrive late or may be found unsuitable when they arrive. Machines may break down. Any number of things can happen to disrupt what appears to be an optimal schedule.
5. Even if the previous four conditions did not make scheduling and controlling a job shop difficult, there would still be the difficulty of deciding what should be regarded as an optimal operation, because scheduling decisions require compromises between competing alternative goals. Jobs could be rescheduled to minimize idle facilities, idle people, in-process inventory, or setup costs. Alternatively, they could be scheduled to deliver the maximum number of jobs before their due date or the maximum dollar value of jobs as soon as possible. All of these criteria have some appeal, and not all of them can be achieved at the same time. But scheduling and control must take place with some goal or goals kept in mind.

Estimation and Precontract Planning

Most job shops are custom manufacturers and bid competitively for a large percentage of the work they receive. Such a job shop will prepare a bid to perform work defined in a set of blueprints and specifications submitted by a potential customer's purchasing department. This process is the other side of the purchasing cycle discussed in Chapter 5.

Much of the planning in a job shop must be performed before a bid is submitted and before the company knows if it will be awarded a contract for the job. Sometimes considerable time and effort are expended in planning and estimating jobs that the company never receives. Nevertheless, this overhead expense is necessary. If the company misses something in the estimating process, either of two undesirable consequences could result:

1. The estimating process may miss some of the details and operations that are necessary to perform the work in compliance with customer specifications. The bid would be low and the job shop would receive the contract, but it would probably lose money on the work. Obviously, a job shop cannot afford to receive much business of this type.
2. In its prebid planning, a job shop may overlook opportunities to plan efficient work methods. Estimates would then be higher than necessary, and the company would not receive the contract.

Winning the Contract without Losing Money   Custom job shops compete on the basis of estimated cost, delivery date, and quality level. Bid packages from potential customers usually contain blueprints and any specifications or documentations necessary to define what they want produced. Estimates are made and bids submitted on the basis of these specifications. Estimating may be performed within a production control department or, if the company is large, in a separate estimating department.

Some companies provide design-and-build service. These companies receive performance specifications and bid for the work of designing a device that will perform the specified functions, in addition to bidding on the manufacturing work. Production personnel work in close coordination with the engineering department in estimating and performing such contracts. Managing the design portion of such a contract is very similar to managing its production stages. Scheduling the stages of design work can be viewed in much the same way as custom manufacturing operations. We shall consider only the manufacturing phase of work here.

People involved in estimating must analyze the work to be done. The *bill of materials* or *parts list,* described in Chapter 7, must be "priced out." Table 8.1 shows a bill of materials that lists all of the components needed to produce a finished item. Each component that is necessary to produce the product must be purchased or manufactured if the contract is received. Many make-or-buy decisions for the job shop are made at this time. The purchasing department will obtain prices of all of the items to be purchased and of the raw materials for all of the items to be manufactured.

Table 8.1
BILL OF MATERIALS OR PARTS LIST FOR LAWNMOWER

Level	Part-No	Part-Name	Unit of Measure	Source (make or purchase)	Usage	Total
1	PCS-003	Mower 20 final asm	EA	M	1.0000	1.0000
2	PCS-0013	Engine/carburetor 3.5 HP	EA	M	1.0000	1.0000
3	PCS-0025	Intake manifold	EA	M	1.0000	1.0000
4	PCS-2035	Galvanized pipe ½ ID	FT	P	0.5000	0.5000
3	PCS-0026	Exhaust manifold	EA	M	1.0000	1.0000
4	PCS-2035	Galvanized pipe ½ ID	FT	P	0.3000	0.3000
3	PCS-2009	Machine screw 10–32 × 2	EA	P	2.0000	2.0000
3	PCS-2027	Carburetor ¼ port	EA	P	1.0000	1.0000
3	PCS-0028	Engine subasm 3.5 HP	EA	M	1.0000	1.0000
4	PCS-0036	Gas tank ½ gallon	EA	M	1.0000	1.0000
5	PCS-2039	Cold rolled steel 18 GA	LBS	P	1.2000	1.2000
4	PCS-2009	Machine screw 10–32 × 2	EA	P	5.0000	5.0000
4	PCS-2037	Engine 3.5 HP	EA	P	1.0000	1.0000
4	PCS-0038	Starter—3.5 HP engine	EA	M	1.0000	1.0000
5	PCS-2044	Rope—nylon ¼	FT	P	1.5000	1.5000
5	PCS-0045	Rope handle	EA	M	1.0000	1.0000
6	PCS-2050	Wood dowel ⅜ OD	FT	P	0.2500	0.2500
5	PCS-2046	Starter solenoid	EA	P	1.0000	1.0000
5	PCS-0047	Gear 6 OD ½ bore	EA	M	1.0000	1.0000
6	PCS-2051	Powdered metal	OZ	P	12.0000	12.0000
5	PCS-2068	Starter spring	EA	P	1.0000	1.0000
5	PCS-0049	Starter body	EA	M	1.0000	1.0000
6	PCS-2039	Cold rolled steel 18 GA	LBS	P	1.3000	1.3000
5	PCS-2009	Machine screw 10–32 × 2	EA	P	3.0000	3.0000
2	PCS-2014	Spark plug M13Y	EA	P	1.0000	1.0000
2	PCS-2015	Shroud—3.5 engine	EA	P	1.0000	1.0000
2	PCS-2016	Paint—forest green	GAL	P	0.2000	0.2000
2	PCS-2017	Label—20 IN 3.5 mower	EA	P	1.0000	1.0000
2	PCS-2009	Machine screw 10–32 × 2	EA	P	3.0000	3.0000
2	PCS-2011	Washer #10 flat	EA	P	3.0000	3.0000
2	PCS-0018	Housing asm—20 IN	EA	M	1.0000	1.0000
3	PCS-2009	Machine screw 10–32 × 2	EA	P	8.0000	8.0000
3	PCS-2011	Washer #10 flat	EA	P	8.0000	8.0000
3	PCS-0029	Foot guard	EA	M	1.0000	1.0000
4	PCS-2039	Cold rolled steel 18 GA	LBS	P	0.8000	0.8000
3	PCS-2030	Cast housing–20 IN MWR	EA	P	1.0000	1.0000
3	PCS-0031	Axle—20 IN mower	EA	M	2.0000	2.0000
4	PCS-2040	Bar steel—rod ½ OD	FT	P	2.3000	4.6000
3	PCS-2032	Mower blade—20 IN	EA	P	1.0000	1.0000
3	PCS-0033	Wheel asm—pneumatic 5	EA	M	4.0000	4.0000
4	PCS-2041	Wheel rim—5 IN	EA	P	1.0000	4.0000
4	PCS-2042	Tire—pneumatic 5 IN	EA	P	1.0000	4.0000
4	PCS-2043	Ball bearing stainless	EA	P	1.0000	4.0000
1	PCS-0002	Parts bag	EA	M	1.0000	1.0000
2	PCS-2009	Machine screw 10–32 × 2	EA	P	4.0000	4.0000
2	PCS-2010	ut 10–32	EA	P	4.0000	4.0000
2	PCS-2011	Washer #10 flat	EA	P	4.0000	4.0000
2	PCS-2012	Plastic bag 3 × 6	EA	P	1.0000	1.0000

Source: Burroughs Corporation, B700 Systems Production Control System I *(Detroit: Burroughs Corporation, June 1976), pp. 3–24.*

For all of the items to be manufactured it is necessary to estimate the labor hours required for all of the operations necessary to convert the raw materials into the finished components and to assemble the components into the finished product. The time for inspection or other quality-control activities must also be included. Sometimes route sheets or crude approximations will be prepared. A *route sheet* is a document listing the routing or the sequence of operations through which an object must pass as it is produced. This document (Figure 8.1) is sometimes called an operations sheet. If the cost per labor hour is different in some work centers, this difference must be taken into account in the estimate. The labor hours are multiplied by the appropriate wage rates to arrive at the direct labor cost. A diagram of the estimating procedure is shown in Figure 8.2.

A completed cost (price) estimate has several components. Direct labor developed by the above (or similar) procedure, direct prices of materials to be

FIGURE 8.1

Sample Operations Sheet, Route Sheet, or Route Card

ROUTE CARD

PLANT	PART NUMBER	CUST. REQ'D DATE	PROM. DATE	LOT NO.	M.O. DATE	MILL ORDER NUMBER
60	LA 6538 XN		9-23		7-22	7-01749

PART SIZE & DESCRIPTION	MILL ORDER QUANT.
1-1/4-7 X 4-1/2 CRSE L-9 HEX CAP SCREW	928

CUSTOMER NAME	CUSTOMER PART NUMBER	CUSTOMER ORDER NO. & DATE

TOTAL LBS. R.M. REQ'D	GROSS R.M. WT. BASIS	FIN. WT./M PCS.	C.O.P.	PROD. LINE	SKETCH NUMBER	SKETCH DATE
2285	2462 91	2123 20	556		2132	00 00 00

NOTES AND SPECIAL INSTRUCTIONS:
FINAL INSPECT & TRACEABILITY

R.M. COAT	RAW MATERIAL	REQUIREMENTS	RAW MATERIAL
	MAT'L CODE/PART NO.	DESCRIPTION	
	04 4130 90	COLD DRAW STEEL BAR 94B30H X 1.237/1.241	
BINS		ALTERNATE	C-3
	04 4135 90	C.D. STEEL BAR 94B30H 1/24371.239	

OPERATIONS

WORK CENTER NUMBER	OPER. SEQ.	OPERATION DESCRIPTION	HRS PER M PCS.	C.I.F. PARTS EMP. NO.	DATE	SCHED. DATE
06 01 000	100	SHEAR	8400			
28 05 000	150	HAND POINT	0816			
06 14 000	200	HOT PRESS HEAD	0300			
06 14 000	250	EXTRUDE ON PRESS	2318			
26 10 000	300	SHOT BLAST	5936			
28 19 000	350	SHAVE	1285			
28 16 000	400	HAND ROLL THREAD	1200			
39 01 000	450	FINAL INSPECT	0000			

FIGURE 8.2

Schematic Overview of the Estimating Procedure

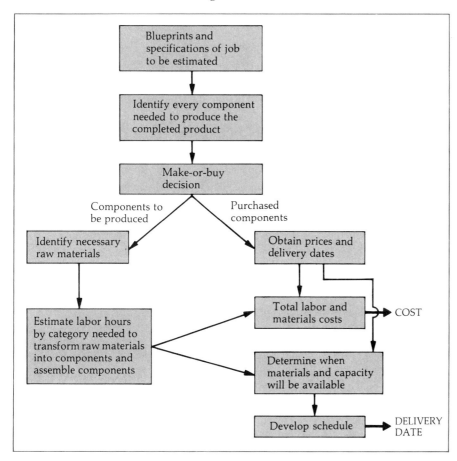

purchased, and the cost of stocked raw materials are added to obtain the direct cost estimate. Overhead expenses (also known as burden or administrative expenses) and a target profit are also added.

The completion date for an estimated project can result from either of two basic approaches to scheduling or from some combination of the two. The first major approach is called *backward scheduling.* In this case the potential customer specifies a required delivery date and the scheduler works backward from the required delivery to determine when (or at least the latest time at which) the necessary production tasks must occur. Backward scheduling was illustrated in Figure 7.9 and was discussed as the scheduling performed in material requirements planning.

If each task can be fitted into the available capacity (total capacity minus the backlog of work already under contract) in some period before its latest

FIGURE 8.3

Sample Backlog Report or Load Report

Work center 16				Weekly capacity 120 hrs.					
Week	1	2	3	4	5	6	7	8	Beyond
Load	120	120	100	65	28	45	20	16	38

allowable date, the requested delivery date can probably be met. If the backlog of contracted work is too great to allow the requested delivery, the job shop must decide whether to quote a late delivery or plan to increase its capacity—through overtime work or adding employees, for example—if it is awarded the job on the basis of the requested date.

The second basic approach is *forward scheduling*.[1] In this approach, each task is scheduled to occur at the earliest time that the necessary material will be on hand and capacity will be available. The earliest completion date, assuming everything goes as planned, could be quoted to the potential customer. Most likely, some buffer time would be added to determine a date that is more likely to be achievable, if the customer will accept such a completion date.

The above discussions of forward and backward scheduling make it obvious that job shop schedulers need valid data about capacity. They need to know how much total capacity each work center has and how much of this capacity has already been sold, that is, the backlog for each time period that is to be scheduled. Figure 8.3 shows a *backlog report* or *load report,* a useful means of keeping records of available and committed capacity. To be valid it must be updated each time work is completed, rescheduled, or canceled. The production control department is usually responsible for obtaining feedback from the production work centers and updating the backlog report or load report.

A job shop often is in a quandary in estimating the delivery date for a customer's work. The available capacity used to estimate the delivery date for one contract probably also was used to estimate other delivery dates. If two or more of these estimates result in contracts, the shop must decide whether to expand capacity by use of overtime or other means or to deliver some product later than it was promised. The shop cannot hold open its capacity in the hope that a quotation will result in a contract; if quoted capacity were reserved in case an order were received, there would be very low utilization of facilities.[2] Also, quoted delivery dates would be far in the future if capacity were not expanded, and the likelihood of receiving contracts would be low. A company would usually not know which work centers would receive the overload. Some companies have a policy of loading only a certain percentage, say 80 or 90

---

[1]Both forward and backward scheduling are used in the network-based scheduling techniques that are discussed in Chapter 10.
[2]This situation is somewhat akin to the problem of overbooking by airlines.

percent, of their capacity. Some may know their previous "hit ratio" for quotations and deduct this percentage of the quoted production time from the available capacity in order to reduce the risk of overquoting.

The sales department or estimating department may compile the materials needed to compute the cost and schedule estimates. In either case, sales personnel probably will contact the potential customer. Various methods can be used to convince the customer that the job shop can be relied on to produce a quality product. A brochure describing the quality-control organization, procedures, and equipment can be enclosed with the quotation. The potential customer can be invited to the plant to observe at firsthand the processing and inspection equipment. Sometimes the names of former customers are given as references to help build the potential customer's confidence that the job shop will produce the product to the specifications.

JOB SHOP SCHEDULING AND PRODUCTION CONTROL

Assume that our hypothetical job shop has been successful in assuring the customer of quality performance and has quoted a reasonable (perhaps minimum) price and delivery time. What happens then? The job shop has made an offer to perform certain work and has been awarded a legal contract. When the contract is received by the sales office it should set into motion all of the activities necessary to fulfill it. The operations function is responsible for producing the product requested by the customer. In this section we shall go through some of the scheduling and control activities involved in producing a product in a job shop. The activities of many shops will differ slightly from those presented here, but this material should provide a general understanding of production control.

The Production Control Department

At any one time, a sizable job shop might have hundreds of jobs in process. Many of these jobs could have hundreds of parts at various stages of completion scattered through a dozen or more work centers. Obviously, no one person can track and coordinate such an extensive array of activities. Such companies usually have a production control group to assist management in planning, organizing, directing, coordinating, and controlling production activities. Production control is usually a staff function that does not directly supervise workers but advises direct-line supervisors.

Planning includes make-or-buy decisions, determining the processing steps that will be used to make the internally produced items, and scheduling. Organizing includes preparing route sheets that assign responsibility for each step of processing to a particular work center. Directing includes dispatching particular jobs to particular work centers at particular times. Coordinating includes constantly assessing the changing priorities of work so that all of the necessary components of a job will be completed when needed. Controlling involves keeping plans and schedules updated, collecting data on actual progress of work, comparing progress to the current plan, and taking corrective action when actual progress is not in reasonable agreement with the plan. Corrective action normally consists of informing line supervisors of problems and recommending courses of action.

Thus good production control depends on:

1. Formulating a good plan and schedule for each job, one that recognizes the needs of other jobs that must use the same facilities.
2. Communicating these plans to all who must help carry them out.
3. Obtaining communication about the actual progress of each job and about the composite situation.
4. Revising the plans and schedules whenever the situation makes improvement desirable or necessary. (This is really a return to step 1.)

It is apparent that good production control involves good communication, that is, the efficient collection and transmittal of data. The production control group serves as the nerve network of a production system, sending signals to evoke action and sensing the results and need for further action.

The massive amount of data accumulated in tracking the numerous parts of all jobs makes automatic data processing essential to sizable shops if timely reports are to be available. Networks of computer terminals can help to coordinate widely dispersed work centers, inspection stations, purchasing offices, and stock rooms. An interactive system such as this makes possible data entry and inquiry from multiple locations. It is desirable to use common data base so as to better coordinate all of the organizational elements involved. Commercial software packages that link many applications into a common data base are available through computer manufacturers and software houses. These packages often integrate other applications as well as production control activities. For example, sales information is related to use of inventory, inventory withdrawal is tracked to see when production should occur, production activities result in material requirements, and materials procurement affects accounts payable. Labor hours are reported to track work performed on jobs, and these same data can be used for payroll preparation. It is apparent that companies are interrelated networks of transactions, and tracking production activities is an important part of this network in a manufacturing company. Figure 8.4 shows the applications that are linked in the IBM Manufacturing Accounting and Production Information Control System (MAPICS).

Scheduling and Controlling Contracts

Scheduling and controlling a contract as it is processed through facilities with perhaps dozens of other contracts involves several organizational components. Numerous activities that are involved in processing one order occur simultaneously with the activities involved in other orders at various stages of processing. The sequence of activities that occur in processing one order, from receiving the order to shipping the item, is outlined below. (Many of these activities are

FIGURE 8.4

Information Flow Between Applications in MAPICS

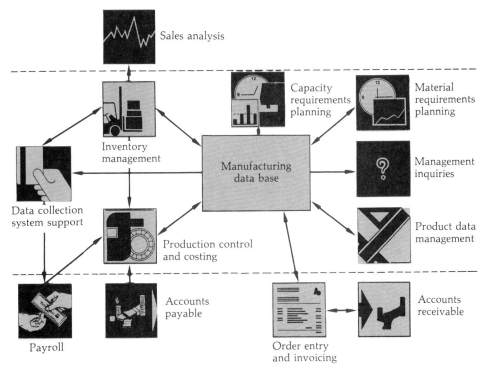

Source: Reprinted by permission from *Introduction to the Manufacturing Applications for MAPICS* (GH30-0221-Z). © 1980 by International Business Machines Corporation.

also shown schematically and numbered in sequence in Figure 8.5.)

The customer places an order with sales. Sales notifies production control to proceed with the job. Production control performs the detailed planning by preparing route sheets for every component to be produced. Requisitions are prepared for all raw materials and purchased components and sent to purchasing. Move tickets may be prepared to instruct materials-handling personnel to move the items to the appropriate next operation after each step of processing is completed. If any special tooling is required, it must be specified and requisitioned to be produced by an internal or external tool-and-die shop. Requisitions for externally produced tooling will be sent to purchasing. The route sheets, blueprints, special instructions or specifications, and move tickets make up what is sometimes called a *traveler package*, which is sent to scheduling.

Scheduling is performed in two stages. The first is called loading. *Loading* is assigning to a particular work center the task to be performed during some gross scheduling period, such as a week. Some desired completion date, however, is usually assigned to each task. Loading of work centers depends on open (available) capacity in the load report and the expected availability of the

FIGURE 8.5

Overview of Production Control and Other Activities That Must Be Coordinated to Produce a Product

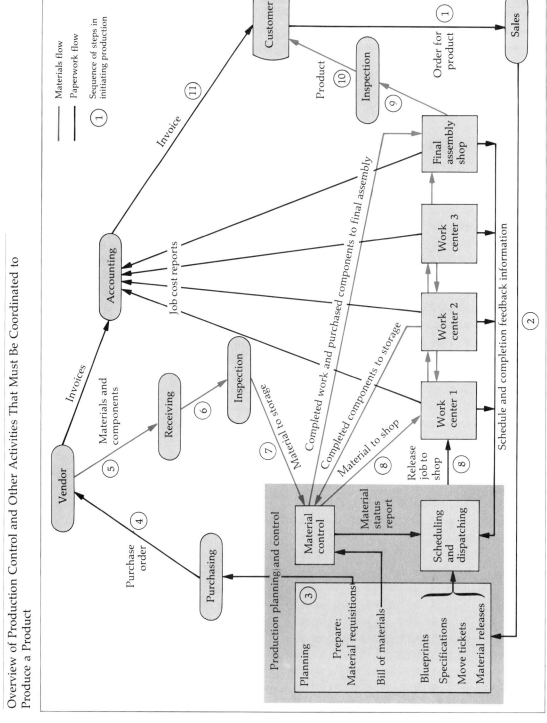

material for the job. If material is available early, it may be held in a material-control area until the period in which the job is to be released to the work center. The jobs loaded to a work center are considered to form a waiting line, or queue, of waiting jobs, even though some of the jobs may not be present physically.

The second stage of scheduling is dispatching. Dispatching is sequencing the tasks that are waiting to be worked on at a work center and releasing them to be performed at a particular time by a specific machine. Dispatching decisions depend on many factors and frequently are made a short time before dispatching is begun so that the current status of these factors can be taken into account.

The planned hours in a task are removed from the backlog, or load, when a work center completes the task. Dispatchers can obtain this feedback by talking with the foremen of the work centers or by collecting move tickets showing that the item has left the work centers. Sometimes computerized information systems are used: Computer cards are returned to a collection point, or electronic data entry terminals are located on the shop floor so that workers can key in the completion of their assignments.

Completed parts or subassemblies are usually held in a material control area until all of the components of a job are completed. After final assembly operations are performed, the job is inspected and shipped to the customer. Naturally, cost data are collected during production. The customer will be invoiced for the contract price of the job, which the company hopes is greater than the total cost.

Load Charts and Reports Companies strive to develop accurate, achievable schedules that smoothly utilize available capacity. Loading each department's capacity depends on accurate information regarding the available capacity throughout the planning horizon and accurate backlog of committed work load. A load report for a work center can be manually prepared or it can be obtained from a computerized system such as MRP (material requirements planning). A sample load report was shown in Figure 8.3 and is repeated in Figure 8.6(a). Capacity is available in week 3 and beyond. A job requiring 20 hours or less of production time in work center 16 could be loaded into week 3 if the materials were available and if its earlier production steps were already completed. A job requiring more than 20 hours would require overtime, or it could be scheduled to be completed sometime after week 3. A bar chart with a vertical or horizontal bar for each week's load can be used to indicate the load shown in a load report. Figure 8.6(b) displays graphically the information in Figure 8.6(a).

Another graphical display that is very effective in indicating the load status of a work center is the Gantt load chart. It can be used to show specific jobs that are scheduled into the work center, as shown in Figure 8.7. Notice that available production time for each machine can be easily spotted. Indicating the detailed load by each specific machine is desirable only if the machine has unique production capability.

Dispatching The dispatcher is production control's representative in the shop. He or she does not have direct authority to assign work to workers, but works

FIGURE 8.6

Sample Load Report and Its Translation into a Bar Graph

(a)

Work center: 16					Weekly capacity: 120 hours				
Week	1	2	3	4	5	6	7	8	Beyond
Load	120	120	100	65	28	45	20	16	38

(b)

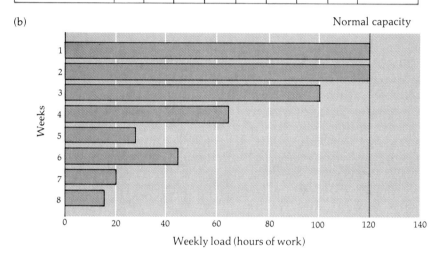

FIGURE 8.7

Gantt Load Chart

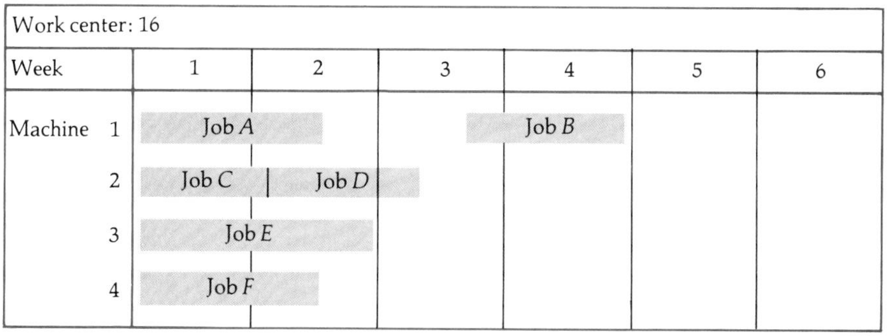

with the foreman to utilize the available capacity in the most advantageous manner and to keep jobs on schedule to the extent possible.

Some of the functions of dispatching may be to:

1. Provide for movement of materials from materials control to the first operation and from operation to operation.

2. Issue instructions for tools, dies, jigs, and fixtures.
3. Issue job orders in accordance with schedules.
4. Sequence jobs.
5. Issue drawings, instruction cards, time tickets, and the like.
6. Provide for inspection.
7. Collect drawings, bills of materials, and so on after each task and return them to production control.
8. Serve as liaison between scheduling and manufacturing in order to monitor work and record start time, progress, and completion.
9. Collect job time tickets.
10. Request action when delays occur.[3]

Job Sequencing (Assigning Priorities) The question of *job sequencing* has received much attention in research and analysis. It rapidly becomes an overwhelming combinatorial problem even when the number of jobs and work centers is small. We shall begin with a very simple problem of n jobs to be sequenced for processing on one machine (i.e., the $n/1$ sequencing problem). There are n jobs that could be selected to be first, $n - 1$ jobs left for the second place, $n - 2$ left for third place, and so on, leading to $n!$ possible sequences. If we had 10 jobs to sequence, that would be $10! = 3,628,800$ possible sequences. If you could evaluate 1,000 in a minute, it would take more than 60 hours to determine the best sequence by enumerating all of them. During this time some jobs could be run even if they were only in a "good" rather than optimal sequence. During this time new jobs would also be received, and some of the other jobs could be canceled. Imagine trying to enumerate all possible sequences of 100 jobs across 10 work centers and then determining the cost of each possible sequence!

Despite the large number of possible sequences, it has been shown that the $n/1$ problem can be optimized. If the criterion is to minimize the average flow time or the average job lateness, the job sequence should begin with the shortest processing time and progress in the order of increasing processing time. Flow time is the total time a job spends in the shop, either waiting or being processed. Job lateness is actual delivery date minus the due date and can be positive or negative. This solution is suitable if there is no significant difference in job priorities or their in-process inventory cost and if the setup costs are independent of sequence.

Johnson's Rule Consider the situation of two work centers, say machine 1 and machine 2, where all jobs flow from the first to the second. If the objective is to minimize idle time and the time from the beginning of the first job until the finish of the last job, scheduling can be optimized by the use of Johnson's rule.[4] The method is suitable when in-process inventory cost and setup cost are independent of sequence.

---

[3]Gordon B. Carson, Harold A. Bolz, and Hewitt H. Young, eds., *Production Handbook*, 3d ed. (New York: Ronald Press, 1972), p. 3.36.
[4]S. M. Johnson, "Optimal Two- and Three-Stage Production Schedules with Setup Times Included," *Naval Research Logistics Quarterly*, (March 1954), pp. 61–68.

Johnson's rule consists of the following four steps:

1. List the processing times (including setup) for all jobs in both production stages.
2. Select the job with the shortest time in either stage.
3. If the shortest time is for the first processing stage, do the job as early as possible in the unfilled portion of the job sequence. If the shortest time is for the second processing stage, do the job as late as possible in the unfilled portion of the job sequence. If the time on the first stage for one job equals the time on the second stage for some other job, fill the earliest slot with the job having this amount of time for the first stage and fill the latest slot with the job having this amount of time for the second stage. If a job has the same time for both stages, it can be placed arbitrarily at the earlier or later end of the unfilled sequence.
4. Delete the job selected in step 2 and repeat the steps until all jobs have been sequenced.

APPLICATION

Job Sequencing by Johnson's Rule

Stan's Furniture Refinishers has five items of furniture to sand and varnish the next day. The times for these two operations are shown in Table 8.2. Stan supervises all refinishing and does not go home until the last operation is finished. Find the sequence that will minimize the time from the beginning of the first item until the finish of the last (i.e., minimize the maximum flow time).

Table 8.2
HOURS REQUIRED TO SAND AND VARNISH FIVE ITEMS OF FURNITURE: FIRST STEP IN JOB SEQUENCING BY JOHNSON'S RULE

Item	Sanding Time	Varnish Time
A	1.50	1.25
B	2.00	3.00
C	1.00	2.00
D	2.50	2.00
E	1.75	1.75

The shortest time for all of the tasks is sanding item C. Since this time is for the first task, job C is placed first in the sequence (Figure 8.8).

FIGURE 8.8

Second Step in Job Sequencing by Johnson's Rule

Sequence

1st	2d	3d	4th	5th
C				

Item C is eliminated from further consideration. The shortest remaining time is 1.25 hours for varnishing item A. Since this is for the last task, item A is placed last in the sequence (Figure 8.9).

FIGURE 8.9

Third Step in Job Sequencing by Johnson's Rule

Sequence

1st	2d	3d	4th	5th
C				A

Item A is eliminated. The shortest remaining time is 1.75 hours for item E. Whether E is performed second or fourth will not change the maximum flow time. It is arbitrarily placed as early as possible (Figure 8.10), but the fourth slot would also be permissible.

FIGURE 8.10

Fourth Step in Job Sequencing by Johnson's Rule

Sequence

1st	2d	3d	4th	5th
C	E			A

Jobs B and D remain and are tied for minimum time for a task. The 2-hour time for job B is at the first stage and favors putting it early, and the stage for job D favors putting it late. The completed sequence is shown in Figure 8.11. Notice that Stan will have to work 11 hours if he is going to be present while all of the work is done.

FIGURE 8.11

Minimum Flow Time Solution by Johnson's Rule

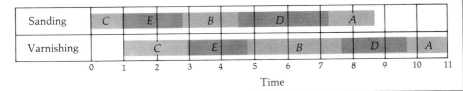

Johnson's rule has been adapted to the three-machine problem in some instances. No simple optimization algorithms are available for problems of greater size, although most job shops contain more than three work centers. In any case, there are other factors to be taken into consideration besides the maximum flow time.

Dispatching would present few problems so long as the work center has excess capacity allowing all jobs to be worked on as they arrive. We previously mentioned that excess capacity is tied to excess capital investment and should be avoided in most instances. Therefore, a queue is likely to form in front of many work centers. There are reasons that a queue may be desirable. It provides a backlog to keep the work center from becoming idle. And it is more likely that a sequence of tasks can be developed that will more efficiently utilize the work center if a number of tasks are available to select from. When work backs up in front of a work center, dispatching decisions must be made regarding which of the waiting jobs should be worked on next.

The question of which jobs to select from the queue and how to sequence them should take current priorities into account. Such factors as the following are sometimes used to help select the next job to be assigned within a work center:

1. The skill of the available worker versus the skill requirements of the waiting jobs.
2. The need for a particular type of job to keep subsequent work centers from having idle time.
3. The possibility that the next work center for some jobs may already be overloaded, making it futile to complete the current stage on these jobs soon.
4. The estimated processing time.
   (a) In ascending order.
   (b) In descending order.
5. The time until the task is scheduled to be complete.
6. The time until the total job is scheduled to be delivered.
7. The total amount of slack time for the item, i.e., work hours until delivery date minus the total estimated processing time.
8. The number of operations remaining to be performed on the item.
9. Sequencing to minimize the total setup cost for changing between jobs.
10. The dollar value of the job to which the item belongs.
11. The importance attached to completing the particular customer's work.

Assume for a moment that the total amount of work in a shop could be sequenced so that it would go through all operations in an optimal fashion, according to some criterion. This sequence would be based on the expected task times for the activities. Yet the actual time for many of the tasks would differ from the expected time. After the first tasks on a few jobs were completed, the actual situation would differ from the plan. Some jobs would arrive at subsequent work centers early and some would arrive late. The numbers of tasks in the queues at these centers would be unequal, and the slack time from many of them would differ from the originally expected values. Besides, new contracts would be received at frequent intervals (the owners hope), bringing new tasks into some of the queues. Also bear in mind the machine breakdowns, late material deliveries, and absenteeism mentioned earlier. This discussion is not intended to indicate the futility of trying to schedule a job shop; rather, it shows why scheduling and sequencing decisions must be based on the current situation. Planning horizons beyond some point in time are mere approximations.

Because these and other factors can influence the best sequencing of jobs, sequencing decisions are not always simple. Keeping priorities current involves deexpediting those jobs that have other components delayed so that they cannot be completed anyway, for example. Collecting all of the data and deciding on the relative importance of these factors for each specific situation can be difficult and time-consuming. Since scheduling in this environment is an inexact science, some researchers and practitioners use simulation and heuristics (rules of thumb) to resolve the problem. The simplest rule of thumb is a first-come, first-served queue discipline. Another widely used method is to select for processing the item with the lowest average slack per operation—that is, the item with the lowest priority, when the priority is the ratio of items 7 and 8 in the previous list of factors.

$$\text{Priority} = \frac{\left(\begin{array}{c}\text{work hours until}\\ \text{delivery date}\end{array}\right) - \left(\begin{array}{c}\text{total estimated}\\ \text{processing time}\end{array}\right)}{\text{number of remaining operations}} \qquad (8.1)$$

Various *dispatching rules* have been evaluated by simulation to see which will perform best according to some criterion. One rule that frequently shows that it will minimize the number of late jobs is the shortest-processing-time (SPT) rule. This rule simply dispatches the queue of jobs at each work station according to their expected processing times. As new jobs continue to arrive, the shorter ones will be worked and a lengthy job may be delayed indefinitely. The longest job would not be worked unless the work center ran out of alternatives. Some of the longer jobs, however, might represent more inventory investment and more potential profit. Consequently, modifications of this rule have been developed. In view of the difficulties, it is doubtful that one simple rule will correctly solve all of the problems that can arise. Considerable research is still being done on this challenging problem.

The Gantt Chart for Tracking Job Progress

The progress of jobs must be monitored to keep them on schedule and to revise schedules as the need arises. Various graphs and reports can be of assistance in this procedure.

One form of Gantt bar chart is often used for planning and monitoring the progress of jobs. The sequence of tasks necessary to complete the total job can be shown on a time-scaled chart. A bar can be used to represent subtasks within a job. The location of each bar indicates the time at which that subtask is scheduled to be performed. Additional information can be included to indicate the planned production hours—say, at the top of the bar. The chart can be marked to indicate actual progress of the job as feedback is obtained from the shops. The chart gives a graphic overview of the job's status, suggesting where corrective action may be desired. An example of a *Gantt schedule chart* is shown in Figure 8.12. The brackets show when a task is scheduled to occur. A solid bar shows the extent of actual progress. The current date pointer at the bottom of the chart indicates that progress on the stand is ahead of schedule and receipt of the compressor is behind schedule.

Several commercial devices display essentially the same type of information as a Gantt chart. They use bars of paper, string, plastic, or metal to represent the bars on the chart. All are visual displays intended to aid in developing a plan or in rapidly inferring the progress of work.

Typewritten or computer-printed reports may also be used to present job status. Lists of completed tasks, remaining tasks, tasks behind schedule, and so on serve to give production control and shop personnel needed information.

FIGURE 8.12

A Gantt Schedule Chart

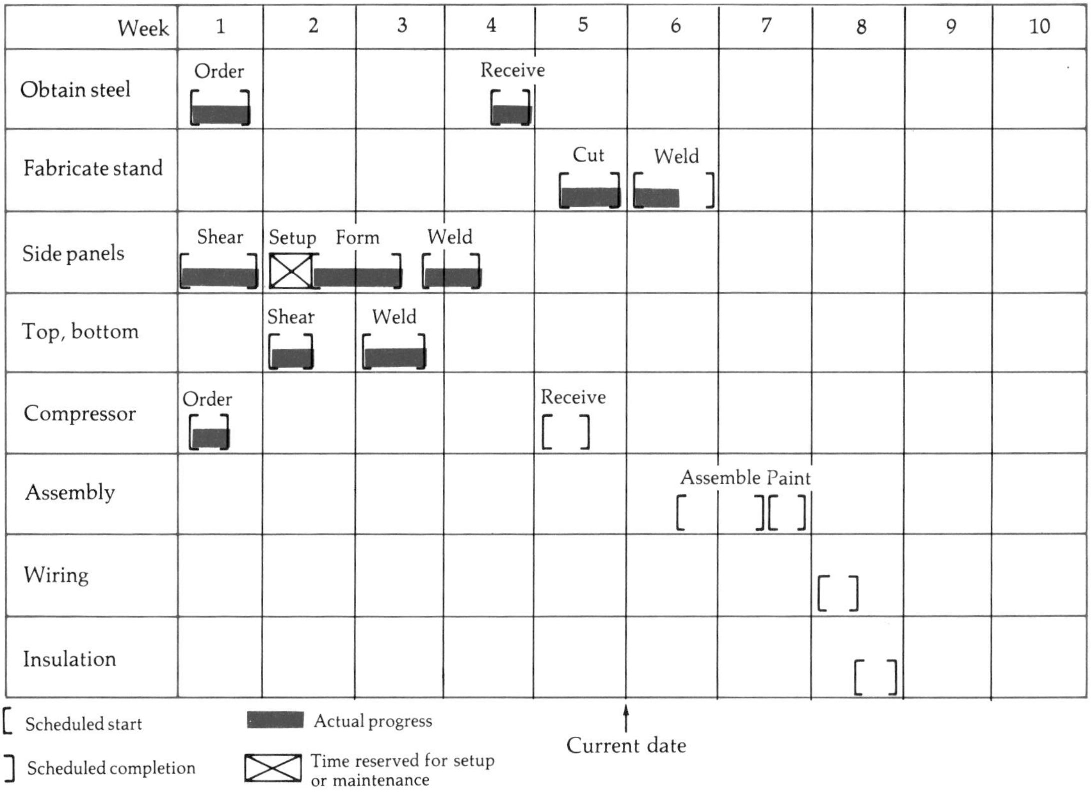

Week	1	2	3	4	5	6	7	8	9	10
Obtain steel	Order			Receive						
Fabricate stand					Cut	Weld				
Side panels	Shear	Setup Form	Weld							
Top, bottom		Shear	Weld							
Compressor	Order				Receive					
Assembly							Assemble Paint			
Wiring								[ ]		
Insulation								[ ]		

[Scheduled start   ▬ Actual progress
] Scheduled completion   ⊠ Time reserved for setup or maintenance
↑ Current date

Computer reports can give very rapid compilation of data to help revise schedules and priorities and respond to dynamic conditions.

Gantt scheduling charts, unless frequently redrawn, tend to compare progress of a job with the originally planned progress. In view of the intrusions that can occur, original schedules may not be the most appropriate to use. Schedules based on current progress are more valid. MRP enables a company to revise priorities in accordance with the current status of other jobs and other components of the same job.

PRODUCTION CONTROL FOR INTERMEDIATE QUANTITIES

The preceding discussion of the job shop presented the challenge of constantly replanning a different set of requirements for every single product. Certainly most companies do not produce only one or two of the same item, yet many do not always produce the same product on a continuous basis. A job shop (make-to-order shop) may have orders to produce dozens or hundreds of perhaps even thousands of the same item for delivery over several time periods. Conversely, a make-to-stock company does not always produce the same item. It may use a production facility or production line to produce some quantity of one item, then switch to the production of some other (probably similar) item for a while. There is a continuum ranging from one per contract to continuous production of the same product, and most companies fall somewhere in the middle. It is estimated that three-fourths of the machined parts produced in the United States are run in batches of 50 or fewer.

PRODUCTION ACTIVITY CONTROL WITH MRP

If an item is to be produced on subsequent occasions, the efforts to construct bill-of-materials files and inventory status files for its components can pay sufficient dividends to make MRP (material requirements planning) even more attractive as a way to manage the dependent components. However, MRP is sometimes used when only one of an item is to be produced. In our discussion of MRP we said it was more than just a way to manage inventory—it provides valuable information for managing production operations. *Production activity control* (i.e., *shop floor control*) requires detailed planning of the necessary operations and accurate information about the current plan and the current status of all components of the jobs that are in progress. The logic of MRP provides a basic core for a system to plan and control shop floor activities.

The objective of shop floor control is to utilize production resources efficiently. In working toward this goal, a company often goes through a series of stages to develop and refine production plans. The planned level of output must be realistic and achievable, yet the planned level of capacity to be made available should not significantly exceed the necessary amount. Aggregate planning provides a first stage of planning whereby intermediate-range plans are developed in approximate terms. Resource requirements planning or another aggregate planning method might be used at this stage to develop a general production plan. This plan is evaluated far enough before actual operations so that the schedule can be revised or capacity can be adjusted to achieve a reasonable match between production commitments and capacity.

The next level of refinement is detailed capacity requirements planning. This gives a truer picture of the capacity requirements, particularly during the near portion of the planning horizon, because it adjusts for the lead-time offsets and deducts available components to determine net requirements. The result of this refinement is a master schedule that can be achieved within the available capacity. Good capacity requirements planning also involves adjusting capacity so that excessive capacity is not made available when it would result in expensive idle time.

After a good master schedule is developed, other detailed refinements are necessary to utilize work center capacities efficiently. Work must be released to the shop smoothly in the proper quantities to avoid drastic shifts between having log jams of work one week and idle time the next. A schedule that results in overtime part of the time and idle workers part of the time is not efficient. The rate of throughput at each work center should be reasonably smooth and adequate to support the master schedule. *Input-output control* is used to release the proper amounts of work to starting (i.e., "gateway") work centers and to spot any blockages or excess capacity in the flow of work through other work centers of the shop.

Performing the proper amount of work in each work center may use the capacity, but it does not necessarily use it most effectively. Jobs can be completed at the proper rate on the average and still miss their schedules. Some jobs may be completed too early, thereby increasing the investment in inventory until they are used or sold. Other jobs can be completed too late, causing delays and idle capacity at downstream work centers or creating customer dissatisfaction. A better approach is to complete each job on schedule (or maybe a little earlier). *Priority control* means keeping the due dates current and dispatching jobs so that work is performed in accordance with the dates that jobs are needed.

In overview, production activity control involves input-output control to see that the proper amount of work is released to the shop floor and performed in each work center. It means dispatching jobs so they will be worked on in the order in which they are needed. This procedure makes the proper amount of capacity available and allocates the capacity to the jobs that have the highest priority. Efficient production must plan and control capacity, and it must plan and control priorities of jobs. Capacity requirements planning, which was discussed in the previous chapter, is used to plan capacity. Input-output control is used to control capacity. MRP, which was also discussed in the previous chapter, is used to plan priorities. Tracking the status of jobs, dispatching, and expediting are used to control the progress of jobs in accordance with priorities indicated by the updated MRP reports. In the following two sections we will discuss further the concepts of input-output control and priority control with MRP to improve the utilization of productive resources.

Input-Output Control

In general, control involves having a plan, comparing actual performance with the plan, and taking corrective actions to keep the plan and the results within reasonable tolerance. The capacity of a work center is the throughput rate, or the rate at which work actually flows out of the work center. Capacity is usually measured in standard hours of work that can be performed per week or in some other time period. Input-output control shows the relationship between the planned and the actual input rate and capacity (output rate) of a work center so that the need for any corrective actions can be readily determined.

Development of a good master schedule is important because, among other things, the planned input rate for starting work centers is determined when the master schedule is established. The actual input rate to work centers that perform starting operations can be varied to some degree by changing the rate at which work is released to the shop. The cumulative deviation between planned and actual input over several periods must not become too great or the master schedule will not be achieved. The master schedule must be revised if the rate of releasing work to the shop is changed significantly from the existing plan. The output rate of a work center is affected by changing the capacity through such means as the use of overtime or additional shifts and adding personnel and equipment.

Changes in the output rate of starting or other work centers will change the input rate at the next downstream work center. It is difficult, however, to determine just when a particular job will reach a downstream work center because the actual processing time may differ from the standard hours estimated for the operation and because the relative priority of the job in a queue depends on what other jobs happen to arrive and wait in line with it. Within a short interval, several work centers may complete jobs that are all routed to the same work center. During another interval no jobs scheduled to flow to a particular work center may be completed. Thus controlling input rates at downstream work centers is difficult, and as a result input rates at downstream centers may be more erratic than input rates at a starting work center. The input at a downstream work center should average the same as the capacity of the center; otherwise, the backlog of work in process will build up or decline over time. Thus input-output control of downstream work centers is mostly capacity control. It is important to recognize that changing the output of some work centers will affect the input rate of downstream work centers.

The backlog changes each week by an amount equal to the actual input minus the actual output that week. Figure 8.13 shows an example of an input-output control report. Notice that the backlog has grown by forty standard hours during the five weeks represented by this report. Work is arriving at a slightly greater rate than has been planned, and the actual throughput rate is less than

FIGURE 8.13

Input-Output Control Report

Week ending	5/31	6/7	6/14	6/21	6/28
Planned input (standard hours)	320	310	315	325	310
Actual input	325	320	310	330	320
Cumulative deviation	+5	+15	+10	+15	+25
Planned output (standard hours)	320	320	320	320	320
Actual output	310	325	310	300	320
Cumulative deviation	−10	−5	−15	−35	−35
Cumulative effect on backlog (standard hours)	+15	+10	+10	+40	+40

the planned rate. If the capacity of the work center is not increased through some means such as the use of overtime or additional personnel, the backlog will accumulate and work will not reach the downstream work centers when it was planned to arrive.

Input-output control can affect several important factors. Input-output control can also be thought of as backlog control, or queue-size control, because it controls the size of the queue of jobs that wait at a work center. A decrease in the input rate and/or an increase in the output rate will reduce the queue of jobs waiting at a work center and therefore reduce the average time required for a job to get through the queue. Alternatively, if inputs are greater than outputs over several periods, then the backlog will grow and the investment in work in process will increase. The lead time through several work centers might become so long that the production system will not be able to respond to changes as rapidly. If production lead times are long, demand must be forecast further into the future, and such forecasts are likely to be less accurate. Consequently, companies often try to maintain control over the capacity at each work center to prevent the average lead time at each center from becoming too long.

Effective input-output control achieves the proper rate of flow through each work center so that the desired production rate to support the master schedule will be achieved. Input-output control also keeps the average queue length at each work center to some reasonable size. Some dispatching rule or some system of logic must be used to select from the queue the job that should be worked on next—that is, when capacity becomes available at the work center, some logic is needed to determine which job in the queue should be allocated the available capacity. In the next section we discuss the priorities of jobs in the queue.

Planning and Controlling Priorities with MRP

It was pointed out earlier that a company can have the proper average lead time at its work centers and still have some jobs completed too early and some jobs completed too late. To avoid this situation it is important to have a means to determine which job in the queue should be worked on first when capacity becomes available. Several dispatching rules were discussed in the previous material on job shop production control. The dispatching logic that is frequently used in shop floor control is to establish priorities on the basis of the need date for the completion of each operation.

The logic in MRP involves offsetting by the planned lead time for each level of fabrication and assembly that must be performed to produce the end item. This backward scheduling process provides a date (time bucket) when each stage of production must be completed if the planned lead time to perform the subsequent operations is to be available. The cumulative lead time—that is, the stacked lead time—for all operations on an item determines when processing should begin to complete end items as originally scheduled. Of course, the planned lead times that are established must be based on realistic considerations of the available capacity—or to state it more accurately, the capacity must be controlled so that the planned lead times are achieved.

The average actual lead time for the jobs that pass through a work center should equal the planned lead time for that operation (or a little less). With a symmetrical distribution of lead times, approximately half of the actual lead times will be less than the mean and half will be greater. Priority control is the effort to know which jobs are needed first and to dispatch these jobs so that they are among the jobs completed in less than average lead time. Input-output control ensures that the right amount of work is done and that the length of the waiting line is neither too long nor too short. Priority control, in turn, ensures that the right jobs are given priority. Jobs with the earliest need date for the next operation to start normally should be at the front of the line. Following this procedure at each work center can help control the actual cumulative lead times so that they will be about equal to the planned cumulative lead time for each item. If a job gets behind schedule, it will be placed near the front of the line; if it is ahead of schedule, it will be moved further back in the line.

Components of Lead Time   Some of the writing about production gives the impression that lead times are fixed and known. There usually are several components to the lead time that occur at each work center. Each of these components can be controlled to some degree, but often each component has some unpredictable variation. The components of lead time that usually occur for each work center are shown in Figure 8.14.

Processing, or run, time is a technological requirement for the operation to be performed. Sometimes the duration of the process can be changed. Two

FIGURE 8.14

Frequent Components of Lead Time

Move to work center	Queue time	Setup time	Run time	Wait for move

machines, working simultaneously, can process a batch of items in about half the time; but at the expense of two setups. Moreover, duplicate equipment and workers must be available. When a lot is split into two or more smaller lots, a second operation can be performed on some of the material while the first operation is still being performed on the remainder of the material. This procedure, called *overlapping* or *telescoping,* is another way to reduce the elapsed calendar time or flow time for a job.

Move time is usually not a large portion of the total job time, but sometimes it can be expedited to some degree. People can be kept on standby to move an item as soon as processing is complete, reducing both the wait and move times for the item. If successive stages of processing are performed at different plants, expedited shipments can sometimes save considerable time.

The greatest opportunity to affect lead time can usually be found in queue time, since it may represent 80 percent or more of the total lead time. Some amount of queue in front of a work center is desirable because it helps to smooth out the fluctuations in input rate. A queue helps to ensure that the work center does not run out of work, causing expensive idle time, as the arrival rate of jobs fluctuates. A queue of waiting jobs also provides options for sequencing jobs so that setups can be simplified or their times can be reduced. In some cases jobs can be run together—for example, metals that require the same temperature heat-treating for the same duration can be treated in a furnace together. A queue that lasts longer than the amount of time needed to provide these advantages is not desirable because it represents an investment in idle work-in-process.

As capacity becomes available, dispatching logic should select from the queue the job that represents the wisest use of the available resource. Normally, priority should be given to the job that has the nearest need date, unless there are reasons, such as those mentioned in the preceding paragraph, for doing otherwise. The need date for an operation is the date at which the next operation must start if the amount of time provided for the remaining operations is to be kept equal to the time that was originally planned. These dates are provided by MRP.

Priority Control   A *dispatch list* can be prepared daily for each work center showing the jobs that should be at that work center and giving a current estimate of the need date for each job. The dispatch list for a work center can change at any time, because a new job can appear on the list whenever it is completed at an upstream work center. The priorities—that is, need dates—for jobs can also change each time the MRP package is run, since the master schedule can be changed, new orders can be received, or orders can be canceled. If some key component of an end item is scrapped or will be delivered from a vendor later than originally planned, all other components of the end item will no longer be needed when they were originally planned. Therefore, the priorities for all other components of the end item will change.

Reports that show the updated status of jobs and the workloads at work centers can be prepared manually or with computerized systems. Using the

FIGURE 8.15

A Compact Data Collection Terminal

Source: Digital Equipment Company, *PDP-11 Systems and Options Catalog*, January–March 1985, page 8–7

latter method ensures that the reports will be more timely and that less labor will be needed for their preparation. Some computerized systems use data collection terminals like the one shown in Figure 8.15 to collect data from the shop floor. Such terminals can be placed at various locations in the plant so that timely data can be reported to a memory unit that is accessed by the computer when the update calculations are to be made. A worker provides data at the terminal each time an operation on a work order is begun or completed. The data terminal can automatically read a great deal of data. An internal clock records the start or stop time. A scan of a magnetic strip or bar code can be used to record the employee's identification from a badge and the job number from a route sheet or work order. The employee may need to key in only the number of good units completed and perhaps the number of defective units. Feedback is needed from each work center to make shop floor control effective.

When an item is completed or almost completed at one work center, the shop floor control system should add it to the dispatch list for the next downstream work center. The number of standard hours associated with each completed operation should be added to the actual output of the appropriate work centers so that the input-output report is accurately updated. A labor reporting system should also track the actual labor hours on the job. Actual hours can be compared to the estimated standard hours to determine the efficiency at each work center, so that more accurate future estimates can be made. Each time a component or subassembly of an end item is completed, it affects the number of these items that are on hand. The number of available items, in turn, affects the netting process when MRP is run and can affect the priorities of other shop orders. For example, a scrap rate might be lower than anticipated, and more of an item might become available than was originally planned. An earlier order to produce a few of this item might no longer be needed, and its priority would become very low. Overshipments or undershipments from vendors also can affect the inventory level, thereby changing priorities on the shop floor. Figure 8.16 shows the flow of information that is involved in coordinating shop floor operations with MRP. The feedback of information into the earlier steps of the flow chart illustrates what is meant by closed-loop MRP. The initial process of rough-cut capacity planning to develop a desirable master schedule is not included in Figure 8.16 because it was discussed in Chapter 4.

PRODUCTION CONTROL FOR REPETITIVE MANUFACTURING

Repetitive manufacturing is characterized by long runs of identical or similar discrete items through the same sequence of processing steps. Often special-purpose equipment and tooling are used because the same operations are performed on each item at a particular work center. Economies are achieved by locating each operation very near to the prior operation so that the time and cost involved in moving the products are minimized. When this type of arrangement is used, the result is referred to as a *production line* or *assembly line*. For lightweight objects, the worker might perform the operations and simply hand the item to the next operator. For heavier objects, mechanical assistance such as a conveyor might be used.

Repetitive production of an item presents a different production control problem from that of the job shop. The routings are fixed, so planning each individual job and preparing individual route sheets are not necessary. The processing steps, routing, and work methods are primarily planned when the production system is designed—hence the need for good manufacturing engineering when the system is designed. The waiting time between operations and the work-in-process inventory are both minimal, so that there usually are no queues of different kinds of jobs waiting at a work center and so priorities do not have to be determined, and dispatching at each work center is not necessary.

Individual parts are not scheduled and tracked unit by unit in this type of production. A particular door for a 12-cubic-foot refrigerator will fit any refrigerator of that model, so it is not important to complete a particular door just at the time a particular refrigerator is completed. The important thing is to complete doors for this model at the same rate that the refrigerators are being produced. More realistically, every component of the refrigerator must be completed at a rate that is proportional to the quantity of the component used in the refrigerator. Repetitive manufacturing is often scheduled at daily rates of output, such as 225 units per day for the next two weeks. This is an application of flow control, mentioned at the beginning of the chapter.

FIGURE 8.16

Information Flow for Shop Floor Control

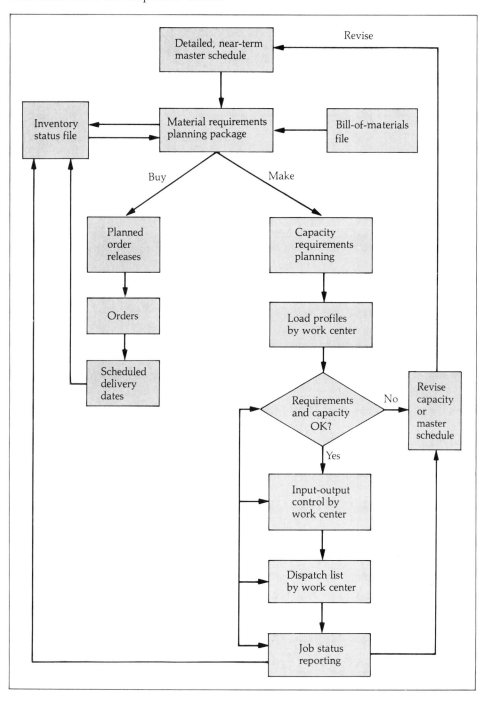

Control of this type of production system would be simple if only one model of product were produced and at a uniform rate. The company could simply build a special-purpose plant with a capacity of the desired output rate and keep it running. The problem is more complicated if the demand rate varies considerably throughout the year. The company can accumulate and deplete inventory, but this option can be expensive at the volume levels typical of many of these companies. The company can vary the output rate by changing the number of workdays per week, the hours per day, or the number of shifts that are worked. Sometimes it is possible to change the number of employees and reassign the work so that a different production rate is achieved. Scheduling and control become even more difficult when several models are produced on the same line and when demand varies so that different product mixes must be made from time to time.

One approach that high-volume, repetitive manufacturing operations can use to meet demand for varying volumes and mixes of products is to have separate facilities for each product and to scale production up or down in response to the demand pattern. Obviously, this would require a high investment in numerous facilities that would seldom be fully utilized. Another approach is to run one large facility on a product for a while, then change to another product for a while. However, the rescheduling and coordinating problems caused by frequently changing from one product to another can be significant. The problem of trying to achieve a balanced assembly line is discussed in a later section of this chapter. An alternative is to stabilize the mix and the production rate for an extended period so that many of the advantages of just-in-time production are more likely to be achieved.

JUST-IN-TIME PRODUCTION

Just-in-time production (JIT), also called *zero inventories* or *stockless production*, is used in repetitive manufacturing by some of the more successful Japanese manufacturers and is being increasingly applied by North American and European repetitive manufacturers. A major objective of JIT is to have only the right item at the right place at the right time; or, to say it another way, to purchase and produce items only a short time before they are needed so that work-in-process inventory is kept very low. The practice not only reduces working capital requirements, it also reduces the need for floor space and shortens the flowthrough time because material spends very little time in queues. Numerous other benefits occur where this practice is successfully employed. JIT has received so much attention in the past few years because it is believed to be a major contributor to the success of many of the Japanese repetitive manufacturers. Many of the advantages of JIT can also be achieved by low-volume or intermediate-volume manufacturers. The following are some of the important elements that frequently are found where JIT production methods are used:

1. A set, uniform production rate.
2. A pull method of coordinating work centers.

3. Purchasing and producing in small lots.
4. Quick, inexpensive setups.
5. Multiskilled workers and flexible facilities.
6. High quality levels.
7. Effective preventive maintenance.
8. Continual work to improve.

These elements are discussed in some detail in the sections that follow.

Uniform Production Rate

An objective of JIT is to achieve a smooth flow of materials from the company's suppliers to the company's customers with no delays or interruptions beyond the very minimum that result from the necessary production processes. Any unnecessary delays or in-process inventory are considered waste, so the work-in-process inventory is kept to a minimum. Inside the plant the objective is to achieve a smooth, synchronized flow of small lots of material at a uniform rate. Since there is no extra inventory in the system, it is not possible to occasionally withdraw and assemble a large lot of material. If there were enough inventory to produce larger lots, but an occasional small lot was produced, the result would be undesired excess inventory. The JIT system works best when the production schedules are kept level. When production levels must be changed, they are scaled up or down in small steps.

Several Japanese manufacturers who use JIT production methods set their production rate for the month equal to the expected demand rate for the month and hold daily production rates at this monthly rate. Within each day, a mix of the models is produced in short repetitive sequences, so that each model is frequently repeated in proportion to its relative demand. The workload within each work center remains uniform within a day and for each day of the month, so neither workers nor work tasks have to be reassigned. Suppose that three models of refrigerators—A, B, and C—are to be produced and that the expected demand for the three models during the next month is 3,000, 2,000 and 1,000 units, respectively. The three models might be produced on the assembly line in the sequence A, B, A, B, A, C. Repetition of this sequence throughout the month will make a uniform work content for all the jobs on the assembly line, even if the work required to assemble a model A is above average and the work required to assemble the other models is below average. Such a repetitive cycle also causes a uniform workload for the work centers that feed the final assembly line, even if there are components in model C that are not in any of the other models.

Pull Versus Push Method of Coordinating Work Centers

Coordinating fabrication and assembly operations through all of the work centers that feed the final assembly line can be complex if a variety of models are being produced on the line, particularly if the product mix is frequently changed. There are two basic approaches to coordinating the feeding of work centers: the push method and the pull method. The push method is much like the production control method described earlier for the job shop: The production control group schedules the necessary quantities of raw material to produce all components of the desired quantities of final assemblies, and the materials are released for work at the starting work centers at the appropriate times. When work is completed at one work center (WC), the parts are pushed to the next WC, where they wait until that WC is ready to work on them.

To understand the pull method, think of the factory as a network of user and supplier WCs. Each WC obtains some less-processed material from a supplier WC, works on the material, and holds an assortment of the various parts it is responsible to make. Each WC holds its "products" until they are called for by some subsequent user WC. The final assembly operation withdraws (i.e., pulls) from the appropriate WCs small containers of each component needed to assemble the scheduled product. Each WC from which these parts were withdrawn will in turn pull a container of the parts it needs from its supplier WCs and produce another container of its product to replace the container that was pulled away. Similar actions occur at the WCs prior to these, and so on down the line. Each WC must hold ready a container of the assortment of products it makes so its customer WCs can have the supplies they need when they need them. Naturally, this system is most suitable where a company repetitively produces standardized products with some reasonable limit to the variety.

It can be seen that with the pull system each WC pulls from the immediately prior WC all of the appropriate materials to produce the components that are being used by the WCs that follow it in the production sequence. The result of this chain reaction is that the appropriate option of every item used in the final assembly will be produced in the correct amount throughout all of the appropriate WCs. With this method of coordination, the production control group has only to schedule the final assembly operation and to ensure that each WC has a means of authorizing its supplier WCs to produce the appropriate feeder component(s). The kanban system is a simple and effective system of accomplishing these authorizations.

The Kanban System

The *kanban system* is a simple information system used by a WC to signal its supplier WC authorizing production and delivery of a particular item to the signaling WC. The kanban system was developed by the Toyota Motor Company where it is used with the pull method just described. A company can perform JIT production without incorporating a kanban signal method, but since kanban was used with the original Toyota system, it is presented here. The Japanese word *kanban* means card or sign. When a card is hung on a wall or rack it becomes a sign that signals to authorize production or movement of items. A company might set up a similar system using flags, lights, or some other signal device, but we will discuss the use of cards because it seems to be a common method. There are a variety of card systems, but the two-card system is a good one to illustrate the concept.

In the two-card kanban system, one type of card, called a production card, authorizes a WC to make one standard container of a particular part specified on the card. The second type of card, called a move card, authorizes the movement of one container of the specified part from a particular WC to another WC as specified on the card. Since these cards are continually reused, they are issued only when production of an item is to be started or changed significantly. The circulation of a move card is illustrated in Figure 8.17. The production card circulates repeatedly between the outbound material location at a WC and the work area where the item is produced. Similar card transactions would link the supplier WC shown in Figure 8.17 and the WCs that supply it. The user WC will also be linked to one or more WCs that it supplies. A series of these linkages connects the final assembly operation with the WC that performs the first operations in making the product. Often even the raw-material vendor is linked with a kanban signal. Kanbans received on one delivery authorize the vendor to make specified items and deliver them on the next delivery.

The kanban system can be a very simple, inexpensive, and effective method of coordinating work centers and also vendors. The organization must be well

FIGURE 8.17

A Two-Card Kanban System

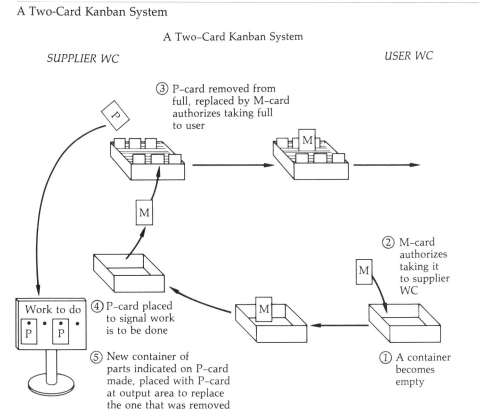

A Two–Card Kanban System

SUPPLIER WC

USER WC

③ P–card removed from full, replaced by M–card authorizes taking full to user

② M–card authorizes taking it to supplier WC

Work to do

④ P–card placed to signal work is to be done

⑤ New container of parts indicated on P–card made, placed with P–card at output area to replace the one that was removed

① A container becomes empty

disciplined so that there is always an authorizing kanban with every container, ensuring that only the appropriate items are produced and excessive inventory does not build up. There is also the opposite danger—that some WC might run out of material and cause work to stop at all subsequent WCs. To make this or any other pull method work well with small inventories, there must be no problems to disrupt production; because there simply is not enough inventory to keep the plant running while a problem is corrected. A uniform production rate and the elements of JIT discussed in following sections interact to make JIT and the kanban signal system work together effectively.

Small Lot Size

With JIT, the size of both production lots and vendor delivery lots is kept to a practical minimum.

Production Lots   Each WC keeps containers of each model of part it makes so that a WC can call for it when needed. Production lots are small—the lots must be small if the in-process inventory is to be kept low—and the items are placed in containers that hold about one hour's work or less. These containers are often likened to egg cartons, in that they are designed with separators to hold items in a specific position for easy inspection, counting, and handling at the next operation. Also, the variety of parts made by a WC cannot be too broad or that too would result in a large inventory of different parts waiting to be pulled. For this and possibly other reasons, JIT manufacturers seem to have "focused factories" that do not try to spread their resources to cover too many missions.

Delivery Lots   With production lots being small, only small amounts of incoming raw materials and components to go into subassemblies are needed at a time. Vendor deliveries therefore also take place in small lots and at frequent intervals. Some vendors of high-volume items make deliveries four or more times per day, and obviously it is desirable for such vendors to locate close to the purchasing plant.

In some cases, the vendor is tied into its customer plant's computer scheduling system and receives printouts of the production schedule to aid in the vendor's planning. The vendor may actually stack the items according to the sequence in which they will be used. For example, automobile seats may be stacked in sequence according to the colors, fabrics, and models that will be assembled that day.

In general, the vendor and the purchasing company have a long-term relationship of mutual support and respect. Each realizes that its future depends on working smoothly together with the other. The vendor works to provide good quality and achieve on-time deliveries, and these efforts improve the chances of success for both companies.

Quick, Inexpensive Setups

One element that is necessary to make production in small lots work well is the achievement of quick, inexpensive setups, since setups will occur often. The traditional approach has been to say that since setups are expensive and delay production, it is better to run large lots and keep setups to a minimum. Yet with infrequent setups, workers never become skilled at them, so setups remain expensive. The JIT philosophy is that the company will have frequent setups, therefore the workers need to get good at setups. A team of workers will try a setup procedure, critique it, revise it, try again, and continue to practice, like an athletic team. At one plant in Japan, the author observed a die change on an injection molding machine that took 50 seconds. This change would take more than an hour in some companies.

Multiskilled Workers and Flexible Facilities

A WC may be called upon to make one item, then a different item. One or more workers in a WC may be available at the time the WC is called on to produce a replacement container of any item the WC supplies. The workers must be capable of performing any operation that is required so that production will not be delayed. Many of the Japanese plants that use JIT have a large percentage of their work force on lifetime employment. The company and these employees work to develop a variety of skills to serve whatever the company's needs are.

Plants often are arranged in cells that facilitate efficient production of any member of a family of various products at a WC. Grouping equipment into "cells" that serve a family of items requiring similar production technology is called *group technology* and is discussed in detail in Chapter 13, which is on plant layout. Since there is little work-in-process inventory and the equipment is grouped into cells, plants can be very compact. Moves of materials between WCs are relatively short and fast, leading to inexpensive materials handling and fast throughput.

High Quality Levels

High quality is both a requirement for JIT to work well and a result of the JIT method. A container of items sent to the next WC contains only a specified number of the item to replace units already withdrawn and committed to work at subsequent WCs. There must be no defective units in the container or a shortage is likely, unless the prior WC can quickly make some more. Little inventory of an item is available in the event that something goes wrong. The objective is to make the system work right and to eliminate the need for the in-process inventory.

Since the small container of parts may have been made only an hour before, there usually is traceability and accountability for items. If a worker at one WC finds defective items in a container, information is usually available regarding who made it, what machine and tooling were used, what the machine settings were, and so on. The workers have a good chance of finding out what went wrong and correcting it before much scrap is made. If one WC in the sequence is making defects, the downstream WCs are stopped, so several workers may be available to assist with solving the problem. The effect of this self-stopping, quick diagnosis, and rapid correction is to ensure that very few defective items are produced. If large lots were produced, it might be a long time before problems were discovered; also it would be more difficult to determine exactly when the defects occurred and therefore more difficult to determine their cause.

Effective Preventive Maintenance

Few equipment breakdowns can be tolerated in a production facility that maintains very little extra inventory to keep it operating while a machine is repaired. Breakdown of one machine could stop the entire plant if it is the only machine that can make a part that goes into every product. Thus it is imperative that equipment be kept in proper working condition. Workers take pride in maintaining their equipment, and they learn to repair some equipment problems themselves. If a machine is not operating, they cannot continue to produce parts, so they spend the time repairing or helping to repair the machine. A set of records about each machine is kept, telling what needs to be done to maintain the machine and how often, when the machine was last repaired, and what was done. Equipment is treated with respect because there is little inventory to operate with while a machine is being repaired and employees feel a vested interest in avoiding breakdowns.

Working to Improve the System

Some Japanese manufacturers have a practice of using kanbans to help them find weaknesses in their production operation so that these weaknesses can be corrected. These manufacturers have a philosophy of perpetual improvement. They reason that if plenty of buffer inventory is available in the production system to protect from problems, those problems may not become apparent. So when the factory is running satisfactorily, a manager might remove a few kanbans from the system, resulting in fewer containers of inventory. If things still run satisfactorily, the manager might remove a few more cards. When a problem appears, it is treated as a treasure. It is an opportunity to improve the system—that is, to resolve a potential bottleneck. Maybe a setup is too long or the production rate is too slow at a WC. Once the problem is identified, the workers can start to solve it. Worker groups, called "quality circles" (discussed in Chapter 11) may become involved in seeking solutions. Through efforts such as these, manufacturers continue to improve quality, develop lower inventories, and achieve more efficient operations.

It is apparent that the JIT approach to repetitive manufacturing can be a very powerful and effective competitive weapon. It achieves a synchronized flow of the correct product mix with very little in-process inventory. It reduces

OPERATIONS MANAGEMENT IN ACTION

Kan Ban? Can Do!

One of the key cost advantages of the vaunted Japanese manufacturing system is *kan ban,* the "just-in-time" parts delivery system used by Japanese carmakers. *Kan ban* allows them to keep inventories—and hence interest costs—low.

The concept of just-in-time delivery is certainly not exclusively Japanese. Back in the 1920s workers at Henry Ford's integrated River Rouge assembly plant in Dearborn, Mich. unloaded ore boats on Monday and converted the ore to steel and then to engine blocks by Tuesday afternoon.

But the Japanese have developed *kan ban* in its modern form. Can just-in-time parts delivery be implemented in the U.S.? Yes it can.

Dana Corp. Chairman Gerry Mitchell says that American suppliers like Dana are even going the Japanese one better by allowing more flexible delivery. "With *kan ban* you don't change your assembly schedule," he says. U.S. manufacturers, he goes on, want more flexibility than that.

But it's interesting to ask why American carmakers need all this flexibility. Think, once again, of Henry Ford. His cheap, reliable vehicles were in such demand that he could afford to let buyers pick any color they wanted, so long as it was black. Perhaps Detroit now runs after the 10-day trends too much, offers too many choices, at a loss of efficiency. It's almost as if American manufacturers have become the swing producers of vehicles in the U.S. market.

Whatever direction U.S. carmakers go, it seems clear that they will be giving increased responsibility to key partsmakers. "Bit by bit," says Mitchell, "we are moving our assembly operations adjacent to car assembly plants. We are taking more responsibility for inventory control. We assemble axles at night that are used the next day. We have 19 regional centers offering overnight delivery on truck parts to truck assembly plants. Often a guy has shipped out a truck and he hasn't even paid us for the parts yet." This kind of speed and service, belated as it is, is one reason Mitchell thinks U.S. partsmakers can compete with low-priced imports. . . . "I don't think," he says, "that you can export from Brazil to the U.S. and have a just-in-time delivery system."

Forbes, January 2, 1984, p. 113, by John R. Dorfman. Reprinted with permission.

---

floor space needs and thus the required plant investment. It enables quality to be more easily improved. It promotes plant flexibility. And it speeds up product throughput, so that manufacturing lead time is reduced and the company can work to a shorter-horizon forecast that is more accurate. Many of the elements of JIT can also be applied in job shops and intermediate-volume manufacturing companies. No wonder a growing number of companies are moving to this production concept (see box).

LINE BALANCING

Scheduling the rate at which work flows through a production or assembly line requires consideration of the work tasks at all of the work stations along the line. The total amount of work to be performed on a line must be broken into tasks and the tasks assigned to work stations so the work is performed in a feasible sequence within an acceptable cycle time. The *cycle time* for a line (time between completion of successive items on the line) is determined by the maximum amount of time required at any work station. Work cannot flow through the line any faster than it can pass through the slowest stage (the *bottleneck* of the line). If one work station has a great deal more work than others, it is desirable to assign some of this work to stations with less work so that there are no bottlenecks in the line.

Ideally, there will be equal amounts of work at work stations—that is, a balanced line. All stations of a balanced line are fully utilized if it is run at its fastest cycle time. If it is run at a slower rate, the idle time on the line will be equitably distributed among all the workers along the line. This idle time might be used as a rest pause and to allow for variability of work requirements from one cycle to another. Consider an automobile assembly line. Installing an automatic transmission may require more time than installing a standard transmission, and the products flowing down the line may have some different transmission requirements. It is desirable to have the average work loads balanced at each station, even though some variation around the expected times will occur.

Line balancing involves selecting the appropriate combination of work tasks to be performed at each work station so that the work is performed in a feasible sequence and approximately equal amounts of time are required at each of the work stations. The objective is to minimize the required labor input and facility investment for a given amount of output. This objective is sought by either:

1. Minimizing the number of work stations (workers) required to achieve a given cycle time (i.e., given production capacity).
2. Minimizing the cycle time (maximizing the output rate) for a given number of work stations.

The first objective is more appropriate when considering the initial scheduling or rescheduling of a line. The second objective is more appropriate if demand equals or exceeds the rate that can be achieved with the available resources (space, equipment, people, etc.)

The total idle time for the line is given by

$$IT = nc - \sum_{i=1}^{k} t_i \tag{8.2}$$

where IT = total idle time for the line
n = the number of work stations, assuming one worker per work station
c = the cycle time for the line
t_i = the time for the ith work task
k = the total number of work tasks to be performed on the production line.

A line is perfectly balanced if $IT = 0$ at the minimum cycle time. Sometimes the degree to which a line approaches this perfect balance is expressed as a percentage or a decimal called the balance delay. As a percentage, the balance delay (d) is found by

$$d = \frac{100(IT)}{nc} \tag{8.3}$$

A well-balanced line has a very low balance delay.

The number of task combinations that could be assigned to a work station rapidly becomes large and unwieldy as the number of work tasks increases. Consequently, algorithms have been programmed to develop approximate or satisficing solutions by use of computers. Line-balancing problems have been solved by various approaches. Some of these are:

1. Trial and error.
2. Heuristic methods.
3. Computer sampling until a good solution is found.
4. Linear programming.
5. Dynamic programming.

Methods 4 and 5 are optimizing methods that will require considerable computation for any reasonable-sized problem.

Before assigning work tasks to work stations, the analyst must take several preliminary steps:

1. Identify all of the work tasks that must be done to produce the product.
2. Identify the amount of time required to perform each task.
3. Identify the precedence requirements for each task; in other words, which task(s) must be performed before a particular task can be performed?
4. Define the target cycle time (which must be greater than or equal to the largest task) or define the target number of work stations. If we know Σt_i and n, then we can find the target cycle time: $c_t = \Sigma t_i/n$.

After these four requirements are completed, the analyst can begin to assign work tasks to work stations. We shall discuss heuristic methods of line balancing. A *heuristic method* uses rules of thumb that lead to a feasible though not necessarily optimal solution.

Some tasks must be performed before others can begin. For example, a hole must be drilled or punched in a piece of metal before a bolt can be put through it. The task that must be performed immediately prior to another will be called its predecessor. Often a precedence diagram is drawn to show the order of performance of work elements to assist in their selection.

Usually tasks are assigned to the first work station, then the second, and so on until the final assembly tasks are assigned to the last work station. A complete set of work tasks will be selected and assigned to one work station before assignments are made to the next station. At any stage of assigning work tasks, some tasks have already had their predecessors assigned and therefore can be assigned themselves. This subset of the total task list is called the *available list*.

A rule or set of rules is needed to guide the selection of tasks from the available list for assignment to the work station that is being loaded with work tasks. A simple rule is to select tasks in the order in which they occur on the list so long as the time required by the tasks is less than or equal to the remaining available work time at the work station. Tasks that are too lengthy are skipped, and assignments continue to be made by working down the list until it is exhausted or until the available time at the work station is filled. Each time a task is assigned, its successor tasks are added to the available list. Once the available cycle time for a work station is filled, assignments to the next are begun.

This or some other heuristic method is usually used to select work elements for assignment, although several computerized line-balancing packages are available, some of which use a combination of rules. Some heuristic methods are:

1. Select from the available list the task with the largest time that will fit within the work station's available time.
2. Select the task with the most successors (so long as it will fit within the work station's available time).
3. Select the task with the greatest sum of the task times of its successor tasks (so long as it will fit within the work station's available time).

Example of Line Balancing

Let's go through an example of a line-balancing problem using heuristic method 1 mentioned above. The company wants to achieve a production rate of 160 units per eight-hour day utilizing a production line. Table 8.3 lists the nine work tasks that must be performed to produce the item and indicates the sequence in which these tasks must be performed. The specified production rate of 160 per eight-hour day is 20 per hour. This rate converts to a cycle time of 3 minutes,

Table 8.3
TASK TIMES AND SEQUENCING
REQUIREMENTS FOR LINE-BALANCING
PROBLEM IN EXAMPLE

Work Task	Predecessor(s)	Time (seconds)
A	none	60
B	A	80
C	none	30
D	C	40
E	B, D	40
F	none	50
G	F	100
H	D, G	70
I	E, H	30

FIGURE 8.18

Precedence Diagram for Line Balancing

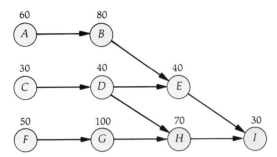

which is 180 seconds per unit. No station can work on the item (or delay it) for more than 180 seconds if the target production rate is to be achieved. If the line is balanced and a minimum number of stations is to be used, each work station should have about this amount of work. The nine work tasks must be assigned to work stations in such a way that they will be performed in the proper sequence, all work stations will have about the same amount of work to perform, and the desired cycle time will be achieved.

For manual solution, it is often helpful to display the sequencing requirements in the form of a network such as that shown in Figure 8.18. Each work task is shown as a node (circle) and the sequences requirements are indicated by arrows. With the time required to perform each task indicated above its node, the entire problem is contained in the network.

Station I Assignments The available list before any assignments are made is *A*, *C*, and *F* because they require no prior work. *A* is selected because the 60-second time is the greatest. *A* is removed from the available list and *B* is added because its predecessor has been assigned.

Next *B* is selected because its time is the longest and it will fit in the unassigned portion of the cycle time at station I. The available list now contains *C* and *F*. Notice that *E* was not added to the available list because only one of its two predecessors has been assigned.

Next task *F* is tried because its time is the longest. *F* is too large, however (its time is longer than the unassigned cycle time at station I). It is found that the next larger time will fit, and task *C* is assigned to work station I.

Assigned tasks: *A*, *B*, *C*.

Total work time: 170 seconds (and 10 seconds idle time).

Station II Assignments The available list is *F* and *D* because their precedence requirements have been fulfilled. The longest task, *F*, is assigned to the second station. The available list is now *D* and *G*. *G* is assigned because its time is longer and it will fit within the remaining time. The available list is D and it will *not* fit into the remaining time.

Assigned tasks: F, G.

Total work time: 150 seconds (and 30 seconds idle time).

Station III Assignments   The available list consists of only task D, so it is assigned to the third station. The available list becomes E and H, so H is assigned. The available list becomes E and E will fit within the available time at the work station, so E is assigned. The available list now consists of task I. Sufficient time for I remains, so it is also assigned to this station.

Assigned tasks: D, H, E, I.

Total work time: 180 seconds (and no idle time).

Evaluation of the Line Balance   The line will be paced by the 180-second time of work station III. The idle time for the line will be

$$
\begin{aligned}
IT &= nc - \sum_{i=1}^{k} t_i \\
&= 3(180) - (60 + 80 + 30 + 40 + 40 + 50 + 100 + 70 + 30) \\
&= 40 \text{ seconds}
\end{aligned}
$$

The balance delay of the line is

$$
d = \frac{100(IT)}{nc} = \frac{100(40)}{3(180)} = \frac{4,000}{540} = 7.41 \text{ percent.}
$$

Other Considerations

We have assigned work tasks to work stations solely on the basis of the amount of time the tasks are expected to take. Sometimes other factors must be taken into consideration. The skills required for one task may be much different from those required for another. Hence, tasks requiring different skills should not be assigned to the same person unless considerable staffing and training difficulty can be tolerated. Regardless of the operator's skills, some processes are incompatible and should be performed in different areas. Grinding and painting probably should be separated. Processes involving flames or sparks, such as welding, should be located away from flammable operations, such as cleaning with solvents. Lines are sometimes zoned into areas, and certain classes of work elements are assigned only within certain zones.

In addition to the technical and physiological considerations, psychological factors should be considered. The worker's need for a sense of accomplishment suggests that the elements assigned to him or her should be somewhat related and should make a recognizable contribution to the total job. Factors of this sort will be discussed in Chapter 14.

Potential for Increases in Production Rate

Various actions are possible if demand increases beyond the capacity of a production or assembly line. If a line is unbalanced, there is potential for increased capacity without modification of the entire line. Many of the work stations in an unbalanced line may have capacity to service demand slightly beyond the capacity of the line as a whole. Remember, the slowest work station determines the minimum possible cycle time of the line. Careful study of the work methods and equipment at the limiting work station may reveal opportunities to reduce the cycle time of the entire line. If the line is balanced but demand greatly exceeds its capacity, it may be replaced by a higher capacity line or complemented by an additional facility. Sometimes the cycle time of a line can be changed by the addition or elimination of work stations and reallocation of tasks.

A balanced line with some manual work stations and some machine-spaced stations may become unbalanced over time. Operators may become more skilled and may develop shortcuts in performing their work. The machine times will remain relatively constant, leading to differences of capacity, or throughput rate. The phenomenon of reduced production time as more and more units are produced is discussed further in the following section.

LEARNING CURVES

When a sizable volume is produced, the direct labor hours required to produce a unit may decrease markedly as more and more units are produced. This reduction frequently is sizable enough so that it should be taken into account in scheduling delivery rates and in planning capacity utilization.

Normally, one would expect the second unit to require less time than the first, because considerable study and thought may be involved in producing the first unit. However, in some industries, such as those that produce aircraft, data processing equipment, and large machines, the reduction has been found to continue for hundreds and even thousands of units. This phenomenon is called a *learning curve*, or sometimes an improvement curve, a progress curve, or a manufacturing progress function.

A learning curve is a graph or equation that expresses the expected *rate of improvement* in productivity as more units are produced. The term *learning* suggests that the reduction in production time occurs because of improved dexterity of workers over time as their skills improve. Actually, increased skill may account for little of the improvement. Employee suggestions for improved work methods, designs for new tooling to assist in performing work, revision of the material or redesign of the product to make production easier, or other innovative work methods and technological improvements may account for much of the reduced production time. Unit production times may be improved in a few large steps or through a collection of numerous small steps. Therefore, the progress or "learning effect" may be somewhat erratic rather than a smooth progression. Given a particular industry and type of product, however, a rather consistent average relationship between unit production time and the number of units produced has sometimes been found. The direct labor hours per unit may be reduced by a fairly consistent percentage each time the cumulative number of units produced is doubled. For instance, with an 80 percent learning curve, the second unit would require 80 percent of the direct labor hours required to produce the first unit. The fourth unit would require 80 percent of the time required to produce the second. The hundredth unit would require 80 percent of the direct labor hours required to produce the fiftieth unit, the two-hundredth 80 percent of the hours to produce the hundredth, and so on.

A mathematical expression frequently used to describe the learning curve is

$$Y_n = (Y_1)n^R \tag{8.4}$$

where Y_n = the direct hours required to produce the nth unit
Y_1 = the direct hours required to produce the first unit
n = the number of the unit for which the time is to be estimated
R = the logarithm of the ratio of the production time for a doubled quantity unit to the production time for a base unit divided by the logarithm of 2. The exponent R is the ratio of two logarithms and can be computed with base 10 logarithms or natural logarithms, so long as both the numerator and the denominator have the same base.

Let us illustrate the use of equation 8.4 with an example. Suppose that a computer manufacturer has experienced an 85 percent learning curve for similar products and expects this same learning rate to apply to a new model. Say it took 3,000 hours to produce the first unit and the company wants to estimate how many hours the fiftieth unit will take. For this problem

$$R = \frac{\log 0.85}{\log 2} = \frac{0.92942 - 1}{0.30103} = \frac{-0.07058}{0.30103} = -0.23446$$

$$Y_{50} = 3,000 \times 50^{-0.23446}$$

$$= 3,000 \times 0.39963 = 1,198.9 \text{ hours.}$$

The fiftieth unit therefore is estimated to take about 1,200 hours.

Equation 8.4 is an exponential equation. When this type of curve is plotted on arithmetic-scale coordinates, it is apparent that the rate of reduction in direct hours declines as more units are produced. Table 8.4 gives the hours required for doubled-quantity units for a 90 percent and an 80 percent learning curve. Figure 8.19 shows four learning curves plotted on arithmetic scales. A learning curve as expressed by equation 8.4 is a straight line when it is plotted on logarithmic-scaled ("log-log") paper. Figure 8.20 shows the same four learning curves plotted on logarithmic paper.

The rates of improvement shown in Figures 8.19 and 8.20 are among the range of curves that appear most frequently. (Appendix II provides the expected

Table 8.4
DIRECT LABOR HOURS REQUIRED TO
PRODUCE DOUBLED-QUANTITY UNITS
FOR 90 PERCENT AND 80 PERCENT
LEARNING CURVES

Cumulative Units	DIRECT LABOR HOURS	
	80% Slope	90% Slope
1	100.00	100.00
2	80.00	90.00
4	64.00	81.00
8	51.20	72.90
16	40.96	65.61
32	32.77	59.05
64	26.21	53.14
128	20.97	47.83
256	16.78	43.05
512	13.42	38.74
1,024	10.74	34.87
2,048	8.59	31.38
4,096	6.87	28.24
8,192	5.50	25.42
16,384	4.40	22.88
32,768	3.52	20.59
65,536	2.81	18.53

FIGURE 8.19

Learning Curves on Arithmetic-Scale Graph

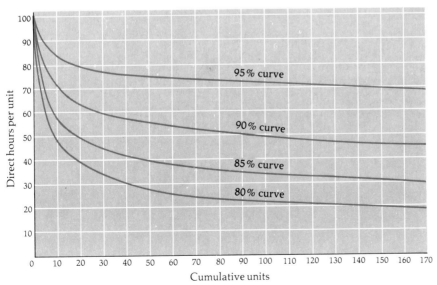

FIGURE 8.20

Learning Curves on Logarithmic-Scale Graph

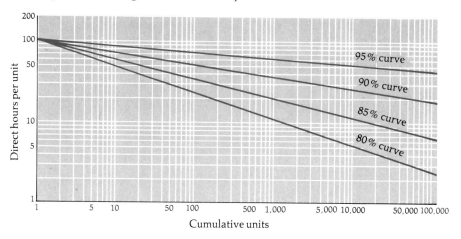

time and cumulative expected time for specific numbers of units.) Most industries strive to achieve improvements in their productivity, for obvious reasons. Governments record and study the changes in productivity on a national scale. At the grass-roots level, learning curves show a company how much productivity improvement it has achieved. After a company has an estimate of its usual rate of improvement, this information can be used in planning. The learning-curve effect may be taken into account in capacity planning, scheduling, or pricing for large-volume production. It also may be used in purchasing large quantities as a means of persuading potential vendors to offer quantity discounts.

SUMMARY

Scheduling and shop floor control present challenges to operations management for several reasons. In job shops, these challenges stem from two major sources of uncertainty:

- Forecast error (the inability to predict future demand) causes uncertainty about the quantity of products or services that will be demanded.
- Since job shops do not make the same item repetitively, there is uncertainty about the sequence of operations that will be required and the amount of capacity in various work centers that each item will require.

Under these circumstances, accurate delivery commitments are difficult to develop and maintain.

If a job shop possessed extreme excess capacity, each job could be worked on as soon as the previous operation was completed. But this amount of capacity is prohibitively expensive. Instead, job shops must attempt wisely to plan, schedule, and control the use of their productive capacity and other resources. They therefore need timely, accurate information regarding the existing work loads (backlogs) in each work center. Jobs are selected from those available in the backlog by some logical procedure or "dispatching rules." Two frequently used dispatching rules are: (1) select the job with the shortest processing time, and (2) select the job with the lowest average waiting time per operation.

Optimization can be achieved only with respect to a few criteria for small problems. Johnson's rule will minimize flow time or average job lateness when there are only two work centers through which a set of jobs must be sequenced.

Shop floor control and production activity control are terms that are used to describe much of the production control activities that occur, particularly when production activities are linked to an MRP system. Shop floor control involves the use of information from MRP to perform detailed capacity requirements planning and input-output control so that the proper amount of capacity is made available and utilized. Dispatching in accordance with need dates determined through the most recent MRP run helps to keep priorities under proper control.

Some of the uncertainty associated with job shop operations is reduced when companies produce standardized products—that is, in repetitive manufacturing. Substantial demand history may provide improved forecasts. The production time for each component is more accurately known because the items have been produced many times. Finished-goods inventory can be used to smooth production since the product is more standardized. Knowing the time required to perform each task enables a company to achieve a better balance between productive capacity and demand at each operation.

Just-in-time production attempts to provide only the right item at the right place at the right time and in the right quantity. Companies using this approach work with small lots and a pull method to keep work centers from running out of material. Quick setups, high quality, multiskilled workers and facilities, preventive maintenance, and uniform production schedules also help make JIT work.

Production lines or assembly lines can be used when very large volumes of identical products are to be produced, because each item has a known flow path and the operation times are known. Line balancing (not to be confused with line of balance) is used to help divide all of the tasks that must be performed so that they may be equally distributed among the work stations along a production line. One approach to line balancing is to fix the cycle time and then determine the number of work stations necessary to balance the work load and achieve the cycle time. An alternative approach is to fix the number of work stations and determine the cycle time that results from balancing the work load among them.

The effect of learning curves sometimes must be considered when large volumes of items are to be produced. The learning curve describes the reduction in direct labor required to produce a unit as more units are produced.

SOLVED PROBLEMS

PROBLEM:

Five jobs are to be run—first on process I then on process II. The jobs are listed below with their time requirements on the two processes.

(a) Sequence the jobs by Johnson's method so that the total flow time and idle time will be minimized.

(b) Show the sequence and durations on

a bar chart, and indicate the time at which each job will be completed.

TIME

Job	Process I	Process II
A	.6	1.3
B	1.5	1.9
C	3.1	.9
D	1.2	1.6
E	2.2	1.8

SOLUTION:

The shortest time in either column of the table is the 0.6 for job A. Since this time is on the first process, job A should be done first. The shortest time for any of the remaining jobs is the 0.9 for job C. Since this time is on the second process, job C should be done last. The shortest time of the remaining jobs is 1.2 for job D. Since this time is on the first process, job D should be done as early as possible in the remaining openings so it will be done just after job A. The shortest of the remaining times is the 1.5 for job B. Since this time is on the first process, B will be placed as early as possible so it will be just behind D, in third place. Job E fills the remaining slot in fourth place.

A Gantt chart showing this schedule for the two processes is shown below.

PROBLEM:

A production line is to be established to produce 300 modems per day (460 minutes). The production tasks, their times, and their precedence requirements are shown in the table below.

Task	Time (min)	Predecessor(s)
a	.6	—
b	.3	a
c	.8	—
d	.7	—
e	.4	c,d
f	.8	b,e
g	.5	f
h	.9	f
i	.2	g
j	.1	h,i

(a) Using a heuristic that assigns the longest available task that will fit within the remaining work station time, assign the tasks to the minimum number of work stations required to meet the cycle time.
(b) Determine the balance delay of the line.
(c) How might the balance be improved?

SOLUTION:

(a) The target cycle time is 460 minutes/ 300 units = 1.533 minutes. A precedence diagram is useful to show how the tasks can be divided.

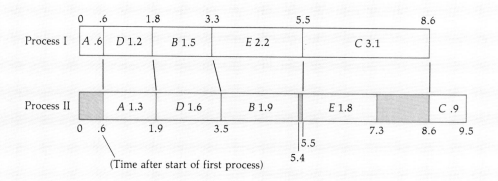

(Time after start of first process)

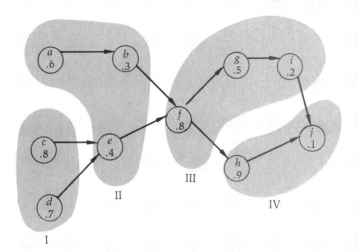

For Station I

The initial available list is $(a(.6), c(.8), d(.7))$, so c is selected. No tasks are added to the available list. Next, d is selected and no other task will fit within the remaining work station time if the cycle time is to be 1.533 minutes. The first station has a cycle time of 1.5 minutes.

Tasks assigned: c, d; Work station time: 1.5 minutes

For Station II

The available list is $(a(.6), e(.4))$, so a is selected and $b(.3)$ is added to the available list. Next e is selected. Task b is the only task on the available list so task b is selected. Task f is added to the available list, but it will not fit in the remaining time at Station II.

Tasks assigned: a,e,b; Work station time: 1.3 minutes

For Station III

The available list is $(f(.8))$, so f is selected and $g(.5)$ and $h(.9)$ are added to the available list. Task g is selected because it is the only one that fits the remaining time. Task

i is added to the available list and it is selected because it will fit in the remaining time.

Tasks assigned: f,g,i; Work station time: 1.5

For Station IV

The available list is $(h(.9), j(.1))$ so h is assigned then j is assigned.

Tasks assigned: h,j; Work station time: 1.0 minutes

It is helpful to mark a boundary around and label the assigned tasks as each station is loaded. These enclosed areas are shown on the diagram above.

(b) The idle time for the line is $nc - \Sigma t_i = 4(1.5) - 5.3 = 0.7$ minutes, if the line is run at its minimum cycle time. The balance delay would be $\dfrac{100(0.7)}{4(1.5)} = 11.67$ percent.

(c) The work at each station would be closer to equal if task a were moved to station I, task d moved to station II and task i were moved to station IV. The cycle time could be reduced to 1.4 minutes if these changes were made.

DISCUSSION QUESTIONS

1. Why is it difficult to select one criterion that will ensure optimum performance of a production system?
2. Briefly describe the steps that are performed in the process of estimating the cost and delivery dates for job shop work.
3. What is a backlog report?
4. Why should production control bother to keep track of the amount of work that has been completed?
5. Is the production control organization usually a line organization or a staff organization?
6. What is dispatching? Describe a few rules of thumb (heuristics) that may be used in dispatching.
7. What problems could result if a company's dispatching rules were always to work on the item with the shortest processing time? To work on the item with the longest processing time?

8. (a) Discuss the objectives of input-output control.
   (b) How can input and output be properly controlled and delivery performance still be mediocre?
9. Why is it necessary to continually replan priorities?
10. Factories that operate with JIT production try to keep a fairly uniform rate of output, and they scale up or down gradually. Why is it difficult to increase quickly the output from a JIT plant?
11. What are seven of the conditions or elements that help to make JIT operate well?
12. What are the two general approaches to solving line-balancing problems?
13. It was stated that inequitable distribution of work along a production line could result in employee dissatisfaction. Can a perfectly balanced line result in employee dissatisfaction? Why or why not?

PROBLEMS

1. The jobs listed in column 1 of the table below are waiting at work center 16. The shop works sixteen hours per day.
   (a) Arrange the jobs in sequence for work center 16 according to the shortest-processing-time rule.
   (b) Arrange the jobs in priority sequence according to the lowest average slack time given by equation 8.1.

Job	Estimated Processing Time at Work Center 16 (hours)	Work Days Until Job Delivery Date	Total Estimated Processing Time Required Including Work Center 16 (hours)	Number of Remaining Operations Including Work Center 16
A	28	14	162	4
B	17	20	270	2
C	6	10	91	3
D	21	8	118	5
E	12	18	205	3

2. Repeat problem 1 for the following set of jobs at work center 41.

Job	Estimated Processing Time at Work Center 41 (hours)	Work Days Until Job Delivery Date	Total Estimated Processing Time Required Including Work Center 41 (hours)	Number of Remaining Operations Including Work Center 41
A	19	8	41	3
B	15	2	30	1
C	19	10	90	4
D	21	12	50	2
E	24	6	35	3
F	16	7	78	4

3. The jobs listed in column 1 of the table below are waiting at work center 4. The shop normally works eight hours a day.
   (a) List the sequence in which the jobs would be done according to the shortest-processing-time rule.

(b) In what order would the jobs be sequenced according to the lowest average slack per operation?

(c) Is there a problem with the scheduling of one job, and if so, what would you do about it?

Job	Estimated Processing Time at Work Center 4	Work Days Until Job Delivery Date	Total Processing Time Required Including Work Center 4 (hours)	Number of Remaining Operations Including Work Center 4
A	6	10	38	3
B	26	20	116	6
C	5	4	37	4
D	1	7	5	3
E	3	6	7	2
F	7	4	18	4

4. Work center 403 is the starting work center for four relatively simple jobs whose route sheets are shown below.

Route Sheet: Job A

Due Date: Shop Day 174

Operation	Work Center	Processing Time (standard hours)	Scheduled Start (shop day)
10	403 Lathes	16	166
20	406 Mills	24	169
30	409 Assembly	3	172

Route Sheet: Job B

Due Date: Shop Day 176

Operation	Work Center	Processing Time (standard hours)	Scheduled Start (shop day)
10	403 Lathes	3	168
20	406 Mills	18	169
30	408 Drills	3	173
40	409 Assembly	6	174

Route Sheet: Job C

Due Date: Shop Day 175

Operation	Work Center	Processing Time (standard hours)	Scheduled Start (shop day)
10	403 Lathes	6	167
20	407 Welding	6	169
30	406 Mills	17	171
40	409 Assembly	4	174

Route Sheet: Job D

Due Date: Shop Day 174

Operation	Work Center	Processing Time (standard hours)	Scheduled Start (shop day)
10	403 Lathes	73	167
20	407 Weld	12	172

Sequence the jobs according to:

(a) The shortest processing time at the current work center.

(b) The shortest processing time at the next work center.

(c) The shortest remaining (also total, in this case) processing time.

(d) The longest processing time at the work center.

(e) The longest remaining processing time.

5. Today is shop day 167 and the backlogs already in queue at each of the work centers through which each of the jobs in problem 4 must flow are presented in the following table.

Work Center	Backlog Currently in Queue	Capacity
403	98	80
406	60	80
407	40	40
408	35	40
409	90	80

(a) Sequence the jobs from problem 4 in order of the scheduled start date at work center 403.

(b) Sequence these jobs in order of the job due date.

(c) Sequence these jobs in order of the smallest backlog at the next operation after work center 403.

6. Bondum Auto Body Shop has five cars that must have their fenders straightened and repainted. Mr. Bondum must be present while the work is being performed, although the person who straightens fenders can work independently of the painter.
   (a) Sequence the cars so that Mr. Bondum's workday will be as short as possible.

Car	Hours of Straightening Required	Hours of Painting Required
A	1.7	2.0
B	2.5	1.6
C	1.5	2.5
D	2.0	1.4
E	1.0	1.8

   (b) How long will Mr. Bondum's workday be if he comes to work when the straightener begins and leaves when the painter leaves?
   (c) How long must the fender reparier work during the day?
   (d) When should the painter come to work and how long must she work if she begins as soon as the first job is available?

7. Sanders Furniture Refinishing Shop has six pieces of furniture to be sanded and varnished tomorrow. Mr. Sanders does the sanding and Mrs. Sanders does the varnishing. They go to work together and leave together and would like to make their workday as short as possible. Sequence the jobs to minimize their time at the shop.

Job	Sanding Time	Varnishing Time
A	1.00	1.50
B	2.50	1.50
C	2.00	1.75
D	1.50	2.00
E	1.25	1.00
F	1.00	0.75

8. Given below is the input part of an input-output control report.

Planned input rate	400	400	400	400	400	400
Actual input rate	317	416	420	331	489	316
Cumulative input deviation						

   (a) Compute the cumulative deviations in input that occurred.
   (b) What is the minimum queue this work center could start with and not run out of work?
   (c) How much capacity should the work center have on the average to keep the average queue at this work center at its starting level?

9. Given below is an input-output control report for a certain work center.

Planned input	400	400	400	400	400	400
Actual input	380	410	415	390		
Cumulative input deviation						
Planned output	400	400	400	400	400	400
Actual output	356	341	372	366		
Cumulative output deviation						

   (a) Compute the remainder of the table for the first four weeks.
   (b) What problem appears to exist?
   (c) What corrective actions can you suggest?

10. The Baud Electronics Company produces electronic calculators and is planning to begin production of a new model. An assembly line is to be developed that will produce 450 units per seven-hour workday. The tasks, task times, and precedence requirements are given below.
   (a) Group the tasks into work stations by selecting the shortest remaining time from the available list at each selection, so long as that time will fit within the remaining available time at the work station.

Task	Time (seconds)	Predecessor
A	30	none
B	35	A
C	15	A
D	20	A
E	35	B
F	38	B
G	12	D
H	16	G
I	31	G
J	20	I

(b) How well balanced is the line? How many work stations are used?

(c) Balance the line by selecting the longest task time that will fit within the available time for the work station. Is this assignment much different from (a)? Why, or why not?

11. Shown below are the tasks, times, and precedence requirements for the work required to assemble a portable video game. The company wants to produce 380 units in a 460-minute shift.

Task	Time (min)	Predecessor(s)	Task	Time	Predecessor(s)
A	.20	—	H	.15	F
B	.60	—	I	.30	H,E
C	.20	—	J	.40	G,I
D	.55	A	K	.40	J
E	.40	B	L	.40	J
F	.85	C	M	.80	K,L
G	.35	D	N	.40	M

(a) Draw a diagram showing the precedence requirements, and list on it the times with the tasks.

(b) Divide the tasks to achieve a balanced line with five work stations. You will see that using a heuristic of selecting the shortest time will not give you a good solution. Using the heuristic of selecting the longest time that will fit in a work station will give you a tie in the first work station.

(c) Describe how you decided to break this tie.

12. The Apollo Toy Company is a small new toy manufacturer. The company is to produce a toy rocket and can assign three people to its assembly.

(a) Develop a three-station assembly line for the following tasks.

Task	Time (seconds)	Predecessor(s)
A	30	none
B	20	none
C	15	A
D	14	A
E	5	B,D
F	20	B
G	18	E
H	6	G
I	16	F
J	20	H
K	12	H
L	6	J

(b) What is the cycle time?

(c) What is the balance delay for the line?

(d) What would be the expected output of this line per eight-hour production shift (assume the line is run at its minimum cycle time)?

13. The Montana Appliance Company is installing an assembly line to produce one of its small appliances, and you have been asked to balance the line. The tasks that are to be performed are listed below, along with the time required to perform each task and its immediate predecessor(s). The line to produce 300 units in a full 8 hours of work.

(a) Assign tasks to work stations by selecting the longest task that can be assigned at each opportunity.

(b) Compute the balance delay for the assignment you obtained in part (a).

Task	Time (seconds)	Predecessor(s)
A	51	none
B	22	A
C	28	A
D	32	A
E	39	A
F	20	B
G	20	C
H	16	D
I	12	E
J	42	F,G
K	44	H,I
L	20	J
M	20	K
N	12	L,M

14. Use the same target cycle time, task times, and precedence requirements given in the previous problem.
   (a) Assign tasks to work stations by selecting the shortest task that can be assigned at each opportunity.
   (b) Compute the balance delay for the line as assigned in part (a) of this problem.

15. The Tuber Aircraft Company has just produced the first of its Model R-80 airplanes, which required 20,000 direct labor hours. The company has experienced an 85 percent learning curve for similar aircraft it has produced in the past.
   (a) How long will the tenth airplane take?
   (b) The twentieth?
   (c) The hundredth?

16. The Peach Computer Company produces computers for home and small business applications. The first of its new model TLC-10 computers required 62 labor hours to complete. The company has experienced an 85 percent learning curve on past models and expects this learning rate to apply to the TLC-10. In the next six months the company plans to produce 3,000 computers. How many employees will be required if each employee can contribute 1,000 production hours during the six-month period?

17. A landscaping contractor has received a contract to plant shrubs for a new subdivision in a nearby city. He intends to send one of his supervisors, who will employ a crew of workers in that city to perform the work.

   The subdivision contains twenty-five houses with basically similar landscape plans. He has been asked to bid on performing the landscaping services for five, ten, fifteen, twenty, and twenty-five houses. He knows from experience that he can expect a 90 percent learning curve. He also estimates that the first house will require twenty hours.
   (a) How much time will the first five houses require?
   (b) How much time will the last five houses require?
   (c) What will be the average number of hours per house if all twenty-five houses are landscaped and a 90 percent learning curve is appropriate? (Refer to the learning curve tables in Appendix II.)

18. Congratulations, you own a job shop manufacturing company. Your company has been requested to quote on a simple assembly: a special-sized metal door for McCall Enterprises. The door assembly consists of the door, the frame, two hinges, and a latch. The door must go to shop 5 for 1 hour and then to shop 9 for 2 hours. The frame must go to shop 2 for 0.5 hours and then to shop 6 for 1 hour. After the above processing, both the door and the doorframe must go to the paint shop for 1 hour of labor and 4 hours of drying time. Next the components must go for 1 hour to assembly, where the hinges and latch are installed and a pasteboard protective crate is strapped around the assembly.

   Raw material for the door and the frame can be obtained with 2 days' lead time. Backlog data for the four shops involved in this job are shown below. Assume adequate time is available in the paint and assembly shops.

available capacity? Remember, a later delivery date may reduce your chance of being awarded the contract.

Backlog Reports

Shop 5				Capacity 40 hours/week			
Week	1	2	3	4	5	6	7
Load	50	35	28	32	20	10	6

Shop 9				Capacity 80 hours/week			
Week	1	2	3	4	5	6	7
Load	100	80	70	50	40	20	16

Shop 2				Capacity 40 hours/week			
Week	1	2	3	4	5	6	7
Load	25	20	18	22	10	5	0

Shop 6				Capacity 40 hours/week			
Week	1	2	3	4	5	6	7
Load	16	25	40	40	25	16	2

In the past few days you have quoted jobs that, *if* they are awarded to you, will require you to use all of the available capacity in all of the shops and a ten-hour overload in shop 9 for the next four weeks.

(a) When can you deliver the doors to McCall Enterprises? Should you quote a little later delivery just in case some of the outstanding quotes are awarded to your company and use some of the available capacity?

(b) Should you quote a price that would include overtime pay, just in case the outstanding quotes are awarded to you and use the available capacity?

(c) Does it concern you that you have people on the payroll in shops 2 and 6 and do not have sufficient work in those shops to utilize their capacity fully? What are you going to do about this situation?

BIBLIOGRAPHY

Biegel, John E. *Production Control: A Quantitative Approach.* 2d ed. Englewood Cliffs, N.J.: Prentice-Hall, 1971.

Buffa, Elwood S., and Jeffrey G. Miller. *Production-Inventory Systems: Planning and Control.* 3d ed. Homewood, Ill.: Irwin, 1979.

Conway, Richard W., William L. Maxwell, and Louis W. Miller. *Theory of Scheduling.* Reading, Mass.: Addison-Wesley, 1967.

Hall, Robert W. *Zero Inventories.* Homewood, Ill.: Dow Jones-Irwin, 1983.

Johnson, Richard A., William T. Newell, and Roger C. Vergin. *Production and Operations Management.* Boston: Houghton Mifflin, 1974.

Mather, Hal, and George Plossl. "Priority Fixation Versus Throughput Planning." *Production and Inventory Management.* 3d quarter, 1978, pp. 27–50.

Mize, Joe H., Charles R. White, and George H. Brooks. *Operations Planning and Control.* Englewood Cliffs, N.J.: Prentice-Hall, 1971.

Monden, Yasuhiro. *Toyota Production System: Practical Approach to Production Management.* Norcross, Ga.: Industrial Engineering and Management Press, 1983.

Niland, Powell. *Production Planning, Scheduling, and Inventory Control.* New York: Macmillan, 1970.

O'Brien, James J. *Scheduling Handbook.* New York: McGraw-Hill, 1969.

Plossl, George. *Manufacturing Control—The Last Frontier for Profits.* Reston, Va.: Reston, 1973.

Powell, Cash, Jr. "Shop Input and Output Control." *Production and Inventory Management,* 2d quarter, 1972, pp. 63–73.

Riggs, James L. *Production Systems: Planning, Analysis, and Control.* New York: Wiley, 1976. Chap. 13.

Schonberger, Richard J. *Japanese Manufacturing Techniques: Nine Hidden Lessons in Simplicity.* New York: Free Press, 1982.

Shore, Barry. *Operations Management.* New York: McGraw-Hill, 1973, Chap 15.

Vollman, Thomas E. *Operations Management: A Systems Model-Building Approach.* Reading, Mass: Addison-Wesley, 1973.

Wight, Oliver W. *Production and Inventory Management in the Computer Age.* Boston: Cahners, 1974.

Chapter Outline
SCHEDULING AND CONTROLLING SERVICE OPERATIONS

UNIQUE CHALLENGES OF SERVICE OPERATIONS
Customer Involvement / Limited Ability to Hold Services in Inventory

STRATEGIES FOR INFLUENCING DEMAND PATTERNS
Maintenance of a Fixed Schedule / Use of an Appointment System / Delayed Delivery / Providing Economic Incentives for Off-Peak Demand

STRATEGIES FOR COPING WITH NONUNIFORM DEMAND
Telephone Services / Banking Services / The Postal Service / *Operations Management in Action:* HOW THE USPS COPES WITH NONUNIFORM DEMAND / Other Services / *Operations Management in Action:* HOW A FAST FOOD RESTAURANT COPES WITH NONUNIFORM DEMAND / *Operations Management in Action:* HOW HARPER-GRACE HOSPITALS COPES WITH NONUNIFORM DEMAND / A Production-Line Equivalent

WAITING-LINE ANALYSIS
The Structure of Queuing Systems / Development of Queues / Mathematical Solutions to Waiting Problems / *Application: Analysis of a Single-Channel Queue* / Constant Service Time / Truncated Queues / *Application: The Effect of a Truncated Queue*

Summary / Solved Problem / Discussion Questions / Problems / Bibliography

KEY TERMS

Customer involvement or contact	Off-peak demand	Single channel	Queue discipline
Front office	Floating capacity or floating staff	Multiple channel	Service time
Back office	Waiting-line or queuing theory	Single phase	Service rate
By-appointment-only		Multiple phase	Utilization factor
		Arrival rate	Truncated queue

Chapter 9

SCHEDULING AND CONTROLLING SERVICE OPERATIONS

Managers of service operations, like managers of manufacturing operations, must wisely use resources to achieve productivity and customer satisfaction. Some service operations face challenges that are quite similar to the challenges in manufacturing—as has been pointed out from time to time in earlier chapters. However, the unique aspects of scheduling and controlling service operations are so extensive as to warrant a chapter devoted exclusively to them.

In this chapter, attention is first directed to some of the features of non-manufacturing operations that make them different from manufacturing. Several examples of nonmanufacturing operations are then presented to illustrate some approaches that are used to deal with the kinds of problems such operations face. Also briefly discussed is waiting-line or queueing theory, which can be useful in analyzing both manufacturing and nonmanufacturing operations.

UNIQUE CHALLENGES OF SERVICE OPERATIONS

Some of the major challenges that make service businesses and organizations operationally different from manufacturing stem from two of the fundamental differences between manufacturing and services that were noted in Chapter 1.

One is that service operations generally have more direct involvement with the customer than do manufacturing operations. A second basic difference is that manufacturing operations can often store their output to have it available in inventory when it is requested, whereas pure services generally are created as they are provided. These two differences greatly affect the ways in which service operations must operate and, therefore, the ways in which managers must plan and direct these operations. Let us now consider some of the implications of these two major differences.

Customer Involvement

Traditionally, one tends to think of services as being more custom-designed and involving more personal contact with the customer in order to assess his or her specific needs and desires. This *customer involvement* or *contact* has an impact on the way that the service operation can be run.

Lack of Standardization Affects Efficiency   Customer contact and involvement affect the degree to which service operations can be standardized and specified for efficiency. Customer involvement provides the opportunity for special requests and instructions to be issued by the customer, which tends to disrupt the efficiency with which services can be provided. In addition, variability in customer preferences makes it difficult to set standards for staffing and to predict how much time it will take to serve a given number of customers.

Capacity Can Be Lost in Providing Nonservice Amenities   Customer contact cannot be strictly limited to the amount of time that is necessary to deliver the actual service—if the provider is to avoid appearing abrupt or rude. Customers often expect a certain amount of conversation—to obtain information, but also to overcome loneliness or have an opportunity to share their interests and concerns.

Perception of Quality Is Subjective   The pure service component of a service operation's output is intangible, and objective measurements of its quality are difficult to obtain. Quality is closely related to the customer's perception of satisfactory service. Customers who feel that they were not treated as important or that their requests were not adequately responded to are not likely to feel satisfied. These customers will tend to rate the service low on quality, even though they may actually have received the same amount of pure service as some other customer—or more. Thus operations employees who work in the areas where customer contact occurs must have sensitivity and customer relations skills as well as the skills required to provide services.

Degree of Customer Involvement Affects Efficiency   Not all service businesses experience the same degree of customer involvement. Table 9.1 lists some examples of nonmanufacturing operations classified according to whether the customer has high, intermediate, or low contact with the system. Also, within a business, some parts of the operations function may experience more customer contact than others.

Table 9.1
DEGREE OF CUSTOMER CONTACT
IN VARIOUS OPERATIONS

Low Contact	Intermediate Contact	High Contact
Mail service	Restaurant	Counseling
Freight truck line	Motel	Dental care
Mail order store	Self-service gasloine	Personal transportation
	Discount store	Full-service retail store

The degree of customer contact often makes a big difference to the way in which an operation can be run. In fact, Richard Chase contends that the degree to which an operation can achieve efficiency is directly related to the extent of customer contact. Table 9.2, which contrasts high-contact operations and low-contact operations, demonstrates the basis of that contention.

Minimizing the Effects of Customer Contact Operations have a variety of methods that can be used to achieve efficiency and still provide the customer with good service. One way in which operations limit the disruption from customer contact—such as unusual requests and changes in customer instructions—is to standardize the services they offer. A limited-menu or fast food restaurant is an example of standardization as well as of other strategies for running a service operation efficiently that will be discussed later. Some service businesses limit customer contact by automating parts of their operations, such as the use of automatic tellers at a bank. This method not only reduces labor costs but also limits the customer's "options" to a particular set of standard transactions.

A common strategy to improve the efficiency of an operation is to keep separate from customers those portions of the operation that do not require customer contact. In a hotel, for example, it is better for the maids to clean the guests' rooms when the guests are absent. This not only avoids disturbing the guests, but the lack of contact also permits the maids to clean efficiently according to a prescribed procedure, rather than acting as personal servants and following the individual instructions of the guests. There is a *front office* operation—involving such functions as the registration clerk, bell captain, and cashier—that is intended to interact with the guests and to provide a friendly personal atmosphere. Workers in the *back office* operations—such as maids and maintenance people—primarily take their directions from the hotel staff rather than from the guests, although they also contribute to the guests' service. There are numerous other services that have some parts of their operation separated from contact with the public so these parts can run with little direction or interruption from the customer. Table 9.3 provides further examples of some operations that have both front and back offices.

Other advantages can result from separating the front office operation from the back office. Since the front office must provide the customer interface,

Table 9.2
MAJOR DESIGN CONSIDERATIONS IN HIGH- AND LOW-CONTACT SYSTEMS

Decision	High-Contact System	Low-Contact System
Facility location	Operations must be near the customer.	Operations may be placed near supply, transportation, or labor.
Facility layout	Facility should accommodate the customer's physical and psychological needs and expectations.	Facility should enhance production.
Product design	Environment as well as the physical product define the nature of the service.	Customer is not in the service environment so the product can be defined by fewer attributes.
Process design	Stages of production have a direct immediate effect on the customer.	Customer is not involved in the majority of processing steps.
Scheduling	Customer is in the production schedule and must be accommodated.	Customer is concerned mainly with completion dates.
Production planning	Orders cannot be stored, so smoothing production flow will result in loss of business.	Both backlogging and production smoothing are possible.
Worker skills	Direct work force comprises a major part of the service product and so must be able to interact well with the public.	Direct work force need only have technical skills.
Quality control	Quality standards are often in the eye of the beholder and hence variable.	Quality standards are generally measurable and hence fixed.
Time standards	Service time depends on customer needs, and therefore time standards are inherently loose.	Work is performed on customer surrogates (e.g., forms), and time standards can be tight.
Wage payment	Variable output requires time-based wage systems.	"Fixable" output permits output-based wage systems.
Capacity planning	To avoid lost sales, capacity must be set to match peak demand.	Storable output permits setting capacity at some average demand level.
Forecasting	Forecasts are short term, time-oriented.	Forecasts are long term, output-oriented.

Source: Richard B. Chase, "Where Does the Customer Fit in a Service Operation?" Harvard Business Review, November–December, 1978, p. 139. Copyright © 1978 by the President and Fellows of Harvard College; all rights reserved.

it needs to be located in convenient, but often more expensive, high-traffic areas. The amount of this expensive real estate that is needed can be reduced by placing all noncontact operations in less expensive areas, and sometimes these operations can be consolidated for economies of scale. Customer-contact areas need to be designed for customer appeal, and employees there need to be more oriented to good customer relations; however, facility arrangement and employees in the low-contact areas can be more oriented to efficiency. Capacity in the customer-contact area must be kept consistently high or scaled up and down

Table 9.3
SOME OPERATIONS WITH FRONT AND BACK OFFICES

Operation	Front Office	Back Office
Bank	Tellers, loan officers	Posting clerks, encoders
Stock brokerage office	Brokers	Transaction clerks, keypunch operators
Restaurant	Hostess, waiters	Chef, cooks, dishwashers
Library	Reference desk	Purchasing, reshelving
Auto shop	Service writer	Mechanics
Laundry	Pickup counter	Pressers, folders

in anticipation of the demand profile if customers are not to be kept waiting. Capacity in the noncontact areas can be kept at a more uniform level, even though demand may vary, and this capacity can be more fully utilized.

Limited Ability to Hold Services in Inventory

The second major difference from manufacturing that affects services is their general inability to hold their output in inventory. Many goods-producing operations can use inventory to decouple their production activities from fluctuations in demand so that production can take place at a more uniform and economical rate. Scheduling and coordinating problems can thus be reduced, and operating expenses can be lower than they would be if manufacturing had to respond instantly to fluctuating demand. Capital investment can be lower and capacity will be more fully utilized throughout the year if a goods producer can accumulate inventory to serve peak demand, rather than being required to have sufficient capacity to produce at the peak demand rate.

Service operations are also more efficient to the extent that they can achieve more uniform operations. Uniform operations would enable the company to serve the same amount of business annually with lower peak capacity, and the capacity would be more fully utilized to spread the investment cost over more units of service. However, services rarely can achieve uniform utilization of their capacity—unless they operate on a *by-appointment-only* basis. When the operation cannot achieve a demand rate that matches its desired capacity level, its objective usually becomes one of developing a capacity profile that matches its demand profile, to the extent that this is feasible and economically viable. Let's now review, in turn, some of the ways in which services attempt to develop more uniform demand patterns and some of the ways in which they vary their capacity so as to serve nonuniform demand patterns more efficiently.

STRATEGIES FOR INFLUENCING DEMAND PATTERNS

Sometimes, through pricing or other policies, a business can influence the times at which demand occurs or the times at which service is provided so that the effect is a somewhat more uniform and manageable rate of service. We will look at four common strategies that serve to some degree to shape the demand pattern so that capacity can be more uniformly utilized.

Maintenance of a Fixed Schedule

Most commercial airplanes do not fly whenever the customer decides to go somewhere. Instead the customer travels at the scheduled time of flight. A form of scheduling is involved in airline, bus, rail, and shipping operations. The time of departure and expected duration of the trip are established and publicized. Demand occurs as people purchase tickets to use some of the previously scheduled transportation capacity. More cars can be added to a train to make the capacity more flexible. Larger planes or buses may be allocated to the routes over which demand is highest.

Airlines face the problem of having their capacity already filled when a customer requests a ticket. Rather than wait for another of the airline's scheduled flights, the customer may switch to another airline. Airlines have some constraints in developing schedules because the departure points, destinations, and timing of their flights must conform to government regulations.

Use of an Appointment System

Some services are provided by appointment. Dentists, for example, set appointments for routine patient care and allow some time for emergency care. The appointments smooth out the utilization of the dentist and his staff rather than having a waiting room full of people who arrived at a time that was convenient for them.

Use of an appointment system permits demand to be moved into available time. The amount of delay between a request for an appointment and the time of the appointment may depend on the backlog or queue of waiting work. The following strategy is similar, except that no appointment is made.

Delayed Delivery

We do not need an appointment to take a watch or small appliance in for repairs and usually have no appointment to get an automobile repaired. The air conditioner repairperson may not get to your house for several days if you call in July, yet in October repair service may be available in a short time. The lead time between a request for service and its delivery depends on the amount of work waiting to be performed. Each request for service waits its turn through the backlog or queue of service requests. Delaying jobs until capacity becomes available serves to make the work load more uniform. Of course, even with the use of overtime or part-time employees, the demand rate may still be so great that some work must be delayed. Routine work may be set aside to make capacity available for rush jobs. This procedure is the equivalent of developing dispatching rules in a manufacturing operation.

Providing Economic Incentives for Off-Peak Demand

Some operations have a heavy capital investment in the capacity they must have to provide their services. The unit cost of capacity that is used only occasionally for peak demand periods is very high. These operations try to keep the demand as uniform as possible by use of economic inducements. Telephone companies, for example, provide discounts for long-distance calls that are made during the off-peak hours. Electric utilities may try to discourage erratic consumption with high peaks by charging rates that are based on the customer's maximum rate of use as well as on the total amount of energy that the customer consumed. But at best such strategies are only partially successful. Nonuniform demand persists.

STRATEGIES FOR COPING WITH NONUNIFORM DEMAND

Telephone Services

In spite of their attempts to promote off-peak demand through economic incentives, many operations still experience highly nonuniform demand patterns. Telephone companies are a classic example. Most business calls are made during business hours, and many people consider it bad manners to make personal calls in the middle of the night. Consequently, the demand for telephone service is extremely nonuniform. Figure 9.1 shows how telephone calls in Long Beach, California, vary from day to day during a month and how nonuniformly the demand is distributed during a twenty-four-hour period.

In the telephone business, price differentials are used not only to influence when calls are made but also to encourage direct dialing so that automated switching can be used almost exclusively. A certain portion of calls, however, will always be operator-assisted. The customer will be kept waiting if the operator staff is not adequate for the volume of business. Maintaining a full-time staff sufficient to handle the peak daily demand volume would be prohibitively expensive.

Scheduling the availability of capacity to cover demand involves constructing work shifts so that the number of operators available at any time matches the demand profile. Willie Henderson and William Berry developed a heuristic method to assign work-shift times for telephone operators. The objective was to find the minimum number of operators required to meet demand that varies throughout the day. This study examined various patterns of assigning work shifts to operators so that the total worker hours available at any time during the day was sufficient for the expected demand. They investigated the practices of varying the number of hours each employee was to work, varying the starting

FIGURE 9.1

Distribution of Telephone Calls in Long Beach, California, January 1972.

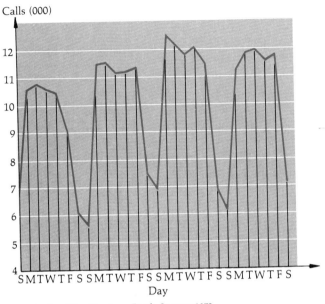

(a) Daily call load for Long Beach, January 1972

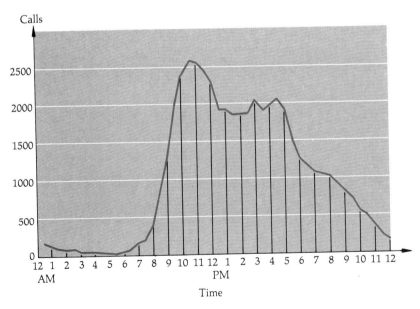

(b) Typical half-hourly call distribution

Source: Elwood S. Buffa, Michael J. Cosgrove, and Bill J. Luce, "An Integrated Workshift Scheduling System," *Decision Sciences*, October 1976, p. 622. *Decision Sciences* is published by the American Institute for Decision Sciences.

times of the first and second sessions, and varying the times of work breaks and the length of the idle session (often a lunch break) between the two major work sessions. The solution method involved linear programming and branch-and-bound logic.[1] Available alternatives (branches) were identified and a reasonable solution (bound) was specified. As soon as a branch appeared to be nonoptimal, it was given no further consideration, thus saving time and computation.

Banking Services

More flexibility to schedule and smooth the work demand is often available for those parts of a service where the customer is not present and the service is provided by working with some surrogate for the customer. For example, consider the back office operation in a bank, where the daily intake of checks dr wn on other banks is encoded for processing. The customer is not present for this work, so it can be delayed or batched, but all checks that will be credited to the bank for a day must be completed by some deadline, say 10:30 P.M. The number of checks that will arrive in a day is a probabilistic variable that is forecast. If some checks are not processed because of insufficient staff, the bank will suffer an opportunity cost because it will not receive credit for the funds for an additional day. The bank will suffer another type of cost, however, if it overstaffs to assure itself of sufficient capacity. Often a part-time work force is scheduled to provide a capacity level that trades off these two risks and matches capacity to the distribution of forecast demand. This problem has been addressed by Vincent Mabert as an integer programming problem.[2] A later study, by Mabert and Charles Watts, used simulation (discussed in Supplement F at the end of this chapter) to evaluate sets of shift schedules under the probabilistic demand patterns in order to select the one that appeared to be best.[3]

The Postal Service

The U.S. Postal Service provides an interesting example of a service that has little contact with the customer but instead performs its service by working with letters and other pieces of mail sent by customers (see box). This service does not try to smooth the profile of demand with which items are mailed. It does, however, offer incentives for flexibility the customer permits in delivery time. Express mail or special delivery requires a premium fee; first-class mail is to be delivered within a specified time; other, less-expensive classes permit more time for delivery.

[1]Willie B. Henderson and William L. Berry, "Determining Optimal Shift Schedules for Telephone Traffic Exchange Operators," *Decision Sciences*, January 1977, pp. 239–255.
[2]Vincent A. Mabert, "A Case Study of Encoder Shift Scheduling Under Uncertainty," *Management Science*, July 1979, pp. 623–631.
[3]Vincent A. Mabert and Charles A. Watts, "A Simulation Analysis of Tour-Shift Construction Procedures," *Management Science*, May 1982, pp. 520–532.

OPERATIONS MANAGEMENT IN ACTION

How the USPS Copes with Nonuniform Demand

The U.S. Postal Service, which is a gigantic materials handling system, has a varying demand for its services. Extra demand occurs at such times as Mother's Day, Father's Day, during the Christmas season, and whenever large mailers send material through the mail.

The system has data going back many years on the volume of mail between bulk mail centers and area distribution centers, and it develops forecasts of demand in each area that are distributed to offices in the system. Whenever local variations are known, forecasts are adjusted by local offices. For example, a mail-order house might notify its local office of a large promotional mailing, or the Treasury Department might notify the office of mailings of Social Security or Veterans Administration retirement checks.

On the basis of these forecasts, the offices can assign additional equipment and have enough people on hand to handle the work.

Mail that is collected at post offices must be sent to area distribution centers, where it is sorted by zip code, packaged according to destination, and loaded on trucks that move it to its proper destination. In some instances sorting schedules have to be coordinated with airline flight schedules—and adjusted if flight schedules change.

Post offices have standards for how much mail can be processed by workers. Hand sorting can accommodate about 850 letters per hour. Mechanical sorting—having individuals key in zip code digits as pieces of mail move through small tracks—can handle about 1,800 per hour. Automatic OCR equipment can sort about 10,000 per hour. From such standards, offices can determine how many employees are needed. The offices have lists of part-time employees and relief clerks who can be called in. They can also call in regular employees who would otherwise be off duty, or have regular employees work overtime.

Mail is color-coded for the amount of time permitted before it must reach its destination, depending on the class of mail and the distance between its points of origin and destination. If the workload is above capacity, mail that is ahead of its required schedule is held while higher-priority mail is processed ahead of its normal delivery rate. Extra trucks are dispatched on routes when extra mail is to be moved between cities. If extra trucks are frequently used, a larger truck or an additional truck will be regularly scheduled.

Thus it can be seen that the postal system uses variable capacity in response to a forecast and the equivalent of buffer inventory to utilize its capacity efficiently and process mail on schedule.

Other Services

The use of part-time employees is a common means of adjusting capacity to higher-than-normal demand rate, particularly if the equivalent to inventory cannot be used. Consider the example of Burger King, presented in the next box. Also, notice that there is a front office for customer contact and a back office that is set up for efficiency. The back office area has a production line or flow line for production of standard components. Standard items are produced at a flow rate. The standard components are assembled in a versatile assemble-to-order area. Notice also that computer simulation (discussed in Supplement F) is used to analyze decisions about staffing levels and scheduling.

The facility capacity in a restaurant must be adequate for the number of customers who are to dine inside. But a drive-through service operation makes it possible to increase the volume of business to levels well above a given seating

OPERATIONS MANAGEMENT IN ACTION

How a Fast Food Restaurant Copes with Nonuniform Demand

Some operations have large variations in their demand rates and cannot use inventory to smooth the work requirements. At Burger King, for example, the maximum shelf life of most of its products is ten minutes, so this operation is extremely limited in how much production it can store in low-demand periods to sell when demand is high.[4] A Burger King restaurant might produce 800 burgers per hour during the lunchtime rush, yet produce only 40 per hour before or after this period. In such restaurants, the design of the facility determines the peak capacity, and the store can be operated at various levels up to its peak capacity.

Customers place their orders at point of sale (POS) stations in the front of the store. The number of POS stations that should be open for a given level of demand is optimized by a computer simulation model. Orders are communicated to the production area by microphone or, in newer stores, by CRT. The production area maintains a flow rate of standard items (burgers and fries) for the level of demand and produces special-order items. In newer stores, production flows from the back of the store, where ingredients are stored,

through the cooking area, then through the sandwich dress and assembly area, to the front of the store where the fry pots and drink stations are located. Counter personnel collect the items to complete an order and deliver them to the customer at the POS stations. The number of employees needed at each of these work areas depends on the level of business.

Labor scheduling is, needless to say, a very important factor in managing a restaurant such as a Burger King. Payroll costs are close to overtaking food costs as the largest expense item. Operating with sufficient full-time staff to meet the peak demand would be prohibitively expensive, so part-time workers are employed. Burger King headquarters in Miami has a simulation model used to determine the staffing levels and job assignments that will best achieve the established service-time standards for any level of demand a store might experience. The output of the model is documented in an easy-to-read format for restaurant managers to use. Savings resulting from this labor productivity program exceed 1 percent of the company's annual sales. And 1 percent of $2.5 billion is $25 million per year!

[4]Information from Richard D. Filley, "Putting the Fast in Fast Foods: Burger King," Industrial Engineering, January 1983, pp. 44–47.

capacity. Services that can use on-call or part-time equipment as well as part-time workers are also less bound by their facilities. A freight line, for example, can contract with independent truck owner-operators to move freight for it. For example, a freight line's terminal may own a fleet of trucks to move some of the loads it ships. Beyond these, the dispatcher at each freight terminal keeps a list of trucks in the area that are waiting for a load to move and can call one of these when a load is to be moved. If there are not enough trucks on the list at a terminal and if that terminal is part of a large truck line, the terminal dispatcher will call the central dispatcher of the truck line to determine if any equipment is in the area or bound into the area that can haul the load. If this does not locate sufficient equipment, the local dispatcher may call local truck stops to find an available truck and driver that can be contracted. Independent owner-operators are looking for loads, and freight companies are looking for trucks. In some instances brokers match shippers in an area with truckers who

OPERATIONS MANAGEMENT IN ACTION

How Harper-Grace Hospitals Copes with Nonuniform Demand

Harper-Grace Hospitals in Detroit (over 1,400 beds and 5,000 employees) has developed an effective and logical approach to scheduling nurses to the various work areas in the hospitals.[5] Near the end of each shift, designated nurses evaluate the patients in each area according to the patients' requirements for nursing care—that is, the "care level." Care levels range from minimal care to intensive care. Management engineers and nurses have developed standards for the amount of work required to respond adequately to each care level. The care requirements for each area in the hospitals are added, and allowances are made for new admissions, discharges, and returns from surgery. About an hour before each shift begins, a scheduler (usually the shift supervisor) can determine how many nurses are required in each area and can then make appropriate assignments. This approach prevents the overassignment of nurses to an area—resulting in nurses distributing linens just to have something to do—or underassignment—resulting in nurses being overworked and frustrated because they cannot render the level of care they feel they should.

As outcomes of this scheduling approach, the hospital reported cost savings, an increase in quality of care for the patients, and improved job satisfaction for the nurses.

[5]Information from Richard D. Filley, "Cost-Effective Patient Care: Harper-Grace Hospitals," Industrial Engineering, January 1983, pp. 48–52.

are looking for a load to haul and charge a fee for this service. Such a means of expanding capacity is equivalent to subcontracting work in a manufacturing operation.

Some services have a maximum capacity that is fixed by the facility, but they can still use part-time employees to scale up or down as some capacity changes appear to be in order. Also, as in the case of a hospital, it might be desirable to have some *floating capacity* that can be shifted from one department to another if the number of patients or the amount of nursing attention required in each department varies.

The scheduling of the nursing staff in a hospital involves assignment of nurses to shifts in various wards. There is considerable variation in the requirements for direct nursing care even though the census in a ward may remain fairly stable. The nursing care requirement depends on the proportion of patients who are designated as total-care, partial-care, or self-care patients. Nursing requirements in one ward are statistically independent of the requirements in other wards, so this type of demand can be served by a stable staff of nurses plus a *floating staff*. The floating staff is moved to the wards that have a high percentage of total-care patients (see box).

A Production-Line Equivalent

In a restaurant or a hospital the customer is present and in most cases is aware of the work that is done in his or her behalf and whether the service is prompt. Some of the other services we have discussed, however, work with a surrogate for the customer. As long as the service involves working with some surrogate for the customer (i.e., as long as it is a very low-contact service), work on one item can be delayed or moved ahead to smooth the use of capacity. The customer is not present and therefore is not offended by being ignored for a while or by having other work performed ahead of his or hers as long as the service is completed within a reasonable time. In some ways working with a surrogate is like having a buffer inventory to smooth the flow of work. This inventory equivalent can be used in the back office operations of some services, resulting in a flow that is much like a production line, especially if the volume is sufficient.

An example of such a situation is provided by the policy issue department of a moderate-sized life insurance company. Several stages of work are involved. Some stages require manual and mental work, others require machine activities such as computer input and response. Some stages perform inspection or quality-control operations and some are equivalent to in-process inventory. Consider an insurance company that receives about 1,000 applications for insurance policies each week. Each application goes through the same steps of review and processing, so they flow along the same route. Table 9.4 describes the steps involved in processing an application, the time each application requires on the average, the number of persons employed at each stage. The equivalent of in-process inventory is held at stage 4. Inspections occur at stages 4 and 6.

The insurance example differs in some respects from an assembly line or production line. Policy applications do not move one at a time but in batches. Some may be held at one station or another, thus allowing applications to pass one another along the way. At one point the policies are held up to await a

Table 9.4
PROCESSING STEPS FOR INSURANCE POLICY ISSUE

Stage	Number of Employees	Processing	Expected Time Per Unit (minutes)
1	2	Log in, check signatures, account for payment	4
2	1	Enter data into automated information system	2
3	2	Check previous insurance history and pull file if company has any records	4
4	2	Check application for medical examination data; hold until medical data arrive from examining physician	3
5	7	Underwriting	10–20
6	3	Check information on computer system to see that it is what underwriter has approved	5
7	2	Prepare policy by printing standard forms; attach riders and amendments	4
8	1	Prepare for mailing	1

medical report, or perhaps more than one if the applicant appears to have some health problem. Each application is unique and must be "assembled" with the specific medical report for its client. A conventional manufacturing assembly line would have ordered materials ahead of time because the people who schedule the operations have specified the number of products of various types they have scheduled to produce. Such planning is not possible with the processing of policy applications because at least one component (the medical examination) is made to order for each individual. The parts are not interchangeable in the processing of policies.

The staffing at the stages in the policy issue department is adequate for the average level of demand. But policy applications do not flow in at a uniform rate. About half of the applications arrive the first two days of the week and the next two have low demand. The average week's work is distributed through the five days of the work week at 25, 25, 15, 15, and 20 percent respectively. This nonuniform demand is managed by flexibility in the skills and capacity of the department in addition to the ability to delay policy applications at any stage. During Mondays and Tuesdays persons from stages 6, 7, and 8 can work parts of the day at the first few stages of the process. Thus work builds up at various stages of the system so that each employee has an adequate supply of work. The line is balanced by a temporary increase in its capacity where demand is high.

WAITING-LINE ANALYSIS

Several examples have been provided to illustrate some strategies that service operations can use to try to match capacity to demand or to try to make demand more compatible with their capacity. You will recognize that these strategies can also be used by many manufacturing operations. Make-to-stock companies can use finished goods inventory in addition to these strategies. Job shops, like service operations, are limited to strategies that utilize the equivalent to in-process inventory or adjustments to demand and/or capacity. They can try to shift demand to make it more uniform, provide excess capacity, miss sales, or adjust the level of some flexible capacity to fit demand.

Not all scheduling problems can be solved by flexibility in scheduling the labor force. Some portion of capacity is provided by the facilities and equipment that are available on a permanent basis. Additions to facilities and equipment often require more lead time and are more difficult to reverse than employment agreements and assignments of working hours. Facilities impose an upper limit on capacity. The amount of capacity that should be made available depends on the expected rate of demand, its variability, and the promptness with which it is to be served.

Waiting-line or *queuing theory* is sometimes useful as a guide in determining the expected waiting time for an arriving patron and the average number of patrons who will be waiting. Queuing theory can provide information useful in determining the amount of capacity that is needed so that waiting times will be reasonable and the amount of space that should be provided for those who are waiting for service.

The Structure of Queuing Systems

Queuing situations may occur in a variety of settings. Several examples are listed below:

Customers at the checkout counter of a grocery, discount, or department store.

An accumulation of jobs to be processed at a work center.

Patrons at bank teller windows.

Computer jobs waiting to be run.

Trucks at a loading dock.

Vehicles at a highway toll booth.

Cargo ships waiting for space at a pier.

Airplanes circling while waiting to land.

Broken machines waiting to be repaired.

A list of patients the doctor is to see as he makes hospital rounds.

Patients waiting in a dentist's office.

A stack of reports and memoranda waiting to be typed.

The basic structure of a simple queuing system is shown at the top of Figure 9.2. Arrivals represent demand for use of the facility. They enter the system from some population of possible arrivals. If the service facility is already occupied (in use), the arrival waits in a queue until capacity in the service facility is available.

The system may contain more than one service facility that may be utilized through various flow patterns within the system. Parallel service facilities may be provided in a multiple-channel system so as to increase the service capacity. Servicing of arrivals may involve more than one stage of processing, so queues may form between these stages. The example at the bottom of Figure 9.2 depicts a combination of multiple-phase processing with a variety of sequences in which the service processing may occur. This structure resembles the flow between queues and work stations that might represent jobs in a job shop manufacturing system, design projects in an architect's office, patient flow in an outpatient clinic, or some similar situation.

In addition to a wide variety of system structures, several other parameters influence the performance of a queuing system. Some important variables are discussed below.

Population Size　The population from which arrivals come may be so small that the number of entities in the system may affect the probability of an arrival. In contrast, the population may be large enough to be assumed to be infinite.

FIGURE 9.2

Types of Queuing Structures

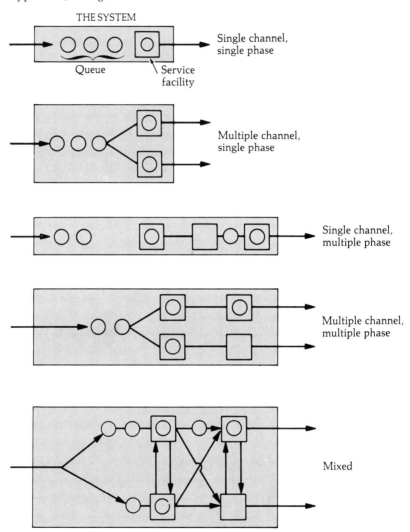

Arrival Rate   The number of units arriving per time period, the *arrival rate,* may be constant or it may be some deterministic or probabilistic variable. Usually arrivals are probabilistic and may occur according to an exponential, Erlang, normal, empirical, or other probability distribution.

Queue Discipline   Arrivals may be selected from the queue to receive service according to one of many possible rules. Priorities may be assigned on the basis of the highest profit attainable, emergency needs, earliest due date, shortest processing time, or some other logic. The most commonly assumed *queue dis-*

cipline and the one used in deriving basic queuing formulas is first come, first served.

Behavior of Arrivals at Queues   In some circumstances, arrivals may balk (i.e., not join the queue) if it is too long when they arrive. People may see a long line at a movie and decide to go elsewhere (balk). Or they may wait for a time, become impatient, and leave (renege). This behavior may not occur in other circumstances. Machines that break down join the queue of machines waiting to be repaired without choice.

Service Time   The time required to provide service may vary considerably. Each repetition of a service may take precisely the same time as every other, as in an automatic car wash. *Service time* may be variable but predictable, or it may be random. Random service times may follow some empirical distribution or perhaps a normal, exponential, Erlang, or some other theoretical distribution.

Development of Queues

A queue or waiting line forms because the short-term demand rate exceeds the short-term service rate; that is, whenever an arrival occurs and the server or servers are busy. If the interarrival times are known, it may be possible to schedule the availability of service capacity so that a queue does not form. Unless these times are constant or nearly constant, however, it might be very expensive to try to adapt capacity to them. When interarrival times are constant, queues can be prevented so long as the time between arrivals is greater than or equal to the service time. If either the interarrival times or the service times are probabilistic, an arrival may occur while the facility is occupied, causing a queue to develop.

Frequently the mean arrival rate, λ (i.e., the reciprocal of the mean interarrival time), is used to express the density of demand. The *service rate,* μ (i.e., the reciprocal of the mean service time), is used to express the system's capacity. If cars arrive at a bank's drive-in window every five minutes on the average, then the mean arrival rate, λ, is twelve cars per hour. If it takes an average of three minutes to serve a car, μ is twenty cars per hour. In random queuing situations, the arrival rate must be less than the service rate or a queue will continue to grow if the customers do not renege or balk.

Mathematical Solutions to Waiting Problems

The variety of waiting situations that may occur is so great that we cannot discuss all of them here. But we shall consider a few situations to illustrate some formulas that can be used in the analysis of waiting situations. It is important to recognize that the equations and figures presented below are for steady-state conditions, which assume that the distributions of arrival rates and service times remain stationary over time and that the system has operated long enough to be in equilibrium. That is, the effects of initial start-up conditions have been overcome and the probability distributions of queue statistics have stabilized about their respective means. If λ is greater than μ, the system may never reach a steady state. In any event, the system may not remain in operation long enough to become stable. If an operation closes down for several breaks during the day, it may not be in equilibrium for much of the day. Simulation often is used to analyze situations that are not in equilibrium or that do not fit adequately the assumed condition of queueing theory. For instance, the probability distributions may not be described by standard theoretical distributions for which equations are available. Sometimes the mathematical complexity is overwhelming when the situation is very involved, as in the mixed structure in Figure 9.2.

Consider the simplest type of queue structure, with one service facility and a single queue from which arrivals are served on a first-come-first-served basis. These models are based on the assumption that arrivals are patient and will wait until service is received (no reneging). Arrivals come from an infinite population with an arrival rate described by a Poisson probability distribution. (Poisson arrival rates are associated with exponential interarrival times.) With a Poisson arrival rate, the probability of x units arriving in a given time period is given by

$$P(x) = \frac{\lambda^x e^{-\lambda}}{x!} \tag{9.1}$$

where λ is the mean rate of arrival and $e = 2.718$, the base of natural logarithms. Other symbols we shall use are given below:

μ = the mean service rate (it is assumed that $\mu > \lambda$)
$\rho = \lambda/\mu$, the utilization factor or traffic-intensity factor
P_n = the probability that n units will be in the system
L_s = the mean number of units in the system
L_q = the mean number of units in the queue
W_s = the mean time a unit spends in the system
W_q = the mean time a unit spends in the queue

The probability that the service facility will be in use is the *utilization factor*, λ/μ. The probability that no unit will be in the system is

$$P_0 = 1 - \lambda/\mu, \tag{9.2}$$

which is the percentage of time that the facility will be idle. The probability of n units in the system is

$$P_n = (\lambda/\mu)^n P_o = (\lambda/\mu)^n (1 - \lambda/\mu). \tag{9.3}$$

The mean number of units in the system is

$$L_s = \sum_0^\infty n P_n = \frac{\lambda}{\mu - \lambda}. \tag{9.4}$$

The mean number of units waiting in the queue will be the mean number in the system minus the mean number being serviced:

$$L_q = L_s - \lambda/\mu = \frac{\lambda^2}{\mu(\mu - \lambda)}. \tag{9.5}$$

The mean time each arrival spends in the system (waiting in the queue and being serviced) is

$$W_s = \frac{L_s}{\lambda} = \frac{1}{\mu - \lambda}.$$ (9.6)

The mean time spent in only the queue, W_q, can be found by subtracting the mean service time from the mean time in the system.

$$W_q = W_s - \frac{1}{\mu} = \frac{\lambda}{\mu(\mu - \lambda)}.$$ (9.7)

Equations 9.4–9.7 approach infinity as λ approaches μ, therefore these equations apply only if μ is greater than λ. The equations for P_o and P_n apply only for $\mu \geq \lambda$. If arrival and service rates are random, we should not expect to get full utilization of a service facility without very long queues because λ/μ must be less than unity. Figure 9.3, below, shows the behavior of L_q and W_q for a

FIGURE 9.3

Mean Queue Length and Mean Waiting Time in Queue for Poisson Arrival Rate and Poisson Service Rate Model

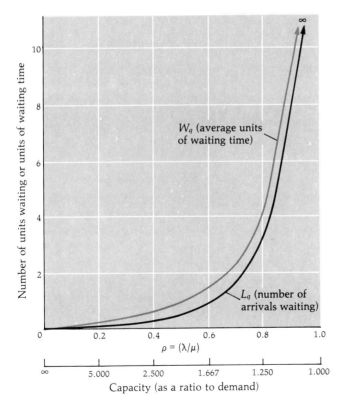

system with Poisson arrival rate and Poisson service rate as the utilization factor, ρ, is increased toward 1. The abscissa of Figure 9.3 is expressed in terms of ρ, sometimes called the traffic factor, which is the ratio of λ to μ. This relationship makes very clear the kinds of waiting lines that can be expected given a particular level of capacity to serve a given arrival rate.

Queue statistics also can be developed for multiple-channel queuing systems. The equations for the mean wait, mean queue length, mean number of arrivals in the system, and so on are more complicated and will not be presented here. The behavior of the mean number in the system as a function of ρ is

FIGURE 9.4

Values of L_s, for Poisson Arrival Rates and Service Times

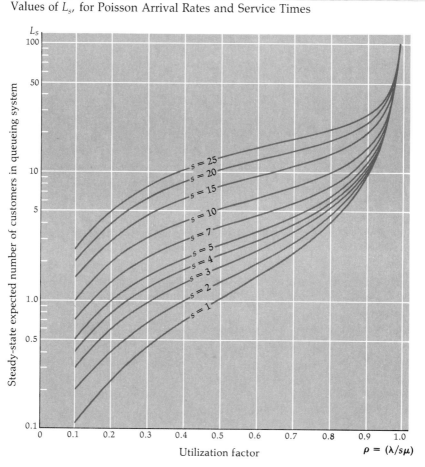

Source: Frederick S. Hillier and Gerald J. Lieberman, *Introduction to Operations Research,* 2d ed. (San Francisco: Holden Day, 1974), p. 402.

shown in Figure 9.4. The utilization factor, ρ, for multiple-channel systems is given by $\dfrac{\lambda}{s\mu}$, where s is the number of parallel channels.

APPLICATION

Analysis of a Single-Channel Queue

The Armstrong Wholesale Grocery Company owns a small distribution center in one of the cities it serves. The loading dock will accommodate only one truck to be loaded or unloaded. Company-owned trucks arrive according to a Poisson distribution with a mean rate of three trucks per day. At present the company employs a crew of two to load and unload the trucks, and the unloading rate is Poisson-distributed with a mean rate of four trucks per day. The company can employ additional persons in the loading crew and increase the average loading rate by one truck per day for each additional employee up to a maximum of six persons who can be utilized effectively in the process. The company estimates that the cost of an idle truck and driver is $20 per hour and the company pays $8 per hour including fringe benefits for each employee in the loading crew.

Daniel Baker, who manages the distribution center, does not want to add any additional employees because he says the utilization of the current loading crew is very low. Actually, the utilization is

$$\rho = \frac{\lambda}{\mu} = \frac{3}{4} = 0.75.$$

His quarterly bonus is based on the profit of the distribution center computed on the basis of its sales minus its costs. The truck costs and drivers are paid by the transportation center. The company's executive vice-president says that the company, overall, would benefit by faster loading and unloading of trucks because the trucks spend too much time at the dock.

The mean wait in the system is

$$W_s = \frac{1}{\mu - \lambda} = \frac{1}{4 - 3} = 1 \text{ day.}$$

The mean number of trucks waiting in the system is

$$L_s = \frac{\lambda}{\mu - \lambda} = \frac{3}{4 - 3} = 3 \text{ trucks.}$$

The daily cost of delaying trucks plus the facility cost is:

Cost for trucks and drivers = 3 trucks × $20/hour × 8 hours = $480
Cost for loading crew = 2 × $8/hour × 8 hours = 128
$608

The executive vice-president and his assistant prepared a table (Table 9.5) and had a meeting with the transportation manager and Dan. It was agreed at the meeting that Dan would hire two more employees to load and unload trucks. He could then try to reduce operating costs by finding additional duties for these people when trucks were not being loaded or unloaded, because the utilization of the crew would be $\lambda/\mu = 3/6 = 0.5$.

Table 9.5
QUEUING ANALYSIS FOR ARMSTRONG WHOLESALE GROCERY COMPANY
(Arrival rate λ = 3 trucks per day)

(1) Size of Loading Crew	(2) Mean Loading Rate (μ)	(3) Daily Cost of Loading Crew	(4) Mean Number of Trucks in System, $L_s = \dfrac{\lambda}{\mu - \lambda}$	(5) Daily Cost of Idle Trucks, $\$20(8)L_s$	Daily Cost of Idle Trucks, Plus Loading Crew, (3) + (5)
2	4	2($8/hr)(8 hrs) = $128	$\dfrac{3}{4-3}$ = 3.0	160 × 3 = 480	$608
3	5	3($8/hr)(8 hrs) = $192	$\dfrac{3}{5-3}$ = 1.5	160 × 1.5 = 240	$432
4	6	4($8/hr)(8 hrs) = $256	$\dfrac{3}{6-3}$ = 1.0	160 × 1 = 160	$416
5	7	5($8/hr)(8 hrs) = $320	$\dfrac{3}{7-3}$ = 0.75	160 × 0.75 = 120	$440
6	8	6($8/hr)(8 hrs) = $384	$\dfrac{3}{8-3}$ = 0.6	160 × 0.6 = 96	$480

Constant Service Time

When the service rate or the arrival rate is constant, the mean queue length or the mean waiting time will be reduced. For a single-channel system with Poisson arrivals and constant service time, the mean length of the queue, L_{qc}, and mean wait time in the queue, W_{qc}, are half what they are when both the arrival rate and service rate are Poisson-distributed.

$$L_{qc} = \frac{\lambda^2}{2\mu(\mu - \lambda)} \qquad (9.8)$$

$$W_{qc} = \frac{\lambda}{2\mu(\mu - \lambda)} \qquad (9.9)$$

The mean number in the system is the mean number in the queue plus the mean number in the service facility, or $L_{qc} + \lambda/\mu$. The mean wait in the system is the mean wait in the queue plus the service time or $W_{qc} + 1/\mu$.

Figure 9.5 shows the number of units in the system as a function of ρ for both single- and multiple-channel systems when the service times are constant.

Assume that a friend of yours is planning to construct an automatic car wash at a location he has selected. The traffic count and market study indicate that a mean arrival rate of six cars per hour can be expected. Assume that arrivals will be Poisson-distributed. Your friend can buy either of two automatic wash-

FIGURE 9.5

Values of L_s, for Poisson Input and Constant Service Times

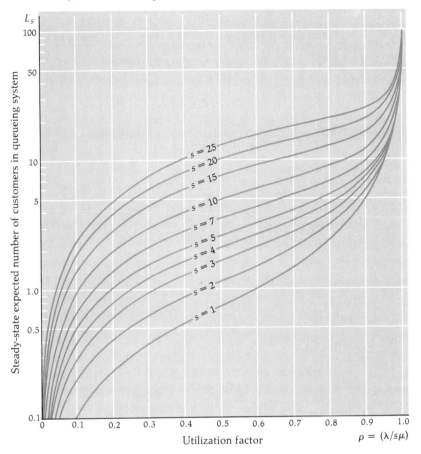

Source: Frederick S. Hiller and Gerald J. Lieberman, *Introduction to Operations Research*, 2d. ed. (San Francisco: Holden Day, 1974), p. 416.

ers, one with a constant service time of five minutes (twelve washes per hour) and a more expensive one with a constant service time of four minutes (fifteen washes per hour). He has established a criterion that the mean waiting time to get into the wash area should not be more than two minutes and will buy the slower machine if it meets this criterion. Which should he buy?

For the slower washer the mean waiting time in the queue will be

$$W_{qc} = \frac{\lambda}{2\mu(\mu - \lambda)} = \frac{6}{2(12)(12 - 6)} = \frac{6}{24(6)} = 0.0417$$

0.0417 hour (60 minutes/hour) = 2.5 minutes

For the faster washer the waiting time in the queue will be

$$W_{qc} = \frac{6}{2(15)(15-6)} = \frac{6}{30(9)} = 0.0222 \text{ hour}$$

0.0222 hour (60 minutes/hour) = 1.33 minutes.

Therefore, your friend should buy the faster washing equipment.

Truncated Queues

The length of a queue may be limited by some factor such as the space allowed for waiting or the impatience of the waiters after the queue has reached a certain length. When the queue is not allowed to reach its normal maximum length at times, the average queue length and average wait will be reduced. The utilization of the facility will therefore be reduced from what it would otherwise have been because some of the arrivals will be turned away.

Let N be the maximum number allowed in the system. Then[6]

$$P_o = \frac{1-\rho}{1-\rho^{N+1}} \text{ for } \lambda \neq \mu \qquad (9.10)$$

and

$$P_n = P_o\left(\frac{\lambda}{\mu}\right)^n. \qquad (9.11)$$

The probability that the system will be full and business will be lost because of lack of a capacity is P_N, and λP_N is the number of persons turned away per unit of time over which λ and μ are measured.[7] These calculations could be used to compute the expected cost of business lost due to insufficient capacity or impatient customers.

[6]Frank S. Budnick, Richard Mojena, and Thomas E. Vollman, *Principles of Operations Research for Management* (Homewood, Ill: Irwin, 1977), p. 471.
[7]Ibid., p. 447.

APPLICATION

The Effect of a Truncated Queue

Sally Cook owns several Star Cook sandwich shops in the concourses of a large international airport. Sandwiches are prepared to order in a small kitchen behind the counter. The mean service rate for preparing and wrapping sandwiches and collecting money is one customer per minute. The distributions for the service and interarrival times are negative exponential. Customers arrive at an average rate of 0.75 per minute or 45 per hour. Sally has noticed that the number of persons in the system almost never exceeds four. Apparently travelers at the airport feel that their schedules will not permit their waiting through a longer line for a snack. Those with more time evidently go to a full-service restaurant farther down the concourse.

Sally thinks it will be more profitable to prepare sandwiches ahead of time and maintain a small inventory on the counter so that customers can select items and pay the cashier. Some customers will still ask for special combinations of ingredients, but this prewrapped service method should accommodate most orders and increase the mean service rate to two per minute.

If the capacity—that is, the mean service rate—remains at one per minute, then, from equations 9.10 and 9.11:

$$P_0 = \frac{1 - \lambda/\mu}{1 - (\lambda/\mu)^{N+1}} = \frac{1 - 0.75/1}{1 - (0.75/1)^5} = \frac{0.250}{0.7627} = 0.328$$

$$P_4 = P_o(\lambda/\mu)^4 = 0.328(0.75)^4 = 0.328(0.316) = 0.104.$$

Sally will miss about 10.4 percent of the potential customers. With $\lambda = 45$ customers per hour and each customer spending an average of $3, she is missing $3 (0.104)(45) = $14.04 each hour.

If the service rate is increased to two customers per minute and customers accept the prewrapped sandwiches and continue to arrive at the previous rate, then

$$P_o = \frac{1 - 0.75/2}{1 - (0.75/2)^5} = \frac{0.625}{0.9962} = 0.630$$

$$P_4 = 0.630(0.75/2)^4 = 0.630(0.0198) = 0.0125.$$

With the increased service rate, Sally would lose only 1.25 percent of her potential business because of balking customers. The loss would be reduced to $3(0.0125) \times 45$ customers per hour = $1.69 per hour. This change should increase revenue by $14.04 - $1.69 or $12.35 per hour. Sally is implementing the new service method in two of her shops.

By now it should be apparent that queuing theory is a complex subject. Formulas are available for solution of problems when the arrival patterns and service times follow certain theoretical distributions. Further, these formulas apply only a steady-state conditions, so that there are many queue situations that have no mathematical solutions. Consequently, simulation is sometimes used in solution of queue problems as well as other types of problems. Simulation is discussed in Supplement F at the end of this chapter. We continue our discussion of scheduling nonfactory operations in the next chapter, which deals with project scheduling.

SUMMARY

When service operations attempt to schedule for efficient utilization of their resources, they face some challenges that do not confront the typical manufacturing operation. Service operations often have more contact with customers than do manufacturing operations, and most service operations cannot hold their output in inventory the way that many manufacturing operations can.

Customer contact tends to reduce the degree to which a service operation can standardize its service. When customers are present they can issue special requests and directions while the service is being provided. Some productive capacity can be lost in trying to foster good customer relations. Services can improve the efficiency of their operations by reducing customer contact or by offering only a limited set of choices for the customer. Some services separate their front offices, where customer contact occurs, from their back office operations, where efficiency can be emphasized. When the service is performed on some surrogate for the customer (the equivalent to in-process inventory) jobs can be delayed, batched, or resequenced to achieve better use of resources.

Most service operations, however, cannot hold a ready supply of their "product." These operations have to deal with nonuniform demand in ways that often are different from those available to manufacturers. One strategy that some service companies use is to try to smooth the demand pattern so it will be more uniform. They may maintain a fixed schedule (as do airlines or bus lines); they may work on an appointment basis (as do dentists), so that capacity is used when it becomes available; or they may offer economic incentives to try to shift some demand to nonpeak periods (as do telephone companies).

Operations that cannot use inventory and cannot shift demand to fit their capacity, may try to vary their capacity so that it more closely conforms to demand. Some services use part-time employees; others maintain a group of versatile employees who serve as floating capacity to be moved to the departments where demand is heavy. Some operations subcontract work to persons or companies who furnish personnel and equipment for short-term use. A further option is to provide an alternative form of service, such as drive-through or carry-out service at a fast food restaurant.

Random arrival patterns and random service times make it almost impossible to schedule so that service capacity is fully utilized without having long waiting lines at times. Waiting-line or queueing theory can be used to analyze some capacity options. Formulas provide estimates for the probability that a specified number of units will be waiting for service. These equations can be used under the appropriate conditions to determine how much service capacity and how much waiting space will probably be needed.

SOLVED PROBLEM

PROBLEM:

1. A hospital's emergency room has one physician on duty full-time. Emergency patients arrive according to a Poisson distribution with a mean rate of 2.4 per hour. The physician can provide emergency treatment until another physician arrives for approximately 3.0 patients per hour. The distribution of the physician's time per case is approximately a negative exponential.

   (a) On the average, how much of the physician's time is utilized in providing emergency care?

   (b) How long, on the average, would an emergency patient wait for the physician?

   (c) If the hospital increased the emergency room staff by one more physician per shift (a two-channel system), what would be the physician's utilization in delivery of emergency care?

   (d) With two physicians available, how

long will the average patient wait for a physician? (Begin with L_s from Figure 9.4)

SOLUTION:

1. $\lambda = 2.4$; $\mu = 3$.

   (a) $\rho = \dfrac{2.4}{3} = 0.80$, so the physician should be utilized 80 percent of the time.

   (b) The mean wait before seeing the physician would be $W_q = \dfrac{\lambda}{\mu(\mu - \lambda)} =$

$\dfrac{2.4}{3(3 - 2.4)} = \dfrac{2.4}{1.8} = 1.333$ hours or 80 minutes.

   (c) $\rho = \dfrac{2.4}{2(3)} = 0.40$ or 40 percent utilization.

   (d) L_s (read from graph in Figure 9.4) = 0.95.

$L_q = L_s - \dfrac{\lambda}{\mu} = 0.95 - 0.8 = 0.15$.

$W_q = \dfrac{L_q}{\lambda} = \dfrac{0.15}{2.4} = 0.0625$ hour or 3.75 minutes.

DISCUSSION QUESTIONS

1. What are two major ways in which service operations differ from manufacturing operations that make a difference in the way services can be scheduled to try to achieve good utilization of their resources?
2. How can some service operations try to shape demand to fit their capacity more closely?
3. How can some service operations try to tailor their capacity to conform more closely to a nonuniform demand pattern?
4. How can nonmanufacturing operations utilize the equivalent to in-process inventory even though they cannot maintain an inventory of finished services?

5. Why might a versatile work force be desirable, even though such employees must be paid more than persons who are not so versatile?

6. Why are waiting lines or queues often desirable to some degree?

7. Briefly describe some examples of queuing situations.

8. How does waiting-line theory relate to capacity decisions? How can the theory of multichannel queues be related to capacity decisions? How might truncated queues be related to a capacity decision?

PROBLEMS

1. Vehicles arrive at Speedy Oil and Lube, a single-channel service facility, at a mean rate of five per hour. The service takes an average of eight minutes per vehicle with the current equipment, staffing level, and operating procedures. The interarrival times and service times are distributed according to a negative exponential distribution.

   (a) What is the utilization of the facility?

   (b) What is the average length of the line waiting to get into the service area?
   (c) What is the probability that more than two vehicles will be in the system?

2. The owner of Speedy Oil and Lube does not have room to expand the facility to more than one channel, but a vacuum evacuator to drain oil and other equipment can be purchased that will reduce the mean service

time to six minutes. Make the same computations made in problem 1 to see if this new equipment will significantly change the system's performance.

3. The owner of Speedy Oil and Lube thinks that the mean service time with the new equipment can be reduced to five minutes by relocating equipment and supplies and training the staff in simplified, standardized procedures. Using this service time, recompute the values found in problems 1 and 2, and compare the results.

4. A small branch bank has a single drive-in window. The customer arrival rate is Poisson-distributed with a mean of fourteen customers per hour. Service times are exponentially distributed with a mean of 3.00 minutes per customer.
   (a) Compute the utilization of the window and the teller who services it.
   (b) How long does the average customer who uses the window spend waiting and being served?
   (c) What is the average number of vehicles in the line (including the one being served)?

5. (a) With regard to the drive-in window in problem 4, what is the probability of more than five vehicles in the system?
   (b) If the teller operations were improved so that they required an average of 2.8 minutes per customer, what would be the probability of more than five vehicles in the system?

6. Assume that the bank in problem 4 has room in its drive for only five cars and that arrivals who appear will not wait if the drive is full.
   (a) Find P_0.
   (b) Compare this with P_0 for the problem if no customers are turned away.
   (c) Compute the probability that the queue will be full.

(d) How many customers per hour will be turned away from the drive-in window?

7. The Armstrong Wholesale Grocery Company, discussed in the chapter as an application of a single-channel queue, is considering the option of adding a second loading dock. The arrival rate for trucks is three per hour, and the service rate for a dock will be four per hour. Both the arrival rate and the service rate follow Poisson distributions. The cost of an idle truck is $20 per hour. The labor cost to run the second dock is $8 per hour for each employee, and two employees will be required. Compare the costs of labor and idle trucks for a single dock with the costs if two docks are operated.

8. The San Carlos copper mine operates an ore-loading dock at Tocopilla, Chile. Ships arrive at the dock according to a Poisson distribution with a mean of four ships per week (seven days). The loading time at the dock is distributed according to a negative exponential distribution with a mean of one day per ship.
   (a) What is the mean number of ships waiting to be loaded?
   (b) How long must a ship spend in the system?
   (c) If the cost of an idle day for each ship is $1,000, how many additional docks, if any, should the company add if the average cost of having a dock is $250 per day? (Use Figure 9.4.)

9. Users of a photocopy machine in a local office arrive according to a Poisson distribution and wait until they obtain the copies they desire. The mean arrival rate is eight users per hour. The service times are exponentially distributed, with a mean service rate of fifteen users per hour.
   (a) What is the utilization of the equipment?

(b) Find the expected number of users in the line.

(c) Find the expected number of users in the system.

(d) What is the cost per 8-hour day for detaining persons to use the copier if the average user's time is estimated to be worth $10 per hour?

10. How much expense for employees' time would be saved by the company in problem 9 if the copy machine could be replaced by a faster one that provided a mean service rate of twenty per hour?

11. On the basis of a traffic count, it is estimated that the number of vehicles using an automatic carwash at a particular location would average eleven per hour. A Poisson distribution is assumed. The owner of the property is considering construction of a carwash and is considering two types of equipment. The first type of equipment is a spray wand that the customer holds and directs while standing outside the vehicle. The service rate for this type of equipment is distributed according to a Poisson distribution with a mean rate of twelve cars per hour for each stall. The second type of equipment is automatically controlled, with a series of spray nozzles that revolve around the car while the driver remains inside. The service rate for this equipment is constant, with a capacity for twelve cars per hour for each stall. The potential carwash owner feels that with an arrival rate of eleven and a service rate of twelve, there will be an average of about one car in the system even if the capacity is large enough that customers will not have to wait in queue.

(a) If manually controlled equipment is selected, what is the minimum number of stalls that should be constructed to achieve about one car in the system under steady-state conditions?

(b) If the automatic equipment is selected, what is the minimum number of stalls that should be built to achieve about one car in the system under steady-state conditions?

(c) What other factors do you think should be considered in the equipment-selection decision?

BIBLIOGRAPHY

Chase, Richard B. "Where Does the Customer Fit In a Service Operation?" *Harvard Business Review,* November–December 1978, pp. 137–142.

Fitzsimmons, James A., and Robert S. Sullivan. *Service Operations Management.* New York: McGraw-Hill, 1982.

Industrial Engineering, January 1983—several articles on service operations.

Mabert, Vincent A. "A Case Study of Encoder Shift Scheduling Under Uncertainty." *Management Science,* July 1979, pp. 623–631.

———, **and Michael J. Showalter.** *Cases in Operations Management.* Plano, Tex.: Business Publications, 1984.

———, **and Charles A. Watts.** "A Simulation Analysis of Tour-Shift Construction Procedures." *Management Science,* May 1982, pp. 520–532.

Sasser, W. Earl, R. Paul Olsen, and D. Daryl Wycoff. *Management of Service Organizations—Text, Cases, and Readings.* Boston: Allyn and Bacon, 1978.

KEY TERMS

Simulation	Hawthorne effect	Attributes	Validation
Steady-state conditions	Face validity	Activities	Statistical comparisons
Non-steady-state conditions	Entities	Stochastic parts of a model	Monte Carlo simulation

Supplement F

SIMULATION

Simulation is more than a single technique. Because a broad variety of models and techniques can be employed in simulation studies it is an approach to problem solving. *Simulation* is the process of experimentation with a model of some real system or situation in order to gain understanding of or solve a problem in the real world. Expressed another way, simulation is a means of gaining artificial experience through the use of a model that gives the appearance or effect of reality. The model is used to generate synthetic data that depict the real system's performance. The model is advanced through time to see what can be expected to occur in the real system under the conditions set for the simulated trial. A simulation model is usually applied to evaluate alternative actions and determine which action probably would be most effective in the real situation.

Because many aspects of the real world might be studied and a model can be anything that is used to represent some part of reality, the potential types and applications of simulation are almost endless. The phenomenon of interest can be a continuous variable, such as the path of a missile in flight, or it can be discrete, such as the number of patrons seated in a fast food restaurant. A simulation model might be physical, as when real water is made to flow through a small-scale replica of a geographical area to study flood control problems, or the model might be a set of mathematical equations that describe the behavior of some characteristics of the real system as a function of the conditions that might occur. Simple simulations can be performed manually, but most utilize a computer. If analog computers are used, certain voltages or amperages in the computer can be used to represent the values of continuous variables in the real system. Usually digital computers are used, and the values of real variables are stored as numerical data. Since the types of simulations that seem most useful in operations management and that are most frequently discussed in the operations management literature are discrete simulations using digital computers, the simulations illustrated in this supplement use digital values for the variables.

ADVANTAGES OF SIMULATION

Simulation can be used for seemingly intractable problems, ones that are too difficult or complex to solve mathematically. Analytical solutions to some issues may not be achievable. Analytical models of the system may not be available, or the model may be so complex as to defy arriving at the optimal solution. Trial-and-error simulations may, however, lead to a near-optimal solution.

Simulation can be a valuable training tool. Through it, a person can gain a better understanding of the system's performance than he or she could achieve by merely solving an equation for the optimal value. An optimization formula may apply only under *steady-state conditions*, but because the actual environment for a system may vary over time, it is often the *non-steady-state conditions* that bear investigating. A bank, for example, might have very high customer arrival rates at certain periods of the day, such as lunchtime and just before closing time, which would increase the need for tellers at the counter during these parts of the day.

Simulation permits study of a system under controlled conditions. A model is not subject to the *Hawthorne effect*, whereby people's behavior is modified because they are being studied. The investigator can select the variables to be changed and the extent to which they are changed. Results can be obtained for various combinations of environmental conditions and internal operation policies that might not occur in the real environment within a reasonable time. Simulation can then project conditions that might occur in the future so that a company can prepare for them.

Simulation may be less expensive and involve less risk to people, property, or a business than actual experimentation. It is often less expensive to change a replica than it is to change some aspects of the real world. If some alternative leads to failure or serious damage to the real system, it would be expensive or even impossible to restore the original conditions so that another alternative could be tried. If actual customers or employees are lost, they may never return to give you a second chance.

Simulation can expand or compress time to provide a more detailed review of events. Data from several years' performance can be simulated and the effects of alternatives can be compared without the delay and the distortions that can occur when one relies on people's long-term memory to recall what outcome resulted from a particular set of conditions. Simulation has also been used to slow chemical or physical phenomena that occur in only a fraction of a second, so that more details can be observed.

LIMITATIONS AND CAUTIONS

A simulation model is a formalized set of assumptions about how the real system behaves. To be workable, the model must give a sufficiently reliable picture of the system that it is assumed to represent. There are obvious dangers in using decisions based on faulty assumptions—whether those assumptions are a simulation model, intuitive mental impressions, or a mathematical optimization model. Simulation models can hide many critical assumptions. It is advisable to document assumptions so that persons who are familiar with the real system can evaluate the *face validity* of the model—that is, the appropriateness of the assumptions and the logic of the model.

Simulation does not optimize; it just shows what the model says would result if a certain alternative were tried under a particular set of conditions. Simulation studies do not guarantee that the best solution will be found. Even with an accurate or valid model there is a danger that the investigator will not try the alternatives that would provide the greatest benefit.

Even if simulation would lead to the best alternative, there might be times when the benefit-cost ratio of a simulation study would make simulation inadvisable. Simulation studies can be very expensive. Development and analysis of a simulation study may require extensive field research, which is time-consuming and expensive. Ideally, there should be a reasonable assurance that the potential benefits of a study will justify the expense, and sufficient funds should be available to conduct a proper study before a simulation study is initiated.

METHODOLOGY FOR SIMULATION

A simulation study involves several stages of activities. The stages that are most likely to occur are shown schematically in Figure F.1 and are discussed in the following material. Some of the stages may be repeated if subsequent stages reveal the need for further consideration in a prior stage.

1. Define the Problem

If you know what you are looking for, you are more likely to find it. The objectives of the study should be defined.

2. Analyze Costs and Benefits

Since simulation can be expensive, it is advisable to review the probable costs and possible benefits of a study before proceeding too far. Some solution method other than simulation might be quicker or less expensive to use. The remaining steps would occur if a simulation study is found to be desirable.

3. Abstract the Real System into a Model

Define the boundaries of the system to be modeled. The system will contain certain *entities,* or components, which are objects of interest in the system. A customer who enters a bank might be an entity.

Each entity can have *attributes,* which are properties of the entity. An attribute of a bank customer might be the type of business he or

FIGURE F.1

Likely Activities in Simulation

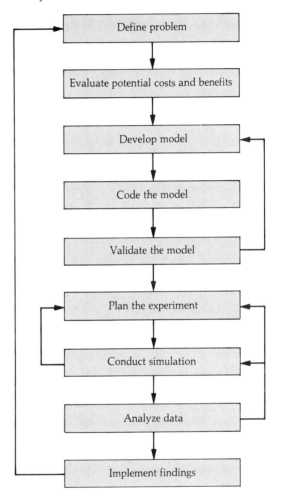

she will transact. The types of *activities* that occur in the system (such as a customer making a bank deposit) should be defined. The activities can cause some change in the state of the system and can affect several interrelated components.

In the development of a simulation model, symbols or objects are chosen to represent the relevant components of the system, and interactions between the components are expressed in some logical, perhaps mathematical, form. The result should be a reasonably close representation of the real system, yet be simple enough to understand and manipulate. Only in this way can the state of the real system be predicted under dynamic conditions. A conflict arises because of the opposing desires to simplify the model yet achieve a good approximation of the real system.

Several approximations can be used to simplify the model. Sometimes two or more components can be combined to reduce the number of components in the system. The mathematical relationships between components can be approximated by less complex functions. For example, within the range over which the variable will be studied, a linear function might be used as a reasonable approximation of the actual relationship, which is mathematically more complex. Sometimes deterministic relationships are used to simplify *stochastic parts of a model* (i.e., parts with values that experience random variation). The model builder must determine where simplifications can be made without losing details that are important in the real system.

4. Code the Model

For computer simulation, the model must be expressed in language that is acceptable to the computer. Several higher-order simulation languages such as GPSS, DYNAMO, and SIM-SCRIPT have been developed for this purpose. Use of a special language can save time, and programs in these languages are more flexible. Simulation languages also provide a standardized terminology for conceptualizing and communicating about systems. The advantage of flexibility provided by a general simulation language may, however, make the computer-run time more expensive.

5. Validate the Model

Unless the model gives results that are adequate approximations of what would occur in the real system, simulation can lead to the wrong answers. *Validation* is achieving a sufficient level of confidence that the model does provide an adequate representation of reality.

There is no single test to prove that a model is 100 percent valid. Face validity can be established by asking people who are familiar with the real system to evaluate the assumptions and results of the model. *Statistical comparisons* of the outputs for the model and the real system under identical inputs can also be made to test the model's accuracy. Goodness-of-fit tests such as the chi square or the Kolmogorov-Smirnov test can be used to compare a distribution of values from the simulation to one from the actual system.

6. Plan the Experiment

The objective of an investigation is usually to learn something about the performance of the real system. Good experimental design should provide a strategy for gathering evidence that will allow inferences to be drawn about the behavior of certain variables. The experiments should determine the variability of the process and make decisions about sample sizes and replications to achieve the desired confidence intervals. Studies often involve sensitivity analysis in which certain parameters are systematically varied over a range of values to determine the extent to which these changes affect the response. The ideal is to obtain the desired information with the least experimentation necessary.

7. Conduct the Study and Collect Data

The types of data to be collected depend on the objectives of the study and the types of analyses to be conducted. During the experimental design phase, the investigators must decide what data should be collected and how much detail is needed. It could be expensive to repeat part of the simulation runs because insufficient data were kept. The model should be programmed so that it collects and summarizes the data needed to analyze the experiment. The model is then stepped through time with parameters set at the desired values, and data are recorded. Parameters may be varied one at a time or in various combinations to gain data from the model. Good experimental design may permit the effect of individual parameters to be determined even though two or more are changed at the same time.

8. Analyze Data and Draw Conclusions

The design of an experiment and the type of analyses that will be performed are related. One should design the experiment with analysis in mind. Tests of statistical significance and confidence intervals can sometimes be constructed to draw inferences from the simulation data. It is advisable to recognize the variability of results that can occur even under conditions that are more closely controlled than the real system can be controlled.

9. Document and Implement the Findings

The value of a simulation model does not end after the first application. True validation of a model occurs over time if actual results are like those the simulation model predicted. A model can become even more valuable after it has been validated by a comparison of its data with actual data. Models that have potential for future use should be documented to record their features, assumptions, and operating procedures so that they can be employed correctly in the future.

The real payoff from a simulation study is that it prevents errors or leads to improved actions in the real system. Although executives usually do not design and construct simulation models, those executives who will decide whether to use simulation results should be involved in the early stages when objectives are defined, and they should be kept abreast of assumptions and findings during the study. These executives are more likely to understand and have confidence in the model and, consequently, are more likely to use simulation data.

MONTE CARLO SIMULATION

Monte Carlo simulation involves the use of some chance process to determine the value assigned to a probabilistic variable during a run of the simulation. For example, if a book is as likely to be checked out of a library as it is to be on the shelf, one could flip a coin to determine which of these two states will be assumed to exist during a simulated call by a library patron. If the probability is 0.30 that the book is not available, then "out" could be printed on three slips of paper and "available" printed on seven slips, and one of these slips could be randomly selected. Some other chance process such as spinning a roulette wheel or rolling dice could be used to set values for a variable. A more common method of selecting a value for a variable, particularly during computer simulation, involves the use of a random number table or a random number generator. A cumulative probability distribution is used to convert the random number to a value of the variable. The following application illustrates the use of random numbers to determine the values of both discrete and continuous variables in a simulation.

APPLICATION

Example of Monte Carlo Simulation

The Mid-American Grain Company plans to locate a small depot in Iowa to receive and store the grain brought in from local farms by truck before it is shipped out

FIGURE F.2

Flow Diagram for Simulation of Daily Grain Accumulation

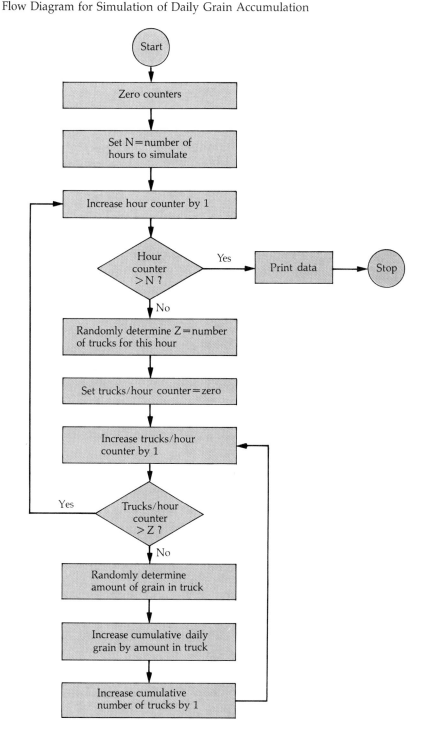

by rail. To determine the capacity required in the facility and to plan how many rail cars to schedule to the depot, the company must know how much grain is likely to arrive during each day of the harvest season. The company wants to simulate the distribution of grain received each day based on a discrete distribution of the number of trucks that arrive each day and a continuous probability distribution of the load in each truck. A flow diagram of the simulation model for this study is shown in Figure F.2.

The Monte Carlo technique is used to select values for the number of trucks that arrive in each hour and to select the amount of grain in each truck. The probability is 0.10 that one truck will arrive, 0.60 that two trucks will arrive, and 0.30 that three trucks will arrive during an hour of a typical harvest day. These data are displayed in a less-than-cumulative probability distribution as shown in Figure F.3. The increase in height of the graph at each possible number of trucks is proportional to the probability that this particular number of trucks will arrive during the hour. A two-digit random number is selected to represent a value of the cumulative probability, and the value of the simulation variable that corresponds to this cumulative probability, is assumed to have occurred. If the random number is 00 through 09, the value of *one truck* is assumed to occur during the hour to be simulated. If random number of 10 through 69 occurs, *two trucks* is

FIGURE F.3

Cumulative Probability of the Number of Trucks That Arrive in One Hour

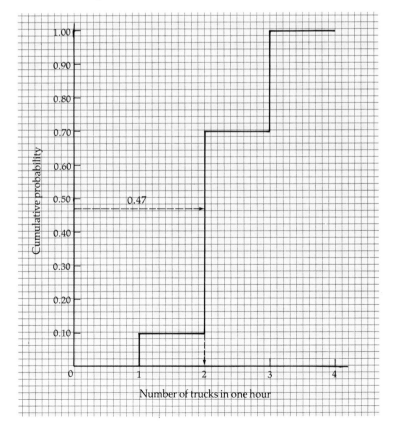

assumed; if a random number of 70 through 99 occurs, *three trucks* is assumed. This procedure causes the relative frequencies to occur randomly in the proper ratios, if the random numbers are uniformly distributed. The value of *two trucks* should occur six times as often as *one truck* and twice as often as *three trucks*. The random number 47 was generated, so it was assumed that two trucks arrived during the first hour, as shown in Figure F.3.

The next question that must be answered is, how much grain was in each truck? The quantity of grain on a truck can vary continuously between 50 and 350 bushels. A cumulative probability distribution for the amount of grain in a truck is shown in Figure F.4. Notice that the curve is steeper between 250 and 300 bushels, so truckloads in this range are more likely to occur. A first random number of 38 was generated, so it was assumed that the first truck delivered 230 bushels. A second random number of 67 was generated, so it was assumed that the second truck delivered 280 bushels of grain. Thus during the first simulated hour the depot received a total of 510 bushels of grain.

FIGURE F.4

Cumulative Probability Distribution of the Amount of Grain in a Truckload

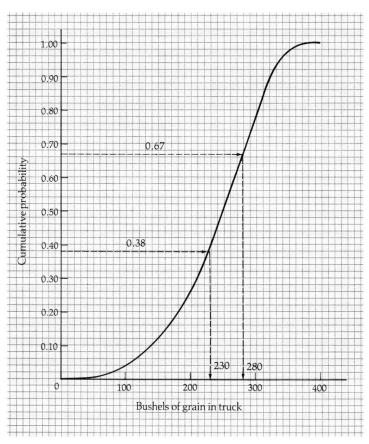

The process outlined in the flow chart of Figure F.2 is continued until the number of hours the depot will be operated during a day, say ten, have been simulated. This provides an estimate of the amount of grain received during one day. A sizable sample of fifty or more days of operation might be simulated to produce the distribution of possible daily receipts of grain. The distribution of grain receipts per day could then be used in planning requirements for operating the depot.

The simulation procedure described in the application could be programmed on a computer to reduce the tedious repetition of many trials. When a computer is used, points along the cumulative distribution can be stored in memory, and the computer can be programmed to generate values of the random number and translate these into values of a simulation variable. The computer could also be programmed to assist in data collection and analysis by collecting statistics from the simulation runs and carrying out various analyses. Obviously, a simulation study could require a large amount of programming time if special-purpose simulation languages such as GPSS, MAP/1, SIMSCRIPT, Q GERT, and GEMS were not available.

GPSS (General Purpose System Simulator) is a commonly used simulation language that is easily applied to queuing situations. Figure F.5 is an example of simple GPSS program used to simulate bank customers arriving and being served at a single drive-in teller window. Some of the summary data normally provided as part of a GPSS output from the run are also included in the figure.

The function statement at the top of Figure F.5 describes for the computer the probability distribution that should be used when function 1 (i.e., FN1) is called. It states that 24 points on a continuous distribution follow, and the coordinates along the curve are then shown. Nine blocks are then shown in the model segment of the program.

Block 1 generates customers with inter-arrival times equal to 4 minutes times a random value for FN1. This simulation is conducted with time units equal to 0.01 minute, so 4 minutes appears as 400 time units. Block 2 places the customers in the queue (queue 1), where they will remain until the teller (facility 1) is available. When the teller is available, block 3 causes the teller to be occupied with a new customer and simultaneously block 4 causes this customer to depart queue 1.

Block 5 says the customer can advance after a service time equal to 3 minutes multiplied by a value randomly selected from FN1. Block 6 then releases facility 1 (the teller) and block 7 "terminates" the customer, i.e., takes the customer out of the simulation.

Segment 2 of the program tells the computer to simulate 480 minutes and terminate the simulation run. The program automatically calls for printout of the type of data shown below the simulation model. Obviously it is much easier to write a program such as the one shown in Figure F.5 than to write one from scratch in a language such as FORTRAN.

Simulation is often used to study more complex situations and provide data under a variety of circumstances. Consider a bank, savings and loan association, or credit union with numerous teller stations. The customer arrival rate will probably vary during the day and from day to day. Management may want to study various conditions to determine the preferred staffing levels under particular demand levels. Table F.1 provides information from such a study in a credit union. Numerous

FIGURE F.5

Example of GPSS Program and Output

```
    1       FUNCTION    RN1     G24
  0         0           .1          .104        .2          .222
  .3        .355        .4          .509        .5          .69
  .6        .915        .7          1.2         .75         1.38
  .8        1.6         .84         1.83        .88         2.12
  .9        2.3         .92         2.52        .94         2.81
  .95       2.99        .96         3.2         .97         3.5
  .98       3.9         .99         4.6         .995        5.3
  .998      6.2         .999        7           .9998       8
  *
  *       MODEL   SEGMENT   1
  *
  1       GENERATE    400     FN1
  2       QUEUE       1
  3       SEIZE       1
  4       DEPART      1
  5       ADVANCE     300     FN1
  6       RELEASE     1
  7       TERMINATE
  *
  *       MODEL SEGMENT   2
  *
  8       GENERATE    48000
  9       TERMINATE   1
  *
```

QUEUE	MAXIMUM CONTENTS	AVERAGE CONTENTS	TOTAL ENTRIES	ZERO ENTRIES	PERCENT ZEROS
TELLQ	9	1.275	113	34	30.0

$AVERAGE TIME/TRANS = AVERAGE TIME/TRANS EXCLUDING ZERO ENTRIES

AVERAGE TIME/TRANS	AVERAGE TIME/TRANS
541.610	774.708

FACILITY	AVERAGE UTILIZATION	NUMBER ENTRIES	AVERAGE TIME/TRAN	SEIZING TRANS. NO.
TELLR	.725	113	308.256	5

other applications of simulation studies are possible, and some are mentioned in the following section.

APPLICATIONS OF SIMULATION

Applications of simulation extend to agriculture, government, military activities, education, sports, engineering and scientific research, social sciences, and business functions other than operations.[1] Simulation has been used in corporate planning to consider broad business issues involving all functional areas.

[1]See, for example, L. Dekka, ed., *Simulation Systems—Eighth AICA Congress* (Amsterdam: North-Holland, 1977).

Table F.1
RESULTS OF SIMULATED TELLER QUEUES UNDER VARYING DEMAND CONDITIONS

Mean Interarrival Time	No. of Tellers	Maximum Content of Any Line	Mean Length of Lines	Members Served (total)	Percent Members Not Waiting	Mean Waiting Time For All Members (min.)	Mean Waiting Time For Those Who Had To Wait (min.)	Mean Transaction Time (min.)
Super-light (1.5 min.)	5*	1	0.04	1643	91.9	0.29	3.57	3.41
	4*	2	0.14	1660	77.1	0.82	3.58	3.38
	3*	4	0.52	1606	50.7	2.32	4.71	3.29
	2*	61	35.40	1590	0.3	106.90	107.20	3.24
Light (.93 min.)	6*	2	0.09	2618	85.0	0.49	3.26	3.22
	5*	5	0.29	2565	69.0	1.33	4.30	3.28
	4	17	4.14	2652	17.0	14.97	18.05	3.36
	3	74	43.10	—	2.1	112.50	114.90	3.22
Medium (.70 min.)	7*	3	0.20	3474	76.3	0.97	4.09	3.37
	6*	5	0.54	3498	56.4	2.22	5.09	3.31
	5	17	6.82	3437	6.1	23.81	25.38	3.44
	4	55	27.00	—	2.8	72.58	74.69	3.34
Heavy (.48 min.)	9*	3	0.25	5053	71.6	1.08	3.83	3.33
	8*	5	0.90	5124	41.5	3.36	5.74	3.33
	7	37	22.45	5145	1.7	73.30	74.58	3.40
Very heavy (.34 min.)	11*	3	0.67	7141	44.9	2.48	4.51	3.34
	10	13	6.21	7142	4.7	20.87	21.92	3.35

*Designates conditions that meet management's acceptable waiting criteria.

Source: George Overstreet, Khris McAlister, and James Dilworth, "A Study in Waiting Line Patterns," Credit Union Executive, Autumn 1979, p. 14.

Applications of simulation in the operations function cover a broad variety of issues in both manufacturing and nonmanufacturing settings. Several applications are mentioned below to illustrate the versatility of simulation methodology and some of the types of applications in which simulation might be beneficial. These applications are illustrative and only begin to show some of the uses of simulation.

Simulation is often the tool selected for the analysis of queuing situations because of the complexity of many queuing problems and because analysts frequently want data for non-steady-state conditions. A wide variety of situations can be formulated as queuing problems. Assembly line balancing problems and conveyor system design studies can be thought of as a problem of a series of queues that feed each other. Work-in-process inventory, or backlogs, can be considered as objects waiting in queues. Simulation can be used to evaluate proposed changes in routings, equipment additions or deletions, and various scheduling or sequencing methods.

Determination of capacity, in terms of manpower and equipment, can be viewed in many situations as adjustments to service rates so that queues will probably remain within acceptable limits. Studies of materials handling systems are quite similar, but the focus is on the volume that flows between processes and the queue capacity that must be provided at each location where the movement of items may be delayed.

Because job shops are so complex and challenging, much of the simulation research on manufacturing systems has involved job shop simulation. A job shop is a series of work centers with queues in front of them. The flow patterns between work centers may have dynamic variation. Simulation studies can be used to determine the proper capacity for each work center, but more often the studies seek to identify a dispatching rule that will optimize the operation according to some criterion. It is unlikely, in the author's view, that one rule will be best for all of the sets of problems that arise in dispatching.

Maintenance operations are often viewed as queuing problems, with the breakdown of a machine considered an arrival that waits in queue until it is repaired. The distribution of times to make repairs is considered as service times. The machine down time is studied to evaluate the effects of changes in the number of maintenance workers or in the way priorities are assigned to jobs that are waiting, or the effect of other decisions.

William Ledbetter and James Cox reported the use of operations research techniques in 176 companies on the 1975 Fortune 500 list.[2] Seventy-three respondents said they applied simulation in at least one area in the production function. The most common areas of application and the percentage of the 73 respondents that used simulation in these areas

are shown in Table F.2. (The percentages do not add to 100 percent because some companies applied simulation to more than one area.) These percentages give some indication of the relative application of simulation within the production functions of these companies.

Many of the nonmanufacturing applications of simulation described in the literature involve service scheduling and personnel deployment. A large percentage of these apply to health care. Simulation has been used to predict the number of nurses needed in each type of unit within a hospital. It has been used to determine the optimal mix of an obstetrical anesthesia team[3] and dental care delivery teams.[4] The effects of patient scheduling procedures have been studied.

Table F.2
SPECIFIC AREA OF SIMULATION APPLICATION WITHIN THE PRODUCTION FUNCTION

Application Area	Percent of Respondents Using in the Area
Inventory Analysis and Control	37
Production Scheduling	36
Logistics	33
Plant Location	32
Plant Layout	26
Production Planning and Control	25
Equipment Acquisition and Replacement	15
Project Acquisition and Replacement	12
Maintenance and Repair	11
Other	10

Source: Ledbetter and Cox, 1977, p. 21.

[2]William N. Ledbetter and James F. Cox, "Are OR Techniques Being Used?" *Industrial Engineering*, February 1977, pp. 19–21.

[3]A. Riesman et al., "On the Design of Alternative Obstetric Anesthesia Team Configurations," *Management Science*, February 1977, pp. 545–556.

[4]James B. Dilworth and Walter J. Pelton, "Computer Simulation of a Dental Practice Using Therapists," *Journal of Dental Education*, June 1972, pp. 35–39.

Materials handling in a hospital has been studied through simulation.[5] One system that was studied consisted of a series of rectangular buggies traveling on a conveyor that connected all parts of the hospital, used to transport drugs, meals, linens, trash, etc. The simulation study was done before the actual conveyor was installed to evaluate different configurations of design in order to avoid bottlenecks, delays, or shortages and to keep costs at reasonable levels.

One nonmanufacturing application described a simulation of the New York Bulk Mail Center.[6] Loads of more than 150,000 sacks of bulk mail and 500,000 parcels per day were simulated. Entities included in the system were trucks, docks, parcel sorters, sack sorters, parcels conveyor containers, and sacks of mail. Three levels of volume were considered: an average level, a Christmas season level (about 25 percent higher than the average), and a peak-day level (about 50 percent higher than the average). The purpose of the study was to provide suggestions for the design of the actual facility and to predict how the system would perform under various loads, with or without certain equipment malfunctions. The simulation showed the percentage of time that equipment was utilized, how much overtime was required to process the specified level of mail, and what queues or delays occurred. The simulation also provided useful operational information about the probable effects of scheduling decisions and resource allocations.

Simulation is well suited to analysis of the inventory levels at various locations in a large-scale distribution system.[7] Various stocking policies, such as the location of safety stock and the quantities to be ordered, can be simulated. The cost of transferring items between locations and other options can also be evaluated. Still more examples could be mentioned, but the ones that have already been described show the versatility of simulation.

SUMMARY

This supplement has provided an overview of simulation, primarily in the context of operations. Some of the advantages and limitations of simulation were reviewed.

A simulation study can involve at least nine stages, some of which may be repeated. These are definition of the problem, justifying the cost of the study, abstracting the model, coding the model, validation of the model, planning a simulation experiment, conducting the study and collecting data, analyzing the data, and documenting and implementing the study.

Monte Carlo simulation was reviewed and illustrated. The Monte Carlo technique is frequently used to generate random values of variables with the probabilities considered to exist in the real system. The technique frequently involves using a cumulative probability distribution for the variable of interest and some random number generator to select values from the distribution of possible values. Monte Carlo simulation often is very useful in analysis of operations. Several applications of simulation in manufacturing and nonmanufacturing settings were described to show the breadth of its applicability.

[5]*Digest of the Second Annual Conference on Applications of Simulation,* New York, December 1968, pp. 262–265.

[6]Orlino C. Baldonado, "Computer Simulation of Mail Flow Through the New York Bulk Mail Center," *Progress in Simulation, Vol. 3, Record of Proceedings, 6th Annual Simulation Symposium:* Joseph G. Sowa, John A. Bolan and Ronald Newmaster, eds. Annual Simulation Symposium, Tampa, Florida, 1973, pp. 165–183.

[7]Michael M. Conners et al., "The Distribution System Simulator," *Management Science,* April 1972, pp. B425–B453.

DISCUSSION QUESTIONS

1. Define simulation.
2. Outline the steps that might be involved in a simulation study.
3. Briefly describe five possible advantages of simulation.
4. Briefly describe four types of situations in manufacturing operations that can be studied by using simulation.
5. Briefly describe four types of situations in nonmanufacturing operations that can be studied by using simulation.
6. Why is there no guarantee that a simulation study will determine an optimal solution to a problem or an optimal set of conditions for the system that is being studied?
7. Discuss some of the trade-offs that must be considered in deciding how detailed and realistic to make a simulation model.
8. In a simulation study, how can the investigator determine when enough observations have probably been made with a particular set of values for the model's parameters?
9. Briefly describe the procedure used in Monte Carlo simulation to select simulated values of a discrete random variable with the same probabilities that were observed in the actual system.
10. Is great proficiency in computer programming necessary for the use of computer simulation? Why?

PROBLEMS

1. (a) Compute the expected value for the number of trucks that arrive in one hour at the Mid-American Grain Company presented as an application within the supplement.

$$\mu = \Sigma[X \cdot P(X)].$$

   (b) Obtain the first twenty two-digit random numbers given at the extreme left of Appendix IV. Use Figure F.3 to convert these random numbers to twenty values of the number of trucks that arrive per hour. What is the mean of these values?

   (c) By what percentage does the value in b differ from the value in a?

2. The time (rounded to the nearest ten minutes) between customer arrivals at a small appliance repair center are distributed according to the following distribution.

Time	Probability
10	0.10
20	0.15
30	0.25
40	0.20
50	0.15
60	0.10
70	0.05

   (a) Calculate the mean of this distribution by

$$\mu = \Sigma[X \cdot P(X)].$$

   (b) Construct a less-than-or-equal cumulative probability distribution suitable for use in Monte Carlo simulation.

   (c) Make a table showing the range of two-digit random numbers that would result in the use of each of the seven time values.

3. Appendix IV contains five major columns of random numbers, each of which contains four two-digit columns. Use the first two digits on the left in the middle major column. Begin at the top of the column of random numbers and translate them into service times by use of the probability distribution constructed in part (b) of problem 2. Each time an observation is obtained, compute the mean of all observations thus far. Continue taking observations until five

consecutive values of the estimated mean remain within ±2 percent of the true mean calculated in part (a) of problem 2.

(a) How many random observations were required to meet this criterion?

(b) Is there a danger from reaching a conclusion regarding steady-state conditions of a system based on only a few runs of a simulation model?

4. Use values from the cumulative Poisson distribution with $\lambda = 2$ as provided in Appendix III. Construct a graph of these values for use with random numbers as the technique for generating random observations. Use the first twenty-five three-digit random numbers found in the right-hand three digits of the middle major column in Appendix IV to obtain twenty-five random observations of the variable.

(a) What is the mean of these twenty-five observations?

(b) By what percentage does this mean differ from the $\lambda = 2$ for the original distribution?

5. Repeat the procedure for problem 4, using the last twenty-five three-digit random numbers in the columns used for problem 4.

(a) What is the mean of these observations?

(b) By what percentage does the mean of the observations differ from $\lambda = 2$ for the original distribution?

(c) Combine the means from problem 4 and this problem to get a mean based on fifty observations. By what percentage does this mean differ from the original $\lambda = 2$?

6. (a) Perform a simulation to determine the amount of grain received in an eight-hour day by the Mid-American Grain Company presented as an application within the supplement. Use the cumulative probability distributions presented in Figures F.3 and F.4, and se-

lect consecutive two-digit random numbers starting any place you select in the random number table.

(b) Compare your results with those of your classmates, and construct a frequency distribution of the daily amounts that were obtained by the class.

7. A distribution center supplies three company outlets. The probability distributions for weekly demand at the three outlets are given below.

(a) Simulate the demand at the distribution center for each week of a twenty-week period, and calculate the mean weekly demand. From Apendix IV, use the top twenty numbers in the left-hand column of two-digit random numbers for the first outlet, the column next to it for the second outlet, etc.

(b) Construct a table showing the frequencies of different levels of total weekly demand at the distribution center.

(c) Compute the mean weekly demand at the distribution center.

OUTLET 1

Weekly Demand	Probability
60	0.20
70	0.40
80	0.30
90	0.10

OUTLET 2

Weekly Demand	Probability
90	0.15
100	0.35
110	0.30
120	0.15
130	0.05

OUTLET 3

Weekly Demand	Probability
50	0.15
60	0.35
70	0.35
80	0.15

8. (a) Compute the mean demand at each outlet and sum them. Compare this mean to the mean obtained in problem 7 above.

   (b) Construct a cumulative probability distribution for weekly demand at the distribution center. If the lead time to restock the distribution center is one week, how much stock should be on hand at the beginning of the week to provide a 90 percent service level?

9. Suppose that the lead time for the distribution center in problem 8 can be either two, three, or four weeks with these probabilities:

Lead Time (weeks)	Probability
2	0.35
3	0.40
4	0.25

   (a) Simulate the amount of demand that occurs at the distribution center for twenty lead times, by using the weekly demand distribution constructed in problem 8 and the information above. Use the two-digit column at the left of Appendix IV, starting at the top, to generate the length of the lead time. Use the two-digit column at the right of Appendix IV to select weekly demand values from the cumulative probability distribution developed in problem 8.

   (b) What amount of the product should be on hand at the beginning of a lead time to provide a probability of 0.90 that stock will not run out?

10. Customers arrive at a small appliance repair shop with interarrival times given by the distribution in problem 2. A customer is there when the shop opens, and new customers are accepted for 7½ hours. The appliances are repaired while the customer waits, with a constant service time of thirty minutes. The shop will remain open until all appliances are repaired. Use the leftmost two digits in the middle major column of Appendix IV, beginning at the top of the column, to obtain the interarrival times for a day of operation.

    (a) Determine the idle time and percent utilization of the service capacity.

    (b) Determine the maximum length of the queue and the average time each customer spends waiting in the queue.

    (c) Compute the mean time waiting in the queue for just those customers who had to wait.

11. A two-stage assembly line is balanced with the expected time at each station equal to four minutes. Assume that the time at each station has a probability of 0.30 that three minutes will be required for the operation and a 0.30 probability that five minutes will be required for the operation.

    (a) Simulate the passage of twenty objects through these two stages of the line. Start at the top of the left major column of the random number table in Appendix IV. Use the two left-hand digits to determine the time on the first station and the two right-hand digits to determine the time at the second station. When the run is begun there will be a job at each station. The first job on the first station will become the second job on the second station.

    (b) Determine the idle time and length of the queue at the second work station.

BIBLIOGRAPHY

Annual Simulation Symposium, *Record of Proceedings,* 1968 through present, Tampa, Florida.

Dekka, L., ed. *Simulation of Systems—Eighth AICA Congress.* Amsterdam: North-Holland, 1977.

Fryer, John A. "Effects of Shop Size and Labor Flexibility in Labor and Machine Limited Production Systems." *Management Science,* January 1975, pp. 507–515.

Godwin, Victor B. "The Dollars and Sense of Simulation." *Decision Science,* April 1976, pp. 312–342.

Gordon, Geoffrey. *System Simulation.* Englewood Cliffs, N.J.: Prentice-Hall, 1969.

Schmidt, J. W., and R. E. Taylor. *Simulation and Analysis of Industrial Systems.* Homewood, Ill.: Irwin, 1970.

Schriber, Thomas J. *Simulation Using GPSS.* New York: Wiley, 1974.

Shannon, Robert E. *Systems Simulation—The Art and Science.* Englewood Cliffs, N.J.: Prentice-Hall, 1975.

KEY TERMS

Project	Program Evaluation and Review Technique (PERT)	Activity-on-arrow (AOA)	Free float
Planning or feasibility phase		Event	Forward pass
Organization phase	Critical Path Method (CPM)	Predecessor activity	Backward pass
Execution phase	Activity	Successor activity	Merge activity
Termination phase	Network	Dummy activity	Burst activity
Work breakdown structure (WBS)	Precedence relationship	Critical path	Optimistic time
Matrix organization	Activity-on-node (AON)	Float or slack	Pessimistic time
			Most likely time

Chapter 10

SCHEDULING AND CONTROLLING PROJECTS

A *project* is an organized endeavor to accomplish a specified, nonroutine or low-volume task. Although projects are not repetitive, they take significant amounts of time to complete and are large-scale or complex enough to be recognized and managed as separate undertakings. Generally, the involvement of an individual or work center in a project is for a longer duration than it would be in a typical manufacturing assignment. Some examples of projects are listed below.

Implementing a new computer system.

Introducing a new product.

Producing an airplane, missile, or large machine.

Opening a new store.

Constructing a bridge, dam, highway, or building.

Relocating an office or a factory.

Performing major maintenance or repair.

Starting up a new manufacturing or service facility.

Instituting a reorganization.

PROJECT MANAGEMENT

Management of a project differs in several ways from management of a typical business. The objective of a project team is to accomplish its assigned mission and disband. Few businesses aim to perform just one job and then cease to exist. Since a project is intended to have a finite life, employees are seldom hired with the intent of building a career with the project. Instead, a project team is pulled together on an ad hoc basis from persons who normally have assignments in other parts of the organization. Persons may be assigned to work full-time with the project until its completion; or they may work only part of their time, such as two days a week, on the project and work the rest of their time in their usual jobs or on other projects. A project might involve a short-term task that lasts only a matter of days, or it may run for years. After the project's completion, the project team members would normally be assigned back to their regular jobs, to other jobs in the organization, or to other projects.

Project Life Cycle

A project passes through a life cycle that may vary depending on the size and complexity of the project and the style established by the organization. The titles of the various phases may differ from organization to organization, but typically a project will pass through the following phases. There is a *concept phase,* during which the organization realizes that a project might be needed or is requested to propose performing a project for some customer. There is an initial *planning* or *feasibility phase,* during which the project manager (and perhaps a staff if the project is complex) plans the project to a level of detail sufficient for initial scheduling and budgeting. If the project is approved, it will enter a more detailed planning phase, an *organization phase,* an *execution phase,* and a *termination phase.*

Sometimes, a work breakdown structure is developed during the planning phase of a project. A *work breakdown structure (WBS),* a document similar to a bill of materials, divides the total work into major work packages to be accomplished. These work packages are divided into major elements, and the major elements are further subdivided to develop a list of all work items that must be accomplished to complete the project. The WBS helps to define the work to be performed and provides a framework for budgeting. It also serves as a framework by which schedule and cost performance can be compared to plans and budgets as the project advances. Table 10.1 shows an example of an abbreviated WBS for an orbital space laboratory vehicle.

The detailed project definition, such as the WBS, is examined during the organization phase of the project to determine the skills necessary to accomplish the project goals. Personnel and other resources to accomplish the project are then made available for all or a portion of the project's duration through temporary assignments from other parts of the organization or, perhaps, by leasing resources or subcontracting portions of the project.

Organization

Companies that are normally involved in a series of projects, and occasionally shift personnel among projects, often utilize the matrix form of organization to achieve the flexibility required in these types of situations. In a *matrix organi-*

Table 10.1
WORK BREAKDOWN
STRUCTURE—ORBITING SPACE
STATION PROJECT

1.0	Command module
2.0	Laboratory module
3.0	Launch propulsion system
3.1	Fuel supply system
3.1.1	Fuel tank assembly
3.1.1.1	Fuel tank casing
3.1.1.2	Fuel tank insulation
4.0	Guidance system

zation, project personnel maintain a permanent reporting relationship that connects vertically to the supervisor who directs the discipline within which they work. At the same time, each person assigned to a project has a horizontal reporting relationship to the manager of a particular project, who coordinates his or her participation in that project. Pay and career advancement within the organization is developed within a particular discipline even though a person is assigned from time to time to different projects. At times this dual reporting relationship can give rise to personnel problems.

Managing a project can be a complex and challenging assignment. Since projects are one-of-a-kind endeavors, there may be little in the way of experience, normal working relationships, or established procedures to guide participants. A project manager might have to coordinate many diverse efforts and activities to achieve the project goals. Persons from various disciplines and from various parts of the organization who have never worked together may be assigned to the project for differing spans of time. Subcontractors who are unfamiliar with the organization may be brought in to carry out major portions of the project. The project may involve thousands of interrelated activities performed by persons employed by any one of several different subcontractors or by the sponsoring organization.

For these and other reasons, it is important that the project leaders have an effective means of identifying and communicating the planned activities and the ways in which they are to be interrelated. An effective scheduling and monitoring method is absolutely essential to management of a large project. Network scheduling methods such as PERT and CPM have proven to be highly effective and valuable tools during both the planning and the execution phases of projects. The remainder of the chapter is devoted to discussing network scheduling methods in order to show the value of these methods and to provide some understanding of the unique features of project management.

NETWORK-BASED SCHEDULING TECHNIQUES

The biggest advance in project scheduling since the development of the Gantt chart in 1917 was made between 1956 and 1958. During this period, two new scheduling techniques were developed that have much in common although they were developed independently. These techniques are PERT (*Program Evaluation and Review Technique*) and CPM (*Critical Path Method*). Both are based on the use of a network or graphical model to depict the work tasks being scheduled. Both were designed to schedule long-duration projects that were to be performed only once or in low volume. Computer programs are available for both PERT and CPM. Computers are helpful in developing timely information about large projects, particularly those that are to be updated or revised several times before completion.

CPM was developed by E. I. du Pont de Nemours & Company in conjunction with the Remington Rand Corporation. Du Pont desired a technique to improve the scheduling of construction and extensive maintenance shutdowns of its production facilities. Most of the activities that were to be scheduled with this technique were similar to previously performed construction and maintenance, so the length of time the tasks were expected to require was treated as though it were a deterministic (known) number.

PERT was developed under the auspices of the U.S. Navy's Special Projects Office working with representatives of Lockheed and Booz, Allen & Hamilton. The technique was developed to assist in managing the development of the Polaris missile-submarine system. This project required the coordination of more than 3,000 individual contractors, suppliers, and agencies—an immense management and scheduling challenge. Since many of the activities involved in this project had never been performed before, the amount of time they might require was uncertain and consequently was treated as a probabilistic variable.

The major basic difference that remains between PERT and CPM is PERT's capability of dealing with probability estimates for activity times. CPM originally included a more detailed analysis of time-cost trade-offs, but this function can be performed with either CPM or PERT. Other differences in network conventions and vocabulary existed in the early years, but the use of the techniques has become so broad that many of these minor distinctions have disappeared. This section outlines some of the advantages of network scheduling techniques and the basic steps involved in their use. Some networking fundamentals are presented, and simple examples are provided. The solutions are developed by manual calculations, but computers are often used with larger problems.

Some Advantages of Network Scheduling

Network-based scheduling techniques can be beneficial in many ways if they are properly used. Like all other scheduling techniques, however, they are not panaceas or substitutes for good management judgment. Since scheduling is an attempt to plan future work, the required work times are estimates. No technique will make poor estimates any better. Scheduling can help plan work, but the accuracy of plans and schedules depends on the accuracy of the time estimates used in their development. Knowledgeable people and/or reliable techniques should be used to provide the time estimates.

Assuming that the estimates for a network scheduling method are as good as those for other scheduling methods, the network techniques may offer some advantages.

1. They lead to planning a project to the selected level of detail so that all parts of the project and their intended order of accomplishment are known.
2. They provide a fairly accurate estimate of the length of time it will take to complete the project and the activities that must be kept on time to meet the schedule.
3. They provide a graphic picture and standardized vocabulary to aid in understanding work assignments and communicating among people involved in the project.
4. They provide a means of tracking progress on a project (that is, show where work is with respect to the plan).
5. They identify and focus attention on potentially troublesome activities to facilitate management by exception.
6. They provide a means of estimating the time and cost impact of changes to the project plan at any stage.

STEPS IN USING NETWORK TECHNIQUES

Three major steps are involved in the use of network scheduling. The steps to be taken are listed below.

1. *Plan the project*
   (a) Analyze the project by determining all of the individual *activities* (sometimes called tasks, jobs, or operations) that must be performed to complete it.
   (b) Show the planned sequence of these activities on a *network* (a graph using arrows and circles to represent the relationships among project activities).
2. *Schedule the project*
   (a) Estimate how long it will take to perform each activity.
   (b) Perform computations to locate the critical path (the longest time chain of sequential activities that determines the duration of the project). This step also provides other information that is useful in scheduling.
   (c) Use this information to develop a more economical and efficient schedule if one is indicated.
3. *Monitor the project*
   (a) Use the plan and schedule to control and monitor progress.
   (b) Revise and update the schedule throughout execution of the project so that the schedule represents the current plans and current status of progress.

PRECEDENCE RELATIONSHIPS

Some activities cannot be performed until other activities have been completed. This type of requirement establishes a technical *precedence relationship*. There may sometimes be options as to the way activities may be performed, but management's prerogatives or differences in costs lead to a particular planned sequence of activities. Other activities may be performed independently. Task independence and precedence relationships should be incorporated into the job plan and indicated on the project network.

Networking Conventions

A network is a graph using circles and arrows to represent the planned relationships among the activities required to complete a project. Either of two conventions can be used to develop a network. One uses circles to represent the project activities, with arrows linking them together to show the sequence in which they are to be performed. This is called the *activity-on-node* (AON) convention, or precedence notation. An alternative is to show the activities as arrows and use circles to connect predecessor and successor activities. This method is called the *activity-on-arrow* (AOA) convention. With this convention, the circles or nodes represent *events* that are points in time at which activities begin or end. An event consumes no resources, whereas an activity consumes time and other resources.

A network is drawn after all of the activities and their relationships have been defined. There is no proven best approach to the identification of activities. Some people start with what they believe to be logically the first activity and proceed in what they believe to be chronological order; others may start with the last activity and work backward; still others list activities in random sequence. After the activities are identified, one may ask:

1. Which activity must immediately precede this one?
2. Which activity must immediately follow this one?
3. Can this activity be accomplished without dependence on some other activity?

The activity that must be performed just before a particular activity is its *predecessor activity;* the one that follows is its *successor activity.*

Methods of showing various relationships among activities are illustrated in Figure 10.1. An activity in the AOA convention is often identified by numbers indicating the starting and ending events. This identification system is called *i-j* notation (*i* represents the number of the starting event and *j* represents the number of the ending event). This notation makes it necessary for every activity to have a unique *i-j* pair. A *dummy activity* (indicated by a dashed arrow) consumes no time or other resources but is used merely to indicate a precedence relationship. A dummy activity has been used in Figure 10.1(g) to keep activities *B* and *C* from having the same starting and ending nodes. With the activity-on-arrow convention, dummy activities also may be needed in other instances to indicate precedence relationships, as in Figure 10.1(f). Activities in the AON convention can be identified by a single number or letter, and there is no need for dummy activities when this convention is used. Generally the AON is easier to learn because it consistently uses arrows only to indicate precedence. In

FIGURE 10.1

AON and AOA Methods of Indicating Activity Relationships on Network Diagrams

Activity-on-node convention
(precedence notation)

Activity-on-arrow convention
(i–j notation)

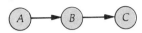 

(a) A must be performed before B, which must be performed before C.

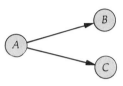 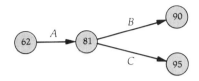

(b) A must be completed before either B or C can begin.

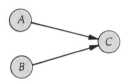 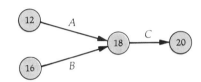

(c) Both A and B must be completed before C can begin.

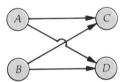 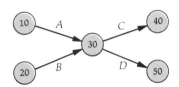

(d) Both A and B must precede both C and D.

(e) A must precede C and B must precede D, but the A–C path is independent of the B–D path.

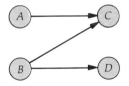 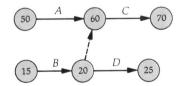

(f) A and B must precede C and B must precede D, but A is independent of D.

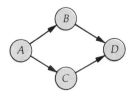 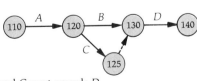

(g) A must precede both B and C. Both B and C must precede D.

437

contrast, some arrows (solid) are activities and other arrows (dashed) indicate precedence requirements when the AOA convention is used.

SCHEDULING

The network is a graphic representation of the interrelationships among all of the activities in the project. Developing the network forces detailed planning of the project and provides a valuable communication tool. After the activities have been identified and the network has been drawn, the next step is to assign expected time durations to the activities. The expected duration depends on the planned crew size, work method, equipment, and working hours. A particular level of resources must be assumed to be available when the work is to be performed. Either of the following conditions may exist when the estimates are made:

1. The person who is in charge of an activity or activities assumes that some customary and reasonable level of resources will be used and specifies an expected duration for the activity. Some completion date is thus determined. This approach is in keeping with the theory of CPM.
2. In some actual applications, a completion time or milestone date is specified and the estimated amount of resources is adjusted so that the duration will be less than or equal to the necessary amount of time.

Critical Path

A path is a chain of sequential activities beginning at the project's start and ending at its completion. Several or many paths may exist through the network. Work may proceed on many independent paths concurrently, but of course work can proceed on an activity only after all of the necessary predecessor activities have been completed. All of the activities, hence all of the paths, must be completed before the project is finished. The path through the network that has the longest expected elapsed time is expected to determine the completion date of the project and is called the *critical path*. Often activities that are not on the critical path can be delayed without necessitating a delay in the completion of the project.

Float or Slack

Total float, usually referred to as simply *float* or *slack,* is the amount of time an activity can be delayed beyond its earliest possible starting time without delaying the project completion, if the other activities take their estimated durations. Float gives some indication of the criticalness of an activity. An activity with little float stands a good chance of delaying the project and should be carefully monitored.

Sometimes, after calculating the float for activities in a network, you will notice that several adjoining activities usually have the same amount of float.

This float is shared by all the activities along this chain. If one activity is delayed, it will reduce by the same amount of time the float for other activities in the chain.

Another type of float is sometimes calculated. *Free float* is the amount of time an activity can be delayed without delaying the early start of a successor activity. To find free float we subtract the early finish of an activity from the early start times for all of its succeeding activities. This type of float is seldom used and will not be discussed further.

Float allows some flexibility in scheduling activities. An activity can be intentionally delayed if the delay would result in a more uniform work load or provide some other advantage. Some amount of float should be retained if possible, because float is like insurance. In days of uncertain material deliveries, possible strikes, delayed drawing approvals, and so on, it is wise to have a cushion where it can be afforded.

More than one activity may require the same resources and may be planned to occur at the same time. Networking and scheduling data provided by the scheduling method will reveal such conflicts so that readjustments can be planned. In order to determine the times at which various activities can occur, it is necessary to calculate the earliest date at which each activity can be performed and how much each activity can be delayed without interfering with the project's scheduled completion.

Calculating Float or Slack   Total float (*TF*), which we shall refer to simply as float, can be ascertained by either of the following equations:

$$TF = LS - ES \tag{10.1}$$

or

$$TF = LF - EF$$

where ES = early start time: the earliest time an activity can be started if its predecessors take the amount of time they are expected to take.

EF = early finish time: the time an activity will be completed if it starts on its ES and takes its expected time.

$$EF = ES + t \tag{10.2}$$

LF = late finish time: the latest date an activity can be finished without delaying the project if its successors take the expected amount of time.

LS = late start time: the latest date an activity can start without delaying the project.

$$LS = LF - t \tag{10.3}$$

t = the duration of the activity under consideration.

The process of calculating ES, EF, LF, and LS requires both a forward pass and a backward pass of calculations through the network.

Forward Pass

The early start and early finish for each activity are found by calculations performed in sequence from the left to the right of the network. This series of calculations is called the *forward pass*. We first assign a project day, usually 0, to the start of the first activity, to represent the *ES* for that activity. Then we obtain the *ES* and *EF* for each activity by making a forward pass through the network, from left to right. The duration of an activity is added to its *ES* to obtain its *EF*. The *ES* of an activity is set equal to the *EF* of its predecessor if there is only one. If an activity has more than one predecessor, its *ES* is equal to the latest *EF* of its predecessors. For example, if the early start for activity *M* in Figure 10.2 is day 10, its early finish is day 15. If the early start for activity *R* is day 12, its early finish is day 18. Even though one of its predecessors (activity *M*) is completed on day 15, activity *P* cannot begin until day 18, when the latest of all its predecessors is finished. The forward pass is continued until we reach the right-hand side of the network. At this point we have the *EF* of the final activity, which is the earliest the project can be completed (if the activities take the amount of time that was estimated).

Backward Pass

The *LF* and *LS* dates are calculated by means of a *backward pass* from right to left through the network. The *LF* of the last activity is usually set equal to the *EF* of the project. Starting with the last activity, subtract the activity duration from *LF* to obtain *LS*. The *LF* for an activity is set equal to the *LS* for its successors if there is only one. It is set equal to the earliest or smallest *LS* of all successors if there is more than one successor.

Example of Scheduling Calculations

Suppose that we are going to construct a small warehouse with an office. The structure will be used to store batteries and will have a large transformer system

FIGURE 10.2
Portion of an Activity-on-Node Network

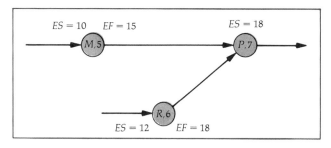

placed in the overhead truss or attic area of the warehouse. This equipment cannot be installed until the steel roof frame is in place but must be installed before the roof is on. The roof is to extend down over the top of the exterior masonry wall and cannot be installed until the wall is completed. Suppose too that the company has decided that it will not put the asphalt paving around the warehouse until the fence has been erected around it and the exterior wall of the warehouse has been completed.

An AON network showing the project plan is provided in Figure 10.3. The expected time in days for each activity is shown in each node. The early start and finish times, found by working from left to right, are indicated above each activity.

The early start date for each activity is equal to the early finish of its predecessor when there is only one predecessor. Notice that activities I, J, and M have more than one predecessor. Such activities are called *merge activities* because paths merge at them. They cannot start until all of their predecessors have been completed. According to this plan, activity I cannot begin until day 21, even though the fence activity (activity D) could be completed on day 6. Remember, the ES of a merge activity is the latest EF of all its predecessors.

Notice that the early finish for the total project is day 30. This time represents 30 workdays. Additions for weekends, holidays, or other nonwork days (such as days of bad weather) must be allowed to convert the workday numbers into calendar dates for the planned occurrence of the activities. Many computer programs used for PERT and CPM have provisions to convert project days to calendar dates automatically.

The backward pass through the network is based on some latest allowable finish date for the total project. If the expected completion time found in the forward pass is acceptable, the latest finish, LF, for the last activity is set equal to this early finish time. We will assume that day 30 is an acceptable finish date and set the LF for activity M equal to 30. The estimated duration of each activity is subtracted from its late finish date to find its late start date. If the latest we can finish activity M is day 30 and it takes one day to perform activity M, then the latest we can start this activity is day 29. The predecessors for activity M must be completed by day 29 if activity M is to start on day 29, so their LF is 29. The late start and late finish dates for all of the activities are calculated by continuing this procedure from right to left of the network.

An activity that has more than one successor is called a *burst activity* because the network spreads in multiple directions after it. The procedure for finding the LF of a burst activity in the backward pass is the reverse of the logic used at a merge activity during the forward pass. The latest time at which the burst activity can be completed without delaying the project is the earliest of all the late starts for its successors. If the burst activity is not finished by that time, it will delay one of its successors beyond its LS. The network for the warehouse project is shown again in Figure 10.4 with the LS and LF dates indicated below each activity.

FIGURE 10.3

Development of Early Start and Early Finish Times by a Forward Pass Through a Network

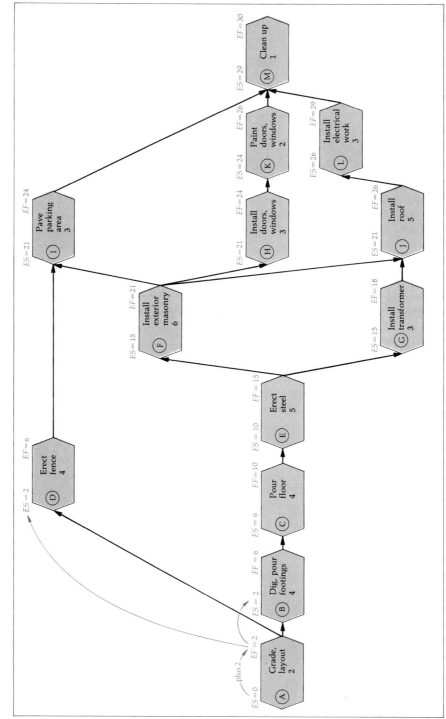

Table 10.2
CALCULATION OF FLOAT

Activity	LS − ES	LF − EF	Float
A	0–0	2–2	0
B	2–2	6–6	0
C	6–6	10–10	0
D	22–2	26–6	20
E	10–10	15–15	0
F	15–15	21–21	0
G	18–15	21–18	3
H	24–21	27–24	3
I	26–21	29–24	5
J	21–21	26–26	0
K	27–24	29–26	3
L	26–26	29–29	0
M	29–29	30–30	0

The slack or float for each activity can be calculated after the ES, EF, LS, and LF dates have been obtained. Float or slack is the amount of time an activity can be delayed without delaying the completion of the project if all the other activities require the estimated amount of time. Float, then, is calculated by subtracting ES from LS or EF from LF. The float for each activity is shown in Table 10.2.

The path of activities from the start to the end of the network with the minimum and identical float is the critical path. This sequence of activities determines the completion date of the entire project and requires careful attention to keep the project from being completed late. The critical path is marked with blue arrows in Figure 10.4. In this example all activities on the critical path have zero float. Activities on the critical path or other paths can have negative float if the project is behind schedule. For example, if the LF for the project had been set at day 28, all activities on the critical path would have −2 for their float. This means that the early finish for each activity would be two days later than the time it must be completed to keep the project on schedule. In such a situation the duration of the critical path would have to be reduced a total of two days to complete the project on schedule. Also, all other activities would have had two days' less float than was found previously. Alternatively, the critical path may have positive float if the project is ahead of schedule. But the critical path has the least float of any, hence the name *critical* path.

Activities that are not on the critical path usually can be delayed without delaying the project. Notice that adjacent activities along a path segment, such as activities H and K, have the same amount of float. This float is shared by all of the activities between the point where the path leaves one path and the point where it joins some other path. If one activity in such a segment is delayed, it uses some of the float available to the other activities in the path segment.

FIGURE 10.4

Determination of Late Finish and Late Start Times by a Backward Pass

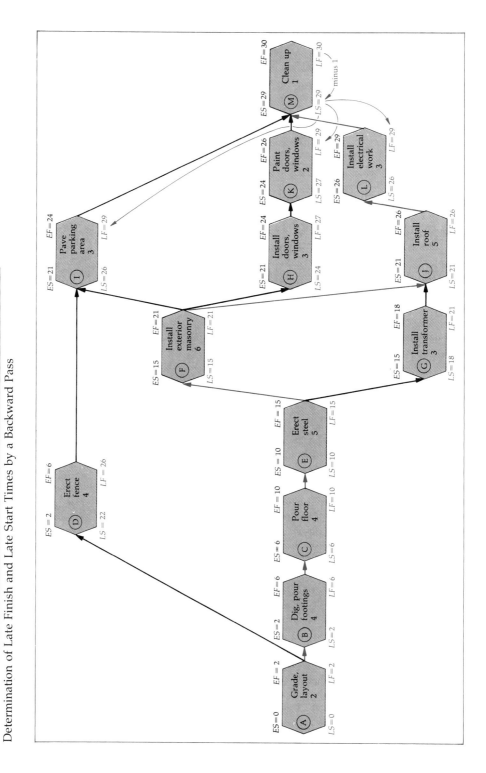

SHIFTING AND ADJUSTING RESOURCES

Working overtime on all activities to expedite a project may involve needless expense. Expediting activities that have considerable float will not change the completion date for the project. A wiser use of resources would be to expedite only the activities on the critical path. The duration of a project can sometimes be reduced by shifting resources (people, equipment, or money) from activities that have excess float to critical activities that constrain the project's completion.

Time-Cost Trade-offs

One feature that frequently is discussed in descriptions of CPM is an analysis of time-cost trade-offs that may reduce the total cost of a project or reduce its duration with a minimum cost increase. This analysis can be performed with PERT also. Time-cost trade-offs focus on the critical path because it is this path that determines the project's completion date. It was mentioned earlier that the availability of a certain level of resources was assumed when activity durations were estimated. Additional resources may be used to reduce the duration of many activities. The relationship between the direct cost of an activity and its duration typically follows the general form shown in Figure 10.5. The direct costs will be increased if the activity is expedited.

     Examination of the time-cost curves for the activities on the critical path may reveal the best combination of activities where additional resources can be applied to reduce the project's duration with a minimum increase in cost. The slope of each activity's cost curve may be different at the currently estimated duration of the activity. The least expensive reduction in the critical path is obtained by first reducing the activity whose cost curve has the least slope, then the activity with the next greater slope, and so on. Suppose that we want to

FIGURE 10.5

Relationship Between Cost and Duration of an
Activity

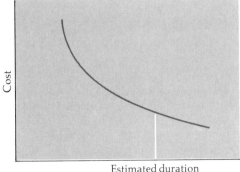

FIGURE 10.6

Possible Relationship Between Project Costs and Project Duration

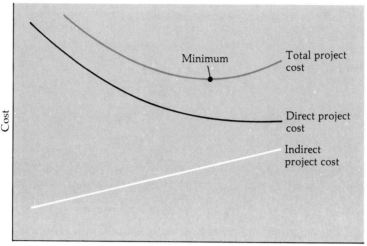

reduce a project's duration by three days. We have three combinations to examine, without considering fractional day reductions of some activities:

1. Reduce one activity by three days.
2. Reduce one activity by two days and another by one day.
3. Reduce three activities by one day each.

Considerable analysis may be required to select the best combination of activities to expedite and to determine just how much each should be expedited, especially if the network contains a large number of activities. The problem becomes extremely complex when a reduction of perhaps ten, fifteen, or more days is desired.

It is sometimes possible to reduce the total cost of a project by reducing its duration. Overhead cost associated with the project may be a fixed amount per day. If the cost of reducing the project's duration by a day is less than the daily overhead cost, then the reduction in duration will reduce the total cost. This is not true, of course, if the overhead expenses continue after the project is terminated. This type of relationship between a project's duration and its costs is shown in Figure 10.6. Time-cost trade-offs may be of particular interest when a company has an incentive clause in its contract or a penalty clause specifying that its profit will be reduced if the project is completed later than some specified date.

PERT: USING PROBABILISTIC TIME ESTIMATES

The previous discussion of CPM has treated each estimated activity duration as though it were a deterministic quantity. PERT has the capability of treating the activity times as though they were probabilistic numbers. Hence PERT is best suited to situations in which there is a great deal of uncertainty or information is insufficient to specify the activity durations accurately. Each activity time is treated as though it will be a random number that comes from a beta probability distribution. The parameters of the beta distribution can be found from three time estimates, described below and illustrated in Figure 10.7.

Optimistic Time

The *optimistic time* (a) is the amount of time an activity will take if everything goes well. The probability that the activity will take less than this amount of time is 0.01.

Pessimistic Time

The *pessimistic time* (b) is the amount of time the activity will take if everything goes poorly. The probability that the activity will exceed this duration is 0.01.

Most Likely Time

The *most likely time* (m) is the time the estimator thinks an activity will probably take. If the activity could be performed many times under the same conditions (no learning), this is the time that would occur most often.

The expected duration of an activity is t_e, the mean of the beta distribution that is defined by the three time estimates. The mean is found by taking a weighted average of the three estimates, using equation 10.4.

$$t_e = \frac{a + 4m + b}{6} \tag{10.4}$$

The standard deviation of the distribution is assumed to be one-sixth of its range. The variance of distribution is given by equation 10.5.

$$\sigma^2 = \left(\frac{b - a}{6}\right)^2 \tag{10.5}$$

FIGURE 10.7

Probability Distribution for an Activity Duration

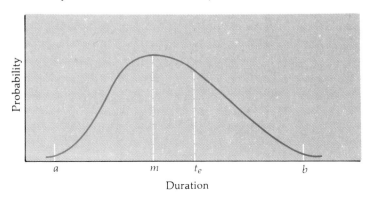

After the t_e for each activity is found by equation 10.4, the critical path and slack or float can be determined by the same logic and calculations used with CPM in the previous section. That is, PERT can be performed by the use of AON (activity-on-node) notation. PERT originally used AOA, however, and this notation is most frequently seen in introductory discussions of PERT. T_E is the earliest an event can be reached and is found by a forward pass. T_L, the latest allowable time an event can be reached if the project is to remain on schedule, is found by a backward pass through the network. T_E and T_L for each event (end of an arrow) provide the same information that was obtained with CPM.

APPLICATION

The Use of AOA and Probability in PERT Network-Based Schedule

The Ajax Leasing Company has employed the services of Buzzwords Unlimited, a computer software company, to develop an information system to keep leasing and maintenance records on its fleet of cars and trucks. Two Ajax employees and members of the Buzzword staff have formed a project team. A PERT network (using i-j notation and activities on the arrows) for the project is shown in Figure 10.8. Notice that a dummy activity is used to indicate that module II cannot be tested until module I and the input/output program are coded. But module I and the input/output program can be tested without module II. The optimistic time, most likely time, and pessimistic time for each activity, as estimated by the members of the project team, are shown in Table 10.3. Equation 10.4 was used to calculate the expected time, t_e, from these time estimates; t_e is shown in column 6 of Table 10.3.

FIGURE 10.8

PERT Network for Ajax Software Project

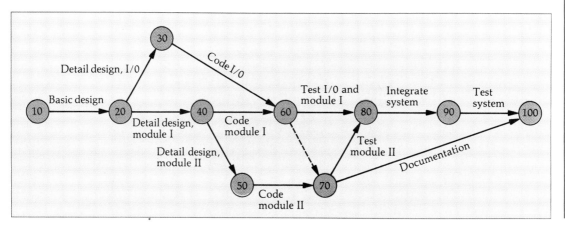

Table 10.3
CALCULATION OF t_e's FOR THE ACTIVITIES
IN THE AJAX PROJECT

i-j Notation	Activity Description	Optimistic Time (week a)	Most Likely Time (week m)	Pessimistic Time (week b)	$t_e = \dfrac{a + 4m + b}{6}$
10– 20	Basic design	2 ·	3	5	$^{19}\!/_6 = 3.17$
20– 30	Detail design, input/ output	3	4	6	$^{25}\!/_6 = 4.17$
30– 60	Code I/O	6	8	11	$^{49}\!/_6 = 8.17$
20– 40	Detail design, module I	5	6	9	$^{38}\!/_6 = 6.33$
40– 60	Code module I	6	8	10	$^{48}\!/_6 = 8.0$
40– 50	Detail design, module II	4	5	6	$^{30}\!/_6 = 5.0$
50– 70	Code module II	5	6	9	$^{38}\!/_6 = 6.33$
60– 80	Test I/O and module I	2	3	4	$^{18}\!/_6 = 3.00$
60– 70	Dummy	0	0	0	$^{0}\!/_6 = 0.00$
70– 80	Test module II	1	3	5	$^{18}\!/_6 = 3.00$
80– 90	Integrate system	4	5	8	$^{32}\!/_6 = 5.33$
90–100	Test system	2	3	5	$^{19}\!/_6 = 3.17$
70–100	Documentation	5	9	11	$^{52}\!/_6 = 8.67$

The network is shown again in Figure 10.9 with the t_e's indicated above each arrow. The same calculations used in the CPM example were performed during a forward pass through the network to calculate the early start and early finish times for each activity. Since a node represents both the end of one activity and the start of another, it is necessary to write the early time for the event only once. This T_E

FIGURE 10.9

Network Calculations for Ajax Project, Showing Critical Path

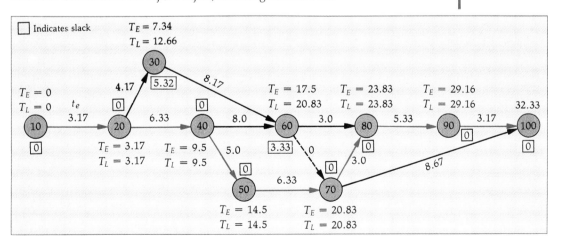

represents both the early finish time for the predecessor and the early start time for the successor at the node. The expected time required to complete the project was determined to be 32.33 weeks.

A backward pass was then performed, and the T_L for each node was determined. The slack, or float, at each node was found by $T_L - T_E$. The slack is indicated below each node of the network shown in Figure 10.9. The critical path connecting the series of nodes with zero slack was determined and is indicated by the series of blue arrows through the network in Figure 10.9.

Ajax assumed that the duration of the total project would be determined by the path that was found to be the critical path in this initial analysis of the project. This assumption is sometimes made if a project does not contain several paths, some of which have only small amounts of slack. The expected completion date for the critical path (i.e., the project), $T_E(CP)$, is 32.33 weeks, which represents the sum of the activity times for all activities on the critical path. The central limit theorem states that the sum (or mean) of independent random variables approaches a normal distribution as the number of random variables is increased. Since the expected duration of the critical path is the sum of several activity durations (which are random variables), the expected duration of the critical path is assumed to be normally distributed. Under the assumption that the critical path will determine the completion of the project, the probability that the project will take longer than the expected duration (i.e., the mean of a normal distribution) is assumed to be 0.5. The probability that the project will take less than $T_E(CP)$ is also 0.5.

The variance of the distribution of possible project durations is assumed to be the variance of the duration of the critical path. The variance of the total critical path is the sum of the variances of all the activities along its route (so long as the durations are considered independent random variables). Therefore the standard deviation for the duration of the critical path or the project is assumed to be determined by equation 10.6:

$$\sigma_{CP} = \sqrt{\sum_{i=1}^{k} \sigma_i^2} \tag{10.6}$$

where σ_{CP} = the standard deviation of the duration of the critical path (i.e., the project)
σ_i^2 = the variance of the ith activity on the critical path
k = the number of activities on the critical path.

To find the probability that a project will be completed in no more than a given duration, D, we must find the probability that a standardized normal variable, Z, will take on a value less than or equal to Z_D given by the transformation equation 10.7:

$$Z_D = \frac{D - T_E(CP)}{\sigma_{CP}} \tag{10.7}$$

where Z_D = a particular value of a standardized normal variable
D = the duration of the project that we want the probability of meeting
$T_E(CP)$ = the early completion time for the critical path
σ_{CP} = the assumed standard deviation of the project duration (i.e., of the critical path)

Ajax Leasing wants the software package completed in less than 34 weeks, so we will determine the probability that this duration will be achieved. The var-

Table 10.4
CALCULATION OF THE CRITICAL PATH VARIANCE

Activity	Optimistic (a)	Pessimistic (b)	$\dfrac{b - a}{6}$	$\left(\dfrac{b - a}{6}\right)^2$
10– 20	2	5	3/6	9/36
20– 40	5	9	4/6	16/36
40– 50	4	6	2/6	4/36
50– 70	5	9	4/6	16/36
70– 80	1	5	4/6	16/36
80– 90	4	8	4/6	16/36
90–100	2	5	3/6	9/36

$$86/36 = \sum_{i=1}^{k} \sigma_i^2$$

iances of the activities on the critical path are determined and summed in Table 10.4. The sum of column 5, $86/36$ or 2.39 weeks, represents the variance of the critical path, that is, the variance of the distribution for the project's duration.

The standard deviation of the project duration: $\sigma_{CP} = \sqrt{2.39} = 1.55$ weeks. The probability that the project will be completed in less than 34 weeks can be determined now that σ_{CP} has been estimated.

$$P(D \leq 34 \text{ weeks}) = P(Z \leq Z_D)$$

$$Z_D = \frac{D - T_E(CP)}{\sigma_{CP}} = \frac{34 - 32.33}{1.55} = 1.08$$

Reference to a standardized normal probability table (Appendix I) shows that

$$P(Z \leq 1.08) = 0.86,$$

so the probability is assumed to be about 0.86 that the company will complete the project within 34 weeks.

A Caution Regarding Probabilities

The probability statements developed in the application are based solely on the critical path. These probabilities do not take into account the probability that some initially noncritical path will be delayed by more than the amount of slack in it. Consequently the probabilities regarding the project's completion are somewhat optimistic. To be theoretically correct, we should consider all paths. The probability that the project will be completed by a specified date is the probability that all paths will be completed by that date. Each path has its own variance and distribution of completion times so we can compute the probability that it will be completed by the specified date. The probability that all paths will be completed by this date is the product of the probabilities for all of the paths. Of course, all of the calculations assume that the estimator actually described the correct probability distributions by providing the correct a, m, and b for the activities.

Simulation of Project Duration

Conventional analysis of a PERT network focuses on finding the critical path and then analyzing its effect on the project's completion. The probability that some other path may be delayed by more than the amount of slack in it is not included in the conventional approach. Finding the probabilities for all paths in a large network is tedious, particularly if several possible dates are considered.

Simulation, taking all paths into account, can be used to develop estimates of the project's completion. Approximations of the probability distributions for each activity's duration are estimated in order to perform PERT. These distributions or more detailed empirical estimates may be used to represent the likelihood that an activity will require various amounts of time. One time from the distribution of possible durations of each activity is randomly selected. The times for all the activities within a path are totaled and the durations for the paths are compared to see which path was the longest and how much time it required. Sometimes some other path might take longer than the conventional critical path.

The procedure of sampling times and determining the longest path and its duration is continued for many trials. Upon completion of the simulation, one can compute the likelihood that a particular path will be critical and can develop a probability distribution for the project's duration. The relative frequency with which a particular path was the longest indicates the likelihood that this path will determine the project's completion date. The relative frequency of various durations, no matter which path was longest, indicates the likelihood of completing the project within a particular length of time. A computer is used to simulate any project of a realistic size because many repetitions are required. A short supplement (F) on simulation is included at the end of Chapter 9.

MONITORING PROJECTS WITH NETWORK TECHNIQUES

Some users of network scheduling techniques have said that networks would greatly improve project management, even if they were thrown away as soon as they were developed, because of the detailed planning that must be done to develop them. This statement may be true, but there is further value to the method. Few if any projects go as they have been planned, no matter how carefully the plan has been developed. A network that is kept updated shows where project is off schedule before it gets too far off. Updating and reviewing the networks or computer reports that represent information obtained from the networks provides management with current information. Continued revision and use of a network technique keeps management up to date on current and predicted project status.

The types of calculations that were made in planning a project may be repeated with current time estimates so that revised plans may be included in the network if necessary. Current estimates of the slack or float for each path highlight the need for management attention. Sometimes a rolling wave of detail is used to plan ahead as work progresses on a lengthy project.

SUMMARY

A project is a complex, often large-scale task that is unique or nonroutine for the performing organization. Management of a project can present unique challenges because of various factors. The project may span several years. The type of work may not have been done previously by the organization. The project may require the efforts of diverse groups, and those groups may be involved in only a part of the project, so there is a lack of continuity to develop skills, understanding, and working relationships that would make coordination simpler.

It is imperative to have an effective means of defining and communicating the work requirements and sequencing involved in a project. Sometimes a work breakdown structure (WBS) is used to identify all the elements of the work to be performed. Network-based scheduling techniques such as PERT and CPM have proven to be very effective tools for both planning and controlling projects.

The major difference between PERT and CPM is that PERT incorporates probabilities into the estimates of activity times and of project completion times, whereas CPM does not. PERT and CPM have numerous advantages. They entail detailed planning of projects, and they provide estimates of completion dates that are as accurate as can be developed from a given level of accuracy in the input data. They furnish a graphic picture of work assignments and their interrelationships, and a uniform vocabulary for communicating about them. Both PERT and CPM identify the critical path, the series of activities that are mostly likely to delay a project. Both techniques provide an effective means of comparing actual performance to the plan, so that the need for

corrective action can be readily recognized and the appropriate corrective action planned.

The procedure for using one of the network techniques begins in the planning stage—with identifying all of the activities that must be performed and the sequence in which they must be performed. A network is constructed to show graphically the sequence of all activities in the project. Either the activity-on-arrow or the activity-on-node convention is used throughout the entire network.

The second major step is scheduling the project. Time estimates must be made for the duration of each activity. A forward pass, from left to right through the network, provides the earliest possible time for completion of each activity. A backward pass, from right to left through the network, provides the latest time that an activity can be completed without delaying the project. The difference between these times is the slack or float—the time that an activity can be delayed beyond its earliest starting time without delaying completion of the project. This information can be used to rearrange the planned use of resources so that resources are more wisely used or so that the project can be completed earlier.

The third major step in using PERT or CPM is to monitor the project as work progresses and to update the network. If the actual work deviates from the plan, management can decide what action would be appropriate—to redeploy resources to get the project back on schedule or to revise the schedule. Network techniques provide useful information to assist in planning actions that seem most appropriate.

CPM is sometimes associated with time-cost trade-offs to determine the lowest-cost way to expedite completion of a project. The original time estimates are based on an assumed crew size, amount of equipment, and length of workday. The incremental cost for saving one, two, three, or more days can be estimated for each activity on the critical path. These estimates can be used to find the lowest-cost way to reduce the duration of the critical path by the desired amount of time.

The expected completion time provided by PERT is assumed to be the mean of a normal distribution of possible project durations that can occur. The probability of completing the project in less than some specified time can be found by converting the time to a z value and finding the probability that z will be less than or equal to that value. In some instances, simulation is used to take into account the possible duration of the critical path and of other paths.

SOLVED PROBLEM

PROBLEM:

Shown below is an AOA network for a small project. The three time estimates, in weeks, for each activity are shown on each arrow.

(a) Compute the expected time for each activity.
(b) Find the expected duration of the project.
(c) Find the slack at the nodes that are not on the critical path.
(d) Compute the standard deviation of the critical path.
(e) Using the standard deviation of the critical path as the standard deviation of the project's duration, compute the probability of completing the project in 35 weeks or less.

SOLUTION:

(a) The expected time for each activity is indicated in column 5 of the table. These times are used to compute the T_E or the earliest expected time for reaching each event (circle) in the network.

(b) The expected completion time for the project is found to be 32.67 weeks, which is the T_E for the last activity (activity H).

(c) The nodes with nonzero slack are nodes 3 and 5, which have 5.17 weeks slack, so the critical path is A-C-E-G-H. The slack is found by calculating the T_Ls in the network by a backward pass through the network. Where they are not equal, the T_E is subtracted from the

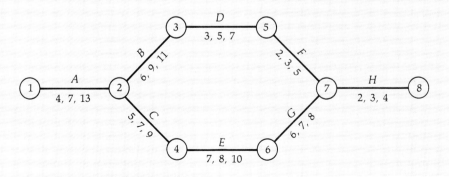

(1) Activity	(2) Optimistic Time a	(3) Most Likely Time m	(4) Pessimistic Time b	(5) t_e $(a + 4m + b)/6$	(6)* Activity Variance $[(b - a/6)]^2$
A	4	7	13	7.50	2.25
B	6	9	11	8.83	
C	5	7	9	7.00	0.44
D	3	5	7	5.00	
E	7	8	10	8.17	0.25
F	2	3	5	3.17	
G	6	7	8	7.00	0.11
H	2	3	4	3.00	0.11
					3.16

*Critical path activities only

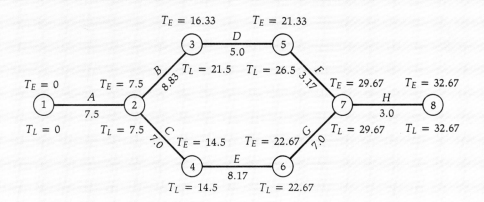

T_L and the result is equal to the slack at that node.

(d) The standard deviation of the critical path is found by summing the numbers in column 6 for every activity on the critical path (A-C-E-G-H) and taking the square root of this sum.

$\sigma^2_{CP} = (2.25 + 0.44 + 0.25 + 0.11 + 0.11) = 3.16$

$\sigma_{CP} = \sqrt{3.16} = 1.778$

(e) $P(D \leq 35 \text{ weeks}) =$

$$P\left(Z \leq \frac{35 - 32.67}{1.778}\right) = P(Z \leq 1.31).$$

By referring to Appendix I, this probability is found to be 0.9049.

DISCUSSION QUESTIONS

1. Why is it particularly advantageous to have a standardized vocabulary and scheduling technique in a company that uses project management to accomplish many of its jobs?
2. How does a project differ from a job that is processed through a job shop or a service facility?
3. (a) What is a work breakdown structure (WBS)?
   (b) Why is a WBS useful?

4. What is the major difference between PERT and CPM?

5. What is free float?

6. What is the theoretical basis for assuming that the duration of a project can be represented by a normal probability distribution?

7. Why does analysis of only the critical path present an optimistic estimate of the probability that the project will be completed within a given time?

8. Why might simulation provide an estimate of the probability of completing a project by a given time that is different from an estimate based solely on the critical path?

PROBLEMS

1. Given below are the precedence relationships among the activities required to perform a project. Construct an AON network for the project.

Activity	Must Precede
A	B, F, C
D, H, E	K
B	L
F	L, G
C	E
L	D
G	H, E

2. Develop an AOA network for the project of problem 1.

3. Given below are the durations for the activities of the project in problem 1. Find the critical path, project duration, and the float for each activity.

Activity	Duration
A	9
B	8
C	8
D	6
E	12
F	16
G	5
H	8
K	7
L	10

4. Given below are the durations of and the precedence relationships among the activities required to complete a project.
   (a) Construct an AON network for the project.

   (b) Determine the critical path for the project.
   (c) Determine the completion time.
   (d) Determine the slack for the activities that are not on the critical path.

Activity	Duration (weeks)	Predecessor(s)
A	4	—
B	6	A
C	5	A
D	9	A
E	8	B
F	2	B,C
G	5	E
H	6	F,I
I	4	D
J	5	G,H

5. A CPM diagram is shown at the top of p. 457 with the estimated times in weeks.
   (a) Find the critical path.
   (b) Find the expected completion date.
   (c) Develop a table showing the slack for each activity.

6. For the project shown in the network in the middle of p. 457:
   (a) Find the expected project duration.
   (b) Find the critical path.
   (c) Find the slack at each activity.

7. The CPM network at the bottom of p. 457 represents a project with the times estimated in weeks.
   (a) What is the expected project duration?
   (b) What is the critical path?
   (c) Find the ES, EF, LS, LF, and float at each activity.

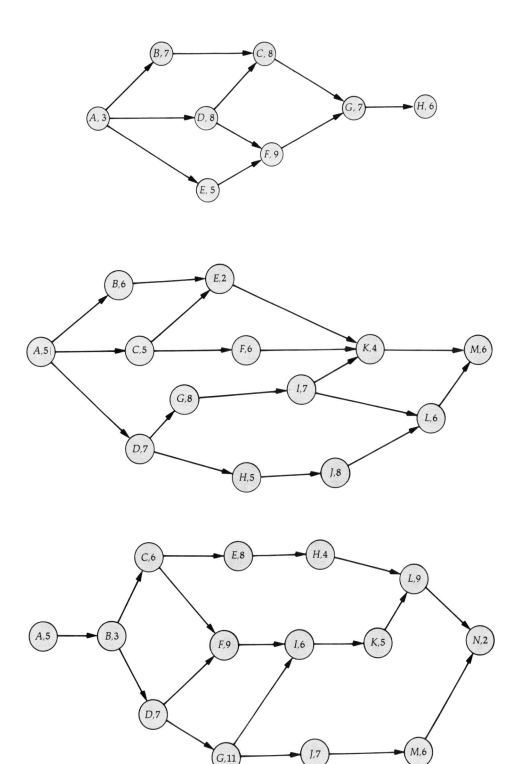

8. Shown below is an AON network for a PERT schedule on a project. The three time estimates, in weeks, for each activity are given in the table below.
   (a) Compute t_e for each activity.
   (b) Determine the expected completion time for the project.
   (c) What is the critical path?
   (d) Give the expected slack for each activity that is not on the critical path.

Activity	a	m	b
A	2	3	4
B	3	5	7
C	4	5	8
D	4	6	8
E	5	6	7
F	2	3	5
G	6	8	10
H	3	5	7
I	3	8	13
J	6	7	8
K	1	2	3

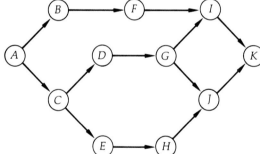

9. At the top of p. 459 is a network showing the sequence of activities that must be performed to complete a contract. The estimated duration for each task, without expediting, is indicated on the network. Because of the revenue generation ability of this project the customer has offered an incentive contract that will pay a $500 bonus for each day that the project is completed ahead of 160 days. The table below indicates the cost to expedite each activity by one, two, or three days.
   (a) Find the critical path and the normal duration.
   (b) Determine which activities should be expedited and by what amount they should be expedited so that the net bonus minus expediting costs will be maximized.
   (c) How much net bonus will be earned?

Job	Cost to Reduce 1 Day	Cost to Reduce 2nd Day	Cost to Reduce 3rd Day
A	500	600	800
B	90	200	400
C	80	200	500
D	100	300	600
E	70	180	275
F	90	200	400
G	250	500	900
H	1,000	1,200	1,500
I	400	600	800
J	100	300	600
K	250	600	1,000
L	90	300	600
M	300	450	700
N	200	400	600
O	400	800	1,400

10. A PERT diagram is shown in the middle of p. 459 with the optimistic, most likely, and pessimistic times in days shown above each arrow.
    (a) Find t_e for each activity.
    (b) Find the slack for each event and find the critical path.
    (c) What is the expected completion time?
    (d) What is the probability that the project will be completed in less than 42 days?

11. Given at the bottom of p. 459 is a PERT network for a project.
    (a) Find the expected duration of each activity.
    (b) Find the expected duration of the project.
    (b) Find the critical path.
    (d) Find the slack at each node.

12. With regard to problem 11:
    (a) Find the standard deviation of the critical path.
    (b) What is the probability of completing the project in two days less than the expected duration?

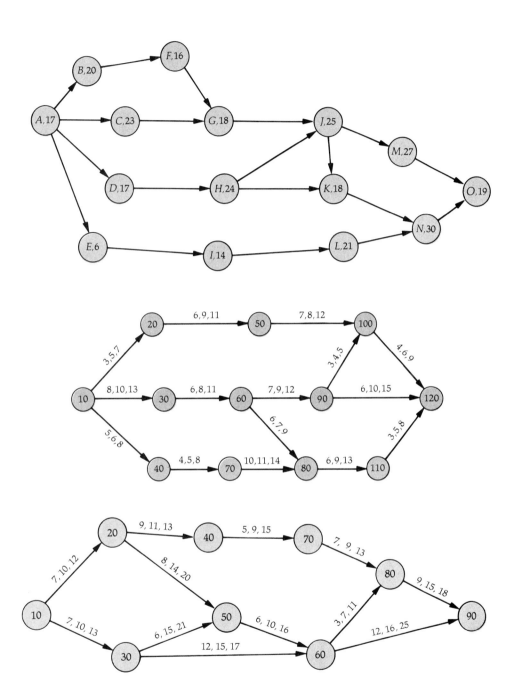

BIBLIOGRAPHY

Antill, James M., and Ronald W. Woodhead. *Critical Path Methods in Construction Practice.* New York: Wiley, 1965.

Benson, Ben. *Critical Path Methods in Building Construction,* Englewood Cliffs, N.J.: Prentice-Hall, 1970.

Budnick, Frank S., Richard Mojena, and Thomas E. Vollman. *Principles of Operations Research for Management.* Homewood, Ill.: Irwin, 1977.

Cleland, David I., and William R. King. *Systems Analysis and Project Management.* 3d ed. New York: McGraw-Hill, 1983.

Clough, Richard H. *Construction Project Management.* New York: Wiley-Interscience, 1972.

Davis, E. W., ed. *Project Management: Techniques, Applications, and Managerial Issues.* 2d ed. Norcross, Ga.: Industrial Engineering and Management Press, 1983.

Hillier, Frederick S., and Gerald J. Lieberman. *Introduction to Operations Research.* 2d ed. San Francisco: Holden Day, 1974.

Horowitz, Joseph. *Critical Path Scheduling: Management Control Through CPM and PERT.* New York: Ronald Press, 1967.

Johnson, Richard A., William T. Newell, and Roger C. Vergin. *Production and Operations Management.* Boston: Houghton Mifflin, 1974.

Kerzner, Harold. *Project Management: A Systems Approach to Planning, Scheduling, and Controlling.* New York: Van Nostrand Reinhold, 1984.

Levin, Richard I., and Charles A. Kirkpatrick. *Planning and Control with PERT/CPM.* (Paperback.) New York: McGraw-Hill, 1966.

Martin, Charles C. *Project Management: How to Make It Work.* New York: AMACOM, 1976.

Moder, Joseph J., Cecil R. Phillips, and Edward W. Davis. *Project Management with CPM, PERT, and Precedence Diagramming.* 3d ed. New York: Van Nostrand Reinhold, 1983.

O'Brien, James J. *CPM in Construction Management.* New York: McGraw-Hill, 1971.

Radcliffe, Byron, Donald E. Kawal, and Ralph J. Stephenson. *Critical Path Method.* Chicago: Cahners, 1967.

Smith, Larry A., and Peter Mahler. "Comparing Commercially Available CPM/PERT Computer Programs." *Industrial Engineering,* April 1978, pp. 37–39.

Wiest, Jerome D., and Ferdinand K. Levy. *A Management Guide to PERT/CPM.* Englewood Cliffs, N.J.: Prentice-Hall, 1969.

Supplement G Outline
MAINTENANCE

PREVENTIVE AND REMEDIAL MAINTENANCE
Preventive Maintenance / Remedial Maintenance

THE IMPORTANCE OF SOUND MAINTENANCE MANAGEMENT

MANAGING MAINTENANCE ACTIVITIES

BASIC MAINTENANCE DECISIONS
Centralized Versus Decentralized Maintenance / Contract Versus In-House Maintenance / Standby Equipment / Repair Versus Replacement / Individual Versus Group Replacement / Amount of Maintenance Capacity / Preventive Maintenance Versus Remedial Repair

EVALUATION OF PREVENTIVE MAINTENANCE POLICIES
Application: Analyzing Costs of Maintenance vs. Repair

Summary / **Discussion Questions** / **Problem**

KEY TERMS

Preventive maintenance   Decentralized   Centralized   Standby equipment
Remedial maintenance   maintenance   Maintenance

MAINTENANCE

The care and maintenance of assets may have an important effect upon sizable investments. Company investments are very large today because increasingly sophisticated mechanization, automation, and other technology is being employed. Companies' operations have become increasingly dependent on the operating condition of their equipment because of the increased productivity that this equipment helps achieve, and many companies have reduced their inventories that could keep the company operating while equipment is being repaired. Poor care of equipment and facilities can be expensive: it allows a large investment to deteriorate, and breakdowns reduce the returns that could be earned. Operations managers must be concerned with the care of assets in their charge.

PREVENTIVE AND REMEDIAL MAINTENANCE

Maintenance operations include all efforts to keep productive facilities and equipment in acceptable operating condition. There are two general types of maintenance, preventive and remedial.

Preventive Maintenance

Preventive maintenance (PM) consists of maintenance activities performed before equipment breaks down, with the intent of keeping it operating acceptably and reducing the likelihood of breakdown. A broad view of PM includes:

1. Design, selection, and installation of equipment and systems so as to achieve acceptable reliability.
2. Periodic inspection and record keeping to assess the condition of facilities and equipment so breakdowns can be avoided.
3. Adequate lubricating, painting, cleaning, and adjusting to maintain operating conditions.
4. Periodic repetitive servicing, repair, or overhauls, even though no breakdown has occurred.

Remedial Maintenance

Remedial maintenance consists of efforts to restore facilities and equipment to an acceptable

463

operating condition after a breakdown has occurred. Automobile care provides a familiar example of maintenance efforts. Tune-ups, lubrication, and waxing are preventive maintenance operations whose timing is subject to some discretion. Repair of something that breaks on the automobile is remedial maintenance. Sometimes the vehicle will not operate until it is repaired, so there is less discretion about the timing of these repairs. Some companies have standby equipment so that breakdowns do not stop production and equipment can be repaired at scheduled times.

THE IMPORTANCE OF SOUND MAINTENANCE MANAGEMENT

Preventive maintenance efforts can interfere with production just as breakdowns can. Maintenance efforts must be managed effectively to keep either type of interference to an economical minimum. Operating a maintenance department costs money, so it should be planned and controlled just as any other department should be. Maintenance activities affect a company's return on investment because they represent an expense and because down time for maintenance may cause missed deliveries. Effective maintenance helps ensure the productivity of a company by influencing the percentage of time that its equipment can operate. It also affects the operation of the equipment, which directly affects the quality of the system's outputs. Maintenance also influences return on investment because it affects the economic lifetime and salvage value of equipment.

The objectives of maintenance management include:

1. Minimizing the loss of productive time and cost because of malfunctioning equipment.
2. Minimizing the loss of productive time and cost because of maintenance efforts.

3. Efficient use of maintenance personnel and equipment.
4. Preserving the company's investment and prolonging the life of assets to increase the time over which investments provide service.

MANAGING MAINTENANCE ACTIVITIES

In many respects, managing maintenance activities is like managing other operations. Preventive maintenance efforts are recurring activities that may be performed at preestablished times. They are much like provision of standardized service or production of a standardized product on a recurring basis. Managing remedial maintenance, however, is more like managing a job shop than a mass-production operation, since the demand for this service often is not repetitive and usually is not forecast. Completion dates for remedial maintenance frequently are expedited, since a breakdown usually means that the equipment was involved in some productive activity that required its service.

Maintenance personnel must perform some work initially in order to diagnose the extent of the problem and estimate the amount and type of work that will be required. This step is similar to estimating in a job shop operation. Further scheduling and planning can be done after the initial diagnosis. Scheduling requires that the steps of work and their sequence be identified. The labor hours that will be required for each skill must be estimated. The tools, equipment, and supplies that will be needed must be identified and obtained if they are not already on hand. If either the appropriately skilled personnel, equipment (capacity), or material is not available, the work cannot be performed. Priorities must be determined if materials are available and a number of jobs are competing for use of the same capacity. These priorities help in planning and controlling the efficient use of maintenance labor. Clearly this procedure is very similar to job shop scheduling. Yet when maintenance work has a long work cycle and is nonrepetitive, it more closely resembles a project than a job shop operation.

Some previous considerations in regard to inventory also apply to maintenance operations. An inventory of repair parts may be maintained to reduce the lead time before repairs can begin. Information from equipment vendors and from past repair records may be used to help forecast the reliability of various components and equipment in the operations system. The costs of down time (lost production and customer ill will) and the savings to be achieved by reducing repair lead time must be evaluated and compared with the cost of keeping parts in inventory. This information can be used to determine the items and amounts that should be held as inventory of repair parts. Spare-parts inventories are subject to costs for obsolescence, taxes and insurance, costs of invested capital, and other costs, like any other types of inventories.

Quality of maintenance work must be ensured if equipment is to be kept running properly. The material on quality in the following chapter applies also to maintenance management.

BASIC MAINTENANCE DECISIONS

Centralized Versus Decentralized Maintenance

Some companies choose to have one large maintenance department, others have a small maintenance department for each part of the company. Individual or *decentralized maintenance* departments may be justified if each part of the company needs a different special skill, special equipment, or very rapid response. However, the work load is more easily distributed with a *centralized maintenance* department.

Contract Versus In-House Maintenance

Some companies do not have enough equipment to justify the expense of a maintenance department. A company with one or two automobiles would not employ a full-time mechanic to repair and service them. Many companies with large fleets of vehicles, however, have their own service garages. Some companies that have their own maintenance departments with facilities to do repair work still use outside contract workers for some of their maintenance. Occasional highly specialized or seasonal maintenance work may be contracted.

Standby Equipment

Sometimes older machines are not sold when they are replaced but are held as *standby equipment* for occasional use in production. One issue related to maintenance is the number of such machines a company should have. Also, newer equipment may be purchased to provide redundancy so that the reliability of the production system is enhanced. The need for extra equipment depends on many factors, such as the reliability of each piece of equipment, the length of time required to perform a repair, the waiting time to begin a repair, the percentage of time that production operations are scheduled, and the cost of lost production time.

Repair Versus Replacement

When a machine breaks down, the best course of action is not always obvious. If equipment is due to be replaced before long, it may be better to replace it than to invest additional money in repairing it. The cash flows required to repair and keep presently-owned equipment may be compared with the cash flows required for the best alternative replacement equipment.

Individual Versus Group Replacement

Some items are used in large quantities—light bulbs, for instance. The saving in labor costs to replace all the bulbs in one section of a building at the same time may more than offset the cost of the good bulbs that are removed. Decisions must be reached also regarding the frequency of replacement.

Amount of Maintenance Capacity

The amount of maintenance capacity a company should have is related to many other issues. The amount and type of equipment to be maintained and the extent to which contract maintenance is used are two basic factors that affect the size of the in-house force. The frequency of requirements for service and the cost of lost production time also are important determinants of the proper capacity.

Insight into this question can sometimes be gained through queuing analysis or simulation. All machines in a facility represent a population from which demands for service may arrive at the maintenance department. The cost of down time while equipment is waiting and being serviced is compared with the cost of maintenance capacity sufficient to provide rapid repair. A balance should be achieved between the cost of delays and the cost of maintenance capacity.

Suppose that a group of machines is large enough to make the probability of an arrival constant and that the interarrival times and service times are distributed according to a negative exponential distribution (Poisson arrival rates). Suppose that the machines break down at a mean rate, λ, of 0.8 per week. One worker can repair one per week ($\mu = 1$ per

week), and the equipment is such that repair time is reduced proportionally as more workers are available, up to a maximum of four. Beyond that number of workers, a second channel in the queuing system would be opened. Maintenance workers are paid $250 per week, and idle machine time is valued at $750 per week. Assume the cost of additional tools is negligible. How many workers should be employed?

If one worker is employed, the cost of tending the facility will be $250. The cost of idle time can be found by the use of queuing formulas. The mean number of machines in the system, L_s, is

$$L_s = \frac{\lambda}{\mu - \lambda} = \frac{0.8}{1 - 0.8} = 4.$$

The total cost with one repair worker would be 1($250) + 4($750) = $3,250. Two workers would raise the service rate to two machines per week, so

$$L_s = \frac{0.8}{2 - 0.8} = \frac{0.8}{1.2} = 0.6667.$$

The total cost would be 2($250) + 0.6667($750) = $1,000. Three workers would raise the service rate to three machines per week.

$$L_s = \frac{0.8}{3 - 0.8} = 0.3636$$

The total cost would be 3($250) + 0.3636($750) = $1,023. The optimum number of repair workers to employ for this situation is two.

Preventive Maintenance Versus Remedial Repair

Should a company spend most of its time on minor tune-ups and preventive work, or should it just wait until something breaks and then fix it? The answer to this question depends on

FIGURE G.1

Cost of Preventive Maintenance vs. Cost of Repair

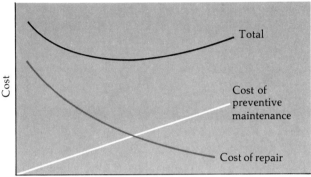

several factors, including the relative cost of prevention versus the cost of repair. Probably some trade-off between the two extremes is advisable, because the costs may follow the pattern shown in Figure G.1.

EVALUATION OF PREVENTIVE MAINTENANCE POLICIES

The absence of preventive maintenance can be expensive because of down time and because the cost of repairs may be more expensive than preventive action. Too much preventive maintenance, however, may be excessively expensive. A balance between the two extremes sometimes can be found by modeling the costs.

Assume that M identical machines are used for a process and that the average cost of a preventive maintenance service is C_p. The cost of a major repair if the machine is run until breakdown is C_R. (Naturally C_R will be greater than C_p or we would not be interested in preventing breakdowns.) Let P_i be the probability that the machine will break down in the ith period after it has been serviced.

The mean time between failures (MTBF)

will be

$$\text{MTBF} = \sum_{i=1}^{n} iP_i$$

where n = the longest number of periods that a machine will go without failure.

The expected cost per period of not providing preventive maintenance will be

$$TC \text{ (no preventive maintenance)} = C_R \frac{M}{\sum_{i=1}^{n} iP_i}.$$

To begin, let us calculate the cost of routine preventive maintenance every period. Part of this cost will be $C_p \cdot M$ to perform the preventive service. In addition, some number of machines, B_1, will break down during the first period after preventive service and be repaired. $B_1 = M \cdot P_1$, where P_1 equals the probability that a machine will break down in the first period after it is serviced. The cost of repairing breakdowns if machines are serviced every period will be $C_R B_1$, so

$$TC(1) = C_p M + C_R B_1 = C_p M + C_R M P_1$$

where $TC(1)$ = the total cost if machines are serviced every period.

We can extend this type of analysis to consider repairing machines every j periods. Let B_j equal the number of breakdowns between preventive services when these services are performed every jth period. Recall that P_i equals the probability that a machine will break down in the ith period after it is serviced. Then

$$B_2 = M(P_1 + P_2) + B_1P_1$$
$$B_3 = M(P_1 + P_2 + P_3) + B_2P_1 + B_1P_2$$

In general,

$$B_j = M(P_1 + P_2 + \cdots + P_j)$$
$$+ B_{j-1}P_1 + B_{j-2}P_2$$
$$+ \cdots + B_1P_{j-1}$$

and the total cost for j periods if the machines are repaired every j period is

$$TC(j) = C_PM + C_RB_j.$$

The average cost per period for this policy will be $TC(j)/j$.

We have examined the type of analysis that may be used to determine preventive maintenance frequency when the P_M cost is compared with the cost of repairing a breakdown. But consideration should be given to other factors as well. Since breakdowns cannot be scheduled, they usually disrupt productive activities and cause additional expenses for

APPLICATION

Analyzing Costs of Maintenance vs. Repair

The Delsoni Laundromat chain has 50 identical coin-operated machines in its facilities throughout the city. The cost of preventive servicing, C_P, is $20, and the cost of repair after a breakdown, C_R, is $100. The company seeks the minimum-cost preventive servicing frequency and has collected the data on breakdown probabilities in Table G.1.

Table G.1
PROBABILITIES OF WASHING MACHINE BREAKDOWN, BY MONTH

Months After Servicing That Breakdown Occurs, i	Probability That Breakdown Will Occur, P_i	iP_i
1	0.10	0.10
2	0.05	0.10
3	0.05	0.15
4	0.10	0.40
5	0.15	0.75
6	0.15	0.90
7	0.20	1.40
8	0.20	1.60
	1.00	5.40

The mean time between failures is 5.4 months, and the expected cost with no preventive maintenance would be $100 $\times$ 50/5.4 = $925.93 per month. The following calculations show B_j, the expected number of breakdowns between preventive maintenance intervals, for the possible intervals that may be considered. The costs of various preventive maintenance intervals are summarized in Table G.2.

$B_1 = MP_1 = 50(0.10) = 5$

$B_2 = M(P_1 + P_2) + B_1P_1 = 50(0.10 + 0.05) + 5(0.10) = 8$

$B_3 = 50(0.10 + 0.05 + 0.05) + 8(0.10) + 5(0.05) = 11.05$

$B_4 = 50(0.10 + 0.05 + 0.05 + 0.10) + 11.05(0.10) + 8(0.05)$
$\qquad + 5(0.05) = 16.75$

$B_5 = 50(0.10 + 0.05 + 0.05 + 0.10 + 0.15) + 16.75(0.10)$
$\qquad + 11.05(0.05) + 8(0.05) + 5(0.10) = 25.63$

$B_6 = 50(0.6) + 25.63(0.1) + 16.75(0.05) + 11.05(0.05)$
$\qquad + 8(0.1) + 5(0.15) = 35.5$

$B_7 = 50(0.8) + 35.5(0.1) + 25.63(0.05) + 16.75(0.05) + 11.05(0.10)$
$\qquad + 8(0.15) + 5(0.15) = 48.72$

$B_8 = 50(1) + 48.72(0.1) + 35.5(0.05) + 25.63(0.05) + 16.75(0.1)$
$\qquad + 11.05(0.15) + 8(0.15) + 5(0.2) = 63.46$

Table G.2
COST OF ALTERNATIVE PREVENTIVE MAINTENANCE INTERVALS

(1) j, Number of Months Between Preventive Services	(2) B_j, Expected Number of Breakdowns in j Months	(3) Expected Cost Per Month to Repair Breakdowns $C_R \cdot B_j/j$	(4) Cost Per Month for Preventive Service Every j Months $C_P(M)/j$	(5) Total Expected Cost Per Month of Preventive Maintenance and Repair (3) + (4)
1	5.00	$500.00	$1,000.00	$1,500.00
2	8.00	400.00	500.00	900.00
3	11.05	368.33	333.33	701.66
4	16.75	418.75	250.00	668.75
5	25.63	512.60	200.00	712.60
6	35.50	591.67	166.67	758.34
7	48.72	696.00	142.86	838.86
8	63.46	793.25	125.00	918.25

A policy of performing preventive maintenance every four months results in the lowest average cost, about $669. This amount is $257 per month less than the $926 expected cost without preventive maintenance. This policy would reduce costs by $257/926 \cdot 100 = 27.75$ percent below the cost of repairing the machines only when they break down.

rescheduling and expediting work. Breakdowns also cause delivery dates to be missed, resulting in customer ill will.

Preventive activities usually can be scheduled to occur when equipment is not normally in operation (such as evening shifts or weekends). We saw in the earlier discussion of queuing that random occurrences of demand make the queuing situation more difficult and cause poorer use of capacity than can be achieved with scheduled arrivals. Thus the use of maintenance personnel can be made more efficient in scheduled preventive activities than in unscheduled remedial activities. It is apparent that in analyzing preventive versus remedial maintenance, factors other than the direct cost of each type of activity should be considered.

SUMMARY

Maintenance activities affect the cost of operations in several ways. There is a direct cost for conducting preventive and/or remedial maintenance work. Maintenance also affects the reliability of the operations system by varying the percentage of its capacity that is productive. Breakdowns often cause extra costs for rescheduling and expediting delayed work as well as those of ill will if deliveries are delayed. Care and maintenance of equipment affect the lifetime and salvage value of equipment, thereby having an impact on the rate of return earned on the invested funds.

In evaluating maintenance policies a company may consider several options and trade-offs, among them (1) centralized versus decentralized maintenance; (2) the use of contract versus in-house maintenance; (3) the number of standby machines to hold; (4) repair versus replacement of defective equipment; (5) individual versus group replacement, when large numbers of similar items are employed in an operation; (6) the amount of maintenance capacity that should be kept available; and (7) the extent to which preventive and remedial maintenance should be used.

DISCUSSION QUESTIONS

1. Discuss the difference between preventive and remedial maintenance. Give examples of each.
2. How might managing a maintenance operation incorporate some of the features of managing both a job shop and a make-to-stock operation at the same time?

PROBLEM

1. The Ecstasy Inn motel has 100 television sets in its rooms. The manager has an opportunity to sign a maintenance contract that calls for an annual payment of $12 per television set. The contract will provide preventive maintenance and adjustments to the sets at six-month intervals. Currently the average repair cost is $25 each time a set is repaired or adjusted. The probabilities of breakdown at various intervals after a repair are given in the table below.

PROBABILITY OF BREAKDOWN
AFTER REPAIR, BY MONTH

(Month)	(Probability)
1	0.12
2	0.08
3	0.08
4	0.08

5	0.08
6	0.08
7	0.08
8	0.11
9	0.13
10	0.16

(a) Should the manager purchase the maintenance service as offered at six-month intervals?

(b) Should he attempt to obtain service at other intervals?

Chapter Outline
QUALITY ASSURANCE

WHY IS QUALITY IMPORTANT?

The Importance of Quality to a Company / *Operations Management in Action:* TOP MANAGEMENT TO PURCHASING: MAKE QUALITY YOUR TOP PRIORITY / The Importance of Quality to a Nation / Breadth of Quality Assurance Activities in a Company

CONTROLLING QUALITY OF DESIGN

Operations Management in Action: IDEAS FROM DR. DEMING

OPERATIONS AND QUALITY OF CONFORMANCE

Interrelated Activities Pertaining to Quality / Where and When to Inspect

STATISTICAL TOOLS TO CONTROL QUALITY OF CONFORMANCE

PROCESS CONTROL

Type I and Type II Errors / The Control Chart: A Stimulus to Corrective Action / Establishing Control Limits for $\overline{X}$ and R / *Application: Establishing Control Limits for $\overline{X}$ and R* / Sampling by Attributes / Control Charts for the Fraction Defective / Control Charts for Defects per Unit / *Application: A Control Chart for Defects per Unit*

ACCEPTANCE SAMPLING

Single Sampling / Double Sampling / Sequential Sampling / Selecting a Single Sampling Plan for Sampling by Attributes / Average Outgoing Quality (AOQ) / *Application: Finding α and β for a Stated Sampling Plan* / Dodge-Romig Tables / Mil-Std-105D

QUALITY CIRCLES

Summary / Solved Problems / Discussion Questions / Problems / Bibliography

KEY TERMS

Quality assurance	Type I error	Central limit theorem	Producer's risk
Quality of design	Type II error	Control chart for the	Lot tolerance percent
Quality of conformance	Control chart	fraction defective or	defective (LTPD)
Quality of performance	Control limits	p chart	Limiting quality level
or service	Control chart for the	Control chart for	(LQL)
Quality circle	mean, or $\overline{X}$ chart	defects per unit, or	Consumer's risk
Inspection	Control chart for the	c chart	Average outgoing
Receiving inspection	range, or R chart	Single sampling	quality (AOQ)
In-process inspection	Chance cause	Double sampling	Average outgoing
Final inspection	Upper control limit	Sequential sampling	quality limit (AOQL)
Statistical quality	(UCL)	Sample size, n	Quality circle or quality
control	Lower control limit	Acceptance number, c	control circle
Sampling by attributes	(LCL)	Acceptable quality level	Pareto analysis
Sampling by variables	Assignable cause	(AQL)	Cause-and-effect
Process control	Specification limits	Operating characteristic	diagram
Acceptance sampling	Warning limit	curve, or OC curve	Facilitator

Chapter 11

QUALITY ASSURANCE

A company's success is greatly influenced by the quality of goods or services the company provides and by the costs incurred in achieving that quality. Consumers assess the value they can obtain by purchasing goods or services from the company, where value is the amount of quality they can obtain for a given price. The quality of the company's goods or services and its reputation for customer service and satisfaction greatly influence the customer's decision. Operations managers and operations personnel have a major responsibility to help the company deliver to the customer a quality product at a reasonable price. In Chapter 2 we discussed quality as one of the performance characteristics that a company considers in selecting its business strategy and operations strategy.

Just what does the term *quality* mean? The quality of a good or service is its fitness for its intended use. A product must be adequate for the application that the customer has in mind. A company might sell an outdoorsman a sleek deluxe model pickup truck with high-traction tires by leading him to believe that it will perform as well off the highway as a four-wheel-drive vehicle. It may be an extremely well-made two-wheel-drive vehicle and beautiful. But if he becomes mired down at a sandy beach or desert or in a muddy swamp he will be just as dissatisfied with it as he would have been with a poorly made four-wheel-drive vehicle.

You can see that advertising and sales personnel, and many persons in the company besides those who actually build a product, have a responsibility for quality. Armand Feigenbaum, a noted authority on quality, defines quality as "the total composite product and service characteristics of marketing, engineering, manufacture, and maintenance through which the product and service in use will meet the expectations of the customer"; and he uses the term "total quality control" to emphasize this broad involvement of the *total* company in quality.[1] The term *quality assurance* as used in this chapter also has this same broad perspective. The glossary of the American Society for Quality Control states: "when quality assurance is used in the total system sense, as it normally is without a restrictive adjective, it has to do with all aspects of quality."[2] In this chapter, the same broad perspective is emphasized; however, primary consideration is given to the part that the operations function plays in achieving quality.

Quality has three major aspects: (1) the product or service must be designed to be of at least the minimum appropriate grade for its use, (2) it should conform to the standards of the design, (3) the consumer should receive the necessary training and service support so that his use of the product is satisfactory within reasonable expectations. These three major aspects of quality can be summarized as

> *quality of design*
>
> *quality of conformance*
>
> *quality of performance or service*

WHY IS QUALITY IMPORTANT?

The quality of goods and services is important for several reasons both at the specific business level and at the national level. First, let us examine the importance of quality for an individual business. Then we shall discuss some reasons that a nation as a whole must be concerned about the quality provided by its production systems.

The Importance of Quality to a Company

Companies compete for consumers' business on several bases. The three most frequently recognized factors that influence a potential purchaser are price, quality, and availability. Basically, quality or the potential customer's perception of quality, which can be influenced by advertising and promotional efforts, is very important. When competing products are available (or can be made available at about the same time), the customer mentally performs an evaluation of the price-quality trade-off. He or she may or may not calculate an explicit cost-benefit ratio, but the concept is very much the same. The basic question is: How much service do I get for my money? A company then has to provide a competitive level of quality at a competitive price in order to have the necessary sales revenue to pay its expenses and leave a profit (see box).

[1]Armand V. Feigenbaum, *Total Quality Control*, 3d ed. (New York: McGraw-Hill, 1983), p. 7.
[2]*Glossary and Tables for Statistical Quality Control* (Milwaukee: American Society for Quality Control, 1983), p. 6.

OPERATIONS MANAGEMENT IN ACTION

Top Management to Purchasing: Make Quality Your Top Priority

We asked a smattering of bright purchasing managers across the country to pinpoint the single most-important demand that top management is now making on their buying organizations. The finding of our informal spot check: Quality is still number one, 100% of the time.

Some sharp-shooters paused for a moment, mentally screening their choices to eliminate the least critical, and replied "quality"—end of conversation. Others, after taking that same pause, would say something like, "I could spend the afternoon telling you what they [management] expect, but if I have to pick one, I guess it's got to be quality." And others went a step further, ranking management demands in terms of importance. Quality, delivery, and pricing emerged the top three.

Here's a Closer Look:

"Quality is free. It doesn't hurt to get it right the first time around," says Stephen D. Morton, purchasing manager at Bendix Field Engineering Corp., a division of Allied Bendix Aerospace in Columbia, Md. He says the big push is to move quality from dock to dock. "We're trying to instill a preoccupation with quality that goes beyond quality systems, that extends to a quality consciousness in employees."

Morton adds that the only way a faulty part should get out of a supplier's plant is via the scrap heap. Morton is most apt to buy from "more highly-automated, more capital-intensive, less people-intensive, suppliers."

All the Angles

Thomas F. Bonnoil, purchasing manager at the magnetic tape division of Ampex Corp., Opelika, Ala, likens quality's rise in importance to triangles. "It used to be an equilateral triangle—with pricing, service, and quality the same. Now it's an isosceles triangle with quality right at the top," he says. There is "immense pressure" on Ampex suppliers to meet specs, and quality meetings are held regularly to ensure it, Bonnoil adds.

While he cites quality performance at the top of the list, Douglas M. Pedder, director of purchasing for the residential group at Aluminum Processing Corp., a division of Lightolier in Fall River, Mass., feels management pressure in other areas, too: cost reduction/avoidance, supplier delivery performance, improved contracting, and negotiation. To get "better pricing and more leverage," Pedder is trying to centralize negotiations with national contracts to service the three divisions for which he's now responsible. He's also concerned with long-term contracts so "the company won't be hurt by any snafu—either supply/demand or strikewise."

Charles Adams, director of procurement at Wright Line in Worcester, Mass., says quality, delivery, and cost are "all vital concerns." Because the plant is operating at full capacity, however, the pressure is more on production, with "purchasing gearing up to support them," says Adams. With the constant pressure to get materials in on schedule, Adams notes it's been difficult to concentrate on cost reduction. "The demands on the plant are just too great right now," he says. There have been some problems in corrugated packaging particularly, as Wright Line requires big, bulky boxes and strives for just-in-time delivery to avoid storage.

Controlling the Flow

J. Robert Connell, PM at the Coca-Cola Foods Division in Auburndale, Fla., says continuity of supply, quality of supply, and pricing ("something you can never turn your back on") are the top three concerns, but quality is "uppermost in our minds, while it may not be in theirs [management]."

In addition to quality, Joe Viva, procurement manager of the test systems group at Fairchild Camera and Instrument Corp. in Latham, N.Y., says this particular industry is having problems with demand changes and getting products in a hurry—"lesser than lead-time, if you will." They're also working to improve costs and find more innovative ways to control inventory. "We're trying to maintain inventory we have here while not showing it on the books. We've developed in-house stores and have distribution stock materials there. It's basically entering into a closer partnership with distribution. And we're still looking for the assurance that a product will be here on the day that it's due," Viva says.

Knotting the Ties

Vern Sawyer, director of international purchasing in PPG Industries in Pittsburgh, Pa., says, "Top management is asking purchasing to establish even closer ties with our key suppliers to ensure they understand our basic strategies and our dependence on them to provide us with: (1) products meeting quality requirements on a consistent basis; (2) technological support as we strive to anticipate changing requirements in our marketplace; (3) timely deliveries to optimize inventory dollars; and (4) pricing that helps us to remain competitive."

Purchasing, *October 4, 1984, p. 23. Reprinted from* Purchasing Magazine. *Copyright by Cahners Publishing Co., 1984*

Product Liability *(caveat emptor, and the company had better watch out, too!)* Product liability is a substantial component in the risk of doing business. A person who is injured because of a faulty product has a right to take legal action against its manufacturer. A product may be considered faulty because of poor design, lack of conformance to the design, or misuse by the purchaser or someone else. Any potential hazards must be designed out of the product if possible. Potential hazards that cannot be avoided must be shielded by guards, and instructions must explicitly caution the user about them. Injuries caused by a product can result in excessive legal expenses and large settlements.

A company must police itself to prevent excessive liability costs. Also it must not allow its product to develop a bad safety reputation, since an unsafe product is less likely to be purchased. The U.S. government has tried to regulate product safety with several laws, one of the more important being the Consumer Product Safety Act of 1972. A major objective of this act is to set and enforce product standards by banning from the marketplace those products that do not meet the standards. A company has to remain aware of the applicable standards and make sure that its product is in compliance if it intends to stay in business.

The Importance of Quality to a Nation

Quality considerations are important to a nation as a whole. If its industry is to compete effectively in the world marketplace, its reputation for quality must be adequate for the price it asks.[3]

A developing nation must produce goods to prevent importation, which drains off wealth, prevents capital accumulation, and provides no employment for its citizens. If industries are to be developed successfully, the goods produced within the nation must compete with those of other nations in price, quality, and availability.[4] Low quality per unit price means low sales and a poor

[3]Centre for Policy Studies, *Quality Control in a Developing Economy: A Case Study of Israel* (Jerusalem, 1970).
[4]Harold L. Gilmore, "Quality Assurance and National Development: A Study of Zambia," *Quality Progress,* January 1977.

economy. A poor economy means little money to train skilled workers and little accumulation of capital to build production facilities that provide jobs and income. If a country purchases all of its goods from outside its borders, it will probably never develop.

Developed nations also need to strive to improve and encourage quality in their industries. The quality, cost, and availability of the nation's goods and services must remain competitive. In today's world of international competition, a nation that lets quality fall behind can suffer severe economic problems. Jobs will be lost, tax revenues will be reduced, and the standard of living will decline.

Breadth of Quality Assurance Activities in a Company

The final measurement of the value of a product to the consumer is made after the product has been designed, produced, and used. Quality is really measured after the customer has had the product for its intended period of service. The customer is the "final inspector" of quality.

As mentioned earlier, the term *quality assurance* is intended to include all of the activities that are performed to ensure that the product performs to the customer's satisfaction, and many parts of the company are involved. Some of the activities that affect quality are listed below.

1. *Reliability engineering,* to ensure that the design will have an adequate useful life.
2. *Value engineering,* to ensure that the product will perform the necessary function at the minimum cost.
3. *Evaluation of usability,* to see that the product will be convenient and safe in the hands of the user.
4. *Process control,* to ensure that the materials, processes, and other inputs to the transformation process are adequate for the intended product.
5. *Product screening* and appraisal, to see that the output that is sold to customers is of sufficient quality.
6. *Service assurance,* to see that the customer is adequately trained to use and maintain the product and that service parts and manuals are made available.
7. Quality feedback to provide *corrective action* when field use indicates inadequate quality.

The activities mentioned above include those aimed at quality of design, quality of conformance, and quality of service. They are not always performed within the quality assurance department of a company. Quality assurance departments have undergone a widening focus through the years, so that their responsibilities may be quite broad.

CONTROLLING QUALITY OF DESIGN

In some instances, a company has little latitude to establish the design of a product it may produce. Some products are considered commodity goods—that is, goods with a basic design and characteristics that are established by commercial codes and association standards. Companies that produce these products compete primarily on the basis of price and service, but the quality must meet the standards and remain consistent. Standard structural shapes of common steel are one example. Custom job shop manufacturers may occasionally be asked which of some design options would be more economical to produce; but typically they have little involvement with design matters. Most job shops bid on and produce according to preestablished designs and specifications. As one condition for being awarded business, the job shop must assure customers that its quality control is adequate. Other types of manufacturing operations perform a fuller range of activities that affect quality.

When a manufacturing company is free to establish the design of its product, the degree to which the design meets its customers' needs depends on the activities of several groups and how well these activities are integrated into an effective system. This integrated interaction is very important (see box, especially point 9) and has been found to be one of the characteristics shared by what are considered to be some of America's best-managed factories.[5] Good marketing research and assessment of consumer behavior should lead to an understanding of customer needs that might be served. These needs, and the product concepts that might serve these needs must be clearly communicated to product development or design engineering personnel so that a quality product (i.e., one that serves the needs) can be developed. As design concepts evolve, it is important that designers work with process development or manufacturing engineers to ensure that the design can be economically produced with little chance for errors. Trial manufacturing runs may be made to test the design and production methods. Analysis of designs and coordination of a possible series of iterations between design and production activities can be improved and speeded by use of computer-aided design and manufacturing, CAD/CAM. Before specifications are finalized, purchasing can also be involved to see that good quality, reasonably priced components and materials are available. Suppliers might suggest some refinements within the areas of their specialties to achieve even better ways of serving the customer's needs. The basic design might be revised through several iterations to achieve a sound one. Designs should be reviewed for maintainability and reliability. Once the design is finalized, specifications can be prepared that clearly spell out what the company intends to produce.

Design in Nonmanufacturing   In some service businesses, the design is already established, much as it is for a commodity product. An electrical utility is a service business with well-established specifications for its output. To achieve customer satisfaction such businesses must produce their product with economy, consistency, and reliability.

Some service organizations might go through a procedure much like the product design process. Consider, for example, a fast food restaurant. Specific

---

[5]Gene Bylinski, "America's Best-Managed Factories," *Fortune*, May 28, 1984, pp. 16–24.

OPERATIONS MANAGEMENT IN ACTION

Ideas From Dr. Deming

Dr. W. Edwards Deming, a statistician and proponent of statistical quality control was one of the Americans who went to Japan after World War II to help reindustrialize that war-torn country. Deming is given much of the credit for the great improvement in the quality of Japanese goods. In fact, the highest award given in Japan each year for industrial quality is named the Deming Award. Deming has been a critic of quality efforts in the United States, attributing most of the problem to the system and saying that managers are responsible for it. Deming has evolved fourteen major points for improving quality, which are summarized below.

Deming's 14 Points

1. Establish the objective of constant innovation and improvement.
2. Adopt a new philosophy, we cannot accept the old mistakes and defects.
3. Cease dependence on mass inspection, require statistical evidence that quality is built in.
4. End the practice of awarding business on the basis of price.
5. Use statistical methods to find the trouble spots.
6. Institute modern methods of training on the job.
7. Improve supervision—do what is right for the company, don't just turn out the required quantity.
8. Drive out fear, so people will feel secure to point out problems and ask for information.
9. Break down barriers between departments and with suppliers and customers so there will be open, effective communication.
10. Eliminate posters and slogans, they don't help people solve problems. Go to work and show people how.
11. Eliminate work standards that prescribe a numerical quota, they disregard quality and put a ceiling on production.
12. Remove barriers between workers and their right to pride in workmanship.
13. Institute a vigorous retraining program to keep up with changes and new developments.
14. Create a top management structure that will push every day for these points.

W. Edwards Deming, Quality, Productivity, and Competitive Position *(Cambridge, Mass.: MIT Press, 1982), pp. 16–17.*

menu items are defined, and the recipes and processing instructions are spelled out to ensure consistent preparation. Standards of decor, cleanliness, and conduct are established so that the atmosphere and service provided to customers will be consistent. Suppliers are informed of the standards for ingredients and supplies so that these will consistently be of the proper grade for the clientele that the restaurant intends to serve. Occasionally, new menu items may appear at some outlets to test the market and the workability of the new product mix.

OPERATIONS AND QUALITY OF CONFORMANCE

Once the target level of quality has been established and a design has been developed, the challenge becomes one of producing items or providing services that conform to the design. Quality must be built in when an item is manufactured or when a service is provided. Thus the operations function plays a vital role in achieving quality of conformance. Operations personnel must take care to see that their actions lead to quality at a reasonable cost. Much of the remainder of the chapter discusses techniques and activities that can be used in operations to control quality and see that it conforms to specifications. Keep in mind that the attitudes and shared values in the organization are also important in encouraging the achievement of quality.

It is very expensive to detect defective workmanship and correct it before a product reaches the customer. Warranty work, product liability, and customer ill will can be even more expensive if defects go undetected and uncorrected. The best way to avoid these problems and expenses is to prevent defects. A large part of the success in preventing defects rests with the worker who produces the product or service. Direct workers are in the best position to detect and correct problems that might degrade the quality of goods or services—as those problems occur. The discussion of just-in-time (JIT) manufacturing in Chapter 8 demonstrated just how effective production workers can be in raising quality.

Companies need to create the right conditions for high-quality production. On the technical side, companies should provide materials and supplies that are adequate to meet the level of quality that is being sought. They should also ensure that equipment is purchased and maintained so as to have the precision necessary to do satisfactory work. Equally important, they must work to achieve the full benefits of employees' skill and creativity. Employees should be selected with care and provided with training to bring their skills up to the necessary level. In addition, companies must create a climate and culture within the organization that motivates workers to achieve quality. If the climate does not support and encourage top performance, persons who take a great deal of pride in their work may quit the company in frustration. Others will just stay on the payroll and do shoddy work.

Employee involvement often helps keep workers motivated to strive for quality in their work. *Quality circles* (discussed in the final section of the chapter) are worker groups that meet regularly to identify and solve problems. These circles have proved effective in many companies. A trend today seems to be to have employees check their own work to some degree, rather than having a formal quality-control organization do all of the checking. No matter what method is used, it is important that top management and the entire organization openly encourage and seek quality.

Before we proceed to a detailed discussion of quality control techniques, let us examine further how these techniques relate to the broader picture of quality assurance.

Interrelated Activities Pertaining to Quality

The previous discussion indicates the importance of design in establishing the level of quality that a company provides. The design is a target level of quality that requires input from several sources inside and outside the company to be properly established. However, numerous other components of the company also play their part in working to achieve and maintain that target level.

Figure 11.1 provides an overview of some of the quality-related activities within a company. The black arrows represent the flow of goods or services and the blue lines represent the flow of communications relating to quality. The scheme is more appropriate for a manufacturing operation, but many parallels to the delivery of services may be found. The figure shows the flow of quality-related information. It indicates that information is obtained from the marketplace, perhaps through interviews with potential customers or through test-marketing of products. Failure reports and warranty claims from repair service centers flow back into the company and affect the design standards or the acceptable quality standards at various in-process inspection points. Information regarding the quality of performance is also obtained from in-process and final inspection stations.

Information obtained through checking the pulse at various points may be used as a basis for decisions about the activities of several departments. Top managers coordinate the activities of the departments so that the company operates as a system. Quality feedback may indicate that a design change is in order. Inspection reports may indicate that the equipment is becoming excessively worn and financial resources must be provided for replacement. A change in maintenance policies may be indicated. Other problems may indicate that some skill levels of the work force are inadequate, and the personnel department may be called upon to raise its employment standards or to institute a training program to upgrade certain skills. Quality is almost everybody's business in many successful companies. Thus the operations manager must be prepared to coordinate the activities within his or her charge with those of other functions in regard to quality as well as in regard to other matters.

The concept of management control was described as involving some standard or target of what is to be performed, a means of measuring actual performance to see if it conforms to the standard, and corrective action if actual work does not conform closely enough to the standard. Quality control follows this scheme. The primary means of checking actual work is called *inspection*. A great deal of inspection is and should be performed by the front-line worker who is doing the work. In other locations within a company, inspection is performed to ensure that good materials are being provided or to verify that the employees and processes are working within acceptable tolerances.

Inspections are shown as blue squares at several locations in Figure 11.1. These inspections provide feedback to persons in the company who either correct problems or see that responsible persons are informed so that the problems can be corrected. Inspections may occur at various points within the total system, but basically there are three types:

1. *Receiving inspection*—checking materials or other inputs to see that they are good before they are used.

FIGURE 11.1

The Involvement of Quality Assurance Activities in the Flow of Information
and Material

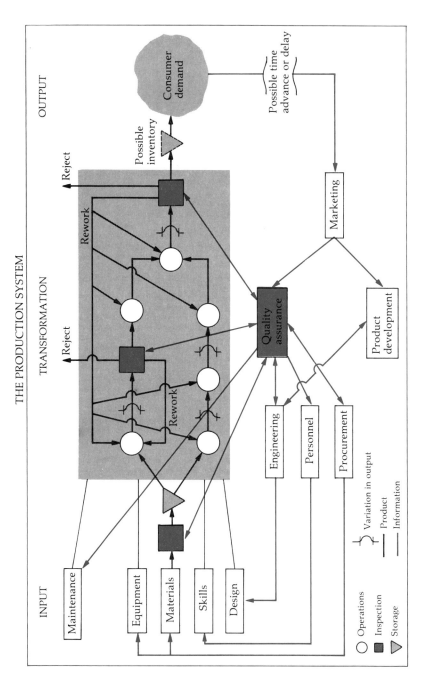

2. *In-process inspection*—checking the output of an operation or a series of operations before further work is performed, or checking on the production processes themselves.
3. *Final inspection*—checking the completed output of the production system before it goes to the customer.

Where and When to Inspect

Some stages of production are more likely to produce defective items ("scrap" or "rework") than others. Those operations that have a high risk should be inspected closely. Generally, a trade-off must be made between the cost of inspecting and the risk of not inspecting. Typically companies spend in the vicinity of 5 percent of their labor cost for inspection. Some general suggestions about when and where to inspect are given below.

1. Inspect a sample of incoming material if it has a chance of being defective and can affect the quality of the final product.
2. Inspect after high-risk or highly variable operations.
3. Inspect before operations of such high cost that the expense of processing a defective item warrants preventing it.
4. Inspect before operations in which defective items might damage the processing equipment or cause injury to workers.
5. Inspect before assembly, painting, plating, and other operations that would cover defects so they could not be detected.
6. Inspect items before they are irreversibly combined or joined to others.
7. Inspect the finished product.

The degree of inspection depends on many factors. Of course, if the test is a destructive one, less than 100 percent inspection must be performed. Electrical fuses might be tested by subjecting them to an electrical overload to see if they burn out. A fuse that works properly is no longer fit for sale. A fuse that survives the test is defective and also should not be sold. Products that could injure someone are subjected to more intensive sampling than products that represent no danger.

The variability of the production process influences the frequency with which the process should be checked. Generally automatic or semiautomatic machines require less surveillance than manual operations. Cost is a part of the trade-off involved in deciding how often to inspect. If the product is expensive relative to the cost of inspection, a larger percentage of the items usually will be inspected. Sometimes when the incidence of defects is no greater than expected, the frequency of inspection will be low; when the process appears to be operating erratically, a higher percentage sample (perhaps 100 percent) will be taken. A relationship such as the one in Figure 11.2 is found in many instances.

Some companies have found that their total costs have declined when they instituted an efficient quality-control program. The key to efficient quality control and improved productivity is to use inspection primarily to maintain a careful watch on processes so that defects are never made in the first place. The

FIGURE 11.2

Costs of Inspection Effort

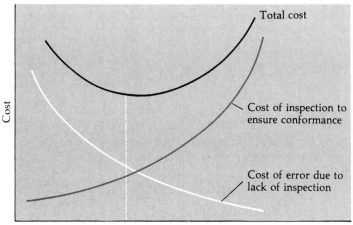

Extent of inspection

cost of making defective parts, inspecting to sort them out, and correcting the problems is often more costly than prevention. Warranty repairs, especially in the field, are expensive and can use a great portion of a company's capacity. Defective work that reaches customers can cause ill will and lost future sales, the full cost of which really cannot be determined.

STATISTICAL TOOLS TO CONTROL QUALITY OF CONFORMANCE

The major means of determining whether goods or services conform to specification is to measure or test them in some way. Customer interviews to determine whether products or services were found to be satisfactory can be annoying to customers and can be expensive. Product testing can also be expensive, particularly in cases where destructive tests are required to evaluate the product. For these and other reasons, quality is often controlled by taking statistical samples—that is, by *statistical quality control*. Samples can be by attributes or by variables. *Sampling by attributes* classifies items as either good or defective or classifies lots of items as acceptable or unacceptable, without regard to the degree to which they exceed or fail to meet minimum requirements. The result is a binary classification that can be performed fairly rapidly in comparison to sampling by variables. *Sampling by variables* is the process of measuring the dimension, weight, or other characteristics of items to determine how far they differ from the quality standard established for the characteristic.

Information from samples can be used for *process control*, that is to infer something about the proper functioning of the processes through which the items have been run. Alternatively, the sample can be used to infer whether the sample was taken from a batch with a sufficient proportion of good items or from a batch with too many defective items. This latter application is called *acceptance sampling.* Process control is very important in quality control because it helps keep processes running adequately so that defects are seldom produced. Process control helps to achieve high-quality operations where quality is built into the product. We will discuss process control in the next section of the chapter. Acceptance sampling is useful for sorting acceptable lots of items from unacceptable lots. Acceptance sampling will be discussed after process control.

PROCESS CONTROL

Process control is the use of statistical sampling for detecting and correcting faults in the production process. Process control is shown schematically in Figure 11.3. It is also a part of the overview presented in Figure 11.1. Information is fed back from inspection operations, is evaluated, and may result in some type of action.

Management control, as you will recall, involves having:

1. Some standard of a desired action or result.
2. A means of measuring and comparing the actual action or result.
3. Corrective action when the result deviates from the acceptable standard.

Management attempts to control quality through these same three steps. In fact, process control is a type of management by exception. The process is carefully set to perform properly, then the status quo is preserved by taking no corrective action unless evidence in the feedback data indicates that the process is not behaving as desired—that is, is "out of control."

FIGURE 11.3

Process Control Involves Feedback

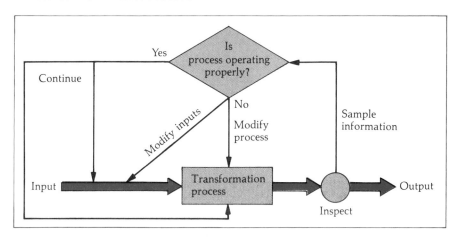

Type I and Type II Errors

Process control relies on sampling information for feedback. Consequently there is the possibility that sampling errors may lead to erroneous conclusions about the process. Process control sampling can lead to two types of errors, a *type I error*, or a *type II error*.

Type I Errors   A sample from the output of a process may lead to the conclusion that the process is out of control when in fact it is operating as intended. Such an error might involve only the cost of rechecking some of the adjustments to the process when there really is no need to. It might also, however, lead to a very expensive and embarrassing result, such as recalling everything produced since the last sample was taken. The probability of making a type I error, α, should be established with due consideration to the cost that would result from such an error.

Type II Errors   A type II error occurs when the process is not working as it should, but sampling error causes one to infer that the process is satisfactory. In a manufacturing plant the risk of a type II error, β, may lead to investing considerable amounts of money in further work on items that are defective. It may also result in product-liability suits if the defects go undetected and the product harms a user as a result of them. The cost of a type II error must be considered in establishing control limits.

Table 11.1 is a contingency table showing the conditions that exist with type I and type II errors. Examples of type I errors are conviction of an innocent defendant, being led by a blood test to believe that one has a disease when one does not, and paying for automotive repairs one does not need. Some examples of type II errors are failure to convict a guilty defendant and getting a false negative result from a blood test. When you fail to notice a leaky automobile transmission and ruin it by driving without enough transmission fluid, you have committed a type II error.

The Control Chart: A Stimulus to Corrective Action

Standards, measurement, and corrective action when it is required are all essential factors in process control. Actually, control is achieved through action,

Table 11.1
TYPE I AND TYPE II ERRORS

	DECISION TO:	
Conditions	Search for Defect in Process and Try to Correct It	Leave the Process As It Is
Process is working properly	Type I error	Correct decision
Process is defective	Correct decision	Type II error

but the first two factors are necessary to indicate when corrective action is needed. Control charts are used as a simple device to indicate when corrective action appears to be in order. *Control charts* are graphs showing the standards, called *control limits,* for a process and a plot of the process measurements obtained from samples over time. Control charts can be used in conjunction with sampling by either variables or attributes.

Sampling by Variables   First consider the use of control charts when the property is measured on a continuous scale. For example, consider controlling a process when the variable of interest is continuous—such as the temperature of a meat-processing cooler or an oven in a bakery, the weight of material used to produce a product, the time it takes for a bank teller to process a customer transaction, or the size of an object leaving a certain production operation. A *control chart for the mean,* or $\overline{X}$ *chart,* and a *control chart for the range,* or *R chart,* often are used to monitor and control processes that are measured in continuous variable units.

     Figure 11.4 shows an example of a control chart used to monitor the mean, $\overline{X}$, of some sample. It could be the average amount of shampoo in a sample of four bottles randomly selected after they have left an automatic filling process. The company does not want to sell less than the advertised contents in a bottle lest customer ill will be created. On the other hand, it does not want to give away its shampoo. The process control chart for $\overline{X}$ provides a graphic display to show if the process is "in control," that is, working satisfactorily as far as the average amount of shampoo it dispenses is concerned. As long as the points are within the control limits, variations in the process measurements are assumed to be the result of *chance causes,* that is, small random variations naturally inherent in the process when it is working correctly. A type II error, however, could occur instead.

FIGURE 11.4

Example of a Control Chart for $\overline{X}$

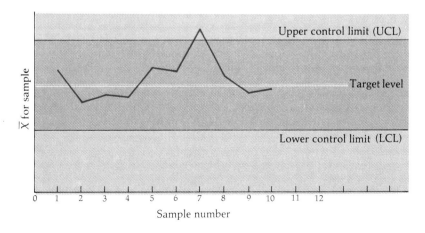

Notice in Figure 11.4 that sample number 7 fell above the *upper control limit* (UCL). Such an event would cause the production personnel to conclude that the automatic filling process was probably "out of control," that is, not working as it should. A similar interpretation would be made if an $\overline{X}$ value fell below the *lower control limit* (LCL). An out-of-control signal would cause the responsible persons to begin looking for an *assignable cause* of the variation and to correct it. Of course, a type I error could have occurred and the process could be working properly.

Usually, a company tries to have its equipment and operator skills good enough so that the natural variability of the process is considerably less than the tolerance band between the limits of the design specifications (i.e., the *specification limits*). When this is the case, it does not necessarily mean that defective products have been made just because the process wandered from the target value and crossed a control limit. Sometimes, particularly if the range between the specification limits is narrow, an upper and lower *warning limit* may be constructed inside the control limits to signal that the process is getting close to a problem. Thus control charts are very helpful in preventing problems—whereas acceptance sampling (which is discussed later) is more useful for sorting out the defective items after the problem has occurred.

The process shown in Figure 11.4 could begin producing defective bottles of shampoo even though the process mean were set at the proper place. The process might become erratic, causing the variability to increase beyond the limits to be expected when it is working properly. A sample of several bottles could have the proper average, yet some of them will be overfilled and some inadequately filled. For this reason, continuous variable characteristics are often controlled through the use of two control charts, one for $\overline{X}$ and another for R, the range. The range, which is the largest value in the sample minus the smallest, is a measure of the variability of a process. Some standard for the range is set and plotted on a control chart for R. If the R for a sample falls above the control limit, one concludes that the process may be out of control, even if $\overline{X}$ is within its limits.

Establishing Control Limits for $\overline{X}$ and R

A process will have some variation in output if it is measured closely enough. Control limits must be set closely enough on either side of this natural variability so that small changes in the distribution will be detected. Having the control limits close together reduces β, the probability of a type II error. Setting the control limits close together, however, increases α, the probability of a type I error. As in acceptance sampling, the only way to reduce both α and β is to increase the size of the samples taken from the population. The central limit theorem provides some insight into the relationship between n and the proper location of the control limits.

The Central Limit Theorem An important foundation of control limits for $\overline{X}$ is the *central limit theorem,* which states that no matter what shape the population has, the distribution of $\overline{X}$'s (the means of samples extracted from the population) will approach a normal distribution as the size of the samples is increased. The mean of the distribution of $\overline{X}$'s will be equal to the mean of the population. That is,

$$\overline{\overline{X}} = \frac{\Sigma \overline{X}}{N},$$

where $\overline{\overline{X}}$ = the mean of the population
$\Sigma \overline{X}$ = the sum of all the sample means; and
N = the total number of observations included in all of the samples.

The standard deviation of the $\overline{X}$'s will be

$$\sigma_{\overline{x}} = \frac{\sigma'}{\sqrt{n}}$$

where $\sigma_{\overline{x}}$ = the standard deviation of the distribution of the sample $\overline{X}$'s
σ' = the standard deviation of the population from which the samples are taken
n = the size of the samples that are taken.

Figure 11.5 shows the relationship between three different distributions and the distribution of sample means (sometimes called the sampling distribution of the mean). Even when the population is not symmetrical, the sampling

FIGURE 11.5

Sampling Distribution of $\overline{X}$ Approaches Normal, and Standard Deviation Decreases, as N Increases

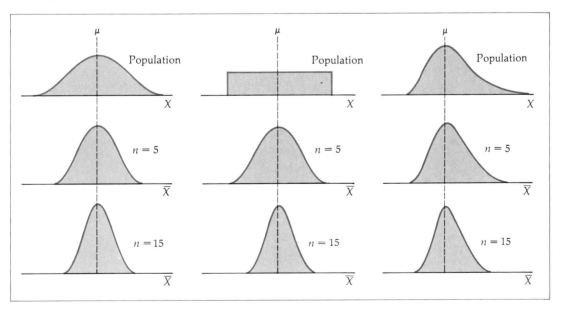

distribution of $\overline{X}$ approaches normality. As long as the population is unimodal and not badly skewed, samples of size $n = 4$ are considered large enough for the central limit theorem to apply. This knowledge that $\overline{X}$ will be approximately normally distributed for most populations when n is 4 or more, enables us to make probability statements about the range of $\overline{X}$'s that will be obtained when the population mean is centered on the target measurement. We shall assume that these conditions exist. When the population is badly skewed, larger samples should be used.

Since the $\overline{X}$'s are assumed to be approximately normally distributed, the probabilities and relationships shown in Figure 11.6 apply. If the control limits are set at $2\sigma_{\overline{x}}$'s on either side of the population mean and the population mean does not move, then the $\overline{X}$'s would be expected to fall within these limits 955 times out of 1,000. The other 45 times we would suspect that the process was out of control when in fact it was not. This would be a type I error. We establish α, the probability of this type of error, when we determine how many $\sigma_{\overline{x}}$'s away from the target value to place the control limits. Control limits do not have to be some integer times $\sigma_{\overline{x}}$ away from the desired measurement. Control limits can be set according to equations 11.1 and 11.2, where $Z_{\alpha/2}$ is selected from a normal probability table such as is presented in Appendix I so that α is the desired probability of a type I error.

$$UCL_{\overline{x}} = \mu + z_{\alpha/2}\,\sigma_{\overline{x}} \tag{11.1}$$

$$LCL_{\overline{x}} = \mu - Z_{\alpha/2}\,\sigma_{\overline{x}} \tag{11.2}$$

Selection of α can be based on the cost of a type I error and the need for tight control. The most common practice, however, is to use μ plus or minus $3\sigma_{\overline{x}}$ for the control limits.

Determining σ'   In order to find $\sigma_{\overline{x}}$ and calculate where $\overline{X}$ control limits should be placed, we need to estimate σ' as a measure of the inherent variability of

FIGURE 11.6

Relationship Between the Population and Control Limits When the Process Is in Control

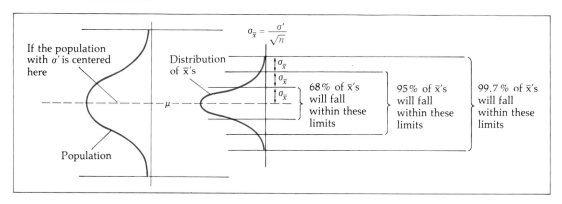

the process to be controlled. The process should be run with close attention to eliminate any assignable cause of variation. Care should be exercised to control incoming material, not to change operating methods, and not to allow any known factors to change. Random observations of the process should yield a distribution of measurements; σ' may be estimated directly by equation 11.3.

$$\sigma' = \sqrt{\frac{\sum_{i=1}^{t} (X_i - \overline{\overline{X}})^2}{t - 1}} \qquad (11.3)$$

where σ' = the estimate of the population standard deviation
t = the total number of measurements (i.e., the number of samples times the sample size)
X_i = each individual measurement
$\overline{\overline{X}}$ = the mean of all the t measurements.

Using the Range to Estimate σ'   Methods have been developed to simplify the calculations involved in monitoring the variability of a process. Simplified methods use R, the sample range, instead of involving computations of squares and square roots. It is much simpler to subtract the smallest observation in a sample from the largest to obtain R.

The ranges of samples from a population depend on σ' and some value of n. Values of R obtained on repeated sampling will vary but will be centered on some expected value, $\overline{R}$. The ratio of $\overline{R}/\sigma'$ is represented by the symbol d_2 and is tabulated in Appendix V for various sample sizes.

Suppose that K random samples of size n are taken from a process while care is exercised to ensure that the process is in control. Generally it is felt that K should be 25 or more. The sample size, n, could be any number, but samples of four or five observations are frequently used. This sample size allows the central limit effect yet does not require the additional expense caused by larger samples. $\overline{R}$ can be found from equation 11.4, and σ' can be estimated by equation 11.5.

$$\overline{R} = \frac{\sum_{i=1}^{K} R_i}{K} \qquad (11.4)$$

$$\sigma' = \frac{\overline{R}}{d_2} \qquad (11.5)$$

Control Chart for R   Having a value of $\overline{R}$ also facilitates establishing control limits for R. The central value of R would be $\overline{R}$. The lower control limit for R, LCL_R, is $D_3\overline{R}$, and $UCL_R = D_4\overline{R}$. The constants D_3 and D_4 are also presented in Appendix V. The LCL_R will be 0 when the sample size is small. You might wonder why anyone would be concerned about the process variability becoming too small since consistency of the process is desirable. A significant reduction of R indicates that the control limits for $\overline{X}$ might be moved closer to the target measurement in order to keep the desired value of α.

APPLICATION

Establishing Control Limits for $\overline{X}$ and R

Pearl Choppers owns a small toothpaste factory in which she uses automatic equipment to fill the toothpaste tubes. The automatic machine can be set to dispense a desired amount and the company is starting to produce a new 6-ounce tube (previously it produced only 12-ounce tubes). Ms. Choppers feels that the variability of the amount dispensed by the machine might be different at a 6-ounce setting from what it had been at the 12-ounce setting. She wants to set up $\overline{X}$ and R charts to help monitor and control the amount of paste in the 6-ounce tubes. If the tubes are too full, toothpaste is wasted and the consumer will get upset because a 5- to 8-inch ribbon of paste will flow out the first time the container is opened. If the container is not sufficiently full, the consumer will be unhappy and the company will be guilty of false advertising. Ms. Choppers wants the probability of a tube's containing less than 6 ounces to be very small.

The machine was set so that approximately 6.35 ounces would be dispensed and the processing was initiated. Samples of $n = 4$ tubes were taken at random intervals during the initial processing. When the data from 25 samples were available, trial control limits were established. The data are given in Table 11.2.

Table 11.2
DATA FROM TWENTY-FIVE RANDOM SAMPLES OF TOOTHPASTE

Sample No.	$\overline{X}$	R	Sample No.	$\overline{X}$	R	Sample No.	$\overline{X}$	R
1	6.36	0.10	9	6.37	0.16	18	6.35	0.13
2	6.38	0.18	10	6.33	0.13	19	6.34	0.18
3	6.35	0.17	11	6.32	0.18	20	6.34	0.16
4	6.39	0.20	12	6.30	0.10	21	6.33	0.12
5	6.32	0.15	13	6.34	0.11	22	6.36	0.09
6	6.34	0.16	14	6.39	0.14	23	6.32	0.17
7	6.40	0.13	15	6.37	0.17	24	6.33	0.10
8	6.33	0.18	16	6.36	0.15	25	6.35	0.20
			17	6.35	0.18			

$\Sigma\overline{X} = 158.72 \quad \overline{\overline{X}} = 6.349 \quad \Sigma R = 3.74 \quad \overline{R} = 0.1496$

$\sigma' = \dfrac{\overline{R}}{d_2} = \dfrac{0.1496}{2.059} = 0.0727$

Before control limits were set for future production, the past data were compared with trial control limits to ensure that the process was in control when σ' was estimated.

Trial control limits for $\overline{X}$ were set at:

$$LCL_{\overline{X}} = 6.35 - 3\frac{\sigma'}{\sqrt{n}} = 6.35 - 3\left(\frac{0.0727}{\sqrt{4}}\right) = 6.35 - 0.109 = 6.241$$

$$UCL_{\overline{X}} = 6.35 + 3\frac{\sigma'}{\sqrt{n}} = 6.35 + 0.109 = 6.459$$

Trial control limits for R were set at

$$LCL_R = D_3(\overline{R}) = 0(0.1496) = 0$$
$$UCL_R = D_4(\overline{R}) = 2.282(0.1496) = 0.341.$$

All of the past data points were within these limits, so the estimates of σ' and $\overline{R}$ were considered valid for controlling future production. If any points had been outside the trial limits (such points are called "outliers"), they would have been removed and new limits would have been computed.

Once an estimate of σ' was available, control limits for future production could be established. Nearly all of the population—99.7 percent—should fall between the mean $+3(0.0727)$ and the mean $-3(0.0727)$. The process mean should be set at least $3(0.0727)$, or 0.2181, ounces above the lower limit of six ounces. Ms. Choppers ordered the machine set at 6.25 ounces with $3\sigma_{\overline{x}}$ control limits established about this value. The control limits were moved to center around 6.25 ounces, which made it very unlikely that tubes would contain less than 6 ounces of paste as long as the process was in control. The new control limits for $\overline{X}$ and R are shown in Figure 11.7. Data for the next fifteen samples are shown, and you will notice that the $\overline{X}$ for sample number 12 was outside the control limits. A search for assignable causes revealed that the orifice was partially clogged, so that the paste could not flow out of the machine at the ordinary rate. After this condition was corrected, samples indicated that the process was back in control.

FIGURE 11.7(a)

$\overline{X}$ Chart for Pearl Choppers' Toothpaste

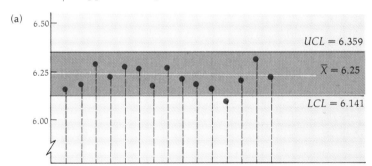

FIGURE 11.7(b)

R Chart for Pearl Choppers' Toothpaste

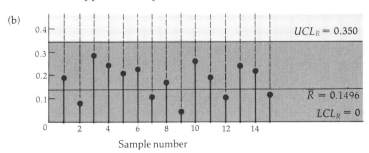

Sampling by Attributes

The process characteristic that is plotted on a control chart depends on the process or operation that one wishes to control. In some cases the characteristic to be monitored is a binary property, so that the item is classified as either good or defective, like a light bulb that either burns or does not or a glass that is either cracked or sound. An indictment results in a court conviction or it does not. An ambulance call results in an ambulance on the scene within six minutes or it does not. In a store either a customer communicates dissatisfaction to a complaint department or does not. In situations such as these a control chart may be used to monitor the fraction defective, designated p.

An example of a *control chart for the fraction defective*, or *p chart*, shown in Figure 11.8. The p chart can be used to see if a process is remaining stable, that is, producing consistent results within normal variation. $\bar{p}$, the target level of p, may be based on historical data from a time when the process was known to be in control, or it may be a target established by management. Care should be taken to establish $\bar{p}$ at attainable levels or people may not take it seriously. In fact, unrealistic goals may cause some animosity. Often p charts are based on full 100 percent inspection. The sample size must be large enough so that it is expected to include at least one defective item, so if $\bar{p}$ is 0.05, the sample size should be at least 20, preferably larger.

Control Charts for the Fraction Defective

Control charts for $\overline{X}$ and R are not appropriate when sampling is by attributes. We are interested in controlling p, the fraction defective produced by the process,

FIGURE 11.8

Example of a p Chart

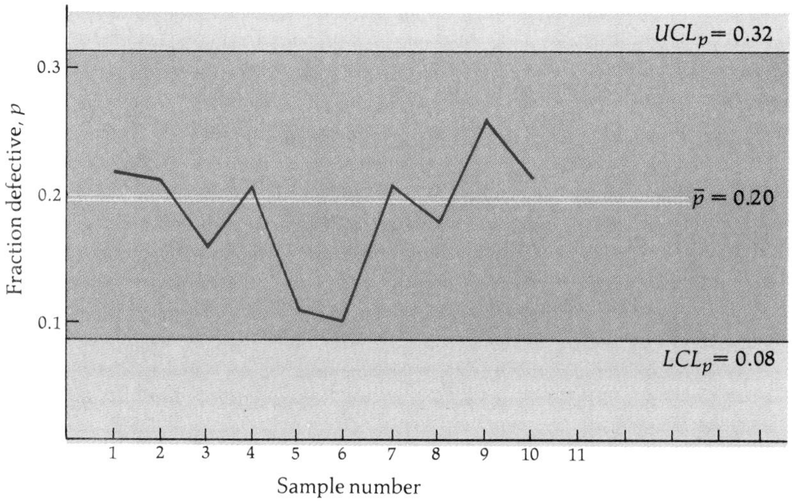

when the output of that process is not measured but is simply classified as good or bad. The 3σ control limits for p should be set as indicated in expression 11.6.[6]

$$\bar{p} \pm 3\sqrt{\frac{\bar{p}(1 - \bar{p})}{n}} \tag{11.6}$$

where $\bar{p}$ = the mean proportion defective for the process
n = the size of samples used in monitoring the process.

Control Charts for Defects per Unit

Another example of an attribute that is counted, rather than a variable that is measured on a continuous scale, is the number of defects found in some specified amount of a product. This discrete variable is often referred to as the defects per unit. A distinction should be made between the terms *defective* and *defect*. A defective item is one that does not conform to specifications. It may contain one or more defects. In many instances, the opportunities for defects in a unit are indeterminable, so the idea of a fraction defective is meaningless. A company may decide to use a *control chart for defects per unit*, or *c chart*, in a situation such as this.

Consider the number of pinholes or small bubbles in the paint on a $4' \times 8'$ sheet of paneling. The number of places where a small defect could appear is countless, yet we can count the number that are detected. One can monitor the number of crimes that occur in a given neighborhood within, say, a one-week period. No one knows the number of opportunities in which crimes could

[6]The probability of a type I error, α, is not the same as provided by the 3σ limits for $\bar{X}$ because the p and c charts are not based on a normal distribution.

APPLICATION

A Control Chart for Defects per Unit

The Mover City Transit Authority receives complaints from customers about the way drivers drive, their lack of courtesy, and so on. On several occasions, the drivers who have received the most complaints have told the manager that they carry many more passengers than other drivers, so they can be expected to receive more complaints. The manager has constructed a control chart for defects per unit, c. In this case a complaint is a defect and a unit of work is 500 fares collected on the bus. The c chart has been posted on the office wall, and the complaints reported are posted each week for each group of 500 fares that the driver collected. An average of 28.2 defects per unit occurred before the chart was posted. Control limits on the chart are

$$LCL_c = 28.2 - 3\sqrt{28.2} = 12.3$$
$$UCL_c = 28.2 + 3\sqrt{28.2} = 44.13.$$

Two weeks have passed since the chart was posted, and the average number of complaints per unit is 17.1. Do you feel that the chart has made a significant difference in the care and courtesy of the drivers?

have been committed. The number of reported crimes per week may be monitored to see if there is a need for additional police patrol, for example. One might monitor the number of errors per page of typing, the number of accidents per month on a given stretch of highway, the number of scratches per yard of picture-frame molding, or the number of leaks per mile of pipe. The c chart is used to display sample data on defects per unit.

Control limits for the defects per unit are based on the Poisson probability distribution, which has a variance equal to its mean. Therefore the standard deviation, σ, is equal to $\sqrt{\bar{c}}$, where $\bar{c}$ is the mean number of defects per unit. The 3σ control limits for $\bar{c}$ are given by expression 11.7.

$$\bar{c} \pm 3\sqrt{\bar{c}} \qquad\qquad\qquad (11.7)$$

where $\bar{c}$ = the mean number of defects per unit of output.

ACCEPTANCE SAMPLING

Acceptance sampling by attributes involves extracting a random sample from some larger lot of material to determine whether to accept or reject the entire lot or whether to subject it to 100 percent screening and separate the good products from the bad. The process may be used in receiving, in-process, or final inspection, but the terminology used is most appropriate for receiving inspection. A rejected lot may be returned to the supplier, or the supplier may be charged for 100 percent screening of rejected lots, after which only the defective items are returned for a refund. A high rate of rejections may be expensive for the supplier even if it does not lead the buyer to find another source of the goods or service. A lot of material may be sampled in any of several ways. It may be evaluated on the basis of one sample through what is called *single sampling*, or on the basis of more than one sample through *double sampling* or *sequential sampling*.

Single Sampling

A sampling plan for a single sample is specified by two numbers, n and c. The number of items that should be included in a single random sample from the lot being inspected is the *sample size, n*. The *acceptance number, c*, specifies the maximum number of defectives that may be found in the sample if the lot is to be accepted. If more than c defective items are found in the sample, the entire lot will be rejected or fully screened.

Double Sampling

Sometimes the quality of a lot of material is so good or so bad that it can be detected by a smaller sample than that normally used in a single sampling plan. Time and expense are spared when such lots are accepted or rejected on the basis of a small sample and only the questionable materials are subjected to larger sampling.

Double sampling plans provide for this procedure. First a random sample of size n_1 is taken. If the number of defectives in n_1 is less than c_1, the lot is accepted. If the number of defectives in n_1 is greater than c_2, the lot is rejected. If the number of defectives in n_1 is between c_1 and c_2, a second random sample of n_2 items is taken. The lot is accepted if the cumulative defectives in the two samples still does not exceed c_2. Otherwise the lot is rejected.

Sequential Sampling

The concept of double sampling can be extended to triple sampling and to other forms of multiple sampling. The limit of reducing the sample size and sampling until a clear decision is reached is sampling one unit at a time. In sequential sampling, units are randomly selected from a lot and tested one by one, and the cumulative sample size and cumulative number of defectives are recorded. If the cumulative number of defectives is above a certain limit for a given cumulative sample size, the lot is rejected. The lot is accepted if the cumulative number of defectives is below some other limit for the cumulative sample size. Figure 11.9 illustrates a sequential sampling plan. Sampling will continue as long as the cumulative number of defectives is between the acceptance limit and the rejection limit for the cumulative sample size taken thus far. Some lots that are close to the borderline of acceptable quality might eventually be sampled 100 percent without being rejected. Some multiple and sequential sampling plans provide for rejection (which may lead to 100 percent inspection) if the cumulative sample size reaches some number without the lot's being accepted. Of course, the lot could automatically be accepted if it still had not been rejected at some cumulative n if the cost of accepting defectives were fairly low.

FIGURE 11.9

A Sequential Sampling Plan

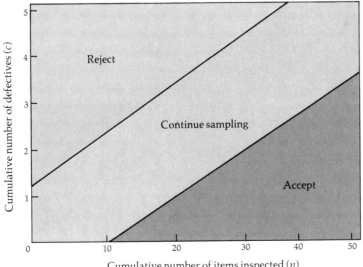

Cumulative number of defectives (c)

Reject

Continue sampling

Accept

Cumulative number of items inspected (n)

Selecting a Single Sampling Plan for Sampling by Attributes

Acceptance sampling is frequently applied to screening of incoming purchased items. Sampling is particularly appropriate when the cost of inspection is high in relation to the cost of allowing defectives to enter the operation or when inspection requires destructive testing. It is generally expected that lots will not always consist of 100 percent good items and that lots with some fraction of defectives will be accepted. Suppose the acceptable fraction or percentage of defectives in a lot is 3 percent. If the inspection process were perfect, 100 percent inspection would provide a probability of 0.0 for accepting lots with more than the acceptable fraction of defective items. The probability would be 1.0 that a lot with less than the acceptable fraction of defectives would be accepted. The discrimination ability of 100 percent sampling with a perfect inspection process when the acceptable fraction of defectives is 0.03 is illustrated in Figure 11.10.

Inspection by sampling yields something less than perfect discrimination owing to sampling error, even if we assume that the test is 100 percent accurate. There is a chance that the random sample will contain much less than the average percentage of defectives in the lot and cause us to conclude that the lot is good when it is not. On the other hand, a random sample may occasionally contain much more than the average percentage of defectives in the lot and cause a good lot to be rejected. The desirability of a sampling plan may be judged by how closely it approaches ideal discrimination. A plot of the probability of acceptance versus the fraction of defectives in a lot will provide what is called the *operating characteristic curve*, or *OC curve*, for a sampling plan.

The Operating Characteristic Curve   As Figure 11.11 illustrates, the operating characteristic curve for a sampling plan will not be a sharp stairstep like the OC curve for 100 percent sampling and no inspection error. Larger sample sizes make the curve steeper when the acceptance number is kept at the same proportion of the sample size. Increasing n for the same c will steepen the curve

FIGURE 11.10

Perfect Discrimination of Inspection Process

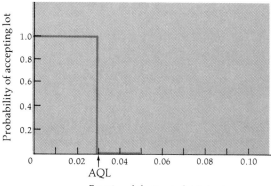

FIGURE 11.11

Effect on the OC Curve of Increasing the Sample Size and the Acceptance Number

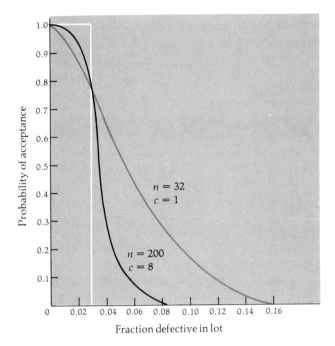

and move it closer to the origin. So will decreasing c for the same n. To approach the ideal curve, a sampling plan would have a large n so that it would have a high likelihood of representing the composition of the lot and a c large enough so that lots of acceptable quality or better would have a high probability of being accepted. The effect of changing both the sample size and the acceptance number is shown in Figure 11.11. The best sampling plan to use at a given inspection station depends on a trade-off of the cost of inspecting a larger sample versus the risk that results from smaller samples.

Producer's Risk and Consumer's Risk Because a random sample does not always reproduce the exact composition of a lot from which it is taken, there is some risk in using sampling data as a basis for acceptance of an entire lot. One might mistakenly reject a good lot (a type I error) or mistakenly accept a bad lot (a type II error). These two kinds of risk are taken into account when a sampling plan is selected. The *acceptable quality level* (AQL) is the maximum percentage (or fraction) defective that is considered satisfactory as the overall average for the process. The AQL must be greater than zero. The producer wants a high probability that lots of this quality will be accepted. There is, however, some probability—called the *producer's risk* and symbolized by α—that a lot as good as the AQL will be rejected by use of a particular sampling plan. All lots will not have the same degree of defectiveness as the process average—

some will be better and some will be worse. There is some upper limit to the percentage of defective products in an individual lot that the consumer is willing to tolerate, even if the process average is acceptable. This limit is called the *lot tolerance percent defective* (LTPD) or *limiting quality level* (LQL). (We will use the term LTPD even though we may at times be referring to a fraction defective.) The *consumer's risk*, symbolized by β, is the probability that a lot with the percentage (or fraction) of defective products equal to the LTPD will be accepted by a sampling plan.

How do we find a sampling plan that will meet the desires of the consumer and the producer? A combination of α and AQL specifies a point that should fall on the operating characteristic curve. Specifying a value of β at a particular LTPD defines another point that should be on the OC curve for the plan we seek. The objective then is to find a plan with an OC curve that passes through or almost through these two points. Bear in mind that if the AQL and LTPD are close to the same percent defective, the OC curve will have to be steep, which means the sample size, n, may be too large to be practical. Figure 11.12 shows an OC curve with the values of α, β, AQL, and LTPD on it.

Searching for a sampling plan with an OC curve through the desired points could lead to many trials and errors. One might have to solve the appropriate probability equation many times to find the sampling plan that had the desired characteristics.[7] Fortunately, tables are available that permit one to find a suggested sampling plan in most instances without detailed calculations.[8] Since a sampling plan uses integers for n and c, the OC curve for a particular plan may not go exactly through the specified points; but a plan should be available with characteristics fairly close to those desired.

The calculations performed in the application can be greatly reduced when a table of Poisson probabilities is available. Such a table is presented in Appendix III. In order to find the probability of accepting a lot, one would look in the row for the expected number of defectives in the sample and read the probability of finding c or fewer defectives.

Average Outgoing Quality (AOQ)

Consider that a process produces an average fraction defective, p', and that items move from production to an inspection operation. The average level of quality leaving the inspection operation is called the *average outgoing quality* (AOQ). The AOQ leaving an inspection station would have to be better than p', the incoming level of quality, or there would be no reason to perform the inspection. (If p' is zero, naturally there will be no improvement and AOQ = p'.) Consider that 100 percent of the items in rejected lots are inspected and

---

[7]The hypergeometric distribution is appropriate, but it can be approximated by the Poisson distribution if the sample is not a significant portion of the lot size. Joseph Juran suggests that the sample size should be at least 16, less than 1/10 the lot size, and p should be less than 0.1 (Joseph M. Juran and Frank M. Gryna, Jr., *Quality Planning and Analysis*, 2nd ed. [New York: McGraw-Hill, 1980], p. 412.

[8]H. F. Dodge and H. G. Romig, *Sampling Inspection Tables*, 2d ed. (New York: Wiley, 1959).

FIGURE 11.12

An OC Curve Showing α, AQL, β, and LTPD

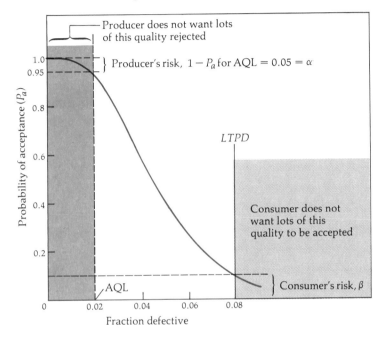

APPLICATION

Finding α and β for a Stated Sampling Plan

The Granite Isle Insurance Company is interested in buying 10,000 simulated granite paperweights to give to new customers. Rocky Davis, a new Granite Isle buyer, got two quotations that he felt were too high. Hoping to get a better price, Rocky said that he did not expect to get perfect quality and would consider 3 percent defectives as reasonable. He requested that the two potential vendors give new quotations with the understanding that a random sample of 60 items would be taken from each lot of 1,000 units, and if no more than 2 defectives were found, the lot would be accepted. The potential vendors asked him for an LTPD that was higher than the 3 percent defectives he considered reasonable. Rocky replied that 5 percent would be acceptable. The vendors said they would use 0.02 for the AQL. When the new quotations arrived, Rocky was surprised to find that the price was the same as before.

     Assume that Rocky knows you are familiar with quality control and has asked for your help. He wants you to find the producer's risk and consumer's risk for the plan he proposed and explain why the price was not reduced.

     The Poisson probability distribution can be used because the sample is small in comparison with the lot size and the probabilities of interest are less than 0.10. The approximate probability of finding x defectives in a random sample is given by the Poisson expression:

$$P(x) = \frac{(np)^x}{x!} e^{-np}$$

where x = the number of defectives for which we wish to find the probability

n = the sample size

p = the actual proportion of defectives in the lot

e = the base of natural logarithms = 2.71828.

In order to find the producer's risk, α, you would subtract from 1.00 the probability that a lot with 0.02 defectives would be accepted. The probability that the lot will be accepted is $P(0) + P(1) + P(2)$.

$$P(0) = \frac{(0.02 \times 60)^0}{0!} e^{-(0.02 \times 60)} = \frac{1}{1}(0.3012) = 0.3012$$

$$P(1) = \frac{(0.02 \times 60)^1}{1!} e^{-(0.02 \times 60)} = \frac{1.2}{1}(0.3012) = 0.3614$$

$$P(2) = \frac{(0.02 \times 60)^2}{2!} e^{-(0.02 \times 60)} = \frac{1.44}{2}(0.3012) = 0.2169$$

The probability that a high-quality lot with only 0.02 defectives would be accepted is $0.3012 + 0.3614 + 0.2169 = 0.8795$. The producer's risk, α, is the probability that a lot as good as the AQL of 0.02 will be rejected, which is $1 - 0.8795$ or 0.1205.

The consumer's risk, β, is the probability that a lot with 5 percent defectives will be accepted by the plan. To find β we must find $P(0) + P(1) + P(2)$ when the fraction defective is 0.05, the LTPD.

$$P(0) = \frac{(0.05 \times 60)^0}{0!} e^{-(0.05 \times 60)} = \frac{1}{1}(0.04979) = 0.0498$$

$$P(1) = \frac{(0.05 \times 60)^1}{1!} e^{-(0.05 \times 60)} = \frac{3}{1}(0.04979) = 0.1494$$

$$P(2) = \frac{(0.05 \times 60)^2}{2!} e^{-(0.05 \times 60)} = \frac{9}{2}(0.04979) = 0.2241$$

Therefore the value of β for the sampling plan that Rocky arbitrarily proposed is $0.0498 + 0.1494 + 0.2241 = 0.4233$. This is the probability that Granite Isle would accept a lot of paperweights that contained 5 percent defectives.

Rocky considered the risk to both parties. He could understand that a vendor would not reduce his price if there were a 12 percent chance that very good products would be rejected. Rocky decided that in the future, instead of arbitrarily selecting a sampling plan, he would examine the operating characteristic curves for several plans and propose one that had a reasonable amount of risk to both parties.

defective items are removed. The outgoing quality will be improved if the defective items are simply removed or if they are replaced by perfect items to bring the lot sizes up to the original amount.

If defectives are removed as they are found but not replaced, then:

$$AOQ = \frac{P_a p'(N - n)}{N - (np') - p'(1 - P_a)(N - n)} \tag{11.8}$$

where P_a = the probability of acceptance read from the OC curve at p'
      p' = the fraction defective in incoming lots
      N = the lot size
      n = the sample size.

If defectives are replaced with good items, then:

$$AOQ = \frac{P_a p'(N - n)}{N} \qquad (11.9)$$

A useful curve, called the AOQ curve, is obtained when the average out-going quality is plotted against the average incoming quality, p', each as a fraction of defectives or percent defective. An example of an AOQ curve is shown in Figure 11.13. As you can see, the fraction defective in the outgoing quality increases as p' increases, then it reaches a peak and declines to low fractions of defectives (higher levels of quality). For low levels of p' an increase in p' results in an increase in AOQ, just as one would expect. At some higher levels of p', however, there is a great increase in the probability that a lot will be rejected and subjected to 100 percent screening. Thus these high levels of p' will result in much higher levels of AOQ than would slightly better incoming quality.

Each sampling plan presents a different probability of rejection of various levels of quality and consequently will have a different AOQ curve. The AOQ for a sampling plan is based on the long-run average outgoing quality, assuming that many lots are inspected. The peak on an AOQ curve corresponds to the highest average fraction defective or the lowest average quality for the sampling plan. This peak on the AOQ curve is called the *average outgoing quality limit* (AOQL). One method of evaluating and selecting sampling plans is to compare the AOQL's for various plans and select one that gives sufficient protection in the long run.

FIGURE 11.13

An AOQ Curve

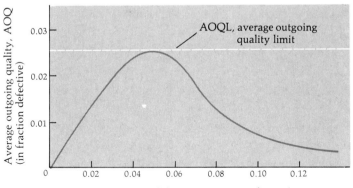

Fraction defective in incoming lots, p'

Dodge-Romig Tables

The Dodge-Romig sampling tables, cited in footnote 8, are organized so that the user can select a sampling plan based on either of two criteria. Some of the plans are arranged so that the user can select a plan based on choice of AOQL; others are arranged so that the user can select a plan based on choice of a particular LTPD that will give a consumer's risk of 0.10.

If only occasional lots of an item are purchased, the purchasing company might prefer to select a plan based on the LTPD to provide the specified degree of protection from accepting a bad lot. For higher-volume items that are purchased in a continuing series of lots, the company might be primarily interested in controlling the average level of quality and might select a plan on the basis of the AOQL.

Mil-Std-105D

Other sampling plans can be found in Military Standard 105D, a quality standard prepared for government procurement and sometimes used for commercial contracts. This standard provides plans based on AQL and is oriented to specifying the producer's risk. Single, double, and multiple sampling plans are given. The plans provide for normal sampling under normal circumstances, with a shift to tightened sampling if quality appears to have deteriorated. The plans permit reduced inspection if quality is very good for a series of prior samples and the process is running at a steady rate.

You can see that a company has a variety of methods for trying to screen out bad lots of items. Process control, likewise, can be applied in various places and with different degrees of sampling. Again, the most desirable approach to quality control is to keep processes in statistical control so that defective items are not produced. Process control charts are most effective in preventing defectives when they are used by the direct worker, because the person who performs the work is the one who can most quickly spot trouble and take corrective or preventive action. Direct employees are also being involved very successfully in the quest for quality in other ways, such as by participation in quality circles.

QUALITY CIRCLES

The typical worker who is directly involved in production has little influence over the quality of design, since that is established when the company sets standards for the type of product or service it will offer. In many instances, however, the responsibility for quality of conformance to design specifications does rest with the individual worker when a product is produced or a service is provided. Since the customer is often present when a service is provided, it is frequently impossible to inspect services and permit only good service to reach the consumer. However, some types of manufactured items can be inspected and the defective items screened out so that only good products reach the consumer. Poor quality is unproductive and expensive because of the initial cost of producing defectives, the cost of inspecting and reworking products, and the potential cost of customer ill will. Consequently, a great source of potential improvement in quality and productivity lies within each individual employee.

Quality circles, or *quality control circles*, represent an organized effort to make constructive use of workers' intimate familiarity with their own work problems by focusing the workers' creative capabilities on finding solutions to those problems. A quality circle is a group, usually made up of five to twelve workers from the same work area, that meets regularly (in many instances, once a week) and voluntarily solves problems related to the work in their part of the company. Often the employees are paid for the time they spend in these meetings, which may last an hour or more. A few points are basic to the success of a quality circle program.

- The quality circle must work on the right problems. This means that communications should be open and the circle should have access to data pertaining to its work.

- Employees should be motivated to contribute their talents. All levels of management should openly and actively support the quality circle program. Circle members should be given recognition for their developments, and the circle should be given financial support, making it possible to implement worthwhile solutions developed by the group. If bonuses are paid to the workers, they are usually small and represent recognition rather than pay for any savings that result. (Participants in the quality circles with which the author is familiar seem highly favorable, even excited, about the circle activities.)

- The participants must have the necessary problem-solving skills. This means that training in certain basic problem-solving techniques is a major part of instituting a quality circle program.

Numerous techniques are employed by quality circles. A few appear as common items in the training that circle members are usually given and will be discussed briefly.

1. *Data collection and analysis techniques* are taught to circle members. Such techniques as compiling checklists and frequency distributions are used to help identify what the problems are. Sometimes control charts are also used to help spot problems.

2. *Pareto analysis* utilizes the Pareto principle, or 80–20 rule, as it is sometimes called. It is based on a theory expressed by an Italian economist that 20 percent of the people control 80 percent of the wealth. This same idea was discussed regarding inventory items (*ABC* classification), since a small percentage of the items usually deserve special attention because they account for a large percentage of the annual expenditure for all items. Pareto analysis determines the relative frequency of various problems or causes for problems so that primary attention can be focused on the most

important ones. If the problems do not result in about the same cost, the frequencies can be multiplied by the average cost of that kind of problem. Such a procedure can help to establish priorities in terms of the costs caused by the problems. Suppose that a quality circle decided to investigate an excessive scrap rate for Part 1088-2. The circle members want to identify the major reason the part is being scrapped. A Pareto diagram of their data, which is useful for displaying this type of information, is presented in Figure 11.14.

3. *Cause and effect diagrams* are useful in identifying and isolating the cause, or the major causes, of a problem. This diagram, sometimes called a "fishbone diagram," lists the problem at one end of a horizontal line. Diagonal branches are drawn from this line for each major category of possible causes. More specific, contributory causes are added to the branch for each category. An example of a cause-and-effect diagram for Part 1088-2 is shown in Figure 11.15.

4. *Brainstorming* is a useful technique for generating ideas about problems on which the circle might focus its activities, about possible causes of problems, and about potential solutions to problems, once they have been identified. The objective of a brainstorming meeting is to generate a large quantity of ideas on a particular subject. No criticism of ideas is permitted during brainstorming because it might stifle creativity, thought flow, and expression. The good ideas are selected later, so that judgments are not

FIGURE 11.14

A Pareto Diagram for Part 1088–2

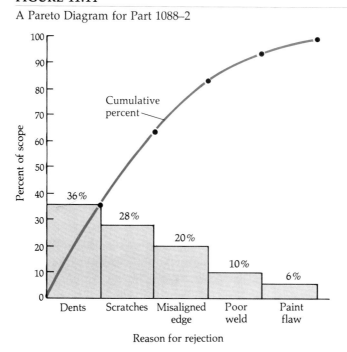

Reason for rejection

FIGURE 11.15

A Cause-and-Effect Diagram

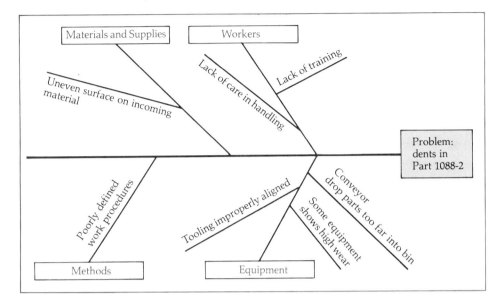

passed while creativity is the objective. One seemingly useless idea may stimulate another one that is valuable.

Through a series of meetings the circle can apply techniques such as these to develop a solution to the causes of the problem. If the recommended solution is approved, the circle will then implement their solution and start the process again to identify and solve another problem. The stages of circle activities in problem solving are summarized in Figure 11.16.

The quality circle is not just a quick fix for a particular problem but an ongoing effort to improve quality, productivity, and safety or to solve other problems. Circles usually operate under the direction of a steering committee composed of top managers and representatives from throughout the company. The steering committee provides broad planning and evaluation of circle activities and decides what matters, such as salaries and grievances, are better left to other units for solution. Each circle has its own leader to coordinate its internal workings and to represent the circle to outside entities. Often a line supervisor serves in this capacity so that no new communication channels or reporting requirements are needed. A person called a *facilitator* is frequently involved to coordinate the activities of circles, to train circle leaders, to help leaders train circle members, and to assist the circles in carrying out their activities. Quality circles have proven to be valuable in Japan, and their use is growing in many countries. Savings as high as five or six times the cost of running the circle program have been reported.

FIGURE 11.16

Stages of a Circle's Work on a Problem

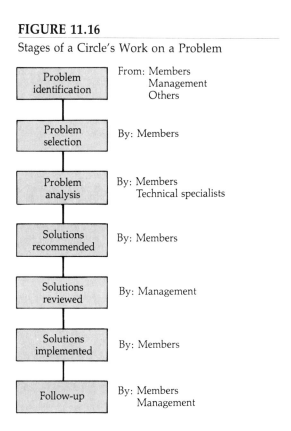

SUMMARY

Quality assurance involves all of the activities necessary to ensure that the customer receives satisfactory performance, including assurance that the product or service is adequately designed and conforms to the design. It may also include efforts to train consumers in proper use, to design safeguards to prevent misuse, and to ensure that reasonable service and repair capabilities are available to the user.

Inspection is the major means of determining quality of conformance. Critical products or critical stages in production often use 100 percent inspection of the output. Sampling, either by attributes or by variables, may be employed in situations that are less critical or where testing is expensive or destructive. Statistical sampling or statistical quality control

may be used for acceptance sampling or for process control. Acceptance sampling is used to infer the acceptability of the particular lot or batch from which the sample was extracted. Process control applications are employed to infer whether the processing operations are being performed adequately.

Both acceptance sampling and process control may be based on sampling by either attributes or variables. Sampling by attributes simply classifies the inspected good or service as acceptable or unacceptable. Sampling by variables involves measuring the extent to which an actual characteristic varies from the target specification for that characteristic. Acceptance sampling requires some sampling plan, such as single, double, or sequential sampling. Since sampling cannot guarantee 100 percent accuracy in the assessment of quality, there is some risk to the producer that good products will be rejected and some risk to the consumer that defective products will be accepted.

Process control relies on control charts and limits to indicate the adequate (or otherwise) performance of the processes that produced the measured characteristic. Control charts for $\overline{X}$, the mean, and R, the range, are used for control when sampling is done by variables. Process control for sampling by attributes may employ a control chart for p, the fraction of the items that are defective, or a control chart for c, the number of defects within some amount of output.

Process control is a very effective means of preventing defective work. Hence it often improves both quality and productivity. Process control can be effectively performed by direct employees—those who perform the processing. Quality circles are becoming more commonly used as a means of organizing and motivating direct workers to use their familiarity with processes and their problem-solving abilities to improve quality.

SOLVED PROBLEMS

PROBLEM:

Incoming steel to be used in processing is tested to see that it is of the right chemical composition before it is machined. Dimensions of the machined parts are inspected prior to the heat-treating operation. An automatic heat-treating furnace is set at a temperature which hardens the parts. The temperature is set so that the average force required to break the part is 32,000 pounds. The inherent variability of the heat-treating process produces a standard deviation of the breaking force of 3,000 pounds. Establish the control limits for $\overline{X}$ so that $\alpha = 0.10$ when samples of size $n = 4$ are taken.

SOLUTION:

$$\sigma_{\overline{x}} = \frac{\sigma'}{\sqrt{n}} = \frac{3,000}{\sqrt{4}}$$
$$= 1,500 \text{ pounds}$$
$$Z_{1-\alpha/2} = Z_{.95} = 1.645$$
$$UCL_{\overline{x}} = \mu + Z\sigma_{\overline{x}}$$
$$= 32,000 + 1.645(1,500)$$
$$= 32,000 + 2467.5$$
$$= 34,467.5 \text{ pounds}$$

$$LCL_{\overline{x}} = \mu - Z\sigma_{\overline{x}} = 32,000 - 2,467.5$$
$$= 29,532.5 \text{ pounds}$$

PROBLEM:

Establish the 3σ control limits for R for the process described above.

SOLUTION:

From Table 1 of Appendix IV, we find that d_2 for samples of size $n = 4$ is 2.059. Since $d_2 = \overline{R}/\sigma'$, we can find an estimate of $\overline{R}$ for samples of 4 taken from this process.

$2.059 = \overline{R}/3,000$, so $\overline{R} = 2.059(3,000) = 6,177$.

From Table 2 of Appendix IV we can obtain the constants D_3 and D_4 for samples of size 4. Using these values, we can compute the control limits for R.

$$UCL_R = D_4\overline{R} = 2.28(6,177) = 14,083.6$$
$$LCL_R = D_3\overline{R} = 0(6,177) = 0.$$

PROBLEM:

The radiology department at a large hospital has an average retake rate of 8.8 percent, that is, 8.8 percent of its X-rays must be repeated because the picture is not sufficiently clear. Errors can occur because of incorrect patient measurement, improper calibration or setting of the machine, poor film quality, incorrect film processing, or other reasons. During the past month 9,000 X-rays were taken and 11.2 percent had to be repeated. Does the process appear to be within its 3σ limits, or does it appear that there may be some assignable cause for variation?

SOLUTION:

$$\bar{p} = 0.088.$$

Control limits for p when a sample of 9,000 is taken are

$$\bar{p} \pm 3\sqrt{\frac{\bar{p}(1 - \bar{p})}{9,000}} =$$

$$0.088 \pm 3\sqrt{\frac{0.088(1 - 0.088)}{9,000}}$$

$$= 0.088 \pm 0.00896 = 0.0970 \text{ and } 0.0790.$$

The value of 11.2 percent defective is very much outside the 3σ limits for the process.

PROBLEM:

Twenty samples were taken from a cable-weaving machine while it was being operated under closely controlled conditions. The number of defects per 100 meters for the samples are recorded in the chart below. Determine the control chart limits for the machine.

4	4	5	3
6	2	2	4
5	3	4	2
3	2	4	5
5	7	5	3

SOLUTION:

$$\bar{c} = \frac{\Sigma c}{n} = \frac{78}{20} = 3.9$$

Control limits for the number of defects per 100 meters are $\bar{c} \pm 3\sqrt{\bar{c}} = 3 \pm 3\sqrt{3.9} = 0$ and 9.8.

DISCUSSION QUESTIONS

1. What is quality assurance?
2. What economic factors should be taken into account in establishing the quality of design?
3. What economic factors should be taken into account in establishing the degree of conformance control?
4. In general, when should inspections be made?
5. Discuss the relationship of quality of design and quality of conformance to quality of performance.
6. (a) What is meant by the consumer's risk?
   (b) What is meant by the producer's risk?
7. Vendor selection and vendor relations are considered important to the purchasing department. Should the quality assurance department ever become involved in these issues? Why, or why not?
8. Under what conditions would a p or c chart be used instead of $\bar{X}$ and R charts?
9. How does the precision or exactness of the testing or measuring method used affect the applicability of control charts? What does variability in the testing method do to α? to β?
10. Would it ever be advisable for control limits to be placed much beyond the $3\sigma_{\bar{x}}$ control limits? When?
11. (a) Can you inspect quality into a product? Explain.

(b) Can extreme care in production offset a poor design? Explain.

12. Can proper application of quality control methods actually reduce costs while improving quality? Give a reason for your response.

13. Briefly describe what is meant by a quality circle.

14. What are some of the tools and methods that quality circles use in performing their activities?

PROBLEMS

1. Rocky Davis has stated that a sampling plan of $n = 100$, $c = 4$ will be used for purchasing simulated granite paperweights. Find the probability that a lot with the AQL of 0.02 defectives will be rejected. Find the probability that a lot of 0.03 defectives will be accepted. Find the probability that a lot with the LTPD of 0.05 defectives will be accepted. Use the Poisson table in Appendix III. How do these probabilities compare to those shown in the Granite Isle application presented within this chapter? Why?

2. Develop the OC curve for the sampling plan $n = 20$, $c = 2$, and for the plan $n = 40$, $c = 4$. Assume that the Poisson distribution can be applied. What are the α's for the two plans if AQL = 0.02? What are the β's for the plans if LTPD = 0.08?

3. A single sampling plan uses $n = 30$, $c = 1$. What is α at AQL = 0.01? What is β at LTPD = 0.06? Assume the Poisson approximation can be used.

4. A single sampling plan uses $n = 60$ and $c = 2$. Assume that the lot size is large enough so that the Poisson table in Appendix III can be used. Construct the OC curve and the AOQ curve for this sampling plan. What is the AOQL for the plan? Assume that defectives are replaced.

5. The supervisor of a stenographic pool is developing control charts for typing reports and memorandums. Random samples of 30 pages of the daily output have been selected and proofread. The fractions defective for 15 samples were recorded as follows: 0.067, 0.10, 0.067, 0.133, 0.067, 0.0,

0.10, 0.133, 0.10, 0.033, 0.067, 0.167, 0.200, 0.167, 0.033. Does the process appear to be in control? (Use 3σ control limits.) Under what circumstances would a chart of these control limits be useful?

6. Silverware at the Riverview Restaurant is washed by an automatic washer. It is inspected as employees select 24 pieces of tableware to set a table and return any that are not satisfactorily cleaned to a container for dirty silver. Normally this procedure averages 1 unsatisfactorily cleaned item out of 24. Today an average of 4 out of 24 were unsatisfactory. Does this suggest that something is amiss in the washing process—that is, does 4 fall outside the control limits for samples of 24?

7. A sharpening machine at the Carolina Electric Razor Company sharpens the blades on rotary cutter heads for electric razors. If there is a burr on any of the cutter blades, the razor will not operate properly, so random samples of 25 parts are inspected regularly to see if the machine is operating properly. The results of 10 samples are 0.08, 0.08, 0.04, 0.12, 0.20, 0.24, 0.04, 0.12, 0.08, 0.04. Establish the 3σ control limits for the proportion defective for this process.

8. A production process makes large sheets of plate glass with an average of 2.38 defects per sheet. Establish 3-σ control limits for the defects per unit for this process.

9. A process produces microminiature circuit chips with a reject rate of 32.9 percent when it is operating satisfactorily. During a day

when the process was operated using materials from a new supplier, 30 defective chips were found in 50 randomly selected chips. Is there cause to suspect that the process is not functioning properly?

10. A police department wants to establish control limits for the number of crimes per week within certain neighborhoods so that they will recognize when and if patrol protection should be increased. If an average of 4 crimes per week occurs within a neighborhood, establish 95 percent control limits for the crime process.

11. Spools of wire have been tested and found to contain an average of 3 defects per spool. Establish the 3-σ control limits for the defects per unit when the wiremaking process is in control.

12. Ten bolts of printed fabric have been carefully examined to determine the number of defects in each bolt. The number of defects found in each were 4, 6, 5, 3, 7, 4, 8, 4, 8, and 6, respectively. Careful attention was given to see that the process was in control when these samples were taken. Establish limits to determine if the process remains in control.

13. An experienced operator has operated a machine over several days, being careful to keep assignable causes of variation absent from the process. Twenty-five random samples of $n = 6$ were taken during this time and $\Sigma \overline{X} = 88.43$ cm and $\Sigma R = 7.35$ cm. Compute control limits for $\overline{X}$ and R that are 3 standard deviations from their expected value. Assume the process mean was correctly set.

14. A process is known to have a σ' of 1.27 kilograms. Control limits have been established at 3 standard deviations on either side of a target weight of 20 kilograms for samples of size $n = 4$. What is β if the process is actually centered at 19.82 kilograms?

15. Samples of size 5 were taken from a process while it was operated under carefully controlled conditions, and the following measurements were found: $\overline{X} = 4.71$ cm and $\overline{R} = 0.0012$ cm. Establish 3-σ control limits for the mean and the range.

16. A process is to produce a product that will stand an average force of 22,500 pounds. The variance of the product's strength is 750,000 pounds-squared.
    (a) Specify the control limits for $\overline{X}$ so that $\alpha = .05$, when samples of size 4 are to be used.
    (b) Establish control limits for $\overline{X}$ when samples of size 5 are to be taken and the desired probability of a type I error $= 0.03$.

17. The specifications for a shaft diameter call for it to be 2.000 inches with a tolerance of ± 0.005 inch. The processing equipment has an inherent variation that is normally distributed with σ' $= 0.002$ inch.
    (a) When the process is correctly set at 2.000 inches and maintained in control, what percentage of the products will fall outside the product tolerance?
    (b) What percentage will fall outside the product tolerance when the process is centered at 1.997 inches?

18. Specifications for an item call for it to have a strength of at least 900 kilograms per square centimeter. The ingredients and processing that raise the item's strength are expensive, so the intent is to center the process so that the mean strength will be 1,100. The process has a σ' of 100 and is normally distributed.
    (a) Construct 95 percent control limits for $\overline{X}$ when samples of size 6 are taken.
    (b) What portion of production will be below the specifications limit if the process is properly centered?

19. Find the probability that the $\overline{X}$ of a random sample of six observations will fall inside

the control limits for $\overline{X}$ that were found in problem 18 if σ' remains equal to 100 kilograms but the mean of the process shifts to: (a) 1,050; (b) 1,000; (c) 950.

20. Refer to the data in problem 18. Suppose that the process is correctly centered at 1,100 kilograms but σ' increases to 150. What portion of production will be below the specifications limit?

*21. (a) Construct a spreadsheet template to compute the 3σ control limits for $\overline{X}$ and R from 15 samples of size $n = 3$. You will need 15 rows and 3 columns to record the data given in the table below. Determine $\overline{X}$, Max., Min., and R for each sample; then compute $\overline{\overline{X}}$ and $\overline{R}$. Store the appropriate constants in

*This problem requires more detailed computation and is intended for programmable assistance such as that provided by a microcomputer.

the program so that the limits are calculated and displayed.

(b) If graphics are available, plot the control limits and the $\overline{X}$ and R values from the samples.

Observed Dimensions (cm)

Sample 1	4.843	4.863	4.859
2	4.925	4.882	4.891
3	4.866	4.914	4.873
4	4.852	4.883	4.880
5	4.920	4.884	4.821
6	4.915	4.902	4.898
7	4.887	4.892	4.858
8	4.868	4.888	4.842
9	4.904	4.863	4.866
10	4.921	4.920	4.894
11	4.914	4.884	4.899
12	4.892	4.896	4.887
13	4.866	4.829	4.880
14	4.850	4.875	4.872
15	4.867	4.900	4.885

BIBLIOGRAPHY

Deming, W. Edwards. *Quality Productivity, and Competitive Position.* Cambridge, Mass.: MIT Press, 1982.

Dodge, H. F., and H. G. Romig. *Sampling Inspection Tables.* 2d ed. New York: Wiley, 1959.

Duncan, A. J. *Quality Control and Industrial Statistics.* 4th ed. Homewood, Ill.: Irwin, 1974.

Enrick, Norbert L. *Quality and Reliability.* 7th ed. New York: Industrial Press, 1977.

Feigenbaum, Armand V. *Total Quality Control.* 3d ed. New York: McGraw-HIll, 1983.

Glossary and Tables for Statistical Quality Control. Milwaukee: American Society for Quality Control, 1983.

Grant, Eugene L., and Richard S. Leavenworth. *Quality Control.* 5th ed. New York: McGraw-Hill, 1980.

Gregerman, Ira B. "Introduction to Quality Circles: An Approach to Participative Problem-Solving." *Industrial Management,* September–October 1979, pp. 21–26.

Gryna, Frank M., Jr. *Quality Circles: A Team Approach to Problem Solving.* New York: AMACOM, 1981.

Ishikawa, Kaoru. *Guide to Quality Control.* Tokyo: Asian Productivity Organization, 1976.

Juran, Joseph M., Ed. *Quality Control Handbook.* 3d ed. New York: McGraw-Hill, 1979.

———, **and Frank M. Gryna, Jr.** *Quality Planning and Analysis.* 2d ed. New York: McGraw-Hill, 1980.

PART III
DESIGNING PRODUCTION SYSTEMS

Because production systems exist in a dynamic environment influenced by many factors, they may need to be revised or redesigned occasionally. Part III, which contains the last five chapters of the book, deals with topics relating to the design of production systems. Chapters 12 and 13 focus on the physical facilities that may constitute part of a production system. Some of the factors that should be considered and some of the methods that may be used in selecting a location for a physical facility are discussed in Chapter 12. Chapter 13 deals with the factors that should be considered in locating components within a facility.

People are a vital component in production systems and are affected by a variety of factors, including the location and arrangement of facilities. The following two chapters focus on the human element in production systems. Chapter 14 discusses designing jobs that will be performed by people employed in operations. Chapter 15 discusses the importance of productivity at the overall level and at the individual worker level. Individual worker productivity is measured through time standards, which enable employees to know what is expected of them and serve in determining capacity, scheduling work, and estimating the cost of work. The chapter also presents some ideas about compensation of employees.

The book concludes with Chapter 16, a consideration of the production system at a macro level. This final chapter discusses some of the relationships that may exist between areas within the production system and between the production system and its external environment.

Chapter Outline
FACILITY LOCATION

THE IMPORTANCE OF LOCATION
Competition / Cost / Hidden Effects

LOCATION DECISIONS
The Systems View

LOCATION FACTORS
Market-Related Factors / Tangible Cost Factors / Intangible Factors

LOCATION EVALUATION METHODS
General Steps in Location Selection / Grouping of Service Areas / Cost-Profit-Volume or Break-Even Analysis / Point Rating / The Transportation Method / *Application: The Use of the Transportation Method in Location Analysis* / Simulation / *Application: A Nonmanufacturing Location Analysis*

Summary / **Discussion Questions** / **Problems** / **Cases** / **Bibliography**

KEY TERMS

Logistic chain	Intangible factors	Market-oriented	Cost-profit-volume
Vertical integration	Centroid	location	analysis
Systems view	Materials-oriented	Satisficing solution	Point rating
Market-related factors	location	Distribution costs	
Tangible cost factors			

Chapter 12

FACILITY LOCATION

In our consideration of design-related issues, we will first discuss the location of operations facilities. In its strategy formulation, a company determines what types of goods or services it will offer and in what markets it will compete. It makes demand forecasts to estimate the demand that can be found in various market areas. Part of the company's strategy consists of selecting the location from which potential markets will be served. The location of a nonmanufacturing operation helps determine how conveniently customers can conduct business with the company. Location of manufacturing and nonmanufacturing operations can have a great impact on operating costs, thereby affecting profit and perhaps the price at which goods or services can be offered.

Long-range forecasts and capacity plans might reveal the need for additional capacity in some areas. If a company has excess capacity in one location or excess shipping costs to some areas, relocation of some facility or facilities may be desirable. At least four aspects of the facility question must be addressed—the types of facilities needed, the location of these facilities, the necessary capacity, and the design or layout of the facilities. Capacity planning has been discussed in previous chapters. The layout of components within a facility is discussed in the next chapter.

Companies that can select the location at which their operations are performed may face decisions about location and arrangement at various times. A new company may begin operating in a leased facility, later decide to build or buy its own, then expand to multiple locations, and so on. Shifts in the location of demand and the addition of new products or services to those already offered may necessitate the relocation of some facilities or the complete design and construction of new ones. In a dynamic market for its goods and services an organization may expand, relocate, or add new facilities, which means that location decisions are made occasionally throughout the life of a company.

This chapter discusses some of the factors and methods involved in selecting locations for operations activities. As will be seen, these decisions often depend on inexact approaches. Naturally, such considerations are appropriate only when the company is free to select the location at which its service is to be provided. Some service operations (e.g., emergency medical or fire fighting, carpet cleaning, and on-site repair services) do not select the location of the actual sites where their services are provided. In such service operations, decisions are influenced more by the equipment to be used and by the locations of the bases from which they operate than by where the services are delivered.

THE IMPORTANCE OF LOCATION

Location decisions are important and warrant management's careful attention for several reasons. Three important reasons for care in the selection of facility locations are as follows:

Competition

A company's location affects its ability to compete and influences many other aspects of its operations. In manufacturing companies, location affects direct costs by influencing transportation costs to and from the facility as well as the cost of labor and many supplies used in the production process. In service operations location can affect the demand for the services and the effectiveness of the entire operation. Location can also affect morale, employee relations, and public relations. The layout or arrangement of facilities also has an impact on the cost of the operation and on ease of supervision and coordination, as well as on morale and employee relations. Its effects are discussed in Chapter 13.

Cost

Failures to make good location decisions are expensive and have long-lasting consequences. Decisions to purchase land and construct a building involve significant amounts of money; mistakes may be literally set in concrete. Time and effort spent in doing something wrong and then correcting it will never be recovered. Perhaps even more expensive—if less obvious—is the cost of making a poor location decision and not correcting it.

Hidden Effects

The effects of location are insidious. Since they are not directly observable, management must always be alert to the need to evaluate location. The cost of a poor location is an opportunity cost and therefore is hidden. No checks are written for the opportunity costs; they do not show up in accounting reports.

Consequently, they come to the attention only of those who periodically examine and critically evaluate operations.

LOCATION DECISIONS

Location decisions usually deal with service facilities or with manufacturing
facilities to be located at some site other than the site of the mineral deposits
that provide the basic raw materials. For most companies, the scope of options
is confined to domestic locations to serve markets near and within the firm's
home country. Even if we restrict potential locations to one country, there are
numerous communities large enough to staff various types of production and
service operations. The scope and magnitude of location problems are enor-
mous, even when considerations are confined within national boundaries.

Sometimes plant locations are based on very little in the way of formal
location studies. A new or young company may be in its present location just
because it is where the owner lived when he or she decided to start the business.
Additional branches may be located at sites the owner felt were easy to oversee
along with other operations. Perhaps a site is one that the owner already owned
or could acquire from a friend or relative. You may think of several other reasons
that some operations are where they happen to be. Most of the methods to be
discussed here, however, are based on the objective of an adequate gain for a
given level of investment and risk.

The Systems View

When considering the location of facilities, a broad systems view is necessary.
The problem may encompass many interrelated factors, and one should be
careful to see that all major ones are included in the analysis.

A production operation is part of a larger system, the company. The company in turn is part of a larger system, a logistic chain. Previous discussions of
materials management (Chapter 5) brought out a manufacturing company's
dependence on suppliers for inputs and its need to supply its outputs to customers. Thus several companies or several divisions of a large company may
be linked together in a *logistic chain* (Figure 12.1). A metallic product may be
produced from ore mined at one location, transported to a smelter to be refined,
converted to mill products at another factory, fabricated into components at yet
another factory, assembled into a finished product at an assembly plant, then
shipped to a warehouse. A company is said to be *vertically integrated* if it owns
several of the links in the logistic chain.

The location of one component in the logistic chain depends on the location of suppliers, consumers, and other facilities involved in the production-
distribution process. Ideally, a company should make location decisions to accomplish the entire production-distribution process at maximum profit or minimum cost, at least for that portion of the logistic chain under its control. A
systems view examines all of the components and their interrelationships to try

FIGURE 12.1

The Logistic Chain

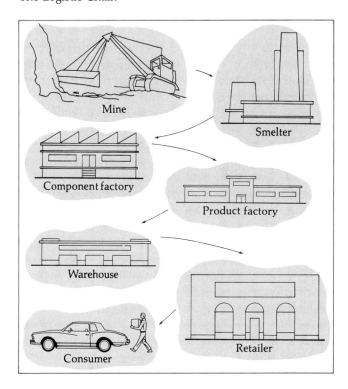

to arrive at an optimal location for all components of the chain. Most companies, however, own only a small portion of the total logistic chain and have little or no control over the location of other components. Even when companies own several links in the logistic chain, several facilities already exist when a decision is to be made about the location of a new one. Consequently, location decisions are usually, by necessity, made piecemeal, in the light of many existing components of the logistic chain.

Nonmanufacturing organizations are also part of logistic chains in that they must obtain input services and supply consumers with their services. Service companies must consider the availability of inputs and the location of demand. Many services require direct contact with customers, making location critical to the success of the enterprise. Often operations of this type concentrate on market-related factors, which will be discussed next.

LOCATION FACTORS

Location decisions often involve a broad array of factors that can influence revenue, cost, or both, and consequently may affect profits. Other factors may have a less measurable effect on profits but still are important in location considerations. Several operations location factors are discussed below and for convenience are grouped into three general categories:

1. *Market-related factors*—locations of demand and of competition.
2. *Tangible cost factors*—transportation, utilities, labor, taxes, site costs, construction costs.
3. *Intangible factors*—local attitude toward industry, zoning and legal regulations, room for growth, climate, schools, churches, hospitals, recreational opportunities, and so on.

Market-Related Factors

Market strategies often must be considered in locating facilities. Demand forecasts help determine where goods or services are most likely to be sold. A *centroid*, or weighted center of demand, exists for each product or product family. A decision on the location of the facility that supplies this demand must take into account the level and location of demand for each product, both now and in the future. The location of competitors will also affect the desirability of a location. Some companies consider it necessary to be located near competition. Other companies wish to avoid competitors. The convenience or inconvenience of a location may affect the number of potential customers and thus revenue. Marketing strategy is an important factor to be considered along with operations factors when a location is to be selected.

Some companies, particularly those that make high-volume purchases over a long term, are changing their purchasing practices to favor suppliers who are located closer to the purchaser's plant. These companies, seeking the advantages of just-in-time (JIT) manufacturing and intending to operate with much less inventory, may require that vendors be located within, say, two hours' driving distance. Or they may stipulate that the vendor must make multiple deliveries of small quantities of products each day. The purchasing company may offer longer-term contracts in exchange for these extra deliveries and a commitment to high quality. The result is that suppliers who want this business may have to locate within an acceptable range of a particular customer.

Tangible Cost Factors

Many items necessary to the operation are costly. Location decisions should take such items into consideration. Long-range forecasts of costs should be used, since facilities may last forty or fifty years or more.

Transportation   Availability of multiple modes of transportation can provide flexibility and minimum-cost means of transporting various materials. Shipping rates per ton-mile vary from one location to another and with the type of material to be transported. The relative weights and freight costs for inbound and outbound items may influence location decisions.

Any link in the logistic chain will receive inputs from some source or sources and distribute its product to some subsequent users. Input factors may be regarded very highly by some companies in making their location decisions. If a company is located near its source of materials, it is said to have a *materials-oriented location.* A manufacturing company will tend to be materials-oriented if it has a single source of raw material and ships its products in many directions or if the raw material is cumbersome or heavy. It is easier to ship paper than to ship trees and water, so a paper mill is usually located near a body of water and in regions with abundant forests. A location near the source of materials may be essential to the securing of the inputs. Quarrying and mining operations must be located near the sources of materials. Few people would donate blood if they had to travel to some remote location and back; a blood drive minimizes the donor's effort and lost time by coming to places of employment for groups of donors.

Some manufacturing operations may locate near the consumer—that is, select *market-oriented locations*—if their products are perishable, extremely heavy, or bulky. When rapid delivery is a condition of sales, companies are more likely to select market-oriented locations. When most of a company's product is consumed within a small region, its plant location is likely to be market-oriented, particularly if the raw materials come from several regions and are inexpensively shipped. Retail and finished-goods warehousing operations are market-oriented. Most service operations are market-oriented, since contact with the consumer is usually necessary.

Labor Availability and Costs   Labor-intensive companies may place more emphasis on the cost of processing materials than on the cost of transporting them. Companies that employ a large labor force may relocate to places with lower wage rates. Productivity per hour may further affect the cost of providing services or producing goods. Union work rules governing crew sizes and work rates may have some bearing on location preferences.

Employee absenteeism and turnover rates affect the number of people who must be on the payroll and the cost of hiring and training. Still another consideration is the ability of a locality to provide sufficient applicants for jobs to facilitate growth and to replace promoted, retired, and released employees.

Energy Availability and Costs   Many manufacturing plants use large amounts of energy sources, such as electricity or natural gas, to operate production processes. Nonmanufacturing facilities use these resources for heating or air conditioning the workers' environment. Fuels have become scarce and expensive in many locations and will play an increasingly large part in companies' location selections. To ensure the possibility of future expansion, it is wise to examine the power company's expansion plans and future allocations to the gas company from its sources.

Water Availability and Costs   Processes that require large amounts of water are restricted to locations where abundant water resources are available. Water shortages occur in some locations and will probably become more common. If the process overheats or chemically contaminates the water, then the availability of locations will be further restricted; some sites may even be forbidden. Availability of water and the cost of water treatment and pollution control must be considered by operations that make extensive use of water.

Site and Construction Costs   One cost directly related to facility location is the cost of purchasing the site and building the facility. The cost per acre of land varies widely from site to site within a region and from region to region. The cost per acre is sometimes deceptive, because less costly land may require greater expenditures to prepare the site and construct a building.

Taxes   Some localities use tax incentives as a motivator to attract business and industry. Tax reductions or exemptions may be allowed to new businesses. Property taxes may be sizable for a company with a multimillion-dollar investment in facilities and inventory. The extent of a company's investment will influence the relative importance of taxes in selection of a location.

Intangible Factors

Not all measures of a location's desirability can be expressed in dollars and cents. People must be induced to come to work there, so the appeal of a locality as a place to live and rear a family is important. The local political environment may also have important effects on a company.

Zoning and Legal Regulations   Local, state, and federal pollution-control regulations may limit the locations available to some companies. Zoning regulations control the types of businesses that may operate in certain areas. Since zoning and legal regulations may restrict the types of future diversification a company can undertake, long-range plans should be considered from both the company's and the community's standpoint.

Community Attitudes   Community relations should be an integral part of location decisions. Public opinion in some areas may be unfavorable to particular types of businesses, even though there is no formal legislation against it. A company locating in such an area runs the risk of future restrictions, excessive taxes, or other undesirable public reactions. Problems may arise if the public becomes aroused by unexpected smoke, noise, odor, or some other undesirable impact. It is wise to meet with community leaders and sample opinion before making costly commitments.

Expansion Potential   A site for a manufacturing or nonmanufacturing facility should offer some flexibility and room for expansion. The size and contour of the plot of land should allow for expansion of the facility without a sacrifice of efficiency. Room for expansion of utility service capacity should be available. Access roads and transportation facilities should also be capable of accommodating increased volume.

Living Conditions   Often a company's top-echelon personnel are obtained from other branches or other companies. Today some people decline promotions with their own company or offers from other companies because they do not want to move to the job location. The costs of living—housing, food, clothing, power, and other essentials—are important to all employees. And areas noted for high crime rates, to mention another example, are not conducive to easy recruiting.

A location's appeal to potential employees may be an important consideration. People are interested in the environment in which they and their families will live. Many want above-average schools for their children and opportunities for further study for themselves. The climate and recreational facilities may also influence the appeal of a location.

LOCATION EVALUATION METHODS

The number and diversity of factors mentioned above should make it obvious that a formal, generic location model would be very difficult to develop. There is no single, cut-and-dried method. A search for all available sites and an evaluation of all of them would be prohibitively time-consuming and expensive. Instead of optimal decisions, satisficing decisions are developed by approximation. It is important to remember that location decisions are long-range decisions and therefore are based on forecast (estimated) consequences of locating at each site. We are talking not only about conditions today but also about conditions in ten or twenty years. The labor force must be adequate, and there must be some assurance that enough trained people will continue to be available in the area to provide for future growth. Since approximations and inferences are used, satisficing decisions, rather than proven optimal ones, often are sought.

The term *satisficing solution* is used because there are perhaps many optimal or almost optimal solutions to a location problem. The difference between an optimal solution and an almost optimal one may be negligible. If there were only one clearly optimal solution, very little analysis or consideration would be necessary. But there are plastics manufacturers in many locations throughout the country. Electronics manufacturers and insurance companies may be found in dozens of places. Apparently they can succeed in a variety of settings.

The issue of location has an important impact on a company's ability to compete and on its exposure to risk from external factors. A manufacturing company, for example, might elect to have one central plant that produces all products in the company's product line. This decision would perhaps provide economies of scale. The volume of some operations will reduce the unit cost because equipment is better utilized and fixed costs can be spread over more units. However, transportation from a single location to broadly dispersed customers can be expensive, and obtaining inputs from broadly dispersed suppliers can also be expensive. A strike or a disaster such as a fire or flood could completely halt all company operations.

A second alternative is to have several smaller plants. Each plant could specialize in one product in the product line. The risk from fire, flood, or a strike would be reduced. Although most of the transportation problems mentioned above might still exist, some products might be made nearer to a con-centration of customers for that product or nearer to the source of materials. However, the volume at each plant might not be sufficient to fully utilize some equipment that must be available at each location, and the company would probably have more fixed costs because of the multiple locations.

Another possibility is to have each smaller plant specialize in production of a particular type of component or components of the product line—such as a transmission plant that produces the transmissions for all of the cars an au-tomobile company produces. The company would still be vulnerable to the risk of a strike or disaster, which could prevent its having some component essential to all products. Economies of scale in production could be achieved, however, with this type of decision. Components would have to be shipped from each production facility to the locations where assembly is performed, then the final product would be distributed from these locations. This deployment of facilities could result in significant shipping costs.

The above discussion illustrates some of the factors that must be taken into consideration before a company begins to select a location or locations for its facilities. Each possible decision will have some advantages and some dis-advantages. The company must determine which option is best suited to the products it offers, the location of its customers and materials, and other con-ditions of the specific company.

How does one person or a group of people arrive at a location selection? No doubt there are many methods—almost an infinite number—when one con-siders how many different types of people could be assembled into a group of decision makers and how many different kinds of location decisions could be assigned to a group. Not all of the group dynamics and personal interactions that might result can be described. We shall focus on a few formal frameworks to illustrate some of the features of the location problem and some possible approaches to its solution.

General Steps in Location Selection

The process of selecting a location may follow many steps of evaluation. The sequencing of these steps may vary with the situation, but a frequently used sequence is this:

1. Select the general region.
2. Select generally acceptable communities.
3. Select appropriate sites within the communities.
4. Determine a method of evaluating community-site combinations.
5. Compare sites and select one.

Step 2 may sometimes be omitted; an organization may search for sites within the desired region and proceed to steps 3 and 4. General approaches other than the one outlined above may be followed. Marketing considerations, *distribution costs*, wage rates, and the availability of raw materials may lead to selection of a general region. An evaluation of available labor skills, highways, railways, waterways, docks, or airports will lead to a list of communities within the region. Intangible factors may eliminate some or move them to the bottom of the list. The company can then survey the acceptable communities to determine if suitable sites are available.

Grouping of Service Areas

When the company produces more than one product or provides several services, the problem of location becomes rather complicated. Managers must decide whether to have small plants and warehouses located in areas ideal for each product or to group products into larger facilities in locations that represent a compromise for some items but are best for the group as a whole. Trade-offs must be evaluated to decide which products to group and where to locate facilities. Economies of scale must be compared with the cost of nonoptimal locations.

As the volume of products handled by a regional warehouse is increased, the warehouse cost will be spread over a greater volume. Hence the warehouse cost per unit will decrease. Introducing additional products into the facility, however, means that a broader geographic area must be covered by it, and delivery costs will therefore be increased. A graphical model of these costs has a generally familiar appearance, as shown in Figure 12.2. The same structure may be applied to service operations by comparing travel costs for a location to the facility savings that result from combining smaller regions.

Sound judgment is a vital part of any decision. A broad array of models or techniques is available to assist those responsible for reaching a decision. Four of the models or techniques that may be beneficial in reaching a location decision are discussed below.

FIGURE 12.2

Transportation Costs vs. Facility Costs for a Distribution Center

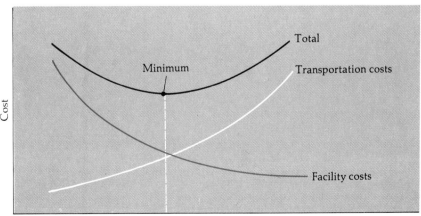

Volume (area served)

Cost-Profit-Volume or Break-Even Analysis

Since the volume of business available is one of the variables that affect a location's desirability, *cost-profit-volume analysis*, sometimes called *break-even analysis*, may be a useful tool in selecting a location. Some of the costs of having a facility in a location will be fixed, and some will vary with the volume of business. The cost structures will probably be different for each location being considered. So will the volume of sales. A graphical model such as Figure 12.3, showing the relationship of cost and volume in two locations, may therefore give a significant insight into the situation. Only one revenue line is shown, since it is assumed that the product will sell for the same price no matter which location is selected. As long as the location does not affect the volume sold and the volume is above V_0, then location 1 is preferable to location 2, because TC_1 is lower than TC_2 for all volumes greater than V_0.

One should not conclude that the lowest-cost location will always be the maximum-profit location, unless the price and volume are to be the same for all locations. Some location other than the one with minimum costs might result in sufficient additional volume to increase revenue more than costs. Figure 12.4 shows the same costs as Figure 12.3. Assume, however, that the company will experience a sales volume of V_2 in location 2 and a sales volume of V_1 in location 1. For this particular set of conditions, the higher-cost location will result in a greater profit.

Many manufactured products are purchased by people who don't know where the goods were manufactured or stored before they were shipped to the point of purchase. Location of a factory or warehouse has no effect on the volume of demand. Location may have a great effect, however, on the volume

FIGURE 12.3

Relationship of Cost and Volume at Two Locations

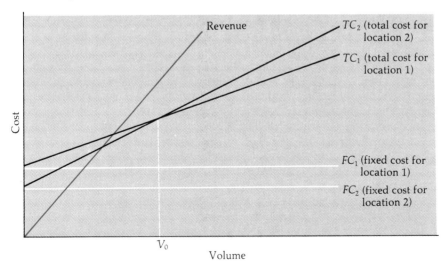

FIGURE 12.4

Higher Cost Locations Can Provide Higher Profit

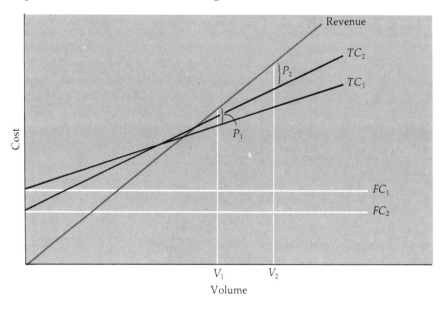

of sales for a retail establishment or a service operation. Consider, for example, a laundry and dry cleaning establishment. A customer has to make two trips, one to leave dirty clothes and another to pick them up after they have been cleaned. A convenient location can often increase volume significantly, and the effect on profit must be considered.

The discussion in this section has been simplified to illustrate the basic idea of cost-profit-volume analysis in relation to location selection. The method can be used to compare more than two possible locations, and the curves representing costs and revenue can be more complicated than straight lines.

Point Rating

In selecting a site companies have several objectives, but not all are of equal importance. The relative weights a company assigns to each type of objective or to each location factor may be represented by the number of points a perfect site would receive in each category. Each potential site then is evaluated with respect to every factor a company is looking for, and points are assigned to each factor. The site with the highest total number of points is considered superior.

Of course, implementing an organized system such as this for evaluating multiple goals requires careful judgment. As the *point rating* has been described thus far, a high score in any factor can overcome a low ranking in any other. However, because some factors may be essential, any site that does not have at least a specified number of points for that factor will be excluded from further consideration. For example, the existing labor force may be sufficient, but the projected growth of other businesses in the area may be so large that the company foresees a lack of growth potential or an expensive wage-payment contest. Another matter that must be worked out to implement a point-rating system is the relative importance of tangible cost factors compared to intangible factors. Points are usually assigned only to the intangible factors, and an evaluation is made to determine whether the difference between the intangible scores is worth the difference, if any, between the tangible costs of the competing locations.

Consider this example: After evaluating two potential sites by comparing costs and finding them approximately equal, a pipe manufacturer decided to evaluate the intangible factors for the sites, A and B, by point rating. Comparative ratings were assigned to major location factors to determine the relative importance of each. Each site was assigned a percentage of the maximum possible points, and these points were totaled. The results of the point rating, presented in Table 12.1, indicate a slight preference for site B.

The Transportation Method

When only one source will be used to supply the location under consideration, the cost of supplying it can be found by adding the production cost at the supply point and the shipping cost from there to the potential location. When a network of several supply points can supply a potential location, however, the cost is more difficult to compute. Interaction between existing facilities and the proposed facility must be considered. The total cost for one location must be compared with the total cost for another location. In order to make this type of comparison, we must first find the best match of capacity and demand for one potential location, then the best match for another, and so on for every location under consideration, so that the costs and profits for all of them can be compared.

Table 12.1
POINTS ASSIGNED TO ALTERNATIVE LOCATIONS

Factors Rated	Maximum Possible Points	LOCATION	
		A	B
Future availability of fuel	300	200	250
Transportation flexibility and growth	200	150	150
Adequacy of water supply	100	100	100
Labor climate	250	220	200
Pollution regulations and tax stability	30	20	20
Site characteristics	50	40	30
Living conditions	150	100	125
Total		830	875

The transportation method of linear programming, discussed in supplement E, can be used to match capacity and demand. Recall that this method derives its name from its ability to minimize the cost of transporting products from source locations to distribution centers. The transportation method can be used to allocate productive capacity at various factories to a group of field warehouses, to allocate materials at field warehouses to customer accounts in various cities, and to assign service accounts to service centers, each of which has some specified capacity.

The location of a facility may affect its operating cost. The location of a repair center, for example, will affect the cost of transporting all of the necessary repair parts. If several sources of supply are available and several other existing repair centers also are to be supplied, the best allocation or distribution of the repair parts probably will not be obvious. If revenue is not affected by location, its contribution to profit and overhead can be maximized by finding the minimum-cost location. Here the transportation method may be put to good use, though a computer might be employed to solve large-scale problems.

APPLICATION

Use of the Transportation Method in Location Analysis

The Atlantis Pool Supply Company began with a factory in Phoenix in 1951. It produces and distributes a line of swimming pool accessories that are sold to pool supply stores in many major cities, primarily in the South and Southwest. Soon after starting the company, Splash Gordon, the owner, expanded by opening a distribution warehouse near Glendale, California. Next he opened a second factory in Little Rock, Arkansas, and a distribution warehouse just outside Dallas, Texas.

Splash has just returned to the company's Phoenix headquarters from getting operations under way at a new factory in Columbus, Georgia. He has decided that he will open a distribution warehouse in the Southeast. Splash and several of his upper-level managers have gone through a point-rating evaluation of several cities and have concluded that either Atlanta or Charlotte will be suitable. We shall look over his shoulder as he compares the cost of operations in the two cities.

In order to use the transportation method, Splash first obtained the costs for shipping from all the sources to all the possible destinations. He also estimated the amount of capacity available at the sources. The estimated demand was 700 in Glendale and Dallas, and 700 at Atlanta or Charlotte. The other data are presented in Table 12.2

Table 12.2
PLANT CAPACITY AND SHIPPING COSTS TO ACTUAL AND HYPOTHETICAL DESTINATIONS, ATLANTIS POOL SUPPLY COMPANY

Plant	Capacity	SHIPPING COST TO:			
		Glendale	Dallas	Atlanta	Charlotte
Phoenix	800	$ 5	$9	$16	$17
Little Rock	800	9	4	8	9
Columbus	600	15	8	3	5

FIGURE 12.5

Optimal Solution to Atlantis's Transportation Problem if Atlanta Is Used as a Warehouse Location

Plant	Warehouse				
	Glendale	Dallas	Atlanta	Dummy	Capacity
Phoenix	700 〈5	〈9	〈16	100 〈0	800
Little Rock	〈9	700 〈4	100 〈8	〈0	800
Columbus	〈15	〈8	600 〈3	〈0	600
Demand	700	700	700	100	

In certain instances, this type of problem could be solved by including both Atlanta and Charlotte in the same transportation-method tableau and adding a dummy source. If either of the proposed locations is excluded from the solution (i.e., receives only dummy products), it is obviously the wrong location. When the optimal solution indicates that both proposed locations should receive some actual product and some dummy product, it is not clear which location is preferred. Splash decided to solve this problem by considering each proposed location separately.

First, the problem was worked under the assumption that Atlanta was chosen. The final solution is shown in Figure 12.5. Notice that the plants have 100 units of excess capacity, so a dummy location requiring 100 units is included in the tableau. The cost of supplying the dummy location from any plant is zero. The total cost of this allocation can be found by multiplying the amount in each occupied cell by the unit shipping cost for that cell and summing these amounts for all of the occupied cells. The monthly shipping cost if Atlanta is used as a location will be 700($5) + 700($4) + 100($8) + 600($3) + $0 = $8,900.

The procedure was then repeated, using the appropriate numbers for Charlotte. The optimal solution is presented in Figure 12.6. This tableau indicates the same shipping pattern, but the total monthly shipping cost if Charlotte is selected

FIGURE 12.6

Optimal Solution if Charlotte Is Used as a Warehouse Location

Plant	Warehouse				
	Glendale	Dallas	Charlotte	Dummy	Capacity
Phoenix	700 〈5	〈9	〈17	100 〈0	800
Little Rock	〈9	700 〈4	100 〈9	〈0	800
Columbus	〈15	〈8	600 〈5	〈0	600
Demand	700	700	700	100	

as the warehouse location will be 700($5) + 700($4) + 100($9) + 600($5) + 100($0) = $10,200.

After going through these calculations, Splash asked his assistant to find the name of a good industrial real estate firm in Atlanta and to place a call to it. He then left to go to the product testing laboratory for a quick swim.

Simulation

The previous application of LP considered only the inbound transportation cost for the swimming pool equipment. The Atlantis Company may feel that the rise in outbound freight cost caused by moving a location in one direction will be offset by an equivalent reduction in the cost of freight going in the opposite direction. Besides, Atlantis charges the outbound delivery cost to the customer.

A company must take a more holistic, systems view when both the inbound and outbound freight costs are relevant to a location decision. In multiple-location operations, materials may be moved around from one warehouse to another because demand is greater than expected in some areas and less than expected in others. Inventory levels within each facility fluctuate with a probabilistic demand. Different levels of safety stock may be required at different locations. When in addition a company stocks and sells hundreds or thousands of products, analysis of the system requires considerable time and effort. Several variables and their interaction must be considered.

Computers have made possible the storage of vast amounts of data and the rapid computation necessary to keep track of the many variables involved in such complex problems. Simulation is sometimes used as a tool in selecting the location for such complex systems. Further, simulation can provide useful information about the system in addition to indicating the results of alternative locations. Simulation can also be used in analysis of operations that do not distribute or manufacture tangible products. An introductory overview of simulation is provided in Supplement F.

APPLICATION

A Nonmanufacturing Location Analysis

Manufacturing firms and some other companies that must transport tangible items are concerned with transportation costs. So are the operators of emergency vehicles, such as ambulances. Their major concern, however, is with the time required to make a trip (response time) rather than the cost. Such factors as the skills of the ambulance personnel and the type of equipment used are important in the ability of the system to meet its objectives. Given some number of ambulances with a particular set of equipment and skilled crews, the effectiveness of the system is determined by the expected response time, which is determined by the location of the vehicles.

Suppose that we want to determine the most desirable locations for a group of ambulances that serve a county. The measure of desirability for a set of locations is the expected response time of the ambulances. People do not select the time

FIGURE 12.7

Sequence of Events Following an Emergency

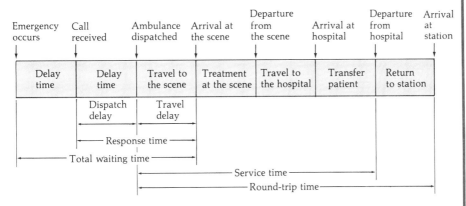

Source: A. W. Drake, R. L. Keeney, and P. M. Morse, eds., *Analysis of Public Systems* (Cambridge, Mass.: MIT Press, 1972), p. 140. Copyright © 1972 by the Massachusetts Institute of Technology. Reprinted by permission of the MIT Press, Cambridge, Massachusetts.

and place at which they will suddenly need medical attention—an ambulance may be called at any time from any point in the county. The variable that can be controlled by the deployment of ambulances is the expected or average elapsed time between the moment an ambulance is called and the time it arrives on the scene. Service time is affected by the number of hospitals in the county and their locations. Several small hospitals might provide care more quickly in emergencies than one large one, but we are assuming that the hospitals are already located. (This is like having part of the logistic chain already in place for a manufacturing company.) Figure 12.7 shows the important events and time delays that occur after an emergency call. Only the response time that is related to the ambulance location is considered here.

Richard Volz developed a computer model to predict the mean response time if the ambulance with the shortest driving time is dispatched every time an emergency call is received. He assumed that the ambulances not on service calls would be redeployed to optimal locations every time an ambulance went on a call. Thus he had to find the best location for one ambulance, for two, for three, on up to the total number available, N. It was assumed that there would always be at least one available ambulance.

Volz applied his model to Washtenaw County in southeastern Michigan (Figure 12.8). The twenty-four-by-thirty-mile county was divided into one-mile squares. It was assumed that all calls from locations within a square came from a single representative point. Fifty-nine major intersections were identified, and the driving time between each pair of intersections was computed. Three surrounding intersections were selected as possible entry points for each one-mile square.

The driving time from one point to another depended on the time to get from the origin to the best entry intersection for the target square and then to the representative point within the square. It was assumed that if the origin and destination were close, the ambulance would stay on a direct route, using city streets or unpaved roads. Travel time was computed by adding the miles traveled on each type of road and dividing the result by the mean velocity for travel on that category

FIGURE 12.8

Washtenaw County, Michigan

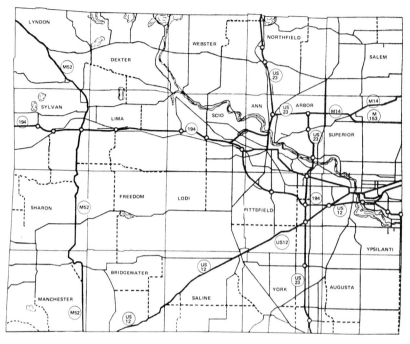

Source: Richard A. Volz, "Optimum Ambulance Location in Semi-Rural Areas," *Transportation Science 5*, no. 2 (May 1971): 196. Reprinted by permission of the publisher.

of road, as displayed in Table 12.3. The driving times between possible origins and destinations were determined and stored.

The unknown variable was the location of the ambulance when a call was received, given a particular number of available ambulances. Various alternative locations were evaluated by an iterative computer search, starting with some ar-

Table 12.3
AVERAGE AMBULANCE SPEED
ON FOUR TYPES OF ROADS

Type of Road	Average Speed (MPH)
Expressways	73.2
Other paved highways	58.1
City streets	25.6
Unpaved county roads	29.6

Source: Richard A. Volz, "Optimum Ambulance Location in Semi-Rural Areas," Transportation Science 5 (1971): 193–203. Reprinted by permission of the publisher.

bitrary point and successively improving it until no further improvement in expected response time could be found. The problem was solved first for one available ambulance, then for two, then for three, and so on.

To get the expected response time for each trial, the point-to-point driving time for a location pair was multiplied by the probability that a call would be received from the destination. This figure was multiplied by the probability that K ambulances would be in service, where K takes on integer values between 1 and $N - 1$. Since the county was divided into discrete one-mile squares, all points could be considered by iteration of the integer values. With each iteration, the search algorithm moved the location in the direction that appeared to cause the greatest reduction in expected response time.

The search was started with the assumption that only one ambulance was available at any time. The solution to the problem provided the location and the expected response time if only one ambulance were owned by the system, if two ambulances were owned and one was on another call, if three were owned and two were busy, and so on. With this information the computer could then solve for the best locations for two available ambulances, and so on. The process was continued until an optimum deployment for all ambulances was determined. Table 12.4 shows the locations selected for various numbers of available ambulances. The locations are indicated by a pair of numbers within parentheses. The first number in each pair represents the miles east of the lower left-hand corner of the county, the second the number of miles north of that point.

Table 12.4
SOLUTIONS TO THE UNCONSTRAINED AMBULANCE LOCATION PROBLEM

Number of Ambulances	Ambulance Locations	Average Response Time (minutes)
1	(23, 9)	—
2	(19, 14), (27,11)	—
3	(9, 17), (20, 14), (27, 11)	9.48
4	(9, 17), (20, 14), (27, 11), (23, 9)	8.64
5	(6, 17), (13, 18), (20, 14), (27, 11), (23, 9)	8.03
6	(6, 17), (13, 18), (20, 14), (27, 11), (18, 6), (22, 13)	7.52

Source: Richard A. Volz, "Optimum Ambulance Location in Semi-Rural Areas," Transportation Science, 5 (1971), pp. 193–203. Reprinted by permission of the publisher.

SUMMARY

Location decisions are important because they may affect cost, profit, and even success or failure of operations. They are likely to be complex, often involving myriad factors and interrelationships among numerous components of a total system. The impact of location on operations is not always obvious because some cost components represent opportunity costs rather than out-of-pocket costs. Since facilities generally are long-term investments, decisions regarding their locations usually have long-term effects.

Three major categories of factors have important influences on location decisions:

market-related factors, tangible cost factors, and intangible factors. These factors may have varying degrees of influence, depending on the type of operation. Since a service operation is likely to involve direct contact with the consumer, its location, even the aesthetics or appearance of the facility, can have a significant impact on demand. Manufacturing operations usually have less direct contact with customers, so their location is usually based on operating costs.

Several models and techniques may be used in evaluating potential locations. Four of these techniques are cost-profit-volume analysis, point rating, linear programming, and computer simulation.

DISCUSSION QUESTIONS

1. Why should location decisions be considered from a broad systems view?
2. Why can location seldom be selected on the basis of tangible cost alone?
3. What three major categories of factors influence operations location?
4. How may tangible costs and intangible factors be compared to arrive at a location decision?
5. Why do various organizations emphasize different location factors?
6. What is a market centroid?
7. What trade-off is made as the area serviced by a distribution center is expanded?
8. When should profit be considered in location analysis? Discuss the usefulness of cost-profit-volume analysis in locating a service operation.

9. What are the general steps in solving the location problem?
10. Is monetary cost or profit always the appropriate criterion for location decisions? Why?
11. Which of the factors discussed in the chapter are most important in determining the location of the following? Briefly explain the reason for your answer.
    (a) A garment plant.
    (b) A paper mill.
    (c) An automobile repair shop.
    (d) A distribution warehouse.
12. (a) What factors would lead a company to be market-oriented rather than materials-oriented in selecting its location?
    (b) What factors favor a materials orientation?

PROBLEMS

1. Rank the four sites shown in the table below on the basis of the total weighted points for each site.

Factor	Weight	A	B	C	D
Site and construction cost	0.10	60	80	90	85
Operating cost	0.15	80	90	90	80
Traffic count	0.25	90	85	60	70
Convenient access	0.20	75	90	80	90
Parking area	0.20	80	90	90	80
Surrounding population	0.10	90	85	60	70

The "Site" label spans columns A, B, C, D.

2. Donald Donavan is comparing two sites for his sales and repair shop which he has decided to relocate from its present location in a declining downtown business district. Both the sites he is considering have high traffic counts, which Donald feels is an important factor. From reading trade magazines and talking with people in similar businesses, he estimates that the average number of customers each day will be about one-half of a percent of the daily traffic count. Donald estimates that the value of the average sale per customer will continue to be $20 worth of goods and services—the average value of goods and services sold at his

present location. The average cost of the goods and services he sells is equal to 70 percent of the retail price.

Donald wants to recover the building and site costs over 10 years with a 16 percent return on the unrecovered investment. The capital recovery in 10 years with a 16 percent return will be treated as a fixed annual cost equal to 20.69 percent of the initial investment. Donald's cost estimates and traffic count for the two sites are shown below. The business will be operated 260 days per year. Compare the annual before-tax profit for the two sites.

Factor	Site I	Site II
Average weekday traffic count	20,260	24,870
Cost of site	$ 90,000	$135,000
Site preparation	$ 10,000	$ 14,000
Building cost	$100,000	$100,000
Operating costs (clerical, maintenance, insurance, taxes, utilities, etc.)	$ 50,000	$ 50,000

3. Your company is considering expanding into the Sun Belt. Your industry is heavily dependent on water transportation, so the preliminary research has narrowed the location to three sites near port facilities in Memphis, New Orleans, and St. Louis. On the basis of the following data, which site is preferable? Show your computations.

Relevant factors	Memphis	New Orleans	St. Louis
Variable costs per unit	$2.00	$2.00	$1.00
Fixed costs	$150,000.00	$300,000.00	$400,000.00
Price per unit	$3.00	$3.00	$3.00
Volume	300,000	250,000	200,000

Note: Suggested format for solution:

	Memphis	New Orleans	St. Louis
Revenue (volume × price)			
Variable costs (volume × VC per unit)			
Fixed costs			
Total costs			
Profit			

4. The Michael Corporation has plants in three cities. It distributes products from these plants to some customers and to two distribution centers. The company is planning to open a third distribution center in either Oklahoma City or Amarillo. The costs of shipping products from the company's plants to its present and prospective distribution center locations are given in the following table along with the plant capacities and requirements for each distribution center.
   (a) Determine the best distribution pattern if Amarillo is selected as the location for the new distribution center.
   (b) Determine the best distribution pattern if Oklahoma City is selected.
   (c) Compute the total distribution cost for parts *a* and *b*, and determine which location results in the lowest total distribution cost.
   (d) What other factors might be important in the selection of a location for the new distribution center?

Shipping Costs, Production Capacity, and Demand at Current and Potential Locations for Distribution Centers

Plant	Capacity	St. Louis	Phoenix
San Jose	800	$17	$6
Salt Lake City	900	13	9
Little Rock	800	5	11
Demand		900	700

Plant	Amarillo	Oklahoma City
San Jose	$9	$10
Salt Lake City	8	7
Little Rock	7	7
Demand	600	600

5. Nancy Andrews is president of the Andrews Electronic Company, which assembles pocket calculators and minicomputers. The company currently has plants in Los Angeles, California, and Richmond, Virginia. Ms. Andrews is evaluating the merits of opening a third plant in a more central part of the United States. She wishes to compare Denver and Omaha as potential locations.

Up to 1,000 units of raw material each month can be obtained from any of three locations: Oakland, Dallas, and Minneapolis. The montly requirements for each of the present and potential locations are given in the following table along with the combined cost to purchase a unit of raw material at a specified source and ship it to the indicated plant location.

| Source of Materials | Cost per Unit at Destination | | | | Total Units Available at Source |
	Los Angeles	Denver	Omaha	Richmond	
Oakland	$ 6	$9	$10	$12	1,000
Dallas	$ 9	$8	$ 7	$ 8	1,000
Minneapolis	$11	$9	$ 7	$ 9	1,000
Requirements	600	550	550	500	

(a) Decide whether the selection of Denver or Omaha would minimize the company's total cost of obtaining raw materials.

(b) How much will these costs be if Denver is selected? If Omaha is selected?

(c) What other factors do you think should be considered in reaching the decision?

6. The Theodore Corporation supplies its entire market from its location in Kansas City. Orders of sufficient size are shipped by rail where rail service is available at the destination. Mr. Theodore is considering a revision in the way smaller orders are transported. All smaller orders (about 30,000 tons) are now delivered by truck from the Kansas City warehouse. Mr. Theodore is considering opening distribution centers in Salt Lake City and Pittsburgh to serve the western and eastern regions, respectively. These distribution centers would be supplied by rail from Kansas City and would then serve small-order customers in their regions by truck. The company would continue to serve small-order customers in the central region by truck from Kansas City. Under the new plan each of the three locations would have a volume of about 10,000 tons of small orders.

If the distribution system is changed, some equipment will be moved to the new distribution centers. Under the current system, the Kansas City operation has fixed costs of $1,000,000 per year. These costs would be reduced to $800,000 if the distribution centers were opened. Each of the two new distribution centers would have fixed costs of $300,000. Under the present system, the Kansas City operation carries an average inventory of 800 tons of product at a cost of $240 per ton per year. This inventory could be reduced to 500 tons if the distribution centers are operated. Each distribution center will carry an average inventory of 200 tons, and the carrying cost is estimated to be $240 per ton per year at these locations also. If the distribution centers are used, there will be additional costs of $4 per ton to load the rail car loads and $4 per ton to unload and handle the product at the distribution centers. A cost of $5 per ton to load the truck shipments will be paid under either distribution alternative.

A major cost difference will result from shipping by rail rather than by truck from the plant to the distribution centers. The cost to ship from Kansas City to Salt Lake City is $3.31 per cwt (hundredweight) by rail and $7.90 per cwt by truck. The cost to ship from Kansas City to Pittsburgh by rail is $2.03 per cwt; by truck it is $2.48 per cwt. It is assumed that the truck costs for delivery from the distribution center will be approximately the same as the distribution costs in each region if the items were shipped directly instead of going through the distribution centers.

(a) Compare the costs of the two alternatives.

(b) What factors other than costs might be important in this comparison?

7. A company is performing a simplified analysis to determine approximately how far apart it should locate its warehouses. The company estimates that the fixed costs of operating a warehouse are $400,000 per year. It wants to determine how large an area to serve with the warehouse. The company estimates that 10 orders per year will be received per square mile served by the warehouse and that the shipping cost is $0.02 per mile for each order.

(a) Begin with a fifty-mile radius around the warehouse and compute the number of orders to be served. Assume that each order in this circle will be shipped an average of twenty-five miles. Compute the total cost and cost per order in this fifty-mile radius area to be served by the warehouse.

(b) Add a ring to the service area by extending the radius an additional fifty miles. Assume the order within this ring must be shipped an average of seventy-five miles. Compute the cost per order if the warehouse services a one hundred-mile radius.

(c) Continue adding rings until you determine the radius at which the cost per order is minimized. What is the best radius?

(d) In what ways would an actual analysis differ from the simplification used in this analysis?

CASES

1. THE DOWNTOWN NATIONAL BANK

The Downtown National Bank (DNB) is located in a city of about 500,000. Mr. James, the chairman of the board, was the major force behind the chartering of the bank five years ago. He had been president and chief executive officer of one of the other top five banks in the state—the Empire Trust Company.

Empire had become so large, with mergers throughout the state through its holding company, that Mr. James felt that its business and personal customers were becoming dissatisfied with the resulting "impersonal" relationship between them and the bank. With these and other circumstances in mind, Mr. James was convinced he could start a new bank that within a short time could compete with the top banks in the state.

The result was awe-inspiring; DNB's growth was nationally heralded. Within the first two years the bank's assets had grown to fifteen times the original capitalization. Mr. James's bank had exceeded even his own optimistic expectations. At the most recent board meeting he complimented everyone in the bank for believing in his convictions and making them work so effectively. Every person associated with the bank felt a personal pride and hoped to be able to take a breather after this accomplishment.

Mr. James, however, announced a plan to seek new personal accounts as aggressively as the bank had sought—and would continue to seek—accounts with correspondent banks and businesses. Mr. Chase, who had spearheaded the marketing department in its initial record-breaking program, was selected to devise a plan of attack on the new expansion policy. Currently the DNB operates from a single downtown location, and everyone knew that the new policy meant suburban branches. Mr. Chase was directed to find the three best suburban locations.

In narrowing his general criteria, Mr. Chase defined his goal as finding those locations that could provide the greatest potential for personal deposits. Going a step further, he evaluated his product—money; there was no doubt that money was the basic product. But money from one bank was the same as money from another. Service—what a bank did with money, how and when it received and disbursed it, and the related services it provided—made the important difference. He made a mental note to check the services offered by competing branch banks, but he rationalized that site selection should be unrelated to services. Regardless of location, the bank would determine the services it would offer as an independent issue. Going back to his basic product, Mr. Chase tried to evaluate its nature. People use money daily, so it is a convenience good rather than a durable good. He needed the three most convenient locations—convenient to the best deposit potential!

Mr. Chase decided to take a personal survey of some of his friends and neighbors to find out what they felt were the requirements of a convenient location for a branch bank. His responses re-

vealed three criteria for convenience:

1. It must be near where I live.
2. It must be near where I shop.
3. It must be near where I work.

Mr. Chase realized that his survey responses described any area in the county. Slightly frustrated, he decided to see what other banks were doing in terms of branch locations. He obtained a map and located every branch bank in the county. Recognizing that competing branches tended to cluster in certain areas, primarily shopping areas, he decided to segregate the clusters into market segments. He then went through the tedious process of determining, through census data, the number of families living in each segment and the amount of average family income earned per segment. Mr. Chase then developed the information shown in Table 12.5,

Table 12.5
BRANCH BANKING MARKET SEGMENT ANALYSIS

Market Segment	No. of Banking Facilities	Total Annual Family Income (in millions of dollars)	Average Total Family Income Per Banking Facility (in millions of dollars)	Family Income Per Branch With One Additional Branch Bank (in millions of dollars)	Growth rate (percent)
Valley Hills	2	$ 98.6	$49.3	$32.9	+48.8
Woodland	2	86.8	43.4	28.9	− 2.2
Crestville	2	80.2	40.1	26.7	+ 3.2
Gardenside	1	34.0	34.0	17.0	+24.5
East Thomas	1	32.2	32.2	16.1	−12.5
Pleasant Grove	1	31.1	31.1	15.5	+16.2
Five Points West	4	122.4	30.6	24.5	−11.4
Cahaba	1	28.9	28.9	14.5	+10.5
Trusstown	1	28.3	28.3	14.2	+12.2
Avondale	1	27.6	27.6	13.8	+ 5.7
Ironwood	4	103.2	20.6	20.6	+ 8.9
Hueyville	2	49.0	24.5	16.3	+11.7
Herbert	3	67.5	22.5	16.9	+52.8
Tarrance	2	40.4	20.2	13.5	−11.7
Montdale	4	76.4	19.1	15.3	+42.9
Forestdale	2	34.8	17.4	11.6	+19.2
Wyman	3	49.8	16.6	12.5	− 1.1
Homeville	6	90.6	15.1	12.9	+5.3
Graysville	1	15.1	15.1	7.6	+14.3
Centerville	3	38.7	12.9	9.7	+27.8
North Morgan	2	24.2	12.1	8.1	−16.5
Downtown	22	182.4	8.3	7.9	−52.3

which identified the total number of branches in a segment and the total annual income of those families per bank branch. He also noted on the table the population growth rate for the previous ten years for each segment and the family income per branch if a new branch were added in the segment.

He reasoned that for two given segments with the same total annual family income, the deposit potential of a new branch would be greater where more potential deposit funds were available.

1. Is a bank materials-oriented or market-oriented?
2. Discuss the "systems approach" as it relates to this case.
3. What other data would you suggest that Mr. Chase evaluate before making his recommendations?
4. Which three market segments would you recommend as the best locations on the basis of the information presented in this case? Why?
5. Within each of Mr. Chase's three recommended market segments, what criteria would you use in selecting the actual sites for the branches?

2. A LOCATION DECISION USING A POINT-RATING SYSTEM

A growing chemical processing company, Excellent, with its home office in Tulsa, Oklahoma, is considering opening an oil refinery on either the Atlantic Coast or the Gulf Coast. Company executives have selected two potential sites for location of the new facility, one near Norfolk, Virginia, and the other near Mobile, Alabama.

Shipment from the rich oil fields of the Middle East would be less costly with a Norfolk location, and currently most of the company's oil comes from the Middle East. But the prospects of future availability of this supply at competitive prices are not encouraging. The possibility of further restrictions on tanker shipments, import duties, and another oil embargo make investment with the Middle East supply in mind less desirable. The potential on the Gulf Coast is much better. In fact, recent testing indicates that the Alabama site may be within a few hundred miles of one of the most productive oil fields of the 1980s.

It is obvious that proper evaluation of this situation is crucial to the success of the company as a whole. Much time and money must be spent to resolve the issue. But this is not the only location consideration; other costs must also be considered. What would be the comparative costs of such things as construction, utilities, transportation, and labor?

Property and labor have been found to be less costly in Mobile. Indeed, almost every cost is lower in Mobile. Mobile is located farther from the manufacturing centers of the North, however, and therefore most materials and supplies are more expensive there as a result of the additional shipping and transportation costs.

After construction is completed, operating costs will become crucial. They may make the difference between success and failure for the new plant. For Excellent the most important of these costs are labor, materials, utilities, transportation, pollution control, and taxes. Data have been collected and statistical forecasts made to determine the possible future impact of each of these factors on operating costs. Mobile has been found to have lower total operating costs.

Norfolk, however, is located nearer much of the planned market and therefore shipping costs would be less from an Atlantic Coast plant. In addition, less competition exists along the Atlantic seaboard. Several refinery plants have been opened recently along the Gulf Coast, and regional competition for everything from product demand to professional employees will be more difficult there.

If Excellent goes through with its proposed expansion, many key personnel from the Tulsa office will be asked to transfer to the new location. A poll of those employees indicated that most would prefer to move to Norfolk. Data from the Norfolk Chamber of Commerce shows that there are more hospitals, schools, and recreational opportunities there.

In sum, more than 200 factors and considerations have been studied. Those of prime importance are outlined above. Other considerations of some relevance are labor union strength, climate (Mobile is located in a potential hurricane path and Norfolk could have winter storms that would completely halt operations and cost Excellent many thousands of dollars), public opinion, and water supply.

After this exhaustive study, the company executives are still undecided as to which location to

Table 12.6
POINTS ASSIGNED TO TWO LOCATIONS, BY FACTOR

Factor	Maximum Possible Points	LOCATION	
		Norfolk	Mobile
Availability of raw materials	1,000	700	800
Construction and site costs	500	300	400
Operating costs	1,000	700	900
Relevant market factors	900	800	600
Living conditions and desirability	400	300	200
Labor union strength	50	40	30
Climate	100	70	80
Public opinion	50	40	40
Water supply	70	60	50
Total		3,010	3,100

select. But one of the top executives at Excellent has worked out a point-rating evaluation of relevant factors for Excellent, using statistical methods plus his own personal judgment. The results of his ratings are listed in Table 12.6 and indicate that Mobile is a slightly more desirable location for Excellent's new plant. The executive realizes that this conclusion is, of course, based on the proper assignment of points. So he has explained the system and his point assignments to several other executives in the Tulsa office and most agree with his findings. This conclusion is based primarily on the lower operating and construction costs in the Mobile area. The potential availability of an adequate supply of domestic crude oil also contributes significantly to the decision.

1. Should Excellent locate in Mobile on the basis of this study?
2. Is the total point difference between Norfolk and Mobile significant?
3. Do you agree with the point assignments?

BIBLIOGRAPHY

Ballou, Ronald H. *Business Logistics Management: Planning & Control.* 2d ed. Englewood Cliffs, N.J.: Prentice-Hall, 1985.

Bowersox, Donald J. *Logistical Management: A System Integration of Physical Distribution, Management, and Materials Management.* 2d ed. New York: Macmillan, 1978.

Brown, P. A., and D. F. Gibson. "A Quantified Model for Facility Site Selection—Application to a Multiplant Location Problem." *AIIE Transactions,* March 1972, pp. 1–10.

Carlson, Richard A. "What You Should Know Before Choosing New Office Spaces." *Administrative Management,* June 1981, pp. 28–30.

"The Checklist of Expansion Planning and Site Selection." *Site Selection Handbook,* vol. 24, no. 1, February 1979, pp. 12–31.

Cooney, James L. "Expand or Move: Some Intangible Factors in Making the Choice." *Industrial Development,* May–June 1980, pp. 2–4.

David, Warren E. "A Primer on Locating Facilities in Foreign Countries." *Industrial Development,* May–June 1979, pp. 10–14.

Doyle, P., I. Fenwick, and G. P. Savage. "A Model for Evaluating Branch Locations and Performance." *Journal of Bank Research,* Summer 1981, pp. 90–95.

Francis, Richard L., and John A. White. *Facility Layout and Location: An Analytical Approach.* Englewood Cliffs, N. J.: Prentice-Hall, 1974.

Freed, Sherwin, and William Best. "Future Challenges to the Site Selection Expert." *Industrial Development,* July–August 1981, pp. 9–13.

Khumawala, B. M., and D. C. Waybark. "A Comparison of Some Recent Warehouse Location Techniques." *The Logistics Review* 7, no. 31 (1971):3–19.

Lambert, Douglas M., and James R. Stock. *Strategic Physical Distribution Management.* Homewood, Ill.: Irwin, 1982.

Markland, Robert E. "Analyzing Geographically Discrete Warehousing Networks by Computer Simulation." *Decision Sciences,* April 1973, pp. 216–236.

Reed, Rudell. *Plant Location, Layout, and Maintenance.* Homewood, Ill.: Irwin, 1967.

Smith, David M. *Industrial Location: An Economic Geographical Analysis.* New York: Wiley, 1971.

"Stress Distribution Planning as Warehouse Numbers Grow." *Chain Store Age Executive,* October 1979, pp. 23–25.

Chapter Outline
LAYOUT OF FACILITIES

OBJECTIVES OF A GOOD LAYOUT

MATERIALS HANDLING
Major Materials-Handling Methods / Selecting a Materials-Handling Method

CLASSICAL LAYOUT TYPES
The Flow-Line Layout / Layout by Process / Layout by Fixed Position

HYBRID LAYOUTS
Manufacturing Operations / Nonmanufacturing Operations

MANUFACTURING CELLS
Group Technology / Some Common Cell Arrangements / *Operations Management in Action:* A CUSTOMIZED, ROBOTIZED MACHINING CELL

FLEXIBLE MANUFACTURING SYSTEMS
Advantages of FMS / Limitations of FMS

FACTORS THAT INFLUENCE LAYOUT SELECTION
Volume of Production / Other Factors

SUPPORT SERVICES

METHODS OF ANALYZING LAYOUT
Layout by Product / Layout by Process / Transportation Cost as a Criterion for Layout / Nontransportation Factors / Computer Packages for Layout Analysis

ARRANGEMENT OF FACILITIES WITHIN DEPARTMENTS
The Need for Versatility / *Application: Example of a Nonmanufacturing Layout*

Summary / **Discussion Questions** / **Problems** / **Bibliography**

KEY TERMS

Layout *or* plant layout	Cranes and hoists	Layout by process	Flexible manufacturing
Materials handling	Industrial robot *or* robot	Manufacturing cell *or*	system (FMS)
Conveyor	Flow-line layout	cell	Transfer line
Industrial truck	Layout by product	Group technology (GT)	Dominated flow pattern
Automatically guided	Production-line *or*	Rabbit-chase cell	Nondominated flow
vehicle (AGV)	assembly-line layout	U-line cell	Nearness priorities

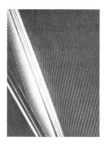

Chapter 13

LAYOUT OF FACILITIES

One way to help achieve productivity of resources is to see that physical facilities are arranged for efficient work. The efficiency of people and the efficient use of equipment can be affected by the way that manufacturing and nonmanufacturing facilities are arranged. The term *layout* (or *plant layout*) is often used to refer to the selection of a location for each department, process, machine, support function, or other activity that will be part of the operations within a facility.

OBJECTIVES OF A GOOD LAYOUT

Layout is important for many reasons. Any or all of the following objectives might be achieved through a good layout:

Reduce bottlenecks (congestion) in moving people or material.

Minimize materials-handling costs.

Reduce hazards to personnel.

Utilize labor efficiently.

Increase morale.

Utilize available space effectively and efficiently.

Provide flexibility

Provide ease of supervision.

Facilitate coordination and face-to-face communications where appropriate.

With multiple objectives to accomplish, it is apparent that experience and informed judgment are useful guides to layout decisions. Computer models have been developed to assist with the factory or office layout problem. Other models also are available to assist in some of the analyses preceding the selection of a layout.

The type of operation to be performed in a facility influences the facility's needs and layout. The amount and type of equipment involved, the volume of transactions to be accommodated, and many other variables influence layout selection. For efficient operations, facilities must be designed for the purposes of the organization. Nonmanufacturing operations require different facilities from manufacturing operations. Often service customers are participants in the service transactions, so convenience and appearance of facilities may influence the sales volume as well as the efficiency or cost of operations.

The needs of operations that deal with tangible items also vary. Even if the objective is simply to display items for sale, as in a retail or wholesale store, customer convenience is still important. Manufacturers of tangible products must consider efficiency of moving products from one work station to another. Production of heavy products places heavy emphasis on materials-handling capabilities.

MATERIALS HANDLING

Efficient *materials handling* is important to manufacturing operations. Just as transportation is important in the location of manufacturing facilities, it is an important factor in the internal layout of manufacturing facilities. Materials must be unloaded, moved through inspections and production operations to storage areas, and finally to the shipping department. These movements do not add value to the product but they do add cost. Some manufacturers spend between 20 and 30 percent of their factory payroll on materials handling. The best amount of materials handling is usually the least amount possible to complete the operation.

Materials-handling methods and plant arrangement enhance one another. A good plant layout enables an operation to use the most efficient handling method. Efficient operation of appropriate materials-handling methods reduces costs and enables maximum capabilities to be derived from a production facility.

Major Materials-Handling Methods

There are five major categories of materials-handling equipment: conveyors, industrial trucks, automatically guided vehicles, cranes and hoists, and industrial robots.

Conveyors   *Conveyors* are fixed pieces of equipment that transport materials along their path (see Figure 13.1). Movement along this path may be continuous or intermittent, but otherwise conveyors offer little flexibility. They require con-

FIGURE 13.1

Types of Conveyors

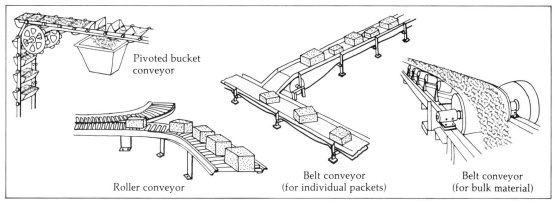

Courtesy of Conveyor Equipment Manufacturers Association

siderable investment and occupy space continuously. Their main advantage is that most do not require operators, will move a large volume of product, and are inexpensive to operate.

Industrial Trucks   *Industrial trucks* are wheeled vehicles that can travel variable paths (see Figure 13.2). They may be pushed or pulled by muscle power or be powered by electricity or combustible fuel. One disadvantage of industrial trucks is that they may require considerable aisle space so that they can be used when materials are to be removed into and out of an area. Moreover, conventional trucks require an operator when they are in use, and they are more costly than conveyors to operate. However, they are more flexible and often require less investment. Fork trucks offer an additional advantage over conveyors, in that

FIGURE 13.2

Types of Industrial Trucks

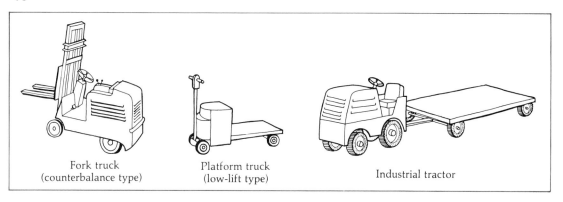

they can be used to stack materials in high bins and racks, permitting more material to be stored in a given amount of floor space.

Automatically Guided Vehicles   Materials handling equipment producers have developed the *automatically guided vehicle* (AGV), which does not require an operator and provides a great deal of flexibility in the paths it can travel and the functions it can perform. These vehicles usually are powered by batteries that can easily be removed and recharged while a fresh battery is being used. The AGV is controlled by signals sent through wires embedded in the floor or inductive tape on the floor surface. New tape paths can be installed very easily.

A remote control computer is used to store directions for one or more vehicles working in a particular area. This computer and possibly an onboard microprocessor can be used to analyze conditions and direct the vehicles accordingly. Signals direct the cart when to raise its lift under a load station, where to move and at what speed, and when to lower its lift under an unload station. The computer keeps track of all the vehicles under its control, so it can prevent congestion or collisions. As a safety feature, such a cart usually has sensors connected to a soft bumper protruding from it, and the vehicle will stop if an object is contacted. The AGVs can share aisles that are used by pedestrians or other vehicles.

The automatic control feature of AGVs removes the need for an operator to be with each vehicle, as is required with conventional mobile equipment. Use of AGVs does not require the erection of permanent obstructions such as conveyors. A photograph of an AGV is shown in Figure 13.3. Japanese producers are experimenting with optical guidance for AGVs so the carts can be more precisely located and will have more flexibility in changing paths.

Cranes and Hoists   *Cranes and hoists* are materials-moving devices mounted in the overhead structure of a building, as illustrated in Figure 13.4. Their use frees

FIGURE 13.3

An Automatically Guided Vehicle (AGV)

Photo courtesy of Eaton-Kenway, Salt Lake City, Utah.

FIGURE 13.4

Types of Cranes and Hoists

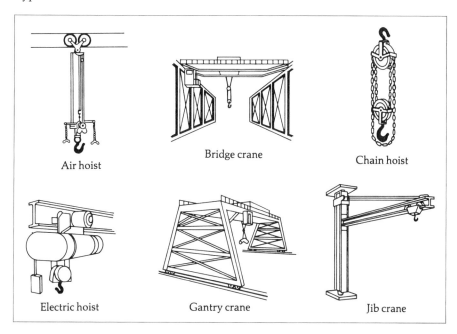

Air hoist

Bridge crane

Chain hoist

Electric hoist

Gantry crane

Jib crane

Source: *Material Handling Engineering Directory and Handbook.* (Cleveland: Industrial Publishing Corp., 1958).

floor space for other uses and provides a great deal of flexibility. Cranes and hoists are limited, however, in that they can serve only the space where they have tracks to travel. They facilitate the handling of heavy work items by setting them on and off machines and placing them in storage areas.

Industrial Robots An *industrial robot* or *robot,* pictured in Figure 13.5, is simply a mechanism which has a movable armlike projection with a gripper on the end that can perform a variety of tasks repeatedly. Robots usually have a built-in control that can be reprogrammed, so they are very versatile. Some robots can be programmed by switching them into a "learn mode" and pushing the gripper through a motion pattern. When switched out of the learn mode, the device can repeat the motions it has been "taught." Some robots are taught by keying in instruction codes that are stored in their memories.

Robots can perform many of the materials handling tasks and value-adding work performed by humans. In addition, robots are very flexible, since they can easily be reprogrammed. For materials-handling tasks, they can maneuver into awkward positions, lift greater loads than humans, and perform strenuous work repeatedly without fatigue. In addition, they can work in hazardous or unpleasant conditions—doing such work as removing hot castings from a die-

FIGURE 13.5

Industrial Robot

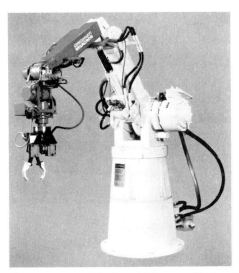

Photo courtesy of Cincinnati Milacron, Cincinnati, Ohio.

casting machine, placing them in a quench tank, and then moving them to another operation. The percentage of operating time for robots, even in multi-shift operations, is in the high nineties. At the present stage of development, only limited "vision" is available for robots and they have a limited ability to deal with a wide variety of shapes. Also, it is unsafe for people to work near large robots because robots move through their programmed motion pattern even though something or someone may be in the way.

Selecting a Materials-Handling Method

The most appropriate materials-handling method depends on numerous factors, including size, shape, and physical and chemical properties of the materials to be handled. The mixture of products to be moved within a facility dictates the requirements for flexibility and will influence the method selected. The volume of materials to be handled will determine the investment in equipment that can be justified. The distance materials must be moved (i.e., the facility layout) also influences the selection of materials-handling methods.

Automatic or semiautomatic materials-handling equipment, such as conveyors, can be used more appropriately when the facility has:

1. A relatively constant path of movement.
2. A stable product line or a family of products with the same move sequence.
3. Sufficient volume to justify the investment.
4. A fairly uniform production rate.

Some conveyors have programmable logic and can vary the paths through which objects are sent depending on coded messages, such as bar codes on the part or pallet.

CLASSICAL LAYOUT TYPES

The activities involved in carrying out the production of a product or provision of a service may be grouped and arranged in a variety of ways. Three classical types of layout represent extremes or pure examples: flow lines, process layout, and fixed-position layouts. Any one facility may encompass a blend that embodies features of two or three of the classical layouts. If the company produces more than one product or provides more than one service at the same facility, a hybrid layout may be preferred.

The Flow-Line Layout

Flow-line layout involves the arrangement of the necessary activities in some sort of line along which the service receiver or product-in-process moves. This type of layout is called *layout by product*, or *production-line* or *assembly-line layout* when used in reference to tangible-item production. Machines or pieces of assembly equipment are located along a route over which the product travels and are arranged in the sequence required by the production plan or route sheet. The path of flow may follow a straight line or a variety of shapes, some of which are shown in Figure 13.6. Layout selection depends on such factors as the available building space, other operations in the same building, ease of supervision, materials-handling needs, and the location of utilities and support operations. Flow-line layout in a manufacturing facility is best suited to fixed-path materials-handling equipment, such as conveyors, because the flow of materials is standardized. Of course, the layout and materials flow are not confined to the flat plane of the factory floor. Conveyors may also be used to move products overhead to another level of a multistory facility.

Advantages   Some of the advantages of flow-line layout in a manufacturing operation are:

1. Reduced materials handling.
2. Small amounts of work in process.
3. Reduced total processing time.
4. Simplified production planning and control systems.
5. Simplification of tasks, enabling unskilled workers to learn tasks quickly.

Disadvantages   Some of the disadvantages of flow-line layout in a manufacturing operation are:

1. Lack of process flexibility: a change in product may require facility modification.

FIGURE 13.6

Some Shapes of Flow Lines

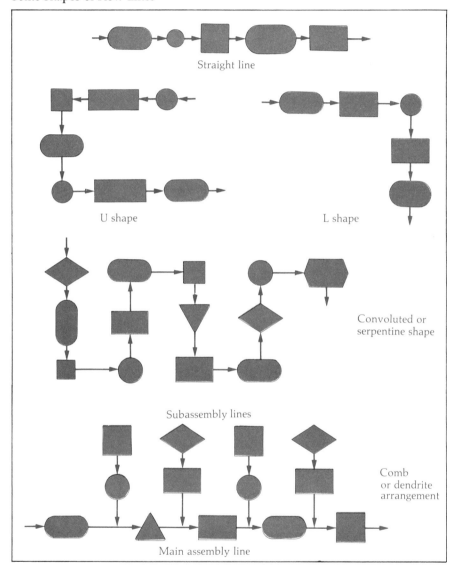

2. Lack of flexibility in timing: the product cannot flow through the line faster than the slowest task can be accomplished unless that task is performed at multiple stations.
3. Large investment: special-purpose equipment is used, and duplication is required to offset lack of flexibility in timing.
4. Dependence of the whole on each part: a breakdown of one machine or absence of enough operators to staff all work stations may stop the entire line.

5. Worker monotony: workers may become bored by the endless repetition of simple tasks.

Applicability to Nonmanufacturing Operations Some nonmanufacturing operations also are arranged in a flow-line layout. When you go through a cafeteria line you pass from one type of operation to another (silverware to salad to entrée, and so on). When large numbers of people are to give blood, the facilities are arranged so that donors move from one station to another: medical history to blood pressure to temperature check, and so on. When a large number of people are to be served through successive steps, some advantages may be gained by use of such a flow-line arrangement.

Flow lines reduce the amount of time people must spend in going through all the steps and reduces backtracking. Fewer people must wait, and each waits a shorter time. It is simple to direct people through the facility because the flow and sequencing are built into the arrangement of the facilities.

Layout by Process

Many organizations arrange facilities so that all people and equipment that perform the same function are grouped together. Such arrangements often are called *layout by process* or departmental groupings. The steps in making this type of arrangement are:

1. Determining the size of each department.
2. Determining the arrangement of the departments with respect to one another.
3. Determining the arrangement of the equipment and people within each department.

An example of a layout that groups similar machines and processes is shown in Figure 13.7.

FIGURE 13.7

Layout by Process

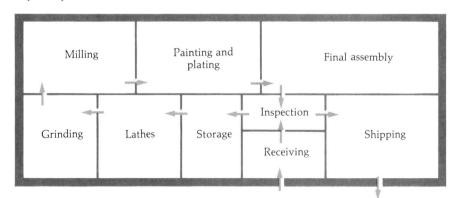

Advantages   Some of the advantages of layout by process are:

1. Flexibility of equipment and personnel.
2. Smaller investment in equipment because duplication is not necessary unless volume is large.
3. Expertise: supervisors for each department become highly knowledgeable about the lower number of functions under their direction.
4. Diversity of tasks: work assignments make work more satisfying for people who prefer variety.

Disadvantages   Some of the disadvantages of layout by process are:

1. Lack of materials-handling efficiency: backtracking and long movements may occur in the handling of materials.
2. Lack of efficiency in timing: work must wait between tasks.
3. Complication of production planning and control.
4. Cost: workers must have broader skills and must be paid higher wages than assembly-line workers.
5. Lowered productivity: because each job is different, it requires different setups and operator learning.

Applicability to Nonmanufacturing Operations   Nonmanufacturing operations also may be arranged according to process. Since materials handling is not an important factor in many such operations, the distances between successive operations and the need for backtracking are not severe penalties. Offices that handle large volumes of paperwork, such as insurance claims, may be arranged to facilitate the high-volume flow of lightweight materials (paperwork). In many offices, however, ease of face-to-face communications and supervision are often more important than the flow of papers. When several people must use the same equipment or have access to the same records, they are usually located in the same area.

Since the customer is often a participant in service operations, customer convenience is important. Facilities should be arranged for easy access and should enable customers to find easily the persons they wish to see so they will not be greatly inconvenienced in dealing with the organization.

Many nonmanufacturing operations arrange facilities by function. Retail stores group all similar products such as hardware, sporting goods, and photography equipment in separate departments for ease of supervision and to enable shoppers to locate merchandise easily. Jobs in offices are grouped into departments or sections, such as accounts receivable and accounts payable. Universities often locate together the separate schools and departments that have frequent communications with one another. Hospitals have obstetrical wards, cardiac units, surgical wards, X-ray departments, and pathology laboratories, with similar functions performed within each department. Automotive repair facilities have designated areas for paint and body work, chassis work, engine work, and transmission work. Since different equipment and skills are needed for these types of work, the functions are separated. Banks frequently have separate components, such as loan and mortgage departments, and sometimes have separate teller windows for savings and checking accounts.

Layout by Fixed Position

For some types of operations, organizations choose to bring the necessary people and equipment to the item being produced or serviced. This method is called layout by fixed position because the work item does not move from one operation to another. Fixed-position layout may be used because the work item is too fragile, too bulky, or too heavy to be moved without complications.

Large manufactured items such as airplanes and large computers may be assembled by bringing the people and equipment to the work item. Shipbuilding and home building are also good examples of work usually performed in a fixed position. Fixed-position work methods necessitate the use of portable equipment.

Advantages   The fixed-position layout has two major advantages:

1. Movement of the work item is reduced to a minimum to minimize damage to the item and the cost of moving it.
2. Since the item does not go from one department to another, there is more continuity of the assigned work force. This reduces the problems of re-planning and instructing people each time a new type of activity is to begin.

Disadvantages   There are some disadvantages to the fixed-position layout:

1. Since the same workers are involved in more operations, skilled and versatile workers are required. The necessary combination of skills may be difficult to find and high pay levels may be necessary.
2. Movement of people and equipment to and from the work site may be expensive.
3. Equipment utilization may be low because the equipment may be left at a location where it will be needed again in a few days, rather than being moved to another location where it would be productively used during the intervening time.

Applicability to Nonmanufacturing Operations   Many nonmanufacturing operations also use the fixed-position concept. Emergency vehicles such as fire trucks, police cars, and ambulances come to the site of need to provide services. An important consideration for these service providers is a location that will enable them to get their services to the site with speed (as we saw in the previous chapter).

Nonemergency services are also brought to the place where they are needed. People who repair furnaces, sand-blast buildings, service oilwells, paint bridges, install new roofs or gutters, or paint stripes down highways move to the place of need or the item to be worked on. No doubt you can think of many other examples of fixed-position layouts. Since such service providers have little control over the actual layout of the item they work on, they attempt to select flexible equipment, adequate to the needs of their businesses. Their bases of operations often are selected to facilitate their movement to work locations and to reduce the cost or inconvenience of the frequent moves necessary in such businesses.

HYBRID LAYOUTS

Each classical layout has certain advantages and disadvantages, as we have seen. Many organizations find that no single type fits its needs precisely, but that a combination of types works well.

Manufacturing Operations

Combinations of layouts are useful in various types of manufacturing operations. The production of flammable, explosive, or toxic substances may be spread out so that they are isolated from other substances and from as many employees as possible. Pesticides and drugs are chemicals that may have some common processing, yet they would not be permitted to be processed where contamination could occur. Precision equipment must be located away from heavy machinery that may cause vibration and should be protected from wide changes in temperature and humidity. A company may process items with a wide range of weights, necessitating some adaptation to this circumstance. Large machines for heavy work pieces may be grouped in an area with a heavily reinforced floor and serviced by an overhead crane; and the area may be located near a shipping and receiving point to reduce the handling of heavy items. Lighter machinery may be grouped in a less expensively constructed area where the service of an overhead crane is not required.

Nonmanufacturing Operations

Nonmanufacturing operations also benefit from a combination of classical layout patterns. Consider a hospital, for example. For some portions of their examination and treatment, patients are moved (or move on their own power) from one department to another. This portion of treatment may be considered as using layout by process. At other times (say, after surgery) the patient is permitted to lie quietly and convalesce while aides, nurses, and doctors make their rounds and perform services. This portion of the treatment may be considered as layout by fixed position.

Banks provide another example. Although all loan officers in a bank perform similar work for the same company, they are often located in separate rooms to provide privacy. Would-be borrowers do not wish to have other members of the public or other bank employees aware of the details of their business or personal finances. Here is a situation in which the needs and convenience of the customer have to be considered in addition to an economical layout.

This section has introduced only a few layout situations in which hybrid layouts are called for; you can think of many others. Each organization will have its own set of objectives and its own budget to guide its layout selection.

MANUFACTURING CELLS

A close grouping of equipment for processing a sequence of operations on multiple units of a part or a family of parts is called a *manufacturing cell* or a *cell*. What we are considering here is the layout not of an entire plant but of only a portion of it as a flow line. Use of cells—cellular manufacturing—affords advantages beyond reduction of the distances that parts must be moved between machines. Since movement is reduced and is therefore not expensive, parts do not have to be moved in large batches to spread the cost of a move over a number of units. Frequently, parts are processed one by one through the steps of production, making the throughput time short and the work-in-process inventory (WIP) low. The cell can be very compact because there is no need for extra space around the machines to hold material, thereby reducing the investment in plant space or freeing existing space for other uses.

The use of cells in repetitive manufacturing plants greatly enhances just-in-time production methods. The use of cells also can provide many of the benefits of flow-line layout to companies that do not produce a large volume of a part but produce moderate volumes of parts with common routings. In companies that have a large variety of parts, group technology is often helpful in selecting appropriate families of parts that can be run in cells.

Group Technology

Group technology (GT) is the analysis and comparison of items to group them into families with similar characteristics. GT can be used to develop a hybrid between pure process layout and pure flow-line layout. GT enables companies that produce a variety of parts in small batches to achieve some of the economies of flow-line layout without product standardization.

The application of group technology involves two basic steps. The first step is the determination of component families or groups. The designs of all components are rigorously reviewed to find families of components that have similar characteristics. The general size and shape of the components in a family should be the same so that equipment of the same capacity and the same type of holding fixtures can be used in working on the family members. Ideally, these parts would also go through the same sequence of operations during the production process. However, some variations from a uniform routing may occur.

The second step in applying group techology is to arrange the plant's equipment into cells, each containing the equipment used to process a particular family of components. The result is a group of small plants within a plant. The processing required by each family can be performed within a cell, where the

FIGURE 13.8

Comparison of Parts Flow Through a Job Shop and an Alternative Cellular Shop

Job shop

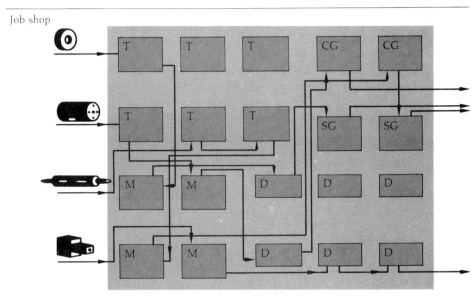

Cell shop

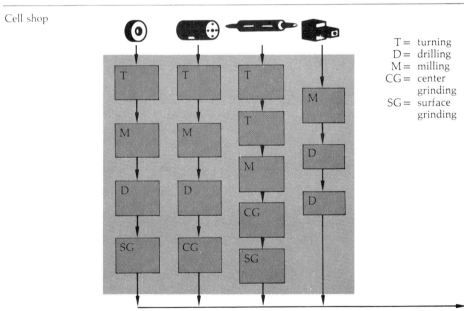

T = turning
D = drilling
M = milling
CG = center
        grinding
SG = surface
        grinding

machines and work stations are arranged to accommodate the common flow pattern for the parts family.

Once implemented, group technology can reduce the production planning time for jobs. It reduces materials handling and in-process inventory because most of the family goes through a common sequence of nearby work stations. Coordination of jobs is often easier because many of the operations can be followed visually. Group technology can also reduce the investment needed for holding fixtures and other tooling, and reduce setup time.

Group technology was applied rather extensively in the Soviet Union and Western Europe in the 1950s and 1960s. At first the concept was not as widely applied in the United States, but applications are increasing. One notable example in the United States is E. G. & G. Sealol, a manufacturer in Warwick, Rhode Island. This company has begun producing 900 parts (about 30 percent of its standard-hour workload) in cells. The company found that WIP was reduced 20–30 percent, the need for floor space declined about 15 percent, and the total output increased about 50 percent. One of the cells processed 324 parts on seven machines, instead of on the twenty-two machines to which the parts had previously been routed.[1] Figure 13.8 illustrates the simplified process planning, materials handling, and production control that can be achieved with a cellular arrangement in contrast to a pure job shop arrangement which would have all grinding done in one area, milling in another, etc.

Some Common Cell Arrangements

One form of cell that often can be used to advantage, particularly if a robot is to perform parts handling, has the machines arranged in the shape of a C, with the robot in the opening of the C. The robot can swing through an arc and reach any machine. The robot loads parts on the first machine, transfers parts between machines, and unloads parts from the last machine. The parts must of course be arranged at locations where the robot has been programmed to find them. An example of a robot used in a C shaped cell is presented in the box on page 560.

Two other forms of cells are frequently used by repetitive manufacturing companies employing multiskilled workers, especially companies that apply just-in-time production methods. These layouts are the rabbit-chase cell and the U-line cell.

Rabbit-Chase Cell   In a *rabbit-chase cell* (shown in Figure 13.10) the machines are arranged in a circle, with the operator side of the machines facing the center. By moving around in a small circle, a worker can operate all of the machines. If the worker must perform all of the operations manually, the cycle time for the cell is the sum of all of the operations' times plus the handling time. The

---

[1]James A. Nolen, "Cellular Manufacturing at E. G. & G. Sealol," Society of Manufacturing Engineers seminar, Dallas, May 1983.

OPERATIONS MANAGEMENT IN ACTION

A Customized, Robotized Machining Cell

At Kurt Manufacturing Company in Minneapolis, a robot handles a 90-pound part between a trio of machine tools to produce a deck that will become part of a hard-disk drive assembled by a subsidiary of Control Data Corp. Kurt, a precision-machining job shop with some 300 employees, bids each year for the contract to make this part and has made the part since 1975. Over the years, Kurt has developed a close relationship with the customer and has recommended design enhancements to improve manufacturability. As the production quantities increased, Kurt Manufacturing moved to a cell to achieve production efficiencies.

The part starts out as a 90-pound aluminum casting, and Kurt performs operations to mill a smooth surface to within 0.0005 inch,

mill other parts of the item, and drill 97 precisely located holes, about 70 of them being tapped with threads for screws. The heavy workpiece would be slow and strenuous for a human operator to maneuver on and off the machines and would require an overhead hoist. Instead, a robot moves the parts between the equipment, arranged as shown in the overhead photograph of Figure 13.9. Two workers operate the cell, where eight were required to operate the cluster of machines previously required to produce the part. One loads the carts and moves them to and from the cell. The other serves as a parts inspector and checks for broken taps or other machine problems.

The robot takes the part from the input cart to the first milling operation, where sev-

FIGURE 13.9

Top View of Robotized Cell

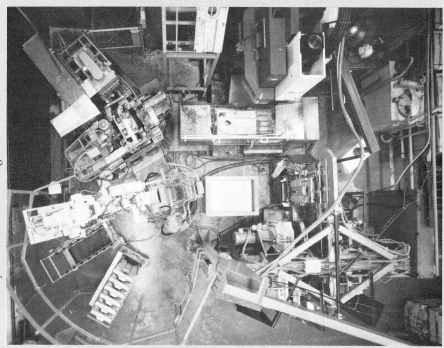

Photo courtesy of Kurt Manufacturing Co.

enteen work spindles operate on five sides of the part. The part is next moved to the ready rack and then to the machining center. The part is removed from the machining center and washed in a custom tank to remove any metal chips from locating surfaces so the part can be precisely located for the final operations. The part is then moved to the drilling and tapping machine. When this operation is complete, the part is washed again and placed in the output cart for shipment to the customer.

The first milling machine and the drilling and tapping machine were custom-designed by Kurt engineers. Kurt also developed the overall system arrangement and programmed the control of the equipment. This robot-tended cell reduces direct labor requirements. You can see how this creative use of a cell also minimizes the move distances and lost time between operations, reduces WIP, and makes very compact use of floor space.

Information courtesy of Kurt Manufacturing Company and from Ingo Wolfe and Richard K. Wallin, "Customizing a Machining Cell," American Machinist, *October 1984, pp. 86–89.*

cycle time can be shortened if some of the machines perform their operations automatically. The worker moves around the circle, loading and unloading the automatic machines, and can perform other work while automatic machines are working. Different parts can be produced in this type of cell by changing the setups on the machines. If an extensive setup is required on some machine for a part that is run fairly often, the machine might be duplicated in the cell. One of the duplicate machines would remain set up with the difficult setup and would be used only when the appropriate part is being run.

Another way to increase the rate of output from this type of cell is by having two workers move around the circle, one behind the other, sharing the equipment. The rate can be increased even further if three or more workers are

FIGURE 13.10

Rabbit-Chase Cell

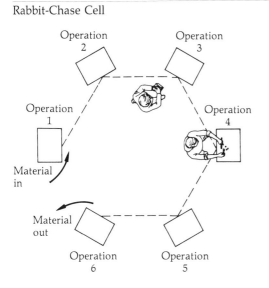

in the chase. But the workers have to be capable of performing all of the operations in the cell. And the work can proceed only as fast as the slowest worker moves around the circle.

U-Line Cell   Sometimes a cell is formed by placing the machines in the shape of a narrow U. A worker with sufficient skills can perform all of the operations on a part by stepping along one side of the U, around the closed end and back up the other side of the U. The rate of output can be increased by having two (or more) workers in the U with each simultaneously performing part of the work cycle. The first worker would process a part through the operations down one side of the U, maybe halfway, then leave the part and turn to the other side of the aisle to pick up a part that had been left by the second worker, and finish processing it back up the other side of the U. The second worker would take the part that had been left by the first worker and process it through the machine down one side, around the closed end of the U, and up the other side, to the place where it is to be picked up and finished by the first worker. A *U-line cell* with the paths that might be followed by two workers is shown in Figure 13.11. Use of multiple workers in this manner can reduce the number of skills required of each worker.

FIGURE 13.11

U-Line Cell

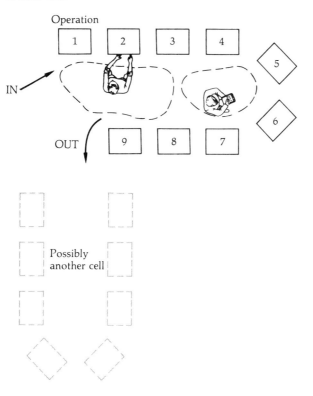

FLEXIBLE MANUFACTURING SYSTEMS

The concept of grouping equipment that can produce a variety of related parts can be extended and automated to form what is often called a *flexible manufacturing system (FMS)*. A flexible manufacturing system is a group of machines with reprogrammable controllers linked by an automated materials-handling system and integrated through a central computer so that the system can produce a variety of parts that have similar processing requirements. An FMS can be constructed with various amounts and combinations of equipment. An example of a small system might be two lathes that share a robot as the materials-handling system. A large system might contain a dozen or more machines connected by an elaborate conveyor network or an automatic guided vehicle system (AGVS) that can move parts from one machine to another in any order. Generally, an FMS will contain at least four machines—to provide enough volume and variety to make the concept really effective and to justify the great amount of work required to develop an integrated system. A diagram of an FMS is shown in Figure 13.12.

FIGURE 13.12

Example of a Flexible Manufacturing System (FMS)

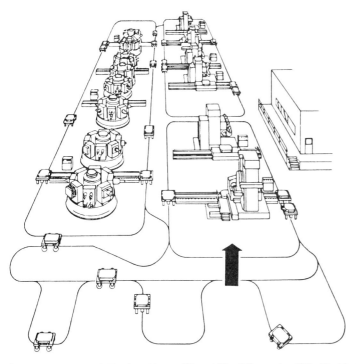

Source: Kearny and Trecker Corp., West Allis, Wisconsin, *KT's World of Advanced Manufacturing Technologies*, 2ND ed., 1983, p. 19.

Since the industrial revolution, the general trend has been toward more specialization of processes to achieve the advantages of automation. A typical and effective way to employ automation has been to use "hard automation" such as a *transfer line*—a fixed-path conveyor with single-purpose equipment mounted along the sides. The conveyor of the transfer line moves the parts on it forward one work station, where they are indexed accurately into position for the machines to perform work; the machines operate; then the parts are all moved forward one more work station. A transfer line is a very economical way to produce large volumes of identical or nearly identical items. An FMS offers more flexibility than a transfer line, but it in turn is not as flexible as individual machinists working with conventional or numeric control (NC) machines. Appropriate applications for FMSs are in companies that produce intermediate volumes of a variety of parts that require the same type of processing. Thus FMSs and nonautomated cells help to fill the gap between individual machines and transfer lines, as shown in Figure 13.13.

Presently, most FMSs are utilized in machining—cutting metal chips away from a block of raw material to leave an item of the desired size and shape. A general overview of the operation of an FMS involves the following steps. The central computer contains the routings for all of the parts that are to be run on the FMS. A person or robot loads a part on a pallet, and the computer is told what has been loaded. The computer retrieves the appropriate routing for the part and directs the conveyor to transport the part to the machine that is to perform the first operation. The conveyor signals the computer when the part

FIGURE 13.13

Combinations of Volume and Variety Best Served by Alternative Production Methods

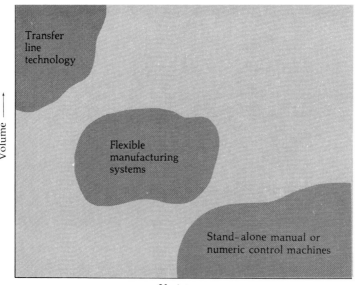

is at the machine, and the computer tells the machine which part is there. The machine then retrieves the appropriate program of instructions to work on that part and steps through the specified tool changes and operations to complete its work. The central computer is informed when this work is completed. The central computer checks the status of the machines that can perform the next operation on the routing and directs the conveyor to deliver the part to an available machine, and processing is continued. When all operations on the part are completed, the part is sent to an unload station, where the part is removed from the pallet and another part can be loaded on the pallet to begin being processed.

Advantages of FMS

Some companies have experienced great success with FMS installations. Many of the early successes were applications with large workpieces, such as axle housings for large earthmovers. Moving these parts between machines and fixturing the parts at each machine would be expensive without an FMS. Parts such as these are expensive and would result in a large work-in-process inventory investment if they were produced in batches. An FMS could be used to make the left housing, the right housing, then the center part. The parts could then be assembled and used, resulting in little accumulation of inventory. More recently, FMSs are being applied to smaller parts.

The advantages of FMS are summarized briefly below.

Reduced direct labor. Reduced fixturing, reduced material handling, and automatic control of machines makes it possible to operate an FMS with less direct labor in many instances.

Reduced capital investment. Machine utilization with FMS can be about three times as high as with conventional machining, so fewer machines are required. Since there are fewer machines, less tooling is required to equip them. Since materials move directly to the next machine, there is a lower investment in inventory. Since there are fewer machines and less inventory, a smaller amount of floor space is required.

Shorter response time. Setup or changeover time is relatively low with FMS, since much of this work is accomplished automatically in response to software commands. With low WIP there are almost no queues to delay jobs. The result is a very short flow-through time. One application reported 1.5 to 3 days instead of the 35 to 90 days required with conventional production.

Consistent quality. Much of the human variability and error are removed, so quality is more consistent. One FMS installation visited by the author reported that the scrap rate had been reduced from 10 percent down to 3 percent.

Better control of work. With few jobs waiting to be worked and a smaller area to survey for problems, it is easier to keep track of the work. Priorities do not change much when jobs flow through in a few days instead of taking months. The flow of much of the work in an FMS is controlled by computer, so it is more consistent.

Limitations of FMS

Not all intermediate variety–intermediate volume situations are suitable for FMS. There needs to be a family of parts that require about the same size machines and the same accuracy, which must be within the tolerances achievable with NC machines. The variety of types and sizes of cutting tools must be kept within the capacity of the automatic tool changers. This limitation may require some standardization of part designs to reduce the number of tools required.

An FMS takes the place of several machines that do not all wear out at the same time. Companies often prefer to make a series of smaller investments over time to replace their machines piecemeal, rather than making a larger investment in a technology with which they are not familiar. FMS requires a long planning cycle and a long development cycle to ensure that the system will be a success. Many managers, however, are oriented to shorter-term decisions and payoffs. The elevated complexity of developing an integrated system may cause some companies to shy away from flexible manufacturing systems. Often the best approach is to evolve into a system. A company can begin using computer numeric control (CNC) machines, then install a linking materials-handling system, and later develop the central computer and software to coordinate the system.

FACTORS THAT INFLUENCE LAYOUT SELECTION

Not every situation will fit exactly the conditions that make one type of layout fully suited to the operation and other types undesirable. Myriad factors should be considered in designing a work facility.

Volume of Production

Volume has great importance in the selection of an appropriate layout. Job shops produce a variety of products, often only one of each type. The volume of production is seldom great, so flexibility is a necessity. Multipurpose equipment and versatile people must be employed in this type of production operation. Fixed-path materials-handling equipment would be inappropriate.

With regard to manufacturing operations, the following generalities often are useful. Usually, as volume increases, so does the cost advantage in favor of layout by product (flow-line production). Layout by process will have a lower fixed cost for facilities and equipment than layout by product, but the variable cost is higher because of increased materials handling, higher wage rates, and lower work efficiency because workers are less familiar with the diverse products. Fixed-position layout has an even higher variable cost because of increased equipment movement, lost production time, and less specialization. Investment in a fixed-position layout is low, however. The three classical layout types may be compared generally by the cost-profit-volume graph of Figure 13.14. If we consider the same product (not too large), the least costly layout would change

FIGURE 13.14

Effect of Volume on Cost with Classical Layouts

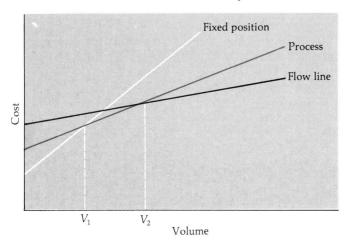

for different volumes. Below V_1 it might be advantageous to use small portable hand tools and move them to the work item. At some volume the additional cost of departments might be justified, particularly if other products were produced also. At some greater volume, V_2, the additional cost of specialized production equipment and materials-handling equipment would be justified for use solely for this product.

Other Factors

Volume is certainly not the only factor to consider in selecting a layout. Each business has many other factors, and their relative importance will vary from one organization to another. Some commonly considered factors are:

The weight of the item to be produced.

The nature of the service to be provided.

The cost of the building to house the operation.

The product mix that must share a facility.

The fragility of a product or component.

SUPPORT SERVICES

No discussion of layout would be complete without consideration of the space necessary for support services. The plant or service facility per se is important, and its layout influences profit. Support activities must be carried on in such a way that the direct operations can function smoothly. It is estimated that about one-third of a plant or department may be devoted to support facilities.

Floor space in any facility costs money. The space required for direct production is always considered justified, but all other space is sometimes considered an unnecessary expense, even though support services are essential to the primary operation. The space occupied by support services should be arranged with care to ensure their efficiency, so that indirect expenses are no greater than necessary. Crowding a department into such small quarters that its operations are hampered is false economy.

Some support services need ready access to the direct work areas whereas others do not. Some of the ancillary departments to be considered in a layout are:

Inventories of components, materials, and supplies.

Toolrooms or tool cribs.

Inspection and quality control.

First aid.

Shipping and receiving.

Maintenance.

Supervisory offices.

Washrooms and locker facilities.

Refreshment areas and cafeteria.

Security and safety.

Clerical and bookkeeping.

Design and development.

The inventory storage area is one service area whose layout has received considerable attention. When a manufacturing operation has 100,000 or more different inventory items, the movement of such items into and out of inventory involves much materials handling. The primary activities of some operations, such as distribution centers, are materials handling and storage. Warehouse design has changed in recent decades, with increased use of high-rise storage, stacker cranes, and computer-directed storage and picking of stock. Storage racks may be eighty feet or more high, with several layers of storage lines above the floor level. The objective is to achieve the maximum amount of storage per square foot of floor space. An example of high-rise storage and stacker cranes is shown in Figure 13.15.

Layout considerations involve three dimensions in high-rise storage. Items may be stored in any location as long as the bins are large enough to accommodate them. High-rise stacker cranes may be operator-controlled or automatically controlled through a punched card, magnetic tape, or computer input. Storage may be random, so that a locator file must be maintained to identify the location of each item. With automated storage and retrieval systems, the computer stores in memory the address at which it stored an item. When the item is to be retrieved, the computer will search its memory, find the item's

FIGURE 13.15

Automated Storage and Retrieval in a High-Rise Warehouse

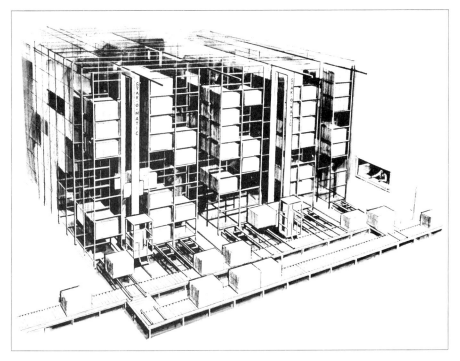

Source: Conoco, Mendota, Illinois.

location, and dispatch the crane to pick it from the rack. Generally, more frequently used items should be stored at the lower levels near the front in order to reduce storage and retrieval time. Energy can be saved by storing heavier items at the lower levels.

METHODS OF ANALYZING LAYOUT

Layout by Product

Designing a layout by product is fairly straightforward. The layout depends on the steps required to produce the product or to provide the service. The necessary stages in production or service may be arranged in a straight line or in various other configurations to suit the available space or fit the necessary system into an economical enclosure suitable for the proposed site. The number of stages and the number of steps to be performed at each stage depend on the rate of output for which the facility is designed. These decisions were discussed under "Line Balancing" in Chapter 8.

The options for sequencing stages along a flow line are already determined by the required product routing. The most desirable processes should be determined in the very early stages of the development of a new product.

Mathematical models such as line-balancing models are useful in determining the grouping of tasks into work stages. Graphical models such as scale drawings are useful in comparing possible arrangements. Sometimes movable templates are cut to scale to facilitate trying various arrangements on a scale drawing of the facility. Some of the shapes that a product layout (flow line) may take were presented in Figure 13.6.

The number of layout options is greatly reduced when the product is designed and the manufacturing processes are selected. The number of options available for layout by process is much greater and will be discussed in more detail below.

Layout by Process

Determining Department Size   Layout by process is generally associated with versatile operations that must·provide nonstandard products or services. The typical product mix must be forecast in order to determine what sort of facility will be appropriate for the operation. Facility decisions may be based on those products that are most frequently produced or most greatly affected by the layout.

After a forecast is made, it must be converted into the space required in each department, much as in capacity requirements planning, discussed in Chapter 4. For a manufacturing operation, the routing of each product or component must be determined. The number of production hours required for each product (i.e., "time standards," which are discussed in Chapter 15) or component should be multiplied by the expected number of items to be produced each month to arrive at an estimate of the number of production hours needed in each department. The production hours per month indicate generally the number of people and machines that should be available. Of course, some provisions are needed for seasonal and random fluctuations in work load that may occur. This additional capacity also allows for catch-up work needed because of scrap, absenteeism, equipment breakdowns, and other causes.

Determining Department Location   After the necessary department sizes have been determined, they can be arranged within an existing structure (if space permits) or in a desired pattern in some new facility. The relative location of departments depends on such factors as the space required, the shape of any existing structure, and the sequence of steps through which each product must be processed. Some structural shapes are more economical or better suited to the site than others. This stage of layout by process presents an extremely large number of options and makes the layout process very challenging.

To illustrate the wide variety of arrangements that can be made, consider the example shown in Figure 13.16. Assume that we are to arrange six equal-

FIGURE 13.16

Six Square Department Spaces in a Rectangular
Building

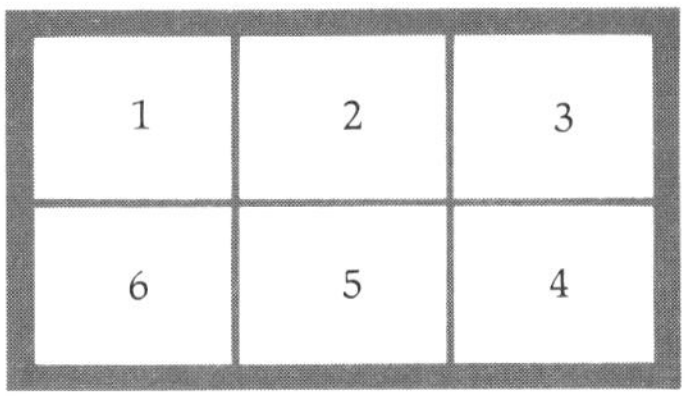

sized departments (*A* through *F*) in a building, and to simplify the matter consider only square departments. Assume that the building is rectangular. There are six spaces in which we could place department *A*. Once *A* is placed, there are five spaces available in which to place the next department. The next department would have four available spaces, and so on. In all there are 6! or 720 ways we could arrange this facility. If we added one more department we would have 7 × 720 = 5,040 ways. The number of ways we can arrange *n* square departments is *n*! Of course some of these arrangements are mirror images (left-to-right or top-to-bottom reversals) of other arrangements. If we begin to change both the shapes and the locations of departments, however, the number of options becomes limitless. You can see that identifying and arranging a realistic number of departments would take a long time unless we used some heuristic (rule of thumb) to limit the options we try. Of course we would need some criterion or objective before we could know which alternative to select, and this criterion would reduce the number of options that must be evaluated.

Transportation Cost as a Criterion for Layout

A large number of factors usually influence the final selection of a layout. A frequently used factor, although it is seldom the sole factor considered, is transportation. To begin with, let us concern ourselves only with transportation cost. The cost of transportation between two departments may arise because of the need to move material or correspondence between departments or the need of personnel to walk from one department to another to confer, to inspect, to supervise, or to perform direct work activities.

It is frequently assumed that transportation costs for a given type of object are proportional to the distances between two departments—at least, the incremental costs that can be influenced by layout. In a factory, for example, the load and unload cost is fixed if the size of the lot to be moved is fixed. Manufacturing layouts often are selected by finding the layout that minimizes the total movement, *M*, the product of the volume, *V*, times the weight, *W*, times the distance, *D*, as shown in equation 13.1.

$$M = \sum_{i=1}^{N} \sum_{t=1}^{T_i} (V_{it} \cdot W_{it} \cdot D_{it})$$

(13.1)

where M = the measure of materials handling

i = the product or component

N = the number of products or components that must be considered

t = the individual transfers that must be accomplished between departments

T_i = the total number of transports that must be accomplished for the ith product or component.

Sometimes only those items produced or used in large volumes or those of great weight are considered. Computer programs are available to perform this step. Flow matrices may also be used. Some of these methods are discussed in more detail later.

The only way to change transportation cost once the layout is established is to change the volume of products moved in each trip, thus also changing the number of trips necessary between two departments. The cost per unit of distance moved will sometimes be different at different stages of production. In the Layback Chair Company, for example, it is more expensive to move a load of wood for chair frames than to move the frame padding. When costs per unit of distance vary, we can work with dollars rather than distance.

Dominated Flow Pattern   We shall consider first a fully *dominated flow pattern*, then a flow that is not fully dominated by any pattern. Assume that we wish to lay out a contract sewing facility. There is no standardized product; the company bids to manufacture a specified number of garments. Each contract can be for a different garment in a different quantity, in different colors and sizes. The material for every contract is received, stored, released to the cutting room, cut, sewn into garments, packaged, stored until a truckload is accumulated, and then shipped. The inspectors move through the plants and inspect each operation where it occurs. Since every movement from any department always goes to only one other department, we can minimize transportation cost by making those departments adjacent. The resulting arrangement could be a straight line of departments. Since shipping and receiving activities are carried out by the same department, however, an O or U shape would be better (see Figure 13.17). The sizes of the departments may vary with the capacity required and the shape of the building. For this type of operation, we are arranging entire departments along some path in the same way that we would arrange machines or work stations along a flow line.

Nondominated Flow   When flow is equal among all departments, no particular arrangement is superior to any other as long as they all fit into the available space—unless, of course, some moves are more costly than others. We shall consider a company that has some reason for desiring a particular layout but for which the most desirable layout is not so obvious as in a fully dominated situation. Job shops have such a broad variety of jobs that the flow of work leaving any department may go in any of a number of directions.

Assume that we have a forecast of demand throughout some reasonable portion of the lifetime of a facility. Knowing the anticipated product mix and

FIGURE 13.17

Layout for a Dominated Flow Pattern

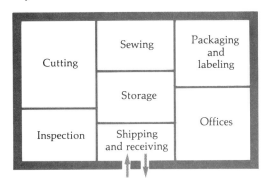

quantity enables us to know the necessary size of each department and the anticipated average number of trips, say per month, between the departments. Figure 13.18 shows a hypothetical number of trips among six departments to be housed in a new facility. Next, we need the cost per unit of distance (per hundred feet, per thousand feet, per hundred meters, whatever) to move the average-sized load between each pair of departments. This information is shown in Figure 13.19. Notice that Figure 13.19 uses all of the matrix except the diagonal. If cost were considered proportional to distance from each department to every other, we could use only the portion of the matrix above or below the diagonal. But a variety of objects are to be handled (because a different transformation is made in each department) and each department's output may be handled by a different method and in a different load size. We shall therefore not assume that the cost to move a load from department A to department D is equal to the cost to move a load from department D to department A, and so on.

FIGURE 13.18

Average Number of Trips per Month Between Departments

From \ To	Departments					
	A	B	C	D	E	F
A	0	217	418	61	42	180
B	216	0	52	190	61	10
C	400	114	0	95	16	20
D	16	421	62	0	41	68
E	126	71	100	315	0	50
F	42	95	83	114	390	0

FIGURE 13.19

Cost per Hundred Feet to Move an Average Load (in Dollars)

From \ To	A	B	C	D	E	F
A	0	0.15	0.15	0.16	0.15	0.16
B	0.18	0	0.16	0.15	0.15	0.15
C	0.15	0.15	0	0.15	0.15	0.16
D	0.18	0.15	0.15	0	0.15	0.16
E	0.15	0.17	0.16	0.20	0	0.15
F	0.15	0.15	0.16	0.15	0.15	0

Multiply the number of trips in the trips matrix (Figure 13.18) by the number in the same cell of the cost-per-unit-of-distance matrix (Figure 13.19). The resulting product represents the cost of each hundred feet of travel from one department to another. When we add the numbers below the diagonal, for cost of movement in one direction, to the numbers above the diagonal, for cost of movement in the opposite direction, we determine the cost per month for each foot of distance between pairs of departments.

The numbers in Figure 13.20 were developed by multiplying the hypothetical numbers in 13.18 and 13.19. The numbers below the diagonal in Figure 13.20 were added to those above the diagonal to find the monthly moving cost per unit of distance, as presented in Figure 13.21. If the cost to move a unit of distance were the same between each pair of departments, we would not have needed matrices 13.19 and 13.20; we could have looked at the number of trips to determine which departments should be near each other. Since the cost to

FIGURE 13.20

Monthly Cost per Hundred Feet Between Departments (Direction of Movement Considered)

From \ To	A	B	C	D	E	F
A	0	32.6	62.7	9.8	6.3	28.8
B	38.9	0	8.3	28.5	9.2	1.5
C	60.0	17.1	0	14.3	2.4	3.2
D	2.9	63.2	9.3	0	6.2	10.9
E	18.9	12.1	16.0	63.0	0	7.5
F	6.3	14.3	13.3	17.1	58.5	0

FIGURE 13.21

Total Monthly Moving Cost per Hundred Feet Between Departments

Between / And	Departments					
	A	B	C	D	E	F
A	0	71.5 ③	122.7 ①	12.7	25.2	35.1
B		0	25.4	91.7 ②	21.3	15.8
C			0	23.6	18.4	16.5
D				0	69.2 ④	28.0
E					0	66.0 ⑤
F						0

move a unit of distance varies between pairs of departments, Figure 13.21 provides a basis for locating departments so as to minimize transportation cost.

The *nearness priorities* (transportation costs) are indicated by circled numbers in cells of Figure 13.21, in descending order. If transportation cost were our only criterion, we would want (1) department A near C, (2) B near D, (3) A near B, (4) D near E, and (5) E near F. Using these heuristics (rules of thumb) as guides, we could develop a resulting layout that looks like Figure 13.22. The double arrows indicate the nearness priorities. We could have several arrangements that would place departments with high nearness priorities adjacent to each other.

Nontransportation Factors

One department may be placed near another or away from another for many reasons other than transportation cost. In a hospital we would want contagious diseases away from the nursery and the surgery wing. Obviously we would want the recovery room near the operating room. In a factory, we would want

FIGURE 13.22

Layout to Satisfy Transportation Cost Nearness Priorities

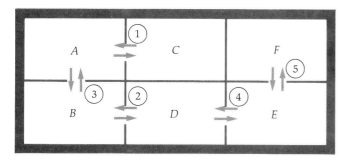

FIGURE 13.23

Nearness Priorities in a Muther Grid

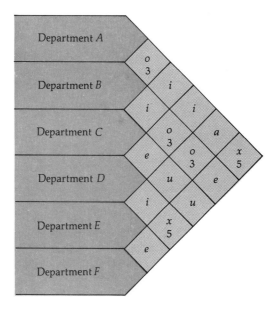

Nearness Priority Code	Degree of Importance	Reason Code	Possible Reasons
a	Absolutely necessary	1	Use same equipment
e	Very important	2	Use same records or personnel
i	Important	3	Work flow facilitated
o	OK, ordinary importance	4	Ease of communication or supervision
u	Unimportant	5	Unsafe conditions
x	Undesirable		

a painting department (with flammable solvents) located away from the welding department (with its sparks and flames). Common sense will provide a few guidelines to prevent the need to try all possible arrangements.

Richard Muther developed a convenient format to indicate nearness priorities, taking into account factors other than transportation costs.[2] His method uses a half matrix or a similar equivalent grid to display location priorities (Figure 13.23). The diamond-shaped boxes at the right-hand side of the figure are used to indicate the desired relationships between the two departments that intersect there. A letter (a, e, i, o, u, or x) is used to depict the desired relationship and a number is used to indicate a reason for the relationship.

[2]Richard Muther, *Practical Plant Layout* (New York: McGraw-Hill, 1955).

FIGURE 13.24

A Layout of Square Departments that Meets the
Priorities of Figure 13.23

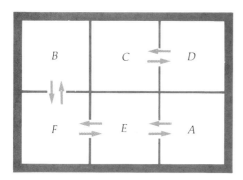

The *a* in the matrix of Figure 13.23 indicates that it is absolutely necessary that departments *E* and *A* be near each other. The *e*'s indicate that department *F* should be near departments *E* and *B* and that department *C* should be near *D*. The *x*'s indicate that department *F* should not be near *D* or *A*. An example layout of a facility that meets these conditions is shown in Figure 13.24.

Computer Packages for Layout Analysis

The person performing a layout analysis must ascertain how much space each department requires and any special shapes that must be provided or avoided. Through ingenuity, he or she arrives at a layout that accommodates the nearness priorities, provides the needed space if possible, and fits within an economical or existing enclosure. The number of departments does not have to be large to present an overwhelming number of arrangements. Recall that the number of options for equal-sized departments was *n*! So for ten departments there are 3,628,800 alternative arrangements. Every time we add the *n*th department, the problem becomes *n* times larger because *n*! = n[(*n* − 1)!]. You can see that there are many possible ways to lay out a sizable number of departments.

Computer programs have been developed to assist the layout analyst in identifying layouts that appear to meet some specified criterion. The user can specify a matrix of the anticipated number of trips between departments (Figure 13.18) or a ranking of nearness priorities such as the Muther scale (Figure 13.23).

In 1963, Gordon Armour and Elwood Buffa presented a computerized layout program called CRAFT (Computerized Relative Allocation of Facilities).[3] This heuristic program could handle up to forty departments. The program required as input a description of an existing or some arbitrary layout and a

[3]Gordon C. Armour and Elwood S. Buffa, "A Heuristic Algorithm and Simulation Approach to Relative Location of Facilities," *Management Science* 9 (1963): 294–309.

matrix of nearness priorities (such as number of trips and material movement costs).

The program operated by iterations or successive improvements. At each step, the original program computed the cost improvement that would result if two departments were interchanged, made the best interchange to develop a new layout, and went back through the evaluations and interchanges until no improvement could be found.

The original CRAFT program reduced computations by considering interchanges of two departments at each step. A more recent version will consider three department interchanges.[4] As an example of the reduction of computations achieved through evaluating pair exchanges, consider that ten departments are to be located. The number of possible interchanges to be evaluated at each stage is C_2^{10} or 45.[5] The program will stop if no improvement can be achieved through one of the interchanges. If improvements are possible, the program will make the best exchange and go on to possible two-way and three-way pairs of interchanges for the curent layout. CRAFT makes successive improvements until no further improvement can be found. If an optimum layout were submitted initially, the program would make only 45 evaluations. In contrast, if one had to compare the initial layout to all other possible layouts, the number of evaluations would be 10! or 3,628,800. A capability is provided in the CRAFT program to fix some departments so they will not be moved in case some features of an existing or proposed layout are necessary for some reason. A summary flow chart of CRAFT is shown in Figure 13.25.

The output of CRAFT may not be optimal because all possible layouts are not considered. But the program produces a layout that cannot easily be improved. Because of the simplifying assumptions made in the program, an exact optimal solution to the problem may not be an ideal solution to the real-world situation anyway, but it should be close.

The CRAFT program works on the assumption that movement between departments occurs along straight lines between the centroids of the departments. It also assumes that costs vary linearly with distance. The model has been applied to both manufacturing and nonmanufacturing organizations.[6]

Other computerized algorithms have been presented in the literature. ALDEP (Automated Layout Design Program) has the capability of laying out up to sixty-three departments.[7] It uses a matrix of letter codes similar to the Muther rankings to specify nearness priorities. These rankings are converted to a quantitative scale to facilitate the evaluation of trade-offs. The program can deal with multistory facilities.

[4]Richard L. Francis and John A. White, *Facility Layout and Location: An Analytical Approach* (Englewood Cliffs, N.J.: Prentice-Hall, 1974), p. 128.

$$^5C_2^{10} = \frac{10!}{2!(10-2)!} = \frac{10 \cdot 9 \cdot 8!}{2 \cdot 8!} = 45$$

[6]Elwood S. Buffa, *Modern Production Management* (New York: Wiley, 1977), pp. 266–275.

[7]Jarrold M. Seehof and Wayne O. Evans, "Automated Layout and Design Program," *Journal of Industrial Engineering*, December 1967, pp. 609–695.

FIGURE 13.25

Descriptive Flow Chart for CRAFT

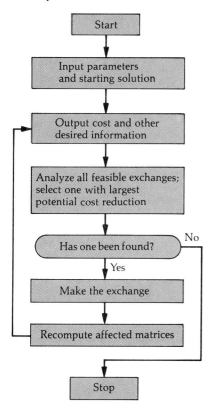

Source: L. P. Ritzman, "The Efficiency of Computer Programs for Plant Layout," doctoral thesis, Michigan State University, 1968.

CORELAP (Computerized Relationship Layout Planning) can lay out up to forty-five departments.[8] It requires that the user specify the sizes of the departments and the length-to-width ratio of the structure to house the layout.

PREP (Plant Relayout and Evaluation Package) is another heuristic layout program. PREP can analyze up to ninety-nine departments at one time. The program bases the results on actual distances traveled by materials-handling equipment (rather than assuming straight lines between department centroids) and can work with different handling equipment in different paths. The user may specify that the program bypass consideration of certain departmental exchanges. The program can also analyze multistory facilities.[9]

[8]Robert S. Lee and James M. Moore, "CORELAP (Computerized Relationship Layout Planning)," *Journal of Industrial Engineering*, March 1967, pp. 195–200.
[9]David M. Anderson, "New Plant Layout Information System," *Industrial Engineering*, April 1973, pp. 32–37.

ARRANGEMENT OF FACILITIES WITHIN DEPARTMENTS

As mentioned above, one of the first major steps in layout analysis is to determine the space needed in each department. This is accomplished by the conversion of a sales forecast into capacity requirements. A second major step is determining the relative location of the departments by seeing how well each arrangement meets some established criteria. This second step can be assisted by computer analysis. The remaining step is arranging equipment and people within the departments.

Arranging facilities within a department may be looked upon as a miniature layout problem. One must consider intradepartmental as well as interdepartmental flows. Actually much of the intradepartmental layout may be determined before the relative departmental locations are considered. Earlier analysis of the layout within departments will help identify their desired size and shape and perhaps reduce the number of alternative arrangements to be considered in arranging their location.

The placement of individual pieces of furniture within a clerical department or of individual machines within a factory may be determined by use of graphical models. Scale drawings of the space and equipment or movable scaled templates may be used to evaluate alternative arrangements. Sometimes templates are used during deliberations and drawings are made after the layout is decided upon. An example of a factory layout drawing is shown in Figure 13.26.

Computers may be used to assist in the layout within departments, though most applications probably do not justify the effort. The layout analyst would need to treat each major piece of equipment within a department as though it were a department. Flow between these subcomponents of departments or nearness priorities for the subcomponents must be identified, just as for other applications of computerized layout packages.

The Need for Versatility

Mass communications, mass marketing, broad travel, and other factors have led to rapid shifts in consumption patterns and operation methods. Change is a part of the life of any organization in a dynamic economy. Factories are designed with broad open areas that can be adapted to a wide variety of uses. Because of their flexibility and economy of construction, metal buildings have become popular as factories, showrooms, warehouses, and even offices.

Office Layout   An integrated approach that makes use of several computer programs has been applied to office layout. This approach involves considerable interaction between the analyst and a series of three computer programs to develop candidate layouts. The initial phase involves the collection of data by questionnaire to determine communication patterns and the use of common data, equipment, or meeting areas. These data are obtained both for individuals and for subunits of the organization.

FIGURE 13.26

Section of Sketch of Equipment Layout Within a Department

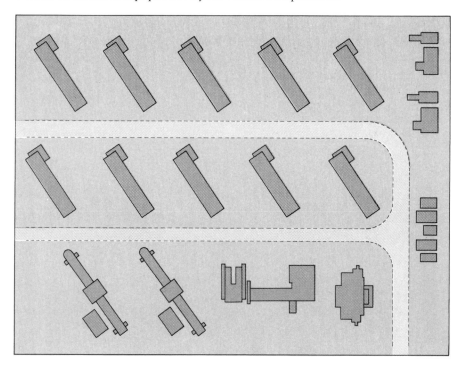

The next phase of analysis involves grouping entities into clusters that have a high degree of interaction. A great deal of flexibility is afforded by the system. The analyst can select from five different heuristic procedures to partition up to 100 entities into groups. Entities can be selected to be individuals, sections, departments, or other organizational subunits. The system supplies data to compare the number of intergroup and intragroup interactions. The analyst must use judgment to determine when desirable groupings have been determined.

The last phase of the approach supplies alternative office layouts for location of the groups. The analyst must supply the input used to determine the floor space required by the groups and must specify any locations that must remain fixed. An expanded version of the CRAFT program is used to generate block-diagram layouts, using the product obtained when interactions are multiplied by the distances between the interacting entities to measure effectiveness.[10]

[10]F. Robert Jacobs, John W. Bradford, and Larry P. Ritzman, "Computerized Layout: An Integrated Approach to Special Planning and Communication Requirements," *Industrial Engineering*, July 1980, pp. 56–61.

Offices have also become more flexible. Many companies are using an "open plan" concept with modular office partitions erected to separate work stations. This concept offers more economy and flexibility than fixed-partition construction. Care must be taken to use sound-absorbent materials, however, to keep noise below annoying levels. Some modular office partitions are shown in Figure 13.27.

FIGURE 13.27

A Modular Office: Action Office®

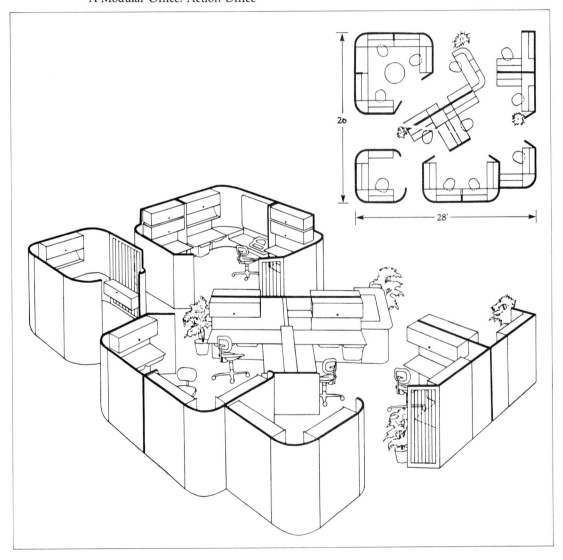

Source: Herman Miller, Inc., Zeeland, Mich.

APPLICATION

Example of a Nonmanufacturing Layout

Noah Sark owned and managed a small brokerage firm. His company had out-grown its offices, so Noah planned to move into new facilities. He had found an ideal location but was not sure that the available space would provide everything that he desired. Besides, the area was square—a different shape from that of the space his company had been occupying.

Noah discussed the situation with his son, Alec, when he was home from school for a weekend. Noah said that he had thought about the layout for some time but just did not see how it could be achieved in the square office space that had such an ideal location. He had to sign a lease on the space early the next week if he wanted it. Noah explained his many objectives, some of which appeared to conflict with others. His senior brokers all wanted privacy and quiet, yet wanted to be able to see the ticker display from their offices. Both the senior and junior brokers wanted to be able to see the customer reception area so they could greet customers who came in. Noah wanted the receptionist area near the entrance and near his office so the receptionist could also serve as his secretary. Noah believed there should be a customer seating area where customers could watch the ticker display, and that his area should also be near the brokers' offices. The operations and bookkeeping department should be near Noah's office and easily accessible by all of the brokers. A large storage room for records and office supplies should be near bookkeeping. Noah also told Alec that the employees needed a lounge for coffee breaks, snacks, or lunch. He would also like a conference room, but he

FIGURE 13.28

Matrix for Sark Layout Analysis

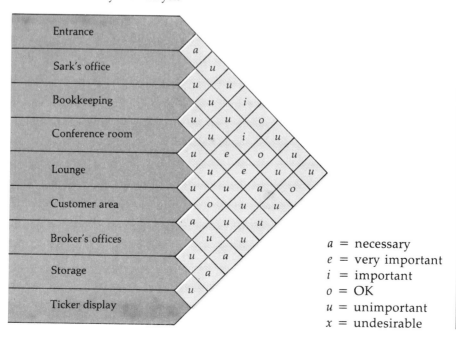

a = necessary
e = very important
i = important
o = OK
u = unimportant
x = undesirable

might not be able to have that and all his other objectives too. If a conference room was added, it should be near the lounge so that coffee could be served easily. Alec developed a matrix to express the priorities that should be observed in the designing of the office (Figure 13.28). He then went to work designing the office.

The available office space was an open square area with the entrance near one corner and restrooms at the opposite corner. Alec knew his father's office should be near the receptionist, so he put it at the corner near the door. The bookkeeping office should also be adjacent to his father's office. The storage area was located in the corner adjoining the bookkeeping office, so, at this stage, that wall of the office area was completely utilized. The ticker display, which displays stock quotations on a wall, is the center of attention in a brokerage office. Any wall where the ticker is located is not suitable for brokers' offices, because the ticker would not be visible from them. Therefore Alec placed the ticker along the outer wall of the bookkeeping office. He then located the lounge and conference

FIGURE 13.29

Alec Sark's Layout

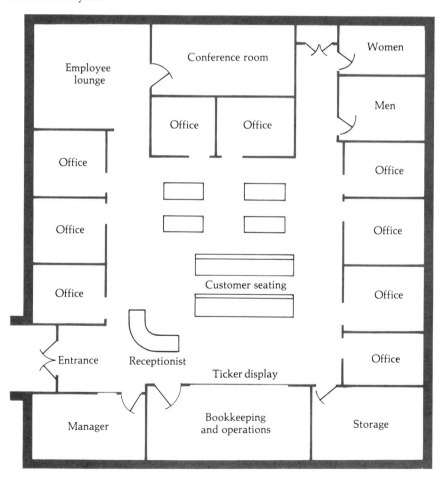

room on the opposite wall, leaving a large open space, from any point in which the ticker display was clearly visible. Alec then drew nine offices along the sides of this space. Each office could be open or it could be separated from the open space by a glass partition without loss of view of the ticker display. The remaining space was left open so that customers could sit and observe the ticker display, yet have easy access to brokers or to the bookkeeping department.

The next morning Alec told his father how silly he was for not being able to develop a layout that met all of his objectives. Alec handed his father the layout presented in Figure 13.29 and said that any student in his class could do almost as well, but none, naturally, quite so well. Noah looked at the layout and marveled at how smart Alec was.

SUMMARY

Layout is the arrangement of the various departments, support functions, and equipment within a facility. Some of the objectives of a good layout are the minimization of the cost of moving materials and people from one department to another and ease of supervision and communication.

Materials-handling methods influence transportation cost and layout selection in manufacturing operations. Five classes of materials-handling methods are conveyors, industrial trucks, automatic guided vehicles, cranes and hoists, and industrial robots. Conveyors are appropriate when a company has a relatively stable pattern of materials flow with sufficient volume to justify the investment. Cranes are advantageous when heavy work items frequently must be lifted on and off machines or moved over variable paths between locations that are not widely separated. Industrial trucks are appropriate when loads are moved longer distances over variable paths.

Three classical types of layout are the flow-line layout, layout by process, and fixed-position layout. Each can be used in manufacturing or nonmanufacturing operations. Flow-line layouts are suitable for large-volume operations that have fixed sequences of activities in producing goods or providing services. Process layouts are suitable when flexibility is desired or when volumes are not large. Fixed-position layouts are used when the work item cannot be moved or when it is too heavy or fragile to be moved economically. Cellular arrangements can sometimes provide many of the advantages of flow lines to companies that perform moderate-volume production of similar items.

The location of equipment in a flow line is dicatated by the necessary sequence of production steps. The location of departments in a process layout may depend on the compatibility of processes, requirements for utilities or ventilation, ease of supervision, employee safety, or transportation (i.e., materials-handling) costs. Transportation costs are frequently calculated in the evaluation of potential layouts. The moving cost that is to be minimized is considered to be proportional to the product of the number of moves times the weight to be moved each trip times the distance for each trip.

Computer algorithms have been applied to the solution of layout problems. CRAFT, ALDEP, CORELAP, and PREP are four of the more publicized heuristic programs that may be used in analyzing layouts. These programs evaluate transportation costs under several simplifying assumptions. Although such programs do not guarantee an optimal solution, they may greatly reduce the amount of time required to arrive at a very good and acceptable layout or to generate alternatives for further evaluation.

DISCUSSION QUESTIONS

1. Define layout.
2. Under what circumstances might a layout study or evaluation be warranted?
3. Discuss some of the objectives of a good layout.
4. Describe five major types of materials-handling methods, and discuss some advantages of each.
5. What are three classical types of layout? Provide an example of each.
6. What are four advantages and four disadvantages of layout by product (flow line)?
7. What is a manufacturing cell or "cellular manufacturing"?
8. Briefly describe how a U-line cell operates.
9. Briefly describe how a rabbit-chase cell operates.
10. What are some of the potential advantages of a flexible manufacturing system (FMS)?
11. Differentiate between manufacturing and service layouts.
12. Several factors should usually be taken into account in the attempt to develop an optimal layout. What are some of these factors?
13. What contribution has the computer made to layout planning?
14. Why are some offices utilizing the open plan with broad expanses of space that have no permanent partitions?
15. Why are many factories utilizing large preengineered metal buildings with broad expanses of unobstructed floor space?
16. Why are many offices being built as multistory buildings whereas single-story factories seem to be more common?

PROBLEMS

1. Arrange six square departments in a grid like the one shown, so as to meet the objectives listed below:

> Department A near E
> A near D
> A near C
> B near C
> B near D
> F near D
> E near F

2. The grid shown here is an initial layout of four square departments within a square office building. The number of moves each week between departments is as follows: $A - B = 200$, $A - C = 300$, $A - D = 400$, $B - C = 200$, $B - D = 500$, $C - D = 100$. All movements are assumed to occur from the center of the sending departments to the center of the receiving departments. These moves are made along aisles that run parallel to the exterior walls. Therefore the average move distance between diagonally located departments is assumed to be 200 feet, and between adjacent departments it is assumed to be 100 feet. Enumerate the layouts that can be made through pairwise interchanges, and determine the total movement distance that results from each layout. Which layout minimizes movement?

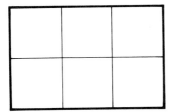

3. Arrange six square departments in a 2 × 3 grid like the figure in problem 1 so that the nearness priorities shown in the matrix below are satisfied.

   a = absolutely necessary
   e = very important
   i = important
   o = OK, ordinary importance
   u = unimportant
   x = undesirable

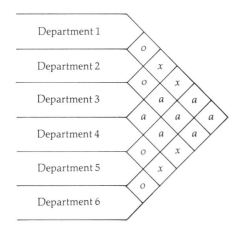

4. Draw the resulting layout for each possible pairwise interchange of departments that can be made in the departmental arrangement shown below.

A	C	E
B	D	F

5. You are called in as a consultant for a firm that produces sporting goods. The manager wants you to arrange the plant to minimize transportation. The number of trips between departments and the cost per unit of distance for the typical load are given in the table below. Develop the nearness priorities for the departments.

Movement		Expected Number	Cost Per Unit
From	To	of Trips	of Distance
A	B	300	$0.10
A	C	150	0.10
A	D	200	0.10
A	E	150	0.10
B	A	75	0.18
B	C	80	0.18
B	D	80	0.18
B	E	90	0.18
C	A	100	0.08
C	B	25	0.08
C	D	80	0.08
C	E	100	0.08
D	A	50	0.12
D	B	75	0.12
D	C	300	0.12
D	E	200	0.12
E	A	200	0.16
E	B	50	0.16
E	C	90	0.16
E	D	100	0.16

6. Departments A, C, D, and E should be 40 feet × 40 feet. Department B should be 40 × 80 feet. Arrange these five departments in an 80 × 120-foot space so that the layout meets the conditions specified in the matrix.

   a = absolutely necessary
   i = important
   x = undesirable

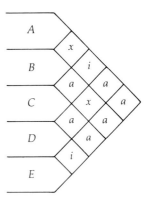

7. Locate nine square departments in a 3 × 3 grid so that the priorities in the matrix below are satisfied.

> a = absolutely necessary
> e = very important
> i = important
> o = OK, ordinary importance
> u = unimportant
> x = undesirable

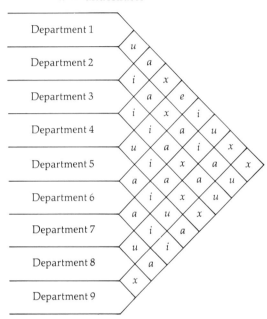

8. Six equal-sized rectangular departments are to be placed in locations I through VI in the building sketched below. Aisles and corridors will be parallel to the exterior walls so that no diagonal travel will occur, and it is assumed that all travel will be from the center of one department to the center of another. For example, the following distances between locations are assumed: I to II = 80′; I to III = 60′; I to IV = 80′ + 60′ = 140′; I to V = 60′ + 60′ = 120′; and I to VI = 80′ + 60′ + 60′ = 200′. The cost per unit of distance moved is the same for any move. Estimates of the average number of trips per week between departments are provided in the table below.

(a) Make an initial assignment of depart-

ments A-F to the six locations so that it appears that the travel distance will be minimized.

(b) Exchange the locations of departments E and D, and compute the net effect on the total move distance.

Weekly Number of Trips Between Departments						
From To	A	B	C	D	E	F
A	—	90	50	90	80	20
B	30	—	20	60	30	60
C	50	20	—	90	90	30
D	70	30	80	—	20	60
E	80	30	60	60	—	10
F	50	80	10	60	30	—

|←— 80ft —→|←— 80ft —→|

I	II	60ft
III	IV	60ft
V	VI	60ft

9. Determine which of the following two layouts will result in a lower product of trips times distance traveled per year if the numbers of trips between pairs of departments are as given in the table above the layouts. Assume that all movements are between the centers of the specified departments and are made parallel to the walls of the building and all turns must be at right angles, since there are no diagonal aisles.

Exchanging Departments	Loads Per Year
A–C	4,500
A–B	4,200
D–E	4,100
C–D	3,700
A–D	3,100
B–C	2,400
B–D	2,000
A–E	1,500
C–E	1,200
B–E	1,000

Layout A

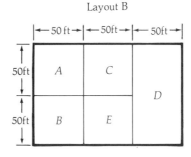

Layout B

10. The MTL Company wishes to arrange stock within its warehouse (see layout below) so that the items with the highest usage-times-weight (about 20 percent of the items in this company) are in zone *A* nearest the loading dock. Items with the next highest usage-times-weight (about 30 percent of the items) will be stored in zone *B*, and the remainder in zone *C*. Select from the items listed in the table (at right) the items that should be in zones *A*, *B*, and *C* respectively.

Item Number	Orders/ Month	Weight	Item Number	Orders/ Month	Weight
1	610	410	11	25	17
2	320	107	12	71	52
3	500	12	13	490	51
4	840	29	14	55	3,000
5	900	650	15	900	1,160
6	250	400	16	250	18
7	560	19	17	120	73
8	1,000	84	18	50	91
9	350	63	19	370	217
10	770	59	20	1,700	318

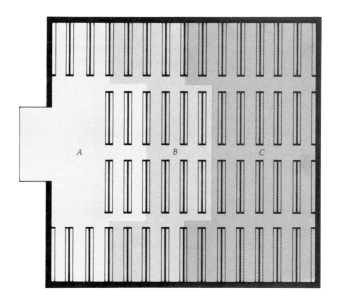

11. The Gingersnap Company is interested in designing a new plant. Forecasts of the future product mix and future demand levels indicate the floor-space requirements for the six production departments shown in the table below. The company does not want the space occupied by any department to be more than twice as long as it is wide. The company plans to use a metal building that has a width of 120 feet and can be constructed in any length. The building site will accommodate a building up to 300 feet long.

Floor-Space Requirements
for Six Departments

Department	Space Required (sq. ft.)
A	4,000
B	5,000
C	3,600
D	7,500
E	2,500
F	4,000

The expected numbers of trips among the departments each week are indicated in the figure below. Assume that the transportation costs per foot traveled are equal between all pairs of departments. Suggest a layout of these departments that will fit the building, provide the desired floor space, and minimize transportation costs.

12. The Marengo Machine Company is a job shop that produces a great variety of items. Flow within its plant is varied. Some departments deal with heavy items that are expensive to transport. The materials usually transported between some departments require only hand trucks, while a large industrial truck is usually required for the items moved in other parts of the plant. The costs for moving between various pairs of departments are shown in Figure A. The expected number of trips between the departments is shown in Figure B.

Figure A.   Cost per Unit of Distance between Departments (in dollars)

From \ To	Lathe	Mills	Drills	Casting	Finishing	Assembly
Lathe	—	0.02	0.02	0.02	0.02	0.02
Mills	0.05	—	0.05	0.05	0.05	0.05
Drills	0.03	0.03	—	0.03	0.03	0.03
Casting	0.08	0.08	0.08	—	0.08	0.08
Finishing	0.05	0.05	0.05	0.05	—	0.05
Assembly	0.10	0.10	0.10	0.10	0.10	—

Figure B.   Expected Number of Trips between Departments per Week

From \ To	Lathe	Mills	Drills	Casting	Finishing	Assembly
Lathe	—	300	100	10	100	100
Mills	200	—	300	10	150	150
Drills	50	150	—	10	200	300
Casting	50	350	300	—	50	100
Finishing	20	20	20	10	—	500
Assembly	10	10	10	0	0	—

(a) Develop a matrix of nearness priorities by computing the cost the company will incur for each unit of distance between the various departments.

From \ To	Departments					
	A	B	C	D	E	F
A	—	80	10	5	2	20
B	20	—	5	90	6	10
C	6	0	—	6	0	120
D	10	18	100	—	0	30
E	20	16	20	2	—	18
F	4	20	25	18	95	—

(b) Assume the departments are equal-sized squares and arrange them in a 2 × 3 grid so that the transportation costs will be minimized.

13. A small college is designing a new campus and has studied the average flow of students between buildings as classes change. The number of students moving between buildings is shown in the matrix below. Arrange the eight buildings around the perimeter of a square block so that the amount of walking between buildings will be near minimal.

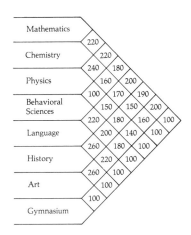

BIBLIOGRAPHY

Buffa, Elwood S., and Jeffrey G. Miller. *Production-Inventory Systems: Planning and Control.* 3d ed. Homewood, Ill.: Irwin, 1979.

Bylinski, Gene. "The Race to the Automatic Factory." *Fortune,* February 21, 1983.

Francis, Richard L., and John A. White. *Facility Layout and Location: An Analytical Approach.* Englewood Cliffs, N.J.: Prentice-Hall, 1974.

Hall, Robert W. *Zero Inventories.* Homewood, Ill.: Dow Jones-Irwin, 1983.

Hughes, Tom, and Don Hegland. "Flexible Manufacturing—The Way to the Winner's Circle." *Production Engineering,* September 1983, pp. 54–63.

Hyer, Nancy L., and Urban Wemmerlöv. "Group Technology and Productivity." *Harvard Business Review,* July–August 1984, pp. 140–149.

Jacobs, F. Robert, John W. Bradford, and Larry P. Ritzman. "Computerized Layout: An Integrated Approach To Special Planning and Communications." *Industrial Engineering,* July 1980, pp. 56–61.

Moore, J. M. "Computer Program Evaluates Plant Layout Alternatives." *Industrial Engineering* 3, no. 8 (1971): 19–25.

Muther, Richard, and K. McPherson. "Four Approaches to Computerized Layout." *Industrial Engineering,* February 1970, pp. 39–42.

Reed, Rudell. *Plant Location, Layout, and Maintenance.* Homewood, Ill.: Irwin, 1967.

Riggs, James L. *Production Systems: Planning Analysis and Control.* 2d ed. New York: Wiley, 1976.

Saphier, Michael. *Office Planning and Design.* New York: McGraw-Hill, 1968.

Schonberger, Richard J. *Japanese Manufacturing Techniques: Nine Hidden Lessons in Simplicity.* New York: Free Press, 1982.

Vollman, Thomas E., and Elwood S. Buffa. "The Facilities Design Problem in Perspective." *Management Science,* June 1966, pp. B450–B468.

Chapter Outline
JOB DESIGN

KEY TERMS

Job design	Division of labor	Sociotechnical systems	Therbligs
Technical feasibility	(specialization)	Quality circle	Human factors
Economic feasibility	Motivator factors	Job rotation	engineering
Behavioral feasibility	Hygiene factors	Job enlargement	(ergonomics)
Industrial robot	Expectancy theory	Job enrichment	Anthropometric data
Multiple-activity chart	Extrinsic rewards	Motion study	Job redesign
	Intrinsic rewards	Micromotion study	Flow process charts

Chapter 14

JOB DESIGN

A company's strategy and its success in accomplishing its strategy depend on many conditions. One of the greatest assets a company has is its human resources. The greatest strategy can be successful to its fullest extent only with the committed efforts of individuals throughout the entire organization. Since the operations function must produce the goods or provide the services that a company offers and since the largest portion of a company's employees often are found within the operations function, it is important to consider the jobs people perform within operations. In this chapter we examine some aspects of job design. Although volumes could be written about job design, we will provide only an overview of some important topics.

People's jobs make them part of a system that also contains the equipment or technical processes with which they work, the physical surroundings (layout, noise, temperature), the social environment (supervisor relations, peer relations), and perhaps other factors. Many factors affect this system and are affected by it. However, we have no clear understanding of how jobs influence the level of employee motivation. According to Richard Steers and Richard Mowday, "a conceptual model is needed to guide research and provide greater insight into motivational implications of changes in the nature of jobs."[1] This chapter examines some of the job design factors and theories that relate to workers.

[1]Richard M. Steers and Richard T. Mowday, "The Motivational Properties of Tasks," *Academy of Management Review*, October 1977, p. 645.

ASPECTS OF JOB DESIGN

Job design is specifying "the tasks, methods, and relationships of jobs in order to satisfy technological and organizational requirements as well as the social and personal requirements of the job holder."[2] Many parts of an organizational system affect workers, and all should be taken into consideration when jobs are designed. They may be grouped in two broad categories:

1. Technical-physical factors.
   (a) Task content—the operations that must be performed to convert inputs to the desired output.
   (b) Physical context—the heat, light, noise, fumes or pollution, appearance, and safety precautions that surround the jobholder.
2. Sociopsychological factors.
   (a) Social factors—the personal interactions that occur because of the organizational structure and job assignments.
   (b) Intrinsic factors—the internal psychological feelings that are engendered as a result of performing the job.

Objectives

A job usually is a long-term assignment of tasks by means of which a person is to contribute to the organization. It also is a long-term definition of the social interactions that the jobholder will have or not have with the remainder of the organization and the way in which he or she will be affected by some of the factors mentioned above. A company is dependent on its employees for its success. Anything that affects the employee's job performance should be of interest to management because it is management's responsibility to get work accomplished through others.

There are three main objectives that a manager should strive for in specifying jobs: *technical feasibility*, *economic feasibility*, and *behavioral feasibility*.

Technical Feasibility   A job is a set of tasks or duties assigned to be performed. The person who holds the job must be capable of performing the assignment with the equipment and systems available, and the job must make the necessary transformations of inputs into outputs. A job must not be beyond the reasonable limits of a person's skills or physical and mental endurance. Proper selection of processes and equipment as well as proper selection and training of employees helps ensure technical feasibility.

Economic Feasibility   The cost of performing the job should not be too high. Overall a business must be able to collect for its services more than the cost of providing them so that some revenue will be left to pay for the use and risk of the owners' and lenders' capital. Since many businesses and other institutions

---

[2]Louis E. Davis, "The Design of Jobs," *Industrial Relations*, October 1966, p. 21.

must perform in a competitive environment, they are subject to some pressure to keep prices and costs at reasonable levels. Regulated monopolies such as utilities are subjected to pressures to keep their rates low. Government agencies compete with each other for funds, which it is hoped are limited by the taxpayers' representatives. As a whole, the collection of jobs within an organization must remain solvent. Some jobholders may be paid more than the value they add to the product or service. There is a limit, however, to the amount of money a company can pay for the jobholders, support equipment, and facilities necessary to effect the desired transformation processes.

Behavioral Feasibility   Some characteristics of a job may affect the jobholders' perception of themselves, their perception of others, and their relationships with others. A task role may give people a feeling of great worth—of being an important part of the organization. The feelings that people derive from a job affect their motivation to perform it. Since a job is often more than just a set of mechanical motions to be performed, it requires motivation and mental stimulation if it is to be performed successfully. Unstructured jobs often require so much of a person's creativity and mental attention that a good attitude is vital to its satisfactory performance. Even routine, structured jobs require that a person be motivated enough to be present at the job and contribute the necessary effort.

Beyond the individual, jobs carry with them social interactions that may lead to group reactions. Informal organizations or work groups have a large impact on the effectiveness of an organization, for either good or bad. Attitudes are contagious, and peer relations or peer pressure may be responsible for many of the motivational reactions of workers.

The Balancing of Objectives

An organization must achieve economic feasibility in order to survive. This pressure may cause a company to stress technical efficiency at the expense of employee satisfaction and motivation. On the one hand, jobs may become so unrewarding that they go unfilled or are filled by employees who are not motivated or cooperative. Half-hearted effort on the job, absenteeism, high labor turnover, and/or strikes may lead to excessive costs and even to lack of economic feasibility. On the other hand, a company cannot afford to make jobs too inefficient just to make them satisfying. One objective in making jobs satisfying is to add to the worker's motivation so that there is no reduction in efficiency, and perhaps even an improvement in quality and cost performance. The relationship between the three types of feasibility is shown schematically in Figure 14.1. The shaded portion represents the objective sought in job design.

Behavioral scientists and managers are still seeking answers to the question of how to achieve optimal job designs that balance technical objectives and social or behavioral objectives. One promising approach is called the sociotechnical systems approach because it involves the interrelationships between the social needs of workers and the technical needs of the task to be performed.

FIGURE 14.1

Objectives of Job Design

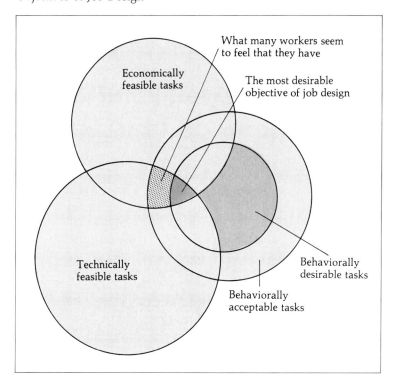

The Role of Machines

The role of industrial workers has changed since the beginning of the factory system. In early manufacturing, people were the providers and controllers of energy. As the age of mechanization advanced, manufacturers increasingly relied on machines to provide the energy or power required to perform work, while the worker still served as the controller of that power. Workers fed material into machines, operated them, and removed processed material. The development and use of automation have lessened the need for workers to control equipment through each production cycle. Now they set up equipment and act as tenders while the equipment performs much of the work. This change creates a need for a larger percentage of skilled workers who can maintain and operate complicated equipment.

Service operations have increased greatly in the past few decades, causing a shift in the composition of the work force, as we saw in Supplement C. Technology and mechanical support have become more common in the delivery of services. In some cases the customer deals directly with a machine, such as an automatic bank teller, a food and beverage vending machine, or an automatic car wash.[3] People involved in providing services are supported by such machines as automatic potato peelers and computer terminals. Both manufacturing and nonmanufacturing operations have increased their use of machines. The first aspect of job design that we shall consider is the question of where machines can be used most appropriately.

When Should Machines Be Used?

Machines can provide assistance in many operations, but many tasks are still best performed by people. Machines were originally applied as mere extensions of human senses and limbs, yet today machines function as extensions of man's perceptual and cognitive processes as well. Today, then, many human functions are candidates for automation. Job design must evaluate the question of where machines are to be used in operations. The lists in Table 14.1 compare some of the capabilities of people and machines. Generally people are more adaptive and flexible than machines; they have the ability to use judgment and think creatively. Machines generally have less flexibility, but they are much more consistent than humans.

Industrial Robots   The capabilities of industrial robots are reducing the general lack of flexibility of machines relative to humans. An *industrial robot* is a machine with reprogrammable internal controls that is capable of numerous manipulations to perform a variety of tasks. Instead of resembling a metallic human of science fiction, a robot usually has a configuration consisting of a support pedestal holding a pivoting armlike projection with a handlike gripper on the end. These machines are sometimes applied to very boring, repetitive jobs, or they are used in settings that would be dangerous or uncomfortable for humans. Some applications, however, are justified purely as cost reductions—robots can work up to twenty-four hours per day without a break, and they don't require overtime pay, vacations, or other fringe benefits. Robots are used for machine loading, forging, heat treating, die casting, welding, painting, assembly, packaging, and other applications. Research and development is expanding the capabilities of these machines to include tactile and visual sensors, and the number of robots in use is rapidly increasing. (See Figure 13.5 on page 550.)

Machine-Worker Interaction

Often jobs are designed to use humans and machines in combination so that the better features of both can complement each other in performing tasks. In addition to considering when machines can best augment people in their work, a job designer may wish to determine how to make the worker-machine combination more productive. A simple example of the interaction of a person and a machine may be found in many kitchens. Suppose a member of the family loads an automatic dishwasher, adds detergent, and turns the machine on. The

[3]Theodore Levitt, "Production-Line Approach to Service," *Harvard Business Review*, September–October 1972, pp. 41–52.

Table 14.1
RELATIVE CAPABILITIES OF HUMANS AND MACHINES

HUMANS ARE GENERALLY *BETTER* IN THEIR ABILITIES TO:

- Sense very low levels of certain kinds of stimuli: visual, auditory, tactual, olfactory, and taste.
- Detect stimuli against high-"noise"-level background, such as blips on cathode-ray-tube (CRT) displays with poor reception.
- Recognize patterns of complex stimuli that may vary from situation to situation, such as objects in aerial photographs and speech sounds.
- Sense unusual and unexpected events in the environment.
- Store (remember) large amounts of information over long periods of time (better for remembering principles and strategies than masses of detailed information).
- Retrieve pertinent information from storage (recall), frequently retrieving many related items of information; but reliability of recall is low.
- Draw upon varied experience in making decisions: adapt decisions to situational requirements; act in emergencies. (Humans do not require previous "programming" for all situations.)
- Select alternative modes of operation, if certain modes fail.
- Reason inductively, generalizing from observations.
- Apply principles to solutions of varied problems.
- Make subjective estimates and evaluations.
- Develop entirely new solutions.
- Concentrate on most important activities when overload conditions require it.
- Adapt physical response (within reason) to variations in operational requirements.

MACHINES GENERALLY ARE *BETTER* IN THEIR ABILITIES TO:

- Sense stimuli that are outside the normal range of human sensitivity, such as X-rays, radar wavelengths, and ultrasonic vibrations.
- Apply deductive reasoning, such as recognizing stimuli as belonging to a general class (but the characteristics of the class need to be specified).
- Monitor for prespecified events, especially when infrequent (but machines cannot improvise in case of unanticipated types of events).
- Store coded information quickly and in substantial quantity (for example, large sets of numerical values can be stored very quickly).
- Retrieve coded information quickly and accurately when specifically requested (although specific instructions need to be provided on the type of information that is to be recalled).
- Process quantitative information following specified programs.
- Make rapid and consistent responses to input signals.
- Perform repetitive activities reliably.
- Exert considerable physical force in a highly controlled manner.
- Maintain performance over extended periods of time. (Machines typically do not "fatigue" as rapidly as humans.)
- Count or measure physical quantities.
- Perform several programmed activities simultaneously.
- Maintain efficient operations under conditions of heavy load. (Humans have relatively limited channel capacity.)
- Maintain efficient operations under distractions.

Source: Ernest J. McCormick, Human Factors Engineering *(New York: McGraw-Hill, 1970), pp. 20–21.*

dishwasher can be left unattended while the person is free to go about other business. The objective of using automatic dishwashers and other automatic machines is to reduce the amount of labor required so that a person can perform tasks more suited to humans while the machine performs routine work that can be programmed.

No complicated analysis is needed when only one dishwasher is to be operated. It is obvious that the family members can perform more productive work while the dishwasher takes care of the necessary but routine task of washing dishes. But if we are analyzing a factory, which may have hundreds of machines of various types, some thought is required to determine how many machines of which type can best be operated by each worker.

Multiple-Activity Chart

A company may determine the best number of machines for a person to tend by use of a *multiple-activity chart*, sometimes called a man-machine chart. This chart is used to record the activities of a worker in one column and those of a machine (or machines) in another. The same type of chart may be used to record the activities of a crew or team of people, with the activities of each person shown in a separate column.

An example of a multiple-activity chart is shown in Figure 14.2. The example used is an office where a large stack of identical letters are prepared on an automatic typewriter. The letters must be given individual addresses and salutations on a standard typewriter while the automatic typewriter completes the content of the letter, which is always the same. One typist operates the two machines simultaneously.

The multiple-activity chart has two purposes. First, it serves to describe a work method that is under consideration so that its feasibility may be evaluated. Second, it provides a basis for analysis so that improvements may be suggested and compared to see which is the most desirable.

SPECIALIZATION

Along with the widespread use of machines, there has been an increase in the applications of more sophisticated and complicated technology. The technical efficiency of the *division of labor (specialization)* has stimulated the trend. In addition, the level of technology has risen until it is almost impossible for one person to understand the myriad technical processes involved in many operations. Specialization has become a normal part of most enterprises, as indicated by the fact that more than 20,000 occupations are listed in the *Dictionary of Occupational Titles,* published by the U.S. Department of Labor.

Specialization has made it increasingly necessary for managers to be effective coordinators. They must coordinate the work of large teams of people, each of whom performs only a small portion of a job. Specialization has not only posed additional challenges for management, it has also caused some prob-

FIGURE 14.2

Multiple-Activity Chart

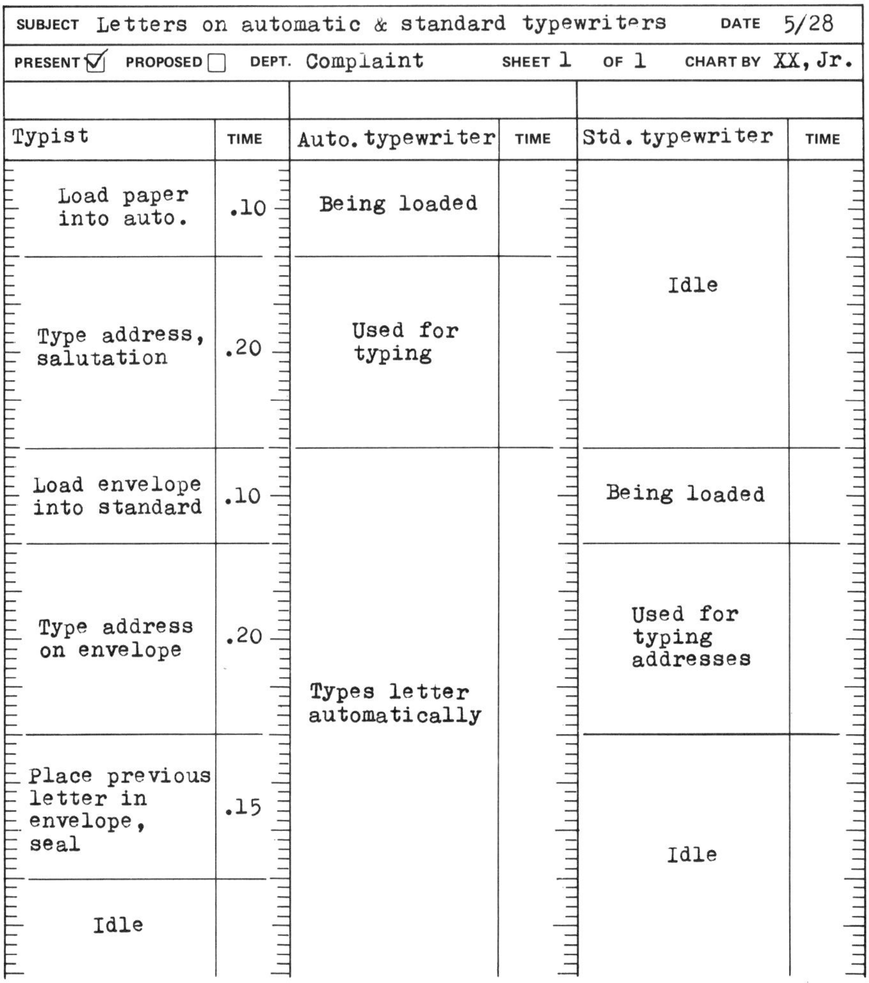

SUBJECT Letters on automatic & standard typewriters				DATE 5/28	
PRESENT ☑ PROPOSED ☐ DEPT. Complaint			SHEET 1 OF 1	CHART BY XX, Jr.	
Typist	TIME	Auto. typewriter	TIME	Std. typewriter	TIME
Load paper into auto.	.10	Being loaded		Idle	
Type address, salutation	.20	Used for typing			
Load envelope into standard	.10			Being loaded	
Type address on envelope	.20	Types letter automatically		Used for typing addresses	
Place previous letter in envelope, seal	.15			Idle	
Idle					

lem in the extent to which some people find satisfaction in their work. Specialization, like many other aspects of life, is a mixed blessing. Table 14.2 summarizes some of the beneficial and adverse consequences of extreme job specialization. Managers must take both the technical and behavioral aspects of specialization into account when they design jobs.

An interesting dilemma arises when the worker already possesses expensively acquired skills of a general nature. In a large hospital radiology department, for example, all of the staff radiographers (X-ray technicians) enter the job with general radiographic skills learned in a two-year training program, but not all of the jobs in the department involve general radiography. There are

Table 14.2
POSSIBLE ADVANTAGES AND DISADVANTAGES OF JOB SPECIALIZATION

ADVANTAGES

Qualified workers are easier to find because fewer skills are required.
Worker training time is shorter.
Production time is shorter due to the "learning curve effect."
Wage rates are generally lower because skill level is lower.
Production instructions and production control are simpler because worker
  assignments are consistent.
Scheduling completion times and labor requirements is more predictable because the
  worker has performed the work before.
A higher degree of mechanization or automation is possible.

DISADVANTAGES

Flexibility is reduced; it is difficult to shift workload to available workers if they do not
  have a variety of skills.
Alternatively, workers may be overqualified for jobs and may lack self-esteem for
  accomplishing them.
Workers may feel less sense of accomplishment because the job makes a small
  contribution to the product or service.
Workers may experience boredom because they perform the same operation
  repeatedly.
Workers may manifest feelings of dissatisfaction through high absenteeism, high
  turnover rates, grievances, demands for higher wages, strikes, sabotage, etc.

other, more specialized areas where complicated examinations of the circulatory and nervous systems are performed. Radiographer error in these procedures may be life-threatening to the patient. In many hospitals, the most expert radiographers are assigned solely to these special procedures. An unfortunate consequence is the deterioration of the generalist skills the radiographer previously possessed, so that the specialist may require a period of retraining before being reassigned to the routine procedures. In other hospitals, all radiographers rotate so as to perform the special procedures regularly, resulting in an increased chance of error in highly special procedures, but maintaining overall skill levels and giving the department much greater flexibility for such contingencies as vacations and sick leave.

THEORIES OF JOB SATISFACTION AND MOTIVATION

Maslow's Needs Hierarchy

Several theories of job satisfaction and motivation have been developed, but none has been proven by rigorous controlled experiments to be a complete explanation of job motivation in all circumstances. Some of them, however, provide useful insight into motivation, and ideas from these theories are being successfully applied in some companies (see box). As far back as 1954, Abraham

OPERATIONS MANAGEMENT IN ACTION

Companies Widen Worker Role in Decisions: Management Turns to Sharing Decisions with Workers for Benefit of Both

At the General Motors Corporation's battery plant in Fitzgerald, Ga., self-managing work teams make many decisions once reserved for management. Practices that have historically represented distinctions between blue-collar and white-collar workers have in part been eliminated, including time clocks, reserved parking and private dining rooms.

This was not the way things had been done at the company, nor the way things are done at all of the company's plants today. But new management methods have become exceedingly important at General Motors.

Today, numerous General Motors plants have some form of "quality of work life" program, and experts who have compared the plants that have the most intensive programs with other automotive plants have found the ones with the worker programs achieving lower absenteeism and labor costs, better manufacturing quality and greater customer satisfaction.

As the General Motors plant shows, substantial success is being achieved in American industry as companies adopt new management science practices that stress a lessening of authoritarianism and hierarchy.

The work reform movement, as it is called, stressing participative management, is not widespread. Experts like Jerome M. Rosow, president of Work in America Institute Inc., a private research institute, said many programs were established for publicity value or because executives wanted to make workers believe they were being consulted, although no real decision-sharing with workers took place.

But where efforts are genuine, according to company and union officials, as well as academicians who specialize in the programs, workers find themselves consulted about how work should be performed. They see themselves, in turn, as participants in company affairs and are more committed to their work.

Managers say they find that company decisions are often better made when the workers, who have the best understanding of how the work should be done, make decisions. In many cases, the experts say, costs have been cut and jobs saved.

"Genuine employee participation is turning Taylorism upside down. The effect is to put the head of the employee back on the body," said John Simmons, professor of labor-management relations at the University of Massachusetts at Amherst. He was referring to the authoritarian management style named for Frederick Winslow Taylor, a pioneer in scientific management.

In a few instances workers are participating in highly important company decisions: how work should be organized, work hours, quality standards and hiring of subcontractors. Employers find substantial reductions in absenteeism, tardiness, grievances and strikes. The quality of the product is superior and pilferage is reduced.

American management philosophy has undergone numerous developments. Through much of the 19th century employers believed in complete authoritarian control. Early in this century Mr. Taylor began devising his system of scientific management, which held that workers were "stupid and phlegmatic" but that production could be improved if the work was scientifically organized and if the workers were given enough instruction and pay.

Human Relations Stressed

Beginning in the 1920's the "human relations school of management" began to develop, holding that production could be improved if managers simply paid greater attention to workers and improved their workplace conditions. The rise of the industrial movement in the 1930's led to the workers' being guaranteed various contractual rights.

Over the last decade or so, the present management science movement has emerged, holding that workers and managers should work together, with workers allowed to function autonomously in many cases and make numerous decisions that were once the sole province of managers.

A New York Stock Exchange survey found

that 14 percent of American companies with more than 100 employees had reform programs. A Government study found that 44 percent of companies with more than 500 workers had groups in which workers and supervisors discussed plant operations.

But Mr. Simmons, co-author of "Working Together," a new book on workplace reform, estimates that 15 percent of the workers participate in the programs at companies that have such groups, known as quality circles.

'Work Humanization' Programs

Only a small percentage of American workers are involved in meaningful work reform projects, he says, adding that few workers participate in their companies' most important decisions, such as product choice, plant location and investment.

Most programs, says Robert Schrank, a private work consultant, are "work humanization rather than work democratization."

Some labor advocates say most workers' gains have been won through aggressiveness and that the natural relationship between labor and management is adversarial. Work reform represents "mostly a surface effort which frequently barely masks a corporate effort to dump collective bargaining obligations," said Howard D. Samuel, president of the Industrial Union Department of the American Federation of Labor and Congress of Industrial Organizations.

Still, authorities said, work reform, known by such names as job redesign, work humanization, employee participation, workplace democracy and quality of work life, is viewed by many as necessary now that the nation is engaged in vigorous international competition and is undergoing profound economic change. James J. O'Toole, professor of management and organization at the University of Southern California's School of Business Administration, calls work reform "the new management."

Innovators in Work Reform

"This innovation is the key to successful competitive operations," says Shoshana Zuboff, assistant professor of organizational behavior at the Harvard Business School.

Companies that use modern developments in management science begin with what Professor O'Toole calls the "old list of small companies," generally regarded as innovators in work reform. They include Lincoln Electric, a manufacturer of arc welding equipment in Euclid, Ohio; Donnelly Mirrors, a mirror manufacturer in Holland, Mich., and Harmon International Industries in Bolivar, Tenn.

Other companies, including some of the nation's largest, have now instituted work reform programs. Among them, besides General Motors, are American Telephone and Telegraph, Citibank, Cummins Engine, Dana, Ford, General Foods, Herman Miller, Hewlett-Packard, Honeywell, the International Business Machines Corporation, Jones & Laughlin, Martin Marietta, Motorola, National Intergroup, People Express, Polaroid, Procter & Gamble, Texas Instruments, Westinghouse and Xerox.

Generally, however, the programs at these companies cover relatively small portions of the work force.

At the General Motors plant in Fitzgerald, worker-management teams select their leaders and help determine their own budgets, schedules, proficiency and maintenance standards. In part, the teams, which get together whenever the need arises, mete out their own discipline, although when that fails conventional discipline mechanisms are used.

The company says it is extremely pleased with the project, and experts like Mr. Rosow say it could be emulated by plants across the country.

"Where these efforts are happening, they are happening in an incredibly serious way," Miss Zuboff said. "It's a religion, a way of life."

There have been many efforts to alter work patterns in America: the paternalistic programs, often colored by strict authoritarianism, of such entrepreneurs as Henry Ford or George M. Pullman; the "scientific management," still a part of American management, of Frederick Winslow Taylor; the formation early in this century by Samuel Gompers, the labor leader, and Mark Hanna, the industrialist, of the National Civic Federation to foster "right relations between employers and workers."

Democracy in the Workplace

After World War II, another approach began to emerge: the philosophy that stressed giving attention and respect to workers. Some exponents of this philosophy said jobs could be enriched if managers were inventive and shared authority. Others went further, calling for democracy in the workplace.

In the 1960's and 1970's, two other developments occurred. In Europe, a movement evolved under which workers, unions, managers and the government began to share some power. But Mr. Rosow said of this co-determination movement, "People in labor and management in this country were frightened."

At the same time, when the Japanese vigorously entered American markets, many academicians began touting Japanese management methods, which stressed the cooperation of workers and managers and strict emphasis on quality. It was the Japanese model that began to be used in America.

Today genuine work reform begins with shop floor participation as it did a decade ago, Mr. O'Toole said, but is now extends to a reduction of authoritarianism, an increase in product quality and job security, a community spirit that includes where to locate plants and perhaps subsidies to workers and communities when plants close. "We're talking about changing the entire culture of the corporation," he added.

William F. Whyte, professor emeritus of industrial relations at Cornell University, said both labor and management must be willing to alter zealously guarded rights. "If you don't touch the labor contract, don't touch management prerogatives, you don't go far," he said.

Yet there have been numerous failures or experiments that never achieved the success attributed to them. "Most managers have the rhetoric of worker participation," Professor O'Toole said. "In almost every case where there is a tradeoff or a tough decision to make, most managers revert to the direct, authoritarian mode."

Pressure on work reform programs will come with economic recovery, Mr. O'Toole said, adding that he feared managers would no longer seek cooperation with workers and unions.

"Progressive management is hard work," he said. "When times are bad, managers hustle and do extra things. When profits come and people get comfortable, it's easy to let things slip. I'm already seeing some backsliding."

Maslow postulated a general hierarchy of needs that appear to guide human activity (Figure 14.3). These needs are presumed to have a specific order in which they dominate the need structure of an individual. Once the lowest level of needs is satisfied, the next level will become predominant, and so on. At the lowest level are such physiological needs as hunger, thirst, sex, and sleep. At the second level is the need for security and freedom from threat. At the third level is the need to belong—to feel accepted and loved. At the fourth level is the need for esteem—for achievement and self-respect. The highest level of needs is that of self-actualization—the utilization and development of one's unique talents, abilities, and creativity.

Today's work force is better educated than that of earlier generations, and a greater percentage of workers have job expectations at the higher levels in the need hierarchy. Minimum wage, social security, and unemployment insurance legislation have helped reduce the importance of the lower levels as the motivating needs of the worker. A large percentage of today's work force views work as more than a means of economic survival, and many theories of motivation recognize these higher level needs.

FIGURE 14.3

Maslow's Hierarchy of Needs

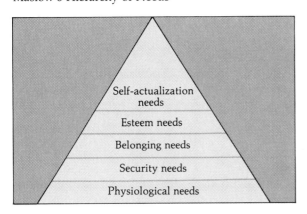

In 1973 and 1974 the National Opinion Research Center conducted two nationwide surveys to determine worker preferences in job characteristics.[4] Door-to-door interviews were conducted with white males over age eighteen, yielding the results in Table 14.3. The results of this survey certainly support theories that workers seek more than just the financial rewards of their jobs. The high percentages of respondents who preferred advancement and meaningful work suggest that many of the needs of the work force (both white-collar and blue-collar) are at the higher levels in Maslow's hierarchy.

Herzberg's Two-Factor Theory

In 1966, Frederick Herzberg proposed that motivation is determined primarily by *motivator factors* that are intrinsic to the work being done. Recognition,

Table 14.3
PERCENTAGE OF WORKER PREFERENCES AMONG FIVE JOB CHARACTERISTICS

Job Characteristic	PERCENTAGE PREFERRING CHARACTERISTIC		
	White Collar (N = 355)	Blue Collar (N = 326)	Average (N = 681)
High income	12.96%	19.63%	15.75%
No danger of being fired	3.66	11.96	7.61
Short work hours	3.94	7.06	5.34
Chances for advancement	17.46	19.02	18.42
Important and meaningful work	61.98	42.33	52.88

[4]J. R. Hackman, "Is Job Enrichment Just a Fad?" *Harvard Business Review,* September–October 1975, pp. 129–138.

achievement, responsibility, advancement, and personal growth are some of the factors that are believed to be effective in motivating employees to superior effort. If these factors are absent, the employee may be satisfied to come to work but will not be motivated to excel. Dissatisfaction, Herzberg theorized, is caused by a deficiency in a separate group of factors that he called *hygiene factors*, or satisfiers. The hygiene factors are extrinsic to the job; that is, they relate to the environment in which the job is performed. Company policies, working conditions, supervision, salary, and relationships with peers are some of the more important hygiene factors. Herzberg's theory suggests that a worker will be motivated only to the extent that the motivator factors are designed into the work itself.

Herzberg's theory is important in that it suggests that motivation is intrinsic to good job design. Several researchers have criticized the methodology by which the theory was developed, but it still has been used as a basis for several successful job redesign programs. This theory is a basis for job enrichment, which will be discussed later.

Expectancy Theory

"Expectancy theory represents one of the most comprehensive motivational models developed to date. For this reason it is valuable for explaining why variations in task characteristics influence an employee's motivation to perform."[5] *Expectancy theory* posits that motivation depends on the valence (subjective utility) to workers of the *extrinsic* and *intrinsic rewards* for their efforts, and workers' estimates of the probability that their efforts will lead to the reward. It is theorized that people will be motivated to perform a job well if it is structured with enough variety and challenge so that they can reward themselves when they perform well.[6]

Sociotechnical Systems Theory

The term *sociotechnical systems* recognizes the interrelationships between the technical system required to perform tasks and the social organization in which the tasks are performed. Any production system is both a social system and a technical system. The system must provide some technology to convert its inputs into the desired outputs. But the system also is a group of humans who interract in some way to carry out its function. Operations managers must be interested in both aspects of the sociotechnical system, since they are responsible for coordinating the efforts of groups of people to perform technical tasks.

Designers of an organization should take into account four requirements of a social system. If these social requirements are not met by the formal system, they will be met in other ways. They may, however, be met in a way that will

---

[5]Steers and Mowday, "Motivational Properties of Tasks," p. 653.
[6]William E. Gallagher, Jr., and Hillel J. Einhorn, "Motivation Theory and Job Design," *Journal of Business*, July 1976, p. 365.

Table 14.4
DESIRABLE TASK CHARACTERISTICS POSITED IN FIVE MOTIVATION THEORIES

Sociotechnical Theory (Trist, Davis)	Two-Factor Theory (Herzberg)	Need Hierarchy (Maslow)	Requisite Task Attributes Model (Turner, Lawrence)	Job Characteristics Model (Hackman, Oldham)
Reasonably demanding content	Responsibility	Esteem	Knowledge and skill	Skill variety
Variety	Growth	Actualization	Variety	Feedback
Learning opportunity	Recognition	Belonging	Responsibility	Autonomy
Discretion in decision making	Advancement	Security	Autonomy	Task identity
Relationship to social life	Achievement		Required and optional interactions	Task significance
Feeling that job leads to some desirable future	The work itself			

Source: Compiled from Richard M. Steers and Richard T. Mowday, "The Motivational Properties of Tasks," Academy of Management Review, October 1977, pp. 645–658.

thwart rather than facilitate the planned technical functions. The requirements are that the organization (1) attain its goals; (2) adapt to its environment; (3) provide for continuing the essential roles through recruitment and training; and (4) integrate the activities of the people in the organization—which includes resolving organizational, task, or interpersonal conflict.

Some principles have been recommended to help support the social requirements of organizations. The job characteristics listed in the first column of Table 14.4 are sometimes cited. Some additional recommendations are that the job design should carry only minimum specifications about how the job will be done, that variances should be controlled as close as possible to their origin, and that feedback information should be provided to the place where the action occurs. The system of social support should reinforce the behavior the organization desires. Selection, training, conflict resolution, work measurement, performance assessment, timekeeping, payment, promotion, leave allocation, separation policies and methods, as well as management philosophy and action should all be consistent with the behavior desired by the oranization.[7]

Several theories of motivation have been proposed. So far these theories are supported by a meager amount of empirical data; more research is needed to develop a complete understanding of the mechanism through which task characteristics affect motivation.

Desirable Job Characteristics

It is interesting to note the similarity of job characteristics recommended by various theories, even though the theories themselves may differ greatly. Table

[7]Albert B. Cherns, "The Principles of Sociotechnical Design," *Human Relations,* Vol. 29 no. 8, 1976, pp. 783–792.

14.4 summarizes some of the desirable task characteristics posited in five theories. Some methods of incorporating desirable characteristics are outlined below.

Quality Circles   One means of providing workers an opportunity for more job satisfaction through participation has received considerable attention recently. It is the use of *quality circles*. A quality circle, as was explained in Chapter 11, is a small, voluntary group of employees who meet on a regular basis to identify, investigate, and recommend solutions to work problems. An effective quality circle program causes workers to become intimately involved in designing some aspects of their own work. The types of problems may include quality, safety, productivity, or any others the group feels are important. Typically, a circle will involve five to ten workers, and the group members will be paid for the time that they meet. But the cost to the company is usually recouped through improvements devised by the group. In fact, savings as high as five or six times the cost of the program have been reported.

Today's more highly educated workers often seek more from their jobs than their predecessors did in terms of intrinsic satisfaction and participation. Their higher level of education and training also makes them able to perform the broader activities involved in participatory approaches such as quality circles. Through these circles the company can tap the education, experience, and creative talents of the workers, who are most familiar with the problems of their jobs. The use of circles puts managers and workers on the same team and improves communication. Circles can cause workers to have more understanding of managers' problems and managers to recognize more of the workers' capabilities. This means circles have the potential to aid in the development of mutual respect and trust. Circles also can improve the workers' self-images and build feelings of being recognized because their opinions are sought. These small-group improvement activities also make the workers more quality conscious and more alert to productivity improvement opportunities. Circles are being used extensively in Japan and are becoming more common in the United States. These programs are also being used in several other countries such as Taiwan, Singapore, Brazil, Mexico, South Korea, and the Netherlands.

All of the behavior-oriented theories propose that workers be given variety and/or discretion of decision making to overcome the boredom and monotony associated with highly specialized jobs. Several methods have been used to increase job variety; we will discuss three of the more common methods.

Job Rotation   *Job rotation* involves having a worker periodically exchange jobs with another worker to break the monotony of performing the same job day in and day out. Some investigators view with skepticism the notion that performing two highly specialized, boring jobs is really better than performing one. But sometimes a job rotation program may add job challenge and improve worker esteem by helping workers develop several new skills.

Job Enlargement   *Job enlargement* is an attempt to counteract oversimplification and permit the worker to perform a whole unit of work so that he or she can recognize a meaningful contribution to the production process. Enlargement usually means a horizontal expansion of a job—the addition of other related tasks—without the addition of prework planning steps or postwork inspection.

Job Enrichment *Job enrichment*, like job enlargement, increases the number and diversity of tasks a worker performs. In addition, it involves vertical loading; that is, adding responsibility for planning and/or inspection. Job enrichment therefore embraces the philosophy of participative management along with many aspects of job enlargement. Additional variety and responsibility are intended to make the job afford such satisfactions as achievement, recognition, and growth. The underlying assumption or hope is that increased satisfaction will be an important source of motivation and will lead to improved performance. Other objectives are to reduce labor turnover, absenteeism, and tardiness.[8]

JOB-ENRICHMENT PROGRAMS

Many firms have used job enrichment successfully—IBM, Texas Instruments, Travelers Insurance, AT&T, Zeiss, Volvo, Saab, and several Japanese firms among them. Not all attempts have been successful, however. Successful applications may involve less than 20 percent of a company's work force. Some unskilled workers prefer specialized tasks because they fear they lack sufficient ability to handle enlarged or enriched jobs.[9] If they wanted diversity and challenge, they probably would not have remained unskilled in the first place. One study concluded that, rather than being alienated from the work environment, urban blue-collar workers were alienated from such middle-class values as seeing work as an end in itself and striving for a responsible position.[10]

Managers should realize that job enrichment is not some magical elixir that will cure all of their motivational and employee problems. Many factors affect the feasibility of a job-enrichment program for an organization. Among these factors are:

The job itself and the technology involved.

Worker attitudes, interests, and skills.

Union attitudes.

Management's willingness to give up some supervisory tasks.

In determining the feasibility or likelihood of success of a job-enrichment program, a company should review the following conditions within the organization:

1. It is technically possible to change the job? Is the work structure flexible enough to permit changes?

[8]William J. Paul, Keith B. Robertson, and Frederick Herzberg, "Job Enrichment Pays Off," *Harvard Business Review*, March–April 1969, pp. 88–89.
[9]William E. Reif and Fred Luthans, "Does Job Enrichment Really Pay Off?" *California Management Review*, Fall 1972, p. 32.
[10]Charles L. Hulin and Milton R. Blood, "Job Enlargement, Individual Differences, and Worker Responses," *Psychological Bulletin* 69, no. 1 (1968): 50.

2. Will employees respond favorably? Are there reasons to believe that employees will perceive an enriched job situation as an improvement over the existing one?
3. What kind of impact might job enrichment have on the work organization? What kind of measurable results might be expected from job enrichment?
4. Are any general organizational problems, such as personnel policies, authoritarian supervision, perceived inadequate compensation, or inadequate training resources, serious enough to hinder a job-enrichment effort?[11]

Questions such as these must be answered to determine if an organization is suitable for a job-enrichment program.

Organizational change of any kind is a complex and difficult task. Those who undertake job enrichment must do more than just understand its principles. They must prepare all persons involved for the change and must "sell" the idea of change beforehand. They must also be well versed in diagnosing potential problems and capable of quickly correcting them as changes are made. Unsuccessful programs may have encountered pitfalls that were not overcome, or perhaps the jobs were not suitable for enlargement in the first place.

Generally, a job-enrichment program is most useful and constructive when the following conditions exist:

1. Workers are bored with their present jobs.
2. Error rates are high, quality is low.
3. Workers are ignorant of the total production process.
4. Customer complaints are high.
5. Absenteeism and turnover rates are above normal.[12]

Even when a job appears suitable for enrichment, the way it might be enriched is not always obvious. Although the research on job design has not converged on universally accepted formulas, some general guidelines have been offered. One article provided an appendix with forty requirements that are representative of the concerns and objectives of job design.[13]

WORK EFFICIENCY AND MOTION ECONOMY

Jobs, whether specialized, enlarged, or enriched, must remain economically efficient. Inefficient companies may survive if they have little or no competition, but most companies must achieve at least a moderate degree of efficiency. Most employees do not enjoy making wasted motions, particularly if they result in

[11]Lyle Yorks, "Determining Job Enrichment Feasibility," *Personnel,* November–December 1974, pp. 18–25.

[12]Louise A. McNulty, "Job Enrichment: How to Make It Work," *Supervisory Management,* September 18, 1973, p. 11.

[13]James S. Dyer and Marvin Hoffenberg, "Evaluating the Quality of Working Life: Some Reflections on Production and Cost and a Method of Problem Definition," in *The Quality of Working Life,* Louis E. Davis and Albert B. Cherns, eds. (New York: Free Press, 1975), vol. 1, pp. 134–149.

unnecessary fatigue. The interest of scientific management in the technical side of a job is still valid today, just as it was when motion study was first developed.

Motion study and micromotion study usually are applied through analysis of the work performed at a fixed location, as opposed to the study of the flow or movement of work, which will be discussed later. The movements of each of the worker's hands are noted and recorded on a chart called an operations chart, or left-and-right-hand chart. The hand motions may be listed with a different degree of detail, but frequently the elements of reach, grasp, transport, position, and assemble are used to describe them. The chart may include a sketch describing the workplace, and distances the hands move may be indicated on the chart to assist in describing and analyzing the work.

The objectives of *motion study* are to examine the motions performed by a worker and to find improvements that will lead to a more productive (i.e., less time-consuming) and/or less fatiguing pattern. A systematic attempt is made to eliminate all unnecessary elements and to arrange the remaining elements in the best sequence. Each step should be examined to see if it can be eliminated, simplified, combined with some other step, replaced by a simpler motion, or rearranged so that an improved motion pattern is achieved.

Figure 14.4 shows an example of a left-and-right-hand chart, or operations chart, for an improved method of assembling a lock washer, a flat steel washer, and a flat rubber washer on a bolt. In the method used previously, the left hand held the bolt while the right hand slipped each washer on it. Use of a hand as a holding device is poor motion economy when a mechanical device can be used. (See principle 12 in Table 14.5.) The hole in the rubber washer is slightly smaller than the diameter of the bolt so that it will not slip off unless intentional force is exerted. In the improved method, the worker produces two assemblies simultaneously by making a stack of washers with each hand, then forcing a bolt through each. This new method utilizes principles of work efficiency 2, 3, and 4 by having both hands work simultaneously and by using fixed locations.

The fifteen principles of work efficiency listed in Table 14.5 are useful criteria to guide the development of efficient motion patterns. These rules or principles may be profitably applied to shops, services, and office work alike. Although not all are applicable to every operation, they do form a basis for improving efficiency and reducing fatigue in manual work.

Micromotion Study

Micromotion study is a much more detailed form of motion analysis that sometimes is used to examine high-volume jobs. Micromotion analysis uses a "simo chart," which is like a left-and-right-hand chart except that the activities are described in terms of seventeen basic elements of motion called *therbligs*. Therbligs are very small parts of motions that can be sequenced to form any task, just as various combinations and sequences of only twenty-six letters can be used to form any word in the English language. *Therblig* is derived from Gilbreth spelled backward; the name recognizes the contributions of Frank and Lillian Gilbreth to the early development of time and motion study.

FIGURE 14.4

Left-and-Right-Hand Chart of Bolt and Washer Assembly—Improved

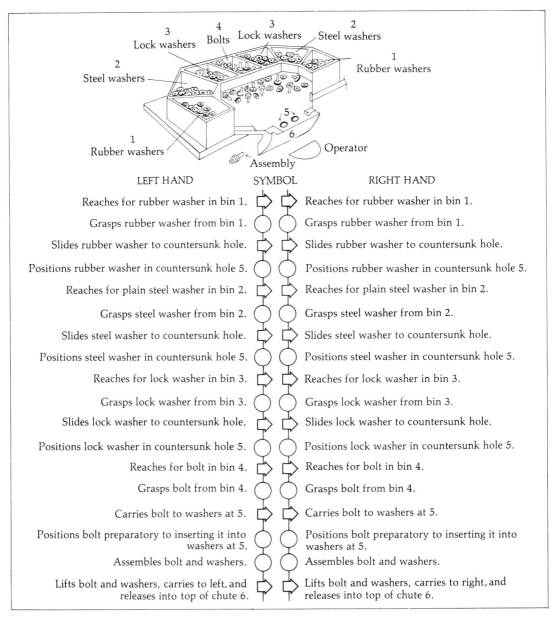

LEFT HAND	SYMBOL	RIGHT HAND
Reaches for rubber washer in bin 1.		Reaches for rubber washer in bin 1.
Grasps rubber washer from bin 1.		Grasps rubber washer from bin 1.
Slides rubber washer to countersunk hole.		Slides rubber washer to countersunk hole.
Positions rubber washer in countersunk hole 5.		Positions rubber washer in countersunk hole 5.
Reaches for plain steel washer in bin 2.		Reaches for plain steel washer in bin 2.
Grasps steel washer from bin 2.		Grasps steel washer from bin 2.
Slides steel washer to countersunk hole.		Slides steel washer to countersunk hole.
Positions steel washer in countersunk hole 5.		Positions steel washer in countersunk hole 5.
Reaches for lock washer in bin 3.		Reaches for lock washer in bin 3.
Grasps lock washer from bin 3.		Grasps lock washer from bin 3.
Slides lock washer to countersunk hole.		Slides lock washer to countersunk hole.
Positions lock washer in countersunk hole 5.		Positions lock washer in countersunk hole 5.
Reaches for bolt in bin 4.		Reaches for bolt in bin 4.
Grasps bolt from bin 4.		Grasps bolt from bin 4.
Carries bolt to washers at 5.		Carries bolt to washers at 5.
Positions bolt preparatory to inserting it into washers at 5.		Positions bolt preparatory to inserting it into washers at 5.
Assembles bolt and washers.		Assembles bolt and washers.
Lifts bolt and washers, carries to left, and releases into top of chute 6.		Lifts bolt and washers, carries to right, and releases into top of chute 6.

Source: After Ralph M. Barnes, *Motion and Time Study: Design and Measurement of Work*, 6th ed. (New York: John Wiley, 1968), p. 114. Copyright 1937, 1940, 1949 by Ralph M. Barnes. Copyright © 1958, 1963, 1968 by John Wiley & Sons, Inc. Reprinted by permission of John Wiley & Sons, Inc.

Table 14.5
PRINCIPLES OF WORK EFFICIENCY

USE THE HUMAN BODY THE WAY IT WORKS BEST

1. Work should be performed by machines if machines are more suitable or if the work is unsafe for humans.
2. Tools and materials should be placed in fixed locations in a sequence that permits a natural rhythm of motions and close together so movements are short and eye fixations are minimized.
3. Hands should begin and complete motions together when possible, and both should not be idle except during rest times.
4. Simultaneous arm motions should be in opposite directions with symmetrical patterns.
5. Smooth continuous arcs of motion are preferable to straight-line movements involving abrupt changes in direction.
6. Motions should be confined to the lowest classification to involve as few muscle groups as are required to perform the job satisfactorily. The ascending order of motion classifications is
   a. Fingers only.
   b. Fingers and wrists.
   c. Fingers, wrists and lower arms.
   d. Fingers, wrists, lower and upper arms.
   e. Hands, arms and body.

ARRANGE THE WORKPLACE TO IMPROVE PERFORMANCE

7. Worker safety is a primary consideration in workplace design.
8. Chairs, tables, ventilation, illumination, and all features of the workplace should be suitable for the task and the worker.
9. Gravity feed chutes or other automatic conveyance devices should be used where appropriate to deliver objects close to the point of use.
10. Tools, materials, and controls on equipment should have set locations, close to the point of use and arranged to permit the best sequence and paths of motion.

USE EQUIPMENT TO IMPROVE HUMAN PRODUCTIVITY

11. Computers, automation, and mechanical assistance should be employed where they can improve productivity.
12. Vises or clamps can be used to hold work precisely and relieve the hands for performing more valuable work than simply holding.
13. Mechanical guides might be used to reduce the time, effort, and attention required to position work.
14. Automatic controls and foot-actuated devices should relieve the hands for higher-value work or to reduce fatigue, where practicable.
15. Mechanical systems should be designed to require minimal operator motion and only reasonable amounts of force to use them.

Source: Based on ideas from Frank C. Barnes, "Principles of Motion Economy: Revisited, Reviewed, and Restored," Proceedings of the Southern Management Association, 1984; and Ralph M. Barnes, Motion and Time Study, 7th ed. (New York: Wiley, 1980).

Seventeen therbligs, or minute basic elements of motion, are listed below.

1. Search—locate an object visually or by groping for it.
2. Select—choose one part from among several.
3. Grasp—close the fingers around a part.
4. Transport empty—motion of the empty hand.
5. Transport loaded—motion of the hand while carrying an object.
6. Hold—manual support or control of an object.
7. Release—relinquish manual control.
8. Position—locate an object in specific position.
9. Preposition—orient object correctly.
10. Inspect—compare object with standard.
11. Assemble—unite mating parts.
12. Disassemble—disunite mating parts.
13. Use—manually implement production procedure.
14. Unavoidable delay—idle beyond operator's control.
15. Avoidable delay—idle for which operator is responsible.
16. Plan—mentally determine next action.
17. Rest to overcome fatigue—a periodic delay due to operator fatigue.

The first fifteen micromotions are so short that they might go undetected in normal observation. For this reason, micromotion study is performed by use of slow-motion photography. A checklist that suggests questions that may lead to improvements in the motion pattern is shown in Table 14.6.

Table 14.6
A CHECKLIST FOR REVIEWING THERBLIGS

WITH REGARD TO SELECT:

1. Is the layout such as to eliminate searching for articles?
2. Can tools and materials be standardized?
3. Are parts and materials properly labeled?
4. Can better arrangements be made to facilitate or eliminate select—such as a bin with a long lip, a tray that prepositions parts, and a transparent container?
5. Are common parts interchangeable?
6. Are parts and materials mixed?
7. Is the lighting satisfactory?
8. Can parts be prepositioned during preceding operation?
9. Can color be used to facilitate selecting parts?

WITH REGARD TO GRASP:

1. Is it possible to grasp more than one object at a time?
2. Can objects be slid instead of carried?
3. Will a lip on front of the bin simplify grasp of small parts?
4. Can tools or parts be prepositioned for easy grasp?
5. Can a special screwdriver, socket wrench, or combination tool be used?
6. Can a vacuum, magnet, rubber fingertip, or other device be used to advantage?
7. Is the article transferred from one hand to the other?
8. Does the design of the jig or fixture permit an easy grasp in removing the part?

WITH REGARD TO TRANSPORT EMPTY AND TRANSPORT LOADED:

1. Can either of these motions be eliminated entirely?
2. Is the distance traveled the best one?
3. Are the proper means used—hand, tweezers, conveyors, etc.?
4. Are the correct members (and muscles) of the body used—fingers, forearm, shoulder, etc.?
5. Can a chute or conveyor be used?
6. Can "transports" be effected more satisfactorily in larger units?
7. Can transport be performed with foot-operated devices?
8. Is transport slowed up because of a delicate position following it?
9. Can transports be eliminated by providing additional small tools and locating them near the point of use?
10. Are parts that are used more frequently located near the point of use?
11. Are proper trays or bins used and is the operation laid out correctly?
12. Are the preceding and following operations properly related to this one?
13. Is it possible to eliminate abrupt changes in direction? Can barriers be eliminated?
14. For the weight of the material moved, is the fastest member of the body used?
15. Are there any body movements that can be eliminated?
16. Can arm movements be made simultaneously, symmetrically, and in opposite directions?
17. Can the object be slid instead of carried?
18. Are the eye movements properly coordinated with hand motions?

WITH REGARD TO HOLD:

1. Can a vise, clamp, clip, vacuum, hook, rack, fixture, or other mechanical device be used?
2. Can an adhesive or friction be used?
3. Can a stop be used to eliminate hold?
4. When hold cannot be eliminated, can armrests be provided?

WITH REGARD TO RELEASE LOAD:

1. Can this motion be eliminated?
2. Can a drop delivery be used?
3. Can the release be made in transit?
4. Is a careful release load necessary? Can this be avoided?
5. Can an ejector (mechanical, air, gravity) be used?
6. Are the material bins of proper design?
7. At the end of the release load, is the hand or the transportation means in the most advantageous position for the next motion?
8. Can a conveyor be used?

WITH REGARD TO POSITION:

1. Is positioning necessary?
2. Can tolerances be increased?
3. Can square edges be eliminated?
4. Can a guide, funnel, bushing, gauge, stop, swinging bracket, locating pin, spring, drift, recess, key, pilot on screw, or chamfer be used?
5. Can armrests be used to steady the hands and reduce the positioning time?
6. Has the object been grasped for easiest positioning?
7. Can a foot-operated collet be used?

WITH REGARD TO PREPOSITION:

1. Can the object be prepositional in transit?
2. Can tools be balanced so as to keep handle in upright position?
3. Can holding device be made to keep tool handle in proper position?
4. Can tools be suspended?
5. Can tools be stored in proper location for work?
6. Can a guide be used?
7. Can design of article be made so that all sides are alike?
8. Can a magazine feed be used?
9. Can a stacking device be used?
10. Can a rotating fixture be used?

WITH REGARD TO INSPECT:

1. Can inspection be eliminated or overlapped with another operation?
2. Can multiple gauges or tests be used?
3. Can a pressure, vibration, hardness, or flash test be used?
4. Can the intensity of illumination be increased or the light sources rearranged to reduce the inspection time?
5. Can a machine inspection be used to replace a visual inspection?
6. Can the operator use spectacles to advantage?

WITH REGARD TO ASSEMBLE, DISASSEMBLE, AND USE:

1. Can a jig or fixture be used?
2. Can an automatic device or machine be used?
3. Can the assembly be made in multiple? Or can the processing be done in multiple?
4. Can a more efficient tool be used?
5. Can stops be used?
6. Can other work be done while machine is making cut?
7. Should a power tool be used?
8. Can a cam or air-operated fixture be used?

Source: Ralph M. Barnes, Motion and Time Study, *7th ed. (New York: John Wiley, 1980), pp. 158, 160, 163, 165, 166, 168, 171, 172. Copyright, 1937, 1940, 1949 by Ralph M. Barnes. Copyright © 1958, 1963, 1968, by John Wiley & Sons, Inc. Reprinted by permission of John Wiley & Sons, Inc.*

Micromotion study is not widely used because the extra expense is not often justified and because filming is likely to distort the observed work and distract other workers. Most workers do not want to have such detailed prescriptions of their work.

Inefficient uses of the hands can be detected by motion study and micromotion study. Analysts look for such things as idle time, long or unnecessary transports, and the use of hands for activities that could be performed by such mechanical devices as jigs and fixtures. Revision of the motions may result in more productive and/or less fatiguing work.

HUMAN FACTORS AND ERGONOMICS

In addition to the psychological effects of work, discussed under specialization, physical effects of work on the worker should be considered in job design. Some of these effects are taken into account in the design of the equipment that workers use. Additional allowances for the physical effects of work are taken into account in work measurement and in the setting of work standards. *Human factors engineering,* or *ergonomics,* endeavors to apply relevant information about human characteristics and behavior to the design of things people use, the methods by which they are used, and the environment in which people work and live.

Human factors engineering is applied in two major areas:

1. The physical devices that people use in performing work.
2. The environment in which work is performed.

Design of Physical Devices

It was stated earlier that a worker is part of a system containing many elements, including the tools and equipment he or she uses. These combinations sometimes are called machine-worker systems because they are interrelated components that form a subsystem in the total collection of factors that affect operations. Since the human part of the machine-worker system cannot be redesigned and reconstructed in an effort to increase its effectiveness, the machine must be adapted to the worker. For a person to be able to operate a piece of equipment, he or she must be able to sense the operating conditions, to reach the controls, and to apply the necessary force to them. The average person is capable of reaching many locations, but the speed of reach and accuracy of adjustment are affected by the location of the thing for which one is reaching; therefore, a determination of the best location requires considerable investigation and understanding of human capability and limitations.

Anthropometric Data   People vary in size, weight, strength, and skill. Considerable *anthropometric data* on the dimensions of various parts of the human body have been collected and serve as a basis for the design of tools and systems. Investigators have tabulated data on the reach, range of motion, speed of response, strength, sitting height, working height, and other variables in the machine-worker relationship. The reach required to operate a piece of equipment should be no greater than the shortest reach of all persons who are expected to operate it.

All controls and information displays should be located for clear access and visibility. Switches should be located so that all of the off positions are in the same direction. Gauges should be arranged so that the indicators point in approximately the same direction when the device is operating normally. Thus the operator can quickly spot deviations from normal. Levers and hand wheels should be of the proper size and located so that sufficient operating force may be applied in the appropriate direction.

The Work Environment

The environment in which people work can affect their comfort, health, and productivity. Some environmental variables to be considered are temperature, noise, and lighting.

Temperature   Humans can perform under a variety of combinations of temperature, humidity, and air movements. The effects of these variables depend on the strenuousness of the work task and individual adaptation to the conditions. A comfortable temperature may range from 65° to 80° F. (26.4° to 38.4° C.), depending on other conditions (humidity and air movement, for example).

Noise   Unwanted sound in the workplace not only may be distracting but may even cause damage to the worker's hearing. The intensity of sound is measured in decibels (db); an increase of ten decibels represents a tenfold increase in sound intensity. Workers may become so accustomed to a low level of noise that it does not impair their ability to perform mental or physical tasks. The Occupational Safety and Health Act of 1970 regulations state that workers should not be exposed to noise above 90 db for more than 9 hours at a time. A lathe or a motorcycle emits a noise intensity of about 90 db. Higher sound intensities are permitted for shorter exposures, but no sound as high as 130 db (a painful intensity) should be experienced. Ear-protection devices should be worn and/or the duration of exposure should be limited when sounds are above 85 to 90 db.

Lighting   Good illumination on work items or on the work surface is necessary for proper work performance without eyestrain. The color content of light and the amount of glare are also important. The recommended illumination for various tasks is shown in Table 14.7.

METHODS ANALYSIS AND IMPROVEMENT

How is the operation being performed now? How can it be performed better? Thomas Edison, Henry Ford, George Westinghouse, and many others asked these questions. They also had the dogged determination to work on the second question until they had an acceptable answer. These men are known today because they succeeded in developing new methods and new products that helped their companies to become successful. To be successful today, companies need new ideas about work methods and products.

Good managers in marketing, finance, and operations must be ever watchful for improvements in operating methods. Good managers want their subordinates to be relentless, trained critics who seek and find improvements when improvement is possible, yet who do not cause strife or resentment as they look for them. Methods improvement involves examination of any aspect of a job and work to redesign it to a more efficient level. The basic aim is to develop a more efficient system for producing goods or providing services, taking into account both the technical and behavioral aspects of the job. Often a company's objective is to achieve a cost saving, but other objectives, such as improved quality, may cause the undertaking of a methods study. A company operating near capacity may try to increase its production without enlarging its facilities or investing in expensive capital equipment.

Table 14.7
**ILLUMINATION STANDARDS RECOMMENDED BY THE
ILLUMINATING ENGINEERING SOCIETY (IES) FOR SEVERAL
SELECTED TYPES OF SITUATIONS AND TASKS**

Situation or Task	Recommended Illumination (in footcandles)
Assembly:	
Rough easy seeing	30
Rough difficult seeing	50
Medium	100
Fine	500
Extra fine	1,000
Machine shops:	
Rough bench and machine work	50
Medium bench and machine work	100
Fine bench and machine work	500
Extra-fine bench and machine work, grinding—fine work	1,000
Storage rooms or warehouses: Inactive	5
Offices:	
Cartography, designing, detailed drafting	200
Accounting, bookkeeping, etc.	150
Regular office work	100
Corridors, elevators, stairways	20
Residences:	
Kitchen, sink area	70
Kitchen, range and work surfaces	50

Source: Ernest J. McCormick, Human Factors Engineering, *3d ed. (New York: McGraw-Hill, 1970), p. 459. Copyright © 1957, 1964, 1970 by McGraw-Hill, Inc.*

Any of the topics discussed earlier with regard to job design can also be applied to methods improvement, which is *job redesign.* Simplification, specialization, mechanization, job enlargement, and motion economy may prove helpful in redesigning jobs so that the overall operation is improved.

Opportunities for improvement may result from any of several circumstances, some of which are:

1. A change in the demanded volume of a product at a particular location.
2. A change in some other product that shares the use of some of the same facilities.
3. Introduction of a new product or service.
4. A change in the product's design.
5. A change in technology, making available some new method or equipment.
6. Consolidation or departmentalization of the organization.
7. Dissatisfaction with some aspect of the operation.

Quality circles may be utilized to achieve improvements in operating methods or products. Suggestion programs are often instituted to generate ideas for possible methods improvements. Evaluation committees composed of managers and/or rank-and-file workers sometimes are established to evaluate suggestions. Posters and other means of publicity are used to solicit suggestions, and often bonuses are awarded for profitable suggestions that are implemented. Of course ideas may occur without a formal suggestion program. Trade magazines or equipment salesmen may suggest ideas that a company would find beneficial. Once targets for improvement have been identified, the study may follow a procedure much like the one below.

Methods-Improvement Procedure

The overall procedure for performing a methods-improvement study may be summarized in the five basic steps listed below:

1. Observe and understand the current method.
2. Document the current method. It is usually helpful to have a detailed description of a method to be studied. Charting methods such as the left-and-right-hand chart or multiple-activity chart, discussed earlier, may be useful. The flow process chart, discussed below, is also helpful.
3. Critically evaluate the current method and any proposed changes in it. This is the most important step in a methods study because it is here that any ideas for improvement will occur. Creativity, ingenuity, and persistence can pay off at this stage. A broad, total-system view is helpful and should include consideration of the layout, training or retraining, required investment, and any other factors that may affect performance and costs.
4. Implement the improvement. Naturally, ideas alone will accomplish little; an improvement must be put into effect before any benefit will be achieved. Someone must specify a plan of action, assign responsibilities, and follow up to see that the new method is used. Any new method that is implemented should show promise of a potential cost savings or an improvement in quality that is at least large enough to pay for its cost.
5. Reevaluate the new method after sufficient time has passed to see that it is working as intended.

Flow Process Chart

A methods-improvement study may focus on a job performed at a fixed location, such as the motions of the worker's hands. A more general overview, however, may reveal a trouble spot where concentrated study appears to be justified, or the possibility of improvement in the overall linkage of individual jobs. *Flow process charts* are useful in documenting the flow of people or materials in some operations. A material flow process chart displays actual or potential movements of material. Each activity that is performed is classified as one of the five types shown below with their symbols.

Operation: ◯ An operation is an intentional change in the physical or chemical characteristics of an object; the receipt or dissemination of information; the making of calculations or plans.

Inspection: ☐ An inspection is the examination of an object or group of objects to verify that they have certain characteristics or to ascertain their quantity.

Transportation: ▷ Transportation is the movement of an object from one location to another; it does not include movements that are part of an operation or inspection.

Delay: D A delay is any occurrence that prevents the immediate performance of the next planned activity.

Storage: ▽ Storage is an intentional delay in which an object is kept and protected against unauthorized removal.

APPLICATION

Use of a Flow Process Chart

The Ace Construction Company had a procedure for paying invoices that sometimes led to excessive delays. Some invoices offered a discount on the amount due if it was paid within ten days. The old procedure involved making copies of the invoice and coding it so that it could be entered into the automatic data processing

FIGURE 14.5

Old Procedure for Reviewing and Paying Invoices

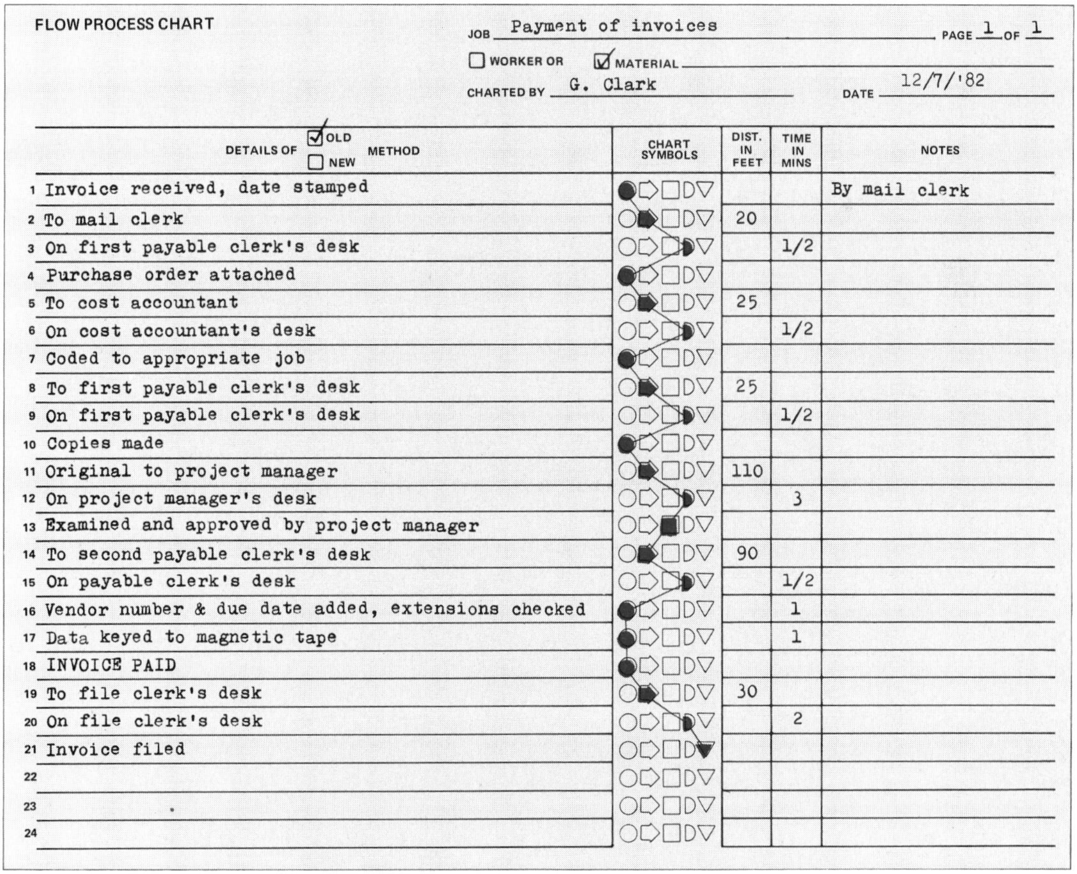

FLOW PROCESS CHART

JOB __Payment of invoices__   PAGE __1__ OF __1__

☐ WORKER OR ☑ MATERIAL _____

CHARTED BY __G. Clark__   DATE __12/7/'82__

DETAILS OF METHOD (☑ OLD ☐ NEW)

#	DETAILS OF METHOD	CHART SYMBOLS	DIST. IN FEET	TIME IN MINS	NOTES
1	Invoice received, date stamped	●▷□D▽			By mail clerk
2	To mail clerk	○▶□D▽	20		
3	On first payable clerk's desk	○▷□▶▽		1/2	
4	Purchase order attached	●▷□D▽			
5	To cost accountant	○▶□D▽	25		
6	On cost accountant's desk	○▷□▶▽		1/2	
7	Coded to appropriate job	●▷□D▽			
8	To first payable clerk's desk	○▶□D▽	25		
9	On first payable clerk's desk	○▷□▶▽		1/2	
10	Copies made	●▷□D▽			
11	Original to project manager	○▶□D▽	110		
12	On project manager's desk	○▷□▶▽		3	
13	Examined and approved by project manager	○▷■D▽			
14	To second payable clerk's desk	○▶□D▽	90		
15	On payable clerk's desk	○▷□▶▽		1/2	
16	Vendor number & due date added, extensions checked	●▷□D▽		1	
17	Data keyed to magnetic tape	●▷□D▽		1	
18	INVOICE PAID	●▷□D▽			
19	To file clerk's desk	○▶□D▽	30		
20	On file clerk's desk	○▷□▶▽		2	
21	Invoice filed	○▷□D▼			
22		○▷□D▽			
23		○▷□D▽			
24		○▷□D▽			

system before the entire package was sent to the project manager for approval. Since the project manager was usually at a construction site or sites, it sometimes took three or four days to obtain his approval of an invoice. The company did not want to pay invoices unless the project manager agreed that the material had been received at the job site and was of acceptable quality.

Ace has adopted an improved method that shortens the time between receipt and payment of invoices. A copy is sent to the project manager before all of the coding and checking are done. The invoice can wait or be checked by the project manager while the additional accounting work is being performed. If the project manager disapproves an invoice—he rarely does—the payment may be stopped. Otherwise the trade discounts are obtained.

The old method is shown on the flow process chart in Figure 14.5 and the new procedure is shown in Figure 14.6. The revised procedure has reduced the length of time for processing invoices from nine or ten days to four or five days. A time reduction of a few days results in a significant reduction in the cost of materials and supplies for the company and is no more costly to perform than the old one.

FIGURE 14.6

Current Procedure for Reviewing and Paying Invoices

FLOW PROCESS CHART

JOB: Payment of invoices   PAGE 1 OF 1
☐ WORKER OR ☑ MATERIAL
CHARTED BY: G. Clark   DATE 12/7/'82

#	DETAILS OF ☐OLD ☑NEW METHOD	CHART SYMBOLS	DIST. IN FEET	TIME IN MINS	NOTES
1	Invoice received, date stamped	●▷□D▽			By mail clerk
2	To first payable clerk's desk	○▶□D▽	20		
3	On first payable clerk's desk	○▷□▶▽		1/2	
4	Purchase order attached, coded, copies made	●▷□D▽			
5	Copies to project manager	○▶□D▽	110		Original to 2nd clerk
6	On project manager's desk	○▷□▶▽		3	
7	Approves payment	○▷■D▽			
8	To second payable clerk	○▶□D▽			
9	On payable clerk's desk	○▷□▶▽		1/2	
10	INVOICE PAID	●▷□D▽			
11	Original to second clerk	○▶□D▽	10		
12	Vendor number & due date added, extensions checked	●▷□D▽		1	
13	Keyed to magnetic tape	●▷□D▽			
14	To file clerk	○▶□D▽	30		
15	On file clerk's desk	○▷□▶▽		2	
16	Invoice filed	○▷□D▼			
17		○▷□D▽			
18		○▷□D▽			
19		○▷□D▽			
20		○▷□D▽			
21		○▷□D▽			
22		○▷□D▽			
23		○▷□D▽			
24		○▷□D▽			

SUMMARY

Engineers and managers must realize that when they select and combine components of a technical system to be used by humans, they are designing a social system. This chapter has presented material on several physical and behavioral aspects of job design and redesign. A job may be examined before it is assigned to a worker or reexamined at any time during the life of a company. Important questions should be raised regarding both the technical-physical and the sociopsychological aspects of a job.

Several theories of motivation and job satisfaction were discussed, and the job characteristics that help achieve motivation were pointed out. Job enrichment is a program of adding variety and decision making to a job.

Motion economy and human engineering are more traditional approaches to designing efficiency into jobs and concentrate primarily on the technical-physical aspects of the job.

Efforts to improve methods should never cease. Managers should strive constantly to encourage members of their organizations to look for improvements. Changes in technology, volume, product mix, and human inventiveness lead to opportunities for improvement. Competitive pressures and/or potential growth of profits encourage methods studies.

DISCUSSION QUESTIONS

1. What is job design?
2. What three criteria should be considered in job design?
3. Discuss the relevance of feedback in job design.
4. How do you think most jobs are designed today?
5. What are some of the hygiene factors mentioned in Herzberg's two-factor theory?
6. What are some of the motivators?
7. How do motivators and hygiene factors compare to extrinsic rewards and intrinsic rewards?
8. Name three methods used to provide variety in jobs.
9. Discuss the use of quality circles.
10. Discuss some of the differences between horizontal job expansion and vertical job expansion.
11. Under what conditions is job enrichment likely to be successful?
12. Can all jobs be enriched successfully? Briefly discuss the reasons for your answers.
13. Discuss briefly some of the physical factors that should be taken into account in job design.
14. How are anthropometric data and human engineering useful in the design of some jobs?
15. What are the objectives of motion study?
16. How is it possible to perform micromotion study at the extremely detailed therblig level?
17. Briefly describe the steps involved in methods analysis and improvement. Why might this activity be referred to as job redesign?

PROBLEMS

1. Go through the following list of tasks and indicate alongside each whether it would be better performed by a human or a machine.

Make rapid and consistent responses to input signals.

Recognize patterns of complex stimuli that may vary from situation to situation.

Adapt decisions to situational conditions.

Retrieve coded information quickly and accurately.

Develop entirely new solutions.

Detect small amounts of light or sound.

Store coded information quickly and in substantial quantity.

Perform repetitive activities reliably.

Select alternative modes of operation if certain modes fail.

Reason inductively, exercise judgment.

Apply great force smoothly and precisely.

Store information briefly and erase it completely.

Develop concepts and create methods.

Perform many different functions simultaneously.

2. Prepare a multiple-activity chart to show the activities involved in preparing two pieces of bacon, two scrambled eggs, two pieces of buttered toast, and four cups of coffee with a coffeemaker, an oven, a stove, and one skillet. Use estimates of the amount of time required for each of the activities. Compare your time estimates with those of other members of your class.

3. An office of the state employment service in a city is responsible for interviewing persons seeking employment, placing the applicants' qualifications in a file, and searching a file of job openings to determine if a suitable match between job and applicant can be found. The three persons presently employed in this activity enjoy interviewing clients more than they enjoy searching files. Employees are displeased because they are overloaded with work, have shortened their breaks, and work some unwanted overtime.

During the typical eight-hour day, clients arrive with an average interarrival time of eight minutes. The times required to perform the interviews are normally distributed with a mean of thirty minutes and a standard deviation of five minutes. Searching the list of job openings requires approximately seven minutes for each applicant, to review files that are in a room next to the interview rooms. No more than three persons can use the files at the same time.

The office manager is planning to add the necessary personnel. She also is considering how to assign work to individuals. All of the employees could continue to interview applicants and perform the associated file searches. Or one or more employees could be permanently assigned to interview applicants, and one or more could be assigned permanently to search files. As a third alternative, the jobs could be rotated each hour, half day, day, week, or month.

(a) How many employees should be assigned to the office to perform the average workload without overtime? Employees are paid for eight hours but are permitted a fifteen-minute break in the morning and in the afternoon.

(b) Discuss the advantages and disadvantages of the alternative ways that work can be assigned to structure jobs in this office.

CASES

1. EAGLE MOUNTAIN RADIOGRAPHY DEPARTMENT

The Eagle Mountain Hospital has recently added a new wing to its older, overcrowded building. The Radiology Department was one of the most crowded in the old facility. The department occupied three diagnostic examination rooms and one darkroom, all of which adjoined a large office with a desk for each radiographer. The six radiographers kept a coffeepot in this office and enjoyed a congenial relationship extending to social activities outside the hospital.

The new radiology department is located at the end of the hall on the first floor of the new wing. Each radiographer has a small office opening to the hall and there is a lounge halfway down the hall. There are four examination rooms, two on each side of the hall, with a darkroom between each pair of examination rooms.

The supervisor in this department has assigned three radiographers to each pair of examination rooms and suggested that they could rotate the assignment of working in the darkroom. The supervisor is not pleased with the performance of the radiographers. They spend too much time down the hall in the lounge and are seldom in their offices when she wants to talk with them or when patients arrive. Despite the attractive surroundings, the employees seem less happy and less motivated than they were before the move. One radiographer has submitted his resignation and the others have complained about having to do so much more walking in the new location.

The supervisor is wondering what can be done to improve the situation in her department. What do you think may be hurting the efficiency and morale of the department? Can you suggest some improvements?

2. ELMOR PRODUCTS, INC.

Elmor Products, Inc., employs 500 people in producing a variety of products, one of which is a small electric saw. The company has been experiencing unusually high absenteeism and employee turnover in several of its departments, and productivity is low. The problem is most serious in one of the older departments. The pay scale in this department is equal to the pay scale in the others. David Emhoff, the new assistant manager, has studied one work center within this department and has identified several relevant facts.

The layout for the saw assembly work center is shown in Figure 14.7. Although the work areas are well lighted, there is little control of the temperature in the room. The workers use considerable movement during the assembly process. All of the work tasks except the drill press operations are per-

FIGURE 14.7

Saw Assembly Layout

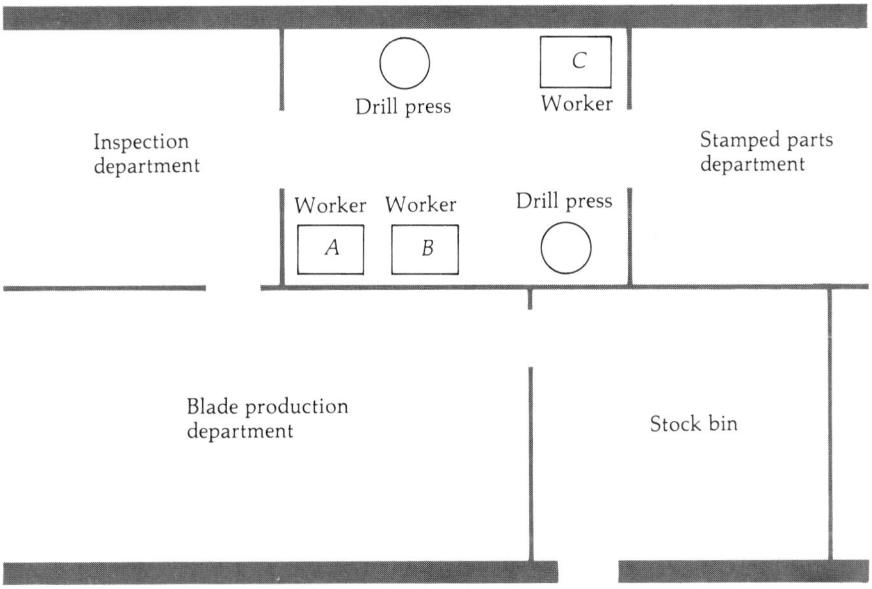

formed by hand. Each worker has a work table that is thirty inches high (about the height of a desk).

The assembly process consists of the following six steps:

1. Worker A walks from his assembly table to the stamped parts department and returns carrying a box of twenty frames. He then hand-files all of the rough edges left from the stamping process.
2. Worker A then drills six holes of two different sizes using the two drill presses.
3. Worker B obtains a set of retaining pins from the stock bin. While worker C holds the frame in position, worker B presses the retaining pins into the frame.
4. Worker C then carries the frame to her work table and attaches a handle, which she obtains from the stock bin.
5. Worker B then takes the frame and attaches a saw blade, which he obtains from the blade production department.
6. Worker C then carries the completed assembly to the inspection department.
   (a) What improvements in the physical arrangements can you recommend?
   (b) What improvements in the work assignments can you recommend?
   (c) Why do you think employee turnover is high in this work center?

3. ALK MANUFACTURING, INC.

ALK Manufacturing, Inc., is a medium-size manufacturing firm making arc welding equipment, elec-tric motors, and generators. The plant design is a typical assembly-line layout: various components are added to the item as it moves down a conveyor line until the completed product is assembled. Each worker is assigned to a work station along the as-sembly line and performs a specific task on the item at his or her station. The tasks are extremely repe-titive with little flexibility for the employee.

The manufacturing facility itself is large, noisy, and poorly ventilated (hot in the summer and cold in the winter). There is little interaction among the employees or the supervisors during the day. Man-agement style has always been authoritarian, and since the plant is a nonunion shop, there is no em-ployee representation to management. Product quality has always been a problem at ALK but has gotten out of hand over the last few years. Returns from distributors have greatly increased, along with customer complaints. Productivity of the workers is well below industry standards for this type of facil-ity. Absenteeism and employee turnover are ex-tremely high, which has begun to hamper the plant's ability to meet production deadlines.

The plant was recently purchased by an out-side investor group, the former owner having de-cided to sell the business because of the problems outlined above. You have been hired as the new plant operations manager, with a firm directive from the investors to improve all phases of operations. Suggest some specific methods you would employ to accomplish the objectives given you by top man-agement.

BIBLIOGRAPHY

Barnes, Ralph M. *Motion and Time Study.* 7th ed. New York: Wiley, 1980.

Davis, Louis E., Albert B. Cherns, and asso-ciates. *The Quality of Working Life.* New York: Free Press, 1975.

————, **and James C. Taylor, eds.** *Design of Jobs.* 2d ed. Santa Monica, Calif.: Good-year, 1979.

Ford, Robert N. "Job Enrichment Lessons from AT & T." *Harvard Business Review,* January 1978, pp. 96–106.

Friedrich, Otto. "The Robot Revolution." *Time,* December 8, 1980, pp. 72–83.

Hackman, J. Richard. "Is Job Enrichment Just a Fad?" *Harvard Business Review,* Septem-ber–October 1975, pp. 129–138.

————, **Greg R. Oldham, Robert Janson, and Kenneth Purdy.** "A New Strategy for Job Enrichment." *California Management Re-view,* Summer 1975, pp. 57–71.

Herzberg, Frederick. "Job Enrichment Admits Disparity Between Promise and Reality."

Industry Week, November 24, 1975, pp. 44–45.

Journal of Contemporary Business, **Spring 1977.** This issue contains several good articles related to job design.

McCormick, Ernest J. *Human Factors Engineering.* 3d ed. New York: McGraw-Hill, 1970.

Niebel, Benjamin W. *Motion and Time Study.* 6th ed. Homewood, Ill.: Irwin, 1976.

Parke, E. L., and C. Tousky. "Mythologies of Job Enrichment." *Personnel,* September 1975, pp. 12–21.

Pasmore, William A., and John J. Sherwood, Eds. *Sociotechnical Systems: A Sourcebook.* La Jolla, Calif.: University Associates, 1978.

Powers, Jack E. "Job Enrichment: How One Company Overcame the Obstacles." *Personnel,* May 1972, pp. 18–22.

Rief, William E., and Fred Luthans. "Does Job Enrichment Really Pay Off?" *California Management Review,* Fall 1972, pp. 30–37.

Scott, W. E., and L. L. Cummings. *Readings in Organizational Behavior and Human Performance.* Rev. ed. Homewood, Ill.: Irwin, 1973. Pp. 126–233.

Steers, Richard M., and Richard T. Mowday. "The Motivational Properties of Tasks." *Academy of Management Review,* October 1977, pp. 645–658.

————, **and Lyman W. Porter.** *Motivation and Work Behavior.* 2d ed. New York: McGraw-Hill, 1979. Pp. 391–473.

Tresko, John. "Myths and Realities of Job Enrichment." *Industry Week,* November 24, 1975, pp. 39–43.

Yorks, Lyle. "Determining Job Enrichment Feasibility." *Personnel,* November–December 1974, pp. 18–25.

Chapter Outline
PRODUCTIVITY, WORK MEASUREMENT, AND COMPENSATION

PRODUCTIVITY

The Importance of Productivity / Historical Review of Productivity / Reasons for the Decline in Productivity Improvement / Reasons for the Revival of Productivity / *Operations Management in Action:* WE PRODUCE MORE ON JOB, SLOW INFLATION / Productivity and Measurement

WORK MEASUREMENT

Uses of Time Standards / Where Work Measurement Can Be Applied

METHODS USED IN SETTING STANDARDS

Time Study / Standard Data / Predetermined Motion Times / Historical Records / Work Sampling / Employee Self-Timing

ASPECTS OF COMPENSATION

Intrinsic and Extrinsic Rewards / Time-Based Pay or Incentive Pay

SOME TYPES OF WAGE INCENTIVE PLANS

Piece-Rate Plan / Standard-Hour Wage Plan / Gain-Sharing Plans / Recommendations

GROUP INCENTIVE PLANS

Direct-Wage Group Incentive Plans / Profit-Sharing and Cost-Reduction Plans / The Scanlon Plan / The Lincoln Electric Plan

Summary / Solved Problems / Discussion Questions / Problems / Bibliography

KEY TERMS

Productivity	Coefficient of variation	Allowance	Measured daywork
Total factor productivity	Performance rating	Standard data	Wage incentive plans
Labor productivity	Normal work pace	Predetermined motion times	Piece-rate plan or piecework
Work measurement	Normal time	Methods-time measurement (MTM)	Standard-hour wage plan
Work standard	Actual time		
Time standard	Standard time	Motivation	Gain-sharing plans
Time study	Personal allowance	Intrinsic rewards	Profit sharing
Work elements	Fatigue allowance	Extrinsic rewards	The Scanlon Plan
Constraining element	Delay allowance	Daywork	The Lincoln Electric Plan
	Ratio delay studies (work sampling)		

Chapter 15

PRODUCTIVITY, WORK MEASUREMENT, AND COMPENSATION

Managers in all parts of a company are responsible for the wise use of resources. Wise use includes working toward the correct objectives and achieving efficiency as these objectives are pursued. Because operations managers often direct the largest portion of a company's human and capital resources, they play a major role in keeping resources productive.

PRODUCTIVITY

The amount individuals, firms, or nations produce—that is, their output—depends on the amount of input and the efficiency with which those inputs are transformed into the desired output. The ratio of output to input provides a measure of the relative efficiency of the process often referred to as *productivity.* Productivity continues to be an important matter to businesses and to the nation as a whole.

The Importance of Productivity

Productivity of a nation's economy is important for several reasons. As a nation's productivity improves, the nation's ability to compete in international markets improves, leading to sustained economic growth. This economic growth gives the nation a bonus that can be spent to enrich the lives of its citizens through an improved standard of living. With increased productivity, fewer inputs are needed for a given amount of output, which helps offset the effects of inflation.[1] When increases in hourly wage rates are greater than gains in productivity per labor hour, the unit labor costs for goods or services increases. Increased costs in turn lead either to reduced profits or higher prices, both of which contribute to inflation.

Changes in productivity often are calculated by comparing ratios of output per worker-hour utilized to produce the product or service or output per unit of labor and capital employed to produce the product or service. If only the labor input is measured, a change in the ratio may be misleading because the change in productivity may have resulted from a change in the amount of equipment per worker rather than increased worker efficiency. The term *total factor productivity* is used when the ratio is based on both capital and labor inputs. The term *labor productivity* is sometimes used if the ratio refers to labor hours as the only input.

Historical Review of Productivity

Figure 15.1 shows the changes in productivity in the United States over a thirty-year period. During the two decades from the end of World War II until the mid 1960s, the United States enjoyed a sustained growth rate that averaged about 3 percent a year. Then the rate of improvement seemed to languish and decelerated to a relatively anemic rate of about 2 percent per year through the 1970s. During the decade of the 1970s, output per worker in the United States grew only 20 percent, while it grew 145 percent in Japan, 75 percent in Germany, and 77 percent in France.[2] Figure 15.2 shows the comparative rates of growth in manufacturing productivity during the 1970s and the early 1980s. U.S. productivity was once far ahead of these nations; but with their more rapid rate of improvement, most of the gap has been closed. In 1984, output per hour in the United States was only 10 percent higher than in Japan and 15 percent higher than in continental Europe.[3] The United States has begun to realize that it is now competing among equals in the world market and that it will soon fall behind if other countries sustain their more rapid rates of improvement. Consequently, an all-out effort to improve productivity has ensued, and a turnaround seems at last to be taking place.

Reasons for the Decline in Productivity Improvement

Why did the rate of improvement decline by so much for this extended period? Many factors affect productivity on a broad national level, and no doubt there

---

[1]*Productivity in the Changing World of the 1980's:* Final Report of the National Center for Productivity and Quality of Working Life, Washington, D.C., 1978, p. 5.
[2]"The Revival of Productivity," *Business Week,* February 13, 1984, p. 92.
[3]Sylvia Nasar, "Good News Ahead for Productivity," *Fortune,* December 10, 1984, p. 42.

FIGURE 15.1

Productivity in the Private Domestic Business Economy, 1948–1978

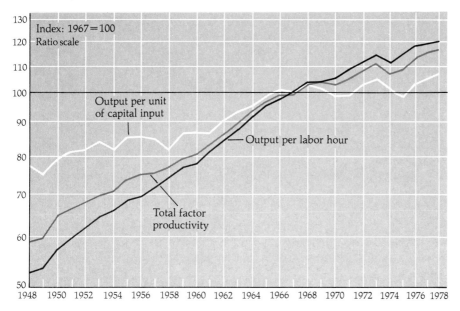

Source: John W. Kendrick and Elliot S. Grossman, *Productivity in the United States: Trends and Cycles* (Baltimore: Johns Hopkins University Press, 1980), p. 30. Data from U.S. Department of Labor; U.S. Department of Commerce; Conference Board.

are several causes for the decline in the rate of improvement. Among the reasons offered for the problem are the following:

- The price of oil increased tenfold as a result of oil embargos and restricted supplies.
- Inflation and interest rates went into double digits.
- New governmental regulations caused businesses to invest heavily in environmental protection and safety equipment.
- With the increased costs and shifting of investments, businesses spent less on research and development and on equipment to improve productivity.
- Many new people were added to the labor force, which lowered the average experience of the work force and reduced the ratio of capital to labor.

Reasons for the Revival of Productivity

Managers and government officials in the United States have noted the country's declining competitiveness with a newly found modesty and a growing sense of urgency. Simple survival has been a big motivator in many instances. Competitive pressures, both domestic and foreign, have stimulated management and labor to look for new improvements. Many businesses have re-

FIGURE 15.2

The U.S. Trails Its Foreign Rivals in Productivity Growth

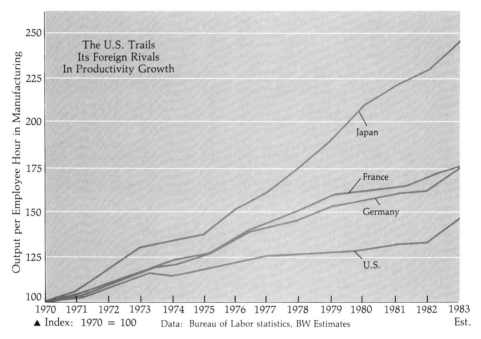

▲ Index: 1970 = 100   Data: Bureau of Labor statistics, BW Estimates   Est.

Source: "The Revival of Productivity," *Business Week*, February 13, 1984, p. 95.

sponded remarkably (see box). Recent rates of improvement in manufacturing productivity seem to be exceeding the banner years of the late 1950s and early 1960s. Projected growth rates for the late 1980s and the 1990s are in the range of 2.7 to 2.9 percent, more like the rates of the 50's and 60's.

What is happening to cause this rise in improvement rates and competitiveness? Healthy anxiety and harder economic times in general have encouraged managers to manage more diligently and to seek greater efficiency in their companies. Also, workers are cooperating in new ways to help make the companies for which they work more successful. Dramatic increases in productivity do not result from a new machine or two or a few quality circles. Significant results usually require significant changes.

Many manufacturing companies are turning to cellular arrangements (Chapter 13), JIT production (Chapter 8) and purchasing (Chapter 5), quality circles (Chapter 11), total quality control (Chapter 11), value analysis (Chapter 5), worker involvement and quality-of-worklife programs (Chapter 14), and improved work flow or other work methods (Chapter 14), among other approaches, to improve their performance. In some cases, companies are building smaller, more "focused" factories, realizing that economies of scale alone do

OPERATIONS MANAGEMENT IN ACTION

We Produce More on Job, Slow Inflation

The USA is "back on track" for long-term gains in worker productivity—the key to lower inflation and rising standards of living, experts say.

The Commerce Department said Monday that productivity—output per worker—grew at a 4.7 percent rate in the April-June quarter, the best gain in a year.

It was the eighth straight quarterly increase, capping the longest string of productivity gains in a decade.

"The productivity slowdown of the 1970s is over and we're back on track with a more normal trend," said John W. Kendrick, a George Washington University economist. "I would expect strong productivity for the rest of the decade."

When productivity grows faster than wages, as in the second quarter, labor costs can fall. The payoff is slower price increases and more income.

"That's how we raise living standards, through rising productivity and stable prices," said Audrey Freedman, labor economist for the New York-based Conference Board.

Keeping productivity high:

- Stiff competition from imports drives both manufacturers and workers.

- Investment is strong: Spending on plant and equipment is rising at a 16.5 percent rate, compared to 10.9 percent in an average recovery, said economist Robert J. Christian of Provident National Bank, Philadelphia.

- Research spending is providing "a greater flow of innovations," Kendrick said.

- The "youth bulge" and greater numbers of women have been absorbed in the work force; those workers are more experienced and more efficient than in the 1970s.

- Labor-management relations have improved.

Source: Mike McNamee, USA Today, August 28, 1984. Copyright, 1984 USA Today. Reprinted with permission.

not build competitiveness. Large plants can become bureaucratic and often are harder to coordinate and to adapt to new products or new work methods.[4]

There are opportunities for improvement at all levels of organizations. Better teamwork among groups and employee involvement help to achieve improvements and are often also important outcomes of improvement efforts. Coordination among marketing, design, and production helps to reduce costs and to improve competitive performance. Companies such as Xerox, Hewlett Packard, and AT&T have reported that the time required to develop and introduce new products has been reduced to half of what it was formerly—which is approaching current Japanese standards. The rapid introduction of new products provides a valuable strategic advantage and reduces costly engineering effort.[5]

Productivity increases outside of manufacturing have been less spectacular. The nonfarm, nonmanufacturing sector has been gaining at 0.9 percent since 1979—which is a giant improvement over the 0.3 percent rate of improvement between 1973 and 1979 but is less than half of the rate that was achieved during the 1950s and early 1960s. In the services sector, many companies are looking

[4]"Small Is Beautiful Now in Manufacturing," *Business Week*, October 22, 1984, p. 152.
[5]Nasar, p. 44.

to the computer to improve productivity. An example is provided by the claims workers at Traveler's Insurance Company. Each claims worker processed an average of 21,000 claims in 1984, compared to only 5,200 seven years earlier, before the company began computerizing its operations. In Chicago, another insurer, the Kemper Corporation, has computerized its claims operations and achieved a $24-million annual savings. On the basis of these productivity gains in its clerical staff, the Kemper Information Services Group is now focusing on redesigning the jobs of higher-salaried staff. The group is looking for changes in the way that insurance services are provided. Some parts of the underwriter's job—such as filing, photocopying, and analyzing applications for assigned-risk pools—may be reassigned to lower-paid employees.[6]

Banks are seeking improved productivity through such means as replacing tellers with ATMs and using computers to perform analyses for loan applications and for personal financial planning. Since 1980, Northwest Corp., a Minneapolis-based holding company with eighty-six banks, has raised its efficiency in almost every facet of operations, from streamlining check processing to down-sizing some branches, and has eliminated about 1,900 jobs. The company uses employee involvement teams that include employees up into the senior level of management.[7]

Productivity and Measurement

Companies can never afford to become complacent about efficiency. Operations managers must work to achieve and improve productivity in the operations function. Quite often, however, the cost of materials and purchased components accounts for as much as half of the cost of a manufactured product. In some repetitive manufacturing operations, labor costs may be only 10 to 20 percent of the cost, so more gains can sometimes be made by improving supplier relations and materials management than can be achieved by concentrating on labor productivity. Nevertheless, efficiency should be sought wherever it can be found. Custom job shops and service operations are more labor intensive and may yield greater improvements in labor costs. Some avenues to improved productivity—improved work flow, new processes, improved work methods, computerization, and materials management—have been discussed earlier. But to know how well it is progressing in its attempts to improve productivity, a company needs to keep some measurement of productivity.

Generally, productivity is measured by a ratio of output produced to resources used. An index for monitoring the overall relative productivity of labor can be provided by a ratio such as equation 15.1.

$$LP = \frac{OMP/LMP}{OBP/LBP} \qquad \textbf{(15.1)}$$

---

[6]"The Revival of Productivity," p. 99.
[7]Nasar, p. 44.

where LP = labor productivity index
    OMP = output during measured period
    LMP = labor hours during measured period
    OBP = output during base period
    LBP = labor hours during base period

The outputs of nonmanufacturing activities can often be measured more easily and described in more meaningful terms if measurements are made at an intermediate or final-product level instead of focusing on small elements of a task. The number of letters or reports completed in a typing pool is usually more relevant than the number of keystrokes made. A steakhouse operator may want to know how many customers are satisfactorily served rather than how much time is needed for each motion involved in preparing a steak. If the owner only counted the number of steaks cooked and ignored a subsequent large increase in the percentage of customers who sent their steaks back for replacement or further cooking, the apparent increase in productivity would be erroneous. When outputs are considered at an intermediate or final-product level, there is an assumption that the difficulty of processing and the level of diligence required to perform satisfactorily have not changed since the base data were taken.

WORK MEASUREMENT

Overall company productivity, of course, is the result of the productivity achieved by all components of the company. In order to achieve high productivity, managers must be concerned about the productivity of all resources. At the individual worker level, labor productivity is often determined by work measurement. *Work measurement* is the application of techniques to determine the amount of time necessary for a qualified worker to perform a particular task.

The amount of time that a job is expected to take is expressed as a "time standard," "work standard," "production standard," or simply "standard." A *time standard* states the amount of time a qualified worker, working at a normal rate of speed, will require to perform the specified task. It may be expressed as minutes per unit of output, units of output per hour, or some other ratio of time to work.

Uses of Time Standards

Standards can be used in both planning and controlling several aspects of operations. Previous parts of the book discussed several areas in which standards are useful. Standards are useful in aggregate planning to determine the capacity required to provide the amount of production called for by a master schedule. The level of staffing required to produce a given level of output can be determined. Standards are useful in scheduling to determine how long it will take for a given set of jobs to be completed. A product's cost is a function of the amount of material and labor inputs required to produce it. Time standards, therefore, provide a basis for establishing cost information. With time standards, workers' performance can be based on objective data rather than on personal assumptions or biases. When the amount of time required to perform a job is known, it provides a basis for comparing alternative work methods to see if improvements can be made. Time standards also provide bases for more equitable compensation rates or incentive wage plans.

Where Work Measurement Can Be Applied

Many jobs in offices and factories may be studied and measured. There are four basic criteria for measurable jobs:

1. The work must be done in a repetitive, reasonably uniform manner.
2. The work must be homogeneous in content over a period of time so that it is consistent from one period to another.
3. The work must be countable, that is, it should be describable in precise quantitative terms: so many cases, forms, letters.
4. There must be a sufficient volume of work, done in a regular manner, to make it worthwhile to count and maintain records.[8]

A 1977 survey of industries in the United States and Canada showed widespread use of work measurement in manufacturing operations. Nearly 1,500 usable responses to the survey were received and 93 percent of the manufacturing industries indicated that they used work measurement.[9] A much smaller percentage of nonmanufacturing operations use work measurement.

Slowness in making use of work measurement in nonmanufacturing settings has been attributed to several characteristics, generally related to the fact that the work is typically more variable and much of it is mental. It is difficult to count mental work or to performance rate it.

The service sector is now in the labor-intensive stage that manufacturing industries were in when time study began. Services are of necessity labor-intensive and thus may offer fertile ground for methods-improvement studies and work measurement. For example, Joan Glazer reported a savings of $700,000 a year from work measurement used in conjunction with a methods-improvement program at the Union Trust Company bank in Stamford, Connecticut. The program helped identify situations where work flow and work processing methods could be improved and led to more productive staffing levels. Bank-wide productivity increased 10 percent overall and as much as 45 percent in some departments. The savings in one year represented almost 5 percent of all salaries and benefits paid.[10]

[8]Elmer V. Grillo and Charles J. Berg, Jr., *Work Measurement in the Office* (New York: McGraw-Hill, 1965), p. 10.

[9]Robert S. Rice, "Survey of Work Measurement and Wage Incentives," *Industrial Engineering*, July 1977, pp. 18–19.

[10]Joan B. Glazer, "Case Study: How Work Measurement Can Control Costs," *ABA Banking Journal*, August 1980, pp. 93–95.

Table 15.1.
PERCENTAGE OF STANDARDS SET BY FIVE
WORK-MEASUREMENT METHODS

Work Measurement Method	Percentage of Standards Set Using Method
Time study	46
Standard data	23
Predetermined motion times	12
Historical records	14
Work sampling	3

Many early methods of work measurement in manufacturing involved determining the time needed to perform small elements of a task. When a tangible process is being observed, it is often easier to determine what elements are involved and necessary. In nonmanufacturing operations it is more difficult to measure the quantity and quality of output. Consequently, new approaches to work measurement are being applied to nonmanufacturing activities. The trend in work measurement is toward macro-measurement of indirect workers instead of micro-measurement of direct workers. In many instances, a computer is employed.

METHODS USED IN SETTING STANDARDS

Several methods of work measurement have been used in setting standards. Five of these methods are listed in Table 15.1, with the approximate percentages of standards that were set by each method, as indicated in a 1977 survey.[11] Each of these methods as well as self-timing by employees will be discussed in the following sections.

Time Study

Fundamentally, stopwatch time study or *time study* is performed by timing a worker as the job is performed, summing the times for the necessary elements of the job, adjusting this time if an abnormal work pace was observed, and then adding time for personal or rest breaks.

Analysts who perform time study should select an operator who is properly trained and uses the proper work method. They should tell the worker that they want to observe and time the job through a considerable number of cycles and should try to allay fears or suspicions the worker may have. After the analysts have observed the job sufficiently to identify the necessary work involved in the job, they list the necessary *work elements* and begin to record the amount of time each element requires.

[11]Rice, "Survey of Work Measurement," p. 21.

Reasons for Dividing the Job into Elements   Frequently the total job is divided into elements so that times are collected for each element rather than for each completed cycle. There are several reasons for this practice:

1. The listing of elements and their times helps to describe the work method and shows how the time for performing the job is distributed among the elements. Longer work elements often are the targets for methods-improvement efforts because they account for the greatest portion of the total.
2. A worker's rate of performance may not be the same for all elements of a job. The time-study analyst must adjust the operator's time to represent the time that the average worker would take. If the operator is much faster than the average worker for some work elements, these elements should be given a different performance rating than those that are performed more slowly.
3. Machine-paced elements should be separated from those that are under the control of the operator.
4. Some elements may not be repeated every cycle but may recur every tenth cycle, every sixteenth cycle, or at some other interval.
5. Times for similar work elements from several jobs may be compared to help keep standards uniform.
6. Element times can be collected and cataloged into "standard data" that can be combined to arrive at standards for some jobs without the need for stopwatch time study.

Figure 15.3 shows a time-study observation form for the task of posting inventory records. Notice that the task has been divided into elements and that one of the elements was not repeated during every cycle that was observed. It is important to estimate accurately the proportion of total cycles in which occasional elements occur, so that the standard will allow the proper amount of time to perform these elements. It was observed in this study that element 3 occurred during only about 8 percent of the inventory transactions that were processed. Therefore, 0.08 times the time to perform element 3 was added to the standard. The study period must be long enough to obtain a good estimate of the delays and interruptions that confront workers who are to perform the job.

The example in Figure 15.3 is simpler than the typical work task that one might subject to time study. The usual task has more than the four elements included in this example, and the typical time study would contain more observations than are recorded here.

Determining the Number of Cycles to Time   The number of cycles that should be timed increases with the degree of accuracy desired for the standard and with the variability of the observed times. After 10 or 15 cycles have been timed and some preliminary calculations have been made, the total number of cycles that should be timed can be determined by use of a formula or graph. Extreme time values for any element should be discarded and not used in estimating the variability of data because they might represent erroneous readings.

FIGURE 15.3

Example of Time Study Observation Sheet

Operation: Posting Inventory Records
Department: Inventory Control
Part:
Size:

Date 3/9/81
Shift 1
Study 1 of 1
Sheet 1 of 1

Operator B. Ratliff
Observer R. Baker

REMARKS Telephone interruptions and delays during study = 9.6%

ELEMENT DESCRIPTION	1	2	3	4	5	6	7	8	9	10	11	12	13	14	15	Rating	Normal Time	Minutes per Cycle
1. Read part number from record, find and pull card	0.14	0.15	0.21	0.17	0.19	0.14	0.17	0.18	0.18	0.21	0.18	0.17	0.18	0.20	0.18	1.10	$(2.65/15)(1.10)$ $= 0.1943$	0.1943
2. Transfer usage or receipt from requisition or receiving report to card and compute new inventory balance	0.45	0.42	0.50	0.51	0.43	0.48	0.54	0.44	missed	0.49	0.43	0.49	0.50	0.43	0.48	1.00	$(6.59/14)(1.00)$ $= 0.4707$	0.4707
3. Write purchase requisition if on hand and on order below reorder level (8% of transactions)	0.88	0.92	1.06	0.90	0.82											1.00	$(4.58/5)(1.00)$ $= 0.916$	0.0733
4. Replace inventory record card in file	0.07	0.08	0.11	0.09	0.05	0.07	0.06	0.08	0.06	0.05	0.05	0.07	0.11	0.05	0.06	1.10	$(1.06/15)(1.10)$ $= 0.0777$	0.0777
																	NORMAL	0.8160
																	$\times$ 1.206	
																	STANDARD	0.9841

ALLOWANCES:
Personal & fatigue 11.0%
Delays 9.6%
20.6% TOTAL ALLOWANCE

Formula for Sample Size   Assuming that a normal probability distribution applies, a confidence interval may be constructed that has a given probability (i.e., "confidence") that the interval will contain the actual mean time to perform the task. A 95 percent confidence interval means that intervals developed by this procedure will contain the actual mean in about 95 percent of the cases. Since we are dealing with a random variable, the probability is 0.95 that the actual mean is estimated within the desired accuracy, A, expressed as a decimal fraction of the actual mean. The equation for the required number of observations is:

$$n = \left(\frac{Zs}{A\bar{x}}\right)^2 \tag{15.2}$$

where n = the total number of observations that should be taken to provide the desired accuracy

$\bar{x}$ = the mean of the times already collected

A = the accuracy desired expressed as a decimal of the true value

Z = the standardized normal deviate that has $\frac{1}{2}(1 - \text{confidence})$ as the area remaining in the tail of the distribution beyond the value of Z

s = the estimated standard deviation of the distribution of element times, based on the observations already made.

A time-study analyst would observe several cycles, say ten or fifteen, and compute n on the basis of the data obtained at that stage of the study. Sampling then would be continued until n observations were obtained. If the element times are to be used to develop a catalog of times required to perform given parts of the cycle, the calculation of n should be based on data for the most *constraining element*: the one that yields the largest value of n—that is, the one with the largest coefficient of variation.

Suppose we are interested in estimating the actual mean time to perform element 4 of the task represented in Figure 15.3. Assume that we wish to provide 95 percent confidence that the true mean time to perform element 4 is estimated within 10 percent accuracy. To simplify the calculations, only the first six observations are used, even though at least two or three times this number of observations probably would be used in an actual study. The observed times for the six observations are shown in Table 15.2. The calculations used to estimate the sample size required to yield 10 percent accuracy with 95 percent confidence are also shown.

This sample size is twenty-six observations. The analyst would continue sampling and might calculate a better estimate of n after twenty-five or thirty observations. Otherwise a sample size of twenty-six would be used.

Determining Sample Size by Graph   The sample size required for a given confidence and precision, expressed as a fraction of the true value, is related to the coefficient of variation of the variable. Trial calculations of the mean and standard deviations of the total task time can be made after about ten or fifteen readings. The *coefficient of variation* (i.e., the standard deviation divided by the

Table 15.2
OBSERVED ELEMENT TIMES FOR
SIX OBSERVATIONS

Observation	Observed Element Time, X_i	X_i^2
1	0.07	0.0049
2	0.08	0.0064
3	0.11	0.0121
4	0.09	0.0081
5	0.05	0.0025
6	0.07	0.0049
	0.47	0.0389

$$\bar{x} = \frac{\Sigma x_i}{n'} = \frac{0.47}{6} = 0.07833$$

$$s = \sqrt{\frac{\Sigma x^2 - \frac{(\Sigma x)^2}{n'}}{n' - 1}} = \sqrt{\frac{0.0389 - \frac{0.47^2}{6}}{5}}$$

$$= 0.0204$$

$$n = \left(\frac{Zs}{A\bar{x}}\right)^2 = \left[\frac{1.96(0.0204)}{0.10(0.07833)}\right]^2 = 26.06$$

where $n' = $ the number of observations already made

mean cycle time) determines the number of observations that should be made to estimate the mean cycle time with a given confidence interval. Figure 15.4 shows the number of observations that should be made to establish a given confidence that the true mean cycle time has been estimated within plus or minus 5 percent.

Suppose that we had taken ten observations of some task and the trial mean was 4.21 minutes with a standard deviation of 0.73 minutes. The coefficient of variation for these data is $0.73/4.21 = 0.173$ or about 17 percent. Referring to Figure 15.4, we see that approximately 40 observations should be taken to establish 95 percent confidence that we have estimated the true mean cycle time within 5 percent of its value.

Adjustment for Worker's Pace   The objective of a time study is to arrive at a standard that is suitable for the normal employee; yet the employee who was timed may not have been working at a normal rate of speed. An adjustment, which may be called *performance rating*, efficiency rating, leveling, or normalizing, is made to adjust the observed times to the time required by someone working at a "normal" pace. Rating is the process of comparing the worker's rate of performance with the observer's concept of a normal work rate. Notice that each element of the task in Figure 15.3 was assigned a rating before the normal time was computed.

The most controversial step in work measurement is that of performance rating because it is largely subjective. There is no universal criterion for what is normal. Each company may have its own concept of a normal work pace, but there are a few benchmarks that help guide the selection of a normal pace. For example, walking at a pace of three to three and a half miles per hour is considered normal. The normal pace is not some optimal rate that only the best workers can achieve. Generally a standard is established so that most employees can achieve it without overexertion. A *normal work pace* should be one at which qualified workers can work all day without undue fatigue. Workers who are being time-studied sometimes may try to add extra steps to a job or work at a

FIGURE 15.4

Chart for Estimating the Sample Size Required to Obtain Maximum Confidence
Intervals of ±5 Percent for Given Coefficient of Variation Values

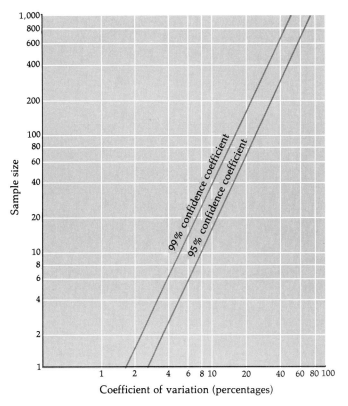

Source: Adam Abruzzi, *Work Measurement* (New York: Columbia University Press, 1952), p. 161.
Reprinted by permission of the publisher.

slow pace so that the standard will be set rather "loose." The observer should,
however, include in the standard only the time for the elements that actually
are part of the job and should make allowance for the worker's slower pace.
You can see that there is some amount of judgment and subjectivity in the time-
study process.

Even though it is a company's prerogative to determine what it considers
a normal pace, it is important that the company be consistent in its rating so as
to provide equitable expectations for all its employees. The time-study analysts
in a company should check and compare their concepts of normal against some
standard work pace at least once a month. The usual method of checking their
rating is to observe films of measured work paces and see if they can correctly
judge the performance rate without prior knowledge.[12]

[12]Larry N. Sitnek, "Performance Rating," *Industrial Management*, January–February 1977, p. 16.

Normal Time   The *normal time* for a job is the time it should take a qualified worker to perform the essential elements of a job while working at a normal pace. The *actual time* is the amount of time taken by the particular worker who was studied, at the pace he or she worked during the study. The normal time (NT) can be found by multiplying the observed actual time (AT) for the essential elements of the job by the overall performance rating for the job as a ratio to the normal efficiency rating (usually 100 percent).

$$NT = AT \times \left(\frac{\text{performance rating}}{\text{normal efficiency rating}} \right) \qquad \text{(15.3)}$$

A worker who was working 15 percent faster than what is considered a normal pace would be given an efficiency of 115 percent. Equation 15.3 would add 15 percent to this worker's time to determine the time that would be expected for the job when a worker was working at the normal pace. If we assume that an analyst had measured an actual time of 4.23 minutes for this job, the normal time would be

$$NT = 4.23 \times 1.15 = 4.86 \text{ minutes.}$$

Working at the normal pace, a worker would be expected to take 4.86 minutes to perform the job.

Allowances   Even though it would take only 4.86 minutes to perform the above job at a normal pace, a company would be unrealistic to allow only this amount of time for each job cycle. Workers need rest breaks during the day, and some delays are bound to occur. *Standard times* that are used for scheduling and pricing products should include time for delays, personal time, and rest time to relieve fatigue. *Personal, fatigue,* and *delay allowances* are added as a percentage of the normal time so that the standard time (ST) is found by equation 15.4.

$$ST = NT(1 + \text{allowances}) \qquad \text{(15.4)}$$

where the allowances are expressed as a decimal fraction of the normal (NT). Some general guidelines for personal and fatigue allowances are shown in Table 15.3.

Delays   Delays may occur on a job through no fault of the operator. He or she may have to wait for an inspector to come by and check one operation before proceeding, for a crane to come and remove a work item from the machine and place another on it, for a computer to respond, or some other unavoidable delay. A company should incorporate time for unavoidable delays in standards. Conversely, time for avoidable delays should not be included in a standard. The percentages that should be allowed for unavoidable delays can be determined by a method called *work sampling* or *ratio delay studies.*

Determining Delay Allowances by Work Sampling   Work sampling has been used extensively to determine allowances used to convert normal times to standard times. An *allowance* is a percentage of the normal working time that is allowed for unavoidable delays. Work sampling involves observing a worker at random

Table 15.3.

PERCENTAGES TO BE ADDED TO THE NORMAL TIME FOR AN ELEMENT TO MAKE ALLOWANCES FOR ITS WORK CONDITIONS

1. Constant allowances			(b) Well below		2
(a) Personal allowance	5		(c) Quite inadequate		5
(b) Basic fatigue allowance	4	E.	Atmospheric conditions (heat and		
2. Variable allowances			humidity)—variable		0–10
A. Standing allowance	2	F.	Close attention		
B. Abnormal position allowance			(a) Fairly fine work		0
(a) Slightly awkward	0		(b) Fine or exacting		2
(b) Awkward (bending)	2		(c) Very fine or exacting		5
(c) Very awkward (lying, stretching)	7	G.	Noise level		
C. Use of force or muscular energy			(a) Continuous		0
(lifting, pulling, pushing)			(b) Intermittent—loud		2
Weight lifted, pounds			(c) Intermittent—very loud		5
5	0		(d) High-pitched—loud		5
10	1	H.	Mental strain		
15	2		(a) Fairly complex process		1
20	3		(b) Complex or wide span of attention		4
25	4		(c) Very complex		8
30	5	I.	Monotony		
35	7		(a) Low		0
40	9		(b) Medium		1
45	11		(c) High		4
50	13	J.	Tediousness		
60	17		(a) Rather tedious		0
70	22		(b) Tedious		2
D. Bad light			(c) Very tedious		5
(a) Slightly below recommended	0				

Source: Benjamin W. Niebel, Motion and Time Study, *6th ed. (Homewood, Ill.: Richard D. Irwin, 1976), p. 365.*

times during the day and noting the type of activity in which he or she is engaged. The basis for work sampling is sampling theory, according to which an adequate-sized random sample should contain observations of various subcategories of work effort in the same proportion as the proportion of time consumed by these subcategories. A work-sampling study to determine the proper allowance should include observations of workers at random times to note whether they are engaged in normal work activities, unavoidably delayed, or involved in some other activity such as breaks or other avoidable delays. The subject of interest is the ratio of unavoidable delay time to normal work time, so we will know how much time should be added to the normal time to allow for delays over which the operator has no control.

Suppose that an analyst observes a lathe operator at 150 randomly selected times. During some of those times the operator may be waiting for a supervisor or inspector to give directions or check the work, waiting at a toolroom to get some tool or attachment needed to perform the job, waiting for someone to help lift an object on or off the machine. These times are recorded as unavoid-

Table 15.4.
OBSERVED FREQUENCIES
OF ACTIVITIES

Activity	Observed Frequency
Normal work activities	112
Avoidable delays	22
Unavoidable delays	16
Total observations	150

able delays. At each observation the analyst makes a tally mark in one of three categories, indicating the activity of the operator at that moment. Suppose that the total tally marks in each category are as shown in Table 15.4. Obviously an allowance must be provided for delays that cannot be prevented. This allowance as a percentage of the normal work time for the observed job is $16/112 = 14.3$ percent.

Standard Data

Several jobs in a company may contain the same work element. It is not necessary to time these work elements in every job if a reasonable standard already has been determined from one or more previously-studied jobs. A company can maintain a data base of work element durations obtained through previous time studies conducted at its facilities (i.e., *standard data*). If the times required for all of the elements of a new job are available in standard data, they can be totaled to arrive at the normal time for the job. Personal, fatigue, and delay allowances have to be added to the normal time to arrive at a standard for the new job.

Sometimes an element time is determined by interpolation of standard data between existing element times. A company might plot the time required to sand the surface on each of several different sizes of wooden shelves. The graph, as shown in Figure 15.5, could then be used to determine the time for sanding various other sizes of shelves.

Standard data have some advantages over stopwatch time study. Since the standards from which the data base of element times are taken will have been used previously, a company can have some assurance that the times are acceptable to both management and workers. Standard times can save the cost and interruption involved in having a time-study analyst go to the workplace, talk with the operator, and study the job. Besides, some workers resent being timed as they work. Another advantage of standard data is that standards can be determined for jobs that are not yet in operation. Production of new products or potential changes in work methods can be evaluated without the time, disruptions, and expense that would occur if they all had to be tried. Table 15.1 indicated that this method is used to establish about 23 percent of the standards in the responding companies.

FIGURE 15.5

Standard Data for a Work Element Graphed to Facilitate Interpolation

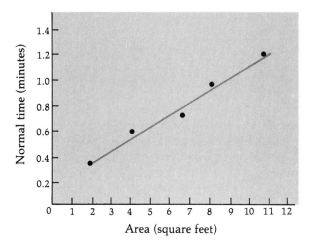

Predetermined Motion Times

Any manual task is composed of basic motions such as reach, grasp, move, turn, or other short motions arranged in a particular sequence. Just as any word in the English language can be composed from only 26 letters of the alphabet, most manual tasks can be described by a list of the sequence in which relatively few basic motions occur and recur. Through thousands of measurements under controlled conditions, researchers have recorded the time required to perform each of the basic motions. By summing the appropriate entries from tables that list these *predetermined motion times* an analyst can determine the time required to perform various manual tasks. It does not matter whether a person is reaching for a pencil, a scapel, or a wrench; the time required to reach a certain distance is approximately the same. Some adjustments may be required to allow for the particular conditions under which the reach occurs.

Predetermined motion times differ from standard data in that the predetermined motion time technique breaks a job into much finer detail than the job elements that are used for standard data and the times for these minute parts of a person's motions were determined through observing a large number of persons outside the using company. The advantages for predetermined motion times are similar to those for standard data and were presented in the discussion of that technique. Table 15.1 indicates that predetermined motion times were used to establish about 12 percent of the standards in the responding companies.

Methods-Time Measurement (MTM)   One of the better-known predetermined motion-time systems is *methods-time measurement.* Figure 15.6 shows MTM tables for some basic motions and the conditions under which these motions

FIGURE 15.6

Methods-Time Measurement Application Data (Times in TMUs)

METHODS-TIME MEASUREMENT
MTM-I APPLICATION DATA

Do not attempt to use this chart or apply Methods-Time Measurement in any way unless you understand the proper application of the data. This statement is included as a word of caution to prevent difficulties resulting from mis-application of the data.

1 TMU = .00001 hour
    = .0006 minute
    = .036 seconds

1 hour = 100,000.0 TMU
1 minute = 1,666.7 TMU
1 second = 27.8 TMU

TABLE I – REACH – R

Distance Moved Inches	Time TMU A	Time TMU B	Time TMU C or D	Time TMU E	Hand In Motion A	Hand In Motion B	Case and Description
3/4 or less	2.0	2.0	2.0	2.0	1.6	1.6	**A** Reach to object in fixed location, or to object in other hand or on which other hand rests.
1	2.5	2.5	3.6	2.4	2.3	2.3	
2	4.0	4.0	5.9	3.8	3.5	2.7	
3	5.3	5.3	7.3	5.3	4.5	3.6	**B** Reach to single object in location which may vary slightly from cycle to cycle.
4	6.1	6.4	8.4	6.8	4.9	4.3	
5	6.5	7.8	9.4	7.4	5.3	5.0	
6	7.0	8.6	10.1	8.0	5.7	5.7	
7	7.4	9.3	10.8	8.7	6.1	6.5	**C** Reach to object jumbled with other objects in a group so that search and select occur.
8	7.9	10.1	11.5	9.3	6.5	7.2	
9	8.3	10.8	12.2	9.9	6.9	7.9	
10	8.7	11.5	12.9	10.5	7.3	8.6	
12	9.6	12.9	14.2	11.8	8.1	10.1	
14	10.5	14.4	15.6	13.0	8.9	11.5	**D** Reach to a very small object or where accurate grasp is required.
16	11.4	15.8	17.0	14.2	9.7	12.9	
18	12.3	17.2	18.4	15.5	10.5	14.4	
20	13.1	18.6	19.8	16.7	11.3	15.8	
22	14.0	20.1	21.2	18.0	12.1	17.3	**E** Reach to indefinite location to get hand in position for body balance or next motion or out of way.
24	14.9	21.5	22.5	19.2	12.9	18.8	
26	15.8	22.9	23.9	20.4	13.7	20.2	
28	16.7	24.4	25.3	21.7	14.5	21.7	
30	17.5	25.8	26.7	22.9	15.3	23.2	
Additional	0.4	0.7	0.7	0.6			TMU per inch over 30 inches

TABLE II – MOVE – M

Distance Moved Inches	Time TMU A	Time TMU B	Time TMU C	Hand In Motion B	Wt. (lb.) Up to	Dynamic Factor	Static Constant TMU	Case and Description
3/4 or less	2.0	2.0	2.0	1.7				
1	2.5	2.9	3.4	2.3				
2	3.6	4.6	5.2	2.9	2.5	1.00	0	
3	4.9	5.7	6.7	3.6				**A** Move object to other hand or against stop.
4	6.1	6.9	8.0	4.3				
5	7.3	8.0	9.2	5.0	7.5	1.06	2.2	
6	8.1	8.9	10.3	5.7				
7	8.9	9.7	11.1	6.5	12.5	1.11	3.9	
8	9.7	10.6	11.8	7.2				
9	10.5	11.5	12.7	7.9	17.5	1.17	5.6	**B** Move object to approximate or indefinite location.
10	11.3	12.2	13.5	8.6				
12	12.9	13.4	15.2	10.0	22.5	1.22	7.4	
14	14.4	14.6	16.9	11.4				
16	16.0	15.8	18.7	12.8	27.5	1.28	9.1	
18	17.6	17.0	20.4	14.2				
20	19.2	18.2	22.1	15.6	32.5	1.33	10.8	
22	20.8	19.4	23.8	17.0				
24	22.4	20.6	25.5	18.4	42.5	1.39	12.5	**C** Move object to exact location.
26	24.0	21.8	27.3	19.8				
28	25.5	23.1	29.0	21.2	42.5	1.44	14.3	
30	27.1	24.3	30.7	22.7	47.5	1.50	16.0	
Additional	0.8	0.6	0.85				TMU per inch over 30 inches	

TABLE III A – TURN – T

Weight	30°	45°	60°	75°	90°	105°	120°	135°	150°	165°	180°
Small – 0 to 2 Pounds	2.8	3.5	4.1	4.8	5.4	6.1	6.8	7.4	8.1	8.7	9.4
Medium – 2.1 to 10 Pounds	4.4	5.5	6.5	7.5	8.5	9.6	10.6	11.6	12.7	13.7	14.8
Large – 10.1 to 35 Pounds	8.4	10.5	12.3	14.4	16.2	18.3	20.4	22.2	24.3	26.1	28.2

TABLE V – POSITION – P

Class of Fit		Symmetry	Easy To Handle	Difficult To Handle
1–Loose	No pressure required	S	5.6	11.2
		SS	9.1	14.7
		NS	10.4	16.0
2–Close	Light pressure required	S	16.2	21.8
		SS	19.7	26.3
		NS	21.0	26.6
3–Exact	Heavy pressure required	S	43.0	48.6
		SS	46.5	52.1
		NS	47.8	53.4

SUPPLEMENTARY RULE FOR SURFACE ALIGNMENT

P1SE per alignment: >1/16 ≤1/4"   P2SE per alignment: ≤1/16"

Source: Copyrighted by the MTM Association for Standards and Research. No reprint permission without written consent from the MTM Association, 16-01 Broadway, Fair Lawn, New Jersey 07410.

can occur. A trained analyst would break a manual task into the basic motions required to perform it and judge the conditions under which each motion will occur, then sum the appropriate predetermined times for all of the basic motions involved.

Historical Records

Standards are sometimes developed by counting the output of a department, person, or work center over some time during which a consistent type of work is being performed, then dividing the output by the number of worker hours expended. The method is simple, but it tends to be less accurate than most other methods because it disregards adjustments for the worker's pace and for delays. That is, it is assumed that the level of diligence while the records were collected was satisfactory.

The accuracy of standards set by this method can be improved by conducting work sampling while historical data are being collected so that the work pace and percentage of time lost to delays can be estimated. The data can then be adjusted for delays or an abnormal work pace. Table 15.1 indicated that approximately 14 percent of the standards set by the respondents were established by using historical records.

Work Sampling

Work sampling is sometimes suggested as a means of setting work standards. The survey reported in Table 15.1 indicated that only about 3 percent of the standards in the responding companies, which primarily were manufacturing operations, were set by this method. The percentage of standards set by work sampling in nonmanufacturing operations is probably somewhat higher.

Some of the advantages and disadvantages of work sampling are presented in Table 15.5.

Number of Observations Required   The number of observations required to estimate the proportion of time that is spent in delays or in any element of a job depends on the accuracy desired and the variability of the data. We may wish to know the proportion of work time spent in an activity within some given percentage of its true value. To keep the relative accuracy the same, the absolute accuracy must be increased if an activity represents only a small portion of the total time. Very large samples must be taken to estimate small proportions accurately.

Frequently a normal distribution is used as an approximation to the binomial distribution of a proportion. If we assume a normal approximation, the sample

Table 15.5
SOME ADVANTAGES AND DISADVANTAGES OF WORK SAMPLING IN COMPARISON TO CONTINUOUS TIME STUDY

Advantages
Does not require extensive training to perform
Can simultaneously study several operators
Takes less of the observer's time and is less costly
Observations are made over a more extended time, so they are more likely to take variations into account

Disadvantages
Does not permit as detailed a breakdown of types of activities
Study of a group provides an average but no measure of individual differences
Workers might intentionally change activity upon seeing the analyst, whereas this distortion is more difficult to produce under the continous observation of time study

size needed to provide a specified accuracy and confidence is given by equation 15.5.

$$n = \frac{Z^2}{A^2}\left(\frac{1-p}{p}\right) \tag{15.5}$$

where A = the accuracy desired as a decimal of the true proportion
p = the proportion
Z = the value from a standardized normal distribution required to give the desired confidence interval
n = the sample size.

A small random sample of fifty or so observations can be used to make an initial estimate of p. Then equation 15.5 can be used to see how large the total sample should be. Sampling is then resumed until the total sample is large enough to give the desired accuracy.

Suppose that work sampling in a hospital has been conducted, and 16 of 100 observations have shown a nurse to be working with charts and other papers. Suppose we want 95 percent confidence that we have estimated the true proportion within 10 percent. The proportion is preliminarily estimated to be 0.16 so

$$n = \frac{1.96^2}{0.10^2} \times \frac{1-0.16}{0.16} = \frac{3.84}{0.01} \times 5.25 = 2,016 \text{ observations}$$

A random-number table could be used to select, say, 100 or so times during a day that observations should be made. One would hope that several nurses would be observed at each of these times so that the study would not be continued for an extremely long time. If the nurses' activities vary from day to day during the week or during the month, however, the observations should be spread over a representative time span.

Employee Self-Timing

Sometimes standards, usually for office workers, may be established by asking the workers to record the time required to perform their jobs. A simple form showing two columns, one for time of day and another for activities, is sufficient for recording data. Some companies make lists of possible activities and assign a code to each activity so that the recording of data is simplified. Each time a different activity is started or completed, the employee indicates the time and a code or brief description indicating the type of activity. A record of the number of units processed during each activity is also made. Later the time data are summarized to construct a distribution or ordered array of the time required for each activity. Management then must decide which value of the distribution of times to use as a standard for each task—the mean, the mode, the 66th percentile, or whatever.

This method of developing standards is simple and requires little training. It provides a general index of work preformed during a period of time. However, the method does not make allowances for inefficiencies or interruptions that might have occurred during the data-collection period. Data collection may also upset the normal work routine because the employees do much of the data collection and considerable time is required to sort out all of the data.

ASPECTS OF COMPENSATION

Employees of a company can exhibit a wide range of commitment and performance, ranging from the bare minimum necessary to remain employed to their full maximum effort. Operations depend on the efforts of employees to produce the products or services they offer for sale. Managers are responsible for gaining employees' cooperation in seeing that the company's objectives are achieved and hence, are interested in directing their behavior. Human behavior is energized, directed, and sustained by *motivation.* An employee's motivation is to some degree related to the rewards the employee receives through participation in the organization.

Intrinsic and Extrinsic Rewards

It is generally recognized that people may receive two major categories of rewards from work. One category is *intrinsic rewards,* which are rewards that are internal to workers and which they give themselves. Intrinsic rewards include self-esteem, a sense of accomplishment, and a feeling of growth or development of special skills and talents. Many of these rewards are derived from the work itself. Because intrinsic rewards are related to the worker's perception of the job, and hence are affected by job design, this type of reward was discussed in Chapter 14.

A second category is *extrinsic rewards,* which are external to workers and are given by the organization or someone else. Extrinsic rewards include direct pay and such fringe benefits as insurance, vacations, company cars, payments to retirement plans, and so on. Being an extrinsic reward, compensation is more easily controlled by managers than are intrinsic rewards. This chapter reviews several aspects of employee compensation methods, with particular attention to wage incentive plans.

Time-Based Pay or Incentive Pay

Organizations may elect to pay employees by either of two major types of pay plans. Employees may be paid on the basis of the amount of time they spend on the job or on the basis of the production they achieve. Obviously, to be paid according to their production, employees must be involved in some activity for which there is some objective means of measuring the employee's output. For this and other reasons, which are discussed later, most employees are paid on the basis of time. Employees are said to work on a *daywork* plan if they are paid by the hour, day, or other unit of time without any production standards or any measurement of their output. The pay plan is called *measured daywork* when production standards are used and output is measured but pay remains at a fixed hourly rate for some period of time.

Companies may, on the other hand, elect to pay employees by some type of incentive program, which ties employees' pay to some measure of individual or group output. *Wage incentive plans* are methods of remuneration by which employees, individually or as a group, are paid automatically and promptly an amount related to their output according to some preestablished and stated formula.

It is estimated that slightly more than 25 percent of the manufacturing work force is paid under some type of individual incentive plan.[13] Few office workers are paid on incentive plans, so that less than 20 percent of the total work force receive individual wage incentives. Survey results indicate that the use of individual wage incentives has declined over the past two decades in most industries except iron and steel and footwear.[14] Yet the use of indirect bonuses through profit sharing appears to be increasing. Certainly, direct incentives are not suitable for every situation, but incentive plans, such as the ones presented in the remainder of the chapter, are used by many companies.

SOME TYPES OF WAGE INCENTIVE PLANS

Employees' pay may be related to their productivity in innumerable ways. We shall briefly discuss some payment plans that relate an individual's pay to output.

Piece-Rate Plan

A *piece-rate plan* or *piecework* pays the employee a stated amount per unit produced, regardless of the number of units produced. This is probably the oldest type of payment plan; it was used in ancient days before clocks were widely available, and it became widely used in the early days of the scientific management era. The primary advantage of piecework is simplicity: neither the company nor the employee have any difficulty computing the worker's pay. The piece-rate method is not common today because of government minimum wage requirements. The *standard-hour wage plan* is more common.

Standard-Hour Wage Plan

The standard-hour incentive plan is like a piece-rate plan except that each employee is guaranteed some base wage even if his or her average hourly output during a pay period is less than the standard. Output can be expressed as the number of standard hours of output produced. Pay for the period is equal to the base rate times the number of standard hours of output produced during the period.

---

[13]Eric Seiler, "Piece Rate vs. Time Rate: The Effect of Incentives on Earnings," *Review of Economics and Statistics,* August 1984, p. 364.
[14]Ibid.

If the standard production is 8 units per hour and an employee produces 10 units, he or she will have 1.25 standard hours of production. If the base wage for the job is $10.00 per hour, the employee will receive $10.00(1.25) = $12.50 for the hour. It is more likely that the production will be counted for a day or a week, as long as the employee is working on the same product during the time period. The standard-hour plan is a one-for-one plan, since the employee is paid 100 percent of the pay per unit that would be received at the standard rate for each unit above standard.

Not all one-for-one plans begin paying incentive bonuses at 100 percent of standard, however. One objective of incentive wage plans is to have worker earnings on the sloping portion of the wage line so that they benefit from increased effort. A worker who usually performed at 85 percent of standard would have to increase his or her production by 16 percent to receive a 1 percent wage bonus if the bonus began at 100 percent. A worker in this situation may be frustrated rather than motivated to produce more. For this reason, some companies begin paying bonus payments at some lower levels of production; say, 60, 75, or 80 percent of standard. The relationship between production and wages that begin at 100 percent of standard (standard-hour plan) is shown in Figure 15.7(a). Figure 15.7(b) shows a one-for-one plan that begins at some level of production less than 100 percent of standard.

Workers who are employed under a one-for-one plan and produce above the level at which the bonus is paid receive pay just as though they were being paid at a piece rate. The pay per unit is equivalent to the unit pay for the production level where bonus earnings begin. Suppose that a worker is em-

FIGURE 15.7

One-for-One Standard-Hour Plans

(a) Bonus beginning at standard

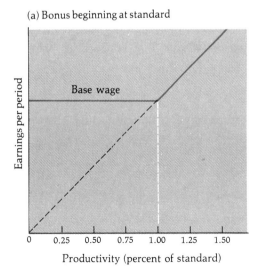

(b) Bonus beginning at less than standard

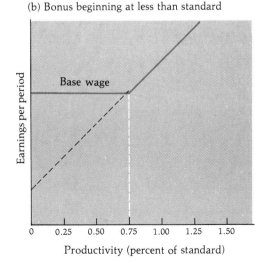

ployed under an agreement that provides a one-for-one bonus for all hourly production above 80 percent of the standard rate. The worker would receive 1.5 times the base rate for production that was 120 percent of the standard. The pay at any level of performance above the point at which incentive pay begins is found by the following equation:

$$\text{pay} = \frac{\text{base hourly wage} \times \text{hours worked} \times \text{actual production rate}}{\text{production at which bonus begins.}}$$

Or, for production below the rate at which bonus pay begins, the worker's pay is:

$$\text{pay} = \text{base hourly wage} \times \text{hours worked.}$$

Gain-Sharing Plans

A *gain-sharing plan* guarantees a base rate, but the wage is increased less than 1 percent for each percentage point that the employee produces above standard. Thus the employee and the company *share* the gain or bonus for work above standard. The employee may receive 70 percent, 50 percent, or some other percentage of the bonus earnings; the remainder may be retained by the company to help defray the cost of setting standards, counting production, and other administrative expenses associated with the incentive plan. Sometimes the part of the bonus that the direct worker does not receive is divided among the foremen and indirect employees who support the production worker.

Like one-for-one plans, gain-sharing plans may begin paying a bonus at some level of production other than 100 percent of standard. Pay may be determined by multiplying the percentage of sharing by the amount of bonus production, then adding this amount to the base pay for the period. For example, if an individual produced 130 percent of the rate at which bonus pay begins, then he or she would have a 30 percent bonus production. Under a 60 percent sharing plan the worker would be credited with 0.6×30 percent or 18 percent bonus pay for the period. If the employee worked 8 hours at the job while achieving this average level of output, then he or she would be paid for $8 \times 1.18 = 9.44$ hours at the base rate. The relationship between production level and wages for some gain-sharing plans is shown in Figure 15.8(a) and (b).

Some wage incentive plans are based on nonlinear relationships between production and wages. It is apparent that an infinite variety of plans can be devised by having different slopes and changing the relationship between pay and productivity at different levels of productivity. Usually this type of plan provides for a decreasing rate of bonus as output increases, so that bonus earnings will level off at, say, twice the standard wage. Such a plan might be used by a company fearful of runaway incentives caused by a standard mistakenly set much too loose. Step bonuses may sometimes be paid if the employee achieves some level of productivity. Figure 15.9 shows the relationship between productivity and hourly pay for a plan that combines a step bonus and a declining bonus.

FIGURE 15.8

Gain-Sharing Plans

(a) Bonus beginning at standard

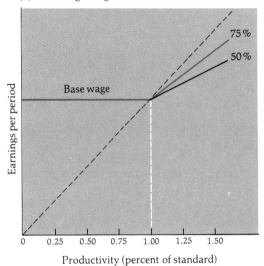

(b) Bonus beginning at less than standard

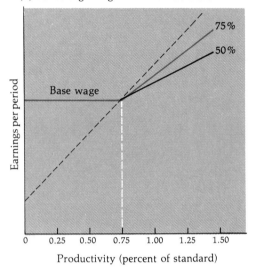

Recommendations

Several recommendations for successful implementation of wage incentive plans can be found in the literature. Five are summarized below:

1. The plan should permit earnings above the base rate. Good performance should pay at least a 30 percent bonus.
2. The plan should benefit both the company and the employee.
3. The plan should be simple and understandable.
4. The standards should be protected from capricious and indiscriminate rate cutting.
5. Earnings should not be affected by factors beyond the control of the operator.[15]

It is important to remember that many factors other than pay have significant effects on motivation and performance. Social interactions with other workers influence workers' attitudes and behavior. Influential fellow workers become opinion leaders, head informal organizations, and have more direct contact with workers than the official managers of the formal organizations. Contacts with peers influence the worker's attitude and the degree to which he or she accepts the company's expectations about performance. This peer pressure can overcome many of the positive or negative effects of a wage program. Social pressure

[15]H. K. von Kaas, *Making Wage Incentives Work* (New York: American Management Association, 1971), pp. 7–8.

FIGURE 15.9

Declining-Rate Incentive Plan with a Step Bonus
Beginning at Standard

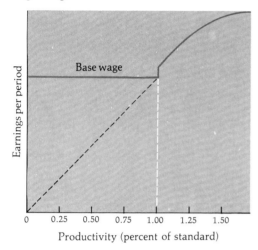

is sometimes applied to any worker who exceeds an informally established quota that sets what is considered a "reasonable" level of work above the company standard. Workers may fear that managers will raise the standard if the workers exceed the standard by very much. Obviously, mutual trust between workers and managers is necessary if an incentive plan is to succeed.

GROUP INCENTIVE PLANS

Financial incentives may be paid to individuals or to groups. Group plans simplify the measurement and compensation decisions, particularly when a group of employees works as an interdependent team to produce a product or service.

Direct-Wage Group Incentive Plans

Any of the individual plans discussed previously could also be applied to groups of employees. Group incentive plans that determine the direct wages on the basis of the output of the group simplify the production counting and administration process and reduce overhead expenses. A group incentive plan divides the bonus among the group members in proportion to each member's base wage. Such plans may lead to peer pressure from members of the group to see that each group member does his or her share of the work. Group plans still depend on the efforts of management, however, to motivate employees. No wage incentive plan should be viewed as a substitute for management efforts. Some proponents of wage incentive plans favor individual plans in settings where a worker performs independent work because they feel that it strengthens the incentive appeal.

Profit-Sharing and Cost-Reduction Plans

Companies are interested in earning enough profits to ensure that they can survive and grow. These objectives should be shared by owners, managers, and workers alike. Many companies have instituted profit-sharing plans to help secure the interest of workers in the soundness of the company and its profit picture. Profit sharing simplifies the job of administering an incentive plan because it does not require that each employee's contribution be measured. Since it is less likely to cause employees to feel a direct relation between their effort and their financial reward, profit sharing is as much an employee relations program as an incentive program.

Profit sharing is defined by the Council of Profit Sharing Industries as "any procedure under which an employer pays or makes available to regular employees, subject to reasonable eligibility rules, in addition to prevailing rates of pay, special current or deferred sums based on the profits of business." Profit-sharing plans have become increasingly popular in recent years. They may pay a bonus quarterly, semiannually, annually, or at some other interval. Some plans pay the bonus as direct income, others pay the employee's share into a retirement fund or provide a combination of payments.

Profit-sharing plans can be influenced by variables other than employee efficiency—variables beyond the control of workers. Changes in demand level, in product mix, in technology, in the cost of materials, and in executive salaries and bonuses affect the amount of revenue left to be divided among owners and workers. In some years employees may do well with no extra effort while in other years they may work extra hard and have no bonus. The business cycle and competitive maneuvers are facts of life for entrepreneurs and can also become unpleasant facts for employees who are on profit-sharing plans.[16] Cooperation with management and other workers, however, can lead to improved production methods that give the company a sounder position in the marketplace, enabling everyone to enjoy better security in the long run and perhaps more pay in the short run.

The Scanlon Plan

The Scanlon Plan was initially developed by the late Joseph Scanlon in 1936, but World War II postponed its implementation at Lapointe Machine Tool Company until 1947. Scanlon, who had been a union official, proposed the plan as a means of keeping a financially troubled company afloat. The initial use was successful and numerous other companies have adopted some form of this plan. The Scanlon Plan is as much an employee relations plan as it is an incentive plan.

[16]"Employee Wrath Hits Profit-Sharing Plans," *Business Week*, July 18, 1977, p. 25.

It is based on a philosophy of building a single team of management and labor striving for increased productivity by reducing cost and improving efficiency. Labor is to share in the savings effected by reduced labor cost per unit of output. The employee's bonus is based on a ratio of total labor cost to the sales value of production. As labor cost declines in relation to sales value, the bonus increases. Since increases in material costs, taxes, fuels, and other expenses can reduce the proportional value of labor costs even when labor efficiency has not increased, the base ratio must be revised from time to time. By collective bargaining and negotiation, management and labor agree on a normal proportion of total cost to represent labor cost. Management may be included in the bonus or may be considered to benefit from increased sales and output relative to plant overhead.

Employee participation is an important aspect of the plan. One major component of the plan is the use of production committees to review suggestions for improved operations. Each production committee can implement improvements that involve no other departments and that require no capital expenditures. A second major component is the use of a screening committee composed of employee representatives and members of the top plant management group. The screening committee reviews and approves suggestions that involve more than one department or capital investments.

The Lincoln Electric Plan

The Lincoln Electric Company of Cleveland, Ohio, has a broad incentive plan that includes elements of profit sharing, participative management, and job enlargement. The basic concepts of the plan evolved between 1914 and 1934 under the direction of James F. Lincoln, the company's president, and no doubt the plan still undergoes occasional refinement. The objective of the plan is for management and labor to work together to produce the best product at the lowest price. Employees serve on job-evaluation committees that seek suggestions for improvement in productivity. Lincoln's philosophy is that making money for someone else has never been a great motivational tool, so several methods of distributing financial rewards to the employees are used.

The Lincoln Electric Plan has three major components: (1) a piecework system, (2) a yearly bonus, and (3) a stock-purchase plan. In addition to these components of the pay scheme, the company provides enriched jobs and participation in decisions. Employees serve on evaluation committees involved in the plan. Independent work groups plan their own production processes and perform their own quality control evaluations.

The employees at Lincoln Electric are among the highest paid factory workers in the world in their lines of work. They also are among the most productive. Some of Lincoln's products sell today for little more than their prices in the 1930s, despite the dramatic inflation in material prices since that time. The Lincoln system has achieved some results that many companies should find worthy of serious study.

SUMMARY

Productivity is vitally important to competitors in the marketplace. They must keep their prices reasonable and competitive and they must be able to respond quickly to changes in demand. The productivity of both labor and capital is important in keeping companies competitive. In recent years the rate of productivity improvement in several industrialized nations has exceeded that of the United States, and many U.S. companies have lost part of their market. Both manufacturing and nonmanufacturing companies in the United States are working to increase their rates of productivity, which in turn has improved the current and projected rate of improvement in the country's overall productivity.

At the individual worker level, the productivity of labor is measured in terms of a work standard, sometimes simply called a *standard,* that expresses output per unit of time. Work standards are determined through some means of work measurement—such as stop watch time study, standard data, predetermined basic motion times, historical records, work sampling, or employee self timing. Stop watch time study, simply called *time study,* is the most common method of establishing standards. After informing the worker of the study, a time study analyst observes the worker long enough to understand the elements of the job and to see that proper work methods are being used. The analyst times the necessary elements of the job for a sufficient number of cycles. The normal time for the job is the actual time adjusted for any difference between the observed worker's pace and a normal pace. Allowances for fatigue and unavoidable delays are then added to the normal time to determine the standard time.

Individual or group wage incentives are used in some companies as a means of motivating employees and as a way to share with employees the benefits of their productivity. Individual incentives may pay the full labor rate for units that the employee produces above the standard. An alternative is gain sharing, which pays less than 100 percent for units above the standard. Profit sharing or other group incentives are used in some instances, such as where administration of individual incentives would be cumbersome or where work depends on interrelated activities of worker groups. Two group incentive plans that have been acclaimed as highly successful in some installations are the Scanlon Plan and the Lincoln Electric Plan.

SOLVED PROBLEMS

PROBLEM:

A job has been time-studied for twenty observations. The mean actual time was 5.83 minutes, and the standard deviation of the times is estimated to be 2.04 minutes. How many total observations should be taken for a 95 percent confidence that the mean actual time has been determined within 10 percent?

SOLUTION:

$$n = \left(\frac{Zs}{A\bar{x}}\right)^2 = \left[\frac{1.96(2.04)}{0.10(5.83)}\right]^2$$

$$\left(\frac{3.998}{0.589}\right)^2 = 6.858^2 = 47.03.$$

Therefore a total of forty-seven observations should be made. Since twenty observations have already been made, only twenty-seven more are necessary.

PROBLEM:

An analyst has observed a job long enough to become familiar with it and has divided it into five elements. The element times for the first four cycles and a performance rating for each element are given in the following table.

Element	Cycle 1	Cycle 2	Cycle 3	Cycle 4	Performance Rating (percent)
1	1.246	1.328	1.298	1.306	90
2	0.972	0.895	0.798	0.919	100
3	0.914	1.875	1.964	1.972	100
4	2.121	2.198	2.146	2.421	110
5	1.253	1.175	1.413	2.218	100

(a) Do any of the times look like "outliers"—that is, probable errors in reading or recording data that should not be included in the analysis?

(b) Compute an estimated normal time for the job based on the data available at this stage of the study.

(c) On the basis of the data available, what size sample should be taken to estimate the time for element 2 within 5 percent of the true mean time with 95 percent confidence?

SOLUTION:

(a) The times for element 3 in cycle 1 and for element 5 in cycle 4 are suspect and should be disregarded.

(b) The following estimates are made using the remaining times:

Element	Mean Actual Time	Performance Rating (percent)	Normal Time
1	1.295	90	1.166
2	0.896	100	0.896
3	1.937	100	1.937
4	2.222	110	2.444
5	1.280	100	1.280

Normal time for total job = 7.723.

(c) For element 2:

$\bar{x} = 0.896$ and

$$s = \sqrt{\frac{\Sigma x^2 - \frac{(\Sigma x)^2}{n'}}{n' - 1}}$$

$$= \sqrt{\frac{3.227174 - \frac{3.584^2}{4}}{3}} = \sqrt{0.005303}$$

$$= 0.0728.$$

$$n = \left(\frac{Zs}{A\bar{x}}\right)^2 = \left[\frac{(1.96)(0.0728)}{(0.05)(0.896)}\right]^2$$

$$= (3.185)^2 = 10.14$$

The analyst probably would want to use more than 10 observations so that workers would have more confidence in the standard. A company might make it a general practice to use at least, say, 15 or more observations.

PROBLEM:

Employees in the manufacturing department of Mammoth Metals Company are paid on a one-for-one incentive plan beginning at 85 percent of standard. Bob Grevanti works in this department and earns a base wage of $7.80 per hour for a 40-hour week. The standard for Bob's job is 20 units per hour. Last week Bob produced 980 units.

(a) How many standard hours did Bob earn last week?

(b) How much gross pay did Bob earn for this work?

SOLUTION:

$(980 \div 20) \div (0.85) = 57.65$ standard hours.
57.65 standard hours $\times$ $7.80 = $449.67.

PROBLEM:

The Tircon Company pays its workers on a 60 percent gain-sharing plan, with bonus pay beginning at 80 percent of standard. The standard is 400 units per 40-hour week. Mary Romaraz, whose base pay is $7.10 per hour, produced 430 units last week.

(a) What is Mary's gross pay for the week?
(b) What is the unit labor cost at 60 percent of standard?
(c) At standard?
(d) At Mary's rate of work last week?

SOLUTION:

(a) Standard is 10 units per hour. Bonus begins at 8 units per hour (i.e., the participation point). Mary produced 430 ÷ (400 × 0.80) = 134.375% of the participation point. She will be paid for 60 percent of her production above the participation point or 0.60 (34.375%) = 20.625%.

Mary will receive 1.20625 × 40 hours = 48.25 hours pay: 48.25 × $7.10/hour = $342.58.

(b) At 60 percent of standard, the unit labor cost is $7.10 ÷ 6 units = $1.183 per unit.

(c) Incentive earnings begin at 8 units per hour. Each unit above that pays 0.6 ($7.10 ÷ 8) or $0.5325. At 10 per hour the unit labor cost will be [7.10 + 2(0.5325)] ÷ 10 = $0.8165.

(d) At Mary's rate of work the unit labor cost is $342.58 ÷ 430 units = $0.7967 per unit.

DISCUSSION QUESTIONS

1. What is a work standard? State two ways that standards may be expressed.
2. What are four basic criteria for determining jobs that are most suitable for measurement?
3. What are the steps in performing a stopwatch time study?
4. What factors should be considered in the determination of a standard?
5. Why do time-study analysts break jobs into elements?
6. Distinguish between actual time, normal time, and standard time.
7. What are predetermined motion times?
8. Distinguish between work sampling and time study.
9. How can historical records be used in the development of standards?
10. (a) What are standard data?
    (b) What are some advantages of using standard data?
11. What are some of the characteristics that differentiate office work from factory work?
12. Do people seem to be less important to organizations in this age of technology than they once were? Why or why not?
13. Why is motivation important to organizations?
14. Briefly describe two categories of rewards that people may derive from their jobs.
15. Define a wage incentive plan.
16. For what reasons might a company elect to use a wage incentive plan?
17. Distinguish between a piece-rate plan and a standard-hour plan.
18. What is gain sharing?
19. Under what conditions is a group incentive plan generally more appropriate than an individual incentive plan?

PROBLEMS

1. A job has been time-studied for thirty observations. The mean actual time was 3.66 minutes, and the coefficient of variation was found to be 20 percent ($CV = 0.20$). How many total observations should be taken for a 95 percent confidence that the mean actual time has been determined within 5 percent?

2. A job has been time studied for several cycles and the mean actual time was found to be 2.13 minutes. The standard deviation of the actual times was estimated to be 0.38 minutes. How many observations should be taken in order to estimate the true actual time within 10 percent with 95 percent confidence?

3. Time study observations of a job have been completed, and the mean actual time was found to be 6.28 minutes. The analyst estimated that the observed worker had a performance rating of 110 percent during the study. Personal and fatigue allowances of 13 percent are appropriate for the job, and unavoidable delays are estimated to be 10 percent.
   (a) Compute the normal time for the job.
   (b) Compute the standard time for the job.

4. An analyst has become familiar with a job and has divided it into four elements. The element times for the first four cycles are given in the table below with a performance rating for each element.

Ele-ment	Cycle 1	Cycle 2	Cycle 3	Cycle 4	Performance Rating (percent)
1	1.38	1.58	1.71	1.49	100
2	.29	.35	.30	.38	120
3	.46	.58	.41	.44	105
4	.77	.82	.74	.88	90

   (a) On the basis of the times observed through four cycles, determine the normal time for the job.

(b) How many observations would be required to estimate the true time for element 1 within 10 percent with 90 percent confidence?

5. An analyst has observed a job long enough to become familiar with it and has divided it into four elements. The element times for the first five cycles are shown in the following table with a performance rating for each element.

Ele-ment	Cycle 1	Cycle 2	Cycle 3	Cycle 4	Cycle 5	Perfor-mance Rating (percent)
1	1.51	1.63	1.48	1.55	1.72	100
2	2.46	2.34	2.33	2.36	2.30	90
3	1.79	3.02	1.84	1.78	1.77	95
4	1.25	1.11	1.40	1.15	1.29	115

   (a) Compute an estimated normal time for the job based on the data available at this stage of the study.
   (b) On the basis of the data available, what size sample should be taken to estimate the time for element 1 within 5 percent of the true mean time with 95 percent confidence?

6. The analyst in problem 4 performed a work-sampling study for the same task and recorded the counts shown in the following table for three categories of activities. What allowance should be made for unavoidable delays?

Activity Category	Observed Frequency
Normal work activity	116
Avoidable delays	17
Unavoidable delays	14

7. The analyst in problem 5 performed a work-sampling study for the same task and recorded the counts shown in the following table for three categories of activities.

What allowance should be made for una-voidable delays?

Activity Category	Observed Frequency
Normal work activity	120
Avoidable delays	25
Unavoidable delays	16

8. Ajax Car Rental Service has attempted to streamline the process of completing a rental contract so that customers may obtain cars with minimum delay. The manager has timed twenty transactions from the time the agent begins talking with the customer until the customer is handed the keys and a completed agreement. The mean time is 11.2 minutes, and the estimated standard deviation is 3.3 minutes. How many observations are required to estimate the mean time with 95 percent confidence within an accuracy of 1 minute?

9. Arrow Airlines has attempted to streamline the process of booking flight reservations in order to service the maximum number of on-site customers. The manager has timed forty transactions from the time the agent begins talking with the customer until tickets are prepared and paid for and luggage is checked in. The mean time is 5.8 minutes and the estimated standard deviation is 1.8 minutes. How many observations are required to estimate the mean time with 95 percent confidence within an accuracy of 0.50 minute?

10. The Donnelly Company owns 100 machines for lease by the day to customers. Randomly selected records of twenty-five days show that an average of forty-two machines are rented each day. How many records should be observed to estimate the utilization of these machines within 15 percent accuracy and with 95 percent confidence?

11. The Blitz Corporation employs 6 workers in painting stripes on parking lots. The employees are paid by a daywork plan at $6.80 per hour. On the basis of past contracts, the manager, Ruby Smith, has established a standard of 50 yards of striping per hour for each painter. The company has just accepted a contract for a new shopping center parking lot with 6,600 yards of stripes.
   (a) Determine the labor cost for the contract if the painters work at efficiencies of 85 percent, 95 percent, 105 percent, and 115 percent.
   (b) The manager is concerned about completing the contract before the new shopping center opens. She can use only three painters, so she has offered to pay $0.12 per yard for each yard of striping above standard. What will be the labor cost if the three workers finish the lot in a 40-hour week?
   (c) What will each painter earn per week, before deductions? How does this figure compare with the pay for an ordinary 40-hour week?

12. The Eagle Mountain Hospital pays employees in its laundry according to a standard-hour plan. The standard rate of ironing is 30 bedsheets an hour. Currently employees in this department are paid $5.75 per hour as a base wage and work 40 hours a week. Ellie Davis, one of the more skilled workers in the department, regularly irons 36 sheets per hour. Determine her weekly (40 hours) pay if she works at 90 percent of standard, a pace that is easy for her; at 100 percent; if she works a little harder, at 110 percent; if she really applies her skill and achieves 120 percent of the standard.

13. Darnell Corporation pays employees in its billing offce according to a one-for-one standard-hour plan with a bonus beginning at 100 percent of standard. The standard rate of billing is 22 bills an hour. Currently employees in this department are paid $6.50 per hour as a base wage and

work 40 hours a week. Jeff Baker, one of the more skilled workers in the department, regularly types 27 bills an hour. Determine his weekly (40 hours) pay if he works at 90 percent of standard, a pace that is easy for him; at 100 percent; if he works a little harder, at 110 percent; if he really applies his skill and achieves 120 percent of the standard.

14. Employees in the manufacturing department of Michael Metals Company are paid on a one-for-one incentive plan beginning at 85 percent of standard. Bob Darver works in this department and earns a base wage of $8.50 per hour for a 40-hour week. The standard for Bob's job is 20 units per hour. Last week Bob produced 890 units.
   (a) How many standard hours did Bob earn last week?
   (b) How much gross pay did Bob earn for this work?

15. Employees in the assembly department of McDaniel Microwave Corporation are paid on a one-for-one incentive plan beginning at 90 percent of standard. Tom Minor works in this department and earns a base wage of $9.20 per hour for a 40-hour week. The standard for Tom's job is 7 units per hour. Last week Tom produced 310 units.
   (a) How many standard hours did Tom produce last week?
   (b) How much gross pay did Tom earn for this work?

16. Sam Smith works 40 hours a week at the Cato Custard Company. Sam is paid on a 70 percent gain-sharing plan, with bonus earnings beginning at standard. The base wage for Sam's job is $7.25 per hour and the standard is 38 units per hour.
   (a) What is Sam's weekly (40 hours) pay if he works at standard, and what is the company's labor cost per unit?
   (b) What is Sam's weekly pay if he produces 1,800 units in the 40 hours? What

is the labor cost per unit at this production rate?

17. Charles Curtis works 40 hours a week at Sunnydale Dairy. Charles is paid on an 80 percent gain-sharing plan, with bonus earnings beginning at standard. The base wage for Charles' job is $6.75 per hour, and the standard is 43 units per hour.
   (a) What is Charles's weekly (40 hours) pay if he works at standard, and what is the company's labor cost per unit?
   (b) What is Charles's weekly pay if he produces 1,950 units in the 40 hours?

18. The Bio Company pays its workers on a 70 percent gain-sharing plan, with bonus pay beginning at 85 percent of standard. The standard is 400 units per 40-hour week. Caroline Demarco, whose pay is $7.10 per hour, produced 425 units last week.
   (a) What is Caroline's gross pay for the week?
   (b) What is the unit labor cost at 60 percent of standard?
   (c) At standard?
   (d) At Caroline's rate of work last week?

19. The Omega Corporation pays its workers on a 75 percent gain-sharing plan, with bonus pay beginning at 85 percent of standard. The standard is 1,200 units per 40-hour week. Leslie Blount, whose pay is $6.90 per hour, produced 1,385 units last week.
   (a) What is Leslie's gross pay for the week?
   (b) What is the unit labor cost at 70 percent, 85 percent, and 100 percent of standard?
   (c) What is the unit labor cost at Leslie's rate of work last week?

20. Alton's Auto Repair pays mechanics one-half of the labor bill charges for the repair work they perform, or $8 per hour, whichever is higher. Repair work is billed at $24 per hour for each standard hour as stated in a reference catalog. A skilled mechanic

can perform 48 standard hours of work in a 40-hour week. Mechanics at this shop are not paid a percentage of the price for parts they install. Barton's Auto Repair charges $22 per standard hour and pays mechanics $10 per hour plus 10 percent of the price for parts used on the repair work they per-form. Each of Barton's mechanics installs an average of $2,400 worth of parts in a week.

(a) What are the average earnings at each shop?

(b) Where would you prefer to have your automobile repaired and why?

BIBLIOGRAPHY

Adam, Everett E., Jr., James C. Hershauer, and William A. Ruch. *Productivity and Quality: Measurement as a Basis for Improvement.* Englewood Cliffs, N.J.: Prentice-Hall, 1981.

Barnes, Ralph M. *Motion and Time Study,* 7th ed. New York: Wiley, 1980.

Brisley, Chester, L., and Royal J. Dossett. "Computer Use and Non-direct Labor Measurement Will Transform Profession in the Next Decade." *Industrial Engineering,* August 1980, pp. 34–43.

Bullock, R. J. and Edward E. Lawler. "Gainsharing: A Few Questions and Fewer Answers." *Human Resources Management,* Spring 1984, pp. 23–40.

International Labour Office. *Introduction to Work Study.* Rev. ed. Geneva, 1974.

Mundel, Marvin E. *Measuring and Enhancing the Productivity of Service and Government Organizations.* Tokyo: Asian Productivity Organization, 1975.

Nadler, Gerald. "Is More Measurement Better?" *Industrial Engineering,* March 1978, pp. 20–25.

Pryor, Frederic L. "Incentives In Manufacturing: The Carrot and the Stick." *Monthly Labor Review,* July 1984, pp. 40–43.

Rice, Robert S. "Survey of Work Measurement and Wage Incentives." *Industrial Engineering,* July 1977, pp. 18–31.

Seiler, Eric. "Piece Rate vs. Time Rate: The Effect of Incentives on Earnings." *Review of Economics and Statistics,* August 1984, pp. 363–376.

Sitnek, Larry N. "Performance Rating." *Industrial Management,* January–February 1977, pp. 11–16.

Von Kaas, H. K. *Making Wage Incentives Work.* New York: American Management Association, 1971.

Chapter Outline
A GLANCE AT THE BIG PICTURE

NEED FOR A BROAD SYSTEMS VIEW

EXTERNAL INFLUENCES ON OPERATIONS

Political, Social, and Economic Influences

FUTURE TRENDS IN OPERATIONS MANAGEMENT

Operations Management in Action: THE FUROR OVER AMERICA'S ABILITY TO COMPETE

Bibliography

KEY TERMS

Just-in-time production (JIT)

Computer numeric control (CNC) machines

Flexible manufacturing system (FMS)

Fixed automation

Factory of the future

Computer-integrated manufacturing (CIM)

Computer-aided design (CAD)

Group technology

Computer-aided process planning (CAPP)

Automatic storage and retrieval system (AS/RS)

Computer-aided manufacturing (CAM)

Chapter 16

A GLANCE AT THE BIG PICTURE

NEED FOR A BROAD SYSTEMS VIEW

A great deal of the material in this book has discussed methods used by operations managers to utilize operations resources efficiently in order to help accomplish corporate strategy. The operations function plays an important role in the strategy of most companies because it must provide the goods or services that the company offers in the marketplace. Of course, other functions are also vital to the success of a company. Consequently, operations managers must work to coordinate the efforts of their function with those of other parts of the enterprise, in addition to coordinating the various activities that occur within the operations functions. As they attempt to do this, operations managers need to keep in mind the relationships among these activities, because each may directly or indirectly affect the others. The extent to which one activity depends on another (within or outside of the operations function) varies from organization to organization and over time within the same organization. Let us examine some of these interdependencies to gain some insight into the kinds of relationships that operations managers should consider when they make their decisions. Figure 16.1 helps to summarize some of these dependencies. The figure depicts the degrees of relationship that might exist among several types of activities within a manufacturing company that produces a standardized product; it is not intended to convey the actual situation in every type of or-

FIGURE 16.1

Types of Relationships Between Some Operations-Related Activities

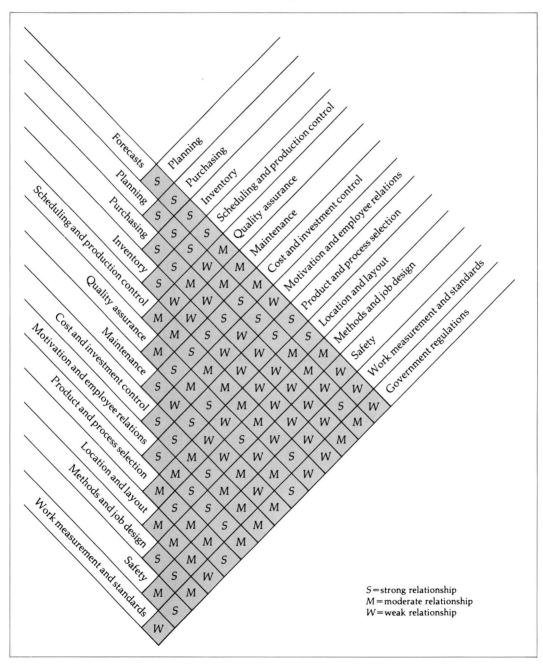

S = strong relationship
M = moderate relationship
W = weak relationship

ganization. You might construct a similar matrix for some other type of operation with which you are familiar.

Notice the extensive number of relationships that can exist even when only two topics are considered at a time. Figure 16.1 shows rankings of relationships, even though some activities have been omitted and some lines combine more than one of the topics discussed in the book. An *S* at the intersection of two diagonal rows indicates that there generally is a strong direct effect between the factors listed at the ends of the diagonal rows. The relationship between two topics may be one-way or reciprocal. For example, forecasts have a direct influence on plans but plans have little direct effect on the demand forecast. A strong direct relationship probably would be found between process selection and product quality and between job design and motivation. The fundamental importance of forecasting is indicated by several *S*'s, which indicate the dependence of plans, purchasing, schedules, inventory levels, location, layout, and production methods on some inferences about the future.

An *M* at the intersection of two diagonal rows indicates a moderate direct relationship between the factors in at least one direction or some indirect relationship that is of moderate importance. For example, responsiveness to production schedules and control efforts may depend to a moderate extent on the processes being used, the way in which work is divided (i.e., job design), and the motivation of the work force. Quality may be affected by many factors, including maintenance, job design, motivation, and the time allowed for tasks.

A *W* at the intersection of two diagonals indicates that one factor usually has a weak or little influence on another. For example, maintenance activities normally have little effect on inventory. In the event that extensive maintenance operations are to be performed, however, some extra inventory may be required so that other operations or sales will not be interrupted. Location and layout usually do not affect quality.

The relationships shown in Figure 16.1 make it apparent that when a decision is to be made, a manager must take into account many more factors than the one that immediately concerns him or her. Seventy-three of the entries in the figure (about 70 percent) are *M*'s or *S*'s, an indication that any one factor may depend on several others within the organization.

EXTERNAL INFLUENCES ON OPERATIONS

Some of the factors that affect decisions within the operations function come from outside the operations function, perhaps even from outside the firm, because businesses function within a complex web of relationships, both internal and external. The community, the nation, and indeed the whole world marketplace can have an effect on an enterprise, and failure to take these relationships into account may jeopardize the very existence of the operation. Changes in technology, population trends, competition, labor movements, personal desires for goods and services, personal job expectations, and domestic and foreign governmental action may have serious effects on an organization.

Operations managers must respond to events outside their organizations as well as those within it. Operations take place within a social system, with all its values, attitudes, goals, customs, and regulations. The operations function interacts with this surrounding environment in many ways beyond the mere supplying of goods or services to people outside the organization. Thus increasingly large portions of the top management's time must be spent in dealing with matters of the external environment.

An organization might be related to the surrounding political and cultural environment through several linkages, such as those depicted in Figure 16.2. Each linkage is represented by two arrows, one aimed in each direction, because there is a two-way interaction between the organization and each of the other entities. Workers supply labor and skills in exchange for pay and employee

FIGURE 16.2

Relationships Between a Domestic Organization and External Entities

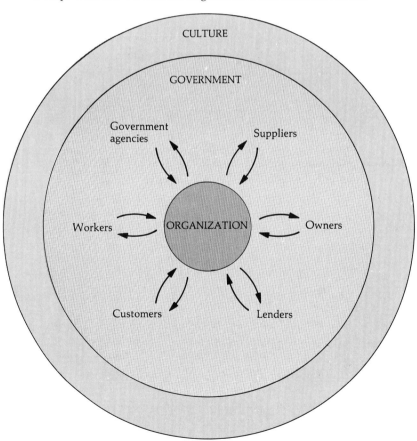

benefits. Suppliers provide resources in exchange for payments. Owners supply risk capital in exchange for prospective dividends, while lenders provide capital in exchange for interest payments and collateral. Customers supply revenue in exchange for goods and services. Government extracts taxes and provides military protection, a stable political and economic climate, and regulation of organizations within its domain so that the rights of various parties are protected. How far the rights of each party extend is a topic that is frequently debated and will be discussed later.

The marketplace for the goods and services of many companies is worldwide. Multinational firms must consider customs, culture, and language in addition to monetary exchange rates, tariffs, and trade quotas. A multinational firm has relationships with two or more governments and two or more cultures, as shown in Figure 16.3. The owners, suppliers, and other parties involved can be in either country, so that the situation for an actual multinational corporation might vary widely from that shown in the figure.

In Figures 16.2 and 16.3 all of the arrows representing interaction of an organization with other entities are drawn to pass through at least one background circle that represents government. Indeed, governmental laws and regulations affect the organization's dealings with employees, lenders, customers, suppliers, and owners. Other laws, naturally, shape the relationship between the organization and the government itself. The role of government as a regulator of business and other organizations has increased over time. Table 16.1 shows the numerous regulatory agencies of the United States government and a brief statement of each agency's mission. No attempt will be made to discuss all of these agencies, but the table should make it apparent that many operations activities are influenced by government.

Governmental regulations influence the jobs that managers must perform and the ways in which those jobs are performed. Businesses have complained about some of these restrictions—in particular about the costs of complying and the paperwork involved in meeting the reporting requirements. Governmental administrators sympathetic to some of the complaints have on occasion reduced reporting requirements.[1] One of the stated intentions of President Reagan on assuming office in 1981 was to attempt to curb the size and influence of the federal government's regulatory agencies and to bring about some deregulation. Among the goals of these efforts were the reduction of paperwork, the use of the least expensive method of regulation, and the use of regulation only in instances where the benefits exceed the costs. The questions of whose benefits are being measured against whose costs, and how you measure them, will certainly continue to be a source of controversy for years. But deregulation has made significant changes in numerous industries such as banking, transportation, and telecommunications.

Business takes place within an environment of values, attitudes, and customs that often are not uniform in location or over time. At least four compo-

---

[1]"OSHA to Lay Off Small Businesses," *American Business*, October 1977, p. 3.

FIGURE 16.3

Possible External Relationships of a Multinational Organization

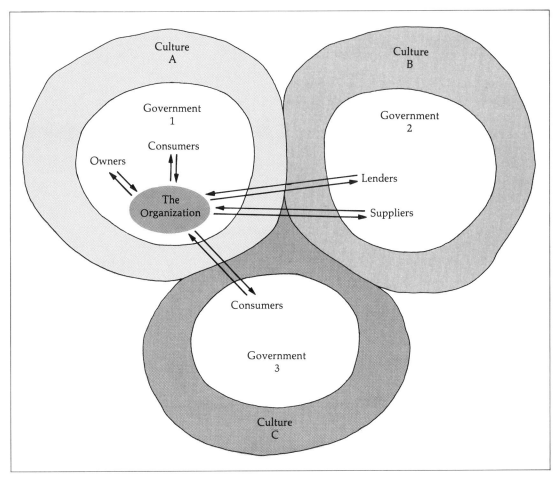

nents of the environment—political, social, economic, and technological—serve to keep businesses in general from becoming too settled. Actually one may find a wide variety of viewpoints on almost any issue.

Political, Social, and Economic Influences

In a pluralistic society, managers often deal with pressure from many diverse groups. Six important issues that relate to society's pressures and regulations on operations are:

1. Environmental protection
2. Social responsibility
3. Consumer protection

Table 16.1
MAJOR REGULATORY AGENCIES OF THE UNITED STATES GOVERNMENT

Independent Agencies

1887	Interstate Commerce Commission	Regulates rails, trucks
1913	Federal Reserve Board	Regulates banks, monetary policy
1914	Federal Trade Commission	Administers antitrust, packaging, advertising
1916	U.S. Tariff Commission	Investigates tariff and foreign trade
1924	U.S. Tax Court	Adjudicates federal tax cases
1926	National Mediation Board	Mediates labor disputes in air and rails
1930	Federal Power Commission	Regulates electricity and natural gas
1932	Federal Home Loan Bank Board	Provides credit reserve for home finance
1933	Federal Deposit Insurance Corporation	Insures deposits, supervises some banks
1934	Federal Communications Commission	Regulates radio, TV, telephone, telegraph
1934	Securities and Exchange Commission	Regulates securities industry
1935	National Labor Relations Board	Regulates unfair labor practices
1936	Federal Maritime Commission	Regulates foreign trade of steamships
1938	Civil Aeronautics Board	Regulates and promotes air travel
1946	Atomic Energy Commission	Regulates and promotes atomic energy
1952	Federal Coal Mine Safety Board	Hears appeals to Coal Mine Safety Act
1964	Equal Employment Opportunity Commission	Investigates discrimination charges
1970	Environmental Protection Agency	Monitors environmental matters
1974	Federal Energy Administration	Regulates energy production and use

Executive Branch Agencies

1824	Army Corps of Engineers	Builds and maintains rivers and harbors
1836	Patent Office	Administers patent and trademark laws
1862	Internal Revenue Service	Administers federal tax programs
1863	Comptroller of the Currency	Regulates national banks
1903	Antitrust division, Justice Department	Enforces antitrust laws
1915	U.S. Coast Guard	Regulates seaworthiness of ships
1916	Packers and Stockyards Administration	Regulates livestock and meat marketing
1922	Commodity Exchange Authority	Regulates commodity exchanges
1931	Food & Drug Administration	Regulates food and drug safety and labeling
1933	Bureau of Employment Security	Administers unemployment compensation
1933	Social Security Administration	Administers federal retirement programs
1933	Commodity Credit Corporation	Administers farm price support programs
1935	Rural Electrification Administration	Administers REA loan programs
1936	Maritime Administration	Promotes merchant marine
1951	Renegotiation Board	Renegotiates defense contracts
1953	Small Business Administration	Promotes small businesses
1958	Federal Aviation Administration	Regulates aircraft and air systems
1959	Oil Import Administration	Regulates petroleum imports
1963	Labor Management Services Administration	Regulates employee welfare and pensions
1964	Office of Economic Opportunity	Administers federal poverty/youth programs
1966	Federal Highway Administration	Administers road building and safety programs
1966	Federal Railroad Administration	Administers high-speed and safety programs
1966	National Transportation Safety Board	Investigates transportation accidents
1971	Occupational Safety & Health Administration	Issues and enforces industrial standards
1972	Consumer Product Safety Commission	Administers federal product safety laws

Source: William D. Brickloe and Mary T. Coughlin, Managing Organizations *(Encino, Calif.: Glencoe Press, 1977), p. 550.*

4. Employee safety and health
5. Employee pressure on wages and work policy
6. Free trade versus protectionism

You will notice discussions of such issues in newspapers, magazines, and trade journals. Interest groups continually exert pressure for actions favorable to them.

Environmental Protection   Environmental protection is one issue that has had a significant impact on operations. In some cases (such as the automobile industry), pollution regulations affect product design, but more commonly they influence the processes and equipment used in manufacturing. Many companies have had to invest vast amounts of money in pollution-control equipment, significantly increasing their payments for debt and equity funds. Since investments for pollution control do not provide additional revenue, these costs must be taken out of profits or added to the price of the product (possibly causing a competitive disadvantage). Some companies have been unable or unwilling to make these investments, and have closed at a time when unemployment was already a problem.

Pollution-control equipment itself can cause some changes in operations. New technology may require additional training programs. Maintenance and scheduled down time for cleaning may cause some additional scheduling constraints. Addition of another processing stage (cleaning of effluents) reduces the reliability of the total system unless duplicate backup equipment is available. If the pollution-control system breaks down, the plant must discontinue some processes until it is repaired or risk legal penalties. The required duplication of some equipment may double the investment of a small business that would normally have only one piece of equipment rather than two. The relative burden of adding a backup unit is smaller for a larger company that already has four or five pieces of this type of equipment.

Social Responsibility   Society today expects managers to have a concern for the welfare of society as well as having a profit motive. A manager's social responsibilities cause him or her to consider human values both within and outside the firm and to make decisions and take actions for reasons that are, at least partially, beyond the company's technological and economic interests. Moreover, business people are opinion leaders and may become involved in civic and social activities.

Society would like business leaders to maintain sound competitive firms that provide stable sources of taxes, employment, and high quality goods or services. In addition, society expects firms to fulfill certain social obligations: to provide equal opportunities, to develop human resources, to locate in areas of high unemployment when possible, to train the unemployed, perhaps to provide day-care programs and scholarships. Business leaders are also expected to contribute their knowledge to help deal with problems of local communities or the nation. Thus business leaders are cast in a variety of roles, with conflicting expectations of altruism, self-interest, and good citizenship.

Consumer Protection   Consumer protection is an effort to give consumers power and a voice, so that no consumer is helpless against the giant business entities that exist today. Protection is provided partly by private associations and partly by governmental agencies that regulate product safety standards and provide drug-testing services. Truth-in-lending and truth-in-advertising help provide the consumer with suffcent information to be in a position to evaluate products or services. The quality assurance efforts of companies also are directed toward fulfilling consumer protection responsibilities.

Employee Safety and Health   Employee safety and health regulations promulgated by the Occupational Safety and Health Administration (OSHA) have had an impact on some operations. Some serious violations of safety have been prevented, and both safe and unsafe operations have had to deal with inspection and reporting requirements.

Employee Influence on Wages and Work Policy   In some instances managers may not deal with employees directly but work with an additional outside entity, as when employees elect to be represented by a labor union. Government regulations establish a framework for collective bargaining to reach agreement about wages, hours, and working conditions. The working agreement may extend to issues of inflation, training, job security, pensions, unemployment benefits, medical benefits, automation, and other issues—such as employee participation in decisions. Issues not included in the contract may be resolved by arbitration if agreement is not reached within a normal work relationship.

The scope of managers' decisions may be restricted in some instances because of contract provisions. On the other hand the position of unions may be weakened by economic conditions, automation, or competition. "The relationships between business and labor have been and are unique, complex, and volatile. The way in which business and labor interact is not something they alone can decide. It is dependent upon government policy, legal decisions, and prevailing attitudes in society, as well as the power of labor and business."[2] The objective of maintaining business and labor agreements is achieved through balancing various influences. This process provides labor relations that are more stable than those that could be achieved through other means without a great deal of government intervention.

Free Trade vs. Protectionism   Competition from foreign trade has aroused quite a stir in several industries. In 1977, within months of winning its largest wage increase, the United Steelworkers union was asking the government for protection from foreign steel imports in order to preserve workers' jobs. The reason: foreign producers, mainly in Japan and Europe, were supplying 18 percent of the U.S. steel market. Imported steel accounted for more than 22 percent of the United States market in 1981 and captured a record 24.2 percent in 1984. In 1983 the total world steel production totaled about 400 million metric

[2]George A. Steiner and John F. Steiner, *Business, Government, and Society: A Managerial Perspective* (New York: Random House, 1980), p. 346.

tons, which is less than two-thirds of the world's rated production capacity. This excess capacity creates tremendous pressure on U.S. producers, whose labor cost is about $154 per ton compared with $105 for Japan and only $22 for South Korea.[3] Japanese imports accounted for 40 percent of the U.S. market for color television sets in 1977 and 87 percent of the U.S. market for black-and-white sets.[4] The share of the U.S. market taken by imported automobiles zoomed from 18 percent in 1978 to more than 27 percent in 1981 and remained at about this level until voluntary quotas expired in 1985.

Due to such factors as higher domestic prices and a strong dollar, imports have remained much higher than exports, resulting in huge trade deficits in recent years. In 1981, the United States had a trade deficit of about $27 billion. By 1983, the trade deficit had grown to about $70 billion. And it was over $100 billion in 1984.[5] Increased productivity and an accompanying decrease in the inflation rate are seen as possible ways to increase the United States' competitiveness and reduce its trade deficits. Foreign trade policy is not made by operations managers but it directly affects them, and consumers as well. International repercussions and restrictions on domestic products must be considered when such policies are established. Even when the government attempts to relieve trade problems, it is not likely to please everyone concerned.

FUTURE TRENDS IN OPERATIONS MANAGEMENT

Today many offices, service facilities, and factories are broadening their use of automation. Many types of business are adopting or expanding their use of electronic data processing, teleprocessing, word processing, electronic filing, electronic mail, and other innovations for performing office activities. Service operations also are implementing more mechanization and using more new technology in their activities.

Some of the trends that exist in manufacturing today will probably continue—both increasing in degree and involving a growing number of companies. The first of these trends is the greater emphasis being given to quality. The belief is growing that a company can reduce cost and improve quality at the same time. As more companies improve quality without increasing their prices, other firms will have to follow.

The trend toward using *just-in-time production* (*JIT*) will probably extend to more companies and change the general approach that manufacturers have to conducting business. Many of the companies presently using this approach will become better at JIT, and their competitors will have to follow. Also, as more companies develop this capability, more JIT suppliers will probably become available, giving further impetus to the trend.

[3]"The Worldwide Steel Industry: Reshaping to Survive," *Business Week,* August 20, 1984, p. 151.
[4]"Zenith at War with Japanese," *American Business,* October 1977, p. 2.
[5]"The Recovery Cheers the GOP," *Business Week,* September 3, 1984, p. 77.

Operations Management in Action

THE FUROR OVER AMERICA'S ABILITY TO COMPETE

A new study by the New York Stock Exchange is likely to be eagerly embraced by those who say there is no need for government efforts to improve the U.S. competitive position. The NYSE concludes, based on an analysis that uses data through 1982, that U.S. manufacturing has not lost international competitiveness. Even the strong dollar and the worsening trade balance—now racing toward a $120 billion deficit for 1984—do not dissuade NYSE economists from their conclusions. "In 1983 and 1984 we may have seen some undesirable short-term trade results," says Mel Colchamiro, chief author of the NYSE's study, "but it's not appropriate to form policies on the basis of one or two years' data."

But other economists—by no means all of them advocates of an industrial policy directed at restoring competitiveness—are challenging the study's findings. They say that the competitive position of U.S. manufacturers is indeed worsening and that it could well continue to do so. For one thing, they say, a rising dollar can influence trade volumes with a lag of up to four years. This means that even if the dollar should begin to weaken, export prices are unlikely to drop immediately, and the dollar's earlier strength will continue to cut into U.S. export volume.

For another thing, market share—the sole gauge used by the NYSE—is not a true measure of competitiveness, the experts argue. They believe that the NYSE should have dug deeper and looked at profitability, productivity, and quality. Had the NYSE done so, they say, it would have found that the ability of U.S. manufacturers to compete in world markets is indeed deteriorating.

Key Losers

The NYSE, with assistance from the University of Maryland, analyzed shifts in the world share—in volume rather than value—of manufacturing exports for the U.S., Japan, Europe, and the rest of the world, and concluded that "our competitive position is much stronger than the conventional wisdom would have it." U.S. manufacturing, the NYSE reports, lost only a small share of U.S. world exports in the two decades ended in 1982. And from 1972 to 1982, the study notes, the U.S. share actually rose from 12.1% to 12.3%.

The study concedes that some key industries—such as autos, steel, and textiles—have lost ground to foreign competitors. "But it would be a great mistake," says William C. Freund, chief economist at the NYSE, "to assume that the travail of those industries applies to all manufacturing." The NYSE relied primarily on disaggregated data for 40 manufacturing industries in nine countries, and it was unable to obtain these data for 1983. But data from the economy as a whole show that the U.S. share of the world market began to erode in 1981 and had really plummeted by 1983, when the dollar took off, says David W. Rolley, an international economist at Chase Econometrics.

Data developed by Chase Econometrics show that merchandise trade exports as a per-

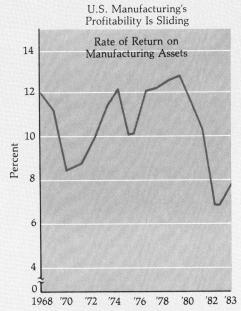

U.S. Manufacturing's Profitability Is Sliding

Rate of Return on Manufacturing Assets

Data: Federal Trade Commission, Data Resources Inc., BW

cent of the total exports for the U.S., Canada, Japan, and the nine largest European nations fell from a peak level of 21.7% in 1980 to 17.3% in 1983. That share is expected to slide even further this year, to about 16.3%. The deterioration was consistent with a sharp acceleration in export prices of the U.S. relative to those same nations. In 1980, U.S. manufacturing export prices averaged 90% of the prices for the 12-nation group, giving the U.S. a strong competitive advantage. By 1983 that figure had risen to 117.2%, and it could top 125% this year.

Even the NYSE's own numbers show that the U.S. is being outpaced by some of its trading partners. The study notes that during the decade ended in 1982, Japan gained a larger export share in 25 industries and lost share in 15, while the U.S. experience was the reverse: It gained share in 15 industries and lost share in 26. "We're not going backward," says Bruce R. Scott of Harvard business school, "but others are running ahead of us."

But Scott's chief criticism of the study is in its use of trade volume as a measure of market share. In the 1970s a weakening dollar meant that the price of U.S. products declined on world markets, and thus the U.S. held market share in volume but lost share in value. (Since late 1981, when the dollar began to strengthen, the pattern has reversed—the volume of U.S. exports has dipped while the value has risen.) Scott notes that the cheaper dollar in the 1970s meant that U.S. exporters were essentially cutting prices and "giving their product away," thereby maintaining volume. And that, he argues, means market share fails to provide an accurate measure of competitiveness.

The study focused on market share in volume terms, says Colchamiro of the NYSE, because "we wanted to think in a straightforward manner, take a businessman's approach, and ask: 'How well did I sell in world markets? How did Macy's do compared to Gimbels?'" But the competitive health and strength of Macy's vs. Gimbels, or the U.S. vs. other nations, rest not simply on the number of units sold but also on the price charged for those units.

A far better measure of whether U.S. business can compete over the longer run is profitability, Scott argues. And the data show that the pretax rate of return on U.S. manufac-

turing assets began to slide in 1980 [see figure]. That year, when the U.S. share of total world exports on a volume basis reached 14.7%, according to the NYSE, the rate of return on manufacturing assets slid to 11.8%, from 13.0% the year before.

Another measure that points to diminished U.S. competitiveness is productivity. While in absolute terms the U.S. still boasts the highest productivity—or unit labor cost—until the recent cyclical upturn, its productivity gains paled when compared with those of its major trading partners. Indeed, a Data Resources Inc. study of U.S. manufacturing indicates that from 1965 to 1981, Japan's manufacturing productivity grew at a rate more than twice that of the U.S., while West Germany's grew one-and-one-half times the U.S. rate.

Eroding Position

Less telling than some of these measures, but still important in determining the competitiveness of U.S. manufacturing, are intangibles such as the quality of U.S. products relative to those made by other major exporters, and the trends in innovation.

A number of recent studies point to an eroding U.S. competitive position based on these qualitative measures. In a study of room air-conditioning manufacturers in the U.S. and Japan, David Garvin, a professor at Harvard business school, found that by numerous measures—from assembly-line defects to service calls required—Japanese companies were far superior to their U.S. counterparts. Furthermore, Garvin found that "quality pays." The highest quality producers also boasted the highest output per man-hour, and the Japanese producers had the lowest overall quality costs.

Significantly, Garvin found these variations were attributable not to differences in technology or capital intensity but rather to differing management policies and attitudes. Seven C. Wheelwright, a professor of management at Stanford University's Graduate School of Business, argues that U.S. manufacturing has lost its competitive edge because "U.S. managers have quit doing a number of things."

For one thing, balkanized organizational structures prevent the research, engineering, and manufacturing staffs from coordinating the introduction of new products. For another, administrators—trained in finance or the law—are more likely to rise to top management positions than are technical experts with thorough hands-on experience in manufacturing. And many executives, says Wheelwright, have made a self-fulfilling prophecy of the notion that "we invent things and somebody else picks them up and runs with them."

Indeed, Scott says this is just what has been happening. Japanese manufacturing, he says, is moving "upscale" and gaining market share in high-technology areas while it is losing it in low-technology areas. He notes that the U.S. is doing its share of research, but that it is failing to capture the returns from innovation.

Another trend that shows promise of continuing and one that will make significant changes in manufacturing is the development and improvement of flexible automation—such as robots, *computer numeric controlled machines* and machining centers, and *flexible manufacturing systems* (FMSs). Since the industrial revolution, the general trend has been toward greater standardization and simplification when automation is used. But flexible manufacturing systems and reprogrammable robots represent a significant reversal of this trend. The fact that *fixed automation* no longer has to be used will bring about several changes in the way that manufacturing companies produce products and compete for business. Generally, although not universally, FMS users agree that most of the potential advantages of FMS mentioned in Chapter 13 can be achieved. There is not full agreement, however, that capital investment is lower with FMS than with conventional equipment. In at least one case, the user of an early system felt that human operators can better measure and compensate for variations in the pallets, fixtures, tools, and machines to produce better and more consistent quality. But adaptive controls for FMSs have been introduced to sense and correct for errors.[6] As these improvements are perfected, both better quality and greater flexibility can be achieved.

Flexible automation technology will be applied to processes other than machining, such as welding, grinding, and painting, and perhaps to processes such as sewing or weaving. Flexible automation will enable companies to use automation at volumes that previously would not justify its use, and product life cycles may become even shorter for some products. Manufacturers will probably compete with a wider variety of custom variations of their basic product and be able to respond more quickly to customer requests, particularly where computer-aided design is used or even coupled to the production process.

Factories are extending automation beyond the use of FMS to incorporate the concept of computer-integrated manufacturing, popularly called *factory of the future*. In *computer-integrated manufacturing*, CIM, computers are used to con-

---

[6]James B. Dilworth and M. Khris McAlister, "Users' Perceptions of FMS Characteristics: A Survey," APICS Spring Seminar, New Orleans, April 24, 1985.

trol on a real-time basis the overall cycle of design, production planning, and manufacturing. CIM integrates and coordinates all of the activities required to go from the input of design concepts to the output of final products. Computers are used to control and link information processing in six different activities:

1. *Computer-aided design,* CAD, which uses *group techology* to take advantage of similarities between parts to reduce both the number of designs needed and the time required to make designs
2. *Computer-aided process planning,* CAPP, which also uses group technology to simplify the planning process
3. Computer-aided management of materials, schedules, and capacity with the closed-loop MRP concept
4. Computer control for the *automatic storage and retrieval system,* AS/RS, and other materials-handling systems
5. *Computer-aided manufacturing,* CAM, to control the processing steps of the production equipment
6. Computer control of robots at various production stages

The CIM concept requires extensive capabilities in information processing. Control of each of the six areas listed above must be mastered before they can be integrated into an overall system. CIM can provide great flexibility in batch manufacturing operations. As this technology becomes better developed and more people develop the capabilities necessary to use it, we will see broader applications of the various parts of CIM and greater integration of these components.

Energy and raw materials will become more important as other nations develop and compete for the world's resources.

Developed nations will have to move increasingly toward the use of advanced technology as the developing countries expand their labor-intensive industries.

As developed nations become more service-oriented "postindustrial states," the operations functions in general will have more contact with consumers, and operations managers will need to take more interest in relations with consumers and with the public in general. Quality of service will become increasingly important as one facet of quality assurance, even for operations that produce tangible items.

More multinational companies and consortiums will be founded to contend with shifting patterns of demand, prosperity, and favorable monetary exchange rates.

Advancing technology will increase the need for trained specialists and will require more frequent retraining of workers and managers.

Management will continue to use staff specialists, quantitative techniques, and computers to deal with increasingly broad and highly technical operations.

Now that the United States is primarily a service economy, productivity advances will be harder to achieve.

The need for large investments to obtain high-technology equipment and the monetary risk to form businesses will be too great for most individuals to bear, so that small manufacturers will become less common. More businesses will be run by professional managers rather than by owners.

With an increasingly well-educated work force, with higher expectations and more mobility, operations managers will need to have even more behavioral competence. People expect to be allowed more participation in decision making, yet an organization cannot follow everyone's preferred course of action. All managers will need to be capable in conflict management and able to gain resolution of differences. One challenge will be to help employees accommodate and adjust to compromises while maintaining *espirit de corps*.

It is to be hoped that government, labor, and business will cooperate to create and preserve jobs and to compete effectively in the world market. The challenge for operations managers (and one of the rewards) will be to participate in improving the quality of life for societies around the world.

BIBLIOGRAPHY

Bureau of National Affairs. *The Job Safety and Health Act of 1970.* Washington, D.C., 1971.

————. *The Consumer Product Safety Act.* Washington, D.C., 1973.

Davis, K., and R. L. Blomstrom. *Business, Society and Environment: Social Power and Social Responses.* 2d ed. New York: McGraw-Hill, 1971.

Hoogenboom, Ari, and Olive Hoogenboom. *A History of the ICC.* New York: Norton, 1976.

Jones, C. O. *Clean Air: The Policies and Politics of Pollution Control.* Pittsburgh: University of Pittsburgh Press, 1975.

Knesse, A. V., and C. L. Schultze. *Pollution, Prices, and Public Policy.* Washington, D.C.: Brookings Institution, 1975.

McFarland, Dalton E. *Management and Society: An Institutional Framework.* Englewood Cliffs, N.J.: Prentice-Hall, 1982.

Redmond, J. C., J. C. Cook, and A. A. J. Hoffman, eds. *Clearing the Air: The Impact of the Clean Air Act on Technology.* New York: Institute of Electrical and Electronics Engineers, 1971.

Rosen, S. J. *Manual for Environmental Impact Evaluation.* Englewood Cliffs, N.J.: Prentice-Hall, 1976.

Samuelson, Paul A. *Economics.* 10th ed. New York: McGraw-Hill, 1976. Chap. 38.

Steiner, George A., and John F. Steiner. *Business, Government, and Society: A Managerial Perspective.* New York: Random House, 1980.

"Zeroing In on Dumping." *Time,* November 7, 1977.

APPENDICES

APPENDIX I

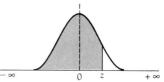

Cumulative Probabilities of the Normal Distribution (Areas under the Standardized Normal Curve from $-\infty$ to z)

z	.00	.01	.02	.03	.04	.05	.06	.07	.08	.09
.0	.5000	.5040	.5080	.5120	.5160	.5199	.5239	.5279	.5319	.5359
.1	.5398	.5438	.5478	.5517	.5557	.5596	.5636	.5675	.5714	.5753
.2	.5793	.5832	.5871	.5910	.5948	.5987	.6026	.6064	.6103	.6141
.3	.6179	.6217	.6255	.6293	.6331	.6368	.6406	.6443	.6480	.6517
.4	.6554	.6591	.6628	.6664	.6700	.6736	.6772	.6808	.6844	.6879
.5	.6915	.6950	.6985	.7019	.7054	.7088	.7123	.7157	.7190	.7224
.6	.7257	.7291	.7324	.7357	.7389	.7422	.7454	.7486	.7517	.7549
.7	.7580	.7611	.7642	.7673	.7704	.7734	.7764	.7794	.7823	.7852
.8	.7881	.7910	.7939	.7967	.7995	.8023	.8051	.8078	.8106	.8133
.9	.8159	.8186	.8212	.8238	.8264	.8289	.8315	.8340	.8365	.8389
1.0	.8413	.8438	.8461	.8485	.8508	.8531	.8554	.8577	.8599	.8621
1.1	.8643	.8665	.8686	.8708	.8729	.8749	.8770	.8790	.8810	.8830
1.2	.8849	.8869	.8888	.8907	.8925	.8944	.8962	.8980	.8997	.9015
1.3	.9032	.9049	.9066	.9082	.9099	.9115	.9131	.9147	.9162	.9177
1.4	.9192	.9207	.9222	.9236	.9251	.9265	.9279	.9292	.9306	.9319
1.5	.9332	.9345	.9357	.9370	.9382	.9394	.9406	.9418	.9429	.9441
1.6	.9452	.9463	.9474	.9484	.9495	.9505	.9515	.9525	.9535	.9545
1.7	.9554	.9564	.9573	.9582	.9591	.9599	.9608	.9616	.9625	.9633
1.8	.9641	.9649	.9656	.9664	.9671	.9678	.9686	.9693	.9699	.9706
1.9	.9713	.9719	.9726	.9732	.9738	.9744	.9750	.9756	.9761	.9767
2.0	.9772	.9778	.9783	.9788	.9793	.9798	.9803	.9808	.9812	.9817
2.1	.9821	.9826	.9830	.9834	.9838	.9842	.9846	.9850	.9854	.9857
2.2	.9861	.9864	.9868	.9871	.9875	.9878	.9881	.9884	.9887	.9890
2.3	.9893	.9896	.9898	.9901	.9904	.9906	.9909	.9911	.9913	.9916
2.4	.9918	.9920	.9922	.9925	.9927	.9929	.9931	.9932	.9934	.9936
2.5	.9938	.9940	.9941	.9943	.9945	.9946	.9948	.9949	.9951	.9952
2.6	.9953	.9955	.9956	.9957	.9959	.9960	.9961	.9962	.9963	.9964
2.7	.9965	.9966	.9967	.9968	.9969	.9970	.9971	.9972	.9973	.9974
2.8	.9974	.9975	.9976	.9977	.9977	.9978	.9979	.9979	.9980	.9981
2.9	.9981	.9982	.9982	.9983	.9984	.9984	.9985	.9985	.9986	.9986
3.0	.9987	.9987	.9987	.9988	.9988	.9989	.9989	.9989	.9990	.9990
3.1	.9990	.9991	.9991	.9991	.9992	.9992	.9992	.9992	.9993	.9993
3.2	.9993	.9993	.9994	.9994	.9994	.9994	.9994	.9995	.9995	.9995
3.3	.9995	.9995	.9995	.9996	.9996	.9996	.9996	.9996	.9996	.9997
3.4	.9997	.9997	.9997	.9997	.9997	.9997	.9997	.9997	.9997	.9998

APPENDIX II

Learning Curve Tables

95%

Unit Number	Time for Unit	Cumulative Total Time for All Units	Cumulative Average Time over All Units
1	1.000	1.000	1.000
2	.9500	1.950	.9750
4	.9025	3.775	.9436
5	.8877	4.6621	.9324
7	.8659	6.4039	.9148
10	.8433	8.9545	.8954
15	.8184	13.0921	.8728
20	.8012	17.1302	.8565
25	.7880	21.0955	.8438
30	.7775	25.0032	.8334
40	.7611	32.6838	.8171
50	.7486	40.2239	.8045
70	.7302	54.9924	.7856
100	.7112	76.5864	.7659
200	.6756	145.6929	.7285
300	.6557	212.1772	.7073
400	.6519	277.0121	.6925
500	.6314	340.6472	.6813
700	.6158	465.2648	.6647
1000	.5998	647.4463	.6474
1500	.5821	942.587	.6284
2000	.5698	1230.3796	.6152
2500	.5605	1512.8486	.6051
3000	.5530	1791.1396	.5970
3500	.5467	2066.0035	.5903
4000	.5413	2337.9672	.5845
5000	.5325	2874.4123	.5749

90%

Unit Number	Time for Unit	Cumulative Total Time for All Units	Cumulative Average Time over All Units
1	1.000	1.000	1.000
2	.9000	1.900	.9500
4	.8100	3.5562	.8891
5	.7830	4.3391	.8678
7	.7438	5.8447	.8350
10	.7047	7.9945	.7994
15	.6626	11.3837	.7589
20	.6342	14.6078	.7304
25	.6131	17.7132	.7085
30	.5963	20.7269	.6909
40	.5078	26.5427	.6636
50	.5518	32.1420	.6428
70	.5243	42.8706	.6124
100	.4966	58.1410	.5814
200	.4469	104.9641	.5248
300	.4202	148.2040	.4940
400	.4022	189.2678	.4732
500	.3889	228.7851	.4576
700	.3694	304.4757	.4350
1000	.3499	412.1718	.4122
1500	.3290	581.4952	.3877
2000	.3149	742.2854	.3711
2500	.3044	897.0392	.3588
3000	.2961	1047.0770	.3490
3500	.2893	1193.3681	.3410
4000	.2834	1336.5057	.3341
5000	.2740	1614.6705	.3229

85%

Unit Number	Time for Unit	Cumulative Total Time for All Units	Cumulative Average Time over All Units
1	1.000	1.000	1.000
2	.8500	1.8500	.9250
4	.7225	3.3454	.8364
5	.6857	4.0310	.8062
7	.6337	5.3217	.7602
10	.5828	7.1161	.7116
15	.5300	9.8611	.6574
20	.4954	12.4023	.6201
25	.4701	14.8007	.5920
30	.4505	17.0907	.5697
40	.4211	21.4252	.5356
50	.3996	25.5131	.5103
70	.3693	33.1664	.4738
100	.3397	43.7539	.4375
200	.2887	74.7885	.3739
300	.2625	102.2301	.3408
400	.2454	127.5690	.3189
500	.2329	151.4504	.3029
700	.2152	196.1344	.2802
1000	.1980	257.9180	.2579
1500	.1800	352.0333	.2347
2000	.1683	438.9276	.2195
2500	.1597	520.8187	.2083
3000	.1530	598.9313	.1996
3500	.1476	674.0355	.1926
4000	.1430	746.6567	.1867
5000	.1357	885.8752	.1772

80%

Unit Number	Time for Unit	Cumulative Total Time for All Units	Cumulative Average Time over All Units
1	1.000	1.000	1.000
2	.8000	1.800	.900
4	.6400	3.1421	.7855
5	.5956	3.7378	.7475
7	.5345	4.8340	.6906
10	.4765	6.3154	.6315
15	.4182	8.5105	.5674
20	.3812	10.4849	.5242
25	.3548	12.3086	.4923
30	.3346	14.0199	.4673
40	.3050	17.1935	.4298
50	.2838	20.1217	.4024
70	.2547	25.4708	.3639
100	.2271	32.6508	.3265
200	.1816	52.7200	.2636
300	.1594	69.6634	.2322
400	.1453	84.8487	.2121
500	.1352	98.8472	.1977
700	.1214	124.3984	.1777
1000	.1082	158.6709	.1587
1500	.0950	209.1580	.1394
2000	.0866	254.3996	.1272
2500	.0806	296.1018	.1184
3000	.0760	355.1843	.1117
3500	.0723	372.2146	.1063
4000	.0692	407.5742	.1019
5000	.0644	474.3001	.0949

75%

Unit Number	Time for Unit	Cumulative Total Time for All Units	Cumulative Average Time over All Units
1	1.000	1.000	1.000
2	.7500	1.7500	.8750
4	.5625	2.9463	.7366
5	.5127	3.4591	.6918
7	.4459	4.3837	.6258
10	.3846	5.5886	.5589
15	.3250	7.3190	.4879
20	.2884	8.8284	.4414
25	.2629	10.1907	.4076
30	.2437	11.4458	.3815
40	.2163	13.7232	.3531
50	.1972	15.7761	.3155
70	.1715	19.4296	.2776
100	.1479	24.1786	.2418
200	.1109	36.8007	.1840
300	.0937	46.9427	.1565
400	.0832	55.7577	.1394
500	.0758	63.6753	.1274
700	.0659	77.7693	.1111
1000	.0569	96.0728	.0961
1500	.0481	122.0917	.0814
2000	.0427	144.6762	.0723
2500	.0389	165.0079	.0660
3000	.0360	183.7078	.0612
3500	.0338	201.1512	.0575
4000	.0320	217.5865	.0544
5000	.0292	247.5119	.0495

APPENDIX III

Cumulative Poisson Probabilities $P(x \le r \mid \lambda) = \sum\limits_{x=0}^{x=c} \dfrac{\lambda^x e^{-\lambda}}{x!}$

λ or np' \\ c	0	1	2	3	4	5	6	7	8	9
0.02	.980	1.000								
0.04	.961	.999	1.000							
0.06	.942	.998	1.000							
0.08	.923	.997	1.000							
0.10	.905	.995	1.000							
0.15	.861	.990	.999	1.000						
0.20	.819	.982	.999	1.000						
0.25	.779	.974	.998	1.000						
0.30	.741	.963	.996	1.000						
0.35	.705	.951	.994	1.000						
0.40	.670	.938	.992	.999	1.000					
0.45	.638	.925	.989	.999	1.000					
0.50	.607	.910	.986	.998	1.000					
0.55	.577	.894	.982	.998	1.000					
0.60	.549	.878	.977	.997	1.000					
0.65	.522	.861	.972	.996	.999	1.000				
0.70	.497	.844	.966	.994	.999	1.000				
0.75	.472	.827	.959	.993	.999	1.000				
0.80	.449	.809	.953	.991	.999	1.000				
0.85	.427	.791	.945	.989	.998	1.000				
0.90	.407	.772	.937	.987	.998	1.000				
0.95	.387	.754	.929	.984	.997	1.000				
1.00	.368	.736	.920	.981	.996	.999	1.000			
1.1	.333	.699	.900	.974	.995	.999	1.000			
1.2	.301	.663	.879	.966	.992	.998	1.000			
1.3	.273	.627	.857	.957	.989	.998	1.000			
1.4	.247	.592	.833	.946	.986	.997	.999	1.000		
1.5	.223	.558	.809	.934	.981	.996	.999	1.000		
1.6	.202	.525	.783	.921	.976	.994	.999	1.000		
1.7	.183	.493	.757	.907	.970	.992	.998	1.000		
1.8	.165	.463	.731	.891	.964	.990	.997	.999	1.000	
1.9	.150	.434	.704	.875	.956	.987	.997	.999	1.000	
2.0	.135	.406	.677	.857	.947	.983	.995	.999	1.000	

λ or np' \ c	0	1	2	3	4	5	6	7	8	9
2.2	.111	.355	.623	.819	.928	.975	.993	.998	1.000	
2.4	.091	.308	.570	.779	.904	.964	.988	.997	.999	1.000
2.6	.074	.267	.518	.736	.877	.951	.983	.995	.999	1.000
2.8	.061	.231	.469	.692	.848	.935	.976	.992	.998	.999
3.0	.050	.199	.423	.647	.815	.916	.966	.988	.996	.999
3.2	.041	.171	.380	.603	.781	.895	.955	.983	.994	.998
3.4	.033	.147	.340	.558	.744	.871	.942	.977	.992	.997
3.6	.027	.126	.303	.515	.706	.844	.927	.969	.988	.996
3.8	.022	.107	.269	.473	.668	.816	.909	.960	.984	.994
4.0	.018	.092	.238	.433	.629	.785	.889	.949	.979	.992
4.2	.015	.078	.210	.395	.590	.753	.867	.936	.972	.989
4.4	.012	.066	.185	.359	.551	.720	.844	.921	.964	.985
4.6	.010	.056	.163	.326	.513	.686	.818	.905	.955	.980
4.8	.008	.048	.143	.294	.476	.651	.791	.887	.944	.975
5.0	.007	.040	.125	.265	.440	.616	.762	.867	.932	.968
5.2	.006	.034	.109	.238	.406	.581	.732	.845	.918	.960
5.4	.005	.029	.095	.213	.373	.546	.702	.822	.903	.951
5.6	.004	.024	.082	.191	.342	.512	.670	.797	.886	.941
5.8	.003	.021	.072	.170	.313	.478	.638	.771	.867	.929
6.0	.002	.017	.062	.151	.285	.446	.606	.744	.847	.916

	10	11	12	13	14	15	16
2.8	1.000						
3.0	1.000						
3.2	1.000						
3.4	.999	1.000					
3.6	.999	1.000					
3.8	.998	.999	1.000				
4.0	.997	.999	1.000				
4.2	.996	.999	1.000				
4.4	.994	.998	.999	1.000			
4.6	.992	.997	.999	1.000			
4.8	.990	.996	.999	1.000			
5.0	.986	.995	.998	.999	1.000		
5.2	.982	.993	.997	.999	1.000		
5.4	.977	.990	.996	.999	1.000		
5.6	.972	.988	.995	.998	.999	1.000	
5.8	.965	.984	.993	.997	.999	1.000	
6.0	.957	.980	.991	.996	.999	.999	1.000

Appendix III   **(Continued)**

λ or np'	0	1	2	3	4	5	6	7	8	9
6.2	.002	.015	.054	.134	.259	.414	.574	.716	.826	.902
6.4	.002	.012	.046	.119	.235	.384	.542	.687	.803	.886
6.6	.001	.010	.040	.105	.213	.355	.511	.658	.780	.869
6.8	.001	.009	.034	.093	.192	.327	.480	.628	.755	.850
7.0	.001	.007	.030	.082	.173	.301	.450	.599	.729	.830
7.2	.001	.006	.025	.072	.156	.276	.420	.569	.703	.810
7.4	.001	.005	.022	.063	.140	.253	.392	.539	.676	.788
7.6	.001	.004	.019	.055	.125	.231	.365	.510	.648	.765
7.8	.000	.004	.016	.048	.112	.210	.338	.481	.620	.741
8.0	.000	.003	.014	.042	.100	.191	.313	.453	.593	.717
8.5	.000	.002	.009	.030	.074	.150	.256	.386	.523	.653
9.0	.000	.001	.006	.021	.055	.116	.207	.324	.456	.587
9.5	.000	.001	.004	.015	.040	.089	.165	.269	.392	.522
10.0	.000	.000	.003	.010	.029	.067	.130	.220	.333	.458

	10	11	12	13	14	15	16	17	18	19
6.2	.949	.975	.989	.995	.998	.999	1.000			
6.4	.939	.969	.986	.994	.997	.999	1.000			
6.6	.927	.963	.982	.992	.997	.999	.999	1.000		
6.8	.915	.955	.978	.990	.996	.998	.999	1.000		
7.0	.901	.947	.973	.987	.994	.998	.999	1.000		
7.2	.887	.937	.967	.984	.993	.997	.999	.999	1.000	
7.4	.871	.926	.961	.980	.991	.996	.998	.999	1.000	
7.6	.854	.915	.954	.976	.989	.995	.998	.999	1.000	
7.8	.835	.902	.945	.971	.986	.993	.997	.999	1.000	
8.0	.816	.888	.936	.966	.983	.992	.996	.998	.999	1.000
8.5	.763	.849	.909	.949	.973	.986	.993	.997	.999	.999
9.0	.706	.803	.876	.926	.959	.978	.989	.995	.998	.999
9.5	.645	.752	.836	.898	.940	.967	.982	.991	.996	.998
10.0	.583	.697	.792	.864	.917	.951	.973	.986	.993	.997

	20	21	22
8.5	1.000		
9.0	1.000		
9.5	.999	1.000	
10.0	.998	.999	1.000

λ or np' \ c	0	1	2	3	4	5	6	7	8	9
10.5	.000	.000	.002	.007	.021	.050	.102	.179	.279	.397
11.0	.000	.000	.001	.005	.015	.038	.079	.143	.232	.341
11.5	.000	.000	.001	.003	.011	.028	.060	.114	.191	.289
12.0	.000	.000	.001	.002	.008	.020	.046	.090	.155	.242
12.5	.000	.000	.000	.002	.005	.015	.035	.070	.125	.201
13.0	.000	.000	.000	.001	.004	.011	.026	.054	.100	.166
13.5	.000	.000	.000	.001	.003	.008	.019	.041	.079	.135
14.0	.000	.000	.000	.000	.002	.006	.014	.032	.062	.109
14.5	.000	.000	.000	.000	.001	.004	.010	.024	.048	.088
15.0	.000	.000	.000	.000	.001	.003	.008	.018	.037	.070

	10	11	12	13	14	15	16	17	18	19
10.5	.521	.639	.742	.825	.888	.932	.960	.978	.988	.994
11.0	.460	.579	.689	.781	.854	.907	.944	.968	.982	.991
11.5	.402	.520	.633	.733	.815	.878	.924	.954	.974	.986
12.0	.347	.462	.576	.682	.772	.844	.899	.937	.963	.979
12.5	.297	.406	.519	.628	.725	.806	.869	.916	.948	.969
13.0	.252	.353	.463	.573	.675	.764	.835	.890	.930	.957
13.5	.211	.304	.409	.518	.623	.718	.798	.861	.908	.942
14.0	.176	.260	.358	.464	.570	.669	.756	.827	.883	.923
14.5	.145	.220	.311	.413	.518	.619	.711	.790	.853	.901
15.0	.118	.185	.268	.363	.466	.568	.664	.749	.819	.875

	20	21	22	23	24	25	26	27	28	29
10.5	.997	.999	.999	1.000						
11.0	.995	.998	.999	1.000						
11.5	.992	.996	.998	.999	1.000					
12.0	.988	.994	.997	.999	.999	1.000				
12.5	.983	.991	.995	.998	.999	.999	1.000			
13.0	.975	.986	.992	.996	.998	.999	1.000			
13.5	.965	.980	.989	.994	.997	.998	.999	1.000		
14.0	.952	.971	.983	.991	.995	.997	.999	.999	1.000	
14.5	.936	.960	.976	.986	.992	.996	.998	.999	.999	1.000
15.0	.917	.947	.967	.981	.989	.994	.997	.998	.999	1.000

Appendix III (Continued)

λ or np' \ c	4	5	6	7	8	9	10	11	12	13
16	.000	.001	.004	.010	.022	.043	.077	.127	.193	.275
17	.000	.001	.002	.005	.013	.026	.049	.085	.135	.201
18	.000	.000	.001	.003	.007	.015	.030	.055	.092	.143
19	.000	.000	.001	.002	.004	.009	.018	.035	.061	.098
20	.000	.000	.000	.001	.002	.005	.011	.021	.039	.066
21	.000	.000	.000	.000	.001	.003	.006	.013	.025	.043
22	.000	.000	.000	.000	.001	.002	.004	.008	.015	.028
23	.000	.000	.000	.000	.000	.001	.002	.004	.009	.017
24	.000	.000	.000	.000	.000	.000	.001	.003	.005	.011
25	.000	.000	.000	.000	.000	.000	.001	.001	.003	.006

	14	15	16	17	18	19	20	21	22	23
16	.368	.467	.566	.659	.742	.812	.868	.911	.942	.963
17	.281	.371	.468	.564	.655	.736	.805	.861	.905	.937
18	.208	.287	.375	.469	.562	.651	.731	.799	.855	.899
19	.150	.215	.292	.378	.469	.561	.647	.725	.793	.849
20	.105	.157	.221	.297	.381	.470	.559	.644	.721	.787
21	.072	.111	.163	.227	.302	.384	.471	.558	.640	.716
22	.048	.077	.117	.169	.232	.306	.387	.472	.556	.637
23	.031	.052	.082	.123	.175	.238	.310	.389	.472	.555
24	.020	.034	.056	.087	.128	.180	.243	.314	.392	.473
25	.012	.022	.038	.060	.092	.134	.185	.247	.318	.394

	24	25	26	27	28	29	30	31	32	33
16	.978	.987	.993	.996	.998	.999	.999	1.000		
17	.959	.975	.985	.991	.995	.997	.999	..999	1.000	
18	.932	.955	.972	.983	.990	.994	.997	.998	.999	1.000
19	.893	.927	.951	.969	.980	.988	.993	.996	.998	.999
20	.843	.888	.922	.948	.966	.978	.987	.992	.995	.997
21	.782	.838	.883	.917	.944	.963	.976	.985	.991	.994
22	.712	.777	.832	.877	.913	.940	.959	.973	.983	.989
23	.635	.708	.772	.827	.873	.908	.936	.956	.971	.981
24	.554	.632	.704	.768	.823	.868	.904	.932	.953	.969
25	.473	.553	.629	.700	.763	.818	.863	.900	.929	.950

	34	35	36	37	38	39	40	41	42	43
19	.999	1.000								
20	.999	.999	1.000							
21	.997	.998	.999	.999	1.000					
22	.994	.996	.998	.999	.999	1.000				
23	.988	.993	.996	.997	.999	.999	1.000			
24	.979	.987	.992	.995	.997	.998	.999	.999	1.000	
25	.966	.978	.985	.991	.994	.997	.998	.999	.999	1.000

APPENDIX IV

Random Digits

52	01	77	67	75	24	63	38	49	35	24	94	21	81	65	44	29	27	49	45
80	50	54	31	64	05	18	81	54	99	76	54	38	55	37	63	82	29	16	65
45	29	96	34	26	89	80	93	96	31	53	07	28	60	26	55	08	03	36	06
68	54	02	00	45	42	72	68	80	80	83	91	40	05	64	18	43	62	76	59
59	46	73	48	01	39	09	22	05	88	52	36	38	21	45	98	17	17	68	33
48	11	76	74	87	37	92	52	17	90	05	97	08	92	00	48	19	92	91	70
12	43	56	35	20	11	74	52	23	46	14	06	05	08	23	41	40	30	97	32
35	09	98	17	01	75	87	53	56	54	14	30	22	20	64	13	62	38	85	79
91	62	68	03	19	47	60	72	15	51	49	38	70	72	58	15	49	12	56	24
89	32	05	05	36	16	81	08	86	43	19	94	20	73	17	90	27	38	84	35
35	44	13	18	45	24	02	84	08	62	48	26	58	26	05	27	50	07	39	98
37	54	87	30	41	94	15	09	18	51	62	32	21	15	94	66	77	56	78	51
94	62	46	11	96	38	27	07	95	10	04	06	92	74	59	73	71	17	78	17
00	38	75	95	71	96	12	82	75	24	91	40	70	14	66	70	60	91	10	62
77	93	89	19	98	14	50	65	63	33	25	37	52	28	25	62	47	83	41	13
80	81	45	17	77	55	73	22	02	94	39	02	49	91	45	23	68	47	92	76
36	04	09	03	80	99	33	71	17	84	56	11	33	69	45	98	26	94	03	68
88	46	12	33	52	07	98	48	66	44	98	83	10	48	19	49	85	15	74	79
15	02	00	99	31	24	96	47	32	47	79	28	55	07	37	42	11	10	00	20
01	84	87	69	87	63	79	19	07	49	41	38	60	64	93	29	16	50	53	44
09	73	25	33	60	97	09	34	10	94	05	58	19	69	04	46	26	45	74	77
54	20	48	05	29	40	52	42	72	56	82	48	47	44	52	66	95	27	07	99
42	26	89	53	18	47	54	06	74	67	00	78	55	72	85	73	67	89	75	43
01	90	25	29	90	36	47	64	76	66	79	51	48	11	62	13	97	34	40	87
80	79	99	70	93	78	56	13	82	60	89	28	52	37	83	17	73	20	88	98
06	57	47	17	73	03	95	71	04	77	69	74	65	33	71	24	76	52	01	35
06	01	08	05	21	11	57	82	31	82	23	74	23	28	72	95	64	89	47	42
26	97	76	02	45	52	16	42	23	60	02	10	90	10	33	93	19	64	50	93
57	33	21	35	76	62	11	39	93	68	72	03	78	56	52	01	09	37	67	07
79	64	57	53	96	29	77	88	42	75	67	88	70	61	74	29	80	15	73	61
99	90	88	96	94	75	08	99	16	28	35	54	85	39	41	18	34	07	27	68
43	54	85	81	53	14	03	33	29	73	41	35	97	11	89	63	45	57	18	24
15	12	33	87	57	60	04	08	97	92	65	75	84	96	28	52	02	05	16	56
86	10	25	91	96	64	48	94	86	07	46	97	20	82	66	95	05	32	54	70
01	02	46	74	43	65	17	70	21	95	25	63	05	01	45	11	03	52	96	47
79	01	71	19	65	39	45	95	92	43	37	29	80	95	90	91	67	35	48	76
33	51	29	69	82	39	61	01	36	78	38	48	20	63	61	04	80	52	40	37
38	17	15	39	91	19	04	25	62	24	44	31	15	95	33	47	20	90	25	60
29	53	68	70	03	07	11	20	86	84	87	67	88	67	67	43	31	13	11	65
58	40	44	01	26	25	22	96	93	59	14	16	98	95	11	68	03	23	66	53
39	09	47	34	61	96	27	93	86	25	10	25	65	81	33	98	69	73	61	70
88	69	51	19	54	69	28	23	11	96	38	96	86	79	90	94	30	34	26	14
25	01	62	52	77	97	45	00	35	13	54	62	73	05	38	52	66	57	48	18
74	85	22	05	13	02	12	48	60	94	97	00	28	46	82	87	55	35	75	48
05	45	56	14	93	91	08	36	28	14	40	77	60	93	52	03	80	83	42	82
52	52	75	80	86	74	31	71	56	70	70	07	14	90	56	86	17	46	85	09
56	12	71	92	18	74	39	24	95	66	00	00	39	80	82	77	17	72	70	80
09	97	33	34	66	67	43	68	41	92	15	85	06	28	89	80	77	40	27	72
32	30	75	75	59	04	79	00	66	79	45	43	86	50	75	84	66	25	22	91
10	51	82	16	01	54	03	54	88	88	15	53	87	51	76	49	14	22	56	85

APPENDIX V

Factors for Constructing Control Charts

Table 1. Factors for Estimating σ' from $\bar{R}$

Number of Observations in Subgroup n	Factor for Estimate from $\bar{R}$ $d_2 = \bar{R}/\sigma'$
2	1.128
3	1.693
4	2.059
5	2.326
6	2.534
7	2.704
8	2.847
9	2.970
10	3.078
11	3.173
12	3.258
13	3.336
14	3.407
15	3.472
16	3.532
17	3.588
18	3.640
19	3.689
20	3.735
21	3.778
22	3.819
23	3.858
24	3.895
25	3.931
30	4.086
35	4.213
40	4.322
45	4.415
50	4.498

Estimate of $\sigma' = \bar{R}/d_2$

Table 2. Factors for Determining from $\bar{R}$ the 3-Sigma Control Limits for $\bar{X}$ and R Charts

Number of Observations in Subgroup n	Factor for $\bar{X}$ Chart A_2	Factor for R Chart Lower Control Limit D_3	Factor for R Chart Upper Control Limit D_4
2	1.88	0	3.27
3	1.02	0	2.57
4	0.73	0	2.28
5	0.58	0	2.11
6	0.48	0	2.00
7	0.42	0.08	1.92
8	0.37	0.14	1.86
9	0.34	0.18	1.82
10	0.31	0.22	1.78
11	0.29	0.26	1.74
12	0.27	0.28	1.72
13	0.25	0.31	1.69
14	0.24	0.33	1.67
15	0.22	0.35	1.65
16	0.21	0.36	1.64
17	0.20	0.38	1.62
18	0.19	0.39	1.61
19	0.19	0.40	1.60
20	0.18	0.41	1.59

Upper Control Limit for $\bar{X} = UCL_{\bar{x}} = \bar{\bar{X}} + A_2\bar{R}$
Lower Control Limit for $\bar{X} = LCL_{\bar{x}} = \bar{\bar{X}} - A_2\bar{R}$

(If aimed-at or standard value $\bar{X}'$ is used rather than $\bar{\bar{X}}$ as the central line on the control chart, $\bar{X}'$ should be substituted for $\bar{\bar{X}}$ in the preceding formulas.)

Upper Control Limit for $R = UCL_R = D_4\bar{R}$
Lower Control Limit for $R = LCL_R = D_3\bar{R}$

All factors in Table 2 are based on the normal probability distribution.

INDEX

ABOUT THE AUTHOR

James B. Dilworth is Professor of Management at the University of Alabama in Birmingham. He received his B.S. at the University of Alabama and his M.S. at Oklahoma State University. Before obtaining his Ph.D. in Industrial Engineering and Management at Oklahoma State University, he worked for eight years in industry, first as an industrial engineer, and later as a manager of production control, an internal consultant, and a manager of the office of public systems. A specialist in production and operations management, Professor Dilworth has published many articles and is certified at the Fellow level by the American Production and Inventory Control Society. He is the author of *Production Observations from Japan* (American Production and Inventory Control Society, 1985) and is the editor of *Strategic and Tactical Issues in Just-in-Time Manufacturing* (Proceedings of the 1985 Conference of the Association for Manufacturing Excellence, in press). Professor Dilworth received the Dean's Teaching Award for the 1984-85 academic year from the University of Alabama in Birmingham.